Church for Every Context

Context

An Introduction to
Theology and Practice

Michael Moynagh

with Philip Harrold

scm press

Published in 2012 by SCM Press
Editorial office
3rd Floor, Invicta House,
108–114 Golden Lane,
London EC1Y 0TG

SCM Press is an imprint of Hymns Ancient & Modern Ltd (a registered charity)
13A Hellesdon Park Road
Norwich NR6 5DR, UK

www.scm-canterburypress.co.uk

British Library Cataloguing in Publication data

A catalogue record for this book is available
from the British Library

978-0-334-04369-0
Kindle edition 978-0-334-04472-7

Typeset by
Manila Typesetting Company
Printed and bound by
Antony Rowe, Chippenham, Wiltshire

To Liz

Contents

Part 3 Bringing Contextual Churches to Birth

Part 4 Growing to Maturity

Acknowledgements

Actors often give credit to their scripts, and I have been fortunate to work to an inspiring script written by numerous church founders in the UK. I have learnt from their experiences largely through being a member of the national Fresh Expressions team, which supports and encourages new and different forms of church. I owe a great debt to stimulating and wise colleagues on the team. Wycliffe Hall, Oxford, has been a kind and friendly place in which to write. I am grateful to Natalie Watson of SCM for encouraging me to write the book.

Thanks are due to Simon Cuff, Christopher Shaw and Cara Singer for being excellent research assistants for periods of time, and to the following who have commented on sections of the emerging draft and are not to blame for any remaining shortcomings: Andy Angel, Ian Bell, Mette Bundvad, Adrian Chatfield, Sylvia Collins-Mayo, Graham Cray, Steven Croft, Simon Cuff, John Drane, Andrew Davison, Bob and Mary Hopkins, Norman Ivison, George Lings, David Lyon, Stuart Murray-Williams, Louise Nelstrop, Andrew Roberts, Christopher Shaw, Janet Tollington, Steve Walton and Joseph Wolyniak. Special thanks to John Flett, who read a whole draft, made innumerable comments and ensured that it became a much better book. Biggest thanks of all go to my wife Liz, whom I admire continually and who has been wonderfully patient, not least when I have been physically present but mentally distant. The book is dedicated to her.

Introduction

New expressions of the church are springing up in many parts of the global North. Going under a variety of names – church plants, emergent church, fresh expressions of church, missional communities and many more – they are making a significant mark on the ecclesial landscape. Though notoriously difficult to count, they have attracted a growing literature, generated extensive debate and changed denominational strategies. It is widely recognized that something significant is afoot. *Church for Every Context* offers a theological rationale of what is becoming a global trend. It proposes some methodologies for starting these new types of churches and growing them to maturity.

A report for the Church of Scotland declared that the emergence of these churches 'has every appearance of being one of the most significant missional movements in the recent history of Christianity in these islands' (Drane and Drane, 2010, p. 3). Alongside an expanding flow of non-academic books, the academic literature is taking steadily more notice of the phenomenon. Academics have begun both to critique it, such as – in the UK – Hull (2006), Milbank (2008), Davison and Milbank (2010) and Percy (2010), and to provide more sympathetic treatments, such as – again using UK examples – Ward (2002), Williams (for example 2006), Dunn (2008) and Drane (2010). Fresh expressions of church have become a topic of study in many of Britain's theological colleges and courses (Croft, 2008a, p. 47), and the subject of a growing number of MA and PhD dissertations.[1]

We begin with an introduction to these new types of church – what I shall call 'new contextual churches'. It describes four ecclesial currents that are giving rise to these churches. It offers a definition of new contextual church, provides some examples and supplies a rationale for the definition. It then summarizes the concerns these churches are raising, and against this background outlines the purpose and shape of the book.

---

1 The Church Army's Sheffield Centre has a hard copy and an electronic database of over 40 of these. See www.churcharmy.org.uk/ms/sc/fxcp/sfc_onlinelibrary.aspx.

Four tributaries

'New contextual church' is used here as an umbrella term to describe the birth and growth of Christian communities that serve people mainly outside the church, belong to their culture, make discipleship a priority and form a new church among the people they serve.[2] They are a response to changes in society and to the new missional context that the church faces in the global North. In contrast to when it dominated society (what is known as 'Christendom'), in most parts of the economically advanced world the church now finds itself in post-Christendom, among populations who increasingly have little or no Christian background. Four overlapping tributaries, representing different responses to this new situation, provide the streams from which new contextual churches are emerging.

Church planting

The first is church planting, which has a long history in the UK. It stretches from churches built in new urban areas during the industrial revolution, to the planting of daughter churches, to the beginnings of a new phase of church planting in the 1970s. During that decade, Patrick Blair started to develop his seven satellite congregations in Chester-le-Street, and Roger Forster began multiplying churches across south London in what became the Ichthus movement.

The tributary started to flow more rapidly in the early 1990s largely as a result of church growth missiology. The latter included an emphasis on evangelism and encouraged a new wave of church planting, inspired by the international DAWN (Disciple a Whole Nation) strategy. The strategy represented a shift from 'come' to 'go' evangelism. Rather than invite people outside church to existing congregations, new gatherings were planted in the hope of attracting those who did not attend.

However, many of these church plants suffered from having a dominant gene[3] that saw church primarily in terms of Sunday worship, albeit done differently. They started down the contextual road, but did not travel far

---

2 This is based on the summary of the definition of fresh expression used by the Fresh Expressions team. See www.freshexpressions.org.uk/about/whatis.

3 Kilpin and Murray (2007, p. 7) describe these plants as clones, but this is unhelpful. A clone would be genetically identical to the parent church, whereas these church plants were not clones in the literal sense of having all their genes in common. They innovated in a number of ways, such as recognizing the diversity of their mission contexts, being lay led with a mission team rather than a single leader, carrying out serious mission audit and in some cases pioneering different forms of worship. I am grateful to Bob and Mary Hopkins for pointing this out.

enough to reach people who were outside the church. Largely for this reason, a number of these plants were short-lived, while others had little effect on the surrounding community. 'Many new churches failed to thrive. Some closed after years of struggle. Many more are small, weak and making little impact' (Lings and Murray, 2003, p. 4).

A deep desire to connect church with people outside, missional reflection on postmodern culture and in some cases 'post-evangelical' angst encouraged more contextual and diverse forms of church planting in the late 1990s, often involving small groups below the radar of the wider church. The momentum has built up since. In addition, churches serving ethnic minority communities have proliferated, but have generally not expanded to include other cultures.

The emerging church conversation

Originating in the United States, this second tributary consists of a smorgasbord of groups and individuals who want to find what they consider to be more authentic ways to live the Christian faith. Found mainly among the Gen X and Gen Y generations, participants in the emerging church conversation seek to connect with popular culture, postmodern practice and philosophy, and reflect a widespread disenchantment with evangelicalism (Cox, 2009, p. 132; Jones, 2008, p. 68). The conversation, in which 'Emergent' is a prominent sub-group, comprises 'a network of networks' (Drane, 2008, p. 90) and has an extensive presence online and in print.

Some of those who would identify with the conversation have started new 'emerging churches'. Based on an extensive study between 2000 and 2005, Eddie Gibbs and Ryan Bolger (2006, pp. 44–5) found that three core practices were common to all these churches – identifying with the life of Jesus, transforming secular space (rather than separating the sacred and secular) and living as community (as a way of pursuing the kingdom within the church and beyond). These central practices combined to create six further practices – welcoming the stranger, serving with generosity, participating as producers, creating as created beings, leading as a body and taking part in spiritual activities.

Many emerging churches have developed alternative forms of worship to re-engage Christians who find existing church culturally alien and unable to speak to them, and are about to leave the church or have recently done so. Others, however, have connected with people who are further from church, and these have tended to put less emphasis on worship as a way to serve people. Especially in the US, emerging churches are generally outside the denominations, are often highly critical of them and in many cases would be suspicious of 'fresh expressions of church', which are emerging *in* the denominations.

Language within the movement has evolved. In 2011, two observers could write that:

> emergence was a word used to communicate the movement as a whole . . . Emergent currently tends to reflect churches inclusive in character of all sorts of conditions of people; emerging is more representative of churches that are evangelical and conservative in nature (Gray-Reeves and Perham, 2011, p. 3).

Doug Gay has asked whether we may be near the end of 'emerging' as a useful term for the church (Gay, 2011, p. xi).

Fresh expressions of church

The third tributary consists of fresh expressions of church. The term was first used in print in the Church of England's 2004 report, Mission-shaped Church, which has been highly influential. The term deliberately echoes the Preface to the Declaration of Assent, which Church of England ministers make at their licensing and which states:

> The Church of England . . . professes the faith uniquely revealed in the Holy Scriptures and set forth in the catholic creeds, which faith the Church is called upon to proclaim afresh in each generation.

The term 'fresh expressions', the report proposed, 'suggests something new or enlivened is happening, but also suggests connection to history and the developing story of God's work in the Church' (Mission-shaped Church, 2004, p. 34).

Since the report's publication, all manner of initiatives have described themselves as 'fresh expressions', including the redesign of a church notice board! So to draw some lines round the phrase, in 2006 the Fresh Expressions team – formed by the Church of England's archbishops and the Methodist Church to encourage and support the development of fresh expressions of church in the UK – offered the following definition:

> A fresh expression is a form of church for our changing culture established primarily for the benefit of people who are not yet members of any church.

> - It will come into being through principles of listening, service, incarnational mission and making disciples.
> - It will have the potential to become a mature expression of church shaped by the gospel and the enduring marks of the church and for its cultural context (Croft, 2008c, p. 10).

Since the report, fresh expressions of church have multiplied across a growing number of denominations, including the Church of Scotland, the Congregational Federation and the United Reformed Church, and overseas. New forms of church – many not calling themselves 'fresh expressions' – are emerging in Australia, New Zealand, North America, other parts of Europe and in some places in the global South.

Communities in mission

'Communities in mission' is my term for groups that seek to combine a rich life in community with mission and do not identify strongly with the other tributaries. They include simple church, which values small, multiplying, home-based churches, minimal structures and relational rather than institutional ties, and organic church, which is very similar but whose leaders put more weight on belonging to a larger movement. Both are less interested in radical theology than in being radical church.

Communities in mission also include mid-sized communities that are being formed in a number of well-established churches. They are clusters of Christians, of varying sizes, which gain purpose from serving a specific group of people outside the church. Each community meets in varying ways and with varying regularity, but does so as a 'congregation'. For example, a small group may gather three times a month and then join with the wider local church on perhaps one Sunday of the month. Larger clusters have small cells that meet regularly for prayer, study and fellowship (Hopkins and Breen, 2007, pp. 29–41).

New monasticism

Within each of these four tributaries are groups that tap into new monasticism, a subterranean source of spiritual nourishment with origins in the monastic tradition and the secular Celtic revival. Ian Mobsby has identified three groups of new monastics – those inspired by monks and nuns who gather for prayer in disused pubs, youth clubs, in places of natural beauty and elsewhere; those who identify with the friar tradition and move into an area either as single households of pioneers or as intentional communities; and a growing number of 'friar monks' who are inspired by both monk and friar traditions (Mobsby 2010, pp. 13–15).

Water flows freely between these four tributaries. A good number of new churches would see themselves as both a church plant and a fresh expression, for example, or as belonging to several tributaries. The result of this energy and innovation has been a bewildering eruption of different types of Christian community and different ideas about what it means to be church in today's world.

Definition

These developments as a whole defy easy definition, and yet some clarity of terms is necessary. I propose to work with a definition based on a summary version of the one offered by the Fresh Expressions team.[4] New contextual churches are new Christian communities that are

- missional – in the sense that, through the Spirit, they are birthed by Christians mainly among people who do not normally attend church;
- contextual – they seek to fit the culture of the people they serve;
- formational – they aim to form disciples;
- ecclesial – they intend to become church for the people they reach in their contexts.

Some examples

New contextual churches can be classified in a variety of ways. One is to describe them in relation to the local church. On this basis, some are closely linked to an existing church. They emerge from within a 'fringe' group – a mission venture or a community project, for instance – so that these initiatives are no longer stepping stones to Sunday church but become 'church' in their own right.

For example, the leaders of a church-run luncheon club for older people invited members to stay behind after the meal for quarter of an hour, at the start of which a candle was lit on each table. There followed some Christian music, a reading from Scripture, a period of silence and some prayers. This became the start of a journey to faith for those involved, and the beginning of a church alongside and in the context of the luncheon club.

Alternatively, a local church may bring a Christian community to birth as part of a new initiative. A Sunday 'Drop In' opened in inner-city Bristol in 2010 to serve a marginalized section of society. There is a cup of tea, some food, pool and table tennis, newspapers and a prayer board. Toward the end of the session, someone invites requests for prayer and a short, informal prayer time follows. Numbers vary from 15 to 25 each week. Some have asked to be baptized. There is cross-fertilization with the regular Sunday congregation. Some of the latter help run Drop In, while a few from Drop In attend church groups or occasional services.

The leaders see Drop In as

an experiment in a new way of being church, at a time when regular church has lost its draw. We do not know where it is leading, or whether

---

4 The definition is a modified version of the one used by Fresh Expressions. See www.sharetheguide.org/section1/1.

it will last . . . We think that we have created something – small and fragile, certainly – where healing and transformation can take place, and a new kind of community can grow.[5]

New contextual churches have emerged within networks that jump local-church boundaries – in a Methodist circuit, an Anglican deanery or among local churches from different denominations acting together. A number of youth congregations have been started through this type of collaboration, such as Eden, a monthly youth gathering in Sussex that breaks into separate youth groups on the other Sundays (Lings, 2007). The congregation is connected to a group of churches in an area rather than to one local church.

Potentially important is a further category. These are gatherings beyond the reach of the local church. They are started by individuals in the context of their daily lives – in a school, among friends or perhaps at work. The initiative comes not from an existing church or group of churches, but from an individual or group who may or may not be recognized by the wider body. A group of women started a monthly event in a leisure centre, for example. Visiting speakers talked about how God had helped them to lead 'fit lives', such as when bringing up a child with handicaps or when facing a crisis. The leaders recognized that when individuals began to enquire about Jesus, this would have the potential to become a church.

Missional, contextual, formational and ecclesial

The definition used here would include only a portion of the many groups and communities in the four tributaries just described. The definition is not intended to put question marks round what is left out, but to provide some discipline and coherence to the language I am using.

The emphasis on mission reflects the prevailing theological understanding that in mission the church joins God's mission to the world.

> 'Church *and* mission' was once the theological frame used by the ecumenical community in an attempt to address this dynamic. It was discovered, however, that the 'and' already bifurcated that which was not to be divided. That is the rationale for using the adjective today, missional. (Bliese 2006, p. 239)

The definition slightly tightens the Fresh Expressions version – from communities that are 'primarily for the benefit of people who are not yet members of any church' to ones that 'are birthed . . . mainly among people who do not normally attend church'. This is intended to give greater precision. It also raises the bar. Often congregations find it harder to work directly with

---

5 *Church Times*, 16 December 2011.

people outside the church than to take action from a distance to support them, such as giving to charity. Yet pushing up the bar is necessary if we are to do full justice to the idea that church is missionary at its heart, a theme that is developed in Chapter 6.

The stress on contextualization (often referred to as inculturation) reflects a consensus that has emerged since Vatican II among theologians across the spectrum from Roman Catholic to evangelical. These theologians agree on the importance of contextualizing theology (and by implication the church), although their understanding of what is involved frequently differs. Stephen Bevans and Roger Schroeder (2004) have shown how historically the church's mission has been carried out through an ongoing interaction between theological *constants* (basic questions that the church has always wrestled with) and a variety of changing *contexts* (the historical circumstances in which the basic questions are faced). A church falls down in its missional task if its witness fails to connect with its immediate setting.

Forming disciples is vital if new churches are to avoid being 'froth expressions' – consumerist expressions of church that fail to encourage an obligation to local people and a commitment to the whole church. 'The ultimate test of any expression of church, whether a fresh expression or a more traditional one – is what quality of disciples are made there?' (Cray, 2010c, p. 3).

The intention to become church marks out new contextual churches from mission initiatives or projects. The aim is not for the initiative to be a stepping stone to existing church but to encourage church to emerge within it. So the luncheon club is no longer seen as a bridge to Sunday church, but as an opportunity for the Spirit to bring church to birth within or alongside the weekly lunch. A youth initiative is not viewed as a youth club, whose members also attend church on Sunday, but as a youth congregation – as church for young people.

Frost and Hirsch have distinguished between 'attractional' churches that relate to the world on a 'you come to us' basis, and 'incarnational' churches that go into the surrounding context and grow new churches within it (Frost and Hirsch, 2003, pp. 41–51). The distinction is a bit sharp because there is a third – 'engaged' – category, which is possibly the most common type of church. 'Engaged' churches go into their communities in loving service, often hoping that the people they serve will be drawn into the church on Sunday (Hopkins and Breen, 2007, pp. 117–21). A project among homeless people might be set up on this basis. Many participants of course never make the journey because the gap between their everyday lives and the church is too great. Contextual churches recognize this and seek to be church in the settings of ordinary life.

'New contextual churches' describes communities within the four tributaries that meet these missional, contextual, formational and ecclesial criteria. They are types of church that should be encouraged for good theological reasons. However, when referring to specific initiatives, the label should be used with care. It may not be clear whether the initiative falls within the definition.

Three approaches to mission by the local church

Attractional

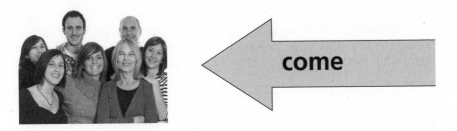

Engaged

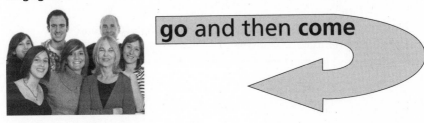

Incarnational

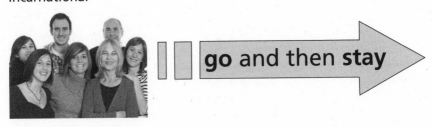

In particular, when a community becomes church varies according to point of view. A team of Christians serving a group of people may see itself as church from the very beginning. But the people the team serves may not consider themselves to be church, and it may be a while before they view themselves in these terms. The denomination or wider institutional body will encourage the initiative as it develops, but not recognize it as a church till it appears sustainable. This of course raises questions, addressed in later chapters, about what is understood by 'maturity' and 'sustainability'.

Scope of the book

The purpose of *Church for Every Context* is to introduce the theology and practice of new contextual churches, drawing on recent British experience. Various rationales for these types of church can be found, for example in Frost and Hirsch (2003), *Mission-shaped Church* (2004) and in the writings of Stuart Murray (for example 2004a and 2004b). But there have also been fierce criticisms, mainly by the writers referred to at the beginning of the chapter. These criticisms reveal a need to articulate a fuller theological justification – not least, of the understanding that these initiatives *are* church.

Though further theological work is needed, one aim of the book is to provide this defence. The book will address a number of concerns, which will be described more fully, including:

- Do these new communities express a full view of the kingdom?
- Can they be regarded as churches?
- Do they reflect a proper understanding of the *missio Dei*?
- In seeking to be contextual, are they also staying faithful to the gospel?
- Can their focus on specific cultural groups be justified?
- What is their relationship to the Christian tradition?
- Are these contextual churches growing disciples with a sense of obligation to the wider church and to others in society, or are they just a form of spiritual consumerism?
- Will they prove sustainable?
- What should be their relationship to the denominations?

A second aim is to contribute to reflection on the practice of contextual churches. The church planting literature, most of which comes from North America, contains a great deal of wisdom. Yet much of it arises from the experience of church planting among existing, but disillusioned churchgoers or among recent church-leavers. In many parts of the global North, such people are a rapidly shrinking proportion of the population. The Church faces a new mission context, in which steadily more people have little or no Christian background.

A number of observers, such as Brian McLaren (2009, p. 17), have claimed that by supporting fresh expressions of church, Britain's denominations are ahead of the rest of the global North in addressing this situation. To many of us in the UK, however, it looks as if we have much to learn from other countries. As part of this mutual learning, there may be lessons from British experience that are worth not only debating in the UK but sharing more widely.

An outline of the book

Church for Every Context argues that as part of recent theology's turn to the church, we should affirm the God-given role of the church as a visible community in all the contexts of life, that methodologies for practising this are beginning to emerge and that the denominations should make new contextual church a priority. The book is in four parts. The first puts new contextual churches into a historical and contemporary context. It shows how the church reproduced in the New Testament, how it has regularly done so since, how in Britain (as in other countries) it is learning to reproduce in fresh ways today and why these new forms of reproduction are sociologically significant.

Against this background, Part 2 offers some theological foundations for contextual church. Chapter 5 asks whether these communities can be properly called church: what is the essential nature of the church and how might we understand maturity in relation to new contextual churches? Chapter 6 maintains that mission should be a first step for the church. Chapter 7 argues that this mission should take communal form in the different places where people now lead their lives. Chapter 8 contends that these communal forms of mission should be thoroughly contextual, while remaining true to Jesus. Chapter 9 argues that being contextual will mean focusing on specific cultures. It suggests that this is consistent with the New Testament vision of a diverse but united church. Chapter 10 claims that these contextual churches are faithful to the Christian tradition.

Part 3 builds on the theology of the earlier chapters. It argues that founding new churches should be viewed as an essential Christian practice, which is beginning to be expressed in new ways. As the beginning of a contemporary description of this practice, Chapter 11 describes what it means for mission to take communal form in the many settings of society. As a crucial step toward this communal expression of mission, Chapter 12 discusses the process of gathering a mission community (the founding team of the new church). Chapters 13 and 14 describe how this mission community can begin to engage in contextual mission – by researching opportunities to serve the context and engaging with potential partners. Chapters 15 and 16 describe two processes – action-based learning and what I have called team awareness – that support the gathering, researching and engaging activities.

Part 4 is about laying down pathways to maturity. It describes the outlines of four such pathways – making disciples, worship, community and sustainability. It points to some of the directions of travel, recognizing that we still have much to learn about the stepping stones within each pathway.

The final chapter argues that contextual churches should grow to maturity within the setting of a mixed-economy church, in which new forms of church and inherited church (churches with inherited structures and patterns of life) exist alongside each other in relationships of mutual support. The book can be read as an extended argument for the mixed economy. New contextual churches are theologically well founded. We are learning how to practise them. This learning should continue within a mixed-economy setting.

In organizing the chapters, I have tried to respond to pleas that training for church founders integrate theory and practice (Croft, 2008a, p. 49). Thus a number of chapters are designed to build bridges between the practice of contextual church and specific academic disciplines. The disciplines include Old Testament (Chapter 19), New Testament (Chapter 1), systematic theology (especially Chapters 5, 6 and 21), church history (Chapters 2 and 10), worship (Chapter 18) and, of course, themes within mission studies such as sociology (Chapter 4), contextualization (Chapters 5 and 6) and evangelism (Chapters 12 and 18).

Resources

Church for Every Context draws on a variety of material. It is informed by over 150 case studies compiled by the UK national team, Fresh Expressions[6], by the Sheffield Centre's important *Encounters on the Edge* series of studies, and by other examples of contextual church with which I am familiar.

It draws on an extensive body of literature arising from the four tributaries of church planting, emerging church, fresh expressions of church and communities in mission. Within this are case studies and case study-based reflections such as Glasson (2006), Male (2008), Gibbs and Bolger (2006) and Gray-Reeves and Perham (2011); contributions to the debate about the validity of these new forms of church, such as some of the essays in Croft (2008b) and Nelstrop and Percy (2008); introductions to specific types of church, such as organic church (Cole, 2005) and mid-sized communities (Breen and Absalom, 2010); studies that address particular themes or issues, such as liquid church (Ward 2002) and new monasticism (Cray, Mobsby and Kennedy, 2010).

Church for Every Context also dialogues with wider streams of theological literature, not least on the nature of the church, the mission of God, contextualization, the church as the carrier of the Christian story, and Old and New Testament studies. In addition, the book plunders insights from commercial and social entrepreneurship to throw light on how contextual churches start and grow, and draws on complexity theory, especially complex responsive process theory, which emphasizes the role of conversations in organizational life.

I write as a Church of England minister who is a member of the UK's national Fresh Expressions team, which since 2005 has encouraged new forms of church for a fast-changing world.[7] This inevitably means that my perspective has something of an institutional feel. However, the church

---

6 www.freshexpressions.org.uk/stories.
7 www.freshexpressions.org.uk/about.

is not primarily an institution, but a variety of interlocking relationships. History is full of ecclesial institutions emerging and dying. There is nothing sacrosanct about today's denominations. So although I write from within one particular institution, which I believe still has something to offer the world, I have sympathy for critical voices outside the denominations. My passion is the mission of the church.

Like many in the emerging church conversation, I have a low-church evangelical background, but in the early 1990s my journey took me to a more sacramental church, where we pioneered – in today's language – several fresh expressions of church. Though my voyage resonates with many in the conversation, I have not travelled to the radical shores a number have reached. Some in the conversation would think me rather tame, whereas several of my evangelical friends would wonder if I was conservative enough.

I have used the phrase 'new contextual church' to span churches founded by people who would describe themselves as conservative evangelicals, Anglo-Catholics, radical emergents, new monastics or some other label, while being willing to stand under this umbrella term. The book is an apologetic for these new types of church within the mixed economy.

Further reading

Gay, Doug, *Remixing the Church: The Five Moves of Emerging Ecclesiology*, London: SCM, 2011.
Lings, George and Stuart Murray, *Church Planting: Past, Present and Future*, Cambridge: Grove Books, 2003.
Mission-shaped Church, London: Church Publishing House, 2004.

Questions for discussion

- Of the four tributaries described in the chapter, which would you most identify with and why?
- What are the advantages and disadvantages of the definition of new contextual church offered here?
- What examples of new contextual church have you experienced or are aware of? In what ways do they fit the chapter's definition?

Part 1

Past and Present

I

Saint Paul's New Contextual Churches

Evangelical critics of the emerging church conversation, such as D. A. Carson (2005), frequently complain that participants are not biblical enough; in their eagerness to connect with contemporary culture, contributors tend to lose their scriptural moorings. Critics from the more Catholic end of the spectrum, such as Andrew Davison and Alison Milbank (2010), accuse fresh expressions of church (and no doubt would include the emerging church conversation) of paying insufficient attention to the church's tradition.

To help ensure that *Church for Every Context* is rooted in Scripture and has a strong eye to the tradition, Part 1 begins with a discussion of Saint Paul's approach to church planting. Chapter 2 provides some historical precedents for contextual church. Chapter 3 recounts Britain's recent experience of fresh expressions of church, while Chapter 4 puts these developments into a sociological perspective. The purpose of these chapters is to place new contextual churches in their historical and contemporary setting, and to show that church reproduction is intrinsic to the church's missional life.

Starting with Saint Paul is no accident. He is widely regarded as one of history's most fruitful church pioneers. So it is natural to ask what his experience can teach us. Eckhard Schnabel (2008) has recently provided a comprehensive description of Paul's approach to mission, while Loveday Alexander (2008), James Dunn (2008), Richard Bauckham (2011) and John Drane (2011) have used New Testament material to reflect on fresh expressions of church and church pioneering.

In following them to learn from the New Testament, we must tread with care. Not all scholars accept the historical accuracy of Acts for example, although plausible reasons exist for assuming that Luke provides a faithful account (Hengel, 1979; Hemer, 1989). We must allow for differences between the New Testament and contemporary worlds, and we must avoid jumping from the New Testament to now as if the church has done no reflection in between.

Discerning in the light of the whole biblical story which actions within the narrative might serve as examples for today is a delicate task. We must also keep in mind that Paul was not the only apostle to found new churches – we just know more about him. Finally, it would be a mistake to plunge straight into Saint Paul's missionary journeys. If we wind back a little, we shall find lessons from an earlier period.

So, we shall look at the shift in emphasis from a 'come' to a 'go' approach to mission, explore lessons for the 'mixed economy' (old and new churches living alongside each other in a denomination), discuss Paul's pioneering teams, speculate a little on some of the processes involved in bringing Paul's churches to birth, consider how far Paul's new congregations were culture specific and examine his transition of leadership.

From mission as 'come' to mission as 'go'

It is often said that there is a shift from the Old Testament's centripetal – 'you come to us' – approach to mission to the New Testament's centrifugal one: 'we'll go to you'. Ancient Israel saw its missional task as being to attract the nations, whereas the first Christians went in mission *to* the nations.

Centripetal mission in Israel

This distinction has been challenged by Walter Kaiser, who has argued that ancient Israel had a duty to go out in centrifugal witness.

> There could be no mistaking where Paul got his marching orders: they came from the Old Testament. The case for evangelizing the Gentiles had not been a recently devised switch in the plan of God, but had always been the long-term commitment of the Living God who is a missionary God. (Kaiser, 2000, p. 82)

If Jewish proselytizers among the Gentiles existed in the first century CE, as scholars used to suggest (De Ridder, 1975, pp. 58–127), this would lend support to Kaiser. It would suggest that there were at least some Jews who recognized a call to mission beyond Israel's borders. Yet Martin Goodman and others have shown that Judaism did not contain a proselytizing tendency before Christian mission began. The later emergence in Judaism of Christian-type proselytizing owed less to impulses within Judaism than to what the *Christians* were doing (Goodman, 1994, pp. 60–91; Riesner, 2000, pp. 211–50; Bird, 2010, p. 11).[1]

---

1 Matthew 23.15's reference to scribes and Pharisees proselytizing, the only ancient source that explicitly ascribes a missionary policy to a Jewish group, can be interpreted in four ways, three of which would not imply Jewish mission to the Gentiles. It may refer to the conversion of other Jews to Pharisaism or the attempt to turn God-fearers into full Jews, for example (Bird, 2010, pp. 66–70).

Christopher Wright points out that the Old Testament contains no explicit command that Israelites should go to the nations in mission. If this had been the expectation, it is surprising that the prophets did not condemn Israel for its failure to do so. The Old Testament emphasis is on God summoning the nations to himself 'in the great pilgrimage to Zion' at the end times (Wright, 2006, pp. 502–3). Zechariah 8.20–3, for instance, pictures people 'from all languages' streaming to Jerusalem. According to Isaiah 61.5–6, when Israel is what it is meant to be Gentiles will join the people of God.

> Only in Isaiah 66 is there explicit word of God sending messengers to the nations, and that is as a future expectation contingent on the ingathering of Israel first. (Wright, 2006, p. 503)

Within this broad sweep are hints of a more centrifugal approach. Jonah leaps to mind of course. Nahum and Amos 1 and 2.1–5 are addressed to the nations, suggesting that Israel should be outward looking. But they are a sub-plot. From a New Testament perspective, they point to what would be fulfilled later in Christian mission.

The emergence of centrifugal mission

The very first Christians in Jerusalem had been instructed by Jesus, assuming the words were from his lips, to be his witnesses 'to the ends of the earth' (Acts 1.8; cf Matt. 28.18–20). Understanding that the end times had arrived, it would have been natural for them to interpret Jesus' command as a fulfilment of Isaiah 66.18–21: as the nations came to Jerusalem, some of the gathered were go to the Gentiles and proclaim the risen Lord.

So why did the apostles at first stay in Jerusalem? Richard Bauckham has suggested that it may have been a deliberate strategy to take the gospel to Jews living outside Israel. Jews from far and wide came to Jerusalem not just for Pentecost, but for all the major Jewish festivals. The best way for the apostles to reach the diaspora Jews was by proclaiming the gospel in Jerusalem and encouraging converts to take the message to their synagogues back home. Gentiles would be reached through the God-fearers, who associated with the synagogues without becoming fully Jews. This helps to explain how the gospel reached Egypt, Rome and elsewhere comparatively early. It was an enactment of Isaiah 66 (Bauckham, 2011, pp. 198–9; cf Gehring, 2004, p. 90).

The strategy was undermined by the persecution that scattered the Jerusalem believers across Judaea and Samaria, making Jerusalem a less secure base for mission (Acts 8.1). At the same time, the Holy Spirit provided a series of unexpected experiences that encouraged the church to become more centrifugal in outlook. Some of the Samaritans were converted (Acts 8.4–25). An Ethiopian eunuch became a believer outside Jerusalem (Acts 8.26–39).

Philip continued preaching in the towns to Caesarea (Acts 8.40). At Caesarea, Peter witnessed the outpouring of the Spirit on the household of the Gentile Cornelius, an event that had a profound impact on the Apostles' thinking (Acts 10.9—11.18). Clearly mission did not require staying in Jerusalem!

To cap it all, in an astonishing break with the past, Jewish converts from Cyprus and Cyrene took the gospel to Gentiles in Antioch. They described Jesus not as 'messiah' but as 'Lord', a term that pagans used for their cult divinities including, notably, Caesar himself. 'From now on the word about Christ, and the faith of Christ, began to work through the vast complex of Greek and Roman thought' (Walls, 1996, pp. 52–3).

Paul developed this process of going out to different cultures and immersing the gospel in them. Schnabel has argued that Paul was not a cross-cultural missionary. He was bi-cultural, a Jew who was also at home in Graeco-Roman culture (Schnabel, 2008, pp. 329–31). But this ignores how Paul crossed social boundaries. Ronald Hock has described Paul's leather-working, which provided financial support during his missionary journeys. It was the work of artisans, whom the elite viewed with hostility and contempt. Hock stresses how difficult this must have been for Paul who by birth came from the elite (Hock, 2007, p. 35). Moreover, as Paul taught from house to house in cosmopolitan centres like Ephesus (Acts 20.20), he would have entered households from a variety of social backgrounds – Roman cities were melting-pots of cultures, classes and ethnic groups.

Paul identified with the contexts he sought to reach. He became all things to all people (1 Cor. 9.22), and allowed the needs (and so cultures) of Jews and Gentiles to inform his behaviour by becoming the slave of his listeners (1 Cor. 9.19). He entered the habits of thought of his audiences and showed what the gospel would look like when it was enacted in their setting. So in Corinth, where people cherished success, sought to climb the social ladder and prized clever rhetoric, Paul had an occupation without status, assumed a servant role and rejected crowd-pleasing rhetoric in favour of standard classical forms (Thiselton, 2006, pp. 6–19). He showed how the gospel was distinctive within a Corinthian way of life.

In identifying with context to be distinctive within it, Paul was imitating Jesus and he expected the small congregations he founded to do the same. Church happened in the midst of the everyday – in the home, which was the centre of day-to-day life. 'Worship and the daily life of the Christian [were] bound together in the household' (Becker, 1993, p. 246). John Drane notes that

> different social contexts enabled the emergence of many different styles of Christian community, and there was never any guarantee that the church in one place would be the same as the church in a different setting. Indeed, this ability to contextualize itself within such diverse cultures is perhaps the one thing that, above all others, explains the attraction of the Christian gospel. (Drane, 2009, p. 196)

Within these different settings, relationships between members of the new gatherings were entirely transformed (or at least meant to be). Distinctions between Jews and Greeks, masters and slaves, and men and women began to be redefined as members saw themselves as brothers and sisters in Christ. The communities that made up the church were living an incarnational life. Immersed in their contexts, they showed how the Spirit could make their contexts very different. When the gospel went out from Jerusalem, it took a different shape in different settings.

For reflection

The shift from centripetal to centrifugal mission is one of the big stories of Scripture. It is consistent with calls today for the church to adopt a 'we'll go to you' rather than 'you come to us' approach to mission. But just as Jesus drew people to himself, so did many of Paul's new congregations. Presumably, that is why they took root and multiplied. They had an attractional, come-to-us dynamic. In a sense these new communities were 'little Israels', attracting people round about, but within a story that had opened an incarnational chapter. Adopting a 'go' strategy, Paul and others gave birth to gatherings whose corporate lives also invited 'come to us'. Has the distinction between 'come' and 'go' mission sometimes been overdrawn? Perhaps we should think of a cycle: a church goes out when it starts a new church, which attracts people. In time the new chuch goes out to start a further church. 'Go' leads to 'come', which is followed by 'go'.

Sustaining the 'mixed economy'

Within fresh expressions circles, there are frequent references to the mixed-economy church, in which inherited church (with its inherited life and structures) and new forms of church exist side by side, in mutual respect and support. But this is not always easy. Are there lessons that can help us from the New Testament church?

Ray Anderson has argued that the Antioch church can be seen as emerging out of the church at Jerusalem. Under Paul's ministry and teaching, it produced an emergent theology, based on the Spirit's revelation about Jesus. This theology was very different to that of the Jerusalem church, which was committed to historical precedent and the tradition of the Twelve. He claims that

> the emerging churches in our present generation can find their ecclesial form and their core theology by tracing out the contours of the missionary church under Paul's leadership based at Antioch. (Anderson, 2007, p. 21)

Unfortunately, Anderson's reading of the New Testament privileges new expressions of church over inherited forms and their traditions. Jerusalem, which in Anderson's reading can be seen as an inherited church, appears to be the big problem. It is 'controlled by a fortress mentality' (Anderson, 2007, p. 27). Anderson underlines the conflicts between Antioch and Jerusalem, but downplays their attempt to stay together and ignores the range of views that existed among believers in Jerusalem (and in Antioch, too, presumably).

Jerusalem can be viewed more sympathetically if we understand the troublesome problem of identity the early believers faced. The key question for the Jerusalem followers of Jesus, as for many in the inherited church now, was how to make space for believers with a very different sense of spiritual identity.

The dispute over identity

The Jerusalem church was born as a reform movement among the Jews. The disciples attended the Temple daily (Acts 2.46) and had a strong sense of their Jewish identity. They saw themselves as the nucleus of a new Israel, living in the last days. As we have seen, they were extremely mission-minded. They assumed that Gentiles would come to faith, but they expected them to do so by becoming Jews.

The conversion of Cornelius challenged that expectation. Peter's vision of clean and unclean animals together in Acts 10 symbolized, for him, the end of Israel separating itself from the nations. The Spirit falling on Cornelius' household convinced him that those present could become Christians as Gentiles without converting to Judaism, and his fellow leaders in Jerusalem agreed (Acts 11.18). This was a very significant expansion of the apostles' sense of spiritual identity: through the Spirit, they were forming a Jewish/Gentile community, not just a Jewish one.

It was of course Paul, deeply immersed in Gentile mission, who did most to reconceptualize the place of Gentile Christians in God's purposes. They were not coming into Judaism but into *church*, a new Israel comprising Jews and Gentiles, whose cornerstone was Jesus. Through him all were made one (Gal. 3.26–9).

This notion of Christian identity was very different to that of the more conservative believers. Until recently, it has been common to distinguish between a 'conservative' Hebrew group of Aramaic-speaking believers, who clung fiercely to their Jewish traditions, and 'liberal' Greek-speaking converts from the Jewish Diaspora, the so-called 'Hellenists'. New Testament scholars now tend to think that conservatives and liberals, if one can use such terms, were drawn from both Hebrew and Hellenistic backgrounds (Witherington III, 1997, pp. 240–7). Indeed, there was probably not a distinct liberal camp in competition with a conservative one: views on such issues as resistance to Rome, temple worship, purity codes, circumcision and eschatological expectations more likely ranged along a spectrum for each issue. These different spectrums may well not have corresponded to each other (Wright, 1992, p. 454).

With that in mind, conservative elements, who treasured their Jewish identity, no doubt saw the baptism of Cornelius without becoming a Jew as an exception rather than the new norm (Dunn, 2009, p. 402). But when the birth of the Antioch church and Paul's first mission showed that Cornelius was far from an exception, the issue of circumcision – Gentile converts becoming Jews – flared up again. In Acts 15 the Council of Jerusalem confirmed that circumcision was not required, yet added an important rider ('the apostolic decree'): Gentile believers were to observe some of the Jewish food laws and certain other stipulations (Acts 15.20, 29).[2]

Though the traditionalists had lost on circumcision, their desire to protect their Jewish identity had been acknowledged – which made sense from a mission view point. If they strayed too far from their Jewish traditions, mission to their compatriots would have become almost impossible (see Gal. 2.9). A way had been found to combine a single identity – one Lord, faith and baptism – with the preservation of distinctive identities (Jewish and Gentile).

Maintaining fellowship

These different trajectories of self-understanding inevitably strained relationships among the early Christians. Yet the believers went to extraordinary lengths to maintain their fellowship. When Gentiles started coming to faith in Antioch, for example, the Jerusalem leaders sent Barnabas to guide and encourage the new church – 'and no doubt bring it under the supervision of the Jerusalem community' (Brown and Meier, 1982, p. 33).

The oversight was done with sensitivity. Barnabas appears to have stayed in Jerusalem after the persecution and was trusted by the Twelve (Brown and Meier, 1982, p. 34). But he was also from Cyprus (Acts 4.36) and so shared an affinity with those who were birthing the new church. His name, 'Son of Encouragement', reflected the spirit in which the accountability was exercised – a lesson for inherited churches today. The Antioch church reciprocated with similar generosity. When famine hit Judaea, they sent Barnabas and Paul to Jerusalem with a financial gift (Acts 11.27–30). There was mutual commitment.

This commitment was tested to near breaking point some time after Paul's first missionary journey. On a visit to Antioch, Peter ate freely with the

---

2 This assumes that the apostolic decree was agreed at the same Council and not on a separate occasion, as some scholars believe. For this alternative, see Gooder (2008, p. 19).

Gentile Christians in the city. He then withdrew from this table fellowship under pressure from newly arrived traditionalists from Jerusalem, who were concerned that Peter was not fully observing the Jewish food laws by eating with the Gentiles (Gal. 2.11–3). This withdrawal implied that the Gentile Christians should be treated as a separate group. They were being pressured to become more Jewish (Dunn, 2009, p. 474). For Paul an issue of identity was at stake. Were Gentile believers to be regarded as distinct from the Jews, or were they members of the one body of Christ, belonging on equal terms?

Two views of the Antioch dispute

The traditional sequence
- Antioch dispute
- *Galatians* letter
- Council of Jerusalem

The sequence as understood by many recent scholars
- Council of Jerusalem
- Antioch dispute
- *Galatians* letter

The episode has been reconstructed in different ways. The traditional view is that it (and the letter to the Galatians) happened *before* the Council of Jerusalem in Acts 15, which is why Paul does not appeal to the apostolic decree in his letter (Schnabel, 2008, pp. 51–6). Indeed, it may have been this dispute that helped precipitate the Council (Acts 15.1–2). On this view, the place of Gentile converts within the Christian community was settled at Jerusalem, with Paul's argument prevailing.

The 'mixed economy', if you like, held together through a process of shared discernment in which both sides in the dispute spoke openly and listened to each other (Acts 15.5, 12), stories were told and interpreted in the light of Scripture (vv. 7–18), the Spirit was seen to be involved (v. 28), and a solution was reached that gave something to both parties. Gentiles were not required to be circumcised, but were to observe some of the Jewish eating practices (v. 20).

The counter view is that the Antioch incident (and the Galatian letter) occurred *after* the Jerusalem Council. In Galatians 2.1–10 Paul describes a meeting in Jerusalem, which Dunn and others assume refers to the Acts 15 Council, and then describes the dispute in Antioch. This is taken to be the sequence in which the events took place (Dunn, 2009, p. 470). Presumably, the Gentile believers in Antioch were observing the apostolic decree, and the Jews from Jerusalem wanted them to go further and obey all the Jewish food requirements.

Rather than Peter backing down and Paul prevailing in his argument as traditionally assumed, probably most New Testament scholars today believe that the Antioch church sided with Peter (Dunn, 2009, p. 491, n. 312). This view rests on Paul's failure to tell us he prevailed. When he won the day at the earlier meeting in Jerusalem, he says so (Gal. 2.6–10). If he had been equally successful at Antioch, why did he not say that Peter, Barnabas and the others agreed with him? This would have greatly strengthened his argument to the Galatians.[3] Instead of Paul persuading the others, it seems that there was a serious breach.

If we take this view, the succeeding story of the 'mixed economy' becomes remarkable. In an astonishing act of magnanimity, Paul after a while suggested to Barnabas, who had sided with Peter, that they go together to visit the churches they had founded (Acts 15.36). Paul must have felt let down by Barnabas and perhaps Barnabas thought that Paul had been unreasonable, yet they were still ready to work together. The partnership broke down because Barnabas wanted to take John Mark, but Paul was concerned about his reliability – he had deserted them on their previous missionary journey (Acts 15.37–9).

Nevertheless, Paul continued his missionary work. Assuming Luke's chronology, after a period he returned to the Antioch church (Acts 18.22–3), even though – due to the outcome of the earlier dispute – he was unable to identify with its Peter-leaning ethos (Murphy-O'Connor, 2002, p. 170). He then established a second base for mission at Ephesus (Acts 19.9–10).

It seems that the two sides in the Antioch dispute permitted some widening of the distance between them. Paul went to the Gentiles and Peter to the Jews (Gal. 2.8),[4] each following the Spirit within their mission spheres. Yet both sides maintained good relationships. When famine hit Judaea, Paul organized a financial gift from his new congregations to the Jerusalem church (1 Cor. 16.1–4). Then he 'tore himself away' from his missionary work (Acts 21.1) to give an account of his activities to the leaders in Jerusalem.[5] The brothers

---

3 For these and other reasons for thinking that Paul 'lost', see Dunn (2009, pp. 489–94). For a different reconstruction of events, but reaching the same conclusion that Paul 'lost', see Hill (1992, pp. 126–47).

4 Paul's second missionary journey was at his initiative (Acts 15.36) rather than, as with the first, at the initiative of the Antioch church, and – again unlike the first journey – there is no sign that he was commissioned by the church. He appears to have been operating on a more independent basis.

5 Unless otherwise indicated, all quotations from Scripture in this and the other chapters are taken from the New International Version, East Brunswick, NJ: International Bible Society, 1978.

there received him warmly, the elders rejoiced in the fruits of his labour and Paul agreed to the elders' request to demonstrate, as a Jew, his willingness to observe the Jewish laws (Acts 21.17–26). Despite their differences, both sides of the Antioch debate worked hard to maintain fellowship.

For reflection

Just as the admission of Gentiles without circumcision challenged more conservative Jewish believers, some Christians today feel that new contextual churches are challenging their church identities. Yet for all its strains, the Jewish–Gentile 'mixed economy' survived by allowing space for two different notions of Christian identity to exist side by side – one with a Jewish and the other with a Gentile flavour. The two sides allowed diversity and gave priority to preserving magnanimous relationships. Ultimately, when identity-charged practices diverged, what held the believers together – through the Spirit – was their determination to relate well at a personal level.

How far does this provide a blueprint for today's 'mixed economy'? It certainly illustrates how different traditions within the church can – and should – maintain fellowship. But does this mean that new and existing types of church must develop relationships within the current denominational structures? While maintaining fellowship has to take some structural form, are those who sit light to the denominations right to question whether fellowship must assume today's institutions?

Paul's use of teams

The literature on entrepreneurs contains calls for less focus on the 'heroic' entrepreneur and more on entrepreneurial *teams* (Cooney, 2005, pp. 226–7). Might this apply also to pioneers of church? Paul's experience is highly suggestive. He was far more than a 'serial pioneer' – founding one church after another: he also mobilized other pioneers, and this was one of the keys to the outstanding fruitfulness of his missionary work.

From mission team to centre mission

Paul followed the pattern of Jesus, who both assembled a team of disciples and sent them to announce the kingdom in pairs (Luke 10.1). He had a strong sense of being part of a team. 'I planted the seed, Apollos watered it, but God made it grow' (1 Cor. 3.6). 'For we are God's fellow workers' (1 Cor. 3.9). He saw himself as collaborating with others both to initiate church and build it up into a 'temple', whose holy living made it a fit place for God's presence (Barton, 2003, pp. 37–8).

On Paul's so-called 'first' missionary journey,[6] he and Barnabas were commissioned as a pair, but they quickly brought in John Mark as a helper (Acts 13.5). It seems that they preferred to work as a three. When they acted as a pair in Galatia, it was because Mark had left them rather than out of choice (Acts 13.13). On his second journey, Paul started with Silas but soon added Timothy (Acts 16.1–2). Being half Greek, Timothy came from a similar background to some of the people Paul was seeking to reach and strengthened the team's ethnic mix (Hopkins, 1988, p. 12). Later, as Paul's teams grew in size they became more culturally diverse, which must have further helped them to relate to the diversity of people they encountered (Acts 20.4).

Members joining or leaving the team frequently did so in pairs – Silas and Timothy in Acts 18.5, Timothy and Erastus in Acts 19.22 and presumably Paul and Luke in Acts 20.6 (Hopkins, 1988, p. 12). This highlights again how teams were central to Paul's approach.

Where possible, Paul seems to have preached the gospel while others on the team did the work of catechesis (Acts 18.5; 1 Cor. 1.14–17). Is this why Luke, on the second and third journeys, became a valued member? Was he perhaps collecting stories about Jesus, which he passed on to the new converts and eventually became his Gospel?[7] Paul's teams expanded as his work matured. On his third journey, he was accompanied by at least eight people for a period.[8] Larger teams enabled Paul to keep breaking new ground while still supporting churches recently established. When disputes threatened the church at Corinth, for example, Paul sent Timothy to help resolve the situation (1 Cor. 4.17).

His teams were largely self-funding – Paul was keen not to depend financially on the people he sought to reach (1 Thess. 2.9). On his first journey, Paul stayed scarcely long enough in one place to get established in his leather-working trade, so it may be that he drew on funds from his wealthy background or that he and Barnabas were supported by the Christians at Antioch and Cyprus.[9] On his second journey, however, he found work in Corinth (Acts 18.3) and later in Ephesus. In Acts 20.34 Paul reminds the Ephesian elders that his paid work helped to support not only himself, but his companions. At times his fellow workers supported him (2 Cor. 11.9). Resources were pooled within the team.

---

6 Schnabel describes additional journeys to Arabia and Syria/Cilicia between Paul's conversion and joining Barnabas at Antioch (Schnabel, 2008, pp. 60–71).

7 I am grateful to Peter Walker for this suggestion.

8 Acts 20.4–5. To the seven names listed in verse 4 must be added Luke, referred to as 'us' in verse 5.

9 For the high social status of Paul, see for example Schnabel (2008, p. 43).

Being financially self-sufficient had many attractions. It modelled sacrificial support for others (Acts 20.35), the workplace almost certainly contained evangelistic opportunities[10] and mission was not held up through lack of funds. Though Paul also received financial gifts from some of his new churches (for example Phil. 4.14–8), it is striking that for much of the time the extraordinary fruitfulness of his ministry depended on activity largely in his spare time (though he might not recognize the language).

The expansion of Paul's teams as his work progressed was a significant strategic development. They drew on 'centre missions' – young congregations, equal in status, networked with each other in major cities, such as Ephesus, and which then became the bases for mission (Gehring, 2004, pp. 180–2). These bases sent workers to help Paul and his permanent colleagues for a limited time. Temporary workers ranged from householders like Stephanas to the slave, Onesimus, from the house of Philemon. Nearly a fifth were women (Schnabel, 2008, p. 251). Here was a very different approach to mission than the centrally organized team sent out from Antioch, travelling from place to place. Co-workers came and went from a variety of congregations, which often acted on their own initiative (for example Acts 18.27).

Like Ephesus, where a missional centre reached out to its hinterland, congregations increasingly engaged in evangelism. First Corinthians 9.1–2 implies that a number of apostles – church founders – emerged (see Eph. 4.11). Gifts of the Spirit to the church included evangelists (Eph. 4.11) and the witness of individual Christians was assumed to be desirable (1 Cor. 7.16; Titus 2.10; 1 Peter 3.1–2). Howard Marshall concludes:

> The strong evidence of Acts is that local congregations expanded and grew through the efforts of their members; the story of the Hellenists who fled from Jerusalem and the growth of the church at Antioch is representative of what must have happened more widely. (Marshall, 2000, p. 263)

In a remarkably short time, Paul's outreach had evolved from mission team to centre mission, based on a growing number of reproducing congregations. At the heart of centre mission was Paul's team, involving a complex web of relationships in which over 50 people made various contributions (Dunn, 2009, pp. 566–71). As Dunn notes, Paul must have been a most accomplished leader who inspired personal loyalty and commitment (Dunn, 2009, p. 572).

---

10 Hock (2007, p. 33) suggests that Paul may well have engaged in spiritual conversations during his leather-work.

Keys to effective teamwork

We know little about the day-to-day life of Paul's teams, but from scattered hints we can detect some practices that made his teams effective. First, Paul took great care over selection. In the dispute about John Mark he was willing to break with Barnabas, with whom he had worked for a long time, to find a companion he could trust. Paul preferred to lose a team (and wait for the right one) than to proceed with the wrong team – a lesson perhaps for church founders today.

Second, if trust was a priority, so were forgiveness and reconciliation. Eventually the relationship between Paul and Mark was put right. Paul later described Mark as being helpful to him in his ministry and sent him to Colossae as his representative (2 Tim. 4.11; Col. 4.10). First Corinthians 9.6 may hint at reconciliation with Barnabas as well. Breakdown in relationships – not untypical in teams – was followed by restoration. Paul urged members of his new congregations to be reconciled with each other (for example Rom. 12.16–19) – and he expected the same of himself and his colleagues.

Third, decision-making was shared. If we take a traditional view of its authorship, the instructions in 1 Thessalonians came from Paul, Silas and Timothy together. Dunn quotes Murphy-O'Connor's calculation that 74 per cent of 2 Corinthians 1–9 is written in the first person plural and only 26 per cent in the first person singular, which suggests that Timothy played an important role in composing these chapters (Dunn, 2009, p. 593, n. 340). Graham Cray notes how often Paul uses 'we' or 'our' when challenging the Corinthian church (2 Cor. 10.3–6; 12.19; 13.4–9). These challenges must have come after consulting others (Cray, 2010a, p. 15).

Fourth, team members shared their lives. They put their earnings into a common purse. Paul's theology of sharing spiritual gifts within the body was presumably forged partly from the experiences of his teams. Hints of this are in Acts 16.6–10, where Paul and his companions are kept by the Spirit from preaching the word in Asia and Paul is called to Macedonia through a vision. Paul likely shared this vision with his team, who exercised their spiritual gifts in a process of discernment.

Fifth, Paul encouraged supportive delegation. He sent Timothy, for instance, as his representative to the Corinthian church and later to Ephesus (1 Cor. 4.17; 1 Tim. 1.3), and he encouraged team members to take the initiative (2 Cor. 8.17). At the same time, he ensured his co-workers were properly supported. The 'pastoral epistles', assuming they were written by Paul, are brimming with instructions and (in 2 Timothy) encouragement. They were the means of mentoring from a distance, as Timothy and Titus 'learnt on the job'. Jesus had invested heavily in training his disciples, and Paul was a trainer too.

Finally, Paul's extended network of associate workers became like a 'holy internet', exchanging news, advice, encouragement and, in particular, good practice (Thompson, 1998, p. 59). The Macedonians' generosity became a prod to the Corinthians (2 Cor. 8.1–7). The Thessalonians' response to the gospel became a model to all the believers in Macedonia and Achaia (1 Thess. 1.6–7). Paul boasted to other churches about the Thessalonians' perseverance and faith in the face of persecution (2 Thess. 1.4).

For reflection

Ralph Winter (1973) argued that throughout history the church has contained 'modalities', believers gathered as congregations, and 'sodalities' that have a specific focus, such as a mission agency or a local men's club. The Spirit has tended to use sodalities to renew the church and increase its involvement in the world, such as the monastic movement and the Wesley revival.

According to Winter, Paul's churches were a prototype of subsequent modalities, while his mission teams were prototypes of sodalities. Paul pioneered a modality/sodality structure that has been of enduring importance in the life of the church. Some people are seeing new contextual churches, and some of the networks that are starting to link them together, as forms of sodality for today.

However, would Paul have drawn this distinction? Would he have been happy with a description that focused mission on sodalities, as if modalities (or congregations) did not have mission obligations as well? Did not his evangelizing congregations blur the distinction between modalities and sodalities? Should we use language that drives a wedge between those parts of the church that are missional and those that are not?

Paul's methods

In Hebrews 2.10 and 12.2 Jesus is described as a 'pioneer'. The word equally means 'trailblazer'.[11] The idea of pioneering is also present in 6.20, where Jesus is described as the one 'who went before us'. Acts can be read as the pioneer Jesus enabling Paul, through the Spirit, to be a trailblazer too. As well as relying on teams, how did Paul go about this task?

Paul's strategy

Paul was strategic, as Dunn highlights. First, Paul had 'a commitment to pioneer evangelism, to pursue his mission only in virgin territory' (Dunn,

---

11 Additionally, it can also be translated as author, captain, founder or originator.

2009, p. 544). In 1 Corinthians 3.6, for example, Paul sees himself as having started something new while Apollos continued the work.

Second, he was determined to take the gospel to Jews first and then to the Gentiles. This was primarily 'a strategic and principled concern' that the gospel was the climax of God's saving purpose for Israel and through Israel (Dunn, 2009, p. 547). But it also made practical sense. In the synagogues were Jews and 'God-fearing' Gentiles, who were attracted to the monotheistic faith of Israel but had not converted to Judaism. These God-fearers were likely to be more open to the gospel than their polytheistic compatriots, and – along with the Jews – had some knowledge of the Hebrew Scriptures on which Paul and his team could build. Jews and God-fearers were well placed to form churches that would draw in Gentiles from outside the synagogues.

Third, Paul had a 'grand strategy to fulfil the mission of Israel to the nations and to fulfil Israel's eschatological hopes in regard to the nations' (Dunn, 2009, p. 543). In his mission, Paul saw himself as acting on behalf of Israel. Dunn follows Rainer Riesner, who argues that the rough direction of Paul's mission matched the principal direction of travel envisaged in the list of nations in Isaiah 66.19. As one influence on him, Paul seems to have viewed his mission as a fulfilment of Isaiah 66. He was going out to the nations at the end times. The financial gift from his churches for Jerusalem may have symbolized the nations gathering at Zion (Riesner, 1998, pp. 245–56).

Was this a view that Paul had from the start of his mission from Antioch, or did it emerge gradually in the light of his experience? If the latter, Paul can perhaps be seen as a practical theologian (in today's language), learning from experience as he reflected theologically upon it.[12]

Paul's fourth strategic priority was to breed in his new churches 'a communal life lived in the light of the coming kingdom – deeply, but not openly, subversive' (Dunn, 2009, p. 555). Not least, the brotherly and sisterly relationships of equality encouraged by Paul contrasted starkly with the hierarchical patron–client structures of the day.

Within this framework of principles, Paul was pragmatic and opportunist like many church founders today. As Schnabel notes, he did not have a rigid plan or method. Led by the Spirit, Paul responded when doors opened. He preached in synagogues, market places, lecture halls, workshops and private homes as the opportunity arose (Schnabel, 2008, pp. 304–6).

Evangelism was much more than preaching

Churchgoers often think of Paul as an evangelist who addressed public meetings. Although he did this (in synagogues and in a sense at Athens), there was much more to his evangelism than that. When he first arrived

---

12 I am grateful to Professor John Drane for pointing this out.

in a city, he familiarized himself with the local culture and seems to have become an acute commentator upon it. The obvious example was Athens, where Paul described how he 'walked around and looked carefully at [their] objects of worship' (Acts 17.23). Living in people's homes and working as in Corinth would have given him plenty of opportunities to listen to people and get to know their ways of life.

Paul seems to have spent considerable time sharing the gospel 'from house to house' (Acts 20.20). To do this he had to be invited, which meant building relationships; he hung out with people. This included developing relationships with 'persons of peace' – people who play a key role in mission by putting the carrier of the gospel in touch with their networks (Luke 10.6). Paul's breakthrough at Philippi begun by meeting with a group of women who had assembled for prayer, in particular Lydia 'who was a worshipper of God' and allowed Paul to use her home as a base (Acts 16.13–5). At Corinth Aquila and Priscilla, Jews who were leather-workers like Paul, provided a bridgehead (Acts 18.1–4). In Ephesus he searched out some 'disciples' and baptized them (Acts 19.1–7).

At Corinth Paul broke his rule of not baptizing people and baptized Crispus, Gaius and the household of Stephanas. This may have been because Paul knew they were prominent people 'who would sponsor his gospel to their dependents . . .' (Osiek and MacDonald with Tulloch, 2006, p. 212). If true, they were classic examples of persons of peace.

The relationships he formed appear to have been strengthened through acts of loving service. 'We loved you so much . . .' Paul reminds the Thessalonians (1 Thess. 2.8). Paul's leather-working trade required tools that could easily be carried with him. This made him 'available for any little job that came along. He could repair the leather sandals, belts, gourds and cloaks of those who walked the roads with him' (Murphy-O'Connor, 2002, p. 194). It is easy to imagine Paul repairing leather goods around the house in return for hospitality (Osiek and MacDonald with Tulloch, 2006, p. 11). Did this help to make him a welcome dinner guest?

Paul recounted how he and his colleagues 'worked night and day' so as not to be a burden on anyone. He described their work as 'toil and hardship' – an experience that would be familiar to many church founders (1 Thess. 2.9; 2 Thess. 3.8). Unlike contemporary orators, Paul did not use rhetorical and other devices to win a fee-paying following (Walton, 2011, pp. 220–33), but laboured sacrificially to demonstrate a life of service and model the gospel (Acts 20.35). He was willing to share what he earned (Philemon 18).

Paul's miraculous healings and exorcisms expressed love and service more dramatically (for example Acts 14.3, 8). Did he heal the sick through the Spirit as he visited people in their homes? This is suggested by the episode on Malta, where as part of his interaction with the household Paul healed the chief official's father. After this, many others were brought to Paul for healing (Acts 28.7–9; cf 19.11–2).

Forming community seems to have been another part of Paul's evangelism. Often it must have started in the homes of people he stayed with. While he lived and worked with Aquila and Priscilla, for instance, one can picture a nucleus of enquirers forming. As individuals returned week by week perhaps, a sense of community would have developed till eventually the 'workshop became a house church' of between 10 and 15 members (Murphy-O'Connor, 2002, p. 195).

Presumably a similar process occurred in the homes Paul visited. It was customary for the wealthy to invite to dinner not only friends of equal standing, but also their dependent clients who had lower social status (Bradshaw, 2009, p. 21) As Paul shared the gospel in such gatherings, it is likely that people who were interested returned on subsequent evenings and over time a sense of community formed. Paul reminds the Thessalonians that he and his fellow workers shared their lives with them (1 Thess. 2.8). In settings where believers and not-yet believers met together (1 Cor. 14.23–5), this sharing of lives must have been part of the process of coming to faith.

Certainly, personal testimony was an ingredient in Paul's evangelism (Acts 22.1–21), and in his letters he repeatedly wrote about the misguided direction of his earlier life and his journey into holiness. As he shared from personal experience, it would have been natural for some of his hearers to share their experiences, laying foundations for the participative worship that developed (1 Cor. 14.26) and for the strong fellowship that existed among the new Christians.

People often needed time to explore Paul's claims. At Pisidian Antioch, those who heard Paul and Barnabas address the synagogue invited them to speak further the next Sabbath (Acts 13.42). Later the Beroeans received the message enthusiastically, but also examined the Scriptures daily to see if what Paul said was true (Acts 17.11). Because people checked out what Paul was claiming, the conversion of entire households at once – in the case of Lydia for instance (Acts 16.15) – was by no means the norm. Several New Testament texts, such as 1 Cor. 7.12–16 and 1 Peter 3.1, suggest that conversion could be more individualized (Osiek and MacDonald with Tulloch, 2006, p. 158). Like today, journeys to faith varied.

Once individuals had made the journey, church took shape in people's homes, which were centres of family, work,[13] everyday leisure (in so far as people had any), and family and friendship networks. 'The Christian churches were probably the only communion in antiquity that had no special place of worship but rather came together in the places of daily life, the private homes' (Becker, 1993, p. 251). Some converts went on to start further congregations, as in the case of Priscilla and Aquila, who were

---

13 Workers might reside on their employer's property, or craftsmen might rent workplaces which were part of their homes (Gehring, 2004, p. 135).

patrons of house churches in three different cities (Osiek and MacDonald with Tulloch, 2006, p. 32).

It would be a mistake to see listening, loving and serving, building community, exploring, church taking shape and then starting another church as a neat linear sequence. Sometimes it may have been, but often the processes must have overlapped, occurred in a different order or in some cases not happened at all. Not everyone, for example, took time in weighing up matters before becoming a believer (for example Acts 13.12). As now, people came to faith in different ways.

For reflection

Paul's apparent practices of listening (including to 'persons of peace'), loving and serving, building community, helping people to explore the possibility of faith and forming new gatherings in the heart of life are all echoed in Chapter 11, which discusses the birthing of contextual church among people with little or no Christian background. Did Paul stumble upon a series of practices that make sense whenever churches are founded in pioneer contexts?

Culture-specific churches?

Were Paul's new churches built around homogeneous people groups – that is, 'a section of society in which all the members have some characteristic in common'? (McGavran, 1980, p. 95) Schnabel believes not. Paul was committed to a church in which all social divisions were overcome. He did not establish separate local congregations for Jews and Gentiles, slaves and freemen, the rich and the poor. He wanted all to be one in Christ Jesus – Galatians 3.28 (Schnabel, 2008, pp. 404–13).

Jerusalem and Antioch

However, a close reading of the New Testament suggests that homogeneous congregations were very much part of the picture. Gehring argues that Acts 2.46 portrays the Jerusalem church both coming together as the whole church in the temple and meeting as small house churches in private homes (Gehring, 2004, p. 83). These house churches were scattered round the city and would have drawn in people from different networks. Families sharing the same courtyard may have broken bread together, for example (Finger, 2007, p. 238).

Jewish synagogues often met in people's homes. The Talmudic assertion that there were 390 synagogues in first-century Jerusalem may have been an exaggeration, but there were certainly a considerable number meeting in various parts of the city and catering for worshippers from different social backgrounds.

> Acts 6.9 may be referring to no less than five synagogues: one for the freedmen, one for the people from Cyrenaica, one for Alexandrians, one for those from Cilicia and one for those from Asia. (Fiensy, 1995, p. 233)

If the first Jewish churches were influenced by the synagogues, which were the closest model to hand, and followed a similar pattern of attracting people from a specific social group, they would indeed have been homogeneous units. Yet importantly, these units also came together 'every day' in the temple courts. Here the different social groupings would have intermingled and the unity of believers been expressed.

The situation in Antioch appears to have been much the same. Gehring believes that Galatians 2.11–4 assumes that a number of house churches existed in Antioch. Peter was accustomed to eating with the Gentiles. When challenged by the Jewish believers from Jerusalem, he began to have table fellowship exclusively with the Jews, a practice made possible by Christians gathering in different homes (Gehring, 2004, p. 112).

Antioch was the third or fourth largest city in the empire and had 18 ethnic quarters (Drane, 2011, p. 160). Jewish synagogues were separated according to ethnic background (Gehring, 2004, p. 113), and it is reasonable to assume that this was true also of the house churches. Ethnic and other social groupings would have lived in different parts of the city, and it would have been natural – if only for convenience – for each house gathering to have drawn in people from its vicinity and from its family and friendship networks.

Gehring does not argue this last point. Indeed, he believes that such separation was improbable because it would have created social barriers in a church that, from its beginning, had been anxious to pull barriers down. Yet as he himself points out (p. 113), the confrontation between Paul and Peter took place in front of the whole Antiochene church – 'in front of them all' (Gal. 2.14). This suggests that, as in Jerusalem, all the house churches gathered together from time to time. It was in this setting that people from different ethnic and social contexts most likely met together and expressed their oneness in Christ.

Rome

In Rome there was a similar pattern of scattered house-based churches. Robert Jewett has suggested that the bulk of the early Christians lived in the slum districts of Rome. Two-thirds of the names in Romans 16 indicate a

Greek rather than Latin background, which suggests they were immigrants. Of the 13 names about which something certain can be said, nine have slave origin (Jewett, 2007, p. 63).

Christians in slum neighbourhoods would have met either in one of the workshop areas on the ground floor of a tenement block, or in a temporarily cleared space on one of the upper floors. The rooms on these floors were too small to accommodate a church, but – according to Jewett – the partitions between rooms were flimsy. Neighbouring families, each occupying one tiny room, may have temporarily removed the partitions to create a large enough space to hold perhaps 10 to 20 people,[14] who would typically have lived nearby and whose social and ethnic backgrounds would have had much in common.

In the wealthier areas of Rome were luxury apartments and for the very rich entire houses. Some churches met in these parts of the city (Jewett, 2007, p. 64–5), drawing on different networks than the tenement churches. In addition to slaves and family members, the head of the household would have had a number of clients, reflecting the ubiquitous system of patronage. Some of these almost certainly would have attended the church.

There is no evidence that the house churches periodically met together, but they were clearly well networked. Paul could address his letter 'to all in Rome' (Rom. 1.7), which implies that the letter was passed from gathering to gathering. If they were not already meeting together, did Paul encourage them to do so when he arrived in Rome?

Paul's churches

Certainly the churches that he founded continued the Jerusalem and Antioch practice of both meeting separately in homes and meeting together. 'The household was much broader than the family in modern Western societies, including not only immediate relatives but also slaves, freemen, hired workers, and sometimes tenants and partners in trade or craft' (Meeks, 2003, pp. 75–6). Patronage networks were important, too. New house churches, therefore, were 'inserted into or superimposed upon an existing network of relationships' (p. 76). In other words, they were largely comprised of homogeneous people groups, formed around hierarchical ties.

It is clear from 1 Corinthians 14.23, where Paul writes of the 'whole church' coming together, that these separate house gatherings periodically met as a single group, probably in a large home such as the one apparently

---

14 Jewett (2007, pp. 54, 64–5). The idea that families could have removed partitions is contested by Gehring (2004, pp. 149–50), though he accepts that churches could have met in a workshop.

owned by Gaius. In the concluding section of Romans, most probably written in Corinth, Paul sends greeting from Gaius, whose hospitality 'the whole church here' enjoyed (Romans 16.23). 'In the Greek Old Testament this expression consistently refers to an assembly of all Israel; thus it must be the totality of Christians in Corinth which is in view' (Banks, 1980, p. 38).

The meeting of the Ephesian elders in Acts 20 is suggestive. Luke says that 'Paul sent to Ephesus for the elders of the church' (v. 17). The reference is to the church as a single unit, a thought echoed in verse 28, where Paul urged the elders to keep watch over 'the flock', again singular. Evidently the house churches in Ephesus, which presumably emerged from the homes Paul visited in verse 20, had a sense of themselves as a citywide entity, a self-perception that would be natural if they periodically met together. The elders summoned by Paul may well have been the leaders of house churches who were used to assembling together (perhaps to plan the wider meetings).

Gehring maintains that recent scholars tend to agree that the early Christians gathered in two church forms: the house church and the whole church at any given location. While these two forms of church were geographically fixed, he suggests that the experience of individual gatherings could have been quite fluid. Congregations may often have lived in an in-between sphere hard to define (Gehring, 2004, p. 173).

New Testament believers appears to have found a way of combining homogeneous people groups with the potential to bridge social divides. This both/and approach held together sameness and diversity, small meetings and larger ones, and intimacy plus exposure to different ideas. Achieving this was far from easy, as the divisions at Corinth demonstrated, but Paul saw it as a priority.

For reflection

Some might say that Paul's house churches were not strictly homogeneous groups. They contained for example slaves and heads of households, who were to relate to each other not in hierarchical ways but as 'brothers and sisters'. Each house church modelled diversity. The only thing that members had in common was that they lived in the same area. Others might question the assumption that members drawn from the same area are not a homogeneous group. Don't geographical divides often reflect social ones?

Is this a question about what counts as a homogeneous group? Or is it about whether, theologically, some forms of homogeneity are to be preferred than others?

Sustainable leadership

A key issue for church-starts is their sustainability, and central to this is encouraging local leadership. Does Paul's practice contain lessons for how quickly and how best this can be done?

Delegation with support

Passing on leadership is a central theme in the writings of Roland Allen. An early twentieth-century missionary, Allen carried on a sustained polemic against the missionary methods of his day and contrasted them with Paul's. His discussion sufficiently reflects the New Testament for Schnabel to commend him (Schnabel, 2008, p. 13).

Unlike missionaries who remained for several generations, Allen maintained, Paul never stayed in one place for more than a few months, or at the most two years. Once a congregation had been established, he selected leaders from its midst and left the fledgling church in their hands. For example in Acts 14.21–3, having been driven out by their opponents, Paul and Barnabas returned to Lystra and Iconium. Opposition seems to have waned sufficiently for them to stay for a while 'strengthening' and 'encouraging' the disciples. But they did not remain for long. They appointed elders, even though the believers had been Christians for only a few months, and left.

The direction to Timothy – to entrust what he had learnt to reliable people who will also be qualified to teach others (2 Tim. 2.2) – clearly reflects a Pauline principle of growing leaders who would instruct other people. The heart of Allen's understanding is that the church lives by faith in Christ, whose gifts – including 'the gift-bearing missionary Spirit' – are sufficient for its life (Paton, 1968, p. 26, 29).

Paul trusted the Spirit to supply whatever an infant church required, and put in place only the bare essentials before moving on: a 'tradition or elementary Creed, the Sacraments of Baptism and the Holy Communion, Orders [that is leadership], and the Holy Scriptures' (Allen, 2006, p. 107). Paul made sure that new leaders had support after he left. 'Between the Apostle and the elders in every Church were the young men whose names crop up towards the end of the epistles – Timothy, Titus, Epaphras, Luke, Onesimus, Silvanas, and all the rest of them.' They made available to the local church resources it did not have (Paton, 1968, p. 37).

Pressing forward into new territory, Paul kept a watchful eye on what happened in his new churches and exercised authority through his co-workers. Writing of 1 Corinthians 9.1–2, Dunn notes that the authority of the 'apostle' was very much tied in to the apostle's role in establishing a church: Paul was not an apostle to others because he had not founded their churches, but he was to the Corinthians because through the Spirit he had brought their church to birth (Dunn, 2009, p. 539).

According to Allen, the early church grew spontaneously by organizing little groups as individuals were converted, handing on to them a simple organization that connected them to the wider church, equipping them with all the spiritual power and authority necessary for their corporate existence and authorizing them to repeat the process (Allen, 1997, p. 143). Speedy delegation was accompanied by continuing support.

This picture needs qualifying, however. There were times when Paul was forced to leave his new churches more quickly than he wanted. In 1 Thessalonians 2.17–9 he wrote of 'making every effort' to see the Thessalonians, having been 'torn away from' them. He was anxious enough to send Timothy to them (3.1–3), and was relieved when Timothy brought back good news (v. 6). When he had the chance, Paul stayed longer in Corinth (for 18 months – Acts 18.11) and in Ephesus (for at least two years – Acts 18.10). Yet even these 'long' periods are remarkably short compared to the five years or more that many founders stay with their gatherings today.

Handing over leadership quickly must have been helped by the composition of Paul's churches. Dunn notes that Paul's letters were addressed largely to Gentile audiences, yet are peppered with quotations and allusions to the Hebrew Bible. Paul must have assumed that these references would have resonated 'in the echo-chamber of a much wider knowledge of Israel's Scriptures' (Dunn, 2009, p. 563). Presumably, the gospel could take root quickly partly because Jews and God-fearing Gentiles knew their Hebrew Bible.

Church took its shape from future leaders

It is also striking how the New Testament church was sculpted round the most pervasive form of leadership in ancient society – leadership within the household. Whereas synagogues moved out of the home as the congregation grew, there is no sign of this happening in the primitive church.[15] Church gatherings remained firmly house bound. Was this partly because finding leaders for new congregations became relatively simple when believers gathered round an existing household, which had leadership already in place?

Gehring, supported by Dunn (2009, p. 571), argues that Paul deliberately concentrated on more wealthy people when he entered a town because they were potential leaders and their homes would provide a base of operations. He did this with Lydia at Philippi for instance (Acts 16.13–5), and also at Corinth. Remarkably, even though most of the Corinthian Christians had comparatively low social origins (1 Cor. 1.26), Paul broke his rule of not baptizing converts only in the case of three households – and these were from the upper economic strata (vv. 14–7).

---

15 Catto (2007, p. 104) notes that purpose-built synagogues were constructed when communities were large and wealthy enough, and had sufficient political leverage to get permission to build.

'The church in the house came with its leadership so to speak "built in"' (Gehring, 2004, pp. 185–7; 194). Among the more wealthy, household heads were educated, had experience of teaching their own families and had financial responsibility for the home. They were well equipped, therefore, to lead a gathering based on their households and to share in the leadership of the church city wide.

Most likely, leadership tended to take the form of 'love-patriarchalism'. The social order was retained, but mutual love based on the gospel was fostered by household heads serving as leaders of the congregations in their homes. In poorer areas, where there was no patron to function as a leader, leadership may have been collective rather than hierarchical (Jewett, 2007, pp. 65–6). Though the author had no connection to Paul, might such a context be in mind in Matthew 18.17, where disputes between brethren are to be taken to the church rather than to church leaders?

For reflection

Knowledge of the Old Testament meant that Paul's Jewish and 'God-fearing' converts had good foundations for Christian faith, which made it easier for Paul to move on rapidly. By contrast in our culture, where increasingly people have little or no knowledge of the Bible, bringing a church to birth is likely to take much longer. Is it realistic to expect church founders to leave anything like as fast as did Paul? .

Paul seems to have founded leadership-shaped churches that took their structure in part from the nature of leadership in their contexts. Might communities that fit the available leadership be crucial in birthing sustainable churches today? If new churches take their shape from the available leadership, what difference would it make? How would this work in poor urban areas where there is often an acute shortage of leadership?

Conclusion

Against the background of a swing in emphasis from 'come' to 'go' mission, Paul strove to maintain good relationships with his fellow apostles and relied on teams. He adopted an 'incarnational' strategy based on being attentive to context, loving and serving, building community, allowing individuals to come to faith at different paces and founding, in the midst of life, churches that were self-reproducing. His churches were culture specific with indigenous forms of leadership.

Paul modelled new contextual church. Yet some of the 'For reflection' boxes warn against making simplistic links between the New Testament and today. Even so, Paul cannot be ignored. By planting churches that started other churches, he modelled church reproduction, which has inspired numerous church planters and much of the church planting literature. To the extent that he is an example to follow, he has set the bar at a challenging height for church founders today.

Further reading

Banks, Robert, *Paul's Idea of Community: The Early House Churches in their Historical Setting*, Exeter: Paternoster, 1980.

Dunn, James D. G., *Beginning from Jerusalem*, Grand Rapids: Eerdmans, 2009.

Gehring, Roger W., *House Church and Mission: The Importance of Household Structures in Early Christianity*, Peabody: Hendrickson, 2004.

Schnabel, Eckhard J., *Paul the Missionary: Realities, Strategies and Methods*, Downers Grove: InterVarsity Press, 2008.

Questions for discussion

- How far can Saint Paul be a guide for today?
- What might we learn about founding new churches from Jesus?
- If you were writing a 'pastoral epistle' to a leader of a new contextual church, what points would you make?

2

Contextual Churches in History

PHILIP HARROLD

The incarnation reminds us that history is essential to Christianity. When the Word became flesh and dwelt among us, history turned in a new direction. In this chapter, we will see how down the centuries the church has translated that divine action into a dazzling array of cultural contexts. As a missionary community the church remembers God's call to be a pilgrim people rooted in the gospel of Jesus Christ. The church is on the move – 'hastening to the ends of the earth to beseech all men to be reconciled to God . . .' (Newbigin, 1953, p. 25).

The history of this movement has defined the church as we know it today, but nonetheless it remains a strange story. Neither the continuities nor the discontinuities should surprise us given what we have already observed about contextual churches in the New Testament. It was there that novelty and innovation mixed with traditional ways of doing things in a process that propelled the church for centuries to come. The unevenness of historical records does not allow us to recognize every aspect of the subsequent church expansion, but looking for missional, contextual, formational and ecclesial features makes the past come alive, as we shall see.

History may not be very good at telling us what to do, but it can stimulate thinking about new possibilities. It is tempting to read the past in order to justify the present or to mould the past into our own perspectives. To avoid this, the chapter will stress both familiarity and strangeness in the long history of new contextual communities. Given that the church is missionary at its heart, it is possible for modern Christians to see a family resemblance in the historic body of Christ, even as it sometimes confounds our expectations. We may then recognize 'a whole immeasurable exchange of gifts, known and unknown' by which we carry on the mission to which we have been called' (Williams, 2005, pp. 25–7).

Recall from the last chapter that in the Book of Acts the mission to Antioch presented the early church with an unprecedented opportunity. The general contours of a new Christian community emerged as the apostles began to acquaint large numbers of non-Jewish people with the gospel. Meanwhile, the Jerusalem church provided leadership drawn from its rich heritage and venerable location. Together, the Jerusalem and Antioch communities comprised a 'mixed economy', existing and new churches in relationship with each other, with Antioch taking the lead in establishing a new mission frontier. The community of believers in Antioch, emerging among the Gentiles, was necessarily contextual and, as a result, the first church founders learned how to do things differently.

This is where our history of new Christian communities will begin. Naturally, we would like to know more about the first mission outpost of the church. How did it reach out? How did it settle into its new surroundings? How did it form people in the image of Christ and make disciples? And how did it imagine itself to be the body of Christ despite its emergent status?

Real presence in Antioch

We can learn a great deal about the new Antioch church from an ancient document known as the *Didache* – or 'The Teaching of the Apostles' – originating, some think, around the years AD 50–70. One of the remarkable actions of these Jewish Christians was intentionally to welcome Gentiles to table fellowship in a house-church setting. This was unheard of in the Mediterranean world, where food and meal-sharing were used to draw strict lines of separation not only between Jews and non-Jews, but between the various class and ethnic divisions in Graeco-Roman society. For Jews, especially, a meal with a Gentile would have been a contaminating experience!

Instead, the Antiochene Christians overcame their fears and prejudices in order to provide hospitality to the strangers in their midst. While ensuring that the food they ate had no connections with idolatry, they sat at table with individuals who had never been circumcised and 'with the people who are righteous and humbled' (*Didache* 3.9).[1] Once the Jerusalem Council gave its authorization, they did what Jesus had often done himself. Quite scandalously, he had associated with some of the most marginal and, yes, *sinful* of people, going so far as to actually dine with them, whether in their homes or in banquet halls.

The Antiochenes knew that sharing a domestic meal with their Gentile neighbours was a personal way of expressing what life was like in the kingdom of God. For their part, the guests would have experienced a family-like atmosphere, with new brothers and sisters in a loving, caring fellowship – perhaps compensating for the loss of family that some had suffered as a result of their conversion from pagan religions.

The *Didache* shows us what it was like to enter into this new way of life. It began with instruction and mentoring in preparation for baptism. That may come as a surprise if we imagine instruction in the modern sense of classroom lectures or book study. Rather this was a time of learning through participation in the daily and weekly patterns of house church

---

1 Quotations from the *Didache* are from O'Loughlin (2010).

life. The apprenticeship terminology of a master-trainer (such as the use of *didaskein* as the verb form for training), the second-person singular address (such as 'my child') and the overall sequence of formative events indicate that an intimate context of one-to-one mentoring preceded wider fellowship in *Agape* meals. In these varied contexts, deep spiritual bonds developed as the newcomers became more fully acquainted with the community (Milavec, 2003, pp. 48–9).

It was often the case in the early house church that the Eucharist was celebrated within the context of the *Agape* meals. We might imagine what it would have been like to have reached the point where the newly baptized were invited to partake of the consecrated bread and wine – with the 'real presence' of the Lord modelled in the fellowship of believers. This was a radically new way to practise the presence of God; nothing quite like this had ever been recorded in the Hebrew Scriptures.[2]

It was an act of hospitality that communicated who Jesus was and what his mission was about at many different levels. There was a sense of gradual initiation in the life of the *Didache* community – a progression of stages and events that led each person into ever deeper and more meaningful experiences of life with God and God's people.[3] One would learn, fairly quickly, that this life was a matter of continued growth in radically new directions, especially in love and trust toward God and neighbour, and in understanding what life was about and where it was headed according to the mission of God. At each point, basic human needs were addressed – the need to eat and drink, most obviously, but also the need for friendship and community.

Here an individual learned the importance of serving others, especially in the preparation of meals and other aspects of hospitality. Each meal that was shared would have been a major communal undertaking, requiring leadership and coordination by deacons/deaconesses. Resources would have to be gathered from members throughout the church membership (not just from the wealthy patrons) and put to the best use.

The community also had to practise *family love*, doing what families do at meal time in a domestic setting. Among the instructions given to each member of the community was that they would 'not turn away from anyone in need but share everything . . . holding back nothing as just your individual property' (*Didache* 4.8). To enter into the atmosphere of this family would have been a profound experience of sharing, acceptance, and participation.

There was also a sense of God's unfolding mission here – what some might call a *realized eschatology* – a sense of what life is like in God's kingdom:

---

2 On the significance of the fellowship meal in the early Christian house church, see Patzia (2001, pp. 216–30).

3 For a detailed study of this pattern, see Milavec (2003).

the gathering of such a mixed assembly, especially at a common table, defied social norms and overcame shameful status, signalling a new way of being together not unlike that anticipated in the eternal banquet with Jesus. In this way, the *Didache* says, 'may your church be gathered together into your kingdom from the very ends of the earth' (9.4).

How had this vibrant community come about? What enabled the early Christians to adjust so quickly to a new culture, a new people? Perhaps the scattered quotations from the prophets that we see in the Book of Acts – the first history book of the church – provide a clue. The newly born church in Antioch was convinced that it was part of an age-old story that was now being fulfilled in a rather strange and marvellous way. It may have heard about the apostle Peter's startling declaration on Solomon's Porch: 'You are the descendants of the prophets and of the covenant that God gave to your ancestors, saying to Abraham, "And in your descendants all the families of the earth shall be blessed"' (Acts 3.25).[4]

Knowing the story was one crucial ingredient in this emerging church, but participating in it was even more significant. In a novel act, the mixed membership of this community re-enacted the story by drinking it in. Gathered at table, the fellowship of believers said the words: 'We give thanks to you, our Father, for the holy vine of David, your servant, which you have made known to us' (*Didache* 9.2). At this point, the common cup of blessing was passed, to be followed by the blessing of a broken loaf of bread, and then thanksgivings and petitions. Among the petitions was a prayer that the Lord would 'remember . . . your church, deliver her from evil, make her complete in your love, and gather her from the four winds into your kingdom you have prepared for her' (*Didache* 10.3).

In effect, a new kind of community had formed by grounding itself in an old story. Listening, loving and serving, and building new relationships were necessary ingredients as Antioch became a new centre of missionary endeavour – moving with the gospel of Jesus Christ in service to God and neighbour.

The word of life from the north to the south of England

Participating in God's story in Jesus Christ continued to be a characteristic feature of Christian communities in the dark and troubled centuries that followed the collapse of Rome. The British Isles were severely impacted by the retreat of Roman authority, leaving Christians isolated and with few resources to endure the social and political instability that followed.

---

4 This and other Bible quotations in this chapter are taken from the *English Standard Version* [*ESV*], Wheaton, IL: Crossway Bibles, 2001.

Saint Patrick worked wonders in Ireland, but it was not until the year 563 that a thriving Christian presence came about in what is now Scotland. An Irish missionary named Columba planted a church on the island of Iona, and for over 30 years it served as a mission outpost to the Pictish tribes. Another Irish monk named Aidan did much the same thing at another 'holy' island, Lindisfarne, in 635, this time serving the Northumbrian and, eventually, Anglo-Saxon populations in northern England.

In both places, incarnational missions were planted in difficult surroundings. It took remarkable leadership, with Aidan described as 'abstemious, ascetic, industrious, fervent, . . . constantly on the move,' and it took remarkable teamwork as well (Moorman, 1980, pp. 18–9). As his monks ventured south into Anglo-Saxon territory, they encountered a culture marked by violent tribal clashes, but also intense loyalty within the tribes and warrior bands. The nomadic people had a reputation for being ferocious, but they also valued hospitality and friendship. As the Celts began to make themselves at home, they learned how relationships were made in these new surroundings, and in the midst of this adjustment the 'Celtic Way of Evangelism' was born (Hunter III, 2000).[5]

We must be careful not to overstate the uniqueness of the Celtic mission. It drew from a spirituality deeply rooted in the Scriptures, in the Desert Fathers and in the forms of organized community life – monasticism – popping-up all over Europe. Still, some distinctive features emerged in the Celtic church that reflected its situation. One important novelty was the highly mobile apostolic team that could pack up and move out, much as the nomadic people it sought to reach with the gospel. Eventually the Celtic Christians settled down like their sponsoring communities at Lindesfarne or Iona, but missionary monks continued to venture forth on long journeys into uncharted territory – travelling light with flexible itineraries.

When they crossed tribal boundaries or moved from one clan to the next, they set up camp close to the local centre of community life, where the chieftains and their inner circles were gathered. The proximity allowed these missionary monks to establish relationships with local leaders, offer them hospitality and render services like health care. They were great fraternizers! This could be a dangerous operation at times, but the monks were effective at winning over their neighbours. Their intentions were clear; the alternative way of life they offered – free of aggression, suspicion, self-interest – was already communicating the love and generosity of their Lord.

One of the most tangible legacies of Celtic adaptability was the vast network of great stone crosses that marked the places where the old was made new, where a people was restored and made whole by the powerful symbol of Christ's victory over death. No aspect of life or creation was

---

5 See also Bradley (2000).

beyond the reach of Christ's redemptive rule. Jesus was the Lord of life, and the Celts let everyone know this in the shape and story of the cross (De Waal, 1997; Sheldrake, 1996).

Too much has been made of the differences between Celtic and later Roman models of evangelization. Certainly after the arrival of Augustine of Canterbury in 597 a new era of Christian activity began in the southern regions of England, and it bore the stamp of Pope Gregory the Great, not Lindisfarne and Iona. The ecclesial intentions were clear.

Still, Augustine had permission to adapt Latin tradition to the English people – even in the liturgy – so long as what was most 'devout, religious, and right' remained intact (Bede, 1.27, 1990, p. 79). This meant that Augustine's mission had to learn many of the same lessons about contextual ministry that had been previously learned by the Celts. Like their apostolic teams, his band of co-workers settled next to the king of Kent, Ethelbert, and quickly established a lasting friendship and a remarkable capacity for listening, loving and serving.

Living in proximity put the Christian way of life on display. Here is what the medieval historian Bede said about this life:

[T]hey began to emulate the life of the apostles and the primitive Church. They were constantly at prayer; they fasted and kept vigils; they preached the word of life to whomsoever they could. They regarded worldly things as of little importance, and accepted only the necessities of life from those they taught. They practised what they preached, and were willing to endure any hardship, and even to die for the truth which they proclaimed. Before long a number of heathen, admiring the simplicity of their holy lives and the comfort of their heavenly message, believed and were baptized (Bede, 1.26, 1990, p. 76).

It was here that the new Christian community provided an alternative to the violence endemic to Anglo-Saxon society. It also cared for the sick and showed the more powerful 'magic' of a God who not only heals, feeds and clothes his children, but redeems them as well.

We're told that the first public introduction of the new faith came at the king's request, in an open-air gathering where Augustine's little community of missionaries sang, carried a beautiful silver cross and a picture of Christ in stately procession. But they carried no weapons! Instead, the monks paraded and Augustine preached. They were armed with the word of God only. This multimedia presentation may have been a startling introduction to the Christian faith, but it seems to have worked.

Pageantry and pomp, boldness and beauty impressed the king and his inner court. Not surprisingly, under his influence, thousands would eventually be baptized into the new faith, including the king himself . . . but only because Augustine, like the Celts before him, learned how to live among the lost, bringing light and life, even beauty, into the strange new culture he was only beginning to understand. Out of this classic mission venture came new churches and, indeed, a new ecclesial outpost – Canterbury – for reaching southern England.

The Celtic and Roman missionaries

- moved out from existing centres to engage people beyond the existing rim of the church;
- combined mission as 'go' with an attractive way of life that beckoned, 'come and join us';
- practised incarnational mission – mission from within the cultures of the people they sought to reach;
- were rooted in the story of God and invited people to join it.

Benedict's guidance of souls

The missionary identity we see in Augustine's mission, with its centrifugal and incarnational impulses, continued in the Benedictines – the most resilient form of Christian community for the next 1,000 years of the church. When the adventurous young Benedict began his communal experiment around the year 525 he had nearly 200 years of monastic wisdom to turn to. He knew the Desert Fathers particularly well, and had also learned of some of the organized communities that had sprung up across southern Europe. But on a rocky hill (Monte Cassino) about 130 km south-east of Rome, he put together a new plan for monastic life that fitted the needs of his own place and time – what became known as the *Rule of St Benedict*.

It was a grim period for the church, with Rome under the control of one barbarian kingdom after another, and many leaders compromised by false teachings about the dual nature of Christ – his divinity *and* humanity. Italy and much of Europe was, in effect, the scene of constant power struggles in both church and society. For this reason and, more personally, to work out his own salvation, Benedict founded what would become the most important expression of Christian community for centuries to come. In a complex and troubled world, he happened on a very simple idea: 'we are about to open a school for God's service,' he declared in the prologue to the *Rule*. He added, 'As our lives progress, the heart expands and with the sweetness of love we move down the paths of God's commandments' (Meisel and Mastro, 1975, p. 45).

So, right at the start, we see how his incarnation of the gospel was a communal endeavour, focused on spiritual growth and serving God out of love. Benedict referred to it as a 'guidance of souls'. While the lonely outpost of Monte Cassino seemed, at first, irrelevant to the troubling social and political realities of the day, it soon became a major attraction to those seeking spiritual renewal, wholeness and stability. Even the barbarian kings came to witness the distinctive life of the monastery. The community formed by the *Rule* was profoundly relevant – the only reminder, over vast stretches of time and place, that there was such a thing as life in the kingdom of God 'under the true King, the Lord Jesus Christ' (Meisel and Mastro, 1975, p. 43).

Not that such an experiment was entirely new. Organized communities had emerged as a natural response to what the earliest Christians referred to as the 'way of the apostles', expressed in Scriptures like 1 Peter 1.13: 'Therefore, prepare your minds for action; discipline yourselves; set all your hope on the grace that Jesus Christ will bring you when he is revealed.' We might also recall 1 John 1.7: 'if we walk in the light as he himself is in the light, we have fellowship with one another, and the blood of Jesus his Son cleanses us from all sin'. The apostle Paul called this 'training in righteousness' (2 Tim. 3.14), and it was taken very seriously by those who thought that following Jesus changed everything.

Benedict had thought long and hard about what this sort of conversion required. After some trial and error, he developed the tools, the patterns and practices, needed to walk with Jesus on a day-to-day basis in the company of fellow disciples. Conversion required a community. The details on how to live well together span the areas of worship, work, and the reading and study of Scripture. Ultimately, a daily rhythm of these activities formed an alternative culture that expressed what one Benedictine scholar has called 'the love of learning and desire for God' (Leclercq, 1961, p. 151). The sevenfold pattern of prayer in a daily cycle was the most conspicuous feature of the new model. At first, it seems the Benedictines were overly attentive to such details, so a closer look is required.

Participation in the carefully structured liturgies was crucial because it was there that a certain kind of knowledge of God was gained. Some call this 'participatory knowledge', because it is about a way of knowing God that comes through the visual, symbolic and embodied actions of worship (Wood, 2001, p. 118). This knowledge does not come individually but corporately, and it is the product of careful coordination or synchronization involving spirit, mind, and body. What is most interesting about this kind of knowledge is that it is more implicit than explicit and it comes by being involved as whole persons. It picks up on the rhythms, the patterns, the structures of communal life and worship, and internalizes them so that we are shaped or conformed to the reality they point to.

For Benedict, this reality was God's love. By entering into the whole experience of the 'hours' members of the community came to a deeper knowledge of their relationship to God and each other. That is because the liturgy ordered these relationships by embodying some of the most fundamental teachings in Scripture on fellowship. It meant adopting practices and patterns of life previously experienced at Antioch, like the Eucharist and table fellowship, as well as a conspicuous focus on the reading and recitation of the Psalms. These activities communicated volumes about the heart and soul of the community in ways that participants could experience with all five of the senses.

It was a matter of some urgency to Benedict that Christians find an alternative script to that of the violence and confusion of the world beyond the monastery. He knew, as did the apostles, that we need a different kind of awareness – an attentiveness to the grace of God, the light of Christ and the peculiar sort of fellowship that only the Holy Spirit makes possible. All of those details that we encounter in the *Rule* produce this awareness of the triune God in action, and the results are quite astounding. Each member of the community becomes more attuned to the needs of others, more pliable in each of their wills and more discerning of God's presence and activity. There is a fresh sense of perspective here – of the order of things and the relation of parts to wholes. Some call this wisdom, and it is a hallmark of Benedictine life to this day.[6]

Little wonder that it was one of Benedict's greatest admirers, Pope Gregory the Great, who sent Augustine, himself a monk formed in the Benedictine way, on that great rescue mission to southern England. Little wonder, too, that in today's conflicted and confusing world, so many weary souls find a peaceful sense of order and spiritual truth in the cloisters of monastic communities. This was yet another 'fresh expression of the church' that incarnated the gospel with transformational, disciple-making vigour in an intensely relational atmosphere of divine love.

Benedictine monasteries, by design, are a cloistered form of Christian community. Yet, they are famous for attracting attention on such a scale that they became missionary extensions of traditional ecclesial structures. William of Saint-Thierry's (d.1148) description of the famous abbey at Clairvaux, France reminds us how the contemplative life 'spoke of the simplicity and humility of the poor of Christ who lived there'. As a distinct community with a conspicuous purpose of prayer and the praise of God, it 'engendered a sense of reverence even among lay people'.[7] On this basis, Clairvaux and other monasteries joining in its renewal movement became important centres of witness and mission to the wider world. They not only attracted, but also sent out people, including preachers like Saint Bernard.

For example, during a period of extensive church reform associated with Pope Gregory VII (1073–85), the apostolic ideal inspired Benedictine communities to preach the Gospel and evangelize under-served or unreached regions of Europe. Out of this, new forms of organized religious life emerged

---

6 An especially helpful perspective on Benedictine wisdom for today is Casey (2005).

7 Saint-Thierry, *First Life of Saint Bernard*, quoted in Casey (2005, pp. 137–8).

with a conscious outward focus, ranging from the Norbertines to the Augustinian canon regulars in the eleventh and twelfth centuries. Ultimately, the thirteenth-century mendicant movements – Franciscans and Dominicans – saw evangelization as essential aspects of their ministry, and this included planting and serving new churches. Many parish churches today owe their founding to this long history of monastic and mendicant church planting.

Benedictine monasteries

- emphasized Christian formation within a communal rhythm of life;
- lived by a different 'story' to the one dominating the world around;
- practised 'go' forms of mission by sending out some of their members to start new communities and plant churches in under-evangelized parts of Europe;
- had a strong attractional dynamic as people came to join these communities.

The Beguines on the edge

Just outside the walls of many northern European towns in the high Middle Ages it was not uncommon to find semi-monastic communities of laywomen known as 'Beguines'. Historians are still unsure about the meaning of the label, but it may have been a slur used to associate the groups with the heresies of the day or, perhaps, with the poor and despised members of medieval society. Certainly the Beguines defied cultural and ecclesiastical norms. As a 'fringe' group, they were the first known woman's movement in the history of the church, and they carved out a distinctive middle way between traditional religious orders like the Benedictines and a wide-ranging popular movement of lay spiritual renewal that swept much of Europe in the twelfth and thirteenth centuries.

They also established their own churches and situated them in the middle of expansive Beguine complexes (called 'Beguinages'). While largely traditional and parochial in operation, the churches were central to beguine spiritual life. Priests were chosen who were willing to provide spiritual direction to the community on a daily basis. They were often selected from the ranks of friars and canons regular who were more in touch with the fervent lay spirituality and renewal of the day. The customary liturgies and sacramental rites were performed, but with an eye to the distinctive mission of each Beguinage. This proximity and contextual awareness enhanced the vitality of church ministry.

Discipleship and spiritual growth were priorities in each Beguinage, and with enough energy and commitment local communities could draw hundreds of women from all classes of a rapidly urbanized society. A large complex, like the Great Beguinage at Ghent, needed two churches, 18 'convents', over 100 houses, a brewery and infirmary to serve its members as well as care for the poor and sick in adjacent neighbourhoods.

Beguinages also featured guest houses, hospitals, community gardens and multipurpose rooms that could be used for a variety of outreach purposes. The number and size of the communities, and the autonomy of their 'secular parishes', bred clerical suspicion and stirred opposition. With the notable exception of James of Vitry (d.1240), a bishop, cardinal and friend to the Beguinage at Oignies in northern France, relations with the wider church became increasingly strained. Despite papal condemnation at the Council of Vienne in 1311, however, the Beguine way of life managed to survive until the nineteenth century.

To understand the origin and expansion of Beguine communities we will retrace the journey of a first-generation leader, Mary of Oignies (1167–1213).[8] Mary and her husband John were part of an emerging movement of spiritual renewal that flourished in the commercial cities of the region. They expressed a desire to incorporate the religious devotion of traditional monastic life into the everyday occupations of 'secular' life, with a particular emphasis on holding the active and contemplative aspects of the Christian life together in a locally organized communal structure. Their vision was one of 'church in life', with a faith expressed in the midst of ordinary occupations and day-to-day relationships.

This required some novel arrangements. Most obviously, the self-governed community formed by Mary and John did not require vows of celibacy. In addition, they did not eliminate private possessions or require huge dowries from single women aspirants (the monastic custom). These accommodations immediately opened the door to the rich as well as the poor. It is also noteworthy that women were especially prominent from the onset. There are at least two reasons for this. First, there were disproportionately larger numbers of single and widowed women in Europe at the time due to the Crusades, and many found themselves in dire situations brought on by lack of any provision for livelihood. Second, new options were just beginning to be imagined for semi-monastic living arrangements, with communities that were not so cloistered, less subject to rigid male-dominated hierarchies of oversight and free of suspicion regarding women's spirituality.

The most distinctive feature, however, of early Beguine life was its emphasis on spiritual growth and renewal. In an age of increasing aspiration among the laity in general, women seized new opportunities to develop their sense of vocation and calling to a deeper religious life. Some were scandalized by growing self-sufficiency and materialism. Others had been turned away

---

8 A helpful resource is Myers (2011). For more general background, see Little (1978).

by existing religious orders that limited the full participation of women. On the positive side, they were often drawn to charismatic figures like Mary of Oignies, whose life was saturated with prayer, who engaged with the Scriptures and who was active in public ministry through evangelistic preaching and caring for those who were left behind in the new economy.

The growing attraction to Mary's life of devotion and service inspired her to develop a flexible pattern of organized community life. Besides the features already mentioned, she instituted a much-needed service to the sick and needy, founding one of the first hospitals in Europe. This gave the community a highly visible missional purpose, marked by a constant flow of traffic between the emerging Beguinage and its immediate context in the town of Oignies. Never before had the surrounding neighbourhoods witnessed incarnational ministry on such a scale by self-governed groups of women. As historian Glenn E. Myers puts it, this was all part of 'battling for the lives and souls of friends and strangers alike' (Myers, 2011, p. 39).

Women from all walks of life were drawn to the community, including many who found safety and freedom from the harsh treatment endemic to single women in the Middle Ages. Some of the married women were able to maintain family ties and obligations while participating to varying degrees in everyday patterns of prayer, work and service at the Beguinage. Perhaps they borrowed this idea from the 'tertiary' option found in some of the monastic and mendicant traditions of the day. This meant that they could retain secular occupations alongside a fervent devotional life supported by the religious community. The opportunities to learn a trade, especially in textiles, or acquire the ability to read or write in a vernacular language were also crucial draws for many women.

The engagement with Scripture was in the local language – another striking and somewhat controversial practice for that day. Vernacular translations of the Bible were sought, and training in those languages became the focal point of literacy – scriptural and otherwise. Beguines were known to memorize vast amounts of Scripture and meditate on it throughout the day, in both personal and communal settings, during their manual labour as well as in their witness and service to others. Little wonder that some were compelled to share their spiritual insights with those whom they served, and some went so far as to preach publically and hear confessions. These quasi-clerical roles were sharply curtailed by the church in the early fourteenth century, especially as the power of the ordained office gained greater power and prestige (Bynum, 1989).

The size of many communities required relocation to the outskirts of town. The innovations in membership and organization led to a form of community life that retained the flexibility and local variety of a movement rather than the uniformity of an established order. In their daily patterns of prayer, work and service they resembled monastic and mendicant traditions, but their fluid structures allowed much more engagement with the workaday world. In this life on the edge, they practised hospitality to single and widowed women who were unable to find a spiritual home elsewhere. The aim was to form disciples who, according to Beatrice of Nazareth (d.1268), were 'ready to serve, so nimble in work, so meek in annoyance, so joyful in trouble'.

> ## Beguines
>
> - brought Christian community into the context of everyday life;
> - the communities were contextualized to laywomen;
> - they served people nearby;
> - they challenged the expectations of the existing church.

Nicholas Ferrar's holy calling

The sixteenth century was revolutionary in many ways – in the fragmentation of medieval Christendom, the increasing use of communications technology and a growing respect for the individual conscience – and these forces continued to bring tremendous change to the Church of England. Church life remained unsettled even after Elizabeth I's long reign and *via media*, such that by the early 1600s it was caught up in the nation's steady drift towards civil war. Grievances against Kings James I and Charles I ran high, within the church and beyond. Partisan division disabled effective communication and heightened tensions. It was a bleak, if not foreboding, time in the spiritual life of the English people.

That is the world in which a successful businessman named Nicholas Ferrar felt a 'holy calling' to leave power and prestige behind, and be ordained a deacon and leader of a semi-monastic community called Little Gidding. He was possessed by the notion that the kingdom of God might best be sought outside the contentious human kingdoms of his day. So, according to a solemn vow, he 'attend[ed] to the one thing necessary': 'to serve God in his holy calling, to be the Levite himself in his own house, and to make his own relations, which were many, his cure of souls'.[9] Reminiscent of Benedict, he accomplished this through the adoption of a very practical rule of life in the context of Christian fellowship and service.

The community founded by Nicholas did not take monastic vows, though members of the community felt a keen sense of obligation to the pattern of life that quickly emerged. The rule of Little Gidding was actually quite unique in this regard. The chief concern was to live as a Christian family, extended in the direction of love to God and neighbour. It did, in fact, begin

---

9 This announcement, recorded on parchment, is quoted in Skipton (1907, p. 85).

with the Ferrar family, but it welcomed others into the household of faith. Eventually, their remote country house north-west of Cambridge became what we might call a retreat centre, attracting the rich and poor, kings and bishops, scholars and ordinary people who sought physical and spiritual healing and renewal. The community also rehabilitated the local parish church as another mode of service to the wider world.

Little Gidding adopted a structured way of life that centred on cooperation and service in an atmosphere of friendship and humility. There were daily hours for communal worship, but also periods set aside for study and work, with particular regard for artistic expression and craftsmanship in the illustration of texts and the binding of large holy books containing Gospel 'harmonies' and the Psalter. Simple meals were prepared for the poor and hungry, and a wide range of other activities in the 'Discipline' of the community produced a rhythm of daily life. One observer noted that the members 'were in the World, not of the World. All their Practice was heavenly . . .'[10]

Among the more interesting developments at Little Gidding was the practice of active reading. Nicholas thought that the gospel narrative should be the unifying story of Little Gidding, but he wanted the story to point to all the other parts of the Bible, especially the Old Testament's prophecies and prefigurations of Christ. This was accomplished by compiling indexes, concordances, commentaries and so on – each a result of the collaborative efforts of the readers. The work was exacting and extensive, becoming something of a spiritual discipline for the community as a whole.

So while the gospel narrative defined the community, there was a simultaneous comprehension of the whole story of God. Each day, a new connection between one passage of Scripture and another might be discovered by a member of the community and recorded in the appropriate book. This attentiveness to the coherence and correlation of the biblical text was a persistent feature of study and devotion at Little Gidding, producing a storehouse of wisdom, especially in regards to the details of Christ's life.

The reading community was, in a sense, read by the biblical text. The Bible had that much power and privileged status in its everyday life. This is why Nicholas and his friend, the poet and pastor George Herbert, saw all of the physical, mental and spiritual activities surrounding the Scriptures as transformative. This occurred, they thought, because the Holy Spirit was given ample opportunity to speak and act – revealing, pointing, stirring and nudging individuals and the community as a whole to respond in particular ways. The responses included the painstaking restoration of a nearby church, the launching of an elaborate programme of religious education for children, the distribution of free meals to the poor and medical care to the sick. Clearly, Little Gidding was not a sequestered community, this despite its quiet resolve to seek first the kingdom of God.

---

10 J. Hacket, quoted in Carter and Carter (1892, p. 247).

In an age of strong anti-Catholic and anti-monastic sentiment, the Little Gidding experiment met with stiff opposition in the Church of England. Rumours circulated about its 'nuns', prayer vigils and 'canonical hours', its richly decorated crosses – both outdoors and indoors – and altar. All of this was associated with the 'adorations, genuflections, and geniculation' of 'superstition and popery'.[11] There was also the charge that too much time was spent in praying, not preaching. Others thought the community's interest in Christian education and the meticulous compilation of Bible study resources departed from more 'orthodox' modes of instruction.

If as a 'Congregation of Saints', Little Gidding was at times a bit 'dutiful and severe' in its manner of life, it remained a vital witness to the transforming power of Christian fellowship – well after the experiment came to an end in 1657 (Ferrar, 1855, p. 349). The community was intent on renewing the church and involving it in the world through attractional and incarnational mission. As often happens, this required a deep level of sharing in the community's inner life even as it adopted new approaches and patterns that invigorated wider commitments to the world beyond.

Today the Little Gidding Trust has begun to revive some aspects of the spiritual vision of Nicholas Ferrar and a growing number of pilgrims are hoping for more Little Giddings to pop up in other places – following the 'good old way' in a fresh expression of gospel light and life.

Little Gidding

- developed a strong communal life;
- centred this life on Scripture, which was read in innovative ways;
- served the surrounding people;
- faced opposition from the existing church.

John Wesley's mirror of God

Another 'good old way' that has been reborn in the Church today is the ministry of small-group fellowship. John Wesley, the great Anglican evangelist and admirer of Little Gidding, is a favourite source of inspiration. A century after Nicholas's death, Wesley was busy with his own experiment, but he shared a common vision with his predecessor: 'I saw a family full as much devoted to God, full as regular in all their exercises of devotion, and at last as exemplary in every branch of Christian holiness' (Wesley, 1872,

---

11 The Puritan pamphlet entitled *The Arminian Nunnery* (1661) is quoted in Parry (2006, p. 120).

p. 333). Wesley is famous for turning this vision of the family of God into reality through his Methodist Societies.

In 1739, the city of Bristol was a rapidly growing commercial centre with a large population of new urban immigrants. It was a crowded and confusing place to live, with many neglected social and economic needs and little or no active church presence. John Wesley arrived on 2 April to share the 'glad tidings of salvation', and for the first time he would preach in the open-air, attracting as many as 3,000 people to his first public event. To preach out of doors was a new thing, and the Anglican establishment viewed it as a seditious act. But Wesley felt that the Spirit of the Lord was upon him – 'to preach the gospel to the poor' – and nothing could stop him.

Wesley's legacy has as much to do with small groups as large crowds, however. His characteristic emphasis on 'deliverance, recovery, and liberty' was most effectively realized in more intimate gatherings. He was something of a celebrity preacher and enjoyed having a large audience, but he learned quickly enough that most people came to faith through close relationships with caring people. In fact, probably more than anyone before him in the modern era, Wesley appreciated that Christianity was essentially *social* in nature.

In one of his sermons, he described the Christian as a *mirror* of God – an image that reflects the *social* nature or Trinity of God. We reflect what we receive: the capacity to love and be loved by others. Just as the divine persons enjoy a bond of fellowship, so do we, especially through the indwelling Holy Spirit. For Wesley, this is what our participation in the divine nature meant. So it made sense to him that Christians would come to faith through the active love of others – through the 'channels of grace' uniquely found in one-to-one relationships and in a community of faith that was mobilized to continually extend its fellowship to others (Wesley, 1951, p. 38).

Wesley was very practical about this. If anyone could make the Trinity and divine love into lived realities in the everyday experience of people, it was this energetic pragmatist. He first drew up a fourfold structure of small groups – each with its own level of spiritual intimacy that corresponded with a particular stage of growth and discipleship.[12] In the 'trial bands' the participants, ideally no more than 12 in number, became more aware of how God had already been at work in their lives – of the grace that had been received even prior to their belief. With this deeper understanding came accountability. Over a period of, perhaps, several months they were expected to learn the basics of fellowship: practising transparency, confession, forgiveness, mutual support and encouragement to live as disciples in all areas of life. Once they learned this, lay leaders – trained by Wesley to serve as overseers – recommended (to his ministers) that band members progress to the next level in the 'United Society' – to larger class structures.

---

12 An early version of this structure appears in Wesley (1831, pp. 176–90).

In the 'classes', the emphasis was on teaching the basics of the Christian faith – 'mind work', as Wesley sometimes called it. The combination of sharing previous life experiences in the trial bands, learning about the faith in the class, and developing stronger relationships day by day with other seekers, prepared the group members for the 'converting grace' of the 'new birth' in Jesus Christ. Wesley was fully prepared to stretch this journey to two years. It was an intricate process and, as always, deeply relational. The more one felt a sense of belonging to the group, the more one came to know at an experiential level what it meant to belong to God. The culmination of this spiritual awareness was a conscious acceptance of salvation and professed testimony of conversion to Jesus Christ.

Next, individuals were recommended by their mentors and overseers to the 'bands'. Here they responded to their conversions with a new resolve to grow in grace, train the will towards God and continue in their support to one another in discipleship. The level of confidentiality increased sufficiently that Wesley thought it was sometimes helpful to break out into smaller and more homogeneous sub-groups based on sex and marital status. Accountability was a major factor here. Finally, in the 'select bands', individuals pursued 'sanctifying grace' – the glow of divine love and a self-denying responsiveness toward others. They practised deep spiritual formation and group fellowship, living out Galatians 3.28 – 'There is neither Jew nor Greek, there is neither slave nor free, there is no male and female, for you are all one in Christ Jesus.'

These four types of group formed all over England and Wales in the mid eighteenth century, and they involved people from all classes of society. Women participated in their leadership as well as men – with everyone 'obedient to their heavenly calling'. Ultimately, this activity led to the great 'revival' that would spill over from the Methodist Society structures into the life of other dissenting groups and also the Church of England. There was plenty of tension and conflict along the way, but over time it became clear that this 'experimental religion' was beneficial not only to the church, but to society as a whole.

Certainly Wesley was a 'trailblazer', and he was strategic, with the nation and, indeed, the world as his parish. No one challenged the parochial model more than this 'methodistic' Anglican. Though he intended each 'society' to link itself to the local Anglican church, the strength and support offered by the emerging Methodist 'connection' proved more effective in sustaining the work of forming disciples. Key to its success were the highly motivated lay leaders and stewards who were more excited by a church that engaged everyday life than a church defined exclusively by Sunday worship events. Here, in 'free conversation', they addressed the 'true state of the soul' as well as concerns regarding 'temporal things' at home and in the workplaces and marketplaces of the day. Wesley even insisted that the hymns, exhortations and prayers of the Methodist groups address these wider spheres of life.

John Wesley became the father of modern evangelicalism because, in part, he was a highly successful 'networker'. He found 'persons of peace' in his lay leaders, ministers and stewards who could reach people where they lived, in all situations, classes and stages of life. He devised a system in which teams of two would fan out across a district or neighbourhood, visiting those who were reported to be in some sort of spiritual or physical need. Wesley selected those he judged to be 'of the most tender, loving spirit' for this ministry. When visiting the sick, in particular, these 'visitors' were, in Wesley's words, to 'inquire into the state of other souls' and to advise them as occasion may require. To inquire into their disorders, and procure advice for them. To relieve them, if they are in want. To do any thing for them, which he (or she) can do' Wesley, 1831, p. 186.

Ultimately, the success of this missional, contextual and formational 'network' would take on ecclesial intensions as well. It was never Wesley's desire that Methodists separate from the Church of England, but soon after his death in 1791 this is precisely what happened. The energy and enthusiasm of the movement could no longer abide by the founder's call to remain as 'living witnesses' *within* the established church.[13] As leadership passed to a new generation, the elaborate – yet highly elastic – structure of small groups gradually turned into circuits of Methodist chapels.

While the history of this separation was marked by conflict and controversy, it offers many lessons and parallels for today's mission-shaped church. Most especially, we recognize that when something 'new or enlivened is happening', it may exceed the capacities of existing structures. The resulting tensions can be healthy and energizing when all concerned remember that it is the church, as a whole, that is 'called upon to proclaim [the gospel] afresh in each generation' (*Mission-shaped Church*, 2004, p. 34). This implies an abiding connection between the historic church *and* the ongoing story of God's mission to the world – a story that will always have its visionary founders and reinvigorated channels of grace.

John Wesley's class system

Individuals progressed through
- trial bands – they learnt the basics of fellowship;
- classes – members learnt the basics of the Christian faith;
- bands – members grew in the faith, practising mutual accountability;
- select bands – individuals pursued 'sanctifying grace'.

---

13 See, for example, John Wesley's 'Reasons Against a Separation from the Church of England', at Project Canterbury: www.anglicanhistory.org/wesley/reasons1760.html.

Charles Kingsley's life in the kingdom

In the century that followed the great English Revival, the Industrial Revolution brought widespread social dislocation and dizzying change to all aspects of life in the British Isles. The population of England expanded from nine million in 1801 to 33 million in 1901. Growth was most dramatic in the larger towns and cities, especially as the agrarian economy of the countryside went into decline. Society was highly segregated, and the working class, in particular, was forced into dense ghetto-like neighbourhoods with overcrowding, poverty, unemployment and inadequate sanitation.

Thanks in part to the Revival, the Church of England had become more aware of these changes. New churches were planted and a wide array of reform societies organized to address the various social, economic and moral ills of the day. A traditional parish might gradually emerge out of rather non-traditional circumstances. Small mission halls or even corrugated-iron structures sometimes served as the first meeting places, often with the assistance of the local people. Sunday schools, day schools, libraries and charities then began their work, and eventually more comprehensive 'settlement' houses offered the whole gamut of services required in the most severely impoverished neighbourhoods (Morris and Macleod, 2000).

What was behind all of this rising church concern for the social conditions of the nation? One of the more fascinating windows into this era is the ministry of Charles Kingsley and his parish church in the village of Eversley in north-eastern Hampshire. This country parson, novelist, labour activist and advocate of 'Christian socialism' worked tirelessly among both the rural and, later in life, urban poor, because he was convinced that in baptism Christians were initiated into the kingdom of God and set free from self-concern to serve others. They were to be a positive force in the world, working toward a good society – much as we have seen at Little Gidding and in the Methodist societies.

When, in 1844, Kingsley first arrived at Eversley, he was told by a local farm labourer that there was an oppressive weight on the hearts of the local people – 'and they care for no hope and no change, for they know they can be no worse off than they are' (Kingsley, 1899, p. 96). As Kingsley got to know those whom he had been called to serve, he became deeply concerned about the grinding poverty and spiritual darkness of their everyday lives. He saw how the circumstances of everyday life can extinguish hope and sap interest in or commitment to change. Kingsley tended to people in their everyday settings, sometimes working beside them in the fields, and calling on them as many as six or seven times a day when illness and other crises hit home.

Equally remarkable, however, was the way Kingsley mobilized his small and impoverished parish to address the needs of its context. It organized cooperatives for the poor, 'shoe clubs', 'coal clubs', a maternal society, a loan fund and a lending library. An adult evening school was established to address the problem of illiteracy, and Sunday schools and weekly cottage lectures were planned for general as well as Christian education. Kingsley's revival of catechesis and confirmation provided a model for the whole Church of England. A church building that had formerly been vacant throughout much of the week was now buzzing with all sorts of activities on a daily basis. In its own way, Kingsley's parish church became 'a school for God's service'.

Learning how to read, having wider access to the Scriptures and gaining a deeper understanding of God's mission in the world remained the chief concerns of the church at Eversley for years to come. These commitments turned an insular country parish into a missionary outpost. Even the dilapidated structure of the church was refurbished and reconfigured with multipurpose spaces to serve the expanding array of ministries. Once again, a church was recovering the vision of how to be a community of the gospel in the midst of life.

It was Kingsley's vision of the kingdom of God that provided the DNA for this outreach, moving the church beyond an exclusive 'come-to-us' mentality that sometimes marginalizes parish life. The recovery of an incarnational ministry had such dramatic effect on the Eversley parish that it was, in effect, reborn as a mission and contextually-shaped church – two of the hallmarks of 'new contextual churches'.

Eversley parish was

- missional – the church served people, including those who rarely attended;
- contextual – it addressed the needs of people in their ordinary lives;
- formational – Kingsley revived catechesis and confirmation, and pioneered Christian education.

Dorothy L. Sayers's pub audience

Among the more innovative aspects of Charles Kingsley's ministry was his popularization of Christian social ideals in novels like *Yeast* (1850) and *Hypatia* (1853). He also knew how to use the print media of the day (magazines and tracts) like we use the Internet – to get the word out, form networks and show how Christians think and act in the modern world. In these ways, Kingsley opened new channels for the gospel that would continue well into the next century.

The next major breakthrough in communication technology, the radio, quickly became such a channel in the 1930s and 1940s, thanks to the missionary vision of Archbishop William Temple and the creativity of writers like Dorothy L. Sayers and C. S. Lewis. Let us conclude our journey through time with a brief look at what Temple called 'one of the most powerful instruments in evangelism' of his day.[14]

Between the two World Wars, Britain experienced a widespread decline of small communities, the expansion of mass media (especially the radio) and a growing interest in new forms of entertainment like the cinema. William Temple, as Archbishop of York and then Canterbury, recognized that while the Church of England had managed to retain a strong institutional presence in society, Christian belief was widely discredited among intellectual elites and disconnected from the everyday realities of the working poor. It was no longer assumed that the church had answers to the questions posed by modernity. So Temple initiated a diverse array of responses that would restore a 'Christian map of life'.[15]

A renewal of crucial ties between Christ and culture came about, in part, through Temple's strong support for religious broadcasting on the BBC. He was active in the founding of the new medium, served on its councils, and encouraged the airing of religious programmes – sometimes meeting stiff resistance from those who worried that this might draw people away from actual church attendance. According to his biographer, F. A. Iremonger, Temple was, himself, 'an admirable broadcaster (1949, p. 556). The map of life he presented to a rapidly growing audience sought integration of religion, art, science, politics, education, industry, commerce and finance. Not unlike Charles Kingsley, he was convinced that Jesus had something to say to the world, through a church that served as herald and foretaste of the reign of God.

Based on this keen sense of social witness, Temple encouraged writers, dramatists and playwrights to offer their gifts to religious broadcasting. Dorothy L. Sayers was among the first to accept an invitation from the BBC to present religious drama for a popular audience. Her debut was in 1938 with the production of a nativity play for the *Children's Hour*. But it was in 1942, with the airing of *The Man Born to be King*, that she received, according to the Controller of Programmes, an 'overwhelming nation-wide response' that would be long remembered as 'one of the great landmarks of broadcasting' (Reynolds, 1993, p. 327). Already famous for her detective novels, now she received some negative publicity as well – this as a result of her emphasis on the humanity of Jesus and use of contemporary language in the script rather than 'talking Bible'.

Temple thought Sayers's work was a 'fine piece of Christian evangelism' and appreciated the need to present a more 'realistic' life of Christ. For her part, Sayers assumed this was all part of what it meant to engage in

---

14 William Temple, quoted in Reynolds (1993, p. 329).
15 William Temple, quoted in Wolf (1979, p. 110).

incarnational ministry. To communicate timeless spiritual truth through 'the arts, all letters, all labour and all learning' was to take up the 'sacramental position' realized by Christ himself, she insisted. This defined the mission and ministry of the church as well – but a Church now communicating the gospel well beyond the traditional parish locale (Reynolds, 1993, p. 336).

Sayers, in fact, found a medium that spoke to people who were not being reached through traditional means. She perceived a gap between the Christian message and a growing audience that no longer found this message credible. Of course, she never imagined herself to be a missionary or church planter in uncharted mission fields, but she aimed to reach people outside the church with the life-changing 'drama' of the Christian message.

One of the unexpected outcomes of her radio broadcasting was the spontaneous formation of networks of listeners around the programmes – even in local pubs! After another nativity play by Sayers was aired on Christmas Day in 1939, she was surprised to learn that a lively discussion on its message had ensued in the 'pub audience'. At a time when the BBC was attempting to sanitize her scripts, she was pleased to note that the conversations generated by her plays were prompted by a deep sense of identity with the gospel story. Sayers had relied on her artistic instincts: 'I felt it important to get people to believe that the characters in the Bible were real people like ourselves, and not just "sacred Personages" apart from common humanity'.[16] From her standpoint, she thought this was the best way for the church to say something 'loud and definite' about Jesus Christ – especially in a world of growing complexity and, as another war approached, conflict.

To think incarnationally, with Temple and Sayers, is to think in a contemporary way about how the Word has become flesh and moved into our world. In the troubled decades of the early twentieth century, materialism and atheism were failing to satisfy many. Incarnational mission engaged people, who were beginning to look elsewhere. The new media of radio formed new networks, as people gathered in the pubs to listen. By working with this technology, Sayers sparked pub discussions that anticipated the churches forming in pubs and cafes today.

Dorothy L. Sayers

- pioneered the missional use of new media;
- reached people outside the church;
- faced criticism from within the church;
- anticipated pub church and cafe church.

---

16 Dorothy L. Sayers to John Rhode, 2 January 1939, in Reynolds (1997, p. 105).

Conclusion

This chapter has shown how the four characteristics of new contextual churches – being missional, contextual, formational and ecclesial – have been repeatedly expressed in new ways during the history of the church. They have not always been present at once. At Little Gidding and Eversley the missional, contextual and formational marks were evident, but because the church was already present in the village, the ecclesial characteristic (existing church giving birth to new ones) lay dormant.

However, 'new contextual churches' were brought to birth on plenty of other occasions. Think of Antioch, the Celtic and Augustinian missions, the evangelizing work of the Benedictine communities and their mendicant successors, the Beguines, and John Wesley. So although the new churches emerging today may – once again – take a different shape to what we have seen in the past, they are nothing new. They belong to a long line of 'mission-shaped church'.

Further reading

Baucum, Tory K., *Evangelical Hospitality: Catechetical Evangelism in the Early Church and Its Recovery for Today*, Plymouth: The Scarecrow Press, 2008.

McLeod, Hugh, *Religion and the People of Western Europe: 1789–1989*, 2nd edition, Oxford University Press, 1997.

Null, Ashley, 'Thomas Cranmer and Tudor Evangelicalism', in Michael A. G. Haykin and Kenneth J. Stewart (eds), *The Advent of Evangelicalism: Exploring Historical Continuities*, Nashville, TN: B&H Academic, 2008, pp. 221–51.

Van Gelder, Craig, *The Essence of the Church: A Community Created by the Spirit*, Grand Rapids, MI: Baker Books, 2000.

Questions for discussion

- Which of the examples in this chapter most spoke to you, and why?
- What themes connect the examples in this chapter?
- What principles of good church practice can we learn from the past?
- How has the history in this chapter stimulated your thinking about new possibilities?

3

Fresh Expressions of Church in Britain

Church reports do not usually become best-sellers. Since its publication in 2004, *Mission-shaped Church* has sold over 30,000 copies, reached an international audience and has been credited with reshaping the Church of England's ecclesiology (Davison and Milbank, 2010, p. 1). It led to the official encouragement of 'fresh expressions of church' in the Church of England and the Methodist Church, and this has influenced other denominations in the UK such as the Congregational Federation, the United Reformed Church and the Church of Scotland.

Brian McLaren, from within the emerging church conversation, has found it amazing that an ancient institutional church should experiment with new styles of church alongside existing expressions – 'to create new wineskins while the existing wineskins were still in use . . .' He believes that 'England provides a tremendous laboratory to test new ideas and learn from them' (McLaren, 2009, pp. 17, 26).

The report pleaded for flexible approaches to the creation of new Christian communities. It urged the church not to rely only on a 'come to us' approach to mission, seeking to incorporate Christians into the current pattern of church life. Rather, the church should seek also to go out to people in innovative ways. It called for new expressions of church, perhaps meeting in unusual places at unusual times, to help people toward transformed lives via fresh commitment to Christ. It sought not the demise of the local geographically based church, but its renewal through other types of Christian community alongside it and linked to it.

These ideas were not new. In 1968, a World Council of Churches report proposed that alongside the 'parish' new churches, taking diverse shapes, should undertake mission in the many contexts of work and leisure where people now lead their lives (WCC, 1968). Four years later John Taylor, General Secretary of the Church Missionary Society, wrote enthusiastically about 'little congregations' of perhaps just two or three Christians, scattered across the settings of everyday life (Taylor, 2004 [1972], pp. 147–52). Lesslie Newbigin expressed similar thoughts five years later (Newbigin, 1977, pp. 115–18).

Yet these ideas were seldom taken up in practice. They seemed very radical, there were few concrete examples to point the way and the need to think about novel expressions of church did not appear urgent to most leaders. By contrast, *Mission-shaped Church* provided examples of new and different types of church. It charted a way forward for a church that not only felt bewildered by the sweeping changes in the cultural landscape (which had been true of the 1960s as well), but had also experienced some 40 years of numerical decline. It captured a mood.

The last two chapters have described how the church has regularly reproduced among people outside the church. This chapter tells the story of Britain's experience of fresh expressions of church, which continue this tradition of reproduction. Although new contextual churches are emerging in a number of countries, Britain's denominations have been at the forefront in recognizing and encouraging them, and so the story may be of some interest to people outside as well as inside the UK.[1] The story will be told within an 'emergence' framework derived from complexity theories. The chapter starts, therefore, with a brief account of the latter, their theological rationale and the model that will frame the narrative here.

Complexity theory

Although far from dominant, complexity theories have gained ground in the social sciences as a helpful lens through which to view aspects of contemporary life (Stalder, 2006, pp. 170–85). Originating in the natural sciences, complexity theories are increasingly being applied fruitfully to organizations (for example, Leifer, 1989; Stacey, Griffin and Shaw, 2000), entrepreneurship (for example, McKelvey, 2004) and social entrepreneurship (for example, Goldstein, Hazy and Silberstang, 2008, 2010).

What are complexity theories?

There is not one complexity theory, but several (see Box).[2] At the heart of them all is that change is not directed from the top but emerges from the system as a whole. It comes about in an unplanned way. It occurs through the amplification of novelty. A chance mutation in nature or a human invention rolls like a snow ball through the system, growing in influence as other elements or individuals in the system react positively to them. In response, agents 'spontaneously' combine to create new patterns of interaction. The emergence of these patterns is unpredictable because they have qualities that are genuinely new.[3]

---

1 What counts as a 'fresh expression of church' is contested. The term certainly includes what I am calling 'new contextual church', but – as used in this chapter – fresh expressions also includes initiatives that would not strictly fit my definition.

2 For an accessible introduction, see Johnson (2002) and Wheatley (2006).

3 This is the strong version, which holds that a system can have qualities not directly traceable to its components but only to how they interact. New qualities

---

Four types of complexity theory

- *Chaos theory* shows how particular parameters, determined outside the system, cause the system's behaviour to move toward a new state called an attractor.
- *Dissipative structure theory* highlights the role of fluctuations, which are small variations in the movement of the entities comprising a system. The amplification of small fluctuations can cause the system to reorganize in an unexpected way.
- *Complex adaptive systems theory* gives more attention to the interaction between agents. Differences between agents and in their interactions lead to spontaneous reorganization.
- *Complex responsive process theory* sees novelty emerging primarily through human communication.

Source: Stacey, Griffin and Shaw, 2000, pp. 85–126; 186–9.

For some complexity theorists, a key concept is the 'edge of chaos'. This is the border between order and disorder. When organizations are too orderly, there is little room for change and novelty. But push them over the boundary to chaos, and they fall apart. A region on the safe side of the boundary, close to but not lapsing into chaos, leaves enough freedom for novelty, for the innovation to be adopted by others, for the new eventually to replace an existing approach (the system reorganizes) and for this new approach to take root within the system.

Complexity theories seek to explain how systems self-organize in this way. From a theological perspective, it can be said that out of love the transcendent God passes the power of fertile self-organization to creation while remaining closely engaged through the Spirit. Theologians, such as Polkinghorne (1995) and Peacocke (1995), have offered conjectural models to describe the Spirit's involvement. Nancey Murphy's (1995) account is particularly helpful. She proposes that God acts at three levels. At the quantum level God activates each particle's movement, while respecting the characteristics and limitations of the entities involved.

---

are irreducible to the system's constituent parts, so that in principle the system is unpredictable. A weak version of emergence holds that new properties arising in a system have characteristics that derive from existing elements in the system, as well as from the interactions between these elements. What emerges is predictable in principle because the new properties have some of their origins in the characteristics of the elements, but it is not predictable in practice.

God is also active in events occurring at all levels of complexity above the quantum level but below free human action. Through the intentional manipulation of each element that constitutes an entity, God maintains the typical characteristics of that entity. So for example God maintains the distinctive features of a billiard ball; the behaviour of the ball in interaction with its environment emerges from the conduct of its constituent parts, whose characteristics God also maintains. Finally, God is active at the human level through his relationships with men and women. In these relationships, as in his interactions with the lower levels, God respects the traits and limitations of the other involved.

Through these levels of involvement, God acts on each piece of the created order to sustain the emergent processes integral to creation and the regular patterns described by 'laws of nature'. Within the limits provided by the 'natural rights' of each constituent of creation, God sometimes governs these components in atypical ways and effects extraordinary behaviours. These exceptions make sense of prayer for events that defy the law-like behaviour of natural processes (Murphy, 1995, pp. 325–57). Thus there is 'a divine self-investment in self-organizing processes' (Gregersen, 2008, p. 92).[4]

A fourfold model

The story of fresh expressions in Britain uses a model developed by Benyamin Lichtenstein and Donde Plowman. The model describes four conditions for 'new emergent order' within an organization (2009, p. 620). The first, disequilibrium, occurs when a system's behaviour is substantially disrupted. An outside threat or new activities within push the system beyond its existing and normally accepted range of behaviours. The second condition is amplifying actions. These enable a small fluctuation in one part of the system to bring unanticipated and substantial changes to the other parts. As information jumps channels, becomes amplified and moves quickly through the system, small changes can cascade unexpectedly.

The third condition is recombination/self-organization. When new behaviours are repeatedly amplified, the system may reach the limit of its capacity. At this threshold, it can either collapse or reorganize. Self-organization (or emergence) occurs when agents or resources within the

---

4 Taking a different approach, Kester Brewin has argued that 'the God who created evolution and dreamt up emergence' has eschewed a purely top-down system of communication and chosen to 're-emerge' within creation, bottom up, through Christ (Brewin, 2004, pp. 44–5). A fuller account than the one here might describe how the Spirit, acting on behalf of God's coming reign, nudges creation toward the kingdom. If self-organization produces ever high levels of complexity, as theorists argue, the kingdom – to which creation is being drawn – can be seen as the ultimate level of complexity.

system recombine in new patterns of interaction, which tend to improve the system's functioning. The fourth condition is stabilizing feedback, which 'dampens' or slows amplification and prevents change spinning the system out of control.

Disequilibrium

In Britain, the fresh-expressions story has its immediate origins in new elements that began to destabilize the status quo. Church was understood in conventional terms, but then some people started to express church differently.

Growing dis-ease with church

According to Goldstein, Hazy and Silberstang, disequilibrium typically begins with a growing realization that 'business as usual' does not work (2010, p. 105). In the British church, this realization – though by no means new – built up steam during the 1990s and intensified in the 2000s. There was mounting interest in how church should respond to the postmodern world, books such as Michael Riddell's *Threshold of the Future*, published in 1998, and later blogs were highly critical of the existing church, and the emerging church conversation had growing influence.

In addition was the stark evidence that church attendance was in decline. Many congregations and clergy could see this in their own churches and experienced the consequences in repeated cycles of reorganization, designed to maintain the church in the face of falling clergy numbers. Christian Research reported that average Sunday attendance in England had fallen from 11.7 per cent of the population in 1979 to 7.5 per cent in 1998. The drop among young people was especially dramatic. Brierley suggested that if the current rate of decline continued the percentage going to church in 2016 would be 0.9 per cent. The church would have 'bled to death' (Brierley, 2000b, pp. 27–8).[5] Though the rate slowed in the early 2000s, the percentage attending church in 2005 was down to 6.3 per cent (Brierley, 2006, p. 20).

According to an extensive Tearfund survey, in 2007 a quarter of UK adults went to church once a year or more – 15 per cent once a month. Among the remainder, 6 per cent belonged to other faiths; 32 per cent had never been to church (except for baptisms, weddings and funerals) and expressed little inclination to go in the future (the 'closed unchurched'); 28 per cent attended church in the past, had stopped doing so and were not very or at all likely to go in the future (the 'closed dechurched'). Thus two-thirds of the

---

5 An alternative way of looking at the figures suggested that the percentage could be 4 per cent, still a sharp decline (Brierley, 2000b, p. 98).

population appeared most unlikely to attend church on current trends. Only 6 per cent of the survey said they did not go to church but were very or fairly likely to do so (Ashworth, Research Matters and Farthing, 2007, pp. 5–7). This set out clearly the scale of the mission task in Britain.

More poignant were the experiences of many churchgoers themselves. The phenomenon of church leaving came firmly on to the agenda. Francis and Richter reported that nearly half of all church leavers found it increasingly hard to believe, did not feel part of the church, disliked the hypocrisy they saw in other churchgoers and claimed that church failed to connect with the rest of their lives. Around two-fifths said that their participation in church had become a chore, they found church boring and they were not interested in the activities on offer. Three-quarters believed that they did not need to go to church to be a Christian (Francis and Richter, 2007, pp. 318–32).

Many of the touted strategies to promote church growth seemed to bear limited fruit. Among evangelicals especially, power evangelism, seeker services, the purpose-driven church and other models appeared to work in relatively few cases. Two notable 'successes' were the Alpha course and church planting-at-scale particularly by Holy Trinity, Brompton in London (HTB). Other churches, however, found that the HTB church planting model demanded too many resources and that Alpha often yielded diminishing returns: numbers fell when the course was repeated.

Combinations of difference

Against this background were spontaneous moves to express church in new ways. Goldstein, Hazy and Silberstang (2010, p. 111) note how novelty occurs through the unexpected combination of different elements. They quote Kary Mullis, Nobel Laureate in chemistry: 'In a sense, I put together elements that were already there, but that is what inventors always do. You can't make up new elements, usually. The new element, if any, it was the combination, the way they were used.'

Novel combinations characterized many new expressions of church before the *Mission-shaped Church* report. Groups experimenting with alternative worship joined elements from popular culture, such as multimedia, to worship in combinations not seen before. In the late 1980s and early 1990s, the Nine O'clock Service (NOS) in Sheffield – a young adults' congregation that peaked at 600 – put alternative worship firmly on the map. Despite the demise of NOS following allegations of sexual and emotional abuse by its leader, a variety of groups such as Oxford Youth Works and Grace Church in West London continued to bring elements from contemporary culture and the Christian tradition together in innovative forms of worship. In January 2011, www.alternativeworship.org listed 37 groups in the UK that were within the alternative worship ethos.

By 2000 perhaps up to 100 youth and teenage congregations of various kinds had emerged (Moynagh, 2001, p. 110). They included the 'Soul Survivor' network of youth churches and Revelation Youth Church in Chichester. Many were combining food, ingredients from contemporary culture, informal interaction and Christian practices in ways that, for the time, were strikingly new. Some were entirely spontaneous and unconnected with groups elsewhere, such as a couple who rented temporarily a vacant vicarage on a council estate, got to know some of the local teenagers (who had never been to church), invited them regularly into their lounge and a year later commented, 'I suppose we've started an emerging church.' For them lounge, church and unauthorized leadership was an unexpected combination.

Other novel combinations included the founding in 1998 of a separate congregation for people who had been through the Alpha course at Holy Trinity, Margate, uniting the concepts of Alpha and being a congregation for possibly the first time. Under the remit of Urban Expressions, in the late 1990s church plants in London's East End brought together home, food and worship in a manner that was certainly not new to the Christian tradition, but was not how most people in the capital experienced church.

By the mid 2000s, unusual combinations had multiplied. In Liverpool making bread was locked together with church (Glasson, 2006). At Haydock, Merseyside, missional clusters were introduced alongside the existing cell model of church. They included *FamLeigh First*, which combined the notion of parish with school: a faith community owned the school as its 'parish' (Hopkins and Breen, 2007, p. 24). The first Fresh Expressions DVD, published in 2006, contained examples of church coalescing with a skateboard park, with surfers and with cafe.[6] Creative expressions of church had joined-up thinking at their core.

Goldstein, Hazy and Silberstang (2010, p. 113) suggest that a further element is needed to generate novelty – the coming together of different perspectives; two or more people tackling a problem pool their different insights. They cite research highlighting the importance of diversity in the creative process. At a national level Archbishop Rowan Williams, an Anglo-Catholic with a liberal ethical theology, injected an element of diversity into the fresh expressions story. As Bishop of Monmouth, Williams was vexed by the disconnection between the church and the bulk of the population, and had direct experience of some imaginative church plants in the diocese. This set him on a path of reflection that prepared him to make *Mission-shaped Church* a priority when it was published soon after his translation to Canterbury.

His support broadened the church-planting tradition in the Church of England, which had been dominated by evangelicals (who also comprised

---

6 *Expressions: the dvd – 1: Stories of church for a changing culture*, produced by Norman Ivison and available from www.freshexpressions.org.uk.

most of the *Mission-shaped Church* working party). It became easier for the whole church to endorse the report. Archbishop Rowan himself contributed the phrase 'mixed economy' to describe different types of church existing alongside each other in mutual respect and support (Croft, 2008c, p. 5).

Disequilibrium has involved

- mounting dis-ease with existing church;
- fresh expressions of church, involving novel combinations, that suggested new ways of practising church.

Amplification

In complexity theory, stable systems tend to dampen innovation.[7] They deploy various strategies to resist novelty. Large changes become possible when the system is less stable – instability is a sign of openness to change. For a system to become unstable, small changes need to be amplified. The stronger the amplification, the more likely it is that resistance will be overcome. Amplification occurs through feedback – the effects of actions feed back through the system and influence future actions. Positive feedback creates a cycle of self-reinforcement, which increases the likelihood of other similar changes (Lichtenstein and Plowman, 2009, p. 620).

Spreading stories

Amplification happens when news about an innovation spreads, encouraging others to innovate too. This has been important in the story of British fresh expressions. In particular, since 1999, the Church Army's Sheffield Centre has played a key role in disseminating stories about new types of church through its quarterly publication series, *Encounters on the Edge*, whose subscription base had grown to 425 by 2011. These publications helped raise awareness in the early 2000s that stirrings were in the undergrowth, and provided an important evidence base for *Mission-shaped Church*. The work of Stuart Murray, a Baptist and leading researcher on church planting, had a similar effect (2004a, 2004b, 2006).

---

7 Theologically, this is interesting. The statement could be challenged if God is seen as a 'stable system', unchanging through and through, for this 'stable' God also innovated in bringing creation into being. On the other hand, if God is unchanging in his character but there is movement in his internal relationships – Fiddes likens them to a dance (2000a, pp. 72–81) – then the statement would be consistent with our understanding of God.

Mission-shaped Church itself, with its huge sales, was a major amplifier. Though some have seen the report as an attempt to institutionalize and control fresh expressions, its authors intended to describe what was happening, provide a theological defence and encourage the church to give appropriate support, including dismantling institutional blocks (pp. xii–xiii). The report sought not to control, but to permit and facilitate. Greatly helped by being endorsed by the Church of England's General Synod and then by the British Methodist Conference, it quickly became an authoritative text. It gave legitimacy to people exploring new ways of being church and encouraged others.

The Fresh Expressions team

Subsequent to the report's publication, the Archbishops of Canterbury and York appointed the Fresh Expressions team, headed by Steven Croft, now Bishop of Sheffield.[8] The team was largely funded by the Lambeth Partners, a charity that raises money to support aspects of the Archbishop of Canterbury's vision. The Methodist Church was a partner from the beginning, the Congregational Federation has partnered for several years and the United Reformed Church has become a partner.[9] A number of agencies, such as the Church Army, are also partners.

The Fresh Expressions team has had amplifying effects in a number of ways. Steven Croft's initial year (in 2005) of listening to pioneers affirmed and legitimized what these 'early adopters' were seeking to do. An online directory of fresh expressions of church had over 750 entries by 2009. Though it is doubtful that all met the team's 2006 definition,[10] the growing number of entries offered a tangible sign that the phenomenon was far from insignificant.

An early tour round a number of Methodist districts and Church of England diocesan synods, followed by a later tour in 2009–11, helped to spread news of what was happening on the ground. Two DVDs, one already referred to and the second in 2007,[11] contained stories of these new

---

8 In 2009, Bishop Graham Cray, who had been Bishop of Maidstone, was appointed the Archbishops' Missioner and Team Leader of Fresh Expressions.

9 At the time of writing, the Church of Scotland seems likely to do so too.

10 'A fresh expression is a form of church for our changing culture established primarily for the benefit of people who are not yet members of any church.

- It will come into being through principles of listening, service, incarnational mission and making disciples.
- It will have the potential to become a mature expression of church shaped by the gospel and the enduring marks of the church and for its cultural context.' (Croft, 2008c, p. 10).

11 *Expressions: the dvd – 2: Changing Church in Every Place* produced by Norman Ivison, available from www.freshexpressions.org.uk.

and different forms of church. The first in particular has been widely used, selling approaching 5,000 copies by 2011, which makes it one of the most popular Christian DVDs to come out of the UK.

To whet people's appetite, Vision Days have provided a story-based introduction to fresh expressions of church. By the start of 2011, 74 had been held, with nearly 5,700 people attending. A downloadable six-week *mission-shaped intro* (*msi*) course for use in small or medium-sized church groups focuses on the 'why' of fresh expressions, and had involved an estimated 25,000 participants in 22 countries by 2011. By early that year, the flagship *mission-shaped ministry* (*msm*) course had been or was running ecumenically in nearly 60 centres across the UK with over 2100 students involved. This 'one-year, part-time course takes participants on a learning journey as part of a supportive community, training them for ministry in fresh expressions of church' (www.missionshapedministry.org).

These and other initiatives (such as a presence on Facebook) have been a megaphone for emerging types of church. Events like Vision Days have given pioneers a platform from which to tell their stories and enthuse their audiences. Stories have legitimized pioneering developments, given others the confidence to follow suit and encouraged the UK churches to give more official support. The Church of Scotland, for example, has been influenced by the spread of fresh expressions in England, as have churches in North America, Australia, New Zealand and parts of Europe.

Official support

Other signs of official support have further amplified the acceptance of fresh expressions, encouraging more people to start one. In 2004, the Methodist Conference identified fresh ways of being church as one of its five priorities and subsequently appointed the Fresh Ways Working Group to take the agenda forward. A succession of presidents, who serve for a year as head of the church, have actively supported the vision, which is now integral to the church's official thinking. 'Venture FX' is a Methodist scheme to identify 20 people with pioneering gifts who will be funded to start 20 Christian communities among young adults with no Christian heritage. It is a powerful symbol of the church's commitment to fresh expressions. A high-level group seeks to overcome institutional blockages as they are identified.

The Church of England has introduced a new category of clergy, Ordained Pioneer Ministers, who are like other ministers (they can perform the sacraments, for example) but are called and trained specifically to develop fresh expressions of church. Seventeen had been ordained by 2009, with another 70 in training in 2010 (*A Mixed Economy for Mission*, 4.6). Fresh expressions have become part of the general curriculum in many ministerial training courses (Croft 2008a, p. 47).

Since 2009, Bishops' Mission Orders have provided an officially sanctioned route for Church of England practitioners to start churches crossing parish boundaries. Twenty-two were in effect in 19 dioceses by October 2011. A number of Church of England dioceses have created part or full-time posts to advise on fresh expressions. In some cases, funds have been made available to support individual initiatives.

Networks

Complexity theorists stress the importance of information-rich networks in creating amplifying feedback – 'to understand networks is to understand self-organization' (Chiles and Meyer, 2001, p. 83). Lichtenstein and Plowman (2009, p. 623) note that amplification is more likely to be present when leaders and members of a system encourage multiple interactions between individuals. Some theorists have gone so far as to suggest that organizations exist primarily in the conversations between their members (Shaw, 2002).

The multiplication of networks has been a key piece of the fresh expressions jigsaw. Between 1989 and 1996 Challenge 2000 was a central player in the Disciple A Whole Nation (DAWN) initiative to plant 20,000 churches in the UK by 2000. The unrealistic nature of these goals and lack of funds strongly contributed to its demise, but Challenge 2000 brought church planting on to the agenda of virtually all the denominations and spawned a number of formal and informal networks.

Through the 1990s and since, Anglican ministers Bob and Mary Hopkins (not least through their training courses and mentoring) have been at the centre of a variety of networks that have accelerated the flow of information about new contextual churches. The Hopkins played an important role, for example, in encouraging the Lincolnshire-based Ground Level Network to be instrumental in planting around 20 churches by 2011.

Networks with a significant impact include Urban Expressions, part of a looser Baptist church-planting network, Church Army's network of pioneers, the networks encouraged by Canon Phil Potter in the Anglican diocese of Liverpool, which has developed one of the most strategic approaches to fresh expressions in the UK, the blah network hosted by CMS (formerly Church Mission Society), the learning communities formed by St Thomas Crookes in Sheffield and by the Holy Trinity Brompton (HTB) network of church plants, the Co-Mission network in London, the missional orders described below and many others. In addition are a host of informal networks, ranging from gatherings of pioneers that have a short but fruitful life to those who follow a specific blog.

The Fresh Expressions team has sought to encourage networking among pioneers. The initial assumption was that these networks would be quite stable and durable, with something of the flavour of St Thomas Crookes' and HTB's learning communities, whose members share their knowledge.

The 'Round Table' of Anglo-Catholic practitioners probably comes close to this. But experience has shown that while durable networks are helpful for some, church founders often rely on well-established personal networks for emotional support and collect information about pioneering from fluid, episodic and fleeting relationships. *Networking* may be just as important as *networks*.

Thus the annual national Break-out conference of pioneers is beginning to play a critical role in enabling practitioners from different backgrounds to broaden their range of contacts. Through such gatherings, church founders can keep extending their networks rather than be limited to their existing ones.

Amplification and the individual

Amplification works at the level of the individual in several ways. Stories of what others are doing can inspire and give legitimacy to individuals' own ideas, creating a bandwagon effect by persuading more people to join the trend. They can also challenge unhelpful preconceptions. 'I thought fresh expressions were about cafe church. Now I see that you have to listen to the context first and that a fresh expression can take many different forms.' As a result, would-be founders make fewer mistakes and their initiatives are more fruitful, which encourages others to get involved.

Stories that spread good practice are an especially important form of amplification. In a complex world, individuals either do not have the time, or the motivation or skill to assess – perhaps by trial and error – what will work in their contexts. 'We're making it up as we go along' may feel exciting for cutting-edge pioneers, but can seem daunting to those coming up behind. Usually people prefer to imitate others – 'it works for them, it will work for me' (Kandori, Mailath and Rob, 1993, p. 31; Dietz, Burns and Buttel, 1990, pp. 159–60). Stories are welcomed as an easy way to learn.

Yet this desire to imitate is problematic where context makes a big difference. If the context is not the same, what worked for them (such as a published evangelistic course) may *not* work for me (perhaps because attendance at organized meetings is erratic). To help avoid unreflective imitation, the Fresh Expressions' *Share* website has sought to draw from pioneers' experience themes – illustrated with stories – that can guide good practice (www.sharethe guide.org).[12] Harnessed through general principles, the experience of others is thus amplified. This makes it easier to pioneer a contextual church and increases the probability of getting it right, which – in a further amplification – is likely to persuade more people to have a go.

It seems that there has been considerable amplification in terms of bandwagon effects, and a fair amount in terms of the 'I hadn't realize that'

---

12 *Share* has now been incorporated in the main Fresh Expressions site (www. freshexpressions.org.uk), but can still be accessed through its original web address.

kind of learning. Through *Share*, training courses from several stables, the Church Army Sheffield Centre, publications and other vehicles, there has been some embrace of helpful methodologies, especially the importance of listening to context, but the spread of good practice remains a challenge.

Amplification has involved

- spreading stories;
- a central team that could act as a megaphone;
- explicit support from church authorities;
- the multiplication of networks;
- spread of good practice.

Recombination/self-organization

In the Lichtenstein/Plowman model, a third group of processes involves recombining the system's elements to reshape the organization. This is *self*-organization because it is not controlled from the centre but reflects a multitude of decisions by individuals and groups. Self-organization occurs when new ways of doing things challenge and then replace existing approaches.

Old and new attractors

Unpacking this, complexity theorists often use the term 'attractor' when describing self-organization.[13] Put simply, an attractor can be understood as something that attracts support. Systems are organized around an attractor, which are ways of doing things that over time have gained support. Emergence occurs when a new attractor, a new way of organizing, gathers enough support to challenge successfully the existing pattern of organization, an old attractor.

Before the new one replaces the old one, the two attractors compete for a while. During this period, the system is no longer stable, dominated by one attractor, one pattern of behaviour. It has been destabilized by the early appearance of an alternative approach, the new attractor. The landscape looks confusing and individuals are uncertain about the future.

Three outcomes are possible. The old attractor wins, or the new one does or the system slides into chaos. In the first and second, once one of the

---

13 The literature distinguishes between different types of attractor. See, for example, Stacy, Griffin and Shaw (2000, p. 87). A good introduction to the concept of 'strange attractors' can be found in Wheatley (2006, pp. 115–34).

attractors has prevailed, the system in theory returns to stability. In practice, in our fast-changing world another attractor is likely to be on the horizon, offering a new challenge, so that the system never feels completely at rest. In the third outcome, the system slips into chaos because the rival attractors tear the organization apart – perhaps (hypothetically) fresh expressions exit a denomination en masse, leaving it seriously weakened.

Theorists describe how one attractor replaces an existing one in various ways.[14] A common notion is the 'edge of chaos'. This is a situation where the old and new attractors are in competition with each other – the system is unstable. The outcome of the rivalry is unclear. The system could lapse into chaos, or one of the attractors could predominate and the organization head toward stability. A system is on the edge of chaos because it is on the stable side of the boundary between stability and chaos.

Parts of the UK church could be described as approaching an edge of chaos state. Fresh expressions of church are beginning to challenge the status quo, but whether and how the denominations will reorganize is unclear. Will the structures accommodate new types of church?

The strength of the old attractor

Despite the amplifying actions just described, many in the wider church are trapped in a 'narrative' of decline. It is a story of shrinking attendance, clergy numbers and finance. Churches are increasingly focused on managing this decline. Diminishing financial and managerial resources are spread ever more thinly over existing congregations, with little left for innovation. Observation suggests that in most discussions about strategy, coping with the effects of decline is higher on the agenda than starting new types of church.

Where decline has become normal, some find innovation threatening. A new church may be accused of drawing people away from struggling neighbours. Shifting resources from existing to new churches is seen as a risk: what will happen if the new gatherings are unfruitful? Will the church as a whole be weakened? Institutions have an instinct for self-preservation. Spending on a new initiative puts resources into something that does not yet exist. No one misses the money if it is not spent. But withdrawing funds from an existing activity evokes howls of anguish (Mannoia, 2005, p. 115).

Amid these head winds are signs that an alternative attractor is starting to take shape. Given complexity theory's stress on unpredictability, it would be rash to anticipate what this attractor will look like, if it prevails. But there are five pointers.

---

14 In addition to works already cited, Chiles, Meyer and Hench (2004) provide a helpful application of the dissipative structure model to organizations. Their article made a significant input into the Lichtenstein/Plowman model.

The mixed economy

One is the idea of the mixed economy, which the Church of England diocese of Liverpool has couched in terms of rivers and lakes. Rivers of fresh expressions flow in and out of the lake of existing church, renewing the waters in the process. Rowan Williams has expressed his hope that over time existing and new forms of church will grow closer together, mutually enriching each other (Podcast, July 2010 extra, www.freshexpressions. org.uk). Crucially, this frames the new attractor not as fresh expressions standing against inherited forms of church, but as a more diverse church in contrast to a narrower version. A mixed-economy attractor is challenging a single-economy church, the old attractor.

Margaret Wheatley notes that 'systems achieve order from clear centres rather than imposed restraints' (2006, p. 132). She suggests that a new centre, a new attractor, should be built on meaning – such as: what does this new way of doing things mean to us in our organization? How does it fit it into the ongoing story of the organization? How does it enable the organization to achieve its goals more effectively? The mixed economy is an example of such meaning. If it is theologically well grounded, weaved into the denomination's values and expressed appropriately, the idea has the potential to help churches interpret positively their journeys to greater diversity.

Corridors

Second, it seems that semi-autonomous 'corridors' are starting to be cleared within the inherited church for new contextual communities. In the Church of England, BMOs (Bishops' Mission Orders) could enable local churches to develop and lead networks of new congregations that jump local-church boundaries. A church in Bristol, for instance, has been given a BMO that allows it to initiate gatherings broadly anywhere in the north of the city. It is not hard to imagine such a church growing new congregations, networking them to provide mutual support, producing its own leaders whom it trains and employs to establish further gatherings, and in time becoming a substantial presence within the diocese.

The CMS (Church Mission Society) has been recognized as an 'acknowledged community', which is a religious order. This allows it to form missional communities within the Church of England that are more independent of dioceses than the typical Anglican church. As an acknowledged community, CMS has a bishop (currently the Bishop of Coventry) who exercises oversight and is entitled to ordain ministers to serve within the community. In 2010, CMS launched a training course for lay (and now ordained) pioneers, and is likely to deploy them in collaboration with local churches and to offer them continuing support.

The Church Army, too, is in the process of becoming an acknowledged community. It currently trains and deploys Church of England evangelists, many of whom are pioneering contextual churches. Given its heritage of supporting lay evangelists, it would not be a large step for the Church Army to host an ecumenical third order of lay church planters, who would have an allegiance to their denomination but receive training and ongoing support under its auspices.

Other dispersed missional orders are emerging as part of the renewed interest in monasticism. They include The Order of Mission (TOM), which grew to over 350 members worldwide between 2003 and 2010 (Kershaw, 2010, p. 80), the 24–7 ecumenical global prayer movement among young people that has expanded to 90 nations in ten years (Freeman, 2010, p. 50) and the Northumbria community, which has been longer established.

Church founders may find it more attractive to bring communities to birth under these BMO or religious-order umbrellas, where the ethos is favourable, than to struggle on their own within the existing structures of the church, where contextual church is often misunderstood and support inadequate. These networks would provide various kinds of support, such as negotiating with the wider church on founders' behalf to clear away misunderstandings and obstacles.

The Methodist Church also has a tradition of religious orders, such as the Methodist Diaconal Order, which uses the language of pioneering to describe its role. Might this Order eventually become a focus for fresh expressions or might a separate 'fresh expressions' order emerge? Churches Together in Lincolnshire are forming an ecumenical lay order of pioneers. What other 'corridors' might open up?

Regional and local cooperation

A third pointer to the new attractor is evidence of growing cooperation between churches at regional and local levels. Fresh Expressions is encouraging the formation of FEASTs, Fresh Expressions Area Strategy Teams. These are groups of key individuals who encourage fresh expressions of church across a wide area. Several are coming into existence, with the Lincolnshire FEAST especially showing how effective they can be.

Although there is a long way to go, the appetite for church collaboration at a more local level seems to be growing. *Hope 08* encouraged churches in 1,500 areas of the UK to undertake joint projects in 2008. Initially viewed as a one-off, the initiative was sufficiently fruitful for its life to be extended as *Hope Together*. The aim is to encourage local churches to work together for mission, in which starting new contextual churches will have a place. Milton Keynes illustrates how churches can cooperate effectively on mission. Among several initiatives, the churches have formed an ecumenical group to oversee the development of Christian communities on new housing estates and elsewhere.

'Temples', 'synagogues' and 'tents'

Fourth, a growing number of contextual churches are emerging in the settings of everyday life – in leisure centres, among groups who share a common interest such as reading books, going to films or outdoor activities, in the workplace or among friends. Some have close links to a parent church nearby, but in other cases the ties are looser.

Fresh Expressions wants to support lay-led initiatives beyond the reach of the local church as a priority in the years ahead. How these new communities connect with the wider body will be of major concern. Will they exist as isolated groups for a while and then wither away through lack of outside stimulus? Or will members attend two 'local' churches, one 'in life' during the week and another, perhaps larger one at the weekend?

In her study of four Church of England fresh expressions, Louise Nelstrop found that a significant proportion of those involved had retained ties to their existing churches.

> Some had intended to leave but the initial fragility of the 'fresh expression' had meant that they had waited to see what would happen. Once they discovered that they could do both, much to their surprise, several actually felt more integrated into the parish system now that their sense of church wasn't limited to it (Nelstrop, 2008, p. 101).

What will happen where communities in everyday contexts, perhaps including people from different denominations, have weaker connections to a local church? Might this be where collaboration between churches becomes crucial? Might 'coalitions of the willing' provide prayer retreats, study days and the like to help new believers grow in the faith?

What seems to be emerging is a reconfiguration of church into 'temples', 'synagogues' and 'tents'. 'Temples' are where individuals connect with the whole body of Christ – conferences, retreats, celebrations, pilgrimages, websites and much else. Like Jesus, believers go up to the 'temple' from time to time. 'Synagogues' are the conventional local church, where worshippers are nourished in Scripture and the Christian tradition. Again like Jesus, believers attend 'synagogue' regularly. These local churches may continue to multiply through fresh expressions.

'Tents' are church in life – small worshipping communities that concentrate on practical discipleship by serving their contexts and drawing others into the faith. Some may not have a long existence because of changing circumstances, but be fruitful for a period. This transience perhaps resonates with the tents the Israelites inhabited as they moved through Sinai.

If this sort of pattern emerges, it will not be a rehash of the church growth cell–congregation–celebration model. It will be more fluid ('tents' will come and go) and the boundaries between the components will overlap.

A large local church may in some respects double up as 'synagogue' and 'temple'. Whereas church growth theorists linked cell and congregation closely together, the ties between 'tents' and 'synagogues' could be looser – members of a 'tent' may attend different 'synagogues'. Central direction in the whole will be weaker and there will be a stronger emergent feel.

Downward causation

This possible configuration of church suggests a fifth characteristic of the emerging attractor. In today's network culture, church will increasingly be characterized by criss-crossing ties. Not least, 'corridors' will intersect with regional FEASTs and local 'coalitions of the willing'. As is already happening, networks of churches will encourage considerable movement – members leaving one gathering and joining another, for example – as individuals and groups access networks and travel along them.

Emergence theorists believe that when new levels of organization come into being, they exert 'downward causation' on the levels below them (Goldstein, Hazy and Silberstang, 2008, p. 105). If church reorganizes along mixed-economy lines, corridors of founders and other new forms of organization will change behaviour throughout the church. Already we are seeing hints of this. One person commented about her local church, 'Introducing fresh expressions two years ago has really changed us.'

Recombination/self-organization may involve

- the mixed economy;
- corridors – networks of fresh expressions that clear space for new churches within the denominations;
- regional and local cooperation, such as FEASTS and 'coalitions of the willing';
- 'temples', 'synagogues' and 'tents';
- downward causation – new levels of organization change the levels below.

Stabilization

A fourth component of the Lichtenstein/Plowman model is stabilization. The more that leaders and members of a system adapt to local constraints, the easier they find it to stabilize the emergent order (Lichtenstein and Plowman, 2009, p. 625). Sensitivity to social rules and values shapes novelties 'in a way consistent with the system's accumulated history and learning, preserving the system's identity and core behavioural patterns' (Chiles, Myers and Hench, 2004, p. 502). Innovations get clothed in the familiar, which makes other people more willing to learn from them and reduces resistance.

Adapting to the denomination

Fresh expressions of church have sought to adapt to local constraints in two directions. One has been the denomination. An example was the Methodist Church's embrace of the Fresh Expressions initiative, which appealed to evangelical Methodists' commitment to evangelism and to Methodists' strong commitment to ecumenism. Ticking both boxes greatly helped the church to get on board. Within the Church of England, Archbishop Rowan has connected emerging church to the parochial system by suggesting that 'both assume that the Church must show itself credible by being where people are, literally and culturally' (Williams, 2006, p. 54). He has linked fresh expressions to the Anglo-Catholic tradition, noting that 'catholic' is 'that dimension of the Christian life which is concerned with speaking the whole truth to the whole person' (Williams, 2009, p. 1).

The suggestion – by the Fresh Expressions team and others – that these new communities will often start with listening, followed by loving and serving, potentially resonates with traditions that emphasize the social responsibilities of the church. The parallel emphasis on evangelism strikes a chord with evangelicals.

In addition, new contextual churches are recovering inherited traditions and 'remixing' them with contemporary cultural trends, such as the use of visual images and symbols from the tradition. The spread of 'new monasticism' is giving an impetus to this. Growth into the tradition often happens in surprising ways. A London-based 'heavy metal' gathering, for example, shares in some of the activities of its neighbouring Anglo-Catholic church.

Explicitly connecting with the tradition is helping new contextual churches to make their home in the body. At the same time, the denominations are finding ways to recognize them and help them be accountable. This is happening reflexively. As fresh expressions are drawn into a denomination's culture, they model different ways of being church. For growing numbers of worshippers, the pattern of church life ceases to be a given and becomes a matter of intent. As individuals look again at what it means to be church, attitudes become more flexible, making it easier for the denomination to welcome the new.

Adapting to the context

In using emergence theory to recount the history of musical theatres in Branson, Missouri, Chiles, Myers and Hench note that key aspects of local culture shaped how the theatres were developed, helping the town to retain its unique character and the theatres to gain support (2004, pp. 512–3). This is a good example of contextualization, which is the second way new contextual churches have sought to adapt to local constraints.

Negotiating these two sites of stability – the church context and the local context – can prove a considerable challenge. Yet a growing number of contextual churches are doing this successfully, despite some of the heartaches involved (see, for instance, www.freshexpressions.org.uk/stories). In so doing, these new communities are finding a place within the values of their sponsoring local church (or group of churches) and through this within the ethos of the denomination.

Some people see this as the inherited church domesticating what is new, blunting the latter's radical edge (Rollins, 2008, pp. 71–7). Were this to happen, it would represent – in the language of complexity theory – the triumph of the old attractor. Alternatively, the reflexive process of stabilization could allow new expressions of Christian community to find a place within the inherited church – and increasingly change it. A new attractor would then emerge, combining novel and existing forms of church in fruitful relationship.

Stabilization involves

- adapting to the tradition, including the denomination;
- adapting to the context of the new church.

Conclusion

New contextual churches are emerging in Britain through processes of disequilibrium, amplification, self-organization and stabilization. Already they are having a substantial influence on ecclesial life, not only in this country but in other parts of the world. Do they represent the early stages in the birth of a new attractor, the mixed-economy church?

There are positive signs. The idea of fresh expressions, even if the term is not used, is taking root in denominations beyond those officially involved in the Fresh Expressions initiative – from the Assemblies of God to the Baptist Church – and overseas (for example Robinson and Brighton, 2009). Denominations associated with Fresh Expressions have steadily deepened their commitment. By 2009 19 out of 43 Church of England dioceses reported that they had created a strategy for encouraging fresh expressions of church and church planting (*A Mixed Economy for Mission*, 3.2).

A telling sign is how church organizations and networks are responding increasingly to the fresh expressions agenda, whether it is publishers, mission agencies or missional networks. Cell UK, for example, is now working in the spirit of '4 life' to underline its focus on encouraging missional communities in the context of everyday life.

The number of fresh expressions continues to multiply. In 2010, the Methodist Church counted 941 fresh expressions, associated with 723 churches out of a total of 5,162 – 14 per cent (*Are We Yet Alive?* 2011, p. 14). In 2011, the Church of England identified at least 1,000 parishes – 6 per cent of the total – with a fresh expression of church.[15] In both cases the definition was wider than the 'new contextual church' one used here. Even so, the relatively rapid spread of the language suggests that, at the very least, the concept of fresh expressions is helping the inherited church to think in more missional terms.

An informed estimate reckons that 50 to 100 churches had or were starting mid-sized communities by 2011, with the number of such churches growing rapidly. If each church had five communities, a not unreasonable assumption, 250 to 500 mid-sized communities – serving people outside the church – would be involved.[16] Many of these may not have been counted as fresh expressions in the Methodist and Church of England surveys.

Despite this progress, a 2009 report to the Church of England's General Synod could identify only three dioceses (out of 43) whose strategies for fresh expressions really stood out. 'Even in these dioceses there is still a long way to go before it could be said that a mixed economy church has been established as irreversible and normative . . .' The majority of lay people were unaware or had only a very partial understanding of the mixed economy (*A Mixed Economy for Mission* 2009, 4.9, 4.28).

Anecdotal evidence and some limited research (for example, Stone, 2010) suggest that most fresh expressions are small, have a significant proportion of people who already go to church, and where they are reaching out are connecting with people on the fringe of church rather than the growing numbers of never-churched. There are encouraging exceptions, but the overall picture is of the UK church being still at the beginnings of a journey to fresh expressions. Despite growing momentum, the vehicle could yet stall.

Further reading

Drane, John and Olive Fleming Drane, *Reformed, Reforming, Emerging and Experimenting*, Report for the Church of Scotland, 2010.
Mission-shaped Church: Church Planting and Fresh Expressions of Church in a Changing Context, London: Church House Publishing, 2004.
Wheatley, Margaret J., *Leadership and the New Science: Discovering Order in a Chaotic World*, 3rd edition, San Francisco: Berrett-Koehler, 2006.

---

15 Press Release, 19 January 2012.
16 Estimate provided by Bob and Mary Hopkins in January 2011.

Questions for discussion

- Much of this chapter has been about official support for new contextual churches. What should individuals and churches do when this support is not present? How far does the spread of new contextual churches depend on official support?
- Do you agree that the mixed economy in Britain could yet stall? If so, what would avoid this?
- What are the lessons from Britain's experience? If you were advising your network or denomination, what strategy would you suggest for multiplying contextual churches?

4

Sociological Perspectives

The last chapter suggested that new contextual churches have emerged largely in response to a growing disconnect between the church and its various contexts. This has begun to generate a state of disequilibrium as church members have sought to respond. However, a number of scholars, such as Steve Bruce (2002) and Paul Heelas (2008), believe that the current gulf between the church and society is too wide to be bridged. Profound social changes are propelling the church into terminal decline, especially in Europe. Though many people are seeking 'spiritualities of life', this demand is being satisfied outside the church, making a resurgence of the church unlikely.

This chapter asks whether such gloomy projections are right. The answer is developed in dialogue with three strands of literature – the secularization debate, discussions around the expressive (or post-materialist) self and Manuel Castells's writings on the 'network society'. These threads describe three 'turns' in society to which the church, if it is to flourish, must respond – an ecclesial turn, an ethical turn, and an economic and social turn. The chapter argues that new contextual churches fit well with these sociological trends.

An ecclesial turn

The ecclesial turn refers to the turning away from church in much of the industrially advanced world. Using data from 22 nations in the European Social Survey, undertaken in 2002/2003, David Voas found that 'Each generation in every country surveyed is less religious than the last . . .' (Voas, 2009, p. 167). Although the most religious countries are changing faster than the least, the fall in religious commitment during the twentieth century has been remarkably constant across the continent. Not only in Europe, but even in the United States with its stronger religious affiliation than Europe, younger age groups are less likely to attend church than older ones (Hollinghurst, 2010, pp. 82–3). Similar trends have been observed in Australia and New Zealand (*Pointers*, 2010).

Secularization

This decline has often been understood in terms of secularization – a slippery term that has been used in different ways. Writers on secularization tend to refer to the decline of religion, which is not exactly the same as the decline of church. The assumption here is that a loss of influence by the Christian religion will be reflected in falling attendance at church. Secularization is taken as referring to the decline in church attendance and influence.

The sociologist, Bryan Wilson, defined secularization 'as the process by which religious thinking, practices, and institutions lose their significance for the operating of the social system'. He added that religion is not destined to disappear entirely: rather, its presence and significance in society will diminish as economies industrialize and become increasingly advanced (Wilson, 1998, p. 49).

Steve Bruce (2002) highlights the rise of rationality and individualism as integral to the process of secularization. Rationality was reflected in the spread of scientific modes of thought, which removed the need for religion to explain the world, made many religious ideas and doctrines implausible and, in particular, created a sense of mastery over fate. Embodying rational procedures within bureaucratic organizations created an impression that order in the world could be maintained without the aid of God.

Individualism has undermined the communal basis of religious life. When, thankfully, society became tolerant of non-Christian beliefs, these beliefs mushroomed and then challenged existing views. It is harder to be confident in an opinion when it is assailed by alternatives. The multiplication of views makes opinions about faith increasingly subjective – religious views become a matter of personal choice. Religion has shrunk from being accepted by the bulk of society to being one lifestyle option among many. The decline is likely to continue.

The inevitability of secularization has been disputed by scholars who note that religious affiliation worldwide is rising (see Davie, 2007, pp. 64–5, 104–9). As the global south has industrialized, the number of religious adherents has not shrunk, as the secularization thesis predicts, but grown – witness, for example, the expansion of the African churches. This is often seen as a knock-down argument against secularization.

However, drawing on four waves of the World Values Survey conducted between 1981 and 2001 and extending to nearly 80 countries, Norris and Inglehart (2004) argue that societies do indeed become increasingly secular as economies develop. More people overall may adhere to traditional religion (including Christianity), but this is because the effects of modernization have not yet become fully apparent.

Besides leading to a decline in religion, modernization also reduces the fertility rate. Better education is associated with smaller families. When birth rates drop in secularizing countries, younger more secular cohorts are smaller than older traditional ones, among whom religious practice is more widespread. The overall decline in religion appears less marked. On the other hand, in countries where modernization is occurring more slowly, higher birth rates produce relatively large cohorts of more religiously committed young people. These two trends together disguise the long-term trend for religion to become less significant.

Shorter and Onyancha (1997) found that 40 per cent of people attended church weekly in traditional rural Kenya, but only 12 per cent did so in the modernizing capital of Nairobi (with 20 per cent attending less frequently). Though church attendance in Nairobi increased as the city's population grew, observers exaggerated the trend because church building did not keep pace with the growing number of worshippers: churches were full to over-flowing. It looked as if the churches were flourishing. In reality, church attendance was falling in percentage terms because the urban population was expanding even faster than church numbers. If attendance was measured as a proportion of the population, the church was losing ground. Nairobi illustrates how the global South appears to be following the secularizing trends of the global North.

Both Shmuel Eisenstadt (2000) and Bruce (2001) have warned against assuming that other countries will tread exactly Europe's path of modernization. In Eisenstadt's phrase, there are 'multiple modernities', each shaped by the history and culture of the country concerned. Proponents of secularization can argue, therefore, that secularization will look different and occur at a different pace from one part of the world to another.

A problem of demand or supply?

The secularization argument rests on the idea that the demand for religion declines as societies modernize. But might the falling demand for religion be due to deficiencies in what the church offers – not shortcomings in the Christian story, but in how the church embodies the story? Has the church lost its appeal because it has failed to adapt to people's changing needs and concerns? By implication, if the church did adapt, might the decline be reversed?

The debate about 'fuzzy fidelity' may point in this direction. Voas has found that across Europe, as religious practice declines individuals retain a casual loyalty to religion – what he calls 'fuzzy fidelity' (Voas, 2009). But religion plays only a minor part in their lives. The pattern is for people to withdraw from church, which leads to an increase in 'fuzzy fidelity', but 'fuzzy fidelity' then falls over a lengthy period. Individuals become steadily more detached from their religious roots.

Grace Davie is more hesitant – 'the role of the churches in western Europe has, in fact, been written off far too soon' (Davie, 2001, p. 101). The church has the tacit support of considerably more people than those who attend regularly. These supporters continue to identify with the church to some extent, they want it to enact the faith on their behalf (what Davie calls 'vicarious religion'), they turn to the church when in need (especially at times of death) and they continue to believe important aspects of the Christian faith, even though they do not actively belong to church.

Unlike Voas who believes that the number of these Christian supporters will inevitably fall, Davie thinks that the decline is not predetermined. Much depends on how the church responds. There is a sizeable constituency of people with some allegiance to the church. They might be prepared to attend more regularly if the church related to them more effectively. Davie (2007, p. 252) notes how in Britain both professional football and cinema attendance declined towards the end of the twentieth century, but then recovered – although patterns changed – as clubs and cinemas found better ways of serving their constituencies.

Similarly, might the church learn to serve people more effectively? It has not always adapted in the past, but at times it has. The Methodist revival in eighteenth-century England allowed ordinary people to 'find and live by their own spiritual style' (Taylor, 2007, p. 455). The Baptists did the same in the rural US and the Pentecostals have done likewise in the global South. Alienated from the formal religion of elites, popular groups have found their voices through more resonant expressions of faith.

A self-limiting church?

The possibility of the church adapting is plausible when we consider three ways in which the church has limited itself. If it can remove these limitations, it might better serve those with a 'fuzzy fidelity' and encourage their more active involvement.

The church has been self-limiting, first, in its *relevance*. It has failed to connect with people's daily concerns. Callum Brown argues that Christian piety was located in masculinity before 1800, but in femininity increasingly thereafter. 'Paeans of praise were heaped on women's innate piety whilst brickbats were hurled at men's susceptibility to temptation' (Brown, 2009, p. 195). Churchgoing decreased from the late nineteenth century, and the fall-off was especially marked among men, whose social pastimes were ignored or frowned upon. Yet men still had their children baptized and attended the major festivals. They stayed plugged into church because their wives remained committed.

In the 1960s, however, the nature of femininity changed radically. Growing numbers of women entered the workplace, while the sexual revolution challenged traditional ideas of courtship and marriage. Women began to see themselves in a different light, but the church was slow to respond. It held on to a traditional view of the family and women, making it seem irrelevant. Women became less involved, and with them their families.

It is precisely because 'the personal' changed so much in the 1960s – and has continued to change in the four decades since – that the churches are in seemingly terminal decay and British Christian culture is in its death throes. . . . The search for personal faith is now in 'the New Age' of minor cults, personal development and consumer choice. (Brown, 2009, p. 196)

Though helpful, Brown sees changes in society as the prime cause of the church's decline, whereas arguably the church's failure to respond to these changes is just as important. The church has been slow to engage with the day-to-day concerns of contemporary women (as well as men), while remaining faithful to the Christian story. Other organizations have adapted to social change, but not the church. The British retailer Tesco, for example, started with supermarkets, developed hypermarkets and then introduced Tesco Local. It has retained the brand while innovating the outlets. By contrast, a gulf has opened up between today's postmodern mood and the modernist feel of the church.

Second, the church has been self-limiting in its *availability*. It has become inaccessible on an everyday basis to swathes of people. Members have tended to set the rules – when they meet, where and the form their meetings take – without much thought for people on the outside. Sunday morning worship, for instance, is almost impossible for people who are in employment at weekends, have sporting commitments at that time or whose family obligations take them away on Sundays.

More important is that *any* worshipping community will put other people off. Identity is based on identifying with particular groups of people and not identifying with others – 'birds of a feather flock together'. This goes beyond older congregations not appealing to the iPod generation. Obvious and less subtle cues, from social background, to educational level, to values and interests, will tell a visitor whether the congregation contains 'my kind of people'. Most people find it difficult to join a group that seems strange and different. Large segments of the population, therefore, will not identify with the church for social rather than religious reasons, and this necessarily makes the church self-limiting.

Rational choice theorists, such as Roger Finke, maintain that the scale of church attendance is linked to the number of options available. Put simply, if the church narrows down the options for people – in terms of when they can worship, the style on offer or the social nature of the groups they can join – fewer will be likely to attend. Well discussed by Grace Davie (2007, pp. 67–88), the theory suggests that where people can choose from plenty of different churches, as in North America, churchgoing flourishes but where the choice is less, as traditionally in Europe, attendance declines. Finke goes so far as to say that an increase in religious supply creates an increase in demand, not the other way round (cited by Davie, 2007, p. 73).

Though the theory has a strong intuitive appeal, it has been remarkably difficult to prove. Daniel Olson has examined attempts to relate the pluralism index – the number of religious groups in an area and the evenness of their sizes[1] – to religious involvement for the whole area. He found that

> just about any measure of pluralism that one can think of is likely to have a non-causal, mathematically necessary component in its relationship with just about any measure of religious participation and belief. . . . This leaves researchers in the frustrating situation of having many theoretical reasons for thinking that religious pluralism should cause religious participation and belief to either increase or decrease, but with no reliable way of studying these effects. (Olson, 2008, p. 101)

Despite the lack of formal proof, it is highly plausible that if you widen choice, individuals are more likely to find an expression of church that appeals to them and get involved. Failure to widen access, it is fair to assume, has put the church in a missional straitjacket.

Third, the church has been self-limiting in its *organization*. Robin Gill (2003) attributes much of the drop in attendance to excessive church building, especially in the nineteenth century. Competition between denominations and over-optimism produced too many churches and churches too large for the local population. In some areas, such as Cornwall, many of the churches could never be full, even if a substantial proportion of local residents attended. Over-provision meant that maintaining buildings consumed excessive resources. Clergy were allocated to buildings – often largely empty in rural areas – rather than to people, so that the deployment of clergy failed to mirror the distribution of the population. Maintaining near-empty buildings discouraged local congregations, which bred disillusionment, which led to decline, which bred further disillusionment.[2]

It was not just that too many churches were built. Gill notes that the rural model of church was unsuited to the urban contexts of the mid nineteenth century. Churches failed to provide the small networks that might have preserved religious communities in urban areas. 'Fragile beliefs depend for their survival upon small-scale communities. In the absence of such communities, religious beliefs soon withered in cities and a gradual

---

1 Evenness of size is important because it affects the amount of competition. To take an extreme example, if 80 per cent of a suburb were Mormon and they had only one place of worship, while the remaining 20 per cent had three alternatives, the amount of choice for the 80 per cent would be less than if there were several Mormon churches.

2 In his well-received report to Britain's Methodist Conference in 2011, General Secretary Martyn Atkins spoke candidly of Methodism having too many chapels, an up-to-date echo of Gill's theme.

demise of churchgoing inevitably followed.' (Gill, 2003, p. 3) Once decline in attendance was well under way, Christian belief followed suit. There was no corporate experience to sustain it (Gill, 2008).

Gill's doubts about the prevailing church model are supported by the mid 1970s research of the Church of England's Urban Church Project (Urban Church Project, 1974; Wasdell, 1977, pp. 366–70). The research showed that membership of the local church as a percentage of its parish population dropped drastically with a rise in population. Small churches in small parishes reached a higher proportion of the population than large churches in large parishes. Large size constrained congregational growth. A greater number of small congregations would make mission more effective. Subsequent research (for example, Jackson, 2002, pp. 108–45; Schwartz, 2006, pp. 48–50) has confirmed that small churches are more likely to grow than bigger ones. The church has had too many buildings, it seems, but not enough congregations.

The Urban Church Project argued that the self-limiting size of congregations was largely due to clergy-based mission. The laity tended to add fewer people than those who died or left a congregation. It was left to full-time clergy to make up the shortfall. If they failed to do so, the congregation would shrink till a balance between gains and losses was reached. Only in rare cases did the clergy bring in more people than the congregation was losing (Urban Church Project, 1974, pp. 8–11).[3]

This was a self-limiting model, first, because it discouraged lay mission. If lay people brought in more people than left the church, the church would grow. But the clergy-dominated model made this unlikely. It discouraged lay people from thinking that attracting outsiders was their responsibility, while it allowed clergy – wanting to stay in control – to block lay initiatives. Lay people were disempowered, which reinforced their belief that growth (if they thought about it at all) was the clergy's job.

Second, extra clergy seemed to produce diminishing returns. A second clergyman typically added 90 Christmas communicants, while a third averaged only 81 (Urban Church Project, 1974, p. 5). Third, there were not enough clergy anyway, especially in the larger parishes. Clergy numbers were actually falling by the 1970s. Fourthly, the amalgamation of parishes to cope with this fall, the Project presciently argued, would force ministers to spend more time on maintaining the institution and less on mission. Attendance would decline further, leaving the church even less sustainable (Urban Church Project, 1974, 1975; Wasdell, 1977).

---

3 The 'Workpaper' recognized that this argument made all sorts of assumptions and that practice would be more nuanced. But using Church of England figures (and proxies) available for annual gains and losses, the number of parishes, the size of churches and the number of clergy, the model predicted that the average congregation would stabilize at around 150, which was a little lower than the national average for a single clergy congregation (Urban Church Project, 1974, p. 11).

In short, for centuries the church has been 'over-capitalized'. That is, nearly all the church's money has been spent on too many and over large buildings, and on maintaining a clergy-dominated model that has self-limitation built in. Despite some notable mission initiatives, increasingly an institution that supposedly exists for the benefit of non-members has devoted the bulk of its resources to maintaining itself. Why should people outside the church feel it is for them?

A *blueprint for change*

Can these limitations of relevance, access and organization be overcome by reimagining the church? In 1968, the World Council of Churches published a prescient report, prepared for its Uppsala conference, by a group of West European theologians. The group argued that originally 'the parish church' in Europe was a missionary structure. Through it the church reached out to small, comparatively isolated communities. The parish church 'represented the whole Church face to face with what was, to all intents and purposes, for most people, the whole of life' (WCC, 1968, p. 29). But people now lead their lives in a variety of arenas. If the church persists in regarding the parish as its normal structure, it will not confront life at its most significant points.

Though the local congregation still has an important role within residential settings, it is failing to connect with people in the mainstream of their existence.

> In this situation many local congregations tend to withdraw into themselves; care is directed towards the 'faithful', largely by the provision of regular opportunities for worship. The justification for the life of the Church is then found within itself, instead of in its mission in the world. . . . the local congregation is carrying the burden of a divine commission which it is not, in the present state of society, able to bear. (WCC, 1968, pp. 29–30)

The report called for new 'functional groups' in different 'spheres of work and living' (p. 33). These 'new congregations' should be seen as 'the Church carrying out the original intention of the 'parish' church' alongside it (p. 30). They should be authentic communities 'in which Christians and non-Christians alike can face the questions which play a determining role in their lives' (p. 23). These new congregations would seek to discern God's activity within their contexts and would enable Christians to participate in mission 'not as an occasional activity but as their very *raison d'etre*' (p. 29).

Some congregations would be large, others small; some permanent, others temporary. They would be ready 'to change and to disband at the right time' (WCC, 1968, p. 33). They would be 'fashioned in very diverse shapes' (p. 29) according to the context, but not at the expense of unity. The different congregations would be in relation with each other. The types and foci of this integration would vary as congregational forms changed in response to changes in society. They would include contacts between groups of the same and different types, encouraged by denominational collaboration. Individuals, whose prime task was to foster integration, would play a key role.

This report, and its companion from a North American Working Group, has usually been criticized for downplaying evangelism and the distinctiveness of the gospel. 'What else can the churches do than recognize and proclaim what God is doing in the world?' the European Group asked (WCC, 1968, p. 15). The report's proposals were placed in a theological framework that emphasized God's activity in the world, independent of the church.

This brought complaints from those who thought that the missional role of the traditional congregation was being downplayed. John Yoder remarked that instead of the missionary structure of the congregation, 'we would have asked to see more about the congregational structure of the mission' (Yoder, 1994, p. 101).[4] The call for a missionary church (on structural lines not so different to the 'temple, synagogues and tents' described in the last chapter) was widely ignored partly because of its theological clothes.

Even so, as noted in the last chapter, the evangelicals John V. Taylor and Lesslie Newbigin picked up some of the report's ideas, as did the Urban Church Project. But this reimagining of the church faded in the face of opposition. It re-emerged, however, in the *Mission-shaped Church* report, which in the very different circumstances of the new millennium returned to many of these earlier themes, but within a different theological framework.

In a sense, *Mission-shaped Church* (2004) is a hypothesis. The assumed hypothesis is that the secularization thesis is wrong; social change does not make church demise inevitable; the problem has been the church's failure to adapt; new contextual churches are the Spirit's means of reversing decline. As yet there is insufficient evidence to confirm this hypothesis, but the new types of church championed by *Mission-shaped Church* are starting to provide pointers. In time, the fruitfulness or otherwise of these new churches will show whether the hypothesis is right.

If the hypothesis is correct and the church acquires a stronger public presence wherever life takes place, the renaissance of the church would provide support for the notion of 'post-secularity'. This fairly recent concept can be understood as 'the renewed visibility of religion in contemporary culture' (Bretherton, 2010, p. 12). It can be related to David Martin's understanding of secularization, which is very different to the story of linear decline told by Wilson, Bruce, Voas and others.

---

4 Yoder's comment is echoed in John Hull's opposite criticism of *Mission-shaped Church,* 'We looked for a mission-shaped church but what we found was a church-shaped mission.' (Hull, 2006, p. 36) I am grateful to John Flett for drawing my attention to the Yoder quote.

Martin argues that 'instead of regarding secularization as a once-for-all unilateral process, one might rather think in terms of successive Christianizations followed or accompanied by recoils' (Martin, 2005, p. 3). He describes four Christianizations, each overlapping the others – a Catholic Christianization centred on the conversion of monarchs, followed by a second in which the friars converted the urban masses; and a Protestant Christianization that effectively corralled Christian people in the nation, followed by one that produced evangelical and pietistic subcultures. Each Christianization encountered social realities inimical to the kingdom, adapted to them and was then forced to retreat by them. As one version of Christianity retreated, another gained ground.

Starting in the 'West', might this historic pattern repeat itself? Might the evangelical/pietistic version of Christianity, still strong in Pentecostalism around the world, slowly give way to a new, yet faithful expression of the gospel, based on Christian communities in every part of society? Might God be calling a reshaped church, fruitfully adapting to social change, to help embody a trend not to secularization but to post-secularity?[5]

The ecclesial turn

- The church is being pushed to the edge of society.
- This largely reflects the church's failure to adapt to social changes.
- The church has become self-limiting in its relevance, availability and organization.
- *Mission-shaped Church* can be seen as a hypothesis – that God will use new contextual churches to help the church be more relevant and available, as it takes shape within all the settings of life.

An ethical turn

A second turn is influencing society. This is 'a turn away from life lived in terms of external or "objective" roles, duties and obligations, and a turn towards life lived by reference to one's own subjective experiences' – a life that may be relational as much as individualistic (Heelas and Woodhead, 2005, p. 2). Individuals pay less attention to divine authority and more attention to their subjective states. Their own needs, desires, capabilities and relationships have become their prime frame of reference.

Charles Taylor has described how following the late eighteenth-century Romantics, the ethic of personal fulfilment was restricted to the intellectual

---

5 For a brief introduction to the idea of post-secularity, see Graham Ward (2009, pp. 117–58).

and artistic elites. For most people, personal fulfilment was constrained by the demands of sexual morality and the values of work and productivity. During the 1960s, however, this ethic leapt out of these constraints and became an overriding goal. 'What is new is that this kind of self-orientation seems to have become a mass phenomenon' (Taylor, 2007, p. 473).

This represents more than an intensified search for pleasure. It is a new understanding of the good: people have their own ways of realizing their humanity. Each person must live out what is true to them. Rather than having to conform to a model imposed by society, the previous generation, religion or political authority, individuals must be given the opportunity to express their authentic selves, provided they do not harm anyone else.

Ronald Inglehart has spent a lifetime arguing that when economies advance, 'materialist' values based on meeting physical security, sustenance, shelter and other needs give way to 'post-materialist', quality-of-life values. Recently, however, he has argued that post-materialist values 'are just one indicator of a much broader cultural shift from survival values to self-expression values'. The latter are changing attitudes to gender roles, sexual orientation, work, religion and child-rearing (Inglehart, 2008, p. 142). This represents a profound ethical turn: the expressive rather than dutiful self dominates society – and increasingly the church.

What lies behind this change?

First, the expressive self reflects post-industrialization, in which subjective opinions are valued more highly (Inglehart and Welzel, 2005, p. 29). This is partly because the post-industrial economy produces unprecedented levels of prosperity, which enhance existential security. Most people now take food, clothing, education and other essentials for granted to an extent never possible before. The proportion of earnings required to secure these necessities has steadily fallen, allowing people to spend more on goals beyond immediate survival. These goals express their subjective selves.

Second, the expressive self is a reaction against an increasingly regulated world. The reaction burst to surface in the 1960s and 1970s. Young people rebelled against the conformity and discipline required by the mass production assembly line and all that supported it, sometimes referred to as Fordism. Postmodernism is 'the culture of Fordism in crisis' (Nilges, 2008, p. 30).

The shift away from mass production has not removed the sense of being controlled. If anything, society has become even more organized. The number of organizations has leapt dramatically – registered companies in California expanded fivefold between 1960 and 2001. Organizations are reaching into the informal parts of everyday life – nurseries are replacing childcare at home; the voluntary sector is less informal. Organizations themselves feel more organized – more regulations, more targets and more accountability (Drori, Meyer and Hwang, 2006, pp. 2–7).

On the one hand, work autonomy expands because tasks are too complex to be controlled by the centre. On the other, management standardizes processes to minimize the risk of accidents, substandard performance and wilful damage. Individuals and teams are ruled by tightly defined discretion, targets and frequent appraisals. Bureaucracies have tightened their grip (Grey and Garsten, 2001, p. 238).

Heelas and Woodhead write about the clash between 'the targeted life' and the subjective self. Individuals wanting to be themselves use their free time to seek liberation from regimented work and become post-institutional in their attitude to religion.

If they engage with associational forms of the sacred, they are therefore much more likely to be involved with freedom-loving spiritualities of life than with role-enforcing . . . religion. Seeking to escape from externally imposed targets elsewhere in their lives, they will not want more of the same in the sphere of the sacred. (Heelas and Woodhead, 2005, p. 128)

Third, the 'creative economy' (Howkins, 2007), in which ideas transform individual talent in novel ways, is producing new opportunities for the expressive self. Initially, growing affluence enabled ordinary people to express their tastes in home furnishings, designer clothes and choice of entertainment to a degree known by the rich alone in previous eras. Now consumers are 'prosumers', using new technology to co-produce, co-design, co-innovate, co-distribute and co-consume with others, often across international borders (Chandra and Coviello, 2010).

The academic literature refers to 'user entrepreneurs' – individuals or groups of individuals who commercialize a product that they themselves use (Shah and Tripsas, 2007, p. 124). But the trend is wider. Trendwatching.com have dubbed it 'minipreneurs': a vast army of consumers turning entrepreneurs, from freelancers to advertising-sponsored bloggers.[6] As life becomes more entrepreneurial, church pioneering feels increasingly natural.

Some characteristics of the expressive self

One is that most people seek to express themselves within an 'immanent frame'. This is Charles Taylor's term for how the different structures in which people now live – scientific, social, technological and so on – are understood on their own terms. They are 'this worldly'. The supernatural is left out (Taylor, 2007, pp. 539–93).

Many people live in the here and now. They are preoccupied with day-to-day concerns. A UK questionnaire-and-interview study of people born after 1982 (Generation Y) found that the sample, who attended church to some

---

6 'Minipreneurs', www.trendwatching.com (accessed 22 February 2011).

extent, had an 'immanent faith'. Family, friends and self were their prime axes of meaning, hope and purpose. Life was focused on the everyday. Individuals tended to think in terms of plans rather than purpose (Collins-Mayo, Mayo and Nash, 2010, p. 89).

Mark Berry, a pioneer in Telford, England, claims that at local mind–body–spirit festivals, where you would expect spirituality to be unusually present, 'spiritual tourists' looking for spiritual growth are rare. More often he encounters 'hurting people, the bereaved, the injured, the lonely and the sick. They do not seem to be in search either of an experience or a belief system, they are looking for healing, for a reason or an explanation for the way they feel' (Berry, 2010, p. 59). While the language of spirituality may be around, for most people the practice of spirituality is lost. They have no time or space for it.

This resonates with the findings of Paul Heelas. He provides evidence that interest in 'wellbeing spirituality' is increasing substantially (Heelas, 2008, pp. 60–78). For example, the proportion of high-street shops in Kendal selling New Age products jumped from 30 per cent in 2001 to 45 per cent in 2003. New Age-related products and practices are 'spiritualities of life' because they are oriented to the day-to-day. They are an example of 'immanent' existence (pp. 21–2).

Heelas argues that the immanent life has an ethical component, which is a second characteristic of the expressive self. Holistic spirituality is not merely the extension of capitalism in which individuals consume spirituality without giving anything back. What practitioners and clients actually say shows that popular mind–body–spirit practices are an ethically charged force for the good life. Individuals tap into them in the hope – sometimes strongly, sometimes faintly held – that they will be helped to live well for themselves and for others.

Heelas points out that much consumption involves more than pleasure: it is about cementing bonds of identity and making life meaningful (Heelas, 2008, pp. 177–8). Within this frame is a strong ethical dimension, such as shopping for others in the household (Miller, 1998) and gift purchases to show appreciation and affection. The immanent life includes the desire to do good.

Expressive selves, third, increasingly live in association with others. An earlier study of Generation Y described their focus on family and friends. Their worldview is a 'happy midi-narrative' that eschews grand ideals in favour of a life centred on family, friends, and the use of popular arts and culture (Savage, Collins-Mayo and Mayo 2006). This probably describes other age groups as well. In 2001 for example, of the adult population living separately from their parents, just over half saw their mother weekly, two-fifths saw their father weekly, while 26 per cent of men and 33 per cent of women saw an adult sibling at least once a week. The figures had been stable since 1995 (Park and Roberts, 2002, pp. 192–3).

Although 'personal communities' of friends and family have always been important, they are now more continuously at the forefront of individuals' lives. Rather than isolating people, as some fear, technology is being used in social ways. iPod owners play new tracks to their friends and compile playlists for family journeys (Standage, 2005, pp. 220–1). Mobile phones allow users to be constantly present to family and friends. 'What is new is the emerging feeling that one should be accessible everywhere and at all times' (Sorensen, 2006, p. 55). Technology is increasing sociability.

Along with the immanent life, its ethical dimensions and personal communities, the fourth characteristic of expressive selves is their particular mode of spirituality. Where spirituality is pursued intentionally, expressive selves favour the quest (Taylor 2007, pp. 507–8). They prefer to be on a journey than to reach a destination. Destination speaks of closure, whereas journey keeps options open. There must be no presumed starting points or exclusions that pre-empt the experience. Individuals must travel their own paths and respect the paths of others. In searching for support, expressive selves would rather have resources for the journey than ready-made answers.

Connecting with an immanent world

Relating to a pragmatic, immanent world is a challenge for churches with their transcendent frames of reference. It is possible that the willingness of well-being spiritualities to downplay the supernatural and prioritize life's concerns has allowed them to corner the market. Maybe, as Heelas suggests, Christianity with its transcendent emphasis cannot compete (Heelas, 2008, p. 21).

Alternatively, if the church became more immanent, more immersed in daily life, without losing the transcendent, might it offer rather more than its rivals? It is striking that the young people interviewed by Collins-Mayo, Mayo and Nash were interested in how Christianity might provide guidelines for living. They valued ethics more than religion (2010, p. 88). In addition, many people still connect with 'thin spaces', including birth, marriage and death, where earth and heaven brush closely by each other. Here may be significant points of contact between the church and contemporary people.

The Christian tradition contains abundant resources that, used creatively and within the framework of divine grace, can add value to individuals' immanent lives. Stewardship connects with issues ranging from money management to ecological threats. Imaginative practices around the Sabbath theme could assist with work/life balance. Practising confession and forgiveness can help to restore broken relationships.

It is in the context of genuinely practical theology that the supernatural may win a hearing. This will become a possibility if the church, through the Spirit, addresses more strongly everyday concerns. The transcendent may add a richness to life which, in the absence of God, can seem devoid of higher purpose. Grace can lighten the burden of *self*-fulfilment, where so much depends on what the individual does. Christian disciplines and practices can help with day-to-day challenges, from parenting to conflicts at work.

The appeal of Christian practices is likely to be increased if they are embodied in ecclesial communities. A more sociable world will be open to relational expressions of spirituality that offer one-to-one and/or collective support for life-enhancing disciplines. Church can be another 'personal community'. In addition, people still enjoy festive events, be they pilgrimages, mass assemblies like World Youth Days or rock concerts and raves. These sorts of events fuse common action and feeling. They take participants out of themselves and create a sense of being in touch with something greater. They may indicate a latent demand for worship that connects the individual to the transcendent (Taylor, 2007, pp. 516–8).

Having awakened a desire to explore, Christian communities will want to support individuals in their spiritual quests by steering between two extremes. On one side are expressions of Christianity that put authority first. By being over-eager to convey the truth, these communities may treat the individual's quest with insufficient respect and push the person to search in a different setting. On the other side are individuals who relish being open to possibilities. They are reluctant to commit, least of all to a transcendent *authority*.

The Taizé community in France offers an example of a middle way. Its ability to attract thousands of young people a year partly lies in how it welcomes them as seekers. They can express themselves without conforming to a predetermined pattern of belief. Yet the centre of the community has clear Christian roots, which are explored through Bible study and liturgy. There is no obligation, but those who want to examine the Christian faith can do so without preconditions (Taylor, 2007, p. 517).

All this amounts to a strong argument for church-in-life – not church confined mainly to the domestic segment of existence, nor believers isolated in their walks of life, but Christian communities in all settings of society, providing practical support for people's immanent lives, connecting with individuals' desire to live good lives, perhaps awakening a hunger for the transcendent and providing a friendly environment for those wishing to tread a spiritual path.

The ethical turn

- This represents a turn away from duty and obligation to the moral value of individuals expressing their authentic selves.
- Expressive selves live within an 'immanent frame', their everyday concerns have an ethical component and relationships with others increasingly dominate their lives.
- New contextual churches may be the Spirit's means of connecting the transcendent to individuals' immanent lives.

An economic and social turn

The Spanish-American sociologist, Manuel Castells, has done perhaps more than anyone to understand the changes represented by this third 'turn'. Felix Stalder, a commentator on Castells, puts him in the same league as the famous sociologist, Max Weber (Stalder, 2006, p. 2). Castells's central contention is that the world is reconfiguring round a series of networks strung across the globe on the basis of advanced communication technologies. The birth of the 'network society', which involves a shift from hierarchies to networks, is transforming every aspect of social existence.

This new world has its origins in three independent processes that began around the late 1960s to mid 1970s: the information technology revolution, the economic crisis of both capitalism and statism and their subsequent restructuring, and the flourishing of cultural social movements such as libertarianism, human rights, feminism and environmentalism. 'The interaction between these processes, and the reactions they triggered, brought into being a new dominant social structure, the network society; a new economy, the informational/global economy; and a new culture, the culture of real virtuality' (Castells, 2000b, p. 337). With Stalder as a guide, three themes from Castells' work have particular salience for the church.

From a mass to a customized world

The economy is the central pillar on which the theory of the network society rests, and for Castells private firms are the main engine for the restructuring of the economy (Castells 2000a, pp. 163–215). At the heart of this restructuring is the transition from mass, 'Fordist' methods of production to 'post-Fordist' flexible production. Adopting broadly a 'post-Fordist' approach, Castells argues that by the 1970s established ways of organizing business were becoming less and less profitable.[7]

For over half a century organizations had been growing steadily more centralized and complex. This made large-scale production possible, using huge assembly lines that lowered unit costs: more items could be produced with the same overheads. But centralized control reduced flexibility – hence Henry Ford's famous comment that customers could choose any colour for their car so long as it was black.

This inflexibility made it increasingly difficult for large, vertically organized firms to manage the mounting complexities of advanced industrial processes and emerging global markets. Consequently, from the late 1970s, less hierarchical, more modular and so more flexible forms of organization emerged. Rather than a resurgence of craft-style enterprises as some expected (Amin, 1994, pp. 13–6), these new types of organization utterly depend on

---

7 Post-Fordism is accessibly introduced by Kumar (1995, pp. 36–65).

economies of scale (to cut unit costs) and of scope (to switch products as markets change). Transnational networks secure these economies by linking multitudes of specialist producers in chains supplying the market.

Networks allow major corporations to exploit the opportunities offered by international markets. They can pool resources by centralizing research, product development and other core functions. By becoming bigger, they can invest more heavily in their central capabilities, not least in coordinating just-in-time deliveries within ever more complex supply chains. By contributing to these networks, independent small firms gain entry to markets and to the benefits of scale economies.

At the same time, these networks enable production units and independent companies to specialize further. Access to a large market makes it economic to scale up core competences and outsource supporting activities, such as legal functions, to specialist suppliers. Within large enterprises, vertical departments have been transformed into horizontal operating units, with more flexibility and responsibility. The overall result has been a shift from vertical bureaucracies to horizontal networks.

Information technology has enabled this networking of scale and specialization. Yet contrary to much business literature, Castells is adamant that technology did not cause the restructuring of organizations (Stalder, 2006, p. 56). Organizations changed to cope with a constantly shifting environment. Once under way, however, the changes were accelerated and enhanced by new technologies.

The combination of scale and specialization represents a shift from mass standardization to what Mathias Nilges calls the 'standardization of difference' (Nilges 2008, p. 30). Whereas under mass standardization scale was used to produce standardized products at prices that more and more people could afford, with the standardization of difference scale is harnessed to produce – alongside standardized offerings – an expanding range of customized goods and services. Consumers increasingly expect organizations to tailor their offerings to the individual's requirements and circumstances. Scale is personalized.

The church of course is very different to business and other secular organizations. Even so, in a more customized culture, the local church cannot expect to relate in the same way to all the varied groups in its vicinity. Niche or focused church is a response to these social realities. Focused churches are the ecclesial counterpart to specialized producers serving market segments. Recognizing that one size does not fit all, focused churches accord individuals with different personality and cultural preferences equal respect and opportunity within the kingdom of God. Mission, community, worship and other aspects of ecclesial life take shape around these differences. The resulting richness and diversity point to the richness and diversity of the kingdom.

Just as other specialist providers network to secure the benefits of scale, focused churches can also work together to make available a wide range of resources for mission and discipleship. Individual churches can concentrate on a narrow set of activities, knowing that support for a fuller Christian life can be found in the larger church. Might the 'corridors' and the local and regional networks, which the previous chapter described, provide some of these supports?

The space of flows

A key concept for Castells is the 'space of flows', which links up places in real time (Castells, 2000a, pp. 407–59). Whereas for over a century places have been getting better connected, what is new is the integration of distant places so they can function as a coherent unit. Locations geographically far apart are linked together, and information is instantly transferred between them as if they are next door.

Castells argues that this compression of space and time brings into existence a new social space with its own dynamics and characteristics, the space of flows. It consists of the electronic circuits and fast transportation corridors that connect distant locations. It enables the movement of information, materials, money or people. It relies on networks that are tied to a series of points or nodes, such as individuals, organizations, cities and nation states.

This space of flows has several implications for the church. First, individuals increasingly live in the space of flows. They facebook, tweet, swap music files, talk endlessly on their mobile phones, follow sport online and much else. Church life is following suit. Between face-to-face meetings, members use the Internet to share news and prayers and sometimes study together. By downloading podcasts, visiting websites and more, individuals and groups give to and receive from the wider church. Current attempts to serve people online – churches in Second Life for example – will become more sophisticated and, as individuals learn from experience, almost certainly more fruitful.

Pete Ward argues that the church increasingly takes the form of networks. These networks are constantly formed and re-formed through communication outside the gathering, as well as inside (Ward, 2002, p. 38; 2008, p. 137). Graham Ward suggests that his namesake's vision is nothing new. Church has always been a network (Ward, 2009, pp. 203–4, n. 32). But the 'talk, talk' society, in which people spend longer in more varied networks, is bringing the network aspect of church to the fore. As more ecclesial life takes place in networks, the church has an opportunity to redeem the space of flows – to show what this space might be like if it was under the lordship of Christ.[8]

---

8 To do this it will have to engage carefully with the critiques of media technology, such as those provided Sherry Turkle (1995, 2011), though she may overstate her case.

The space of flows and the networks within it do not reduce the importance of geography. Most people are embedded in the places where they live. Networks actually enhance physical life (Castells, 2001, pp. 207–46). Community groups employ the space of flows on behalf of locally rooted projects; mobile phones are used to arrange meetings in a *place*; teleworking retains the office, but utilizes it in a different way. Likewise, new network churches often gather people who have a place in common – a sports centre, workplace, school or community centre. 'Local' churches have a long-term future because for most people everyday life remains local. Thus, just as society is both online and physical, church too increasingly has a network and geographical existence.

Second, Castells argues that one effect of the space of flows is to fragment localities. Some of the fragments are integrated into new functional units by being connected to complementary nodes elsewhere. The local convenience store is part of a global supply chain. Individuals meet up with their friends from some distance away. But geographical space is fragmented. The convenience store ignores local suppliers. Well-networked individuals may not know each other next door. In particular the elite strata of 'informational labour', which inhabits boutique hotels, loft apartments and airport VIP lounges, lacks deep roots in a place. The gated community symbolizes the elite's presence in a locality, and yet its distance from it.

By contrast, the poor live outside the space of flows in an existence constrained by geography. Here is a key way that power is exercised in this new society. Networks have a binary logic – you are either in or out. Castells writes of 'networking power', which is the capacity of a network to include or exclude people (Castells, 2009, pp. 42). Who belongs to society's dominant networks and does not becomes a major source of exclusion. This is exemplified by the City of London. It is a node in the networks of financial capital but sits alongside areas of great poverty. Networks create geographical rich–poor divides.

This breaking up of place creates a new context in which the church can live out the reconciling power of the kingdom. Dual church membership, mentioned in the last chapter, and networks that link focused churches at local and regional levels can counter the trend toward fragmentation. Individual churches can become nodes within networks that tie people together across a locality. Might focused churches increasingly join the fragments of society, while ecclesial networks join the fragments up?

To be serious about integration, these networks will have to pay close attention to people who risk being excluded. Networks of the like-minded will merely replicate the inclusion/exclusion dynamic of networks in general. To overcome this dynamic, the church must bring something fresh to the network society. Flying in the face of almost everything, from Facebook's modus operandi to national immigration policies, the church will have to create networks that welcome individuals who are different.

Third, networks enable churches to mobilize and serve the wider society. Networks can address issues that are too large for any one gathering. Martyn Percy is concerned that this will fail to happen. Fresh expressions of church, he fears, will lack 'thick' connections to the wider body and to their neighbourhoods. They will be too self-focused to pursue the social good and to build up the whole church (2008; 2010, pp. 67–79). Without discussing alternative views,[9] Percy sides with commentators who believe that personal networks are spreading at the expense of mass membership organizations, such as Scouts and Guides, trade unions and traditional churches, which socialized their members into being civic-minded. Civil and voluntary associations are giving way to inward-looking family and friendship ties.

Others think that new large-scale forms of solidarity are emerging. Mass movements can be organized on the Internet, while local action becomes easier when arranged online. In support of this second view, there is some evidence that the Internet has expanded individuals' circles of friends and contacts, while the number of close confidants has shrunk.[10] It is conceivable that as people live busier lives, they have less time to make intimate friends, but the Internet partly compensates by enabling them to have more acquaintances.

This extension of 'weak' ties (as against 'strong' ones between close friends) may be good for building social capital and mobilizing people. Information can race along connections to more individuals faster. A number of examples could be cited, such as the 'Arab spring' in 2011. A striking one occurred on Monday 27 March 2006 when, after a weekend of immigrant protests, tens of thousands of American teenagers walked out of class for their own protest. Many were responding to messages on Myspace.[11]

Percy works with a particular assumption about what 'thick' church is like. He ignores the potential for church of the network society. If the space of flows makes local and wider collaboration easier than before, the key question becomes: how can the church – inherited as well as emerging – use this new space to promote the well-being of society and strengthen the whole ecclesial body?

---

9 The range of views is well summarized by Bretherton (2010, pp. 6–10). Percy quotes Putnam (Percy, 2010, p. 73) but not sociologists like Anthony Giddens and Manuel Castells who are more hopeful.

10 A Microsoft survey of over 1,000 British people found that each person's average number of friends increased by an astonishing 64 per cent between 2003 and 2006; nearly a third of the sample had made friends online. ('Britons Make More Time for Friendship than Ever Before', November 2006, www.microsoft.com.) McPherson, Smith-Lovin and Brashears (2006) found that the mean number of people with whom adult Americans could discuss matters important to them had dropped by nearly a third between 1985 and 2004.

11 Danah Boyd, 'Friends, Friendsters, and Top 8: Writing community into being on social network sites', *First Monday,* December 2006, www.firstmonday.org.

Networks and emergence

Castells claims that networks are becoming the preferred way of organizing in almost all spheres of life. Although his definition of networks is annoyingly wide – for example, 'a network is a set of interconnected nodes' (Castells, 2009, p. 19) – his discussion of them brings out what is new. They are very different to hierarchical organizations, which are communication-poor. In these traditional organizations, individuals follow rules and execute orders. Structures are sufficiently simple for managers to insist that procedures are followed in the prescribed way (Stalder, 2006, p. 182–3).

However, when tasks and organizations become too complex for procedures to be determined in advance and enforced from the top, the network form of organizing becomes more effective. Networks are communication-rich. Under their influence, workers increasingly relate not person to machine but person to person. In the past notices would appear, 'Less talk, more work!' but in many cases today talk *is* the work. A number of studies (for example, Felstead, Gallie and Green, 2002, pp. 123–6; Johnson, Manyika and Yee, 2005, pp. 25–6) have shown the growing importance of human interactive skills within network enterprises – 'companies thrive on good company' (Starkey and Tempest, 2005, p. 152). From this, it is not much of a step to view organizations as the sum of the conversations within them (for example, Shaw, 2002).

These conversations give rise to processes with emergent properties. Stalder maintains that 'Castells substantiates, by way of standard empirical research methods and a rather traditionalist terminology, some of the core arguments advanced speculatively by the new complexity-oriented social theory' (Stalder, 2006, p. 185). In conversations, for example, ideas may be combined in novel ways, which can lead to new types of action, which spark new conversations, leading to further novel combinations.

Leadership in particular acquires a bottom-up quality. It is a feature of networks that they have no internal authority able to dictate what happens. Networks and their tasks are too complex for command and control. Top-down orders get reinterpreted or ignored in the conversations that make organizing possible, while people in authority lack the time or knowledge to enforce their instructions. This has contributed to the end of deference, which extends to small, simpler networks where in theory the top can exercise control.

Leadership gets dispersed as different actors take the lead at different times in the conversations to which they contribute (Lichtenstein and Plowman, 2009, pp. 2–3). This means that the appointed leader must foster conditions that will encourage conversations to be fruitful. Coming to terms with this dispersed leadership, however, is difficult when senior management has responsibility for meeting stakeholders' objectives and ensuring that legal requirements are met. As we have noted, management continues to seek new forms of control to secure regulatory compliance and improved performance. Thus emergent processes tend to co-exist awkwardly with top-down regulation. Tension lies between the two.

Bottom-up emergence produces effects at higher levels. The interactions of lower-level agents generate the level above. But these higher levels are largely beyond the control of lower-level agents, they exhibit properties not revealed at lower levels and they influence levels below through downward causation. Networked financial markets, for example, are like a 'mighty whirlwind'. They take on a life of their own. They are beyond the control of agents within them, but have an impact upon them. Governments work within national frames of reference to develop strategies for interacting at a global level. But these interactions create international bureaucracies that have their independent logics. These logics then constrain the actions of governments that brought them into being (Stalder, 2006, pp. 190–2).

In the network society, new contextual churches will have emergent properties. Focused churches will give rise to networks at a higher level, and these networks will exert downward causation on the levels below. The structure of 'temples, synagogues and tents' described in the last chapter can be understood in these terms. Assuming momentum gathers pace, it will bring about a reconfiguration of the church. In addition, if leadership is dispersed and emerges through conversations, it becomes vital that church leaders attend carefully to the minutiae of conversations and help others to do so too – a theme taken up in Chapter 16.

The economic and social turn

- The logic of combining scale and specialization creates opportunities for focused churches that are well connected.
- The space of flows opens doors to network churches that exist alongside geographical ones. It fragments localities, which challenges the church to draw these fragments together. It provides new opportunities for churches to work together to serve society.
- The proliferation of networks makes society more conversational, and conversations give rise to processes with emergent properties. These processes are shaping the cultural context of the church.

Conclusion

Some people, such as Andrew Davison and Alison Milbank (2010), believe that there is no need for new types of church. At its best, inherited church is well engaged with local communities. Clergy are known in schools, youth centres and by the police. They coordinate the local response to racism, lobby about the drains and support local voluntary groups. They encourage the laity to be involved in residents associations, local politics and in the pub darts team. The church meets people at times of crisis and celebration. Evangelism often permeates all these activities.

If this was the whole story, there would be no need to explain the church's decline in much of the global North. Secularization theory exists because the church has contracted. This shrinkage questions any claim that the existing church alone can meet today's missional challenge. As society disengages further from the church, why should more of the same solve a problem that was created by more of the same? The church needs to adapt.

Against many of the secularization writers, however, it is premature to pen the church's obituary. Decline seems to stem from the church's own limitations. With the fragmentation of life, the church has failed to accompany people into the numerous settings where they now live. It has become detached from their concerns, failed to open sufficient doors to newcomers and persisted with an ecclesial model that is self-defeating. The birthing, still at an early stage, of contextual churches in the splinters of society could herald a church that serves people in the ordinary settings of life, and becomes significant to them once again.

To serve these contexts well, new churches will need to connect with expressive selves who lead immanent lives, have a desire to be good, are increasingly sociable and, if they are interested in spirituality at all, prefer it in the form of a quest. Churches will be supportive communities that engage with practical, everyday concerns, respond to ethical desires, connect transcendence more tightly to day-to-day realities and provide a welcoming environment in which individuals can tread their spiritual paths. Churches that do this will be in tune with the network society. They will be focused, serving specific groups of people, but also be networked, pooling resources for mission and discipleship. They will be emergent, displaying the self-organizing properties of networks that now shape society.

All this describes some of the potential contours of church in every context – church in the different settings of life, church that enriches everyday existence in life and church that is responsive to the dynamics of network life. Yet if contextual church is a plausible response to today's cultural landscape, what are its theological foundations? It is to this question that we now turn.

Further reading

Davie, Grace, *The Sociology of Religion*, London: Sage, 2007.

Heelas, Paul, *Spiritualities of Life: New Age Romanticism and Consumptive Capitalism*, Oxford: Blackwell, 2008.

Stalder, Felix, *Manuel Castells. The Theory of the Network Society*, Cambridge: Polity, 2006.

Taylor, Charles, *A Secular Age*, Cambridge, MA: Belknap Press, 2007.

Questions for discussion

- How far should the church adapt to changes in society and how far should it seek to be distinct from society?
- Can it be said that the expressive self is a Christian self minus God? Or is prioritizing the search for fulfilment fundamentally flawed?
- How would you theologically evaluate the network society?

Part 2

Towards a Theological Rationale

5

What is the Purpose and Nature
of the Church?

One of the first questions often asked about new contextual churches is whether they are truly church. Indeed, many of the concerns about these communities arise from calling them church. In offering a theological rationale for these churches, therefore, Part 2 starts with a discussion about the nature of the church. It then considers the place of mission in church, the communal nature of mission in the local church, the extent to which new churches should be contextualized, whether it is legitimate for these churches to focus on a specific cultural group and whether new contextual churches are faithful to the tradition. These chapters draw on, and are intended to contribute to ongoing reflection – still at an early stage – about new contextual churches.

Whereas the traditional approach to evangelism begins with the current church and asks how people can be encouraged to belong, new contextual churches go to where people are and ask what church should appropriately look like in their context. Many young adults think that this is common sense. Meeting with friends to form a new Christian community in everyday life and calling it church seems an obvious thing to do.

It makes all sorts of people nervous, however. Are we playing fast and loose with the language, using 'church' when it does not really apply? Are we taking seriously what mature church entails? Others wonder if all this talk about church risks putting a straitjacket on mission, encouraging practitioners to worry more about being church than about being contextual. This chapter considers the purpose of church, asks what constitutes the essence of the church and discusses what mature church involves.

What is the purpose of the church?

As God's visible people, the church has its purpose in relation to the kingdom of God, which was a central theme in Jesus' ministry. In Luke 4.17–9, for instance, Jesus identified himself with Isaiah's vision of the kingdom. The vision included peace for the entire earth (Isa. 2.4), light where there has been darkness (9.2), harmony in the whole of creation (11.6) and a world of health, justice and abundance (65.17–24). Jesus taught the values of the kingdom, challenged the assumptions of his society from a kingdom perspective and demonstrated the power of the kingdom through his miracles. His life, death and resurrection inaugurated the kingdom, which will be established in full when he returns. In the 'between time' church bears witness to the kingdom. But what does bearing witness involve?

Church-shaped kingdom?

There is a spectrum in how theologians understand the relationship between church and kingdom. At one end are those who say the church is where the kingdom is made real in the present (Higton, 2008, p. 335). This 'church-shaped kingdom' view was assumed in the church-centred approach to mission common in the nineteenth and early twentieth centuries. In the mid nineteenth century, Henry Venn and others in the Anglo-Saxon tradition argued that church planting should be considered a goal of missionary endeavours, alongside personal conversion. Mission came to be seen as church extension overseas (Scherer, 1993, pp. 82–4). The kingdom of God was not discussed in connection with church and mission till the 1930s.

J. C. Hoekendijk, whose solution was not without problems, summarized the prevailing view in 1952:

> The world has almost ceased to be the *world* and is now conceived of as a sort of ecclesiastical training-ground. The kingdom is either confined within the bounds of the Church or else it has become something like an eschatological lightning on the far horizon. (1952, p. 324)

Although theologians have brought the relationship between church and kingdom more sharply into focus since World War Two, the assumption that mission was mainly about church left a legacy. Many Christians today still define the world in church categories, distinguishing – in Hoekendijk's words – 'not-yet-church, already-church, still-church and no-longer church' (1952, p. 324). They see mission primarily in terms of evangelism, of working with God to draw people into his family. The church follows the Spirit into the world to rescue it from sin and bring people into the kingdom. Individuals enter the kingdom when they are born again and become members of the church. Church and kingdom are virtually collapsed into one.

On this view, through the Spirit the church imperfectly embodies the kingdom in its life, not least by explicitly acknowledging the Lord's reign. In some perspectives the kingdom is spiritualized – by entering the church you enter a spiritual kingdom. But increasingly the kingdom is seen in physical terms, as God's rescue of the whole of creation. The church then becomes God's agent and foretaste of a holistic kingdom. It joins the Spirit in pushing back forces that threaten creation's well-being, and conversion includes being converted to this task. The underlying assumption, however, remains the same: the church is the gateway to and the vehicle of the kingdom.

Is this the perspective of *Mission-shaped Church* (2004), which kick-started fresh expressions of church in the UK? John Hull lambasts the report for leaning too heavily in this direction. The lineage of church planting, in which mission was closely identified with church extension, encouraged the working party to become too church centred in its theology. 'We looked for a mission-shaped church but what we found was a church-shaped mission' (Hull, 2006, p. 36). Hull's complaint has some substance. Though the report specifically affirms holistic mission (p. 81), this is not given a great deal of attention.

Roger Walton detects a church-centric undercurrent in much of the literature flowing from *Mission-shaped Church*. Often the literature, he claims, reveals an assumption that the church in mission is always the carrier of Christ, bringing him to the world but rarely, if ever, a recipient of God through the world (Walton, 2008, pp. 42–3). Where in the 'church-shaped kingdom' view is the acknowledgement that time and again it is the *world* that has been good news for the *church*? Outside pressure groups, for example, make the churches sensitive to ecological and social issues and stir Christians' consciences (Moltmann, 2001 [1992], p. 242).

The risk with 'church-shaped kingdom' is that horizons shrink away from the kingdom to the church. The Spirit advances the kingdom by growing the church, with social and ecological issues being seen as ancillary. Though the view is right to emphasize the world's need of salvation, the danger is that not enough attention is paid to what the church is for. Mission degenerates into a rather dispiriting attempt to bring more people into the church so that they can bring more people into the church. Or mission becomes almost exclusively about saving people from divine judgement. Mission fails to connect with God's vision for the whole of creation.

In particular this view can produce, as Martyn Atkins puts it, a 'sloping' attitude to mission. Mission slopes downward from the church to other people because the church starts from an elevated position. It assumes it has a gospel that everyone else needs. This produces a subtle superiority that is out of kilter with the contemporary mood. Atkins calls for a more level approach, supporting and serving people as friends and neighbours, acting as a servant in someone else's house (Atkins, 2007, pp. 124–31). Yet, as Walton notes, we can only take part in such serving if we delight in others' lives and are open to receive from them (Walton, 2008, p. 45).

World-shaped kingdom?

At the other end of the spectrum lies a 'world-shaped kingdom' perspective. Instead of being narrowed to the church, the kingdom is expanded to the world. Theologians holding this view focus on the kingdom's presence outside the church. God's mission is about the Spirit growing the kingdom in society and in creation. The church's task is to recognize signs of this growth, help other people to see it too and work with it. Conversion and the church are means therefore not of entering the kingdom, but of recognizing the kingdom's silhouette in the world (Hiebert, 1993, p. 156). Writers in this vein, such as Harvey Cox (1965), frequently point out that while the kingdom saturates Jesus' teaching, he only mentioned the church twice.

Though the 'world-shaped kingdom' view had its hey-day in the 1960s and early 1970s, especially in the World Council of Churches (Bosch, 1991, pp. 382–5), it continues to have its proponents. In his evaluation of the literature on mission-shaped church, Walton for example endorses Clive Marsh's search for Christ's presence in communities of practice. Marsh sees these as any intentional communities in work, education, family and elsewhere, in which people are formed. When these communities function well they reveal something of God.

For Walton, the church is not so much *the* body of Christ as *a* body of Christ – one of several entities working for God in the world. By means of the Spirit, the church is to be a facilitating agency, making others aware of Christ's presence in healthy forms of social interaction. Believers do not bring Christ from the church to the world but instead celebrate, with believer and non-believer alike, wherever Christ is present in creation (Walton, 2008, p. 49).

In their eagerness to reject a 'church-shaped kingdom', some emerging church leaders have been accused of sliding too far in this alternative direction. 'When a Kingdom approach is embraced then the place of church can be reduced' (Miles, 2007, p. 9). The kingdom has been foregrounded at the expense of the church, it is said, ignoring the balance that Jesus struck between the two. He may not have talked much about church, but – as part of proclaiming and demonstrating the kingdom – he spent much time preparing his disciples to become the nucleus of the church.

'World-shaped kingdom' underestimates the discontinuity between Jesus and the world. 'The gospels make it harshly clear that belonging with Jesus upsets other kinds of belonging – of family, of status, even of membership of the children of Abraham' (Williams, 2000, p. 229). The church is to do more than embrace visible signs of the kingdom: it is to critique their absence and point to salvation in Christ.

Kingdom-shaped church

'Kingdom-shaped church' is shorthand for the church's life being read back from the kingdom, which is partly present in the world and the church but will fully arrive when Christ returns. Thanks to the Spirit, foretastes of the kingdom exist in the world. They are present wherever the Spirit is at work. As in the previous view but unlike the first one, the church is to be alert to traces of the kingdom outside the church.

Anticipations of the kingdom also exist in the church. To adapt John Zizioulas's phrase, the church has 'its roots in the future and its branches in the present' (Zizioulas, 1985, p. 59). As it comes from the future, the kingdom shapes the church uniquely through Jesus, who embodies the kingdom and reigns over it. The church is called through the Spirit to live the story of Jesus, at the centre of which is his death and resurrection. It does this whenever it takes up the cross in evangelism, sacrificial service and in its corporate life. The church is to be a sign, foretaste and instrument of the kingdom in its Jesus-centred life.

Through the Spirit, the 'kingdom-shaped church' is the embryonic first-fruits of the kingdom. It is a nucleus within the universe that is growing in some way to be the universe itself in perfect relation to God. The church is not therefore simply a means or agent of the kingdom, which would make the church dispensable once its job was done. Nor is the church alone the goal of the kingdom, as if the kingdom's presence outside the church did not count.

The church is the foretaste of the kingdom – of something far more expansive and wonderful than exists in the church (or world) now. As a foretaste, the church mediates the future to the world (Moltmann, 1977, pp. 194–5). But it does this imperfectly. 'The church's fellowship is always in transit between the historical minimum and the eschatological maximum . . .' (Volf, 1998, p. 207).

The church's relationship to the world is one of similarity and difference – similarity because the church is part of the world and shares in it, but different because the church explicitly follows Jesus. This means that the church has something, or someone distinctive to offer the world. The offer of Jesus is the offer of forgiveness, of new life, of reconciliation, of creation restored. Through the Spirit Jesus is certainly present outside the church, but it is the church – in the power of the Spirit – that recognizes him, unveils him and helps others to respond to him. As Christ's body, the church has a connection to Jesus that the world does not have.

This relationship between kingdom and church warns against prioritizing the kingdom at the expense of the church – as if we were to say, 'our call to serve the kingdom is too important to worry much about the sort of church our fresh expression becomes, or whether we even use the word church.' Such thoughts ignore how belonging to the church is an essential part of the kingdom – and that what we belong to requires a name. So reflection on what it means to be church, and indeed sensitive use of the word itself, cannot be relegated to second-order status. Both the church and the name itself are integral to the kingdom.[1]

---

1 For some people feeling their way into the church, it may be helpful initially to use language such as 'Christian community'. But at some stage explorers will have to understand that baptism entails membership of the worldwide and historic body of Christ. Not to use 'church' to describe that body, when this is the generally accepted term, risks pretending that the church is something other than it is.

'Kingdom-shaped church' warns, too, against elevating the church at the expense of the kingdom's presence in the world. Though the church offers the kingdom to the world, it receives gifts of the kingdom from the world. Thus mission is not one-way traffic from the church to people outside. Peter's ministry to Cornelius, for example, was a learning experience for the church, as well as for Cornelius. Mission involves giving and receiving.

This makes listening to the context important not just to discern where and how a church might be born. Listening becomes crucial throughout a church's life. What might the church discover from the world and what might it celebrate with the world? Wherever the kingdom is present in creation, through the Spirit the church works to expand it and learn from it – to turn a sketch of the kingdom into a fuller picture.

This view emphasizes the Spirit's 'go-between' roles (Taylor, 2004 [1972]) in bridging the future and the present, and the church and the world. Indeed, if the Spirit brings the kingdom into both the world and the church and if the church's growth into the kingdom includes expansion into the whole of creation, we would expect the Spirit to be working in the here and now to bring the church, world and the kingdom closer together. Might expressions of church that embody the kingdom corporately in the midst of everyday existence point to a future in which church, life and kingdom are one?

The relationship between kingdom and church

- *Church-shaped kingdom*: Through the Spirit, the church makes the kingdom present.
- *World-shaped kingdom*: The kingdom is present in the world and the church points to it.
- *Kingdom-shaped church*: The kingdom, though present in the world, is distinctively present in the church.

The essence of church

What is the essential nature of the 'kingdom-shaped church'? In answering this, it is helpful to keep in mind the distinction frequently made between what is fundamental to the church (the 'esse' or essence of church) and what is for the good of the church (the 'bene esse' or well-being of church).

Mission and communion approaches

Theologians have been far from agreed on what comprises the essence of church. Some have argued that mission – being sent by God to serve the world – is the defining feature of the church. Within fresh expressions circles, Martyn Atkins argues that God has revealed himself to be missionary in his nature. The only way we know God is by encountering him in his missionary activity. Scripture reveals what God is like by relating what God does, which is to go out in mission. The people of God are first the product of God's mission, and then participants in it (Atkins, 2008, pp. 16–28).

This helpfully emphasizes the missionary role of the church but risks being reductionist. Although mission is an essential aspect of God's character, can God be reduced to mission – to the Father who sends, and to the Son and Spirit who are sent (which is the literal meaning of mission)? Is not to describe God as loving to describe him as being more than missionary – more than the one who sends and is sent? Equating love with mission is one-dimensional, and such a view of God may lead to a one-dimensional church. While mission is *of* the essence of the church, it is saying too much to claim that it is *the* essence of the church. The church is more than mission.

To avoid reducing church only to mission, Atkins argues that the church partners the God of mission by being forged into a loving community embodying the kingdom. But the risk is that this becomes an instrumental view of community. Community exists for mission rather than as an end in itself. Yet creating a community of love is one of the purposes of mission. The church bears witness to this future community by anticipating it in the present. By being a fellowship of love, the church commends the purpose for which mission exists. 'It is precisely because she is not merely instrumental that she can be instrumental' (Newbigin, 1953, pp. 147–8).

In recent years, the idea has grown that not mission but community is the essence of church. This has been expressed in a variety of ways, many of which draw inspiration from social conceptions of the Trinity. In his study of four fresh expressions of church Ian Mobsby, a church pioneer in London, found that the most common understanding of the church was in connection to the Holy Trinity (Mobsby, 2007, p. 51).

Mobsby argues that the church participates in the communion of the triune God. The mutual giving and receiving within the church reflects the perichoretic Trinity, a technical term for the persons of the Godhead indwelling and interpenetrating each other. What constitutes the church is participation in the perichoretic dance of the triune God. 'The holy Trinity is beckoning the emerging Church to model a way of being a spiritual community that reflects the very nature of the Trinitarian Godhead' (Mobsby, 2008, p. 68). This is a helpful corrective to Atkins's approach. It is consonant with the New Testament concept of 'koinonia' – joint participation, sharing and intimacy – within the church, and with the direction of ecumenical discussions.

However, a communal description of the church implies that community is more important than mission. (If the description gave equal weight to mission it would be saying something different – it would be a community-and-mission view of the church, perhaps.) Implicitly the Trinity's inner communion is seen as sequentially or logically prior to God's external missionary activity. Mission is what God does in his 'economy' – in his relation to the world. It is not fundamental to the inner life of the Trinity, which has an existence prior to mission. The church then imitates this view of God by regarding fellowship as the heart of its existence. Mission flows out from community, but is not central to the church's life.

From his reading of the literature, John Flett notes 'the absence of reference to the missionary act within communion accounts of the church. Indeed, it is not only possible, but normative' to base theologies of the church on a social account of the Trinity 'and to omit the missionary act as immaterial to the being of the church' (Flett, 2010, p. 207). He cites Volf as an example. At the beginning of his study of the church as the image of the Trinity, Volf states that 'the outside world and the church's mission are only in my peripheral vision' (Volf, 1998, p. 7). He argues that his other publications address how God's coming to creation should inform our practices in the world – 'one cannot say everything at once'. Pulling mission away from the doctrine of the church is precisely the problem. Mission becomes an outworking of the church. From this, mission can easily slide into being an add-on rather than integral to the church's life.

Church as four sets of relationships[2]

How can mission and community both be seen as being the essence of church? One possibility might be to think more closely about the relationships that constitute the church. The church is comprised of four sets of relationships centred on Jesus – to the Godhead, between members of the local church, to the world and between each part and the whole body. In believers' experience, these relationships are what church is. Take any one set of these relationships away, and church would be less than fully church. These four sets of relationships are essential to the being of church.

Seeing these sets of relationships as the essence of church is rather different to the 'mystical communion' account of church, where the focus is on 'the communion (of people) mystically united to God in Christ through the Holy Spirit' (Jenson and Wilhite, 2010, p. 24). For Leonardo Boff, a modern exponent of this view, this divine communion of persons 'enjoys a primacy over the particular churches because it is this church-from-above that exists in them all' (Boff, 2000, p. 19). Mystical communion is the ultimate reality of church, both transcending the relationships that make up the visible church and being present in those relationships.

---

2 I am grateful to Bob Hopkins and George Lings for encouraging me to think on these lines.

However, is this not too abstract a view of the church's essence to be helpful? Is this view saying much more than that the church is the people of God in communion with God? Is that enough to be able to recognize a church? Indeed, does this mystical communion have any reality apart from the relationships in which it exists? And if it does not, why employ the notion at all? Why not focus concretely on the relationships that comprise church?

Most understandings of church would probably take these four sets of relationships for granted, but they tend not to concentrate on them as the defining features of the church. Such a focus, however, has been hinted at in some of the writings of Rowan Williams and in the direction that *Mission-shaped Church* began to travel.

In *Anarchy, Church and Utopia*, Theo Hobson has described the Christ-centred, open, self-critical and social conception of church that emerges from the writings of Rowan Williams. Williams has described the New Testament picture of church as

> what happens when the news and presence of Jesus, raised from the dead, impact upon the human scene, drawing people together in a relationship that changes everyone involved, a relationship which means that each person involved with Jesus is now involved with all others who have answered his invitation, in ways that are painful and demanding but are also lifegiving and transforming beyond imagination. (Williams, 2008–09, p. 13)

Elsewhere he has written, 'Each Christian generation makes itself responsible, as did Jesus' first friends, for bringing people into relation with him and so with each other. When that happens, the Church "happens" . . .' (Williams, 2006, p. 52).

These passages describe church as an event in the context of four sets of relationships – with Jesus (the 'presence of Jesus') and so through him with the Trinity, within the Christian gathering ('drawing people together'), with the body of people 'who have answered his invitation' down the ages and with people outside the church, some of whom the church brings into relation with Jesus. Any part of the church – and any individual within it – is engaged in each of these relationships. Jesus is the hub round which these relationships happen.

In the language of *Mission-shaped Church* (p. 99), these four sets of relations can be described as:

UP relationships through participating in the life of the Trinity
IN relationships through fellowship within the gathering
OUT relationships in love for, and service of the world
OF relationships, as part *of* the whole body, through connections with the wider church.

The report described UP, IN, OUT and OF as 'four dimensions of a journey' that the church is called to walk and used them as a description of the four historic marks of the church. However, in describing these 'dimensions' the report's language made clear that it was describing relationships. Though it did not quite get there, the report was straining towards a 'four relationships' understanding of the church, which can be understood diagrammatically like this:

'Four relationships' understanding of the church

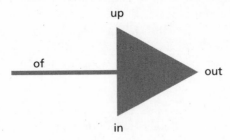

These sets of relationships, although distinct, are of course deeply entwined with each other, enrich one another and have equal weight. The relationship with God, for instance, can be experienced in the gathering, in connections with the living Christian tradition or in going out to the world. The relationship with the whole tradition will be experienced when a gathering shares in the mission of the wider church, grows in its discipleship by learning from another part of the body and prays for the whole church.

These four ecclesial relations echo and participate in the Trinity. The relationship with God is modelled on the Father's giving to the Son (Matt. 28.18) and the Son's obedience to the Father (John 8.28–9). The relationship with the world is a participation in God's mission through the Spirit. Fellowship within the gathering reflects the mutual love of the divine persons.

Relations to the whole church are the ecclesial counterpart to the *perichoretic* relationships within the Trinity – one affects all. Through their *perichoretic* relations, the three divine persons permeate one another without ceasing to be distinct persons. 'In a certain sense, each divine person *is* the other persons, though is such in its own way' (Volf, 1998, p. 209). Volf argues that as Christian communities open themselves to each other in a faint echo of this divine mutual indwelling, they pass on their identifying characteristics to other churches. One church enriches the others by giving something of itself; in accepting what is offered, the recipient churches become more like the giving church (p. 213).

Relationships and practices

This four-relationships approach differs from views that emphasize certain practices as essential to church. Usually the tradition has sought to describe the practices that must be present if any Christian gathering is to be truly church, such as the ministries of word and sacrament and the existence of bishops, priests and deacons. The historic four marks of the church – One, Holy, Catholic and Apostolic – are typically defined in terms of practices.

Yet just as defining marriage in terms of a legal document and having sex would fail to capture the fullness of the relationship involved, so conceiving the essence of church as certain practices omits too much of what it means to be church. Rather than practices, concentrating on the four sets of ecclesial relationships that practices embody provides a richer account of the church's fundamental nature.

Accenting the relational nature of the church does not mean that the content of these relationships is unimportant. Something for better or worse always happens within a relationship. So attention must be paid to practices that promote the health of the relationships that constitute the church. If relationships are the essence of the church, practices are for the good of the church.

It may be helpful to see these practices in a gradation. At one end of the spectrum are practices unique to an individual gathering. At the other are practices expected by virtually the entire church. The latter start to give content to the four sets of relations that make up the church, and include for example:

- word, sacraments and prayer in the Godward relationships;
- care for those in need and evangelism in relationships with the world;
- regular meetings and some form of church discipline in the gathering's relationships;
- use of these practices in the context of relationships to the whole church – word, sacraments and prayer draw on the tradition, for instance.

In the middle of the spectrum are the practices of intermediate structures, such as denominations or networks of churches. The practices of these intermediaries are rooted in specific understandings of the Christian tradition and may be viewed as gifts to the wider church – gifts because they reveal facets of God and provoke other believers to reflect on their own understandings.

Through the Spirit these intermediate practices shape individuals in the faith, and so inevitably they come to be cherished by believers and form a crucial part of their spiritual identities. Because believers value how they express the faith, their thinking will contain an element of 'I wish you believed and did this too.' To an extent, strongly held beliefs necessarily have a universal claim.

The danger is that such claims will subvert the relational nature of the church by closing down space for those who see things differently. Seeking to uphold their view of how the institution should function, defenders of certain practices may use their influence to prevent others 'straying outside the rules'. They will exert their power, for disputes about practices always involve power: whose views will prevail? If those who 'lose' feel deeply hurt or leave the denomination, their relationships will be impaired. Practices will have trumped relationships, damaging the church at its core.

When practices are in dispute, the relational heart of church provides a touchstone about what is ultimately important in the body and helpfully frames the debates – think of Paul's advice on eating meat offered to idols; love was to be the guiding principle (1 Cor. 8.9–13). Emphasizing relationships will encourage differences to be discussed with kindness and generosity. The expression of strong claims – 'this is what everyone should believe' – will be tempered by the recognition that others disagree. If compromise or allowing practices to diverge is impossible and there has to be a parting of the ways, friendly relationships will be sought between the institution and those who leave.

Does this emphasis on relationships give enough weight to practices? Are not relationships actually formed through practices and nurtured by them? Through the Spirit, for example, the practices involved in mission *create* the connection between church and the people outside. While this may be the case, just as a couple who met in a bar go on to form a relationship that transcends meeting in a bar, relationships rather than practices become essential to church once these relationships start to form.

Practices are not unimportant, but they exist for the sake of the four interlocking sets of relationships that comprise the church. They are servants of these relationships, just as the Old Testament law is the servant of the covenant. Walter Brueggemann points out that the covenant works not by grace coming before law, which is a false distinction (1997, pp. 419–20). Grace and law work together. The purpose of the law was to show Israel how to respond in love to the self-giving love of Yahweh. The covenant relationship was the ultimate reality that obedience to Yahweh made concrete.

Since the covenant was of ultimate importance rather than its stipulations, the covenant could alter as historical circumstances changed – worship shifted from the tabernacle to the temple, for example. In a similar way, the relationships at the root of church are ultimate, and practices can vary according to the context. It often happens that when practices no longer serve relationships, they are felt to be lifeless. Worship may feel dead rather than energizing the relationship with God. Or practices may hinder community by seeming inauthentic. Practices must then evolve so that they can continue their serving role.

What about the church's accumulated wisdom about which practices best support these relationships? Don't certain denominational or universal practices have, as it were, a mandatory status because they have been tested by experience? Certainly, to be in relationship with the whole means being drawn into the church's long story of practice and witness. Any gathering that takes seriously its connection to the living tradition will pay careful attention to practices that the wider church has come to value. Where these practices are in dispute, however, discernment will occur through prayerful conversation with the church at large.

Why this four-relationships approach?

A longer study could explore more fully the claim that it is not practices which constitute the church, but four sets of interlocking relationships expressed through practices. The claim is promising for several reasons.

First, it is faithful to the church's New Testament origins. The church began with people encountering the Lord, encountering each other and telling others about their encounters with Jesus. As the church spread, relationships were established between local churches. Practices grew out of these encounters. Holy Communion itself, a vehicle for the church to have an intimate relationship with Christ, was instituted in the context of a community that had been on the road with Jesus for three years.

The New Testament imagery of the church is strongly relational – the household of God, the vine and the branches, and many more. In his classic *Images of Church in the New Testament*, Paul Minear described four controlling images – the people of God, the new creation (which includes the restoration of fractured relationships), the fellowship of faith and the body of Christ. These are all relational pictures.

Second, church as four sets of relationships provides a realistic starting point for reflecting on church. It fits with how church is actually experienced. Believers engage with church through these sets of relationships. How do new Christians, for instance, discover that the word, sacraments and other practices are fundamental to their faith? It is through their relationships with fellow believers. Practices are encountered within these relationships.

Nicholas Healy (1995, 2000) has warned against what he calls 'blueprint ecclesiologies', which are ways of reflecting on church through abstract models. They tend to describe ideal versions of church, which are at variance with the complexities and shortcomings of ecclesial life. There is a disjunction between church as described and church as it is experienced. Starting with the relationships that comprise church helps to avoid this. It allows reflection on church to begin with the story of the relationships that make up the church – a story rooted in the narratives of Scripture. Doctrines can then summon church to be true to its calling without presenting an unrealistic, idealized picture.

Third, the emphasis on the social nature of the church accords with the contemporary understanding of human nature: humans are primarily social beings. In particular, it resonates with the complex responsive process perspective, a branch of complexity theory, which assumes that contemporary organizations are little more than a sequence of conversations (Shaw, 2002; Griffin and Stacey, 2005; Stacey, 2010). Organizations do not exist apart from the formal and informal conversations that comprise them. Take away the conversations, and you would be left with some legal documents and buildings, but no living entity. Legal contracts, vision statements, written procedures and much else are the result of conversations and become ingredients within further exchanges.

Behaviours cannot be imposed on these organizations. If they are accepted within a series of conversations, required behaviours are given meaning in subtly – and sometimes substantially – different ways. They evolve through being talked about. If they are not accepted, they are either ignored or subverted so that they have a very different meaning to the one originally intended.

Understanding church in terms of practices – of gathering round the word, celebrating the sacraments and other expected behaviours – fails to do justice to how any one practice originates in conversation, is constantly being changed through conversation and has a meaning that varies, if only in tiny degrees, from one conversation to another. Church is a myriad flow of communication exchanges, weaving in and out of each other. What makes it distinct from other organizations is that it is embraced within the conversations of the Trinity.

Fourth, practices cannot define the church because Christians are unable to agree about these practices. While the overwhelming majority of Christians see Holy Communion as an essential practice, Quakers and the Salvation Army, for example, do not. As Kathryn Tanner (1997) argues, church can be understood as an ongoing discussion about practices. Practices are continually subject to disagreement and debate as Christians seek to discern which practices are appropriate in the circumstances and in what way. As subjects of conversation, practices are the ingredients of ecclesial relationships rather than firm structures for them.

Tanner argues that this view of practices is authentic to the tradition – it is in keeping with the nature of the practices themselves. Being faithful to Scripture, remembering the Lord's Supper or caring for the poor are too imprecise to translate into single concrete forms usable across the church. The tradition has engaged with ecclesial practices not by employing them in a uniform way, but by discussing them and often being in dispute about them. Tanner notes how the formulation of Christian statements about Jesus has failed to prevent disagreement.

Rather than having the clear definition of rules, these doctrines attempted to resolve disagreements through the use of rather vague and ambiguous expressions (for instance, *homoousion*) into which a variety of parties could read their own positions. These ambiguities then set the stage for further controversy – say, between Cyrilian and Antiochene factions after the Council of Chalcedon, the very factions united in their acceptance of the Chalcedonian creed to begin with. (Tanner, 1997, p. 140)

Liturgy has often functioned in a similar manner. Texts have been compromises that allow different groupings within the church to read the same text in different ways. At best, the church has been able to agree what lies outside the bounds of acceptable belief and practice, but even these boundaries, as the ordination of women illustrates, have not been immutable. Church is more a debate than an agreement about practices.

Fifth, focusing on the four sets of relationships that comprise church has affinities with other relational conceptions of the church, but is broader. For instance, it is consistent with the communal view currently favoured in ecumenical discussions, but it keeps all four sets of relationships in the foreground. The World Council of Churches 2005 statement, *The Nature and Mission of the Church*, provides an example of the tendency to conflate these relationships. It argues that the biblical images of the church 'evoke the nature and quality of the relationship of God's people to God, to one another and to the created order' (WCC, 2005, pp. 22–3). The relationship 'to one another' fuses in one phrase relations within individual churches and between them.

Some evangelicals have done the same by summarizing ecclesial life as 'UP, IN and OUT' – believers' relationships with God, each other and the world. Mike Breen and Alex Absalom's *Launching Missional Communities* (2010) provides a recent example. Where is OF – being part *of* the whole body of Christ?

Failure to distinguish between relationships within a gathering and between gatherings can damage the practice of church. Repeatedly collapsing relationships within the gathering and to the tradition into each other allows one of these sets of relations to be disregarded. Since for most believers the church is more immediately experienced within a specific community than in the relationships between individual churches, it is likely that relations with the wider body will be the set that is overlooked. If an explicit reference to relationships with the wider body is constantly omitted from descriptions of church, believers' commitment to the whole and their sense of Christian identity will suffer. Language shapes thought.

Finally, this approach recognizes that relationships cannot be separated from the practices that embody them, but encourages practices to be tested against the bar of relationships – for example, 'How far would the way we usually celebrate Holy Communion help this particular group of people grow in their relationships with God and with each other?' At the same time, relationships with the whole body can be honoured, 'Would this way of celebrating Communion be recognizable to the larger church?'

A relational approach to practices allows plenty of room for diversity. Just as the conduct of relationships varies at a personal level, so the core relationships of church will look different from one expression of church to another. This provides a basis for welcoming innovative types of church. Novel expressions of Christian community can be regarded as church if they maintain four interlocking sets of relationships with God through Christ, with the world, with the living tradition and within the gathering.

Opening doors to innovation will help the church adapt to changes in its context, while remaining faithful to its heritage. Denominational identities are inevitably a mixture of relationships and the practices that sustain relationships. The more a denomination's identity is fixed on its practices, the harder the denomination will find it to welcome new shapes of community that fit their contexts. Conversely, the more a denomination allows the four relationships of church to qualify its practices and its identity, the more diverse and adaptable it will be.

The essence of church lies in relationships rather than practices

- This view is faithful to the New Testament.
- It fits with how church is experienced.
- It reflects the social nature of human beings.
- It accords with the debated nature of practices.
- It resonates with communal and other relational conceptions of church.
- It allows room for diversity.

Mature church

Understanding the essence of church provides guidance as to whether a mission initiative can properly be described as church. But this is only the beginning. If an initiative starts to engage in the four interlocking sets of relationships that constitute the church, the question naturally arises as to what mature church looks like. What embodiment of church should a new Christian community aspire to?

George Lings and John Drane have discussed maturity in relation to new contextual churches. While recognizing that the notion is elusive and ambiguous, both concentrate on the elements that comprise maturity, such as a church's potential to reproduce (Lings, 2006a, pp. 146–7) and concern for an organic way of being (Drane, 2008, pp. 94–5). These attempts to describe maturity, however, put the cart before the horse. The key question is who decides what maturity looks like. When that is clear, those seeking to discern maturity can fill out what they mean by the concept.

A starting definition

Obviously, we must provide some sort of definition – if only an initial one. A good launch pad is Ephesians 4.13, where maturity is understood as 'attaining to the whole measure of the fullness of Christ'. This involves at least two things. First, as Lings emphasizes (2006a, p. 140), maturity is a relational quality. If church comprises four interlocking sets of relationships, growth into maturity will involve growth in each of these relationships – with God, the wider church, the world and within the fellowship.

Both Lings and Drane maintain that this growth cannot be recognized by referring mainly to what already exists. 'Maturity is not necessarily becoming like your parents. It is growing into what you are' (Lings, 2006a, p. 140). Of course there will be family resemblances. We would hardly expect adults to be totally unlike their parents. Similarly, a new church will share recognizable traits with the whole body. It will participate in the inheritance of the tradition through which the Spirit has been at work. Equally, we would expect the birth of a church to bring something new into the tradition, just as children make distinctive contributions to the family and beyond.

Drane argues that to define maturity mainly in relation to the past overlooks how change in society has become more random, rapid and unpredictable. Unlike in previous centuries, an individual cannot mature into the sort of world inhabited by their parents because that world will have disappeared.

> . . . the nature of maturity is being redefined as a quality that will enable us to live in the future rather than the past. The old maturity was characterized by nostalgia; the new maturity is marked by innovation. The old maturity valued tradition and rationality; the new maturity centres around imagination and creativity. The old maturity found a home in religious performance; the new maturity prioritizes values and spirituality. (Drane, 2008, pp. 92–3)

Though these distinctions should not be over drawn in relation to the church (as if the Spirit's contribution to the tradition has little value), Drane is right to go on and say that this future orientation is deeply grounded in the biblical tradition. The centre of Jesus' proclamation was that 'The kingdom of God is near' – a declaration full of anticipation (Mark 1.15). Paul placed his life and ministry in the story of God's coming kingdom. 'If the dead are not raised at all . . . why do we endanger ourselves every hour?' (1 Cor. 15.29–30).

Thus the second aspect of maturity is its future dimension. The maturity of any church should be judged according to the purpose of the church, just as the maturity of any person must take account of the purpose of human beings. If the church's purpose is to be a sign, first-fruit and instrument of the kingdom, then the maturity of any individual church should be evaluated in relation to the kingdom. How far, through the Spirit, are the church's four sets of constituent relationships pointing to the kingdom, providing a foretaste of it and contributing to it?

Who should decide?

Deciding whether a church is moving toward maturity is a matter of prayerful discernment – but by whom? A way into thinking about this is suggested by a lecture that the Roman Catholic theologian, Karl Rahner, gave in 1979. Reflecting on the Second Vatican Council, which between 1962 and 1965 addressed relations between the Roman Catholic Church and the modern world, Rahner noted that the Council was the first major official event in which the Church acted as a *world church*. There were antecedents and the world church 'made its appearance only initially and diffidently' (Rahner, 1979, p. 717). Even so, 'a world Church as such begins to act through the reciprocal influence exercised by all its components'. The European voice was still dominant, but other voices made their contributions.

Since then, of course, the dominance of the Western church has been eroded by the continued expansion of the church in many parts of the global South, by post-colonialism (in which theologies have emerged in the South partly in response to the legacy of imperialism), by globalization which has integrated the South into the world economy and by the recession which, since 2007, has accelerated the relative economic decline of the global North. The combined impact of these developments has been to make the church in its totality less Western and far more global.

Alongside this de-centring of the Western church has been a second de-centring, one that Rahner did not refer to. This is the de-centring of the church *within* the West, particularly in Europe. This is often described as a shift to post-Christendom. Post-Christendom refers to the culture that emerges when the churches and the Christian story lose their central place in the society they did much to shape. The church is now on the edge of society, needing to reach out to people whose cultures are very different to the cultures that shaped the Western church. As people from these cultures are welcomed into the body, they will join believers in the global South in offering the church new Christian perspectives. The inherited church in the West will be surrounded by an expanding multitude of different voices.

This double de-centring of the Western church has ushered in what Rahner, writing about the emergence of a global church, described as a third theological epoch. The first was the short period of Jewish Christianity. The second was initiated by the conversion of the Gentiles, and was the period of the church in a distinct cultural region – that of Hellenism and Europe. We might nuance this and say that it was the period when the church was *dominant in* a distinct cultural region. The third epoch is 'the period in which the sphere of the Church's life is in fact the entire world' (Rahner, 1979, p. 721). Like the major transition from Jewish to Gentile Christianity, today an equally profound transition is occurring from a Christianity of Europe ('with its American annexes' – p. 722) to a fully world religion.[3]

Thirty years after Rahner's article, we can include in the process he described the emergence of new contextual churches within the West. All across the globe the church has been transplanted into cultures every bit as different to the existing church as the difference between Gentile and Jewish Christianity. Now, we pray, the same is beginning to happen in the West. New cultures have been, are being and, we hope in faith, are about to be admitted to the church. They are starting to change the composition of the church as radically as did the admission of the Gentiles.

Just as Jewish believers had to modify their assumptions about what it meant to be a Christian and how this was expressed in the life of the church, so too the Western church – as it responds to new cultures at home and overseas – must be open to question its inherited life and assumptions. Rahner, without spelling it out quite so bluntly, writes:

> The open question is whether, during such historical breaks as the second one which we are now discussing, the Church can legitimately perceive possibilities of which she never made use during her second major epoch because those possibilities would have been meaningless in that epoch and consequently illegitimate. (Rahner, 1979, p. 724)

If this is a valid understanding of today's situation, three things flow from it. First, we cannot assume that the church the West has inherited is the sole or even the best yardstick of mature church in the cultures outside it. Such a view in today's circumstances sounds presumptuous, even imperialistic. Having passed on the gift of community with Jesus to the global South and as it starts to pass on this gift to cultures within post-Christendom, the church can hardly take back the gift by telling the recipients how the gift is to be received (Williams, 1994a, p. 20–1). As new believers shape church perhaps in novel ways, they will have insights into maturity that the wider body, in turn, can receive as a gift.

It follows, second, that prayerfully discerning what it means for a church to be mature in its context will be a shared process. It will not be undertaken by the new church alone, as if the Spirit has not been active in the church's history and the latter has nothing of value to bequeath. It will certainly

---

3 Rahner acknowledges his assumption that this contemporary transition is more theologically decisive than the transitions from ancient Gentile Christianity in the Mediterranean to medieval and then modern Christianity in Europe.

not be undertaken by the inherited church alone, as if the new Christians – gathered round Scripture and attentive to the tradition – have nothing to contribute. Maturity, understood as growth toward the kingdom within the four interlocking sets of relationships that constitute the church, will be defined and recognized by new and existing believers together, working within whatever structures are appropriate.[4] If the process is sometimes difficult, we must not be surprised. As Tanner says, often the church is more about debate than agreement.

Third, if the 'Gentile analogy' has validity, its implications will be explored imaginatively.[5] For instance, what would be the equivalent of the Jerusalem Council's prohibitions on sexual immorality and various non-kosher meats – prohibitions that were binding on Gentile Christians (Acts 15.29)? Might it be an expectation that the new church engages seriously with the wider body? The admission of the Gentiles was followed by centuries of anti-Semitism in the church. What might be the equivalent danger with new contextual churches, and how might it be avoided?

Conclusion

If Griffin, Shaw and Stacey (cited on p. 112) are right to see organizations as a series of communicative exchanges, focusing on conversations may be a helpful way to draw this chapter together. The kingdom-shaped church is in perpetual conversation about the kingdom and with the world. These conversations are part of an ongoing series of interactions that are not just at the heart of church, but constitute its very existence. Take away these conversations and there would be little left. The conversations that make up the church are with the Trinity, with the world, between different parts of the wider church and within each ecclesial gathering.

New communities can be considered church, however novel their shapes, if they are engaged in all of these conversations. Radical reimaginations of the church become possible. These reimaginations should include a vision for maturity. The vision will centre on how the four interlocking relationships of church can – in the context – become signs, foretastes and instruments of the kingdom. Understanding and recognizing maturity will be the subject of conversation between the new and the wider church. Through

---

4 When the new church is birthed within a denomination or network, this will be within the structures of the denomination or network. When a new church is birthed independently, this may be through consultation with churches in the area that are welcoming of the new church (just as in the period after the apostles, bishops were appointed by the laying on of hands by neighbouring bishops.)

5 The analogy has been used extensively in the homosexuality debate, and principles for using the analogy can be learnt from that debate. See especially Perry (2010).

these conversations, gifts of wisdom and insight will be exchanged. As these conversations display fruits of the Spirit, they will themselves be signs of maturity and foretastes of the kingdom.

Further reading

Croft, Steven (ed.), *Mission-shaped Questions. Defining Issues for Today's Church*, London: Church House Publishing, 2008.

Davison, Andrew and Alison Milbank, *For the Parish: A Critique of Fresh Expressions*, London: SCM Press, 2010.

Tanner, Kathryn, *Theories of Culture: A New Agenda for Theology*, Minneapolis: Fortress Press, 1997.

Volf, Miroslav, *After Our Likeness: The Church as the Image of the Trinity*, Grand Rapids, MI: Eerdmans, 1998.

Questions for discussion

- How does one's view of the relationship between the kingdom and the church make a difference in practice?
- What arguments would you use to support and critique the contention that the essence of church is four interlocking sets of relationships?
- How would you define maturity for the church in your context?

6

Should Mission be a First Step for the Church?

A growing number of new contextual churches are meeting in leisure centres and cafes, emerging among young and older people, forming round interests ranging from surfing to making cards, and gathering in apartment blocks and new housing estates.[1] They raise a number of questions, to which the chapters in Part 2 offer the beginnings of an answer.

Whereas the last chapter asked whether these initiatives are proper church, this chapter challenges a widespread assumption that in the church's corporate life, worship should be primary and mission a second step. Why, for example, should the church's central meeting concentrate on word and sacrament ('we're here to worship God') rather than mission ('we're here to organize how we join God in serving the world')?

The chapter should be read in the context of Stephen Bevans's comment that ecclesiology and missiology have typically focused on different things – ecclesiology on what the church is, missiology on what the church does. The disciplines have tended to bypass each other. Recent movements in the two disciplines, however, have begun to close the gap. In both disciplines today, the immediate starting point is neither the church's nature nor – as used to be the case with missiology – its activity, but the reality of the triune God. Ecclesiology has become more missiological as it realizes that it is God's mission – the sending of the Son and the Spirit – that calls the church into being. Missiology has become more ecclesiological by recognizing that the church is how God's mission takes shape (Bevans, 2005, pp. 45–9).

In the spirit of this convergence, the chapter discusses the missionary priority of God. It introduces the *missio Dei*, the mission of God, and then explores the place of mission in the divine life, the self-giving nature of mission, the goals of mission, the church's participation in the divine mission and some ways that contextual church corresponds to the nature of God's mission. It argues that mission is not a second step for God and should

---

1 Some 150 'fresh expressions of church' are described at www.freshexpressions. org.uk/stories.

not be a second step for the church. New contextual churches provide an authentic echo of God's missional priority.

The mission of God

Since the middle of the last century it has been customary to root the church's mission in the *missio Dei*. Mission first and foremost is an activity of God. Christopher Wright maintains that the Bible reveals a personal God who has a purpose, which is that the whole of creation should give glory to him. Scripture describes humanity with a mission, Israel with a mission, Jesus with a mission and the church with a mission – all with that purpose in view (Wright, 2006, pp. 64–8).

The activity of this missional God means that, in Jürgen Moltmann's words, 'It is not the church that "has a mission" but the very reverse; . . . the mission of Christ creates its own church.' (Moltmann, 1977, p. 10). Rather than the church engaging in mission and asking God to bless it, God engages in mission and asks the church to join it. The focus shifts from the church to God.

The evolution of *missio Dei* theology has been summarized by David Bosch (1991, pp. 389–93) and by Stephen Bevans and Roger Schroeder (2004, pp. 286–95). The modern idea of the *missio Dei* (though not the term) first surfaced clearly at the International Missionary Council's 1952 meeting in Willingen, Germany, and the concept has been developed in many different ways since.[2]

At the core of *missio Dei* is the idea of sending. The Latin can be translated as 'the sending of God'. It is the Son and the Spirit who are sent, and the church in their wake. John Thompson quotes P. T. Forsyth's description of the four 'missionaries' involved in the one divine redemption (Thompson, 1994, pp. 70–4):

- the Father, who is not sent himself but reveals a missionary heart in sending his Son and the Spirit to work for the fulfilment of creation;
- the Son who has redeemed the world;

---

2 Accounts usually stress the initial influence of Karl Barth, who in a paper to the 1932 Brandenburg Missionary Conference described mission as primarily an activity of God himself. Through Karl Hartenstein, who coined the term *missio Dei*, Barth – it is said – had a key influence on the International Missionary Council's meeting in 1952. Barth's contribution, however, has recently been disputed by Flett, who offers a number of reasons for doubting his role, including that 'not a single fragment of textual evidence supports the connection between Barth's 1932 lecture and Willingen's Trinitarian developments' (Flett, 2010, p. 15).

- the Holy Spirit, who shares in the mission of the Father and the Son in creation and the incarnation, and is himself sent to sustain creation and advance the kingdom;
- the church, which participates in God's mission and is enabled by the Spirit to witness to the world.

What is the place of mission?

One question the *missio Dei* raises is the place of mission in the church's life. Is mission an outpouring from worship? If so, mission risks becoming subordinate to worship, a second step for the church. The church's life becomes organized around the requirements of worship rather than those of mission. Or does mission provide the context for worship, being as much a first step for the church as corporate devotion?

Mission as a second step for God?

The answer can be approached by considering the place of mission in the divine life. This involves some complex theology, and the limited space here will not do it full justice. However, one view is to say that the missions of God are the way that the divine processions relate to creation. The processions refer to the eternal begetting of the Son and the eternal breathing forth of the Spirit. They occur within the internal life of God, the immanent Trinity. The divine missions, in this first perspective, happen when the processions flow into the external life of God, the economic Trinity. The Son saves the world; the Spirit sustains it and carries forward the Son's work of salvation.

On this view, there is a correspondence between the processions and the missions, or it can be said that the missions reveal the processions. But such language does not go as far as saying that the missions *are* the processions. Some distinction is implied between them. Stephen Holmes sees Augustine as holding this view. 'Augustine insists that the sending of the Son and the Spirit is merely economic . . . there is no sending or being sent within the eternal life of God. On this account God has a mission, but God is not properly described as missionary' (Holmes, 2006, p. 78).

Whether or not this is a fair depiction of Augustine, any view that sees the divine missions as a consequence or outward expression of the immanent Trinity makes these missions a second step for God. Though mission is said to be in continuity with God's inner life, it is not fundamental to it (Flett, 2010, p. 29). Mission, as the way God relates to the world, may be consistent with God's being in himself, but is logically and sequentially secondary to it. Flett argues that this legitimizes mission as a second step for the church: first the church gathers to worship, then mission flows out into the world. Worship becomes the prime corporate activity of the church; mission is of secondary importance.

Might this be averted by following Karl Rahner, who famously declared that the economic Trinity is the immanent Trinity? 'The economic Trinity is not merely the means of gaining knowledge of the immanent Trinity, but is the same thing' (Rahner, 1970b, p. 305). It follows, he argues, that in the will of God the two immanent processions – the begetting of the Son and the proceeding of the Spirit – can be equated with the two missions: with the sending of the Son and the sending of the Spirit. If through divine decision the immanent Trinity is the economic Trinity, the processions of God are the missions of God.

This appears to bring the missions into the internal life of God, but does it go far enough? One danger is that mission can still be seen as a second step for God. At what 'point' in his eternal life did God decide that the begetting of the Son and the breathing forth of the Spirit was to have a missionary purpose? Even to ask the question is to concede that there was a 'time' within God when the processions did not have a missionary intent. God's turning outward in mission was not a decision from all eternity. It remains a second step – a second step within the immanent Trinity rather than being associated with the economic Trinity.

Mission as an attribute of God

A second view, expressed by Stephen Holmes, is that mission can be seen as a divine attribute. Mission is as much an attribute of God as love (Holmes, 2006, p, 88). Though all the attributes of God are deeply interconnected – they are different lenses on to the same reality – mission should not be seen as an aspect of any one attribute of God, such as love or fidelity, but as an attribute in its own right.

Aquinas maintained that the two processions in the Trinity imply four kinds of 'real relations' – begetting, being begotten, breathing out and being breathed. These relations involve all the attributes of God – omnipotence, omniscience, love, fidelity and so on. There is no reason in principle why mission should not be a characteristic of these relations as well. Begetting and being begotten would be described as having a missional dimension (a dimension that exists from all eternity), as do breathing out and being breathed.

Holmes argues that mission has the idea of intentional action. The sendings within God represent a teleological movement – they are movements with a purpose. 'In and through begetting the Son, the Father intends generosity towards his Spirit; in and through the procession of the Spirit, the Father intends generosity towards his Son.' (Holmes, 2006, p. 88) The Son is a gift to the Spirit and the Spirit is a gift to the Son. The processions have a missionary character because they are sendings with a purposeful intent – they are intended to be gifts. In God's economy, this eternally purposeful movement is directed toward creation.

Love can also be purposeful of course, but purposefulness is just one aspect of love. Mission by contrast is purposeful in its essence, with love as one of its dimensions. Love might be concerned about a struggling village in Rwanda: mission would actively organize to do something about it. Likewise, mission in the service of, say, fidelity might purposefully act on a promise to the village. Mission would occur in conjunction with faithfulness, but would be not the same as it, just as faithfulness may entail purposeful activity but cannot be reduced to this. Like all the divine attributes, mission is bound up with the other attributes, but cannot be equated to any one of them.

Mission is thus not a consequence of God's being. In God's will it is fundamental to God's being. It is an attribute of God, on a par with the other attributes such as love. Just as we speak of God as love, we can speak of God as mission. Mission is an eternal first, not second thought for God. This means that mission reaches into the very heart of God's communal life. The Trinity is the exact opposite of a community that exists for itself. From all eternity the divine communion is looking outward.

It follows that just as mission is not a second step for God, it must not be a second step for the church. If mission does not derive from any other divine attribute but is a characteristic of God in its own right, mission should not flow from any other aspect of the church's life but be an intrinsic dimension of ecclesial life. Mission therefore will not be a consequence of worship, which can easily make mission secondary to worship. Mission will be an activity of the church with the same standing as worship. Just as all the divine attributes are bound together and expressed in God's self-giving, so all aspects of the church's life will combine when the church gives itself to the world.

One problem with Holmes's approach is that the list of the divine attributes is well set within the tradition. Those wishing to protect the tradition will resist the addition of a further attribute. Another difficulty is the manner in which Holmes seemingly reduces mission to sending. Is sending an adequate description of the fullness of God's mission, which ranges from creation to what Jesus has accomplished on the cross? Do we not need a richer understanding of mission?

Mission as an eternal step for God

As a third approach, John Flett draws on Karl Barth's doctrine of election to maintain that in God's will the divine mission to the world belongs to God's eternal nature (Flett, 2010, pp. 198–214). The eternal begetting of the Son and the eternal procession of the Spirit have always been directed outwards. The Son was eternally destined to become a human being because of God's decision from all time to be for humanity (Eph. 1.4). The outward procession of the Spirit opens up the Father and the Son to creatures outside the Trinity, and this too reflects a decision from all eternity.

There has never been a time when God has not been for humanity. It is in the very nature of God, from all eternity, to be for human beings. God does not have to change his being or reduce his divinity to become human. In some sense, the second person of the Trinity was always human.[3] So God creating, reconciling and redeeming is no distortion of his being, but God being what he is truly in himself. We know this because of God's revelation of himself in Jesus. Though whatever we say about the immanent Trinity should be said with proper caution (Collins, 2008, p. 109), Jesus reveals who God is in and for himself.

For Flett, mission is more than a single attribute of God. It is much more than sending (2010, pp. 200–4, 287–90). God's eternal decision to be for humanity includes the Son's willingness to die for it. Mission is the whole of God, in the sense that all the divine attributes have a missionary purpose. Mission is God's self-giving for the sake of humanity. This makes divine giving, not sending, the heart of mission. Rather than self-donation being an aspect of sending, sending should be seen an aspect of the eternal giving within the Trinity. Sending into the world is what happens when God gives himself to the world. If God's eternal heart has always been shaped by this missional giving, mission cannot be a second step for God.

Mission cannot therefore be a second step for the church. The church does not have a mission (which can sound like an afterthought), just as God does not have a mission. The church is missionary in its nature, as God is missionary in his nature. Indeed, mission is so fundamental to the church that it is part of the church's destiny. Mission will not stop with the return of Christ. As a going out to others in the service of God, it will be part of eternal life (Flett, 2010, p. 291).

If the church is missionary by nature, how does mission relate to the other aspects of ecclesial life – to the other sets of relationships (with God, the wider church and within the gathering) that the last chapter described as being fundamental to the church? We must avoid saying that these relationships exist for mission rather than being ends in themselves. This would reduce these other components of church to being means to an end. Surely a Christmas party can be fun in itself rather than being just an opportunity to invite friends who are outside the church? Surely we can praise God for his creativity, as something intrinsically valuable, rather than simply because it has a missional purpose?

Perhaps it is more helpful to recognize that mission plays two roles in the church's life. First, it has an equal standing in the church's rhythm of worship, fellowship and connections to the wider body. Second, as a

---

3 For an exploration of this based on the relevant New Testament texts, see Farrow (1999, pp. 275–98).

disposition of heart – as self-giving with an outward focus – mission also flows into the other sets of relations, expands their character and gives them the flavour of being gifts to the world.

Thus fellowship will be undertaken for itself, but will also have an outward orientation as guests are welcomed. Connections with the wider church will include, but not be reduced to, serving a missional purpose. Worship will centre on the missional God, while recognizing that this is not all that can be said about him. Mission will permeate all the relationships of church without reducing any of the other sets to being instruments of mission.[4] By playing these two roles, mission will be a first step for the church as it is for God.

Three views

- Mission is a second step for God.
- Mission is as much an attribute of God as love.
- Mission is an eternal first step for God.

What is the nature of mission?

Flett's emphasis on divine self-giving is in line with a great deal of contemporary theology. For example, in his exposition of Sergei Bulgakov, the early twentieth-century Russian Orthodox theologian, Rowan Williams writes about the self-giving that lies at the heart of the Trinity. 'The Father gives all that he has and is to the Son, gives over everything to the Son. When the Son comes forth in the Father's begetting, nothing is held back' (Williams, 2008a, p. 22).

Self-giving as the essence of God

In eternally begetting the Son, the Father gives away his divinity to the Son, who receives it not as something borrowed but as something that constitutes his very being. The Father does not cling to his divinity, but empties himself of it all to beget the Son. The process is eternal. Divinity never 'runs out', because the Father has an infinite supply, as it were, to pour into the Son. What is emptied out is given – hence self-emptying and self-giving are interchangeable terms.

---

4 Equally, as noted in the last chapter, the other sets of relationships that constitute the church will also flow into each other. Fellowship within the gathering, for example, will pervade worship, mission and relations with the wider church (such as a bring-and-share meal to raise funds for a partner church). Mission, however, will be the dominant note in the church's life.

The Son's obedience to the Father represents a self-giving back to the Father. As evidenced by his life on earth, the Son gratefully puts his life at the Father's disposal. Though this obedience is revealed by the incarnation, it does not have to 'wait' for the incarnation to be expressed. It is lived out eternally as the Son submits all he has to the Father's will. 'But what is the life of the Son? It is itself a pouring out . . . the Son's life is simply what is given over and over again to the Father.' The Father and Son eternally give themselves to each other (Williams, 2008a, p. 22).

This dynamic between Father and Son is seen not only in the incarnation but at the beginning and 'end' of creation. The created order, brought into being through the Son, is also the Father's gift to the Son – 'all things were created by him and *for* him' (Col. 1.16). Yet at the end of history, when the kingdom is fully realized, the Son will hand the redeemed creation back to the Father (1 Cor. 15.24). The Son will return all that the Father gave him.

The mutual self-giving of the Father and the Son is not just a giving to – a giving between the two of them. It becomes a giving out in the form of the third person. It is an outpouring of love for each other that overflows into the eternal procession of the Spirit. Hans Urs von Balthasar sees this as somewhat akin to conjugal love, in which the sexual self-giving of the spouses may blossom forth in a new life. 'In the Trinitarian life, the love of the Father and the Son opens out to the Holy Spirit. The Spirit is at one and the same time the bond of their union and the opening of their love beyond the Godhead' (O'Donnell, 1991, p. 143).

Just as the self of the Spirit is eternally received from the Father and the Son,[5] it is given back to them when the Spirit shows, communicates and makes concrete what the Father and Son are doing. The Spirit's gift to the Father and the Son is the gift of a life, a life that is entirely dedicated to revealing, communicating and acting on the Father and Son's behalf. The Spirit behaves in obedience, continually pointing to the other two persons. 'To the total gift of self by the Father and the Son, the Spirit responds by making his own equally total gift of self' (Scola, 1995, p. 62). To be filled with the Spirit, therefore, is to be filled with the Spirit of giving.

Self-giving as the essence of mission

If self-giving typifies the life of the Trinity, it is not surprising that self-giving is at the heart of the divine missions to the world. God's decision to be for humanity is reflected in the creation of the natural and human orders. God retains his utter separateness. At the same time, creation is an act of divine self-giving. God puts some of himself into creation, just as we might say of musicians, 'They put themselves into that piece.' They left traces of

---

5 This assumes a 'Western' position on the *filioque*, the credal statement that the Holy Spirit proceeds from the Father and the Son.

themselves in the music they played. Likewise, God leaves traces of himself in creation, not least in humanity.[6]

Divine self-giving continues in the mission of salvation. Eternal self-giving within the Trinity is reproduced in the life and death of Jesus. This life and death, this self-donation, gives birth to the church. The church is distinct from Jesus – it remains on earth when he ascends to heaven. Yet it receives so much of its life from Jesus that Paul can describe it as the body of Christ. The church is God's gift to the world of a community with Jesus.

The church corresponds to the divine self-donation when it, too, gives itself in mission – when it generates new entities that reflect the self-giving character it has received from God. Mission includes the sacrificial bringing to birth of these new forms of life, which may range from events that energize a neighbourhood, to acts of care, to groups for social action or mutual support, to new contextual churches.

Much of the church planting literature takes for granted that the church is called to reproduce. As we saw in Part 1, the church reproduced in the New Testament, it has reproduced at different times and places ever since, and reproduction is beginning to take new shapes today. Mission as giving provides a theological starting point for understanding ecclesial reproduction. When the church reproduces, it offers a piece of itself to others. It forms an embryonic community of believers, and gives this community away to become the heart of a new church. Just as God gives himself to the world, the body of Christ gives part of itself to the world.

Self-giving

- sums up the nature of God;
- sums up the nature of mission;
- sums up the nature of church reproduction.

What is the goal of mission?

In the traditional understanding, mission's goal was to save souls and build the church. It was undertaken largely by experts, by 'missionaries', and it occurred in foreign lands. Through reflection on the *missio Dei*,

---

6 David Cunningham (1998, pp. 84–5) writes: 'We often say that the artist "puts something of herself" into the work that she produces . . . the production of the work of art involves sacrifice and gift. The artist gives up something of who she is (or who she otherwise might be) in order to create the work of art. And often (though not always), the artist uses the work of art as a medium through which to communicate something to others. For all these reasons, the work of art "bears the mark" of the artist; it reflects her character.'

the goal is now seen more broadly. God's mission has the world in view. Understanding what this involves has not been based solely on the concept of sending, which is too thin, but on other theologies – of creation, salvation and kingdom (Flett, 2010, p. 43). This has given rise to a multiplicity of views about mission's purpose – views that have echoes of the discussion about kingdom and church in the last chapter.

Building on Jacques Matthey's classification (2001, pp. 429–30), the 'classical' approach says that God is in mission in the midst of creation primarily through the atonement. The sending of the Spirit enables the church to witness to what the Son has accomplished on the cross. The emphasis is usually placed on the mission of the Son and the Spirit through the church, which gives effect to the atonement. God's active involvement in creation is left in the background. The goal of mission is to help save creation by making the atonement effective through the church.

The 'ecumenical' strand is expressed in a number of ecumenical documents from the 1960s to the 1980s. Unlike the classical approach, it affirms that by means of the Spirit God is active in the social and political events of the world. The Spirit works through people of good will, whether they are Christians or not. The goal of mission is to help save creation by joining the Spirit's activity in the world. Creation is brought to the fore.

An emerging 'balanced' position seeks to retain the focus on creation, while also emphasizing the church's role. It reflects the divine self-giving that brings creation into being, makes salvation possible and continues through the Spirit to make salvation effective in both the world and the church. The balanced view is helpfully reflected in the five marks of mission, which were first formulated by the Anglican Communion but have been endorsed more widely. The church is

- to proclaim the good news of the kingdom;
- to teach, baptize and nurture new believers;
- to respond to human need by loving service;
- to seek to transform unjust structures of society;
- to safeguard the integrity of creation, and sustain and renew the life of the earth.

The church can be said to join in God's mission when it displays these five marks, or goals of mission. Wherever the Spirit is active in personal lives, in social and political developments, in the behaviour of men and women whether followers of Christ or not, the church is called to throw its weight behind what the Spirit is doing. It does this not only by supporting the Spirit's work in the world, but also by offering the gospel of salvation and inviting people into its communal life with Jesus.

New contextual churches have the potential to express this rounded view of mission – in particular, to draw together aspects of mission that have sometimes been separated. Despite the ideal of holistic mission, local church practice can pull the evangelistic/discipling and social/ecological poles apart. Some churches see mission in terms largely of one of the poles, 'evangelical' churches veering toward the first and 'liberal' ones toward the second. Other congregations have a broad understanding of mission, but engage *as communities* mainly in evangelism and forming disciples; the struggle for justice and the care of creation are left to *individual members*. The poles are separated but in a different way.

New contextual churches hold out the promise of bringing these poles together. As they emerge in the fabric of life, some of these churches are active on social, political or environmental fronts.[7] Where they differ from existing churches is that church grows out of a social or environmental concern (rather than the concern growing out of an existing church, as members become aware of the need). This is creating new opportunities to serve people, introduce them to the gospel, form them as disciples and draw them into an expression of church, all as part of a justice or ecological commitment.

Might there be a link here to John Milbank's call for the church to be the site of true society, where relationships are characterized by mutual giving? He urges on the church

> something of a shift in direction away from the [Archbishop] Temple legacy of long reports telling the Government what to do and being admired by the liberal press, while the laity are secretly sceptical. We need a shift instead to a more authentic radicalism in which the Church gets involved in all kinds of processes of welfare, medicine, banking, education, the arts, business, technology, ecology, and more, and seeks to transform them in the joint name of reciprocity and virtue. (*Church Times*, 16 December 2011)

Milbank imagines this involvement in the context of the Anglican parish. But this seems rather unrealistic when so many of the activities he refers to either have no links to their nearest church or skip across local-church boundaries. It may make more sense to see the lay ventures he proposes 'in the world of real work, founded upon a commitment to Christian co-operativist principles', as having the potential to become, or give rise to church where they are.

Why should someone who owns a small business and applies to it Christian values not also, sensitively, lay down pathways to faith for employees who are interested? Why should not more schools with Christian foundations enable pupils, if they wish, to form groups that explore intentional discipleship? A former health visitor training for ordination planned to start a social

---

7 For an example, see Howson (2011).

enterprise that would combine work for the National Health Service with opportunities for people to explore well-being from a Christian perspective, as a first step to forming a Christian community.[8] Other pioneers have formed social enterprises and are now exploring how church might emerge within them.

When the church gives itself to people where they actually spend their lives, it can be more deeply immersed – as a visible community – in the social and political contexts that the Spirit has already entered. Its work of evangelism and discipling new believers can be brought physically closer to the Spirit's mission of loving care, justice and environmental action in settings that are beyond the reach of existing churches. Closer integration becomes possible between the marks of mission, corporate expressions of mission and individuals' everyday lives.

How does the church share in God's mission?

This chapter has steadily filled out the notion of divine mission from sending, to self-giving, to self-giving that ranges from proclaiming the gospel to caring for creation. The church is included in the divine self-giving mission that touches every dimension of life.

This involvement is not just through imitation. The danger with imitation alone is that it puts the accent on what we do. 'It can lead to a human effort to conform to God, whatever appeals are made to the grace of God which assists us' (Fiddes, 2000a, p. 29). Relating to God becomes a matter of knowing him as an external person, as a being to be imitated, and this exalts human consciousness. God becomes subject to human understanding as we seek to get hold of him in our minds, and this in turn violates his transcendence (p. 39).

By contrast, the church is involved in mission mainly through participation, through the church's inclusion in the divine life. The church is drawn into the self-giving mission of God by the Spirit, who enables the church to receive the offer of grace. The way in which grace is received is for the church to obey Christ's command to give itself to the world. Taking part in God's mission is the appropriate response to God's mission (Flett, 2010, p. 290).

John 20.20–3 makes this clear. First, in a powerful visual demonstration, the disciples are reminded that the divine mission entails the giving of self. Jesus shows them his hands and side in verse 20 – a pointer to what he has done for them. Then in verse 21 the disciples are incorporated into this mission. 'As the Father has sent me, I am sending you' (John 20.21). Being sent is the disciples' appropriate response. So in verse 22 they receive the

---

8 Obviously, there are all sorts of issues that would need careful thought, such as maintaining appropriate professional boundaries.

Spirit, who makes their response possible (John 16.7–15). Finally, in verse 23 they are authorized to forgive sins (as Jesus forgave sins). Their actions will be as effective as those of Jesus himself. They will represent Jesus in their acts (Fiddes, 2000a, p. 51).

Being drawn into the missional flow of the Trinity enables the church to embody the missionary God in its life. Mission is the manner in which grace is received and the recipient made like the giver. Worship is the supreme context in which this exchange, this covenant takes place. To receive grace is not just to have a happy experience or to say a heartfelt 'thank you' to Jesus. To receive grace is to donate oneself to a missional God.

This takes concrete form when worshippers, enabled by the Spirit, dedicate their lives to mission as they are drawn into the Trinity. Worship must therefore connect with individuals' missional lives. It is only as worship and the practice of mission are linked together that this exchange – this receipt of grace by offering one's life back to God in missional service – can be explicit and make sense to those involved. Thus worship can never be a self-contained zone separate from the church's mission, let alone a priority over mission. If God is missionary in his essence, to worship God is to worship the One who engages in mission from all eternity. Worship must express clearly that the church is being drawn into God's missional life of self-giving to the world.

Some aspects of the *missio Dei*

- Mission is a first step for God in his inner life.
- This first step involves self-giving.
- The church echoes divine self-giving when it gives itself in mission on a broad front.
- Mission as a first step for the church is a response to grace.

Conclusion

A number of things happen when the church participates in the divine mission. First, if mission is not the result of who God is but *is* who God is, if God is as much mission as love, mission will be central to the church. It will never be a second step. Mission will not be extra to the congregation's life: it will be essential to the congregation's life. Meeting to organize mission will be as important as meeting to worship. This has implications beyond the inherited church, which must consider how mission can be a priority in its life. Mission must be a continuing first step for new contextual churches too.

Second, participating in the Spirit's outward movement into creation will discourage over reliance on attractional approaches to mission. 'A kingdom-like church follows God's mission into the world because that is where God's mission is located. Such a church does not seek to create a "come-to-us" structure . . .' (Bolger, 2007, p. 134).[9] Rather, the church will go to places and networks where it is not already present. It will give a portion of itself – in the form of a new Christian community – away.

Third, by giving itself to people where they enact their concerns, the church as a visible community will be immersed in a variety of social and political settings. Being fully church in these contexts – engaged in Christian formation as well as witness, for example – will enable it to integrate aspects of mission that have often been kept apart.

Fourth, when the church recognizes the Spirit's presence in the world it will be attentive to its context. The church is not 'a self-sufficient reality that has a ready-made message for the world, but an entity that develops its identity and vision *in dialogue with* the world' (Bevans, 2005, p. 31; author's italics). To proclaim the gospel fruitfully, the church will learn before it teaches. As well as from Scripture and tradition, it will learn from the Spirit's activity outside the church. Christian understanding and practice can never reflect the entirety of God. Being questioned by the Spirit's accomplishments in the world will help the church to reveal God more fully.

Attending to the world will alert the church to what is healthy in a setting. Of course the church will also be aware of the fallenness of creation, but this will not produce an over-pessimistic view of the context. If the Spirit is busy in a situation, the church will rejoice in evidence of the Spirit's work. The church will not expect, therefore, to draw individuals from a culture outside God into an ecclesial culture within God. It will seek to form new Christian communities in which the Spirit's work in the context is fused with the Spirit's work in the church. These contextual churches will hint at what the setting might look like were it to be under the lordship of Christ.

Finally, Christians will not adopt an imperialistic approach to starting new churches – as if to say, 'we'll bring what we have and drop it into your midst.'[10] If the missionary Spirit is present in a setting, the outcome of the Spirit's work will well up from within the setting. If that includes the birth of a church, it will be a church from inside the context. Outsiders may have a role of play, as midwives of the church, but only if they have become so

---

9 Bolger immediately goes on to say that a kingdom-like church does not seek to convince others to become members. This understates the church's witnessing role and the call to make disciples of all nations (Matt. 28.19). In resisting a neurotic, excessively narrow approach to mission, evangelism must not be left out of the picture altogether.

10 It could be said that the incarnation is God bringing what he has and dropping it into a culture. On the other hand, Jesus was conceived by the Spirit who was already present in creation. Jesus emerged as a baby from within nature with the aid of the Spirit, who fused the natural and supernatural together.

immersed in the culture as to be part of it. Church will emerge from within the context – to serve it.

Further reading

Collins, Paul M., *The Trinity: A Guide for the Perplexed*, London: T & T Clark, 2008.

Cunningham, David S., *These Three Are One: The Practice of Trinitarian Theology*, Oxford: Blackwell, 1998.

Flett, John G., *The Witness of God: The Trinity, Missio Dei, Karl Barth, and the Nature of Christian Community*, Grand Rapids, MI: Eerdmans, 2010.

Questions for discussion

- What would it practically mean for the local church to avoid making mission a second step?
- Do new contextual churches have more potential to undertake holistic mission than inherited churches, or is it that holistic mission looks different in these new churches?
- What pressures might pull a new contextual church away from mission? How might it resist these pressures?

7

Mission by Individuals or Communities?

Much contemporary theology sees the church as a community that witnesses to the world and forms individuals in the faith. Both happen supremely as individuals gather for worship, during which they are drawn into and shaped by the Christian story. They are then sent into the world as a dispersed but godly community. Chapter 7 challenges this idea that Christians gather for worship and disperse for mission.

It starts by discussing Stanley Hauerwas, whose stress on the formational task of the church has been highly influential, and Lesslie Newbigin, a leading missional thinker in the last century, who emphasized the congregation's evangelistic role. The chapter argues that both writers leave a gap in their approaches – a gap between the church and the world. This gap arises from the assumption that congregations assemble to worship God and scatter to serve the world. New contextual churches have the potential to help fill this gap by being communities in mission.

To support this, the chapter argues that the *missio Dei* is communal in nature. God should be seen as a divine communion-in-mission and this should be echoed in the local church. This transforms our understanding of congregational mission and pleads for communities of mission in everyday life. While the last chapter pulled mission into the communal heart of God, this one draws the communal heart of God into mission.

Stanley Hauerwas and Lesslie Newbigin

Both Hauerwas and Newbigin can be understood as responding to the elevation of the individual in contemporary society. Hauerwas emphasizes the believing community's role in forming Christian character. Newbigin argues that alongside personal evangelism, the congregation plays a critical part in making Christ known to the world. Both writers place their emphasis on the Christian community.

Stanley Hauerwas

Hauerwas – following Alasdair MacIntyre – has argued that there is no neutrality in human thought. Individuals are always embedded in communities, which form how they interpret and live in the world. When believers commit themselves to an ecclesial life, are immersed in the Christian story and learn the practices of the Christian community, they will bear truthful witness to Jesus. The Spirit forms Christian character through the church.

According to Hauerwas, 'the church is God's new language and describes the Christian way by its manner of life' (Thomson, 2010, p. 14). Through its corporate life and the practices of individual believers, the church reveals a story about Jesus that is very different to the story told by the world. The world is humanity that fails to worship Jesus, leaving the world in deep distress. The church serves the world by naming this distress through its witness to Jesus. 'You do not know how to cure a disease until you can name it' (Hauerwas and Willimon, 1996, pp. 58–9). The church, both gathered and dispersed, witnesses to Jesus by embodying holiness in flesh-and-blood life. It narrates to the world the ongoing story of Jesus.

Hauerwas's account of Christian formation and witness has had great influence. It resonates with developments in philosophy since Wittgenstein, who argued that meaning arises from how language is used within a context of shared practices and forms of life. It is consistent with sociological insights into the contextual influences on knowledge and behaviour. It suggests how the church can be both faithful to the story of Jesus and engaged with society.

Yet it is around this last point that some critics have felt frustrated. They have wondered whether Hauerwas does enough to bridge the gap between the church, with its specific narrative and practices, and the world. David Fergusson, for instance, claims that Hauerwas puts so much stress on the church's distinctiveness that it becomes difficult to understand how the will of God may be done outside the church. How may Christians make common cause with other agencies and individuals? (Fergusson, 1997, p. 246)

Hauerwas would say that believers learn practices like truthfulness and peaceableness within the church. As these practices become second nature, they inform behaviour in the world. But what is missing from this account is how the structure of the church, with its weighting toward residential neighbourhoods, works against a distinctively Christian engagement with the world. It is not easy for the church to form Christian lives in work, volunteering and leisure when the formation takes place some distance away. The teaching of practices at church may have a level of generality that fails to engage with the specifics of a person's life.

If, on Hauerwas' own premises, communities shape individuals' thoughts and actions, what happens when worshippers leave church and become immersed again in the communities of everyday life? Communities of the world, in which Christians spend far more time than in church, provide a counter-weight to the ecclesial gathering and dampen its formational effect. This indeed is the experience of many believers. They find themselves caught between competing communities, and – despite the exceptions – often the church is not the most influential.

In particular, these communities are highly organized. The powers arrayed against the kingdom work through social structures. The kingdom – a term that carries the idea of organization – must have structures to respond. Yet when the church in its organized form inhabits the residential segments of life, it leaves individual believers dis-organized in those parts of society, such as work and entertainment, where the powers have their strongholds. How can Christians counter the powers when they have no structured means for doing so?

Margaret Hebblethwaite describes how people forming base communities, small groups of worshipping Christians who serve people around them, often talk of the need to organize. Though 'organization can almost smack of bureaucracy', alone we are vulnerable and powerless.

> Strength lies in numbers. A people is organized when they have worked out how to convert a disorganized crowd into a coherent, coordinated body that can achieve goals. There must be order, not chaos; there must be communication, not ignorance; there must be accepted leaders, not manipulation by a few pushy entrepreneurs; and so on. Any community needs some organization, and the bigger the network of communities, the better the organization needs to be. (Hebblethwaite, 1993, p. 96)

Hauerwas seems, perhaps, to intuit the church/world gap in his theology when he praises Dorothy Day, co-founder of the Catholic Worker movement.[1] In his 2000–1 Gifford Lectures, he praises her as an example of how the church can 'be a witness to the peace that is an alternative to the death that grips the life of the world'. The Houses of Hospitality that she helped to found in the slums of New York and beyond give practical witness to the Jesus story (Hauerwas, 2001, p. 230).

Significantly, Day lived in a small room in one of these houses. Though she attended church daily, her everyday life was shaped by a lay community in the midst of the secular world (Day, 1997, pp. 1–6). Might this suggest how the church/world gap can be bridged? Hauerwas begins to point to this himself when he writes of the need to send out missionaries in pairs. '. . . it is a mistake to send out *a* missionary. Two, at the very least, have to travel together because otherwise those to whom they go would not be able to "see" the gospel' (Hauerwas, 2010, p. 68). In a footnote he says that Jesus' sending of the disciples in twos is a good place to start to rethink the theology of missions. Earlier he comments that the Spirit sometimes forces the church to leave one time and place to go (as a witness) into an unfamiliar time and place (p. 54).

---

1 I am grateful to Joseph Wolyniak for drawing my attention to this.

This creeps close to the idea of church beyond the residential arena – of church as a visible community (sometimes a small one) in all the settings of life. What holds Hauerwas back, possibly, is the church-focus of his theology.[2] In Hauerwas's understanding, to be missionary the church must be holy, at a distance from the world. The holiness of the church shows the world that it is the world – that there is an alternative way of life in which the world does not share. This creates space for witness, which is achieved through the small moral decisions and practices that the church makes each day.

This concentration on the internal life of the church, so as to distance the church from the world, blinds Hauerwas perhaps to the challenge of finding new ways for the church to connect to the world. Though he recognizes that the church must be hospitable to the new discoveries that witness both makes possible and requires (Hauerwas, 2010, p. 59), he fails to follow through the implications of this for the shape of the church. Might these new discoveries include new ways of being church? If the church fails to be present in different contexts, can it be an effective witness to them – both faithful to Jesus and to the people it serves?

Lesslie Newbigin

Whereas Hauerwas emphasizes the corporate aspect of Christian formation, in *The Gospel in a Pluralist Society* Newbigin singles out the corporate dimension of evangelism. He describes the congregation as 'hermeneutic of the gospel' (1989, pp. 222–33). By this he means that the congregation is to interpret the gospel to the world. How can the church faithfully and credibly represent the gospel in society? Newbigin responds, 'I am suggesting that the only answer, the only hermeneutic of the gospel, is a congregation of men and women who believe it and live by it.' Evangelistic campaigns and other efforts to bring the gospel to public life are all secondary to this, and are effective only 'as they are rooted in and lead back to a believing community'. Jesus did not write a book but formed a community (p. 227).

Writing about evangelism in the city, Newbigin distinguishes between evangelism and proselytism. The latter is the natural attempt of every human community to add to its own strength at the expense of others. The former is the activity of a church that cares about the rule of God and not about itself. To communicate the good news authentically, therefore, the local congregation must display its concern not just for itself but for the wellbeing of the whole community. It must be so involved in the secular concerns of the neighbourhood that everyone will realize that nothing is outside God's love. There is no other hermeneutic of the gospel than God being present in the believing, worshipping, celebrating and caring congregation (Newbigin, 1987).

---

2 I am grateful to John Flett for pointing this out.

The problem is that Newbigin, like Hauerwas, takes the existing shape of church for granted. Having in the late 1970s written about the church scattered in places throughout society (Newbigin, 1977), Newbigin pulls back to a conventional position a decade later. Phrases like being 'deeply involved in the concerns of its neighbourhood' and 'the Church gathers every Sunday' (Newbigin, 1989, pp. 228, 230) betray Newbigin's assumptions. The church is the existing local church, not the more radical vision that he flirted with earlier (and which is discussed more fully in Chapter 10).

The result is a physical and cultural gap in his account between the evangelizing congregation and much of the world. How can the church be a communal witness in work, leisure, political and other spheres of life when it is at a distance from them? Believers participate in Christ's priesthood 'not within the walls of the Church but in the daily business of the world' (Newbigin, 1989, p. 230). But Newbigin allows them to enter the world as individuals. They are like lambs before wolves as they confront on their own the collectives of everyday life. They are asked to engage with the world, including through evangelism, without the support of any visible Christian community round them.

Again like Hauerwas, but more explicitly, Newbigin seems to sense that something is missing. He recognizes the 'need for "frontier-groups", groups of Christians working in the same sectors of public life, meeting to thrash out the controversial issues of their business or profession in the light of their faith' (Newbigin, 1989, pp. 230–1). These sound like groups whose members would come together from *different* places. They would not be Christians in the *same* place. Nor would each group seek actively to serve and witness in a place – an agenda that is much wider than meeting to 'thrash out controversial issues'.

Hauerwas and Newbigin both leave a gap between the church and the world. This is because in their assumed model of church, congregations gather for worship and by and large scatter for mission. Having met together, worshippers plunge back into the world as individuals. They mainly engage in mission not as ecclesial communities, but on their own.

Gathered for worship, scattered for mission

This reflects a widespread understanding of the local church. Jürgen Moltmann, for example, distinguishes between the 'gathered congregation', who come together for the sake of the word and sacrament, and 'Christians in the world' who are the dispersed church in families, vocations, work and friendships (Moltmann, 2001, p. 234). 'Christians in the world' are called to join with others in doing 'Kingdom of God work'. This work provides one door into the community of Christ, whether it is undertaken by churchgoers or others. The 'gathered congregation' provides a second door. The horizon spanning both aspects of Christ's community is the kingdom of God (pp. 242–3).

On this view, mission takes communal form when Christians join people outside the church in action and self-help groups that serve the kingdom.

These groups have their origins not in the church, but in social and political needs. They are part of the community of Christ, but are not visibly part of the church (pp. 243–6). When worshippers are sent into the world as individuals, therefore, they are sent to form communities with people outside the church. These communities are to work for the kingdom without an expectation that they themselves be church. The result is to draw something of wedge between the gathered congregation and these kingdom-serving communities in the midst of everyday life.

Of course, the wedge is not a total breach. The congregation itself may bring churchgoers and others together in groups that serve the kingdom. The worship and prayers of the congregation sustain its members in their missional settings. So does the ongoing fellowship of believing friends and relatives. To an extent, church members take the congregation with them into the world. Yet despite this, the felt experience of most Christians is that having gathered for worship, they do go into the rest of life as individuals. Most of their social connections, such as at the school gate or in work, are among people outside church. When relationships are with fellow Christians, individuals typically meet as companions rather than explicitly as church.

Particularly in today's individualistic global North, the result is that Christians feel they must live out their faith by acting largely as individual believers. They may take the congregation with them, but often have little sense of its presence. The congregation is even more hidden to the people Christians encounter. If the church is visible at all, usually through its buildings, it is seen as something that happens on a Sunday. It is not evident, for the most part, in the realities of ordinary life. However, a very different approach is suggested by the notion of community-in-mission, which is rooted in the nature of God, creation and salvation.

Community-in-mission

Augustine of Hippo noted that in speaking of God, we necessarily separate out the words Father, Son and Spirit. You cannot say them at exactly the same time or write them in precisely the same space (Poitras, 1999, p. 34). Our language pulls apart the divine persons. This can mislead churchgoers with little theological background. It becomes easy to assume that when the Son and the Spirit act in the world they act on their own, as if they were individuals. It is then natural to accept that during the week church members should carry forward God's mission also as individuals.

The divine communion-in-mission

Theologically of course, separating the divine persons runs counter to Augustine's famous axiom that, with respect to the persons, 'all the external works of the Trinity are undivided'. There is no external act of God that only one person of the Trinity undertakes. This does not mean that the three persons are so joined together that they lose their distinctiveness. Rather, because the three persons mutually indwell each other, the Son does not act alone and nor does the Spirit. In Leonardo Boff's words, 'Father, Son and Holy Spirit are always together: they create together, save together, and together they bring us into their communion of life and love' (Boff, 2000, p. 9). They are in eternal intimate communion.

Bevans and Schroeder have drawn on Eastern Orthodox theologians to describe the Trinity as communion-in-mission. 'Theologians like Vladimir Lossky, John Meyendorf and John Zizioulas have helped theologians in the West understand the Trinity as an ec-static communion of persons, always involved in the world, always inviting all of creation to share in the triune life of communion-in-mission' (Bevans and Schroeder, 2004, p. 294). The mutual giving and receiving that constitutes the divine communion is reflected in the sending of the Spirit, a gift to sustain creation and help bring it to fulfilment. They are evident, too, in the sending of the Son who is at the centre of salvation. Through these missions the divine communion is turned 'inside out' and revealed to be communion-in-mission (pp. 297–8).

'Communion-in-mission' is preferable to the divine 'community in mission' used on the Fresh Expressions Share website (www.sharetheguide. org/section1/2) and by George Lings (Lings, 2008, pp. 166–9). Communities vary widely and include groupings in which ties are loose. 'Community' therefore has a greater risk of implying tritheism – seeing the Trinity as three Gods – than 'communion', with its stronger sense of mutual participation.

Bevans and Schroeder argue that a Trinitarian-inspired ecclesiology will speak of the church as 'a communion-in-mission' (pp. 298–9). The church is communion because it participates in God's communal character (cf. 2 Peter 1.4). 'The perfect communication and self-giving that is God's very self is the church's deepest reality.' Equally, like the Trinity the church is missionary in its essential nature. Deriving its identity from the mission of the Son and the Spirit, the church as communion-in-mission takes its being from the divine communion-in-mission.

The creation mandate

Might the church as communion (or community)-in-mission also derive from creation? Contemporary theologians often point out that the image of God in Genesis 1 is given to the man and the woman together, in relationship. Genesis 1 portrays the man and the woman not as individuals who then contract to be a community: they are in relationship from the very beginning.

Moltmann provides an eschatological interpretation of the *imago Dei*. Humans are in the process, which is fulfilled when the Lord returns, of becoming like God. This likeness is not an individual's possession, but exists in human relationships that mirror the Trinitarian life (Moltmann, 1985, pp. 215–9). As the image of God on earth, human beings correspond first of all to the relationship of God to humanity and the whole of creation. 'But they also correspond to the inner relationships of God to himself . . .' (p. 77).

The purpose – or mission – of humanity is revealed in the context of the man and woman's relationship with each other. Having been created in relationship, they are jointly given responsibility for creation (Gen. 1.28). The connection between community and 'mission' is reinforced in Chapter 2. Yahweh commands the man to care for the garden in verse 15 and then soon after says that it is not good for the man to be alone. The social nature of human beings is tied directly to their purpose, which is to take forward God's work of creation. The divine communion-in-mission is mirrored in humanity.[3]

Community-in-mission after the Fall

This emphasis on communal mission continues after the Fall – in the vocation of Israel, in Jesus' mission *with* his disciples, in the sending out of the disciples in pairs, in Saint Paul's missionary teams and in the churches in people's homes, which were at the intersections of family, work and – in some cases – public life. Rita Finger notes how city dwellings in the ancient world were packed together, with no glass windows to shut out the noise.

> Many neighbors would have overheard activity around a communal meal in a small room or an open courtyard that was characterized by great joy (singing? laughter?). In the midst of the urban chaos and misery that characterized every ancient Mediterranean city, such a gathering must have sounded inviting indeed. (Finger, 2007, p. 242)

Congregations, as congregations, had a witnessing role, which was supplemented by the work of individual evangelists. Paul assumes that non-believers will sometimes be present in the gathering and expects worship to be ordered with an eye to them (1 Cor. 14.22–5). Mark Keown provides detailed support for the view that Paul has corporate evangelism in mind when he urges the Philippians to 'stand firm in one Spirit, contending as one for the faith of the gospel' (Phil. 1.27). This 'includes all manner of contending for the faith of the gospel including evangelism' (Keown, 2008,

---

3 This resonates, of course, with the Trinitarian reading of Genesis 1.26, 'Let us make man in our image'. On this reading, the divine communion works explicitly as a community to create the man and the woman, who are to undertake their work of mission also in community.

p. 116). Paul is addressing the congregation as a whole. Members are to stand together in evangelism and their other actions as they struggle for the faith.

God's ideal for mission is to work through communities (as well as through individuals). Since the goal of mission to create a Jesus-filled community, God's missional means fit his missional ends. The church is community-in-mission, therefore, because it corresponds to the divine communion-in-mission, it lives out the community-in-mission vocation of men and women and it is the vehicle of God's desire to accomplish salvation through community. When churches act as communities-in-mission, they witness to the nature of God, the nature of humanity and the nature of salvation.

In discussing the church as 'communion-in-mission', Bevans and Schroeder do not draw out the implications for the local church. Yet the implications are profound. If the church is community-in-mission, then – as a normal expectation – the mission of the local church should be undertaken in community. Just as *God's* mission is a communal activity, so the church's mission should be a communal activity; just as *humanity's* mission in creation was to be done in community, so mission in the church should be undertaken in community; just as God's mission of redemption works through *human communities*, the church should enact mission through its communities; and just as community is the *goal of mission*, so community should be the means of mission.

The church is community-in-mission

- as an echo of the divine communion-in-mission;
- as a correspondence to the communal nature of human beings;
- as a communal vehicle and the communal goal of salvation.

Communal mission in the local church

The idea that individuals in a congregation take forward the church's mission on their own is utterly foreign to who and how God is, to how men and women were created and to how God undertakes mission in a fallen world. Today's new contextual churches represent the beginnings of a different approach. They are starting to close the gap between the 'gathered congregation' and 'Christians in the world'.

Scattered and gathered for mission

They are showing that believers can make the gathered church visible at more times of the week and in more places. They are creating new and more opportunities for churchgoers to be not just individuals in mission, but members of an ecclesial community-in-mission. They are enabling the church to be dispersed in society not only as individuals with missional responsibilities, but also as communities that share these responsibilities. They are reflecting the communal nature of the divine mission. In so doing, they are making the communal heart of God more prominent in the missional life of the church.

These new contextual churches may be small groups of Christians or larger church planting teams, but whatever their size community is fundamental to them. Their members share interests and concerns in the context of prayer and simple forms of worship. They have a missional focus. They may work with homeless people, organize 'managing life' events for users of a leisure centre, enable the 'late middle aged' on a new housing estate to get to know each other, teach English as a second language, provide an entrée into workplace spirituality or equip young people for work. At the same time, openings are created for individuals to explore the Christian life.

An example is the mid-sized missional communities that are being formed in a growing number of churches on both sides of the Atlantic. Going by a variety of names such as clusters, connect groups and NETS, these missional groups meet several times a month effectively as a congregation and join with the rest of the local church perhaps monthly. Each community serves a specific group of people currently outside the church. In partnership with the European Church Planting Network, 3DM – based in the United States – had been involved in starting over 725 new churches in just three years by 2010; many were mid-sized communities (Breen and Absalom, 2010).

Examples include communities serving children with disabilities, young adults in the workplace and people with an interest in justice and environmental issues. One group has run a money management course for a Bangladeshi community, another facilitates parenting support groups for mothers and fathers, while a third organizes events on contemporary issues for young adults in a pub. The vision of St Paul's Shadwell, in East London, is that a number of their mid-sized communities will grow and spawn further communities, some of which will multiply again. Their intention is to 'plant pregnant churches'.

Though not always seen as such, these mid-sized communities are more than sub-groups of church. They can be regarded as churches in their own right so long as they are engaged in the four interlocking sets of relationships that constitute the church – with God, the world, the wider church and within the community. Just as the New Testament can use 'church' to describe a meeting in a house, all believers in a city or the whole body of Christ, so church can be an appropriate term for a small missional community, or a large congregation or the wider Christian body.

The potential of communal mission

New contextual churches are exploring how the witness of Christians through the week can have a stronger communal dimension. If these churches are fruitful, their lives of service will help the church to connect more firmly with people's ordinary circumstances. The local church will break out of its mainly residential setting to become a servant in more parts of life. Churchgoers will be able to minister to their contexts more effectively because they will not be doing it on their own. They will have the encouragement and support of other Christians who are in the situation and understand it. The church as a corporate entity will be visible as yeast and light in more segments of society.

Communities that serve their contexts have the potential to draw in people who do not attend church but identify with the group's focus. A community organizing stress, conflict management and other seminars for people at work might attract someone who catches the vision. The group might welcome the person, explaining 'We always start by discussing what we are doing to serve our colleagues, we usually read a story about Jesus (who is known as one of the world's greatest spiritual teachers), we say what we think about it and we finish with some quiet music, during which those of us who believe in God offer silent prayers. You are welcome to join us.'

A contextual church does not have to be small. But when it is, though it will be vulnerable to one or two members leaving, it can also be more sensitive to newcomers than a larger group and more easily adapt its language and agenda to them. Newcomers can be more readily made at home. Welcoming people from the same setting means that group members will always have at least their context in common, and this will help the group to gel. The small size of the group will make it easier for a newcomer to contribute.

The warmth, prayer and witness of the contextual church may encourage individuals to enter the faith. In such cases, they will do so in an environment of service. If the purpose of the church is to benefit others and this is reflected in its life, new members may be engaged in 'mission' before they intentionally follow Christ. Experiencing church as a community of service will influence their perception of what it means to be a Christian. Mission will be in their DNA as they are born again, and from the beginning their discipleship will be in the context of practical, day-to-day self-giving.

This can be true of existing churches, of course, but often members are drawn from a wide area. This dilutes the church's ability to serve a specific context and so weakens the effectiveness of the congregation's corporate mission. A new contextual church is likely to have a more clearly defined missional focus, which makes it easier for members to engage in mission as a community. They can start initiatives together, and better support each other's individual witness because they understand the situation. As a result, newcomers are drawn into a community whose corporate missional life is stronger than many conventional churches.

New contextual churches enable individuals who are attracted to Jesus to experience church in their circumstances. Not having to attend church in a very different setting can make it easier to start learning the communal practices of the faith. Once new believers are comfortable with their experience of church, they can be introduced to the wider body. Possibilities include belonging to a sacramental community at weekends, being invited to prayer retreats and short study courses, joining pilgrimages or attending conferences, accessing resources from the web, or a combination of these. Encounters with the larger church will enable individuals to grow in their Christian identity, mature as disciples and enjoy a richer ecclesial life than is possible in one gathering, especially if it is small.

Threading the church through society

- makes the church more visible;
- makes it easier to draw in people from outside;
- often involves small groups that can adapt more easily to a new member;
- implants mission into the DNA of an emerging Christian;
- involves accessible groups that can be bridges to the wider church.

Some challenges

To help contextual churches bear fruit, it is important to insist that they really are church. Theologically, this is true whatever their size.[4]

How small is church?

Not all contextual churches are small, by any means, but some are. Todd Hunter, for example, has proposed 'Three Is Enough' groups, comprising three friends or colleagues doing three simple and humble activities in places of daily life. Several nurses could band together. Their floor would no longer be merely their place of work. It would become 'the soil of their discipleship and missional engagement with the world' (Hunter, 2009, p. 160). This is close to the vision of Cell UK, which seeks to be '4 life' by encouraging communities of mission in the context of everyday life.

---

4 Of course, they may be described as congregations (or by some other term) if they are part of a local church, but whatever the language the point here is that theologically they can be regarded as being church.

Can such small groups really be church? In terms of what it essentially means to be church, the answer is 'yes'. Many mainstream churches have Sunday or midweek congregations of a handful of members, yet these are considered as much an expression of church as larger congregations. In the tradition, the size of a gathering has never been a mark of church. If the essence of church consists of four interlocking sets of relationships with God, the wider church, the world and within the gathering, then so long as a new community engages in these relationships it can be considered a church. To suppose a small gathering cannot be church is to make a value judgement about size that Jesus never made. The kingdom of heaven is like a mustard seed.

However, the tradition has distinguished between the *esse* and the *bene esse* of church – between the essence of church and what is necessary for the well-being of a church. A micro group may meet the relational criteria for church, but is likely to be too small to provide its members with an ample experience of ecclesial life. Only as it connects to the larger body will members enjoy the fuller blessings of church. The smaller the gathering, the more its health will depend on frequent connections to the whole.

Recognizing these gatherings as churches will help them to take their place alongside existing local churches. If they are seen as being less than church, there is a risk that inherited churches will stifle them unwittingly. Members will continue to think that 'weekend church' should be the focus of their involvement and that in-life communities should have lower priority. Yet if believers undertake mission through the week in community and if they do so through the four sets of relationships that constitute the church, there is no reason to suppose that 'weekend church' is more important than these new churches, or vice versa. Both have equal validity. They can complement each other.

Providing support

As contextual churches become more common, a growing number of church-goers will be less involved in traditional congregations. Some will be fully immersed in their contextual church, while others will have dual loyalties – to their 'Sunday' church and to their 'weekday' one. Financial and other support for inherited churches will be diverted to these new communities.

Will inherited churches react defensively or see emerging churches as an opportunity to reshape and extend their ministries? Potentially, existing congregations could have a new role in equipping their members to take part in and lead contextual churches. They could follow other churches in developing mid-sized communities. Or they could help to provide a fuller church experience for those who come to faith in contextual church and decide for family or other reasons to have dual church membership.

Denominations and networks are beginning to find that they have a new role in supporting communities of mission. Contextual churches increasingly tend to be lay led, and if the number of such churches is to grow their leaders will need resources, opportunities to learn from each other and pastoral care. Experience in Lincolnshire, Liverpool and elsewhere points to the key role of catalysts and connectors, individuals who network, fan the emerging opportunities, bring people together, encourage mutual learning and provide personal support. Finding, releasing and paying for such people when the church is acutely short of resources is a tall order – but not impossible. Churches and denominations have begun to do precisely this.

Support includes helping new churches to connect up. If one task of mission is to draw people into the kingdom via a community of believers, another is to bring these communities into visible communion with the wider church. Christian identity needs public expression, not least as a witness to the world. Moreover, whether emerging or established, no one church can meet all the spiritual needs of its members. This is not just an issue for micro churches. Even with large ones, individuals require various forms of nourishment from the wider body, alongside their 'local' gathering, if they are to grow in the faith.

As Chapter 3 described, pointers to how these connections might be fostered are beginning to emerge. New gatherings can be networked into the body through links with a local church, or through local 'coalitions' of churches that work together on mission and discipleship, or through networks of churches that share a common spiritual tradition, or through networks of pioneers within a monastic order of mission, or through a combination of these. Connecting up is integral to reaching out.

Belonging to more than one church

The inherited local church has a particular responsibility to welcome Christians who belong to more than one gathering. Dual church membership is likely to be increasingly important. If micro churches multiply in the nooks and crannies of life, a growing number of people may have to juggle their church-in-life participation with the involvement of their families in different gatherings. Belonging to more than one church becomes the obvious answer.

Dual church membership will be especially necessary when a full sacramental life is not possible in the new contextual community. Although hopefully these gatherings will celebrate the sacraments,[5] in some cases this may not be feasible. In these instances, the expectation will be that members become committed to a sacramental community elsewhere. The situation will be analogous to some Church of England evensong congregations where baptism and Holy Communion are not celebrated. Members are also involved in a morning congregation where they are. The evensong congregation is deemed a valid expression of church by sharing in the sacramental life of the wider body.

---

5 Ways of addressing this are discussed in Chapter 18.

Theologically, when individuals belong to multiple networks, there is no reason why someone should not contribute to two 'local' churches. If mutual giving is at the heart of Christian community, an individual can contribute to two Christian communities by giving and receiving within them. Both are part of the same body. Indeed, the Church of England's Liturgical Commission has recognized the possibility. It has urged local churches not to try and do everything well but to play to their strengths. 'The corollary is that worshippers may attend more than one church regularly, for different occasions of worship'. This 'dual or triple "citizenship"' should be active and consistent belonging rather than a consumerist pick and mix (Church of England Liturgical Commission, 2007, pp. 25–6).

Remaining missional

A further challenge is for contextual churches to preserve their missional focus. As with inherited congregations, they will be in constant danger of putting their preferences for fellowship or prayer and study ahead of their missional call. This may be a particular risk for interest-based groups that concentrate on their passions and invite others to join in, such as a walking group which welcomes friends. Once the community has a settled membership, mission may shrink to serving people within the group rather than those outside it. The group may become a consumer-type activity rather than a community that gives itself to others.

The danger can be partly addressed by keeping mission central to the main meeting. A sequence of purpose ('how are we getting on with mission?'), pressures ('what issues are we facing?') and presence ('let's attend to God') would ensure that serving others was the first matter addressed when the church met.[6]

Meeting challenges step by step

Contextual churches face a variety of other challenges, such as discerning how to serve others given practical constraints. Having the stamina to keep going can be an issue. The vicissitudes of life, such as a key member leaving or an awkward new person joining, may cause disruption. Christian members may come from different spiritual traditions and have contrasting expectations – about the sacraments, for example. Light-touch accountability may be an issue for some ecumenical groups (to whom do they turn?). Connecting to the wider body may prove easier in theory than practice.

Many of these problems cannot be answered in advance. Solutions will only emerge as contextual churches follow the Spirit, reflect prayerfully on their

---

6 This reverses the 'presence, pressures, purpose' order of the Riverforce fresh expression on Merseyside (www.sharetheguide.org/examples/workplace). Putting purpose and pressures first follows an experience–reflection approach.

experiences and keep talking about the issues they face. The wider church will have to be patient as it uncovers good practice and learns to live with untidiness. Discovering prayerfully how to navigate uncharted waters will take time.

Challenges include

- recognizing communities-in-mission as church even when they are very small;
- providing contextual churches with proper support;
- accepting the practice of dual church membership;
- retaining a missional focus;
- living with untidiness.

Conclusion

Wherever possible, worshippers should practise mission in their ordinary lives as communities of the church. This does not mean that they will undertake mission only in community. They will still witness as individuals outside the gathering, while there will be parts of their lives where no contextual church is present. Nevertheless, God's mission is communal. By participating in the life of the Trinity and sharing in God's hopes for human beings, the church is to be not just missionary in its nature, but communal in its mission. New contextual churches can bring mission and community together – in life.

Further reading

Bevans, Stephen B. and Roger P. Schroeder, *Constants in Context: A Theology of Mission for Today*, Maryknoll, NT : Orbis, 2004, pp. 296–304.
Moltmann, Jürgen, *The Spirit of Life: A Universal Affirmation*, trans. M. Kohl, Minneapolis: Fortress, 2001 [1992], pp. 218–67.
www.freshexpressions.org.uk/stories.

Questions for discussion

- Do you agree that the local church scatters for mission and that this is a problem?
- What is the missional potential of church in the settings of everyday life? What are the practical difficulties and how can they be overcome?
- How compelling are the theological arguments for communities-in-mission? How might they be critiqued and defended?

8

Why Church with Many Shapes?

It is widely recognized that churches in the West cannot go on as if nothing has changed outside their doors. Over the past half century a cultural blizzard has transformed the landscape, and the church must engage with the world as it now exists. This does not mean that inherited forms of church have had their day. Many churches continue to serve significant segments of society. Yet the question presses: whom are these churches *not* serving?

As congregations seek to answer this question, they will be aware of how varied the terrain around them has become – a multiplicity of ethnic groups as more people move across the globe, an ever-widening range of ages as individuals live longer, more rungs on the income ladder as the top pulls further from the bottom, and myriad subcultures generated by pre-recession economic growth, increased consumer choice, more fluid identities and better communications. Whether it is diversity legislation or the Myers-Briggs personality indicator, our culture is intensely aware of difference.

Church no longer has the option, if it ever had, of relating to people as if they were all the same. It has to engage with each of them appropriately, a task that has been described as contextualization. Contextualizing the church is the attempt to be church in ways that are both faithful to Jesus and appropriate to the people the church serves. It assumes that the shape of church can change according to the situation. Churches will look different because they are engaging with different people.

This immediately raises the question of how much can be conceded to the context. Though writing in relation to the marketing of church in North America, David Wells voices concerns that he would no doubt apply to other forms of contextualization. He worries that many churches are trying too hard to connect with culture. They are orchestrating warm feelings that soft-pedal the costly demands of the gospel. Church becomes the smile without the Cheshire cat.

What does Christian faith have to say to a society that is losing its soul in consumption? What does it have to say about the way the meaning of life has been rewritten by the pervasive, ubiquitous, empty, trivializing, entertainment industry? What does it have to say about hope which transcends the narrow focus of privatized, personal experience? Indeed, does it have anything to say that Boomers and Xers do not want to hear? (Wells, 2005, p. 296)

He quotes Rodney Stark and Roger Finke, *The Churching of America, 1776–1990*, as showing that the content of the faith has been vital to the church's success. Rather than doctrine being an impediment to growth as postmodern Christians often argue, growing churches have been those with a high degree of distinction from culture.

The reason for this is that people in the past have been looking for something different, something which is other than and larger than life, something which cannot be had under a secular guise, and churches which have offered this have flourished. Churches which lose their distinction from the surrounding culture have failed and disappeared. (Wells, 2005, p. 298)

Coming from a different tradition, Andrew Davison and Alison Milbank have stressed the importance of the church as a mediator of grace. Mission initiatives, such as those that describe themselves as fresh expressions of church, have a place in the church's life, but they should feed into mature expressions of church that are firmly rooted in the tradition. As believers are immersed in the tradition, their faith will mature.

Expressing concerns that would be widely shared, Davison and Milbank fear that if the church is moulded like plasticine into different shapes to fit different contexts, it will lose the capacity to form new believers in the Christian story. It will unhitch itself from practices that have been honed over the centuries, have become intrinsic to the story and have proved fruitful vehicles for the Spirit. The gospel will become like flotsam, lacking substantive form (Davison and Milbank, 2010, pp. 28–40).

This chapter responds to these concerns in three parts. It provides several arguments in support of some degree of contextualization. It then addresses the question of what boundaries should be placed round contextualization. Following Stephen Bevans (2002), it goes on to argue that contextualization can be undertaken in different ways. Each model has strengths and weaknesses. If new contextual churches use the different models in different settings, they can minimize the weaknesses of each and draw on its strengths. The chapter thus builds on the previous one: mission in community requires the community to be contextual.

Three arguments for contextualization

Since Vatican II, reflection on contextualization has gathered pace across the spectrum from Roman Catholics to evangelicals. The focus has tended to be on contextualizing 'the gospel', often understood as generating 'local theologies', but the issues raised are pertinent to contextualizing the church. Though views differ as to how far churches should be shaped by their surrounding cultures, there would be general agreement about the starting premise: if a church is to serve its context, it must connect to it. This is so easily forgotten in practice that it is worth rehearsing three arguments for some degree of accommodation to context.

Contextualization is part of life

First, accommodation is a normal part of human existence. In conversation, we adjust ourselves to the other person. Likewise, when we go abroad we adapt to the local customs. Public speakers respect their audiences, using different types of illustration according to their hearers' interests. Contextualizing church merely extends these taken-for-granted courtesies.

It also accords with today's understanding of culture. Bernard Lonergan distinguishes between classicist and empirical notions of culture. The classicist notion thinks in terms of a universal 'high' culture. A person of culture is one who is nourished by the world's great artistic and intellectual achievements. The empiricist notion, on the other hand, defines culture as a set of meanings and values that informs a way of life. There are clearly many such cultures. A person is already 'cultured' by belonging to a particular context. Culture is not a single entity 'out there', to be entered into by visiting museums and reading the right books: culture is the sea in which we all swim (Lonergan, 1973, p. xi).

In his interpretation of Lonergan, Bevans suggests that if you work out of a classicist understanding of culture, there can only be one theology – one that is valid for all times, places and cultures. But if you work out of an empirical view, there can be – indeed must be – a theology for every culture, because theology stands between a culture and religion. Theology mediates the meaning and role of religion to a culture (Bevans, 2002, p. 11).

What applies to theology applies even more to being church. If you have a classicist approach, you will think there is a form of church that is valid for everyone. But if you accept the empirical view of culture, which the contemporary social sciences work with, you will recognize that church mediates God to a context. Church will look different in different contexts.

Rather than polarizing these approaches, it may be helpful to see them as a spectrum. Christians nearer the 'empirical' end will allow a greater degree of diversity than those at the 'classicist' one. Across the spectrum, however, it will be recognized that just as people adapt to each other in conversation, the church must adapt – to some extent – to the context it serves. Only then can God be understood and people feel able to respond to him.

God's revelation involves contextualization

Contextualizing the church is important, second, because God reveals himself through everyday existence. The sacramental view of reality believes that the world and all its inhabitants can reveal their creator as actively and lovingly present to creation – 'the heavens declare the glory of God' (Ps. 19.1). Reality can reveal God because it reflects his artistry and because his Spirit is present within the natural order, working with it.

Properly describing the relationship between the natural and the supernatural has long been a challenge for theology. Influenced by Maurice Blondel, Henri de Lubac insisted that goodness is not so present in culture that we have scarcely any need of God. Nor is God so different, so far above culture and hence so puzzling that he fails to evoke a response from us. Rather, human culture is *by nature* oriented to an end – to God – which it is not equipped *by nature* to attain. The supernatural acts on and within culture to enable it to achieve its longing, its potential (Howsare, 2009, pp. 14–16).

This view holds the transcendence and immanence of grace together. God comes to a context from outside, but he then works within it. Charles Kraft's phrase, 'God above but through culture' (quoted by Conn, 1984, p. 156), captures these two dimensions. Through the Spirit, the transcendent inhabits creation in all its diversity, working with what is good to limit, push back or ultimately defeat what is bad. When the church adapts to context, therefore, it adapts to a world in which God is already present.

Scripture is a prime example of God working through culture. The Bible 'belonged in the ancient worlds that produced it. It was not an abstract, otherworldly book, dropped out of heaven. It was *connected to* and therefore *spoke to* those ancient cultures' (Enns, 2005, p. 17, author's italics). The human marks of the Bible are everywhere, thoroughly integrated into the character of Scripture itself. They enable Scripture to convey God's word, which transcends culture.

The Bible was written in the languages of the day – Hebrew, Greek and a little Aramaic. Temples, priests and sacrifices, which were woven into the ancient Mesopotamian world, were very much part of Old Testament life too. Like the surrounding nations, ancient Israel had prophets that mediated the divine will and for much of its history it was ruled by kings. Individual books in the Bible were addressed to specific contexts.

Peter Enns describes the contextual nature of the Bible as an 'incarnational analogy': in its union of the human and divine, Scripture's 'incarnation' is analogous to Christ's incarnation.[1] 'When God reveals himself, he always

---

1 This analogy works so long as it is remembered that Christ's hypostatic union – his union of the two natures – is unique, which of course raises the question as to whether it is so unique that no analogy is possible.

does so to people, which means that he must speak and act in ways that they will understand' (Enns, 2005, p. 20). In taking different shapes according to the context, therefore, the church is simply doing what Scripture does: it is adapting itself to the setting so as to speak from within God's word from outside. Like the Bible, it is only by expressing itself in many different ways that the church can tell the story of Jesus, which transcends context.

The incarnation itself is a key paradigm for contextualizing the church. Jesus was thoroughly immersed in his Jewish culture, speaking Aramaic with a Galilean accent and taking part in his society's celebrations and traditions. He used local resources to do his theology. His parables drew upon the Jewish thought categories and rhetorical traditions of his day (Flemming, 2005, p. 21).

Jesus tailored his exposition of the gospel to his audience, speaking differently to the crowds than the Pharisees, and to Nicodemus than to Peter. Indeed, he was so much part of his context that many never even recognized him as the eternal Word from outside (Kraft, 1979, p. 175). The body of Christ follows the tradition of its head when it, too, is embedded in its context. 'Pioneering ministry cannot be done to a community by someone who knows what they need, it can only be done with a community by someone who shares their need' (Shier-Jones, 2009, p. 123).

Contextualization serves the kingdom

The third reason that contextualizing church is important is that it helps the church to be a sign, first fruit and instrument of God's kingdom. Contextual churches aid faithful discipleship especially when they occur in the midst of everyday life. When the church takes shape where people actually work and pursue their interests, believers have Christian colleagues who can see them in situ and hold them to account, who understand the setting and can help them to discern God's will in it, who can assist them to comprehend the Christian story and apply it to the specifics of the situation, and who together can find ways to serve the context. Appropriate discipleship becomes easier.

As believers live out their faith individually and corporately, they become exhibitors – though imperfect – of what the context would be like if it was under the lordship of Christ. They begin to transform the setting, bringing it more into the kingdom. This both enriches the kingdom and helps the setting to flourish. Through the Spirit, the Christian community joins the fruits of the church's inheritance to the context to create a foretaste of the kingdom – the culture *en route* to being redeemed. The results inevitably vary. How the kingdom appears in the City of London will be very different to among Bengali women five miles away.

It is unthinkable that the church can serve the kingdom without being contextualized. How would a church begin to show what Christ's reign means for a context if it was not immersed in it? How could it start to transform the context if it was not engaged with it? How could it bring gospel and context together if it kept its distance from the latter? When church is not contextualized, it fails to make the connection between the kingdom and culture. It suggests that the kingdom is divorced from ordinary life. In so doing, instead of being an instrument of salvation, it becomes an obstacle.

Why should churches be contextual?

- to show respect to the surrounding context;
- to communicate God to the context;
- to bring the context into the kingdom.

What are the limits to contextualization?

While the case for some accommodation to culture would be widely shared, theologians differ as to what the boundaries should be. Some would say that a gospel core, rooted in Scripture, limits the extent to which a church can be shaped by its context. Others would emphasize the restraining role of the church's practices and traditions.

A gospel core?

The first group of theologians adopt a kernel-and-husks approach. They argue that the shell of the gospel can be contextualized, such as language, illustrations and some of the applications, but that the kernel of the gospel is unchanging. Wells says that the church should address the issues foremost in a culture, but in the language of truth. He has unchanging truths in mind (Wells, 2005, p. 308). Churches in varied contexts may look different, but they should share a core gospel. Contextualization can seep through the church's life so long as it does not penetrate the core.

Kernels-and-husks vocabulary, however, is not fair to the reality of the Christian life. It suggests that central to this life are propositions. These propositions have a core that is eternally valid, though the cultural container can change. But propositions are not central to discipleship. One's walk with Jesus is. The irreducible minimum of the Christian faith is not a body of knowledge, but the person of Christ. We should speak not about a propositional kernel with cultural husks, but about a divine personal centre with relationships.

Just as children will relate differently to the same parent because of differences in personality and situation, so believers have different relationships with Jesus depending on their personalities and contexts. A child's relationship with Jesus will be very different to an adult's. Someone who is well educated may have a more conceptual relationship than a person with little education. When some church traditions speak about having a personal relationship with Jesus, the implication is that each of these relationships is unique. The same is true when individuals come together in Christian communities. Each community has its own distinctive relationship with Jesus, and will express this relationship in its own way.

This does not mean that propositions are unimportant. They tell us things about Jesus and so help to ensure that we are walking with a genuine Christ and not one of our imaginations. They aid our relationships with him. But we must be careful not to squeeze these relationships through a grid of required propositions. A helpful proposition in one context may be unnecessary or even confusing in another. We recognize this in everyday life. It may be important for a teenage fan of motor racing to know that his grandfather is a fan too, but for a three-year-old it may be enough that grandpa loves her.

Norman Kraus, an American missionary in Japan, has illustrated how a proposition in one setting – a Western understanding of the atonement as penal substitution – can have little traction in another. The Japanese do not 'get' penal substitution. Re-reading Scripture in the light of Japan's shame-based culture, Kraus has highlighted how crucifixion in the Roman era was dreaded mainly for its shameful character. It was designed to be an instrument of contempt and public ridicule.

> The cross was the epitome of Jesus' identification with us in shame . . . Because of this identification Kraus can tell the Japanese, and others debilitated by shame, that Jesus knows fully the shameful exclusion they fear. Yet Kraus does more than that. He proclaims to them that Jesus' identification provides us the possibility of identifying with him and overcoming shame. (Green and Baker, 2003 [2000], p. 164)

Instead of excluding themselves from relationships because of their shame, the Japanese are invited to identify with Jesus. They can discover a new self-identity as children of God; '. . . they can be free of the burden of exclusion they have already experienced and free from the fear of shameful exclusion. They have the opportunity for a new start' (p. 166).

Kraus, with his close attention to biblical exegesis, exemplifies how fundamentals about Jesus and his church can be viewed differently in different contexts. Just as relatives may have different perceptions of their family, churches vary in their understandings of Jesus and his family. Their different relationships with Jesus may yield different theories about these relationships, including how the church should be expressed.

If the kernel of Jesus' life, the cross, can be – and has been – understood biblically in very different ways, what then happens to the kernel-and-husks approach? Is kernel to be redefined to include not the interpretation of the cross, but the event itself? In which case, does not the kernel become the facts of Jesus' life known through Scripture – the fact of Jesus? And does this not lead to the view that Jesus is the centre of our faith, with each person and church having a particular relationship to him?

An ecclesial core?

An alternative approach allows a degree of contextualization round a well-defined ecclesial core. Davison and Milbank stress that the gospel cannot be disentangled from culture – being a Christian is cultural through and through. It is the culture of the church, however, that ultimately counts. The Spirit maintains and gradually improves church practices, which come from us and from beyond us. These practices have enough 'exteriority' to be able to judge us and change our perspective (Davison and Milbank, 2010, p. 103). 'Salvation is no abstract, rarefied, or purely spiritual matter . . . it meets us in corporeal and social ways and then it reorders our patterns of life and relations in the world' (Davison and Milbank, 2010, p. 59). Church practices mediate the gospel. They can be contextualized only to a limited extent. An ecclesial mannequin can wear contextual clothes, but the body gives the clothes their shape.

There are a number of difficulties with this. First, the church's tradition does not stand above culture, as it were, coterminous with secular culture but separate from it. The church's culture is not a distinct culture into which people are drawn. Robert Schreiter has described the Christian tradition 'as a series of local theologies, closely wedded to and responding to different cultural conditions' (Schreiter, 1985, p. 93). Christians' understanding and expression of the gospel has been shaped by the worlds they inhabit, from the Hellenistic thought forms of the church fathers to the post-colonial legacies in today's global South.

There is no single, definitive 'church culture'. There are church cultures in the plural – cultures that vary according to their contexts, whether it is an informal gathering in a Chinese apartment or the celebration of mass at St Peter's Rome. Davison and Milbank slide too easily from recognizing the formational influence of a church's culture to arguing for a particular church culture. The two are distinct. Down the centuries, a great variety of church cultures have formed believers in the faith.

Second, we are in theological difficulty if we claim that the bearers of the church have a better understanding of how the church should mediate the gospel in the new context than those who receive the church. This may possibly be true initially, but as the new converts engage with Scripture and the tradition, they will indigenize the church just as church will have been indigenized in the culture of those who brought it. Why should one culture have a superior understanding of the form church should take than another, and be able to dictate that form to the other? Why should the church be indigenous to some contexts but not others? Why should it fit the cultures of Christendom but not be allowed to fit the cultures of post-Christendom? (Stanley, 2007, p. 25).

Third, it is in the nature of giving that we cannot dictate the terms on which the gift is received. Otherwise, we risk offering the gift with one hand and taking it back with the other. So when we offer the gift of community with Jesus, we must allow the manner in which the gift is accepted to be determined by the recipient.

> [W]e may often find that we have offered a gift that is welcome, yet it is not received as we should expect it to be; Jesus is recognizable, yet the responses that to us seem orthodox or obvious are not necessarily made. This demands of us both patience and courage to let go of the gift into the hands of those who receive it. (Williams, 1994b, p. 20)

We must be careful not to assume that we know exactly what is in the wrapping paper of the gift we bring. Our own reception of the gift makes us aware that the gift of Christian identity – of life with Jesus in the church – is not something that we have of ourselves, by our own choice or ingenuity. It is given by divine invitation. It 'cannot be administered by the institution' (p. 21). It only comes home to another through the Spirit. The Spirit is therefore free to offer the gift in whatever form God chooses. The Spirit is free to give the church and its practices in a different manner to how we ourselves received it.

To put it another way, 'the Jesus we proclaim is not bound to our understanding or our images' (p. 21). It follows that how he identifies with another culture, forms community within it and transcends that culture cannot be specified in advance. We cannot constrain how Jesus will act in the new situation. So we cannot predict what the structures and practices of Christ's body will be like in the culture that receives him. Christ may be mediated by an expression of church very different to what we expected.

Thus, fourth, when the church is indigenized, new believers may end up criticizing those who brought them the church. Lamin Sanneh has shown how indigenization gave African Christians the tools to complain about the unacceptable degree of Westernization in the church. Because Scripture had been translated into their own languages, believers were able to argue their position from Scripture.

> With the help of vernacular Scriptures, for example, Zulu Christians found sanction for their habit of dressing in skins (Gen. 3.21), and began to criticize missionaries for not being properly dressed according to the Scriptures. The same criticism was voiced with regard to church services,

with Africans insisting that missionary churches were unfaithful to the Scriptures, which call for dancing and music in worship and praise . . . (Sanneh, 1989, p. 176)

Indeed, critique of those who brought the gospel may be an indication that indigenization is taking place: the Spirit is enabling the new Christians to search Scripture and the tradition for themselves. The bearers of the church, therefore, must not be surprised if their practices are criticized by those who receive the gift. Through the Spirit, the recipients will be searching for practices that best mediate grace in their context.

There is not one church culture to which all churches should aspire

- The church is a series of local theologies.
- The church cannot be indigenized in one context but not another.
- Giving the church includes allowing the Spirit to show the recipients how they should receive the gift.
- A sign of indigenization is that believers criticize the practices of those who brought them the church.

Some criteria

If there are no gospel and ecclesial cores to put limits on contextualization, if contextualization is through and through, does this mean that anything goes? One answer is that the wider body acts as a restraint. Just as people from different language groups find ways to communicate with each other, so churches in varied settings are able to speak across their contexts. Each church's view of what it means to be church can be judged against the weight of theological reflection down the centuries and around the world. Being part of the whole body encircles Christian self-understandings. At the same time, as more insights are brought into the church, truth expands within the body – there is a greater plenitude in the church's life with God (Cook, 2010, pp. 85–9).

The suggestion here is that this emphasis on the larger church should be broadened into the four interlocking sets of relationships that constitute the church, described in Chapter 5. Together, these relationships limit the church's cultural accommodation. Thus within the Godward relationship, accommodation will be subject to what God says through Scripture, read in the setting of prayer and worship. Relations with the wider body will mean that any one church's interpretation of Scripture will be open to scrutiny and question by the tradition.

The relationship to the world will compel understandings to be tested against the church's experience of serving its context. If the Spirit is active in the world, what might God be saying through these experiences? Relationships within the fellowship mean that members of the community will share in the process of discernment. There will be checks and balances as the community listens to God through Scripture, the whole church, the context and through the participation of its members.

Perhaps a new church forms around Jesus with its cultural pre-understanding. But it is not forever bound by this pre-understanding. By listening humbly to Scripture, the wider church, the context and to one another and by being willing to be challenged, members of the community find that their pre-understanding is inadequate. As they adjust their understanding, their perception of Jesus – and what it means to be his body – becomes more congruent with him. Maybe they have a new insight. Sharing this with the wider church expands the whole body's vision of Christ. This enlarged vision, in turn, becomes a fuller resource for churches as they emerge.[2]

Approaching contextualization contextually

There is a fifth control on cultural accommodation – to be contextual in one's approach to contextualization. Stephen Bevans helpfully describes six models of contextualization (2002). These are contextual ways of doing theology in the church. Bevans is clear that no one model can be used exclusively. Each model has strengths and weaknesses. To build on its strengths and minimize its weaknesses, each must be used in conjunction with the others according to the circumstances (pp. 32–3).

If a church operates with only one model of contextualization, it will adopt a lopsided approach. A church working solely with the 'anthropological' model, for example, will emphasize God's presence in the context but ignore the 'counter-cultural' model's stress on bringing transformation. Alternative models knock one another off their pedestals and encourage each to be used only in the proper circumstances. Thus the models check and limit each other. Whereas each cord alone would snap, entwining them produces a stronger rope.

To illustrate this, the rest of the chapter introduces the six models. To strengthen Bevans's claim that all the models are legitimate in appropriate circumstances, the chapter shows how each one was used by Jesus. It concludes by suggesting how a new contextual church might use the models in different situations. Contextualization becomes a finely honed process, which helps to safeguard it from abuse.

---

2 This paragraph adapts material in van den Toren (2010, p. 100).

The translation model

This is concerned with translating Christian truths into the context. Through translation, these truths may look and sound different from their original formulation, but their core will be the same. There is 'something' which must be 'put into' other terms (Bevans, 2002, pp. 37–53). This is the kernel-and-husks approach described above. It is thus open to the critique of this approach. But if the model is reformulated, as suggested, so that *Jesus* is at the centre, translation may have more going for it. The task becomes translating Jesus into different cultures. His parables illustrate how this can be done.

Even with this modification, however, the model has limitations. It underestimates the presence of Jesus in the context. Jesus is to be inserted into the setting, but doesn't the setting give anything back? Might not the context have something to give to the church because Jesus is already there? The giving is too one way.

The anthropological model

This model assumes that God is highly present in the context, sanctifying it. By listening to the context, we can discern God's hidden presence in ordinary life, and discover 'the symbols and concepts with which to construct an adequate articulation of that people's faith' (Bevans, 2002, p. 55). The gospel is pulled out of the culture. In its more radical form, the model sees each context as unique. Each context must develop its own theology, using the categories of thought, images and values of the context.[3]

Mark 7.24–30 provides an example of Jesus learning from his context. In Mark 5 Jesus has entered Gentile territory (the Decapolis), healing a man possessed by a demon, but is urged to depart by the people (v. 17). Does this leave Jesus uncertain about how far he can extend his mission beyond the Jews? Mark 7.24 describes Jesus entering Gentile territory again (the vicinity of Tyre and Sidon), but only to get away from the crowds – 'he entered a house and did not want anyone to know it' (Perkins, 1995, p. 610; cf Bird, 2005, p. 101).

A Syro-Phoenician woman begs Jesus to cast a demon out of her daughter, but Jesus replies that his mission is first of all for the Jews. The woman responds with a clever reply, suggesting that the Gentiles can share the fruits of this mission (v. 28). Unlike in other conversations, Jesus does not correct this response (Ringe, 1985, pp. 67–8). He grants her request, returns to the Decapolis, performs a healing and is well received (vv. 31–7). The feeding

---

3 There is a danger, of course, in pushing the model too far in this radical direction. If each context is totally unique, to what extent can one church learn from another?

of the 4,000 that follows symbolizes his mission to the four corners of the earth (Harris, 2006, p. 135).

The story can be read as Jesus learning from the woman that his mission was indeed for the Gentiles – a lesson that he immediately acts upon.[4] The idea of Jesus learning from his context should not surprise us. The entire process of growing into adulthood required Jesus to learn from others. Why should this learning not have continued as part of his ministry?

Indeed, this is a strength of the anthropological model. It encourages us to learn from context. A weakness is that the model can be too optimistic. It can underestimate the extent to which the context is fallen.

The praxis model

Praxis is a way of doing theology based on reflective action. It assumes that the highest level of knowing is intelligent and responsible doing. Theologically, to know God involves far more than knowing him with our minds. It entails loving obedience. Actions reflect our understanding. Praxis 'is reflected-upon action and acted-upon reflection – both rolled into one' (Bevans, 2002, p. 72).

It involves a continuous spiral of action, reflection upon action and action again. An example is the return of the 72 disciples to Jesus after being sent on mission. They report that even the demons submitted to them in his name. Jesus responds by explaining what has happened. 'I saw Satan fall like lightning from heaven. I have given you authority . . .' He then tells them how to respond: 'rejoice that your names are written in heaven' (Luke 10.18–20). The disciples and Jesus are jointly reflecting on action.

This points to a strength of the model. By asking questions like, 'How would Jesus have reacted to this situation? What would he have said and done?' a community can think theologically about its activities. The model can be a tool to link the transcendent to people's immanent lives. But a danger is that practice always sets the agenda. Why should not God speak an entirely fresh word, unrelated to current practice?

The conversation model

This is one of Bevans's alternative names for the synthetic model. The model looks for a synthesis of the other five models. More important, it also 'reaches out to the resources of other contexts and other theological expressions for both the method and the content of its own articulation of faith' (Bevans, 2002, pp. 89–90). A synthesis develops between one's own cultural view and views from other cultures in the tradition. The form of

---

4 For an alternative view, see Bird (2005, p. 102).

this synthesis is not a mishmash compromise between different perspectives, but the holding of differences in tension.

The model is described here as 'conversation' to emphasize its engagement with different theological viewpoints through dialogue. A good example is Luke 2.41–8. The young Jesus, with his Galilean synagogue background, is portrayed talking with experts from the Jerusalem temple, which was a very different culture.

Conversation across church cultures is one of the model's strengths. A new contextual church would be using this model when it seeks to learn from the experiences of other churches. A weakness is that the model does not say much about challenging others' experiences. Is there too much stress on holding differences in tension rather than on choosing between alternative points of view?

The counter-cultural model

This model treats context with the utmost seriousness but regards it with a good deal of suspicion. Aspects of context will always be inimical to the gospel and must be challenged by the gospel's liberating and healing power. The gospel is seen as a lens through which to interpret, critique, challenge and refashion culture. When the local church does this, it 'is not just *in* a place or *of* a place; it finds its identity in being *for* the particular place . . .' (Bevans, 2002, p. 123).

Jesus' use of the Old Testament to critique Jewish society illustrates the model. In Mark 7 the Pharisees criticize the disciples for eating with unclean hands. Jesus responds in verses 6–7 by quoting Isaiah 29.13: 'These people honour me with their lips, but their hearts are far from me. . . .' Jesus uses Scripture to critique the Pharisaic culture. His whole ministry was counter-cultural – calling Israel to a different way of life. He illustrates the value of the model: it is both faithful to Scripture and engaged with the context. The danger is that it becomes over negative. Proponents can be quicker to criticize than to affirm positives in the context.

The subjective model

Bevans calls this the transcendental model to highlight a basic change, associated with Immanuel Kant in the eighteenth century, in the process of coming to know reality. 'The switch is one from beginning with a world of objects to beginning with the world of the subject, the interior world of the human person. . . . It is in attending to one's transcendental subjectivity, therefore, as it reaches out naturally toward truth, that one finds oneself doing an authentic contextual theology' (Bevans, 2002, p. 104).

The model does not start with the outside world and ask what Christianity would look like in that setting. It begins with the interior world of the believer: how is God being experienced inside the person? Revelation is not primarily in Scripture, nor in culture nor in a dialogue between the two. It is inside the person, as the Spirit works on his or her subjective world.

The key question becomes whether the person has an authentic experience of God. Given the sort of person they are and the influence of their context, is the person's experience of God genuine? What does it mean for me as a white, well-educated, middle-class Englishman to be a Christian? An African-Caribbean woman would ask a similar question. By describing our authentic faith experiences, we help others on their spiritual journeys just as they can help us.

The temptations of Jesus provide an example. The accounts focus on Jesus' inner life. The Father announces that Jesus is his Son (Matt. 3.17). The temptations then take up this theme: what will it mean for Jesus as God's Son to live out his faith and calling? How can he be an authentic Son of God? This reflects the virtue of the model. It has a helpful stress on authenticity, on God at work inside the person. But it risks degenerating into relativity – 'my experience is as good as yours.' By giving pride of place to subjective experiences of faith, is enough said about what is a valid experience of faith?

Using these models in new contextual churches

Being a new contextual church involves a variety of processes. Each of Bevans's models can contribute to a different process – for example:

- *Attending to the context* will be helped by assuming the anthropological model – that God is active in culture. Attending will include looking for signs of God's activity. How can the church join in? What aspects of the culture can the church build upon?
- *Launching out* will benefit from the praxis model – reflecting on experience. Starting a new church can be experimental. The pioneering team may be unclear what will work. The team tries something, sees what happens and reflects upon it before taking the next step.
- *Evangelism* will draw inevitably on the translation model, as the gospel is made intelligible to the culture.
- *Being church*, especially learning how to worship, will require the conversation model – dialoguing with other churches, including churches from the past. 'What can we learn from their experiences of worship?'
- *Making disciples* will involve the counter-cultural model. Discipleship will challenge many behaviours expected by society, and seek to refashion the context so that it reflects the kingdom more fully.
- *The pioneer moves on.* As the founder prepares to leave the new church, the subjective model will come to the fore. Church members

may be challenged about the authenticity of their faith. Are they living the pioneer's faith or their own?

Six models of contextualization

- *Translation* – translate the gospel into the context
- *Anthropological* – context reveals God
- *Praxis* – action/reflection/action . . .
- *Conversation* – dialogue with other churches and the tradition
- *Counter-cultural* – evaluate, critique and transform culture
- *Subjective* – develop an authentic faith.

Conclusion

If the church is to serve people as community in mission, it must connect with them. If it is to connect with them, it must be contextual. Just as individuals adapt to each other in conversation, each church must adapt to its culture. Just as God shows himself through culture, the church must enter its context to reveal God. Just as Jesus modelled the kingdom by taking flesh in a culture, each church begins to enflesh the kingdom within its context.

This accommodation to context is not without limits. Boundaries are established when contextualization occurs within the four interlocking sets of relationships that constitute the church, and when the different approaches to contextualization are allowed to qualify and limit each other. When this happens, new contextual churches will be moulded both by Jesus and their contexts. They will look different in different settings.

This means that reproducing the church is not about multiplying churches that all look the same. Nor is it about copying church models that have been successful elsewhere (as opposed to learning from them). Multiplication is not about replication. It is about non-identical reproduction (Lings, 2008, p. 14). It is about producing offspring that have their own unique characteristics, while retaining a family likeness through loyalty to Jesus. Christ's one church will have many shapes.

Further reading

Bevans, Stephen B., *Models of Contextual Theology*, revised edition, Maryknoll, NY: Orbis, 2002.
Cook, Matthew, Rob Haskell, Ruth Julian and Natee Tanchanpongs (eds), *Local Theology for the Global Church: Principles for an Evangelical Approach to Contextualization*, Pasadena, CA: William Carey, 2010.

Schreiter, Robert J., *Constructing Local Theologies*, London: SCM Press, 1985.

Stanley, Brian, 'Inculturation: Historical Background, Theological Foundations and Contemporary Questions', *Transformation: An International Journal of Holistic Mission Studies* 24 (1), 2007, pp. 21–7.

Questions for discussion

- How strong are the arguments for and against a kernel-and-husks approach to contextualization?
- What does it mean to safeguard truth in a new contextual church, and how would you do it?
- The chapter has suggested that Bevans's models of contextualization can aid different processes involved in birthing a contextual church. Does this ring true to your knowledge of such churches? In what other ways might the models be helpful?

9

Are Culture-specific Churches Legitimate?

If a church is to be contextual, as the last chapter argued, it must start and grow within a specific culture. Only then can it serve that culture. But this idea is highly controversial. It is associated with the homogeneous unit principle, formulated by Donald McGavran. McGavran was concerned with how Christianity could spread among a whole group of people. He famously declared that people 'like to become Christians without crossing racial, linguistic, or class barriers' (McGavran, 1980, p. 223). Human beings are born into thousands of different social groupings. They are helped to become Christians if they are discipled within the group they already belong to.

'A homogeneous unit is a group in which all the members have some characteristic in common' (Gibbs, 1981, p. 116). The characteristic may range from language, age, class or interest to shared values. The homogeneous unit principle includes the idea that, as far as possible, church takes shape within each of these units. This chapter describes three approaches to the idea of culture-specific churches, and argues for a fourth – a focused-and-connected view.

Three views

The literature offers three views of homogeneous congregations. These gatherings can be seen as a missional goal, a missional first step or a missional no-go.

A missional goal

No one sensibly rejects the idea of building bridges between congregations in different cultures, but some writers have put more emphasis on establishing homogeneous congregations than linking them up. McGavran is an example. He argues that people are more likely to come to faith if they are reached within their culture. Once converted, they should seek to evangelize others with whom they have a cultural affinity. The gospel will spread across the cultural unit.

It is true that McGavran speaks about the need to surmount divisions and describes the church as 'a unifying society' (McGavran, 1980, pp. 242–4). But this comes as a short qualification at the end of a chapter arguing for homogeneous congregations. The argument for building links between these congregations is given much less weight. The same imbalance appears, I suspect unwittingly, in *Mission-shaped Church* (2004, pp. 108–9). Homogeneous congregations appear to be *the* missional priority.

This one-sided emphasis is difficult to square with the New Testament vision of Jesus tearing down barriers between people and creating a new single humanity. Surely the church is to be foretaste of this? Is reconciliation not fundamental to the church's mission?

A missional first step

A second view is that homogeneous congregations are a necessary first step in mission, but should not be the last one. Lesslie Newbigin argued that, 'The existence of separate congregations in the same geographical area on the basis of language and culture may have to be accepted as a necessary, but provisional, measure for the sake of the fulfilment of Christ's mission' (Newbigin, 1977, p. 124). In situations of racial conflict, for example, the demand for integration may be a demand for dominance by one group over another.

Where the context requires separate congregations, however, separation must never be final. Saint Paul refused to allow the distinct lifestyles of Jewish and Gentile Christians to be institutionalized in separately organized bodies within the local church (p. 121). The church today should embody Paul's vision for reconciliation by developing 'structures which are explicitly designed to promote the growth in unity of those who are provisionally separated' (p. 125). When culturally distinct congregations exist, regional and national structures should draw the different gatherings together.

The picture, as Newbigin paints it, is that culturally based congregations are regrettable because they are potentially divisive. They should be bridged wherever possible. Yet is he right to be so downbeat about culturally diverse expressions of church? As Peter Wagner asks, in the coming kingdom, 'will Peter still be a Jew? Will the eunuch still be an Ethiopian? Will Cornelius still be a Gentile? Will the woman at the well still be a Samaritan? Or will group identity be wiped out?' (Wagner, 1987, p. 173)

A missional no-go

A third view calls for the creation of heterogeneous congregations. *For the Parish*, for example, argues that culturally mixed churches are part of the very nature of church. The church inherited this pattern from its earliest days.

From the very beginning, the Church stood against the segregation and stratification of society in the ancient world. The Church was perhaps the only place in the Roman Empire where slaves mixed equally with the freeborn, men with women, the old with the young, the educated with the uneducated, the poor with the rich. (Davison and Milbank, 2010, p. 66)

Davison and Milbank accept that cultural diversity is built into creation, but claim that the local church should not be organized on this basis. A congregation can recognize the goodness of cultural difference by making space for distinct cultural groups among its members – a sewing circle for instance. But these groups should be drawn together into a church that reflects the social diversity of its locality. Only in that way will church do justice to the reconciling vision of the New Testament (Davison and Milbank, 2010, pp. 77–8).

The authors articulate a widely held view. Seeing the damage done by culturally distinct churches in *apartheid* South Africa and Northern Ireland, for example, mission scholars have tended to shy away from the homogeneous unit principle. Yet this overlooks the social dynamics at work in the local church. Like any group, a congregation will be diverse to a significant extent. It may contain a mixture of age groups, people from different ethnic backgrounds and individuals with a variety of interests. But poke beneath the surface and you will find that certain cultural traits draw the community together.

They may include shared values, such as a liberal or conservative theology, a common level of educational attainment, a shared cultural preference (for traditional hymns and formal liturgy for example) or common residence ('we come from this side of the village'). It is these commonalities that give the congregation its identity, and identity by definition includes some people and excludes others. A person identifies with some, but not other individuals.

The local church has tacitly accepted this for many years. In an Anglican church where I ministered, people claimed that as late as the 1950s the gentry came to church in the morning and working-class people in the evening. The only time they met together was at the annual harvest supper, which apparently was a nightmare! Davison and Milbank romanticize the heterogeneity of the traditional church.

Echoing Davison and Milbank's concerns but from an evangelical standpoint, David Wells recognizes the difficulty that local churches have in exhibiting the full diversity of God's people. This is especially the case when ethnic, and rich and poor people live in different parts of the city (Wells, 2005, p. 295). But he offers no solution beyond arguing that Christians should not compound the problem; they should not deliberately create different churches for different cultures. He bases his view on the fact that many of the early church's problems arose from the first converts being together despite their diversity (p. 293). Yet he fails to explain how they came together in cities that were socially and geographically divided. The model they adopted suggests a fourth approach.

Focused-and-connected church

Chapter 1 described how the Jerusalem, Antioch, Corinthian and Ephesian churches combined house-based homogeneous gatherings, called church, with larger, probably town-wide assemblies (also called church), which drew these gatherings together. First-century cities were much like today. Distinct ethnic and income groups lived in different areas. So a house church that drew in members of the family and their networks would reflect a specific culture. These culturally focused churches then met together as 'the whole church' (1 Cor. 14.23) from time to time.

New contextual churches follow this model when they focus on a specific culture but also connect up. Both should be seen as equally important. Homogeneity and heterogeneity can then be held together – for instance (echoing trends discussed in Chapter 3):

- A local church might give birth to several culturally different congregations (perhaps mid-sized communities). The congregations would cluster together from time to time.
- Culturally distinct contextual churches might join with other churches in their locality to collaborate on mission and discipleship.
- Contextual churches from different backgrounds might come together in activities organized by a national network sharing a common spiritual tradition.
- Individuals might attend more than one 'local' church.

This focused-and-connected view differs from McGavran's by giving homogeneity and heterogeneity equal weight; connecting up is as important as being culture-specific. It differs from Newbigin by being more positive about homogeneous churches; they are not stepping stones to something better but desirable in their own right, so long as they have ties to culturally different churches. It differs from Davison and Milbank by allowing individual churches to be homogeneous rather than limiting homogeneity to groups within a church. Peter Wagner's book, *Our Kind of People* (1979), contains a similar focused-and-connected view (pp. 135–63), though his arguments mostly differ to the ones here. Focused-and-connected churches will be marked by a welcoming attitude to people who are different – a theme picked up Chapter 19.

An argument from social reality

Focused-and-connected church fits with developments in the network society. Summarizing some of the research on identity formation, Jones, Latham and Betta (2008, p. 332) note that 'the drawing of boundaries is framed by human decisions about what counts as similarity (bringing together) and what counts as difference (setting apart).' Identity is crafted carefully by distinguishing between 'the Me and the Not-Me'.

Research shows that individuals are inclined to be friends if they have an interest that overlaps – the other person is more 'Me' than 'Not-Me'. This inclination strengthens when shared interests are specific. 'Two people who like fencing are likelier to be friends than two people who like football' (Shirky, 2009, p. 200). There is more likelihood, therefore, of community forming in depth if those involved have something substantial in common.

From an evolutionary perspective, individuals identify with a group because instinctively they believe that other members will return favours. This is a means of survival. I'll help you because I know you will help me. A quick and easy way to pick out people who will reciprocate our good turns is if they look and behave like us. We develop an affinity with such people, and to attract favours we do our best to fit in (Wright, 1996 [1994], pp. 189–209). These affinity groups have been described as 'moral circles'. Members of the group feel a moral obligation to each other (Hofstede, Hofstede and Minkov, 2010, p. 17). Focused churches reflect the desire to belong to such groups.

A long tradition in cultural studies sees affinity groups – subcultures – as subordinate to a more dominant culture. Individuals identify simultaneously with a wider group and with smaller groups within it. They might see themselves as both Pakistani and British. Even when members of a group define themselves against a dominant culture, they are still attached to what they resist. If the subculture was totally autonomous, 'the very cultural power they define themselves against would, in fact, no longer be powerful at all' (Hills, 2005, p. 138). Identification with the whole group holds the smaller groups together. It provides a link between groups. A sense, then, of belonging to the wider tradition can connect 'affinity' churches.

Human beings have always valued this wider connectedness. Advances in travel and other forms of communication have repeatedly been used to bring people together. It is happening exponentially today. Technology enables networks to jump long distances rather than be confined to tight geographical areas. Individuals can join a greater diversity of groups, and also networks that connect these groups. (Christakis and Fowler, 2010, pp. 252–86).

A feature of networks is that one often leads to another. You meet someone at a focused church who introduces you to a wider circle of Christian activities. This is most likely to happen if others in the network are well connected themselves and can act as bridges into a separate network. Underestimating these bridging ties is a weakness of McGavran's account of homogeneous units. McGavran concentrates on mission to the edge of each people group rather than on the potential of one group to lead individuals to another (see McClintock, 1988, p. 112).

It is also a weakness of some of the critiques of focused church. Davison and Milbank, for example, fail to recognize that belonging to an affinity group is often the means by which people become more widely connected (Davison and Milbank, 2010, p. 77). Someone is drawn into a church for young adults, and is then invited to a pilgrimage or Christian conference containing a range of age groups. If the person had not been attracted by the homogeneity of the age-based church, they would not have ended up in the more heterogeneous event.

Trends in contemporary society are increasing the number of 'bridging ties' – ties that take people to other networks. They include improved communications, greater population density, the expansion of professional and managerial occupations (people who are most likely to engage in bridging behaviour) and the spread of market mechanisms (Granovetter, 1983, pp. 208, 210). Densely knit, bounded local groups are giving way to sparsely knit, permeable and specialized networks. As a result, American adults seem to be increasing their number of friendships (Wang and Wellman, 2010, pp. 1148–69).

Not all networks are full of bridging ties, however. Where contextual churches have few links to the wider body, steps can be taken to increase the ties. For example, leaders of ecclesial communities can be drawn together, as when leaders of mid-sized communities meet in small 'huddles' (Breen and Absalom, 2010). Leaders then start to become the bridges, leading their churches into the wider body.

In short, focused-and-connected church reflects two human instincts. People naturally gravitate to affinity groups, but they also want to belong to a bigger whole. In certain respects, contemporary developments are making both these aspects of church easier. Better communications help believers to find others of a like mind and associate with them. They also help people to connect up. How do these social realities square with God's intentions for humanity?

An argument from God's purposes

Though belonging to affinity groups and connecting up are deeply ingrained, everyday experience shows that they often conflict. The fear of difference means that either diversity takes precedence and degenerates into division, or unity gets the upper hand and becomes uniformity. Genesis 10 (the Table of Nations) and 11.1–9 (the story of Babel) provide a theological reflection on this tension. Together, they suggest God intends that human beings should both belong to specific cultural groups and be united, and that this intention persists despite the Fall.

The chapters have been read in different ways. For example, von Rad believes that in their origin the Table of Nations and the Babel story are only loosely connected. Despite their antagonisms, however, the chapters must be understood together because they are placed next to one another. The multitude of nations reflects both God's creativity and his judgement on the sinful rebellion at Babel (von Rad, 1972, p. 152). This makes the existence of homogeneous cultural groups, epitomized by differences of language, distinctly ambiguous.

Bernard Anderson, on the other hand, suggests that the chapters have a more coherent meaning. The Table of Nations describes God's intention that the whole world should be peopled from the sons of Noah. The people are one because they have a common origin. This unity was to be combined with their 'scattering' (9.19) through the multiplication of different language groups. God's will for creation is unity and diversity (Anderson, 1977, p. 68).

The Babel story describes how, contrary to God's will, human beings fear diversity and strive for a unity that minimizes difference. They build a tower to make a name for themselves and avoid being scattered (11.4b). But God refuses to let his will be thwarted. Twice, in verses 8 and 9, he insists on scattering them (Anderson, 1977, p. 66). God confuses their language in verses 7 and 9 not because diversity is a bad thing – different languages are clearly a good thing in Chapter 9 – but because in their sinfulness human beings are resisting the call to diversify.[1] The people's offence was to prioritize unity over diversity. Their punishment was to experience the thing they feared – the divisiveness of difference represented by confused languages.

On this basis, the two chapters can be seen as a plea for the creation intention to be kept intact despite the fall, for unity to be combined with difference. The longing to connect to the whole is to coexist with identity in a language group. Unity is not to be at the expense of cultural diversity, nor is diversity to prevent unity. Focused-and-connected churches express this creation ideal.

An argument from election

Focused-and-connected churches are instruments of salvation in a fallen world. They echo the dynamics of election, through which God chooses the particular to reach the universal. Abraham's descendants are to be the recipients of God's blessing in order that 'all peoples on earth' will be blessed (Gen. 12.2). These descendants are brought out of slavery as God's 'treasured possession' so that, as a nation of priests (Exod. 19.5–6), they

---

1 Different languages in themselves need not be a source of division. Throughout history people have learnt to speak in different languages, thereby overcoming division and showing respect for the other culture. The problem at Babel was the *confusion* of languages, perhaps suggesting that people were unwilling to learn each other's tongues.

can perform a ministerial function among the other nations. God chooses a specific entity, Israel, so that other social entities can benefit.

Newbigin points out that election assumes interdependence. Israel depended on the Lord for blessing and other nations depended on Israel to share in that blessing. The Bible consistently sees human life in terms of mutual relationships.

> It follows that this mutual relatedness, this dependence of one on another, is not merely part of the journey toward the goal of salvation, but is intrinsic to the goal itself. . . . There is, there can be, no private salvation, no salvation which does not involve us with one another. (Newbigin, 1989, p. 82)

Culture-specific churches can behave in a similar way. Having received the gospel from one culture, recipients use their 'bridging ties' to carry the gospel to a different culture. Someone who comes to faith through church in a leisure centre, for example, might start church in a workplace. Salvation is transmitted through the relationships between cultures. As Newbigin says, since restored relationships are integral to the goal of salvation, the means fit the end.

The incarnation of Jesus demonstrates the same process. Election is narrowed down to one person, who represents all that Israel was meant to be. He did not go to everyone, but chose a small group of followers to take his salvation to the ends of the earth. Despite their differences, members of the group shared the same Jewish culture. It was in that sense homogeneous. When he rose from the dead, again Jesus did not appear to everyone, but only to this group (Newbigin, 1989, p. 86). These elect were to go to other cultural groups and bear fruit.[2]

It was as they bore fruit that a homogeneous-looking church became increasingly diverse. Davison and Milbank (2010, p. 79) express a widespread fear that a church in every culture will fragment and segregate on the basis of micro-cultures. Certainly there was conflict as diversity increased within the New Testament church. Even so, as we have noted, churches from different networks came together on a citywide basis. Churches were birthed in one social fragment after another without causing disintegration.

What is the secret of the church being both focused and connected? The answer lies in what Sigurd Grindheim maintains is 'the crux of election', which is the reversal of values. 'That which has no outstanding inherent value becomes precious by divine election and that which is not choice

---

2 The extent to which Jesus initiated the Gentile mission has been debated by New Testament scholars. The debate is reviewed by Bird (2005, pp. 83–108), who concludes that Jesus saw the salvation of the Gentiles as intimately bound up with his intended restoration of Israel.

in itself becomes the object of God's choice' (Grindheim, 2005, p. 9). In particular, Paul was convinced that election implied conformity to the cross. 'This conformity means that the elect will share in Christ's sufferings and status loss, and in this way the resurrection power of Christ will be effective in them' (pp. 3–4).

When through the Spirit a homogeneous group takes the time and the trouble to share the gospel with another group, at whatever cost, it starts to bear the cross of Jesus. When it pays the price of working closely with groups who are different, it again carries the cross. Paul Avis notes, 'the opposite of unity is not diversity but division. The opposite of diversity is not unity but uniformity' (Avis, 2010, p. 32). Holding the proper polarities together – unity and diversity – is often difficult and painful. It is the way of the crucifixion. From the crucifixion, of course, comes life.

An argument from the new creation

Focused-and-connected churches are foretastes of the future when all will be perfected. In anticipation of this future, Jesus brought into human history the gift of community centred on himself. During his earthly life he created a single community to which everyone was invited, from people on the margins to those at the centre of society such as Joanna, wife of Chuza, a senior official in Herod's household (Luke 8.3). Anyone who obeyed God's word was Jesus' brother or sister, a member of his one family (Luke 8.21). But within this single community were individual communities that had distinct lives – households such as Mary and Martha, Jesus' mother and brothers, and those who responded to the missions of the Twelve and the 72 and presumably remained in their villages.

This single community with smaller units was paradigmatic of Jesus' gift of community. On the one hand, Jesus offers humanity the gift of one community open to all.

> [T]he unity Christians celebrate is not one we have negotiated by skill and patience, but one given in relation to something never possessed, never wholly within our grasp, a horizon to which we all look. We have been given a kind of 'belonging' that sits at an angle to all particular local loyalties and identities. To be converted is to discover a common perspective, not dependent on a specific group's concern or interest. (Williams, 1994b, p. 8)

On the other hand, Jesus assumes that this gift of community will be received and made concrete in a diversity of ways. The gift is not to be received in a uniform manner. Jesus who was part of Jewish history was not bound by his history. When he spoke to Peter through a vision at Joppa (Acts 10. 9–16), he opened Israel's history to Gentiles, who were admitted while keeping their own histories intact. Israel's boundaries were redrawn, so that other cultures could be included without leaving their histories behind. Jesus' offer of community became the gift of a multicultural community, a gift to be received in a multitude of cultural ways.

This was affirmed at Pentecost. The Spirit enabled those present to understand the apostles not by obliterating language differences, but by hearing in their own languages (Acts 2.5–12). Unity of hearing was combined with diversity of speech. 'At Pentecost the Spirit representatively baptized and sanctified all languages and hence in principle all cultures' (Stanley, 2007, pp. 25–6). Those who responded were drawn into a single community, God's one family. Unity became possible alongside cultural variety.

The same theme is repeated in Revelation's vision of the new creation. The one multitude of saints in 7.9 is drawn from a huge variety of cultures. Revelation 21.3 speaks of God dwelling with his 'peoples'. 'There is no one people of God chosen from among the nations. All are now united in God, but still maintaining their particularities, their individual riches' (Ellul, 1970, p. 193). Later, in verses 24 and 26, Revelation describes the nations (plural) bringing their accomplishments into the new city (singular). Unity and cultural diversity are again combined.

Davison and Milbank acknowledge that the cultural interests of members should be valued within the churches, but arue that churches should not be structured around them (Davison and Milbank, 2010, p. 77). The priority, it is implied, is to bring people together. But this is at odds with the vision of Revelation. When the kingdom is fully present, unity will not have pride of place over diversity, just as diversity will not triumph over unity. The two will be combined on equal terms. Focused-and-connected churches anticipate this future.

Arguments from justice

Finally, focused-and-connected church embodies principles of justice that make the new creation tangible today. If existing members set the terms of church life – when it meets, where, in what style and so on – these conditions will inevitably reflect the interests of those who already belong. As Hirsch and Ferguson point out: 'If we persist with the current status quo, we are in effect asking the nonbeliever to do all the cross-cultural work in coming to church! Remember, we are the sent ones, not them' (Hirsch and Ferguson, 2011, p. 73).

On the other hand, when the church emerges among people outside, the character of the church can be shaped by the newcomers. The more culturally specific the church, the more it can respond to the needs of the people it serves, such as meeting at a time that fits in with shift work or in a convenient place. The interests of a particular grouping are not lost within the diversity of competing claims. Serving specific cultures opens the church's doors. It helps contextual churches both to attract and hold people. The Spirit can then convert individuals to the pursuit of heterogeneity.

Furthermore, as *Mission-shaped Church* argued, experience shows that when two cultures are together in a social context, often a healthy heterogeneous mixture does not result – one tends to dominate the other. The culture of the people with the educational and economic power tends to come out on top. An attempt at diversity becomes dominance (p. 109).

An example is a cafe church with homeless people in London. The middle-class leaders have unwittingly created a style of church, with a sophisticated music band and a sermon, that the homeless people can never hope to lead. Continued dependence on middle-class leaders has been built into almost every aspect of the gathering. By contrast, one reason for the growing number of separate congregations of deaf people is to allow members to be themselves and to share their gifts in ways that are natural for them. When groups meet separately, the indigenous culture can be protected rather than being smothered by an alien, 'imperial' one.

Davison and Milbank complain that this argument allows sociology to triumph over theology. It denies the Spirit's power to help people build communities of reconciliation rather than dominance (Davison and Milbank, 2010, p. 80). Likewise, John Hull protests, 'The marginalized are to be encouraged to form their own churches rather than struggling to overcome their marginalization!' (2006, p. 15)

Almost 30 years earlier David Bosch, writing from his South African experience, maintained that homogeneous churches would allow social divisions to become more deeply ingrained (Bosch, 1983, p. 239). These concerns are widely shared among mission theorists. They spotlight the dangers: distinct cultural churches can legitimize and deepen social divides and inequalities. However, theorists have to answer the practical question: how should marginalization be overcome, and how should different cultural groups be encouraged to build bridges to each other?

In our flawed world, newcomers may find mixing with people who are different in a heterogeneous group too challenging. By refusing to join, they never start the journey toward the embrace of difference. Yet if the dynamics of networks are harnessed, 'bridging ties' can take members of a homogeneous church to other groupings within the body. Individuals who do not find it easy to relate across differences will be able to travel along these networks at their own pace. They will be able to dip their toes in one event with people from other churches, and then attend another as their confidence grows.

The process will be helped if networks encompass a variety of affinity groups. A member of a 'Gen Y' congregation who enjoys sewing might be invited to join a contemplative sewing group with a mixture of ages. Someone else who likes skiing might join a skiing holiday organized by the local churches. Interest groups in the wider body will help to overcome the fear of difference and encourage people to engage with the larger whole. As individuals meet new people, they will receive invitations from within one interest group to attend another and connect more widely.

Bringing different churches together in larger clusters and encouraging events that attract Christians from a variety of backgrounds can begin to create social heterogeneity. Of course issues of power will still have to be faced, as the Corinthian church found. But encouraging people from different churches to come together in a variety of ways will begin to express the gospel vision of reconciliation. Not least, as commonly happens now, churches will be able to use their connections to transfer resources from richer to poorer parts of the body, and to pool resources to combat the unjust structures of society.

Some arguments for focused-and-connected church

- It echoes New Testament practice.
- It flows with social reality.
- It corresponds to God's intentions for humanity.
- It echoes the pattern of election.
- It anticipates the new creation.
- It models the justice that will be found in the new creation.

Conclusion

Against those who argue that the church should not be structured around cultural groupings, the claim here is that one of the most fruitful ways for a church to be contextual is to relate to a specific culture. The more a Christian community focuses on the needs and longings of a single context, whether it is an age group, a locality or a network sharing an interest, the better it will serve people in that setting. A church cannot be contextual in general. When a church seeks to be present in several cultures, it finds it harder to be committed to each of these cultures.

Focusing on a context enables a church to serve the needs of the people in a targeted way. Newcomers will join the community more readily because it contains people like them, and because it is responsive to their specific concerns and aspirations. When a church is immersed in a single culture, it can begin to show corporately what that culture will be like within the kingdom – members can support each other in improving the dynamics of their work teams, for example; they can remove the graffiti on their housing estate; a children's church at school can stand together against a bully. Doing this is much harder, if not impossible, when several cultures are mixed together.

Taking *focus* seriously will mean that communities intending to birth a church will be clear about which context they are called to serve. The more specific they are, the better they will engage the people involved. Taking *connection* seriously may require church founders to spend almost as much time networking in the wider body as among the people they are called to. Establishing these networks – if they do not already exist – will create the infrastructure for connected church. This could lengthen the time it takes to start a church, but will help to ensure that a focused-*and*-connected church is born. The new church will be both contextual and linked to the living tradition.

Further reading

Davison, Andrew and Alison Milbank, *For the Parish: A Critique of Fresh Expressions*, London: SCM Press, 2010, pp. 64–92.

McGavran, Donald A., *Understanding Church Growth*, 2nd edition, Grand Rapids, MI: Eerdmans, 1980 [1970], pp. 223–44.

Newbigin, Lesslie, 'What is "a local church truly united"?', *Ecumenical Review* 29, 1977, pp. 115–28.

Shirky, Clay, *Here Comes Everybody: How Change Happens When People Come Together*, London: Penguin, 2009 [2008].

Questions for discussion

- How fundamental to mission is the homogeneous unit principle?
- What are the practical implications of the principle for birthing and growing new contextual churches?
- Why has connecting to the wider body been found so difficult? Do you think it is becoming easier? What practical steps might your church take?

10

Are New Contextual Churches Faithful to the Tradition?

Chapter 8 argued that contextualization should be 'through and through', controlled by the four interlocking sets of relationships that constitute the church and by the balanced use of different approaches to contextualization. The last chapter maintained that contextualization requires churches to focus on a specific context, while maintaining 'thick' connections to the living tradition. Does this emphasis on contextualization mean that new contextual churches have no ecclesiastical pedigree – that context trumps history, and if so should this be a concern? If a Goth Holy Communion, a gathering in a skateboard park and a fluid community with few set meetings wear the label of church, are they in continuity with the tradition, and if so in what ways? This chapter addresses these questions, approaching them from a mainstream reformed position.

In Oliver O'Donovan's words, the church experiences a tension between an 'outer' and 'inner' identity. Its outer identity consists of the varying offices of leadership, rules and disciplines and the conduct of its visible life. These serve its inner, hidden and universal identity under God's rule in Christ. The 'outer forms' of the church 'are essentially responsive to the historical circumstances in which the Church has to live' (O'Donovan, 2007, p. 186). They must be subject to reformation in the light of its inner identity.

Reformation is a perpetually open question in the church because the church's outward forms must always be answerable to its inner, gospel identity. 'The Church's openness to reformation is first and foremost a matter of appraising and evaluating the service rendered by traditional forms, keeping the subservience of the outer to the inner in view' (O'Donovan, 2007, p. 187). The church's inner identity shapes the outer forms through the church's obedience to Scripture. The church is 'under criticism' by being 'under authority' (p. 188).

Perhaps we can adapt the distinction between the church's 'inner' and 'outer identity', so that the church's 'inner identity' equates to the four sets of relationships that constitute the church. This then offers a framework for testing the validity of new contextual churches. If the church is to be open continually to reform in the light of its inner identity, its current outer forms cannot be the ultimate judge as to whether a new shape of church is theologically valid. New types of church must be evaluated against Scripture, understood through shared discernment, tested against the tradition and take into account the church's mission. Attention to Scripture will include asking whether these communities correspond to the founder of the church, Jesus, as he is revealed in the Gospels.

Advocates of contextual church often appeal to the incarnation. Frost and Hirsch, for example, argue that the incarnation shows that the church must fully enter into its context in mission and identify with the people in it (2003, pp. 35–59). Such writers usually understand the incarnation as Jesus *coming* to the earth. *Mission-shaped Church* (2004, pp. 85–6) explicitly differentiates the incarnation from the rest of Jesus' life. 'The Son himself, through incarnation, atonement, resurrection and ascension, is the sole foundation of the Church.'

This chapter understands the incarnation in terms of the whole of Jesus' earthly and ascended life. Jesus became and remains a human being. The chapter maintains that contextual churches echo the whole sweep of Jesus' life when they mirror not only his identification with culture, but also his mission in community within ordinary life, his community's Good Friday fragmentation and Easter resurrection, his letting go and sending out, and his completion of all 'places' when he returns.

Contextual churches bear the fingerprints of Jesus when they enact these themes. Again going beyond Frost-and-Hirsch-type appeals to the incarnation, this chapter draws on Chapter 2 to argue that we can recognize the presence of these fingerprints at different moments of the church's past. Thus new contextual churches are not faithful to Jesus as if the tradition did not count, nor are they faithful to the latest manifestation of the tradition as if the life of Jesus did not count. By being true to the church's founder, they are faithful to patterns of his life that have reverberated down the ages.

Identifying with the context

The Spirit clothed Jesus with flesh at the incarnation. Following Karl Barth, this was far from being a Plan B. The incarnation was God's intention from before the world was made. According to Barth's doctrine of election, which draws on Ephesians 1.4, the Son was chosen – and also chose – from all eternity to become a human, to die for the world, to rise and ascend as a human, and to remain a human being for all eternity. This was a radical opting for humanity. By not shedding his humanity when he ascended, Jesus showed that – through his free decision – humanness combined with divinity would remain his preferred mode of being. This was the strongest possible identification with humanity.

Jesus did not appear in the form of a general mishmash of all cultures, which would have made him a strangely abstract Christ: he grew up within a specific culture. Markus Bockmuehl (2008, p. 63) notes how till recently Christian commentators tended to draw a wedge between Jesus and Judaism. Jesus had come to replace Judaism with Christianity. The present consensus, by contrast, emphasizes the Jewishness of Jesus. The Gospels highlight this through their descriptions of his genealogy, the calling of the Twelve (who will judge the twelve tribes of Israel), his acceptance of the description 'rabbi', his commitment to Jewish practices, his affirmation of the Torah's authority and much else. Jesus took *Jewish* flesh (Bockmuehl, 2008, pp. 69–71, 75).

Bockmuehl reminds us that Jesus rose from the dead and ascended as a Jew. The church must 'reappropriate the meaning and significance of the Word made – and raised! – Israelite flesh' (2008, p. 76). New contextual churches echo this cultural consistency of Jesus. Just as Jesus did not abandon his Jewishness when he died and rose, converts who are baptized into his death and resurrection do not forsake their cultures. Like Jesus who retains his Jewish identity while sitting next to the Father, through worship new believers enter the Father's presence with their cultural identities. Again like Jesus who refused to identify with his Jewish culture merely for a season, contextual churches do not identify with their cultures just for a while.

This full-blooded identification with a specific culture has been the mark of missional churches down the ages. Chapter 2 provided the example of the Antioch church, where Christian community found expression in the context of a household meal. It described Celtic missionaries, whose mobile apostolic teams packed up and moved on like the nomadic people they sought to reach and who set up camp close to the centre of community life. It recounted how the Beguine communities translated Scripture into the vernacular and taught people to read, practices that were continued centuries later by missionaries to foreign lands. Lamin Sanneh has emphasized how translation is a deeply contextual practice. By involving a search for dynamic equivalences, it requires the translator to explore cultures on their own terms (Sanneh, 1989, pp. 192–209).

Throughout history, churches have sought to make Jesus' identification with the human species, which he demonstrated in one culture, concrete for other cultures. Just as Jesus came to a specific culture and retains this cultural particularity, new churches have been immersed in particular cultures, often becoming more culturally embedded as time moves on. Today's contextual churches are part of this slipstream of history.

Serving a culture

Jesus took a missional community into everyday existence. It is easy to miss the significance of this because we are so absorbed with Jesus as an individual. Yet fundamental to his ministry was modelling the kingdom *with* his followers. Hans Frei points out that Jesus did not first accomplish his earthly ministry and then choose followers to proclaim what he had done. He called his disciples before his mission of reconciliation was complete. Calling and equipping the Twelve was an essential component of how he saw his vocation. It was basic to his obedience to the Father, and so a core ingredient of his identity (Demson, 1997, pp. ix–x).

John Flett quotes Barth as saying that Jesus would not be who he is if he lacked his community and if this community lacked a missionary character (Flett, 2010, p. 218). Jesus involved his disciples in feeding the multitudes. He turned his ministry of healing, preaching and baptizing into a shared community activity. He taught about mutual service in his community and led by example. When, at Cana, Jesus connected the transcendent kingdom to a crisis in a wedding, he was not on his own but surrounded by his disciples.

In community with his disciples, Jesus showed that the kingdom of God lies in the details of life. His parables, which disclosed the secrets of the kingdom, drew attention to God's involvement with ordinary, immanent life. They showed that the kingdom was like a feast, a shepherd who found his sheep and a woman who lost a coin. By his life and teaching *with his disciples*, Jesus demonstrated how the kingdom could make a difference to everyday practices, whether at a meal, or chance encounters on a road, or staying at someone's home, or collecting tax.

The disciples were so important to Jesus that he handed his body over to them – 'Take it; this is my body' (Mark 14.22). Whether Jesus metaphorically handed himself over to his disciples or did so somehow literally as he poured himself into the bread (Ward, 1999, pp. 167–8), the manner of receiving was unlike ordinary food. The body of Christ was not assimilated into the disciples' bodies, but vice versa. By eating the bread they were drawn into Christ's body, which is the bread of life (John 6.35). This communal body was to become food for the world, to be broken, given away and consumed. '. . . the church is most properly the church when it exists as a gift and sustenance for others' (Cavanaugh, 1998, p. 232).

The church continues the ministry of Jesus when it 'breaks off' pieces of the body and 'distributes' them, as new communities, in the fragments of society. Just as Jesus was present in his culture with a community, he seeks to be present in the details of all cultures with church communities. This should not be understood as the church being present in an indirect way through its prayers, for example, or by resourcing members for individual witness (important though these are).

Jesus did not withdraw his disciples from the world, teach and pray with them, and then send them out in mission as individuals. Jesus identified himself with a visible community, he ministered in everyday settings with this community, he sent his followers to ordinary villages in small communities, and he reveals his presence when the church, in continuity with his original community, multiplies into different cultures.

As Chapter 7 pointed out, one reason the church is 'distributing' contextual communities today is to enable believers to organize in the service of others where they live and work. The church stops being 'that building over there which some people go to at weekends', and becomes a tangible presence where ordinary life is encountered. This includes new churches established not just in the cultures of home or work, but in the social cultures that lie between the two – the cultures of hobbies, entertainment, political and social action, and hanging out with friends.

The principle of being church in life is far from new. The first churches, as noted in Chapter 1, were located in the midst of daily life. To be church in the home was to be church at the centre of family, social networks and often work. In excavations at Pompeii, for instance, over half the houses either incorporate shops or workshops, or have horticultural plots (Schnabel, 2008, p. 298).

The tradition continued into the Middle Ages. The medieval rural church was integral to the village where all aspects of life – work, home, friendships and festivals – took place. It was local court, social service and meeting place for the whole people. Chapter 2 offered some specific examples of church in the midst of life. Mary of Oignies, a first-generation leader of the Beguines, sought to combine elements of the communal monastic life with everyday secular occupations. Little Gidding, the seventeenth-century community north-west of Cambridge, served the poor and hungry in the village. In the nineteenth century, Charles Kingsley mobilized the parish church at Eversley to address the needs of its context.

This tradition of being a faithful and visible *community* in life was ruptured by the industrial revolution. Work and then important dimensions of leisure moved some distance from home but the local church remained in its residential place. Yet now, with churches emerging in cafes, schools, leisure centres, workplaces and other settings, the notion that a faithful community can reveal God in the centre of daily existence is once more coming to the fore. New contextual churches are bringing this strand of the tradition up to date.

Dying for a culture

If the church multiplies communities that feel comfortable in their cultures, the task of making Jesus present will hardly have begun. Just as the incarnation and the cross cannot be separated, so embedding the church in the details of life cannot be severed from the costs involved.

Jesus told his disciples, 'As the Father has sent me, I am sending you' (John 20.21). Newbigin highlights the word 'as'. It is the manner in which the Father sent the Son, he argues, that determines the way in which Jesus sends the church. Just before speaking, Jesus had shown his disciples his hands and side. There could be no doubt about how Jesus was sent. Those same scars in the church's corporate life will authenticate it as the body of Christ (Schuster, 2009, pp. 97–8). People will know that Jesus is being made present when they see the church suffering in service of the world.

Mission-shaped Church made an important contribution when it maintained that:

> If it is the nature of God's love to undertake such sacrifice, it must also be the nature of his Church. The Church is most true to itself when it gives itself up, in current cultural form, to be re-formed among those who do not know God's Son. In each new context the church must die to live. (2004, p. 89)

Especially in cross-cultural contexts, this dying to live requires those who birth the new church to let go of their cultural presuppositions so that they can see the culture on its own terms. Letting go includes making space for the context to unfold. Knowledge involves the ability to receive what the other discloses. This reception seems to be the essence of authentic love: 'the higher the ability to receive, the higher the love' (Howsare, 2009, p. 62). In a similar vein, new contextual churches die to live when they give themselves to the welfare of the existing body and to engaging with its structures. They make space for inherited church and receive it into their lives. Dying to live is reciprocal.

The argument of *Mission-shaped Church* can be taken further. Dying to live is more than correspondence to Jesus. It is built into the very foundations of the church. It was experienced by the community of Jesus as part of the crucifixion and resurrection. At the crucifixion, it was not only Jesus who died. His community 'died' as well. It disintegrated. The disciples fled from Gethsemane, Peter denied Jesus and Judas hanged himself. Only fragments of the community, a group of women and the beloved John, are recorded as being with Jesus at his death. For the disciples, it must have felt as if their community had died. Yet this 'death' was reversed after the resurrection. The community regrouped round Jesus, was taught by him, was sent into the world and then reproduced.

This communal death and resurrection was repeated within a few years of Pentecost, when the persecution of the Jerusalem church led to 'all except the apostles' being scattered throughout Judaea and Samaria (Acts 8.1). The form the Christian community took at Jerusalem virtually died. Yet 'those who scattered preached the word wherever they went' (v. 4). They started new churches, including the one at Antioch (11.19–21). A form of death was followed by new birth.

This pattern has recurred in varying ways down the church's history. Both the Beguines' vernacular translation of the Scriptures and the laity's intense Bible reading at Little Gidding provoked opposition from the wider church. The laity was being empowered to draw their own conclusions from Scripture. This threatened the disintegration of the church's existing, clergy-dominated practices. If power ebbed away from those in control, something akin to death would occur within the power structures of the church. Yet it was a death, as some recognized, that promised new forms of communal life.

During the Wesley revival, John Wesley never intended that the Methodists separate from the Church of England. But the new energies of Methodism exceeded the capacities of the existing structures. There was a long-term loss to the Church of England, a death if you like, when the Methodists left. However, their departure helped the new church to flourish. This new life in time included the establishment of mutually enriching relationships between the two churches.

Communal 'deaths' and 'resurrections' continue to occur whenever contextual churches are brought to birth. The departure of the leader to start a new community, the going out of a church planting group, the division of an ecclesial cell for purposes of mission, the partial withdrawal of two people from a congregation so that they have time to start a new missional gathering, the splintering of a congregation into mid-sized missional communities that meet together only once a month, the closing of a church activity to free up resources for mission – all these may be felt as losses or threats to an existing community. They echo the church's primordial 'death' at the cross.

Yet like the first death, which was followed by the reconstitution of the community, these losses or threats need never be the last word. A believing community may fragment as it multiplies, but through the Spirit these fragments are reconfigured round the person of Jesus. When this reconfiguration gives rise to new types of visible connection, the whole church can be enriched by the new. Disintegration (however small) is followed by reintegration, a form of death by new forms of life. When a church bears the cost of reproducing, it shares in the death and resurrection of that first community of Christ. It continues a pattern of ecclesial life that can be traced through the centuries.

The departure of Jesus

It is not enough to speak of the presence of Jesus in the church. When Jesus ascended, he physically left the earth. The result is the paradox that Jesus is in 'a manner present and in a manner absent' (Farrow, 1999, p. 3).

The ascension involved Jesus in a letting go. Jesus entrusted his mission to his disciples – the form it would take, the pace at which it would progress and how faithful it would remain. In fresh expressions circles, Roland Allen is often quoted as a trenchant advocate of missional letting go. Allen based his view on the example of Saint Paul, who quickly handed over his new churches to indigenous leaders. But Paul did not pioneer this practice. Jesus did. His departure at the ascension was inherent to the founding of the church.

Those who were entrusted with Jesus' mission doubted (Matt. 28.17), were fearful (John 20.19) and misunderstood his intentions (Acts 1.6) – reactions that regularly hold people back from mission. Jesus responded neither by refusing to let go, nor by filling up his disciples with more knowledge ('let's send them on another course') but by taking a risk. He passed on responsibility despite the disciples' doubts, fears and misunderstandings. Perhaps he recognized that ultimately these reactions could be overcome only in the practice of mission. Perhaps he knew, too, that in commissioning his disciples as a community he was reinforcing one of the best antidotes to doubt and fear, the security of relationships. Whatever was in his mind, risk was integral to the process of letting go.

Jesus was not foolhardy, however. When he let go, he left his followers with the Holy Spirit, with his teachings and the experience of being trained by him, with their Jewish Scriptures (our Old Testament), with the sacraments of baptism and Holy Communion, with leadership based on the apostles and with ongoing support – the promise of his continued presence. Far from being an irresponsible abdication of authority, letting go was a new way of providing support.

Jesus' letting go was a sending out. The disciples were not commanded to settle down in Jerusalem. When they received the Spirit, they were told to go 'to the ends of the earth' (Acts 1.8). They were to continue the mission they had been doing with Jesus, but on a wider canvas. Previously when Jesus had sent them out in pairs, they had returned to him. But with Jesus' ascension, this centripetal pull was removed. There was no commanding figure physically present for the disciples to come back to. Henceforth, Jesus would be with them wherever they were. The nature of mission had changed. Instead of going out and then regrouping at the centre, there would be a continuous going out because the centre of the community was going out too.

The centre – Jesus – was moving to the rim, turning the community inside out and transforming its entire mode of being. Consolidating and remaining an entity in one place became impossible as the community was stretched by its expanding edge. Instead of being a single community travelling with Jesus, sometimes splitting off in pairs but always re-forming as a single unit, now there would be multiple communities, all travelling outward with their Lord. Dissipating into a plurality of groupings that stayed connected became the community's natural form of existence. The church was to be a movement rather than an institution.

This dynamic is so characteristic of the church that throughout history Christianity has not maintained a single cultural or geographical centre.

It has expanded in a 'serial' fashion, growing and then withering in its heartland. Contrast the position today

> with that of Jerusalem, the first major centre of Christianity; or of Egypt and Syria, once almost as axiomatically Christian as Arabia is now Islamic; or of the cities once stirred by the preaching of John Knox or John Wesley, now full of unwanted churches doing duty as furniture stores or night clubs. (Walls, 2002, p. 29)

These areas of decline have been replaced by new centres of Christian growth, notably today in the global South. Think, too, of the Roman Catholic Church, where the most vibrant centres now lie outside Rome.

In today's global church, new ecclesial centres are starting to return to the old ones in mission, finding there a new rim where Jesus is present. Church founders join this movement when they go to, and beyond, the edge of the local church, to parts of society where the Christian faith has withered, and thereby continue the outward pattern inaugurated by Jesus. They are not the only ones to do this, of course. Hospital and other chaplains also go to the edge, but founders do so in a particular way: they form new ecclesial communities.

Christ will fill all cultures

Ephesians 1.10 describes God's purpose as being to bring all things in heaven and on earth under the headship of Christ. The time will come when Christ fills – or completes – everything in every way (Eph. 1.23). The church is to be a sign, foretaste and instrument of this divine purpose by taking Jesus into all cultures now. Since he possesses 'all authority in heaven and on earth' (Matt. 28.18), there is nowhere that Jesus cannot be. There is no limit therefore to the places and cultures in which the church, through the Spirit, can be his companion.

Church in every place

In a 1977 article, Newbigin asks what it means for the church to anticipate Christ's fullness in every place. He answers that the 'place' in which the church is located 'is not just the latitude and longitude of the spot where the church happens to be . . . The "place" of the Church is not thus its situation on the surface of the globe, but its place in the fabric of human society' (Newbigin, 1977, p. 118). Most people live in several 'places' at the same time – places of residence, work, kinship, political commitment and many others. Whereas in simple rural society these different worlds largely coalesce, in contemporary urban society they pull the same person in different directions and involve a variety of commitments (p. 119).

If the church is to point to, embody and be a means of God's intention to fill all things with Christ, the church must be connected to all the different spheres of life. It must be credible in relation to the secular realities of these various worlds. Individuals must be able to recognize Christ's call to them in words, deeds and patterns of life that can be understood. This will be impossible, the church will not be truly local, if 'its language, worship and style of life belong to another "place"' and so fail to communicate as the authentic call of God in that "place" (p. 120). On the other hand, if the church is too conformed to the 'place' it will not communicate the sovereign judgement and mercy of God.

Broadening out the notion of 'place' is not without precedence in the church. It is normal that in a city with many linguistic groups, congregations exist for different languages 'since it is proper that people should worship God in their own language' (p. 119). It is also common to find congregations organized in relation to a sector of society – university, military, school, hospital and other chaplaincies. The church may need to specialize further in order to fulfil its mission.

There may be parts of society that are culturally so alien to existing church that the latter cannot function as sign, instrument and first-fruit of God's purpose to embrace them in his new creation.

> It is not enough in this situation for the Church to say 'Come – all are welcome.' A few may accept the invitation, but only to become assimilated to the language, culture, style of the already existing congregation. This is not to take seriously the full reality of the 'place'. Those who are left outside have their treasures to bring into the Holy City – their own treasures, not borrowings from others. The existing congregation must be willing to *go* – to go outside the walls of the Church in order to become part of that other reality – in language, culture, style of life. Only so does there appear in the midst of *that* reality the sign and first-fruit of God's all-embracing purpose. (p. 123 author's italics)

When the church threads its way through the multiple contexts of society, it can begin to show – through its life and witness – what these contexts can be like when they are under the rule of Christ. As the accumulated wisdom of the church bears on the details of life and is interpreted afresh, the reign of Jesus becomes tangible. This requires, as noted in the last chapter, that each new church's manner of life be appropriate to its setting while remaining faithful to the gospel. Only in this way can a church show what it means for the context to be converted by Jesus.

Diversity and unity

The whole body becomes more diverse when individual churches take different shapes to engage with different contexts. As Rowan Williams says, mission, kingdom and catholicity belong together (1982, pp. 63–4). The church joins its Lord in mission when it goes beyond the edge of its existence. As it does so and new communities are formed, the kingdom is brought more fully to life in the new setting. Repeating the process, one context after another, makes the church increasingly catholic.

Reproducing contextually creates a dynamic that demands further reproduction. By growing more Christ-like, new believers will become increasingly distinct in their individual and corporate lives. A gap will open up between the context and the shared life of the new church. It may be that as the church becomes more deeply influenced by Jesus, this gap will widen. The church in its collective life will become progressively different. Members will make assumptions about Jesus that will be steadily more distant from their peers. People outside the church will find it increasingly difficult to bridge this expanding gap. A new contextual community then becomes necessary. The church will reproduce again. Diversity breeds further diversity.

As the church enters the different 'places' of life, diversity and unity must be held together. The universality of the church does not cancel out the particularity of each 'place', nor does locality deny universality. Each local congregation must be knit with the wider church through ties of mutual responsibility.

> These bonds must not be so interpreted that – in the name of catholicity – the life-style of another place or time is imposed upon the local congregation as a condition of recognition. True catholicity will not deny but will confirm a proper particularity in the life-style of each local church. (Newbigin, 1977, p. 121)

While the life of Jesus must be allowed to flower in each individual church, these churches will also reflect Christ when they work together. The local nature of these ties was an important theme for Newbigin, who argued strenuously against denominational divisions. The latter encourage 'the divided parts' to develop and emphasize beliefs and practices that distinguish the parts from one another. The result is 'a series of societies, each marked by some peculiarity of tradition', a peculiarity that makes it impossible for any denomination to be the home for all men and women (Newbigin in Weston, 2006, p. 78).

Newbigin saw the United Church of South India, which brought three denominations together in 1947, as somehow pioneering a path for the church worldwide. In 1976, he argued for church life 'so open, so free, so welcoming of variety and even contradiction, that men and women of every kind can be at home in it'. This implies 'the death of all our denominations as we know them'. Unity must be based on a visible and recognizable local expression of what God has done in Jesus (Newbigin, 1976, p. 306).

While there can be a place for denominations, they can never replace the collaboration of different churches at a local level.

By reproducing, the church brings the lordship of Christ into progressively more portions of society. By being contextual, it starts to show what these cultures can be like when they are under the reign of Christ. By reflecting the diversity of these cultures, the church becomes more catholic. By linking these cultures up, the church anticipates the end of time when the *one* Lord will fill *all* places.

This dynamic, expressed at times imperfectly and with insufficient insight, has propelled the church's history. Whether it is Saint Paul's new churches, the communities founded by the Celtic missionaries and then by Augustine of Canterbury, the new communities planted by the twelfth-century Norbertines, the churches that originated with the thirteenth-century mendicant movements, the churches started by the Spanish and Portuguese missionaries, church planters on the North American frontier or the modern missionary movement, the church has been a sign, foretaste and instrument of the coming time when God will be 'all in all' (1 Cor. 15.28). New contextual churches follow in a long tradition.

The church corresponds to the life and ministry of Jesus when it

- identifies with a specific culture;
- forms communities in the midst of people's immanent lives;
- endures a 'death' as it brings forth new life;
- finds that the church's centre has followed Jesus to the rim;
- anticipates the inclusion of 'all things' in the kingdom.

Conclusion

New contextual churches are not a strange infection on the ecclesial body. They are part of the body's DNA. They are faithful to the tradition because they recapitulate the life of the one who founded the tradition. More than that, they resonate with echoes of Jesus that have bounced through the church's history. Thus new contextual churches are not bringing something entirely novel into the church. Nor are they just repeating the past. They are opening a chapter that carries the church's story forward.

This must not be understood in a conservative way. Jesus became human to bring in the new creation. Mary, for example, saw the announcement of Jesus' entry into Jewish society as a sign that God was siding with the humble and poor (Luke 1.46–55). Jesus' communal ministry with his disciples was biased toward people on the social margins. The 'death' and 'resurrection' of the Jesus community enabled it to continue his ministry toward the vulnerable. New Christian communities follow the ascended Lord not only to the edge of the church but to people on the edge of society. When Jesus returns to fill every 'place', he will banish all hurts and injustices from these places. Contextual churches will correspond to the life of Jesus, therefore, not just by being present in the status quo but by transforming it, by pointing to the time when every place will be renewed.[1] They will follow Jesus when they walk his radical path.

Further reading

Langmead, Ross, *The Word Made Flesh: Towards an Incarnational Missiology*, Lanham, MD: United Press of America, 2004.

Newbigin, Lesslie, 'What is "a local church truly united"?', *Ecumenical Review* 29, 1977, pp. 115–28.

Schuster, Jürgen, *Christian Mission in Eschatological Perspective: Lesslie Newbigin's Contribution*, Nürnberg & Bonn: VTR & VKW, 2009.

Questions for discussion

- Is the church's tradition an aid or impediment to mission?
- Besides those in the chapter, in what other ways do new contextual churches echo Jesus?
- How do you respond to Newbigin's vision of church collaboration on a geographical basis? Does this pull away from denominational involvement, and if so does it matter? Have denominations had their day?
- Can you give examples of new contextual churches that illustrate this chapter?

---

1 David Purves, 'How might some recent accounts of the doctrine of the incarnation serve as a resource for the Fresh Expressions of Church?', 2012, available from the author (david.purves@theology.ox.ac.uk).

Part 3

Bringing Contextual Churches to Birth

How Do Contextual Churches Emerge?

Parts of the global North are witnessing a revolution in how churches are brought to birth. Traditional methods of church planting – a team going out from one church and creating another in a similar mould – sometimes remain valid, but are being supplemented by new approaches associated with the emerging church, fresh expressions of church and mid-sized communities. Old and new methods are not in competition, but complement each other and at times have the potential to be fruitfully combined.

Whereas Part 1 placed new contextual churches in their historical and sociological context and Part 2 offered the beginning of a theological rationale for them, Part 3 examines the nature of this revolution and some of the key methodologies involved. It shows how the theology in Part 2 can be turned into practice – how mission can be a first step for the church, how it can be done in community, how these communities can be contextual through and through, and how they can serve a specific context while remaining connected to the whole Christian tradition.

Part 3 should be seen as a series of hypotheses that combine theory and experience-based wisdom. These hypotheses are developed on the basis of around 200 case studies in the UK,[1] the accumulated wisdom of the church planting tradition in North America and Britain,[2] wisdom coming out of the emerging church conversation[3] and insights from the literature on entrepreneurship (remembering that business has a different purpose and values to church). Part 3 provides an initial sketch of some methodologies rather

---

1 These are drawn from the Church Army Sheffield Centre's *Encounters on the Edge* series, case studies published by Fresh Expressions (www.freshexpressions. uk/stories) and personal knowledge.

2 I would commend especially Stuart Murray *Planting Churches. A framework for practitioners* (2008), which draws on his wide UK experience, and Ed Stetzer, *Planting Missional Churches* (2006), which is based on extensive North American experience and research. I have also benefited from conversations especially with Bob and Mary Hopkins and George Lings, though they are not responsible for the conclusions I have drawn.

3 See for example Halter and Smay (2008) and Neil Cole's books (2005, 2009). It should be noted that the distinction between church planting and the emerging church conversation is getting increasingly blurred.

than a fully worked out theology of them, which would require a longer study. Though the methodologies have intuitive appeal, we still have much to learn. Their validity therefore needs systematic testing.

Part 3 is about mission in community – about how small or large groups of Christians can bring new churches to birth, and about how they can do this contextually by attending to the specific group of people they serve. This chapter lays the foundations by describing two models for how contextual churches develop. Chapters 12 to 16 describe five interconnected sets of methodologies that build on these foundations.

The methodologies centre on gathering the community that will practise mission, practising contextual mission through careful attention to those whom the community will serve, engaging partners that will support communal and contextual mission, utilizing action-based learning and – in a departure from much of the literature – on developing good quality conversations within the community that leads the initiative.

The chapter begins with a rationale for Part 3. It uses a conceptual model to explain the value and place of theorizing about the methodology of contextual church, and suggests that the founding of contextual communities should be understood as a church practice. The chapter then proceeds to its main theme. It offers two models for how contextual churches develop – *Worship-first* and *Serving-first*.

The rest of the chapter discusses the *Serving-first* model, not because it is always superior to *Worship-first* (that depends on the context), but because it is much less understood in the literature. Whereas *Worship-first* has been treated extensively in guides to church planting (for example, Malphurs, 2004), *Serving-first* is more recent. It has been articulated within UK fresh expressions circles to describe approaches to reaching people with little or no church background. Used flexibly, it offers a promising methodology for the church to serve an increasingly post-Christian society. The chapter argues that *Worship-first* and *Serving-first* each have strengths, which can be maximized when both models – where possible – are used in tandem. These models, in combination or independently, should centrally inform mission strategy in a post-Christendom era.

Birthing churches as a church practice

Founders find the process of bringing a church to birth messy, opportunistic and full of surprises. 'We're making it up as we go along' is a common refrain. Some pioneering communities start with a blank piece of paper and follow their noses. Others have some initial ideas but then, against expectations, head off in a different direction. Others find that a church emerges almost by mistake; they did not plan to start one, it just happened. Others are in a network where there is a literal 'manual', but as they follow the guidelines the unexpected happens. Any theoretical account of the unfolding of church must do justice to this perceived spontaneity.

Simple, complicated, complex and chaotic contexts

The account here starts with the place of theory in understanding how contextual churches are born and grow. Being clear about the role of theory is necessary because of the random and haphazard way that many of these churches seem to develop. The experiences of church founders might suggest that no such theory is possible. The process is too serendipitous. The counter-suggestion here is that there is a place for theory, but we must be clear about what that place is.

Developed within a complexity theory perspective, David Snowden's Cynefin model offers a helpful framework in which to place theories about the methodology of contextual church. *Cynefin* (pronounced ku-*nev*-in) is a Welsh word signifying the many factors in a situation that influence us in ways we can never understand (Snowden and Boone, 2007, p. 2). Different contexts require different types of decision.

A simple version of the Cynefin framework

Complex context	Complicated context
Chaotic context	Simple context

First, there are 'simple contexts'. These are stable and have clear cause-and-effect relationships, easily discernible by everyone. Decision-makers *sense* (they assess the facts of the situation), they *categorize* the facts (to determine what type of event they are dealing with) and they *respond* on the basis of good practice for dealing with that category of event. Decision-makers need to know what the good practice is. If a denomination gives a grant for a new contextual church, for instance, there are established ways of processing the monthly payments and the church founder needs to understand these. The danger, when things are going smoothly, is complacency. Perhaps the denomination hits a financial crisis; all budgets have to be cut; the grant is scaled back. The contextual church's leaders failed to spot the risk.

Second, there are 'complicated contexts' which, unlike simple ones, may contain several established answers. Though there is a clear relationship between cause and effect, not everyone can see it, which makes this the domain of experts. The expert *senses* (evaluates the facts), *analyses* the different options and then *responds*, using one of the recognized approaches.

There is no single way of worshipping, for example, but there are principles that can be applied flexibly in different situations. Leading worship
requires knowledge of these principles and skills in applying them, and may
be entrusted to individuals with the necessary gifts and the training. The
danger is that the expert is trapped in a given way thinking and is prone to
dominate the domain. Innovative suggestions from non-experts are overlooked. Experts, therefore, need to stay in touch with good practice (in the
case of worship, to keep listening to the tradition) and to attend also to
novel ideas from other people.

When pioneers say that they are making it up as they go along, they may
be operating in a 'complex context', which is a third domain, the domain
of emergence. No recognized solutions are to hand, so the answer has to be
discovered, usually through trial and error. Perhaps a pioneering community
feels called to work with a cultural group that the church has not served
specifically before. This is not like worship, where the challenge is to apply
the appropriate principles. How to serve this particular culture may seem
to be governed by few established principles. The mission community has
to *probe, sense* and *respond*. It must open up discussion so that insights can
emerge, and must encourage dissent and diversity to stimulate fresh thought
(Snowden and Boone, 2007, p. 6).

'Chaotic contexts', fourthly, are the domain of rapid response. This is the
realm of turbulence, where cause-and-effect relationships shift constantly
and no manageable patterns exist – a 9/11 situation. Perhaps two days before
the mission community's first public meeting, permission to use the room
is cancelled. The leader must *act* to establish order (he asks two colleagues
to enquire about a temporary alternative). He must *sense* where stability is
and is not present (he suggests organizations that might have rooms). He
must then *respond* by transforming the situation from chaos to complexity,
where emerging patterns and new opportunities can be identified. The
leader notifies others of the change of room, and suggests that a colleague
be tasked with finding a permanent venue.

Simple, complicated, complex and chaotic contexts may well exist
simultaneously – paying the grant into the bank coexists with the crisis of
not being able to use the room. But Snowden and Boone (p. 8) contend that
many leaders are effective in only one or two domains. Wise leaders will
delegate their leadership in domains where they are less competent – 'help!
We can't have the room on Thursday. What shall we do?' the leader might
ask anxiously. 'Don't worry', responds a colleague, 'I'll take care of it.'

The birthing of church as a 'practice'

The suggestion here is that starting a church is a 'practice'. As this practice is
understood and described, it enlarges the 'complicated context' and shrinks
the 'complex context' domain. Complex contexts will still exist, but founders

will find themselves operating more often in 'complicated contexts', where recognized principles can guide action.

The notion of practice was developed by Alasdair MacIntyre in *After Virtue* (1981), and is helpfully discussed in relation to evangelism by Bryan Stone (2007, pp. 30–7). A practice, first, can be understood as a coherent and distinct set of skills. Baseball, painting, law and medicine are four very different practices. Each requires a different range of technical skills, and these skills are regularly experimented with and sometimes improved upon. Stone (p. 31) quotes MacIntyre as saying that bricklaying is not a practice, while architecture is. Similarly, planting turnips is not a practice, while farming is. A practice is a coherent set of activities that achieve the goal of the practice. Birthing a church can be understood as a practice in that it too employs a variety of skills, arts, techniques and activities.

Second, the criteria for doing well in a practice are determined largely by the practice itself and, indeed, help to define the practice. Stone quotes MacIntyre's example of candy being repeatedly given to a child who wins at chess. So long as it is the candy alone that provides the motivation, the child has no reason not to cheat, provided he or she can do so successfully. The child will never learn to play chess well, even though the child is able to win consistently. In fact by cheating, the child erodes the standards of excellence that define the practice of chess.

These standards of excellence can be understood within a narrative that is able to characterize the practice from beginning to middle to end. The narrative of chess will include how you play the game, but also how you enter and progress through competitions. Clearly the goal, both of the game itself and of progressing through tournaments, is essential to the narrative, and standards of excellence make sense in connection to it. In relation to founding church, the narrative obviously has the goal of bringing a church to birth, but this in turn has to be set within the larger Christian story. It is in the context of the church-birthing narrative, as seen within the bigger story, that standards of excellence for starting a church can be defined.

Standards of excellence for any practice are determined by a tradition of practitioners. This highlights a third feature of a practice – that it is a socially established and cooperative human activity. Individual practitioners subordinate themselves to a community of other practitioners, from whom they learn the standards of excellence and to whom they contribute by sharing their own insights and experiences. Chess players learn from grandmasters.

In the case of bringing churches to birth, the community of practitioners has traditionally centred on church planters mainly in the United States. Scores of books have been written about church planting largely in the North American context. These have defined excellence around themes such as selecting the planter, recruiting a church planting team, preparing to launch the congregation, the public launch of the congregation and much else.

However, a significant expansion and development of the church planting community is currently taking place. Church planters have tended to birth churches among people who are dissatisfied with church and want to find an alternative, or have recently left church. Many continue to work with this demographic. But as Christendom recedes further, a growing number of Christian communities are being founded among people with much less church background. Lessons from working in these contexts are feeding into the church planting community. This is reflected in the writings of Britain's Stuart Murray, for example, and of Ed Stetzer in the United States.

A fourth characteristic of a practice follows from this. It can be systematically extended. The standards of a practice are open to criticism by fellow practitioners. Standards of excellence can be modified in the light of experience. Thus a practice need not be static or finished. It can evolve steadily for a while and then change quite rapidly. The improvement of a practice refers not to advances in a particular skill, such as drilling a tooth in the case of dentistry, but to the systematic advance in the practice itself.

Such an advance appears to be happening in the church planting community. Founders working with people further away from church are introducing systematic improvements to the practice of bringing a church to birth. The improvements include starting 'further back' (not with a worship service but with loving service and building relationships), on not copying pre-existing models but attending to the context, and on allowing the Spirit to shape the church so that it fits that context.

Finally, especially important for MacIntyre are qualities of character that sustain the practice. These virtues are learned and cultivated over time from the community of practitioners who determine the standards of excellence. 'To practice well is to see well. But one can never come to see well by attending to the "how to" of a practice. That is why excellence in a practice requires . . . a virtuous formation . . .' (Stone, 2007, p. 45). It requires courage, justice, liberality and other moral virtues.

A 'good game of chess', for example, assumes that the rules are fair, the game is played creatively, the players deliberate carefully over each move (exercising patience), they take calculated risks (show courage) and they display other virtues. These virtues help to define both the game and how it should be played. These virtues are learned within the community of chess players and make it possible to practice well.

Thus bringing a church to birth, whose purpose must be understood in relation to the whole Christian narrative, will be defined by and will involve the exercise of kingdom virtues, which are learned and nurtured within the church. Starting a church can never be just a technical or pragmatic activity. Stone's comment about evangelism applies equally to birthing a church: 'the prevailing emphasis in our time on technique and effectiveness must be subordinated to a greater emphasis on holy virtues, acquired and formed within the fellowship of the Holy Spirit' (Stone, 2007, p. 45).[4]

Five characteristics of a practice

- It is a coherent and consistent set of skills.
- It has standards of excellence that emerge from a narrative that describes the practice.
- Standards of excellence are determined by a community of practitioners.
- The practice can be improved and extended.
- The practice is rooted in moral virtues.

Some implications

Understanding the birthing of contextual church as a practice has at least five implications. First, it enables us to move on from the rhetoric, 'we are making it up as we go along.' This may be the experience of founders who are breaking new ground and perhaps relish the thought that they are complete innovators. But it can be off-putting to others who may want to assist in starting a church but feel they need some guidance. Standards of excellence – principles of good practice in other words – can provide the help that many desire.

What if birthing a church was more like leading worship than constantly making it up? There would be recognized good practice, but this would provide a framework within which improvisation takes place. The 'complex context' in Snowden's model would shrink and the 'complicated context' would expand. This would fit with the growing attention to learning networks (such as by the European Church Planters Network) and to coaching for church founders. These trends would make little sense if there were no principles to pass on to others or to be coached in.

Second, viewing the birthing of contextual church as a practice will encourage principles of good practice to be learnt. At present the notion of 'pioneer', a term frequently used in fresh expressions circles, tends to be equated with starting a fresh entity (Lings, 2011, p. 31), which then slides into 'being the first to do or see something' (p. 33). Pioneering ends up being seen as innovating, and this accurately describes what many pioneers are currently doing. The danger is that starting a fresh entity and innovating

---

4 If Stone is right to claim that evangelism is a practice and if, as this chapter will argue, evangelism is an aspect of bringing churches to birth which is also a practice, then starting church might strictly be seen as a meta-practice – an overarching practice that embraces other practices. MacIntyre sees politics, for example, as a meta-practice.

become equated with each other. Founding *any* new church is seen to have innovation at its heart.

If this is the case, the practitioner cannot know much about how to do it in advance, for it is in the nature of innovation that it is new and unpredictable. The danger of such a perception is that principles of good practice will not be taken seriously. 'There may be some good practice, but most of it probably won't apply in my case, because I am starting something new.' The value of learning will be downplayed, which will increase the risk that the founder will repeat the mistakes that others have made.

However, if birthing a church is viewed as being more like leading worship, practitioners will be encouraged to learn the principles involved. 'Pioneer' can then be understood as someone who is skilled in the practice, perhaps develops and teaches these skills, but in particular introduces innovations to the practice as a whole. This different view of 'pioneer' would put the accent on learning, and on pioneering new *understandings* in the light of what is being learnt.

Third, understanding these principles will provide a framework within which to fit stories of good practice. It is widely accepted that many people – and church founders are no exception – prefer to learn through stories. Such learning can be enhanced if these stories are connected to principles of excellence. Hearers can use a story to illustrate, challenge or extend these principles. Listening to stories becomes a matter of interpreting each one in the light of received wisdom, which encourages *reflection* on practice.

Fourth, seeing the birthing of contextual church as a practice highlights the importance of a community discerning and sharing standards of excellence. Chapter 3 emphasized the contribution of networks to the development of fresh expressions of church, including learning networks. These networks have the promise to become the skeleton of a larger community of practice.

As learning networks grow increasingly diverse, they have the potential to comprise an informal community whose members exchange knowledge about good practice through personal contact, websites, books, courses and conferences, recognize experts in the field, take seriously their views and debate with them. In particular, as church planters are joined by practitioners working with the never churched, both groups may have much to learn from each other. Different networks need to be in touch with one another so that viral learning can take place.

Fifth, all this implies that descriptions of good practice should be seen as inputs into an ongoing conversation about bringing churches to birth. These descriptions can never produce fixed guides to action, guides that sit over practitioners and tell them what to do. This is because the moment a description of good practice is talked about, it becomes subtly changed by the conversation (like any practice, as we saw in Chapter 5). Some elements will be ignored and others reframed.

So rather than imagining that descriptions of good practice will generate authoritative guides to practice, it may be more helpful to see them as potential ingredients of conversations. These conversations could issue in guides to practice (anything from manuals to a mentor's advice), but these guides will themselves be inputs into further conversations – 'how relevant is this to our context? How would we adapt this suggestion?' Guides will be commented upon, disagreed with and reshaped, according to the situation. Descriptions of good practice can never direct practitioners. They can only inform conversations among practitioners.

Seeing the birthing of contextual church as a practice

- reduces the need to make everything up as you go along;
- puts an emphasis on learning the principles of good practice;
- provides a framework within which to interpret stories;
- highlights the importance of different networks learning from each other;
- implies that principles of good practice should be seen as inputs into conversations among practitioners, not as statements that rule over these conversations.

Journeys to church

To understand the practice of birthing contextual church, it is important to have a picture of how these churches emerge. The value of such a picture is suggested by Bill Bolton and John Thompson (2004, p. 288), who have described the benefits of developing a model of the entrepreneurial process:

- The model enables entrepreneurs to recognize the road they are on and be encouraged.
- It guides inexperienced and less confident travellers so that they can chart their progress and understand what to expect.
- It provides a useful framework for those who would encourage and support potential entrepreneurs.
- It enables strategies to promote entrepreneurship to include interventions at specific stages of the process.

When used as aids to fruitful conversation, models of how new contextual churches develop can bring similar benefits. For example, Chris Russell and his fellow pioneers at St Laurence, Reading, a church with a focus on young people, found that a key moment was when their bishop, Stephen Cottrell, suggested a framework for thinking about their activities. The framework described how individuals could be helped to move from one stage to the next in their journeys to Jesus. The leaders had been doing more and more things to make contact with young people, and had established some good relationships. But few young people had come to faith.

Stephen Cottrell's framework, which is described in the Box on p. 210, helped the leaders to become more intentional about what they were doing. It gave the leaders a structure that has encouraged them to ask of any activity, 'What happens next?' and to consider whether any of the steps from one 'stage' to another are too big. Far from being a constraint, the framework has helped them to stay creative but in a strategic manner.

A *worship-first journey*

Recognizing that new churches come into being in many different ways, two simple models are offered here. They point to some of the dynamics entailed in starting a church in two contrasting sets of circumstances. Like any model, they do not mirror reality, but are generalizations and simplifications of it. They provide insight into some of the processes involved, but do not reflect all the myriad ways in which these processes may be worked out. They offer partial, not complete knowledge. So while the models are to be taken seriously, they are not to be taken literally. Nothing in real life is quite like a model.

The first model is *a worship-first journey,* which over the years quite a few churches have adopted, sometimes with very fruitful results. Once the ground has been prepared, a congregation is planted, perhaps in a church building threatened with closure. The church plant offers worship and/or preaching as a shop window, and members invite their friends. Through a variety of events, such as presentations and discussions on contemporary issues, these friends are encouraged to attend a course in which they can explore the faith further and perhaps make a commitment. As a result they join a small group and get more involved in the church's life.

A *worship-first journey*

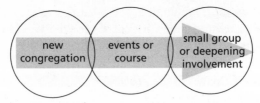

Source: Michael Moynagh and Andy Freeman (2011a, p. 4).

One advantage is that the planting team can scale up quickly. In some versions, a large church might send out a congregation of around 50 with two or three paid staff. As the congregation grows, it rapidly assumes financial responsibility for the staff and adds to their number.[5] The mission of the new church expands on a self-sustaining basis. An alternative version involves a smaller planting team, which organizes events and publicity in preparation for the public launch of the new congregation. The preparatory activities are designed to gain support for the congregation when it starts.

This *worship-first* approach has been influential in traditional church planting. The lifecycle framework, widely used by planters, has traditionally centred on 'birth', when public worship is first held. In one version, two stages (conception and development) lead up to the birth, and three stages follow – growth, maturity and reproduction (Malphurs, 2004). The association of birth with worship reflects the emphasis on planting a worshipping congregation. In the UK, the model appears to be especially fruitful among people who are moving between churches (such as new arrivals to a city), or have stopped attending church but are open to returning. It works, too, if members of the planting team and the new congregation have good networks and use them.

On the other hand, the new church is unlikely to attract many people who are outside its members' networks and have difficulty in identifying with the congregation's culture. The model also seems to be less effective in reaching people with little or no Christian experience, for whom the leap into church is too big. Among such people, friendships with churchgoers may not be enough. Friends do not have all their interests in common. A friend who enjoyed swimming, which I dislike, could never entice me to go too. Friends of churchgoers may feel about church the way I do about swimming.

One pioneer, who led a youth congregation in North-West London, described his hope that their congregation would attract newcomers to church.

> I remember feeling deflated on the first Sunday we hired a community centre for Sunday night worship. As I looked at the 20 people gathered there, I said to myself, 'Why aren't there more people here?' A more appropriate question would have been 'Why should they come?'

He explained, 'In our enthusiasm we bypassed some important stages in the development of Ignite. . . .' (quoted by Lings, 2007, pp. 8–9)

Writing about the United States, Ed Stetzer comments, 'In the country I live in, 70 percent of the population is completely unchurched, meaning they have little or no connection or interest in Christianity. We have already reached most people who are open to the "come and see" approach.'

---

5 This is broadly the approach of Holy Trinity Brompton, London, which has been highly fruitful.

Churches that use this approach are 'effectively reaching only 30 percent of my local neighbourhood, and I live in Georgia!' (Stetzer, 2006, p. 166)[6]

A *serving-first journey*

In the UK we have found that for the 'scarcely' or 'never churched', a different tack is often required, called here *a serving-first journey*. The model has been developed within the Fresh Expressions team to describe what the team was observing. In this model, the starting point for a new church is not a worshipping congregation, preceded by preparation, but loving and serving others, preceded by listening.

A serving-first journey

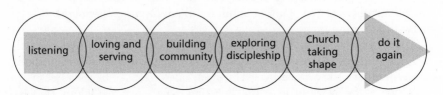

Source: Michael Moynagh and Andy Freeman (2011a, p. 5).

The *journey* starts with listening to God and to the people the founding community feels called to serve, which is an act of love in itself. The community begins to build loving relationships and engage in acts of service, as Jesus did. This might range from a spirituality-at-work group, to hanging out with friends, to a 'Saga group' for the over 50s, to an environmental campaigning group, to a drop-in centre for homeless people, to a regular discussion-over-curry.

An example is the Earlybird Cafe for parents and carers dropping off children at the St Paul's Church nursery in Dorking. By providing a weekday place to chat, it became the first step to a cafe church on the first Sunday of the month, which in 2011 was attracting 80 children and 175 adults (www.freshexpressions.org.uk/stories). As Saint John of the Cross said, 'Mission is putting love where love is not.' This is a love that serves people not by creating dependency, but by enabling individuals to flourish. It is a participation in the self-giving God of love.

Community develops around the relationships and activities the founding team establishes as individuals get to know one another, trust each other and develop a sense of belonging. Building community requires at least:

---

6 In the UK, the term 'unchurched' normally refers to people with little or no church background, whereas in the United States it can include people who used to attend church but are now disconnected from it.

- *That people have something in common.* The more disparate the group, the harder it is to form community, as some pioneers have painfully discovered. Focused-and-connected churches make not just theological, but practical sense.
- *Time to form and gel.* This requires regular and frequent meetings, whether one to one or in groups, face to face or online, or a combination. Groups meeting monthly will take longer to form community than those gathering weekly.
- *Identity* – a sense of being a distinct group. 'This is how we do things, which is different to others.' Shared rituals, such as particular ways of celebrating birthdays, are important. To prevent identity becoming exclusive, it may need to form round the theme, 'This is how we serve other people.' As we saw in Chapter 9, in Scripture election works by one group serving other groups.
- *The exchange of gifts.* Community is where gifts are shared so that the other may flourish. 'The New Testament sees the Church as a community in which each person has a gift that only they can give into the common life.' (Williams, 2007, p. 106) Giving equips and strengthens the other so that he or she can become a giver in turn.

'Building community' is valuable in its own right. It is what Jesus did as he ate meals with his followers, travelled with them and devoted periods of special time to them. But it is also important for mission. Loving relationships reveal something of Christ, they give people a partial (though important) experience of church and they create a climate of trust within which to share the gospel.

Low-key evangelism may continue throughout the initial 'circles', but when the need arises more intentional opportunities will allow individuals to explore becoming disciples of Jesus. Individuals may be mentored on a one-to-one basis; one person may be followed by another, until there is a sufficient number to form a small cell. Or there could be enough people to form an explorers' group. The founding team might use or adapt a published course, or develop its own material. One person invited her friends to explore spirituality: 'Jesus is known as one of the world's greatest spiritual teachers', she said. 'Why don't we look at the stories he told and see if we agree with them?'

Some people may come to faith quickly, others more slowly. Once they start to believe, they will be encouraged to see discipleship as a lifelong process affecting the whole of their lives. They will also consider what it would mean for them to be church in their context. Church guided by the gospel and appropriate to the culture will take shape around them.

Emerging cells may cluster together in monthly or occasional meetings to provide a larger experience of church. Some cells will strengthen the spiritual life of the original group from which they sprang so that the group as a whole becomes more like church: an Alpha cell might take responsibility for future Alpha courses, designed for people in the wider group; a luncheon club, influenced by emerging Christians, might incorporate Holy Communion from time to time.

While the founding community may have seen this as church from the beginning, those being drawn into faith may grow only gradually in understanding themselves as church. Authorities in the denomination will encourage and support the initiative from the start, but may delay recognizing it as church till there is evidence of stability. Once established, the new church will reach out to and serve its context. This may include reproducing – 'doing it again'.

St Laurence, Reading

St Laurence, Reading, is a church with a mission focus on young people. It was started in 2001 and provides a good example of *a serving-first journey*. The leaders began by hanging out round the local schools – 'listening' to what was going on. But it was only when they started to think and pray in terms of the framework below that they started to see people coming to faith in significant numbers. By 2010, St Laurence had nearly 50 young people growing in Christian life and belief, few with any previous church experience.

A serving-first journey

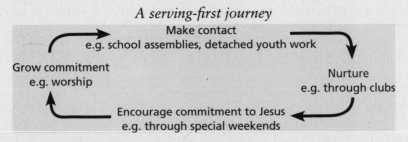

Source: Michael Moynagh and Andy Freeman (2011a, p. 5).

- 'Make contact' involves building relationships and engaging in simple acts of service, such as leading school assemblies or accompanying a person to the courts.
- 'Nurture' has building community at its heart. A variety of clubs attract teenagers not mainly through activities but because the young people want to belong.
- 'Commitment' weekends allow individuals to explore the possibility of following Jesus.
- As they enter the faith and 'Grow in their commitment', church takes shape around them.

Introducing Jesus

Social workers can find that they have to work with their clients to change the nature of the conversation in the client group. The task of social workers may have been socially constructed as a means for society to regulate and control individual behaviour, which influences how clients see social work interventions. The social worker has to understand what the helping process means to individuals, and facilitate a dialogue with and between them to reframe how interventions are viewed (Hardina, 2002, pp. 58–60).

A similar process may be required during the emergence of a new church. The founding team listens to those who are gathering round it to understand how they perceive the Christian faith in general, and how they see the faith of the team in particular. Is Christianity a curious irrelevance? Is it filed under 'fundamentalism' and so a bit sinister? Are individuals worried that the team's benevolence is a device to manipulate them into belief? Are they even aware that team members are Christians? Once the team has understood these perceptions, it will create opportunities for individuals, if they wish, to reframe their assumptions.

This reframing is necessary if people are to travel through the circles of being loved and served and of forming community, to reach a point where they are willing to explore intentionally the possibility of following Jesus. As they make this journey, their conversations about the pioneer community and the Christian faith will begin to change. Indifference, suspicion or even hostility will give way to openness and perhaps interest. Changing conversations is ultimately a work of the Spirit, who may act through a number of channels. Providing these channels is a prime task of the founding team.

Acts of kindness reveal Jesus' heart of love and enable non-believers to catch a glimpse of him. They are more than kindnesses by members of the founding team toward people within the initiative. They are ways in which the emerging community serves people outside it. A lads-and-dads football team might support a family with a disabled son on their housing estate. A book club with a spiritual dimension might provide financial support for a school library in Uganda.

Many people struggle to achieve their aspirations to be good. Belonging to a group that has an altruistic dimension may help them achieve some of the goodness they long for. As their hearts are warmed by being associated with generosity, they may become more committed to the group and more open to God's grace.

Acts of kindness towards people outside the group are especially important when the group gathers round a hobby or shared interest. It instils a tradition of serving others from an early stage. An outward, loving disposition becomes part of the new church's DNA. Individuals who are born into the kingdom do so in the context of this serving community. The Christian life into which they are introduced will extend beyond consumerist personal fulfilment to mission through generosity.

God talk is about sharing the Christian faith in natural conversations and through events that provoke questions about Jesus.[7] These events may include opportunities for people to hear personal stories about faith. A monthly women's luncheon club in a leisure centre featured talks by women who faced challenging circumstances, such as bereavement or raising a child with handicaps. Because the speakers were Christians, they invariably described how God had helped them.

Some cafe churches have a 'God slot' during the morning, a short period – publicized in advance – when someone gives a testimony or short Christian reflection. This provides an explicit pointer to Jesus, which may open up conversations. The risk is that people find it intrusive and stop coming. A less overt approach may encourage larger numbers, but then the challenge becomes how to introduce explicitly Christian content.

Missional worship may be part of the answer. It is designed for people who have little faith or are confused about faith. It creates opportunities for encounters with God that heighten spiritual awareness and encourage individuals to explore more. For instance, some church-run cafes have adjacent quiet rooms, perhaps with lighted candles, where individuals can pray and reflect silently.

Leaders of a retired persons' luncheon club might put candles on the tables after the meal, play some Christian music, invite someone to read a few verses from the Bible, allow time for silent prayer and ask someone else to read a couple of written prayers – lasting 20 minutes in all. Guests could leave straight after lunch or stay behind for this simple act of worship. Some who have led Alpha courses among people with little church background testify to the key role of worship. Worship can be quite 'full on' in these contexts if sensitively led. As church begins to take shape, missional worship can evolve into fuller expressions of Christian worship.

The experience of answered prayer can play an important part in opening individuals to God. In a culture that strongly values experience, answered prayer can give people an experience of Jesus. A number of initiatives use prayer boards, on which individuals post prayer requests. The Christian core incorporates these requests into their prayers. Prayer may include requests for healing. Healing may come through the love of Christian friends, the prayer of Christians (in their personal devotions or corporate worship), specific services for healing or through other kinds of prayer ministry. Some people have called it power evangelism (Wimber, 1985), while for others it is lower key. Being careful not to raise false expectations is clearly important.

Creative expressions of spirituality can help to increase a group's awareness of spiritual issues. Around Christmas or Easter, for example, those served

---

7 Graham Tomlin, in *The Provocative Church* (2002), sees evangelism as a corporate activity in which the church provokes people to ask how life could be different.

by an initiative might be invited to express their spiritual hopes and views through painting, photography, poetry, pottery and in other creative ways. These might not be explicitly Christian, but frequently they will direct attention to God. As talking points, they may help individuals to feel more confident in expressing their spiritual opinions and exploring their beliefs. They can be a means of putting God on the agenda.

Introducing Jesus can occur through

- acts of kindness;
- God talk;
- missional worship;
- experience of answered prayer;
- creative expressions of spirituality.

Some clarifications

A *serving-first journey* describes not an individual's pathways to faith, nor how the internal life of the founding team might evolve, but the action taken to enable a new expression of church to emerge. It is the process encouraged by the founding team to help people move from the edge of the circle in the diagram below to the centre.

From the circle's edge to the centre

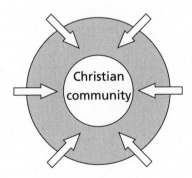

Whether the team is two or three people or larger, the internal and public aspects of the team's life are different. The internal dimension is about what the team does to prepare for and bring to birth a new expression of church. Like conception, what is within the team – the church in embryo – will permeate the new church as it develops. That is one reason why fostering healthy team relationships, the theme of Chapter 16, should be a priority. The public aspect of the team's life, which is the *journey*, is about what prayerfully and contextually results as the team engages in mission.

The *journey* is a sequence of *overlapping* circles. Overlapping is important because it conveys something of the messiness of what is involved. 'Loving and serving' and 'building community', for example, may be so linked that they happen almost at the same time. Though simultaneous, they may nevertheless be distinct processes. A language cafe may serve afternoon tea and encourage migrant women to learn English by giving them topics to talk about at their tables. This is 'loving and serving'. 'Community' might be encouraged by suggesting that the women sit at the same tables for a few weeks so that they can get to know each other.

Having come to the fore, each circle remains present throughout the *journey* – 'loving and serving' does not stop, for example. But the focus shifts from one circle to the next as the *journey* develops. The process may occur quickly, but will frequently take a few years. It will often be longer the less Christian background people have.

. It is vital that each circle has its own integrity. Each can contribute to the kingdom of God. 'Building community' is not valuable just because it can create an environment where people have the confidence to 'explore discipleship'. It is valuable in its own right. 'Loving and serving' should not be reduced to being the means to an evangelistic end. If the rest of the *journey* never took place, that individuals felt loved would be worthwhile in itself. The *journey* should not be a form of spiritual expediency.

Throughout the *journey* it is important that the founding team keeps listening to God and the people it is serving, and remains well connected to the wider church. After all, as individuals come to faith they will be baptized into the whole body of Christ. The team needs to model this Christian identity.

A rationale

A *serving-first journey* has three rationales – an empirical, theological and a strategic one. It has also emerged through a process of reflection and refinement.

Empirical evidence

St Laurence, Reading, cited earlier, is one example of the *journey*. Barbara Glasson's account of her *Mixed-up Blessing* (2006) is a good Methodist illustration. She started by walking the streets of central Liverpool, England for a year, watching and listening. With a group of friends she began baking bread, giving the loaves away. Others began to join this loving and serving core. As they made the bread, community began to form. 'Side-by-side encounters are infinitely less threatening than face to face ones' (Glasson, 2006, p. 39). They started a period of quiet reflection in the side room in the middle of the day. People were invited to comment on a Bible passage but not interrupt each other. There was space for silent prayer and reflection, allowing people to explore the Christian faith if they wished. Church gradually took shape.

Another example is a language cafe for women on a housing estate in North-West London. The women meet in a community centre on Wednesday afternoons and sit in small groups discussing a topic. There is no formal teaching, but the leaders use pictures and other resources to stimulate conversation on the week's theme, enabling the women to develop their English language skills. Though the team has yet to discover if the community will develop into church, it encourages the women to write names of people they are concerned about on a prayer board. The team prays for these concerns after the weekly meeting. The women have provided some encouraging feedback and have started to talk with team members about their situations locally and in their home countries. Offering a version of the Alpha course for speakers of other languages has been the next step.

A further example is TANGO (Together As Neighbours Giving Out), which is a cafe and recycling centre for a Merseyside community. Set up by the local Anglican church in 2000 to bring 'give and take' and care back into the local community, it is a social service that also provides opportunity for Christian witness through action and conversation. Expanding from one day a week to three, Wednesdays developed into a craft day for Golden Oldies.

The team offered the latter a time to get together and pray in autumn 2005, which became TANGO on the QT. This is attended by 20 to 30 Golden Oldies (some churchgoers, others not) every Wednesday for half an hour from two o'clock – an add-on to the craft day. Sometimes the gathering includes a reflection on a Scripture passage (illustrated with stones, candles, a box of chocolates or other objects), sometimes music and quietness, sometimes space for prayer requests. An evening cell held at the home of the leader of Golden Oldies every Wednesday provides the opportunity to pursue faith further.

This sequence of loving and serving, building community, exploring discipleship and church taking shape should not be pushed too far. Not all fresh expressions among the scarcely or never-churched grow in this way – the Spirit cannot be boxed in. There will be times when the circles are taken in a different order or perhaps get missed out altogether. Sometimes, however, if you peek beneath an apparent exception, you will find that the *journey's* sequence is secretly at work. Perhaps for instance some university students decide to run Alpha or Christianity Explored as an apologetics course. They might seem to be starting with 'exploring discipleship'. But look a little closer. By starting with listening and prayer, they may have discerned that this was the best way that they, in their situation, could love and serve their fellow students.

Maybe they redouble their efforts to be good and generous friends to their peers. They want their course to spring out of a network of loving relationships and their invitations to get a favourable response. Though Christian apologetics is certainly present, during the first evening or two the focus is on forming community – through the welcome, the meal, the discussion and much else. The hosts want people to feel at home and come back. Later, although the community dimension remains, attention shifts to encouraging individuals to explore discipleship and make a response. A follow-up course might be the context in which church begins to take shape.

A *serving-first journey* describe many initiatives that Britain's Fresh Expressions team is observing. It is also consistent with what others are noting. Phil Potter, an experienced pioneer in Liverpool, encourages lay Christians 'to share your passion, share your life, share your faith, share *their* journey'.[8] Eleanor Williams suggests a sequence of 'blessing, belonging, believing, behaving' to describe the experience of the urban fresh expressions she studied (Williams, 2007, p. 87). If we replaced 'behaving' with 'being church', this would map well on to the succession of circles.

The *journey* fits the North American examples of 'Missional/Incarnational' churches provided by Ed Stetzer (2006, pp. 163–5), the approach to mid-sized communities advocated by Mike Breen and Alex Absalom (2010) and some of the organic churches described by the American, Neil Cole (2005). Cole has been involved in planting hundreds of cell churches in just a few years.

He describes how a small team might, for example, throw a barbecue for a block of apartments and strike up friendships with some of those who turn up (loving and serving). As part of these friendships, team members share their faith. If someone becomes interested, the team might suggest that the person invites friends and family to his or her apartment to hear more. Those who are interested come back the next week and a small group begins to form (building community). The group explores the Christian faith (exploring discipleship). As members come into faith, they are encouraged to be church in the apartment (church taking shape).

In this example, the four circles overlap closely – so much so that the second and third circles (building community and exploring discipleship) become virtually one. Even so, the underlying dynamic of *a serving-first journey* remains: loving and listening, building community, exploring discipleship and becoming church.

A strategic rationale

As suggested earlier, the *journey* enables founding communities to recognize the road they are on and be intentional in their activities. Teams may be doing an element like 'building community' intuitively. But seeing this as part

---

8 In conversation with the author.

of an overall process may encourage them to give it particular attention – 'Could we do more to strengthen community?'

The *journey* allows inexperienced practitioners to chart their progress and understand what to expect. It provides a framework for coaches and others supporting church founders, and offers a way to measure 'progress'. It enables founding teams to design interventions to move the journey on (as St Laurence, Reading did). Notions of 'progress' and 'moving the journey on', however, must be used with care. It may be that the *journey* stalls with 'building community'. As emphasized already, this would still be a sign of the kingdom and should be valued as such.

The *journey* may have particular strategic value when it is combined with *a worship-first journey*. A church might send out a large planting team, which establishes a new congregation on a worship-first basis. The congregation might then ask: who are we not reaching? It might use a *serving-first journey* as the basis of its mission to these groups. Planting at scale in an area would be combined with planting at depth.

There are signs that this approach is beginning to gain ground. Some of the Holy Trinity Brompton church plants in London are combining a new sizeable congregation with smaller mid-sized communities. These communities comprise members of the congregation who serve a specific group of people outside church. They have the potential to become church in their own right.

Alan Hirsch and Dave Ferguson describe the Community Christian Church in Chicago, which was established in 1989 and had planted about 100 churches and sites by 2011. Its leaders are now being encouraged to 'reproduce micro'. This includes encouraging many of the church's small groups to become 'groups on a mission' – groups with a shared missional purpose to plant new gatherings on a smaller scale (Hirsch and Ferguson, 2011, pp. 306–7).

A theological rationale

Might we discern *a serving-first journey* in Luke's account of Jesus' public ministry? In the early years Jesus is teaching, healing and performing exorcisms. Then, while this loving and serving continues, there is a new focus on the call of the disciples (5.1–11; 6.12–16). Jesus is forming community – he describes his followers as his family (Luke 8.19–21). Building community presumably persists alongside his public ministry, but the focus falls more heavily on the process of making disciples – for example, sending out the Twelve and 72, and the Last Supper. Luke describes how church takes shape in his second volume. Chapter 1 suggested that a similar *serving-first journey* can be detected in Paul's church planting.

Certainly the starting point – of listening, followed by loving and serving – resonates with the command to love your neighbour. But the *journey* also offers a way of combining this 'great commandment' with the 'great commission' (to make disciples). Loving and serving, and evangelism need not be discreet activities, as they often are in church practice. The *journey* brings them together in a way that allows individuals to step toward faith at their own pace, and gives permission for people not to travel if they prefer. This combination of loving and serving with forming disciples makes the *journey* distinctive in its holistic approach to mission – and is one of its main attractions.

In particular, the *journey* demolishes barriers between church and life. Church can be combined with a language cafe, with making cards and with many other 'secular' activities. This makes theological sense. If there is no part of the world where Jesus is not lord, if there is no slice of life that cannot be redeemed within the kingdom and if the church is to be a foretaste of as well as a witness to God's rule, then no situation exists where the church cannot be present. Breaking down barriers between church and life is precisely what Christians are called to do. So long as there is no coercion, no manipulation and no false pretences, creating communities of loving service that are also evangelizing communities is thoroughly true to the church's vocation.

An earlier version

A serving-first journey – original version
Prayer and support

Connection

Source: Croft, Dalpra and Lings (2006, p. 3).

An initial version of the *serving-first journey* was published in 2006 and is summarized in the diagram above. Subsequent reflection within the Fresh Expressions team suggested some modifications, which led to the version described here. In particular:

- 'Loving service' did not fully capture the experience of pioneers who were primarily engaged in building relationships, such as a youth worker hanging out with young people. Some felt the phrase implied projects of loving service. 'Loving and serving' more clearly covers both projects and 'hanging out'.
- 'Evangelism and discipleship' seemed to confine evangelism to a specific stage, after 'Forming community' and before 'Evolving worship',

whereas evangelism can occur throughout the four circles. 'Exploring discipleship' captures the idea of intentionally exploring the possibility of following Jesus.

- 'Evolving worship' in the first version was put at the end to emphasize the difference from the 'worship first' model. But this could be misunderstood as suggesting that 'Evolving worship' was the destination of the process, whereas the journey was toward church (which is much more than worship, but of course includes it). Putting 'Evolving worship' at the end also failed to allow for 'missional worship' earlier in the journey.

- Presenting four *distinct* circles created a risk that the model would be understood as four separate stages – 'Forming community' comes after 'Loving service' and so on. In reality the circles overlap, and once started each circle continues as the next comes to the fore.

A *qualification*

The description of *a worship-first* and *a serving-first journey* comes out of reflection on the story to date of fresh expressions in Britain. But we are still at an early stage. Two reservations may be in order. First, though the distinction between the two journeys appears neat and clear, real life is more complicated. Some initiatives look as if they fall between the two.

Thirst Cafe Church, for example, grew out of relationships formed among parents at St Philips Primary School, Romsey Town, Cambridge. In 2006, 30 people who did not attend church gathered over refreshments in the school lounge. They watched a Rob Bell Nooma DVD, after which a discussion spontaneously began. A few months later, a weekly prayer time was offered, comprising a five-minute talk, followed by discussion on a biblical theme and a spiritual exercise or activity of some kind. A weekly Bible study has since been introduced, incorporating a simple Holy Communion (www. freshexpressions.org.uk/stories). Work:space offers half-hour sessions of 'quiet and contemplative spirituality' in several locations in Poole, Dorset (www.freshexpressions.org.uk/stories).

Are these versions of *a serving-first journey*, following its basic dynamics – listening to the context, finding a way to serve people (by engaging with their spiritual longings), drawing them into community, encouraging individuals to explore the possibility of following Jesus and allowing church to take shape around those who come into faith? Or will they prove to be a distinct category, sharing *worship-first's* explicit focus on Jesus at the beginning but *serving-first's* missional dynamics? In time, might we come to recognize a number of different journeys?

Second, is the assumption that *a serving-first journey* will become the default option among the never-churched unduly pessimistic about the potential of sensitive worship to connect with such people? There is some anecdotal evidence (such as New Song Cafe in Warrington) that initiatives which start with missional worship can be a route into faith for such people, and it may be that a growing number of such churches will be birthed in this way.

A serving-first journey

- seems to describe much of what we are observing;
- can help founding teams to know what to expect and thereby help move the journey on;
- can be combined with *a worship-first journey* to reproduce church at scale and depth;
- enables mission to integrate loving service with evangelism and to connect church to life;
- has emerged from a process of ongoing reflection.

Conclusion

A *worship-first journey* and *a serving-first journey* provide two ways for pioneer teams to discuss how their new church is unfolding. They are not the only paths an emerging church might take, nor should one be seen as always more fruitful than another. They are appropriate for different contexts – the first mainly among people with a church background who are open to returning, and the second mainly among those who are further away from church. In some contexts the two can be fruitfully combined.

A *serving-first journey* can be commended as:

- A *conversational device*: Along with *a worship-first journey*, it is a useful input into the conversations of pioneer teams. It can help a team clarify its intentions and strategy.
- A *missional necessity*: As more people grow up disconnected from church, approaches that start with 'listening' and then proceed via 'loving and serving' and 'building community' could well become the church-start strategy of choice, but we need more research-based evidence to be sure.
- A *theological preference*: A case has been made that *a serving-first journey* is theologically desirable. The *journey* accents loving and serving as the first thing a founding community must do, after listening. This fits with Jesus' prioritizing of the command to love. It ensures that the other person is treated as an object of love rather than merely as an object of evangelism. It illustrates how social action and evangelism can go hand in hand. Might the model be a significant *theological* input into the conversations of founding communities?

Further reading

Glasson, Barbara, *Mixed-up Blessing: A New Encounter with Being Church*, Peterborough: Inspire, 2006.

Morisy, Ann, *Journeying Out: A New Approach to Christian Mission*, London: Morehouse, 2004.

Stone, Bryan, *Evangelism after Christendom: The Theology and Practice of Christian Witness*, Grand Rapids, MI: Brazos Press, 2007.

Questions for discussion

- Which of the two journeys described here comes closer to your experiences of contextual church?
- What variations on the two journeys are you aware of or can you imagine?
- What different leadership gifts are required for each journey?

12

Gathering a Mission Community

Churches can be brought to birth in a host of ways – from traditional church planting to edgy pioneering and from the launch of large-scale congregations to the emergence of micro churches. The last chapter proposed two models for how, in all their variety, contextual churches emerge. The models are an outworking of the contention that, wherever possible, mission should be undertaken in community.

This and the next four chapters explore five sets of methodologies that can aid this birthing of contextual church.

Gathering the mission community
Researching opportunities
Engaging partners
Action-based learning
Team awareness

These are not usually a sequence. They are most likely to weave in and out of each other. Pulling them apart as distinct methodologies, however, can help in understanding what good practice might involve.

Chapters 12 to 16 diverge from the life-cycle framework for church planting, which has been highly influential in the United States. First developed by Bob Logan (Logan and Ogne, 1991), the framework has been expanded to eight stages – conception, pregnancy, preparing for birth, birth (when public worship is first held), infancy, adolescence, maturity and reproduction.[1] It contains check lists of what should happen at each stage, which is a strength, but fails to describe adequately the underlying social dynamics. The framework is also too linear. It suggests there are discrete stages in developing a new church, whereas the experience of many church founders is that apparent stages may overlap and occur out of sequence.

The chapters also differ from the growing number of case studies that suggest approaches to starting and growing specific types of church, such as Neil Cole on the organic church (2005) and Mike Breen and Alex Absalom (2010) on

---

1 www.acpi.org.uk. The version in Malphurs (2004) has six stages: conception, development, birth, growth, maturity, reproduction.

mid-sized communities. The five sets of methodologies described here are intended to apply in varying ways to a wide range of contextual churches.

Recognizing that we have much to learn, the methodologies suggested in this and the next four chapters should be regarded as hypotheses, to be tested by experience and research. To a significant extent, they are adapted from the literature on business and social entrepreneurship. For some, the term 'entrepreneur' speaks of building things, seeing new possibilities and making things happen. Resonances exist between secular and church entrepreneurship (Bolton, 2006). To others such as John Milbank (2008), the term would be tainted with overtones of market capitalism and the pursuit of profit. They would emphasize the distinctive witness of the church. The reality is that the potential crossovers and differences between entrepreneurship and church pioneering are largely unexplored.[2] So the descriptions in these chapters must be viewed as provisional.

This chapter is about the gathering of the mission community, which is the team that forms the core of the new initiative. It is the team through which the Spirit practices 'mission in community' and makes concrete the theological argument of Chapter 7. The term is not to be confused with 'missional communities', used by Breen and Absalom (2010), which I refer to as mid-sized communities and can be understood as one type of contextual church.

Mission communities are the teams that found contextual churches. They vary in size, from a couple of people to a church planting team of 50 or more. They may form with the intention of giving birth to a contextual church, or acquire the intention as church begins to emerge around them. Their boundaries may be well defined or fluid. Though mission community has a clear definition here, the reality is often more messy.

This chapter argues that identity formation is at the heart of gathering the mission community. After discussing two theoretical approaches, it explores this theme in relation to the processes of gathering – the emergence of a mission leader, a mission community, a mission call, a mission focus (the people the new church will serve) and of mission values. Identity formation ties these processes together. In the space available, the chapter does no more than point to some of the theological implications.

Two theoretical approaches

Gathering is about forming a mission community with an agreed purpose. It can be approached from two theoretical standpoints.

---

2 Bolton begins briefly to open up the field with his discussion of the church's entrepreneurial heritage and 'the kingdom entrepreneur' (2006, pp. 5–7, 23–5). Alan Hirsch and Tim Catchin (2012) explore entrepreneurship theory quite extensively, but their book was published after my manuscript went to print.

Rational choice

The first is a rational choice perspective. This is implicit in much of the church planting literature, which deals with a number of the processes described here as gathering, such as the selection of the leader, recruiting a team and developing team values. On this view, individuals make rational choices about these matters. After prayerfully weighing up the advantages and disadvantages, they make decisions that will most benefit the initiative. A church selects the most suitable person to head up the new plant, for example. The literature is designed to provide practical advice. A weakness is that it pays little attention to the influence of social context and relational networks.

The argument here is that gathering is a social process involving the negotiation of identity. This fits with the increased attention sociologists have paid to identity over the past quarter of a century. Influenced by writers like Anthony Giddens (1991), sociologists tend to see identity not as basically fixed, but as a narrative that emerges in the context of social interaction. Through relationships with other people, an individual's sense of self evolves over time. Identity is 'a *formative practice* whereby individuals tell stories of who they are' (Ozkazanc-Pan, 2009, p. 15, author's italics).

In recent years, entrepreneurship has been understood as a process of identity construction (Hoang and Gimeno, 2010, pp. 41–53), and it is not unreasonable to adopt a similar approach to contextual church. Founding a new Christian community – whether large or small, intentional or accidental, formal or informal – is a significant activity for the people involved. So it is bound to affect how they see themselves. Associating perhaps with new people and engaging in a new initiative will to an extent redefine them as individuals. One person's self-perception will rub against another's as the mission community emerges and individuals negotiate its purpose. Individuals' sense of who they are will evolve in the process.

Though identity formation continues throughout the mission community's life, it is especially important in the gathering process and virtually defines it. Gathering can be understood as three identity voyages – the one taken by the leader, the one taken by individuals who join the mission community, and the voyage the mission community takes as it clarifies its call, focus and values.

Identity voyages

Taking this role of identity seriously, the suggestion is that during the gathering process, mission communities come into being with members whose personal identities undergo a transition ('the identity voyage'). These identities evolve from 'starting identities' by way of 'possible identities' to become 'contextual church identities'.

Four ways of understanding the process of identity formation among entrepreneurs

- The *individualistic* approach concentrates on the impact of the individual's personal traits and experience. Applied to the church, for example, what influence does the emerging leader's character and background have on the decision to become a church founder? This ignores, however, the roles of context and relationships in identity.
- The *positivist* view sees the context as a discrete influence. How does, say, the rhetoric of pioneering in the Church of England shape an individual's self-perception as a potential church founder? The influence is one way – from the context to the person. But this pays insufficient attention to how individuals interpret and respond to their contexts.
- The *'reproductionist'* view asks how, in the process of developing their identities, individuals 'reproduce' influences from the external world. Reproduction occurs as individuals interpret these external influences in the light of their situations. The external context can be 'reproduced' in a variety of ways, depending on individuals' construction of their social worlds. So an individual can reinterpret the idea of pioneering. Yet this begs the question of how individuals construct their worlds in the first place.
- An *'interactionist'* (or 'conversational') approach sees the formation of identity as a pluralistic process. Identities and social worlds emerge as individuals negotiate the meaning of their experiences in the social communities to which they belong. The emerging leader's decision to start a church is bound up with the decisions of others to help. These decisions emerge through a series of conversations with different people in a variety of settings. Not just the leader, but all the conversation partners give meaning to the idea of pioneering through their interactions. Each person brings to these conversations patterns of thought, including their self-image, which have emerged from all their previous conversations and will be shaped again through the current one. As these identities-in-process engage with one another, the external context (as understood through conversations) becomes merely one influence on the here and now.

Source: Based on Down and Reveley (2004, pp. 235–7).

The individual's identity voyage

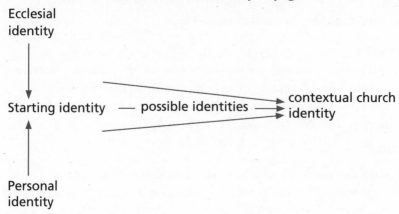

An individual's starting identity is the person's self-image before they begin to explore their involvement in a contextual church. It includes their 'ecclesial identity' (how they see themselves in their existing church setting) and their 'personal identity' (how they see themselves in their family, friendship and work settings). There will be varying degrees of overlap between the two. Contextual church identities are the way individuals see themselves once they have begun to help in bringing a contextual church to birth.

When individuals explore whether to be involved in starting a contextual church, they prayerfully test out in their minds what this would mean for them. They imagine a whole range of 'possible identities', trying them on for size, tinkering with them, discarding outdated images and coming to grips with information that challenges these possible selves. They are like shoppers trying on clothes – what would I look like in this, or in that? How would they fit with the sort of person I am? What would my family and friends think? Through imagining possible selves, individuals may come to see themselves in a new light.

Possible identities represent not what someone is but what he or she could become. They are aspired to but not yet realized identities (Farmer, Yao and Kung-Mcintyre, 2011, pp. 247–8). They are possible future selves that the individual envisages. A person often has multiple possible selves. Individuals are not single selves that evolve. They are many selves, and these multiple identities exist not only in the past and present, but also in the future. Individuals carry in their heads a whole cast of characters that they hope to become or fear becoming (Ibarra, 2004, pp. 35–9).

A key part of the identity voyage is the construction of one or more possible identities – what sort of person would the individual be if they helped with a contextual church? What different roles might they play? Can they see themselves in any of these roles? Is this the sort of person they want to be? Is it consistent with who they are now – with how their friends see them? How does it relate to their church tradition? Whereas someone's contextual church identity is the actual self helping a contextual church to emerge and flourish, a possible identity is the imagined self in that situation. If the individual is considering a variety of options for the future, possible identities in relation to the proposed church may exist alongside these other possible selves.

During the gathering process, three sets of identity voyages occur. First, there is the transition made by the leader. This comprises the recognition of a call to start a church (which leads to an identity based on the call) and the recognition of that call by potential followers, during which the call – and the identity based on it – may be modified.

Second, anyone who joins the mission community undertakes an identity voyage. Through conversations with friends, others who might be involved and so on, prospective members of the mission community develop and refine their possible identities in relation to the proposed initiative. Some people will reject their possible identities and decide not to join the mission community: 'This is not the sort of person I am/want to be.' Others will embrace one of their possible selves and become members.

The third identity voyage is undertaken by the mission community, which prayerfully travels a similar journey. Its starting identity consists of the personal identities of its members. Through discussion centring especially on the nature of mission (its mission call), whom the community is to serve and be served by (its mission focus), and its mission values, members of the community construct a series of possible identities for the community as a whole.

These are shared (or disputed) views on what it might mean for the community to initiate a contextual church. 'We could work with the teenagers on the estate, or we could focus on their parents.' Through discussion, some of these possible identities will be put to one side, while others will be explored further. When the community broadly agrees about its call, focus and values, these possible identities will evolve into the community's contextual church identity, which will continue to develop thereafter.

The mission community's identity voyage

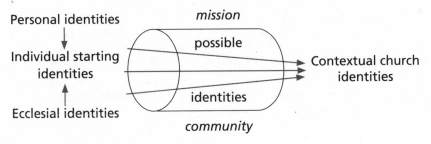

227

The ease with which these three identity voyages are made depends significantly on the distance between starting identities and how contextual church identities are imagined in possible identities. If individuals are to engage with the initiative, a degree of congruence must exist between how they see themselves now and the sort of persons they would become if they got involved.

The greater the distance, the less likely the voyage will take place – for example, when someone is invited to help with an initiative run by people from a very different Christian tradition. Especially important is the distance between individuals' starting identities and the context of the proposed church. Can individuals see themselves in that setting? If it involves crossing cultures, are individuals able to identify wholeheartedly with the different culture?

This initial shot at conceptualizing what happens during the gathering process is a model. Like all models it is an abstraction and generalization. The model will take a variety of shapes according to circumstances. For instance, if the founder initially gathers a core of one or two people who are not Christians, possible identities and contextual church identities will most likely not be understood in terms of starting a church. They will be conceived as helping the founder or joining a project.

Likewise, if the mission community has no clear-cut membership (anyone for example can come to the weekly shared meal where the initiative is discussed), the mission community's identity voyage will be more fluid. The voyage may primarily occur among the de facto core – the two or three people who are regularly present – even though the core is not recognized as a distinct team. Other people will get caught up in the core's journey as they attend the meals.

Understanding these identity voyages can help individuals to be more intentional about the processes involved – to reflect on factors influencing their possible identities and to evaluate them theologically: 'I'm holding back because of what my friends might think. But what does God think?' In a mixed-economy context, recognizing these dynamics will help those in authority to be realistic about the complexities of gathering a team and the timescales involved. Paying attention to identity processes will assist mission communities in steering the initiative in a healthy direction.

The central theological issue is the length of identity voyages. How far are individuals and mission communities willing to travel from their starting identities to identifying with the people they seek to serve – to engaging in mission that is contextual through and through? The issue will re-emerge in the rest of the chapter, as we consider the identity voyages of the leader, members of the mission community and of the community itself (as members discusses their call, focus and values).

> **Both individuals and the mission community make identity voyages, which involve**
>
> - a starting identity, comprising ecclesial and personal identities;
> - possible identities, which are imagined pictures of the self (or the community) helping to birth the proposed contextual church;
> - a contextual church identity, which is the self (or the community) concretely helping to birth the church; it continues to evolve.

The emerging leader

The start of the gathering process is the recognition of a leader. The leader can be described as a pioneer, church planter, founder or go by some other title. Whatever the label, a new contextual church has to be led by someone – usually with a team. Leaders emerge as they undertake an identity voyage, which has two phases. The phases may occur in a sequence or overlap – sometimes substantially.

Recognition of a call

The first entails the recognition of the founder's call to start a contextual church. This involves a shift from the person's starting identity to a new identity, based on their sense of call. This new 'founder identity' is how the person imagines responding to their call. The voyage starts with a process of *disengagement* from the individual's current church involvement.[3] The person thinks about taking on something new in the church, or perhaps feels a growing dissatisfaction with existing church. He or she begins psychologically to disengage with what they are doing in church.

It is followed by a period of prayerful *exploration*, during which the individual toys with a variety of possible identities, such as joining a different church, being ordained, founding a church in the person's spare time and becoming a full-time church pioneer. During this exploration, the individual crafts some trial narratives to explain why he or she is changing (and what stays the same) and to try on various possibilities.

There will also be a process of *confirmation*. This may come through the comments of friends, encounters with God in personal devotions or worship, or through divine 'coincidences'. Often there will be an institutional dimension. A local church or group of churches may recognize that a lay person is called to start a new church. Or the person may feel called to ordination, and go through a selection and training process.

---

3 The concepts used here are taken from Ibarra (2004, p. 55).

Four things may complicate the process. The first is the existence of stereotypes. The rhetoric of pioneering, common in fresh expressions circles, may conjure up pictures of 'baggy shorts, bushy moustaches and manly struggles with alligators' (Moore, 2011, p. 95). Women in particular may be put off by an over-masculine view of what starting a contextual church involves. Other stereotypes may be that starting church is a full-time job, that you have to be ordained, that you need a certain type of personality (see Box), that it all depends on the leader (but what about the team?) and that it involves a Sunday gathering with a building. Such stereotypes are imbibed from the person's church involvement and so form part of the individual's starting identity. They can make it difficult to hear God's unique call to the person.

A second complication can be the person's home church. The latter may try to hang on to the founder (and perhaps to members of the team he or she may be starting to gather). Mother churches are sometimes reluctant to release leaders and team members, expecting them to continue with some form of ministry in the home church. Or they try to retain control over what the new church will look like ('it must have our DNA'), thereby constraining how far it can adapt to the context. This may narrow the

---

Can you define a church pioneer?

It is often assumed that church founders emerge on the basis of their personal qualities. The founder has a latent self with the gifts and experiences to start a contextual church. Through a process of discernment, this latent self is called into being. Charles Ridley's list of 13 characteristics of an effective church planter, which has been much used in North America, exemplifies this view (Ridley, 1988). So do Bolton and Thompson (2004) in relation to entrepreneurs. They have suggested that a combination of 'talent, temperament and technique' characterize potential entrepreneurs.

However, reviews of the entrepreneurship literature suggest that it will be difficult to equate pioneering with specific personal attributes:

1 *Entrepreneurship is a team process.* It involves a variety of activities such as being able to spot opportunities, find creative solutions to problems, mobilize support for an idea, organize practical steps to implement the idea and much else (Deakins and Freel, 2009, pp. 135–7). It requires one or more teams rather than a single person. Entrepreneurs (or leaders) can contribute to the team in many different ways, depending on their capabilities and personal traits.

2 *Entrepreneurship is highly contextual.* Different contexts will require different skills and aptitudes. Being entrepreneurial in the voluntary sector will be different to the commercial world. A start-up phase may require different skills than consolidation (Deakins and Freel, 2009, p. 13).

3 *Entrepreneurial ability may be widespread in the general population*, but remain latent because circumstances do not draw it out. Focusing on entrepreneurial traits may create stereotypes that potential entrepreneurs cannot identify with, and wrongly suggest that only a small minority can be entrepreneurs (Rae, 2007, pp. 28–9).

4 *Researchers have failed to identify a widely accepted list of entrepreneurial traits* (with the possible exception of self-efficacy). They prefer to concentrate on the cognitive processes needed to undertake specific tasks, and which can be learned (Kirby, 2003, p. 116; Mitchelmore and Rowley, 2010).

It may also be premature to define church pioneers as 'being the first to do or see something', 'on the edge', 'disturbers of the peace' and 'bicultural' (Lings, 2011, pp. 33, 39). Such statements may encourage stereotypes that help some people to identify with pioneering but put others off. What does 'being the first to do or see something' actually mean? Is it the first to connect cafe and church? Is it the first to start cafe church in a district? If so, how big is the district? How would we describe the second person to start cafe church in the area? Are they not a pioneer, even if they are serving a different group of people? How 'original' does a person have to be?

Rather than recruiting church founders on the basis of a presumed set of pioneering characteristics, one possibility may be to design posts that can be filled by individuals who have demonstrated four essential qualities. Founders with these qualities would be asked to start a church in ways that fit their capabilities and the context. These qualities would include being:

- *grounded spiritually* – having a faithful walk with God
- *gatherers of people* – being able to gather a team and help to attract round it the people the team serves;
- *gifted in drawing out others* – being aware of their limitations, able to involve people with complementary gifts and willing to release them to use their gifts;
- *a good fit for the culture* – being at home in the context because they either come from the same/similar culture or are gifted in cross-cultural mission.

range of possibilities the individual explores. The Spirit could be calling the person to pioneer in a way the home church does not expect.

Third, the person may feel swamped by the range of possibilities. To reduce the stress, he or she may plump for one too quickly and fail to explore others that could be helpful. Perhaps the person assumes they have to be ordained and ignores the lay alternatives (or vice versa). Being ordained draws the person away from starting church where they are and among people they already know, which might have been the ideal setting.[4]

Fourth, individuals may experience a dissonance between their starting and possible identities. If this becomes too great to bear, individuals may break with their starting identities too firmly. They may reject their past ecclesial life to such an extent that they become over-negative toward it: they become highly critical of existing church, which strains their relationships with it and possibly closes down a potential source of future support.

Alternatively, individuals may hang on to their starting identities too tightly. They develop narratives that are highly congruent with their existing identities. They imagine the new church in terms that borrow heavily from their existing church experience, making contextualization more difficult. The identity voyage feels less frightening because the destination appears familiar. Or perhaps the person belongs to a church that identifies with a mode of church planting involving large teams. The person crafts a narrative around leading such a team. But circumstances may make recruiting a big team difficult. Instead of exploring possibilities using a small team, the person gives up the idea, deciding the time is not right.

Being aware of such issues will enable potential leaders – and those who advise them – to be alert to possible complications. These can then become matters of reflection, prayer and careful management. Stereotypes can be gently challenged. Someone who feels overwhelmed by their possible identities can be invited to narrow down the options, but not too drastically. A person who struggles with the dissonance between their starting and possible identities can be invited to ask what God might be saying through the tension, or allow time to grow accustomed to it.

Recognition by followers

The first phase of recognition is complete when individuals finish exploring possible identities and recognize that they are called to take the lead in founding a contextual church. Possible identities are narrowed down to a founder identity. Even though it has been confirmed by others in the church,

---

4 Though there are plenty examples of this, there are also a growing number of opportunities for ordination training to take places in situ, on a part-time course, which can help to avoid the problem.

this is only an identity in the person's mind. It does not in itself make the person a leader. The individual only becomes a leader when others follow, when they offer to help. This emergence of the leader through decisions to follow is the next, possibly overlapping phase of the leader's identity voyage.

Decisions to follow are taken as individuals meet and talk with the potential leader (and others). Some people will affirm the person's identity as leader by offering to join in, while others will walk away. Individuals prayerfully weighing up whether to support the potential leader will construct images of themselves in the initiative. They will imagine themselves working with the leader. They will ask how well these possible identities fit with their starting identities – with their ecclesial identities for example. Does the potential leader come from the same spiritual tradition? They will also consider the possible match with their personal identities – the people they are in their family, friendship and occupational networks. 'What would others whose views I value think if I joined this person?'

At the same time, emerging leaders will ask how far each potential follower fits with their hopes for the venture and their spiritual values. They will also continue to experience the pull of their starting identities – expectations from their church, home and other backgrounds. (Starting identities can never be fully left behind.) In addition, as they explore the context, they will experience the pull of the people they are called to serve. They may be torn in three directions–The expectations of potential followers, the leader's own starting identity, and the mission context.

Perhaps the founder favours a laid-back style of leadership, but the people offering to help want something more directive. Maybe also the leader and potential members of the mission community come from professional and managerial-type backgrounds, and expect the leadership team to be clearly recognized and have formal meetings. But the people they are called to serve have more fluid, informal and participative expectations: anyone should be able to take part in the decisions. The founder may have to work with the emerging mission community to reconcile these different sets of expectations. They may have to re-evaluate their founder identities in the light of these pulls. They will do so by trying out possible identities. The process culminates in contextual church identities, which is how the leaders see themselves as they start to birth their new churches.

No wonder founders can find the gathering process quite fraught! They will be helped if those who support them – prayer partners, institutional authorities, family and friends – understand some of these tensions. Coaches and others may want to encourage the founder to recognize what is going on and prayerfully negotiate a way through. As founders try out possible identities that might resolve the tensions, they may have to re-evaluate their own expectations. For example, if it is taking a long time to gather a mission community, founders might ask whether they are hanging on to their founder identities – how they imagine their call – too tightly. Are they are putting potential members off? Perhaps someone's founder identity centres on a specific vision for the initiative. Does sticking to this betray an unhelpful lack of flexibility? Or is it faithfulness to one's call?

The emergence of a founder

- The private recognition of the person's call involves an identity voyage – from a starting identity, through possible identities, to a founder's identity (how the person imagines responding to their call).
- The public recognition of the person's call involves a second identity voyage, in which the founder identity may have to be modified as followers gather and in the light of the context.
- Private and public recognition may be sequential stages or overlap.

Forming the mission community

Central to the gathering process is drawing together a mission community. The mission community comprises 'two or more people possessing a common social identification and whose existence as a group is recognized by a third party' (Brown, 2000, p. 19). It brings a contextual church to birth and leads its development. God's comment, 'It is not good that the man should be alone' (Gen. 2.18), applies as much to starting contextual churches as to any human activity.

Traditional church planting has tended to rely on relatively large teams – from a dozen people to 50 or more. This can work well if the envisaged church will be in a network or area where the church already has a strong presence and if it will be drawn from the friends and contacts of team members. The larger the team, the more points of contact it will have. These contacts make it likely that the team will be reaching people with a similar culture to its own.

Where the church is not well represented, a gap is likely to exist between the church and the people concerned. A large team will contain centripetal dynamics that will make it difficult to bridge this gap. The team may develop a preferred style of worship, for example, that is out of sync with the culture of the people it is called to. A smaller team, however, will find it easier to adapt to the context. As it works with people coming into faith, it can adapt its worshipping life to fit the setting.

Small mission communities will look different in different contexts – for example:

- two or three friends who want to serve people in their neighbourhood, leisure centre or workplace;

- an interest group or prayer group that finds itself serving others and becoming unexpectedly a new expression of church;
- a close-knit team that is gathered by a practitioner as his or her work develops;
- a fluid group that gathers over a regular meal to which anyone is invited. An unofficial core of two or three people is always present and comprises the mission community as understood here;
- a dispersed network of support for a practitioner. One person on a new housing estate had a prayer group, a practical support group with financial and other expertise, some friends to cry and laugh with, a nearby church where she worshipped, a spiritual director (to which one might add a coach or mentor), and as the work gathered pace, leaders of mums and toddlers and other groups she had helped to start.

Gathering the community

Research into entrepreneurial teams has found that the two dominant influences on team recruitment are homophily and familiarity (Aldrich, 2008, pp. 9–11). Homophily refers to the tendency of individuals to associate and bond with similar others. 'Like attracts like.' Familiarity refers to the ties that exist between people, such as through work or family. 'Your friend is my friend.' These processes are so ingrained in human behaviour that they are bound to shape the formation of mission communities.

They highlight the crucial role of identity. 'Like attracts like' and 'your friend is my friend' are two of the processes through which individuals construct their identities. 'One of the major consequences of becoming a member of a group is a change in the way we see ourselves. Joining a group often requires us to redefine who we are, which in turn may have implications for our self-esteem' (Brown 2000, p. 28).

Just as there are two overlapping phases in founders' identity voyages, often members of a mission community also experience two phases in their voyages. The first culminates in the decision to join the mission community.

An individual's identity voyage

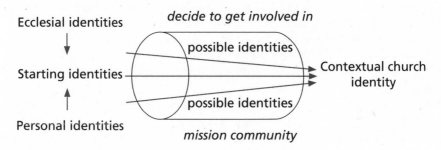

The second is complete when the community is broadly agreed about its purpose and values.

When individuals join the mission community, they have not yet arrived at their contextual church identities (how they see themselves as they start to birth the new church). Through the community's conversations about its purpose and values, individuals will continue to try out possible identities in relation to the imagined outcomes of the discussions. 'If we agreed this, what would it mean for my involvement? What sort of community would this be and how would I feel about it?'

Each person's possible identity in relation to the community will bump up against the possible identities of other members. Indeed, much of the community's discussions will involve negotiating these identities. As the community's purpose and values are clarified and accepted, individuals will see more clearly how they fit it. Thus once they have joined the mission community, individuals' identity voyages will become part and parcel of the community's identity voyage.

The decision to join

Deciding whether to join and remain in the mission community involves three dynamics. One is the strength and nature of individuals' starting identities. Potential members will ask whether they can see themselves making a contribution to the community. They will think about who belongs to it and these people's ideas for the initiative. They will weigh up whether the mission community is too distant from their own starting identities for them to join, or whether it is congruent with them.

Does the community fit with their spiritual tradition (or help them stand out from it)? Is it consistent with how they see themselves in their personal networks – the sort of people they mix with, for example, or the type of activity their friends respect? If they get involved, will they have to make a new set of friends in the context the proposed church will serve? Will this draw them away from their existing friends, and are they prepared for this?

A second dynamic is the way that prospective members construct and test their possible identities. Testing what it might mean to take part in the initiative may include entering into a trial membership of the mission community. This can lead to misunderstanding if others in the community fail to realize this is a trial and think the person has made a commitment. Some mission communities avoid this danger by the obvious device of assuming that everyone initially belongs on a trial basis, [5] or by having a loose understanding of membership whereby individuals are free to come and go.

---

5 An example can be found on www.freshexpressions.org.uk/stories/authentic. Team members are expected to be part of the community for a year before they commit.

A third dynamic centres on how prospective members prayerfully reach a conclusion. They will be sensitive to two barometers (Ibarra, 2004, p. 62). One will be an external gauge, based on the feedback from people around. Do they feel welcomed by the mission community, or are they picking up signals they would not fit in? How are their friends and family reacting to their possible involvement? Would joining enhance or diminish their standing among people who matter to them?

The other barometer will be an internal gauge: Does involvement feel right? Would involvement square sufficiently with the core spiritual beliefs that are part of the individual's starting identity? Can the person envisage not only belonging to the mission community, but being comfortable with the type of mission involved and the context in which the mission will take place?

Leaders and others in the community will be wise to pay attention to these dynamics, so as to help individuals navigate their identity voyages. A well-placed question, for instance, may uncover a person's concern that their spiritual outlook differs from others in the community. This could lead to an honest discussion about members' spiritual 'bottom lines', which might reveal fundamental differences. It may be better for the person to leave the community, with its blessing, than to run the risk that these differences will disrupt the community's work later on.

Some dangers

Problems may arise if members of the mission community are unable to voyage some distance from their starting identities. This does not mean that they will abandon these identities completely (as if that was feasible). But if they fail to develop significantly new identities, the mission community may encounter difficulties later.

A particular danger is that individuals – and hence the mission community – retain an inherited church mindset. Members envisage a church they are used to rather than one that fits the context.

> Congregation is the concrete in which our cultural conception of church is set . . . Congregation is used here in the sense that in our minds this word carries so many of the assumptions about church as a religious event, in a special building, on one day of the week, with a predetermined pattern of activities, leadership and involvement (or lack of it). This concept of church, like any mindset, is subconsciously held through a deep process of socialization and teaching. (Hopkins, 2008, pp. 12–3)

A second danger is that members' friendships remain primarily with their existing networks. This may be a good thing if the networks of members overlap, are similar and if the mission community intends to start the church among them. On the other hand, it may be a problem if the networks are very diverse; individuals from them may be too different to form a viable community. Existing friendships can also become a problem if the intention is to serve a group of people who are not existing friends. There may have to be some loosening of ties so that the mission community's members have time to develop relationships with the people they are called to.

A third danger is that members' personal networks are weighted towards people who have recently left church. Given that like attracts like, unless members 'travel' some distance from these networks, an initiative among the 'once-churched twice shy' may be more likely than among people who have never been to church. Members may have starting identities grounded in their disillusionment with church, and construct possible identities based on being church with others having similar experiences. Unless they intentionally avoid doing so, they will be inclined to gather round them others who are also disillusioned. Disillusionment rather than missional engagement may become the mark of the new church.

Fourth, individuals whose starting identities are moulded by heavy pastoral needs may identify with the mission community in the hope that it will better meet their needs than their existing congregations. They may develop possible identities that envisage their needs being met through involvement with the proposed church. The risk is that these pastoral problems become a distraction, consuming time that the community could have spent on its mission task.

Understanding the risks of not leaving behind starting identities will encourage founders to be explicit about the purpose of the proposed church. This will help individuals to construct realistic possible identities rather than fantasy ones. Reflecting on his seven-year experience of pioneering a church on Northampton's Grange Park housing estate, Charlie Noble commented

If I had communicated a clearer sense of the vision – particularly the focus on Grange Park residents and the fact that the new church would be primarily a church for them, not the dream church of the planting team members – perhaps things may have been easier. Seven years on, only Richard and his two sons remain from the starting team (other than my own family) . . . quite a number left under a bit of a cloud: their expressed reasons were varied but underlying them was the fact that this was not the church they had hoped it would become. (Male, 2011, p. 27)

Four dangers

- Inherited church mindset
- Existing friendships get in the way
- Starting identities are weighted toward disillusioned church leavers
- Starting identities are shaped by heavy pastoral needs

Understanding these processes will also encourage mission communities to avoid being too prescriptive about the gifts they require. Volunteers with needed gifts may be unavailable because they are not in members' networks (familiarity), or they may be unwilling to help because they believe they would not fit in (homophily), or they may be willing to help but are clinging unhelpfully to their starting identities. The distance between starting identities and the initiative is too great.

In these circumstances, recruitment strategies based on 'who' before 'what' may make sense. Is God bringing someone who will be a reliable colleague, and whose preferred possible identity is compatible with the community's emerging vision for the people it seeks to serve and be served by? These attributes may be more important than having the specific gifts the community hoped for. God may use someone with the right personal qualities and a congruent identity, but unsought gifts, to take the community in a surprising yet fruitful direction. Being open to this recognizes the force of identity in the gathering process and works with it.

Who before what?

Practitioners and mission communities might want to look for colleagues who are

- *Faithful* – passionate about their faith and inspired by the Great Commission (Matt. 29.19–20).
- *Available* – They can offer time. They know pioneering can be hard work and discouraging, but they make it a priority.
- *Conscientious* – They work hard. They are reliable. They don't let others down. Often they are unsung heroes – 'She always puts out the chairs'.
- *Teachable* – willing to learn from Scripture, the pioneer context and their colleagues.
- *Servant-hearted* – Willingness to serve the context is the basis of a mission heart.

Source: adapted from Robinson (2007, pp. 42, 46).

Hearing a mission call

As individuals join the mission community, they will join the community's voyage from its starting identity, via possible identities (conceptions of what the community will be like and how it will go about its task) to its contextual church identity (what the community becomes as it helps take forward the initiative). The community's starting identity will consist of the variety of expectations individuals bring with them into the community. These identities will jostle with each other, gradually fuse into a number of possible identities and eventually emerge, refashioned as the community's contextual church identity. The latter will be viewed somewhat differently by each member.

Intrinsic to this journey will be the growth of a shared understanding of the mission call, not least its theological nature. This understanding may emerge through discussion of such matters as the importance of mission to God, the nature of church and the rationale for contextual church. Or it may evolve implicitly and, indeed, remain beneath the surface. Assumptions about the mission call may be shared, even though they are barely discussed. Overt discussion will enable agreement to be negotiated explicitly and avoid differences exploding later, perhaps in circumstances that make them harder to resolve.

A key aspect of the mission call is a willingness to put aside preconceptions and listen to God through the context. For example, often a mission community's members know that in some settings the church must be different. But because it can be hard to imagine what being different means, they hold on to an example they have seen or heard about: 'Let's do messy church'. (Messy Church is a highly creative expression of all-age church in which parents, carers and children eat together, express their creativity, experience worship and have fun together outside Sunday worship, but within a church context. See Moore, 2006.) The example speaks to them because it is exciting and vivid, and they develop possible identities in relation to it.

Part of the process of being called to help found a contextual church is to let the Spirit fill out this understanding. The Spirit takes individuals beyond their initial perception that church must be different to seeing how church could be different for the people the mission community is called to serve. Their imaginations expand from 'this is how church could be fresh' to 'this is how it could be fresh *for them* (including "us")'.

An identity voyage is involved. The mission community starts by thinking in terms of a model – 'they did it over there, so let's do it here' – but this ignores differences in context. Stories of what others have done then become valued not as models to be copied, but as sources of inspiration (see Box). The next step, ideally, is to discover what contributed to the fruitfulness of these ventures (or perhaps disappointments). Themes might emerge from several stories as the mission community asks, 'Are there some principles that we might learn from? How do these principles embody the kingdom? How might we apply these principles in our context?' The community moves from imitating a model, to being inspired by a story, to reflecting on the story. It begins to practise theological reflection.

Stories of other contextual churches can be sources of

- *Encouragement* – 'They felt daunted like we do, but kept pushing on.'
- *Legitimacy* – 'If they can develop a completely different way of being church, why can't we?'
- *Confidence* – 'They had no training and track record to begin with, but learnt what they needed to know as they went along. Can't we do the same?'
- *Ideas* – 'Messy church would never work round here, but it's given me an idea . . .'
- *Warnings* – 'Don't make the mistakes we did.'

Undertaking this voyage need not mean abandoning someone's original idea. The Spirit may keep alive a vision for messy church, but enable the church to take shape in ways that were never expected. But it could be that the Spirit wants the vision to lapse so that a different one can emerge. Maybe the Spirit wants to replace the person's – or group's – love for an idea ('Messy church would be great') with an even greater love for the people the community is to serve ('Their real need is for . . .').

The voyage may be quite straightforward, or it may involve a wrench. The original idea may be associated with the community's ecclesial or personal networks (or both). Perhaps the congregation where some members recently worshipped has run a fruitful messy church. Or some of the members' friends or relatives are involved in one. Through these ties, members may have a personal stake in this way of being church. Messy church is closely bound up with their starting identities. Letting their possible identities travel some distance from their starting identities may not be easy.

Yet this aspect of members' starting identities may have to fall away so that their possible identities can grow in new ways. Individuals may have to give up their initial images of how they would be involved in the new church in favour of the desires, longings and aspirations of the people they seek to serve. The community's possible identities will be allied more closely to the context.

Bringing to the surface the processes involved in this identity voyage may help the community to navigate the journey. As the processes are subject to scrutiny and theological evaluation, individuals may be encouraged to detach themselves from their starting identities and to identify more closely with Jesus. Identifying with his heart of love may enable them, through the Spirit, to identify more closely with the people they are called to serve.

In particular, identifying with his willingness to be crucified so that others can live may help them to allow elements of their starting identities to die so that new possible identities can come alive – identities that have serving others at their heart. Through the Spirit, dying to live is the engine that moves the mission community from its starting identity to a healthy contextual church identity. It enables a truly contextual church to be born.

Developing a mission focus

If forming the mission community involves being willing to move away from starting identities and hearing the mission call requires dying to live, developing a mission focus entails reaching the contextual destination. It requires choosing a possible identity that genuinely identifies with the people the initiative will serve. The mission focus is the people the mission community is called to serve and to be served by. The clearer the focus, the easier it will be to love the people concerned practically and in depth. The community will be able to concentrate resources on them. Initiatives that lack a clear focus often dissipate resources and are ineffective. Chapter 9 offered theological reasons for bringing expressions of church to birth within specific cultures, so long as these churches are well connected to the wider body.

Grace Church, Hackney in London, for example, is explicit about the unreached people group round Shoreditch that it is seeking to engage

- politically left wing;
- socially liberal;
- culturally sophisticated;
- interested in spirituality.

Sometimes identifying with the mission focus is fairly straightforward – for example, if a high degree of congruence exists between starting identities and the people to be served. Existing personal identities may overlap with the mission focus, such as beginning church among friends and contacts. Or if the mission community represents a local church, the focus may be the natural outflow of the church's mission, such as expanding the church's work among young people. A possible identity can be developed in close alliance with a starting identity.

Identifying with the mission focus will also be possible if the Spirit has led the mission community's members through the dying to live process. But sometimes, even when this has happened, tensions may arise between members' starting and possible identities. Churches in the area may resent the prospect of a new youth congregation. 'Will it steal our young people?' Members' identification with the wider church (part of their starting identity) may conflict with their possible identity, focused on teenagers. Sorting out the tension may create delays. Or if the venture goes ahead without agreement (the possible identity pulls away from the starting identity), the new congregation may suffer from other churches' mistrust.

Within the Church of England, a tension may arise from the community's desire to work with a demographic that spreads into the next-door parish. 'The rules say that we can't do it without a Bishop's Mission Order. Do we want to be bothered with all that? Why not set ourselves up as an independent group?' Loyalty to the institution (starting identity) may clash with the desire to hurry on with the mission (the growing strength of one of the community's possible identities). Some in the community may want to work within the structures; their starting identities put firm boundaries round their possible identities. For others, loyalty to existing church may be less of a constraint. Will the issue tear the mission community apart?

In other cases, there may be a failure to identify with the mission focus through lack of imagination. A wealthy church wanted to serve an estate of poor people adjacent to it by founding a congregation 'for' that estate. (The language says a great deal.) Identifying with the church planting tradition, it asked 20–30 members to start a congregation in a school close to, but not on the estate.

Nearly everyone on the estate had been judged failures at school and had left as soon as they could (if not earlier!). Why would they be attracted to a church in a *school*, which was not even on their estate? Starting identities – 'this is how other people we know plant churches (and we are identifying with them)'– swamped contextual considerations. The problem appears to have been not a reluctance to identify with the estate but an inability to do so. No one encouraged the decision-makers to ask the right questions.

At times, failure to identify with the context may be due not to lack of imagination, but to an intentional decision. Perhaps members of a mission community are discussing whether to 'tabernacle' – to move into a neighbourhood that comprises the mission focus. They are still trying out their possible identities. They are asking what their selves would become if they were involved in the cross-cultural venture.

Moving into the neighbourhood would mean living in a much poorer part of the town. How would this square with the 'personal' side of their starting identities – what would their friends and family say? Would it lengthen their commute to work? The mission community's members may never have seen themselves living in this sort of an area. It may be an identity voyage too far. But without moving on to the estate they persist with the initiative, which bears little fruit because the deep work of identification was avoided.

In another case, perhaps church leaders want to invite members who commute to worship from a certain area to form a congregation and serve people near their homes. But before issuing the invitation, they ask, 'Why are these members not attending a church where they live? Is it because they do not identify with the area? If so, will they form a suitable core of the new church?' They discover that the personal and church ties of the people concerned are pulling them away from the area. Individuals are not willing to loosen the ties. Unlike the previous example, the leaders abandon the idea rather than go ahead in a half-hearted way.

Failure to identify with the context may not just prevent an initiative from being fruitful or going ahead at all. It may damage a work that has started to bear fruit. In a small rural town, church began to emerge among a group who had completed a Christian discovery course but continued to meet together. Several church members decided to join them. Their Christian outlooks and how they talked about their faith completely changed the dynamics of the group, which disintegrated. This kind of disruption is not uncommon. Well-established believers are unable or unwilling to adapt their starting identities to the context, and damage what others are doing.

These are examples of failing adequately to complete the identity voyage. They illustrate how discerning the mission focus is much more than deciding which group of people to serve. It demands a willingness to identify wholeheartedly with those people. This may require individuals to adapt and rework their starting identities so that the context becomes a major new source of identity. Individuals will be helped in this by identifying with Jesus and the identity voyage he made in the incarnation, by sharing with one another the struggles involved and supporting each other, and by listening to those the community is called to serve: getting close to other people expands the capacity to identify with them.

Identity voyages are involved in these 'Gathering' processes

- the emergence of a leader;
- the drawing together of a mission community;
- the development of a shared understanding of the call to mission;
- the development of a shared understanding of the mission focus;
- agreeing mission values.

Mission values

Much has been written about values, vision and purpose, and understandings differ. The box below makes some helpful distinctions. 'Mission values' express the identity of the mission community. They are 'emotional rudders' that guide how the community operates, how members talk together and treat one another. Like an iceberg, values often lie beneath the surface. They are taken for granted, assumed and unspoken. Making them explicit allows them to be reflected upon and challenged.

Ethos, values, vision and purpose

- *Ethos* reflects how the community or church *feels* (the ambience of its life).
- *Values* express who it *is* (how the group describes itself).
- *Vision* expresses what it *sees* (in relation to the future).
- *Purpose* expresses what it wishes to *accomplish* (actions that realize the vision).

Source: Murray (2008, pp. 150–5).

Values cannot be determined by the leader in advance. A founder can say that these are 'my' values before the mission community forms, but they only become 'our' values when members of the community reshape and own them. In the gathering process, members will talk about others who might join the community, the mission focus and the nature of their mission call. Through these and other conversations, what they most value as a group will be implicitly defined. The gathering process should include making these values explicit, so that differences can be openly faced and negotiated.

Conversations about these values will be conversations about the community's preferred possible identity. 'How do we see ourselves in relation to our task?' 'What will define us as we undertake it?' Members of the community will have their own possible identities and these must be drawn into a coherent whole. Members will be travelling from their starting identities. If these starting identities are fairly different and members vary in the degree of distance they are willing to travel from them, it may be difficult to reach agreement.

In a 'mixed economy' context, different ways of identifying with the parent church or the denomination may have to be negotiated. Some in the group may have formed their identities strongly against the church they have come from ('it's so out of date!'), while others may have a greater sense of loyalty. In addition, the tradition the community represents will have certain 'bottom lines', such as an understanding of Scripture or celebrating the Eucharist in a specific way. How far will these bottom lines – the tradition's identity – impinge on the community's task? If some members' starting identities have been formed in opposition to the parent church, developing possible identities that accommodate the institution may require considerable grace – or not prove possible. (The latter may not matter too much so long as there is some form of connection to the wider church and peer accountability).

Sometimes agreement will be especially difficult because values touch the heart of who individuals are. Members may feel that in negotiating values they are negotiating their very selves. Issues of power will also be involved. Whose views are to take precedence? Just as Paul and Barnabas parted company after what seems to have been an acrimonious dispute (Acts 15.39), it will not be surprising if someone leaves the mission community after a trial period or two friends decide that they would not work well together. Possible identities may be incompatible. This is not failure: it is part of discerning what sort of person God wants the individual to be. Not serving in one situation releases the person to serve in another.

Conversations about values typically lead to a short statement encapsulating the values the community cherishes. These may include statements such as those in the box below. The statement expresses something of how the community sees itself. However, a statement of values is not an end in itself – something agreed and then forgotten. The worth of the statement lies in the discussions that produced it (the conversations enable differences to surface and hopefully be resolved), and in the discussions that it then gives rise to. Regular reviews of the statement can be opportunities to hold each other to account. Has the community acted consistently with its values? If there are inconsistencies, is this because members have not articulated what is really important to them?

A statement of values (The Net in Huddersfield)

God centred
Bible based
Desiring authentic relationships
Seeker focused
Creating relevant faith
Developing discipleship
Open to change

Source: Male (2008, p. 57).

Though practice will vary, an agreed statement of values can mark the completion of identity voyages. This will be the case if the statement, and the conversations surrounding its production, reflect consensus about the membership of the mission community, the nature of the mission task and the mission focus. The community and its members can be said to have travelled from individuals' starting identities, through the development of possible identities, to arrive at the community's contextual church identity, which is the way members see the community's mission task and enact it. The process of enactment will carry identities on a further journey.

Conclusion

The gathering process involves not a sequence of decisions reached through 'rational choice', but a series of conversations that give rise to identity voyages. The voyages begin with starting identities, which comprise ecclesial and personal identities. These form the launch pad for possible identities, as individuals imagine their future selves. Possible identities give way to contextual church identities, when individuals enact their selves in birthing and growing the church. Navigating identity voyages is a task for the leader, for individuals who may join the leader and for the mission community.

Each voyage normally involves at least four groups of people (some of which overlap) – the church and its various networks, individuals' family, friendship and employment networks, others involved in the initiative and the social context of the proposed new church. Identity voyages occur in dialogue with these groupings. 'If I take part in this venture, how would it fit with what I have been taught about mission? Can I see myself working with the people the initiative expects to serve?'

The variety of groupings makes identity voyages far from straightforward. Individuals have to negotiate the expectations of others, which may tug in different directions. Perhaps church involvement encourages a teacher to help found a contextual church, but some of the school's pupils live on the housing estate where the new community will form. Does the teacher, who likes to keep school and the rest of life separate, feel comfortable? If he pulls out, would he let down the founder, who is a friend?

These tensions mean that the gathering process may take a long time and be quite fraught. Volunteers may not emerge as quickly as imagined. Some may leave after a few months because the initiative is not what they expected – their possible identities and the community's possible identities increasingly diverge. Those who remain may find themselves caught in tensions between their ecclesial, personal and contextual situations. It may take a while to reconcile the three. In a 'mixed economy' setting, therefore, the denomination will need to be realistic about the timescales involved. Likewise, when after a year friends ask the emerging leader, 'Have you planted a church yet?' and the leader thinks, 'I haven't even got a team', the person should not despair. Gathering is a complicated process.

Further reading

Down, Simon and James Reveley, 'Generational Encounters and the Social Formation of Entrepreneurial Identity: "Young Guns" and "Old Farts"', *Organization* 11 (2), 2004, pp. 233–50.

Ibarra, Herminia, *Working Identity: Unconventional Strategies for Reinventing Your Career*, Boston: Harvard Business School, 2004 [2003].

Murray, Stuart, *Planting Churches: A framework for practitioners*, Milton Keynes: Paternoster, 2008.

Questions for discussion

- What key things should be kept in mind when gathering a mission community?
- What components of your 'starting identity' would open doors to developing a 'contextual church identity'? How might your starting identity constrain the type of contextual church you could help to birth?
- In your experience, are contextual churches mostly started in cultures similar to those of the founding community, or in cross-cultural contexts? What are the strengths and weaknesses of each approach?

13

Researching Opportunities

Once a mission community – the founding core of a contextual church – has formed and is clear about the people it is called to, the question becomes how best to serve them. The answer begins to emerge by prayerfully exploring how opportunities and available resources can be matched. 'Researching opportunities' is shorthand for this.

It is a process that is barely discussed in much of the church planting and emerging church literature. For example, Ed Stetzer (2006, pp. 115–23) and Halter and Smay (2008, pp. 61–81) emphasize the importance of understanding culture, but say little about the methodologies involved. Joel Comiskey gives the practicalities just two pages (Comiskey, 2009, pp. 91–3). This neglect, which is especially characteristic of the US literature, may be due to the North American context: new churches tend to be drawn largely from people who have stopped attending or are willing to switch church. Yet as the church increasingly engages with people who have little or no church background, understanding the people the mission community is called to and finding ways to serve them becomes an urgent task. It is fundamental to *contextual* church.

Researching opportunities is not normally a stage in the birthing process – 'we've gathered the mission community, now we'll take the next step'. Because starting contextual churches is intrinsically messy, as with all the five methodologies discussed in these chapters, researching opportunities weaves in and out of the other threads, occurring simultaneously and often overlapping with them. It should be ongoing throughout the life of the church.

This chapter introduces the concept of researching opportunities, asks whom the mission community should research with, what it should seek to discover, how it should go about the research process and what type of results will emerge. Circumstances will of course vary, ranging from a couple of people who want to start church among their friends to a large church planting team on a housing estate. Researching opportunities will look different in different contexts.

What does researching opportunities involve?

Researching opportunities involves identifying and generating mission opportunities among the people the mission community is called to serve. These opportunities will include sharing the gospel but, as Chapter 11 argued, often evangelism will not be the starting point. When steadily more people have little or no church background, the church has to begin 'further back'. It has to start with loving and serving. This will frequently be the initial focus of the research process.

Recognition or creation?

In fresh expressions circles, great emphasis has been placed on listening as a methodology for mission (*Mission-shaped Church*, 2004, pp. 104–5; Croft, Hedley and Hopkins, 2007). This is not dissimilar to the concept of opportunity recognition in the entrepreneurship literature. Opportunity recognition is perceiving a possibility to a create new business or significantly improve an existing one (Lumpkin, Hills and Shrader, 2004, p. 74). The entrepreneur reads the environment to discover new openings.

The assumption is that the environment and the possibilities within it are givens. They are an 'objective phenomenon which cannot be created by the entrepreneur, only discovered and exploited . . . the key to entrepreneurial success is access to and awareness of new and unusual information' (Dunham, 2003, p. 79). Ivan Vaghely and Pierre-André Julien liken the activity to an information processing machine (2010, p. 78). The entrepreneur processes information about the environment to produce as accurate a model of reality as possible.

The alternative view is that entrepreneurs construct reality. Opportunities are not sitting in the context waiting to be discovered. Entrepreneurs bring to the context assumptions and aspirations that influence how they see it. Through interacting with others, they construct ideas that they test and revise. They are more like experimenters than information processors. Opportunities are created through an iterative process of trial and error rather than simply recognized. Opportunity 'should be viewed as a set of subjective expectations of what the entrepreneur thinks can be accomplished' (Edelman and Yli-Renko, 2010, p. 838).

Vaghely and Julien tested the two models on a sample of technology entrepreneurs and found that they used both. Sometimes the environment was read as a source of information, at other times it became the context in which ideas were tested and revised. It seems likely that founders of contextual churches use both approaches, too. At times they process information from the context like a computer and come to recognize opportunities 'out there'. At other times, they behave more like experimenters, trying out possibilities.

Researching opportunities involves observation

Opportunity recognition

Conversations→see patterns in the context→recognize opportunities →input to conversations

Opportunity creation

Conversations→make connections in the mind→test ideas → create opportunities→input to conversations

---

'Research opportunities' captures both these processes. Some aspects of research involve observing a situation and seeing something that perhaps others had not noticed, such as the discovery of a new planet. Other aspects entail linking disparate pieces of information ('making connections in the mind') to generate a hypothesis. The hypothesis is then tested. Both aspects involve conversations with others and within the researcher's head.

'Researching opportunities' is:

- *Attentive*: This is a better word than listening because it includes observation. As individuals attend to their context and talk about it, they may recognize an opportunity.
- *Collaborative*: It involves people talking together and is best undertaken in community.
- *Generative*: Conversations produce new ideas.
- *Creative*: Connections are made between different ideas about, comments regarding and observations of the context (Lumpkin, Hills and Shrader, 2004, pp. 84–5).

If the mission community does not know its context well, researching can be the means by which it makes contacts, develops networks and falls in love with the people. Researching 'begins the process of identification by which we become neighbours to others' (Bretherton, 2010, p. 102). It builds trust. It gives others a chance to see the mission community in action, to evaluate its motives, to discover whether its objectives fit in with theirs and to make a judgement about its character. Trust is the currency mission communities trade in. The more of it they have the better.

Researching as contextual mission

Researching opportunities lays the foundations for contextual mission, whose theological basis was discussed in Chapters 8 and 9. The more members of a mission community talk with people in and who know the situation, the more they will be at home in the setting. The initiative will come out of the context rather than being an imposition on it. Like Jesus, members will be missional not by shouting at people from the outside, but by coming up close beside them.

Becoming a Jew enabled Jesus to conduct his mission in Palestine from the inside. The first action recorded of him is as a twelve-year-old, when he stayed in Jerusalem to listen to the Temple authorities (Luke 2.41–52). In so doing he entered another culture – an adult culture, the Temple as opposed to the synagogue and Jerusalem rather than Nazareth. He established a relationship as he sat respectfully among the religious leaders, meeting them face to face. He asked questions, engaged in dialogue, took time – he was there for three days – and presumably ran a risk: would he incur his parents' anger? Jesus was learning about his context.

Mission communities do something similar when they invest time attending to their contexts. Even close friends will have parts of their lives that are different to the other person, such as tastes in film or music. Getting to know someone well will involve entering these different 'cultures'. This is especially important if, as part of its service, the mission community hopes to lead people into faith.

Rory Ridley-Duff and Mike Bull describe how in some circumstances, social entrepreneurs may need temporarily to become the follower until sufficiently knowledgeable to perform their leadership role effectively. If leadership is not to be coercive or manipulative, it must be exercised from inside a culture (Ridley-Duff and Bull, 2011, p. 207). Attending to the context involves entering the culture more fully.

Sara Savage, a psychologist, has written, 'The experience of being listened to is so close to the experience of being loved as to be indistinguishable.'[1] The longer a mission community spends attending to people, the more love it will show them. That is compelling grounds for not short-changing the research process. By being attentive, a mission community will reveal the heart of Jesus, who lived three decades in his culture before spending a mere three years ministering to it. Researching opportunities has intrinsic value and is not just a means to an end.

Who are the research partners?

The *Mission-shaped Church* report (2004, pp. 104–5) called for double listening – to the people the mission community is called to serve and to the living tradition of the church. To unpack what this involves, the Fresh Expressions team coined the phrase '360 degrees listening'. This is listening in the round – getting your bearings from all four points of the compass. It

---

[1] Beta Course, Session 2. www.beta-course.org.

includes attending to God through prayer and study and to the context. It makes explicit that both the local and the wider churches must be heard. No sequence is intended, since all four 'directions' will occur at varying times or in parallel (see diagram below).

'360 degrees listening'

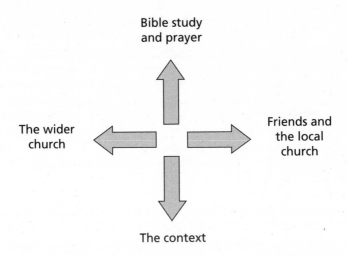

The concept can be developed further. It is not just that there are four audiences to which attention should be paid. These audiences can be seen as research partners. Researching opportunities is a collaborative process, in which the mission community works with God, with praying friends and the local church, with the people it is called to serve and with the wider body. 'With' conveys a sense of exchanging ideas and information. The mission community engages in dialogue with its four sets of partners, and through these conversations, possibilities for action and knowledge of the available resources emerge.

These four 'directions' of conversation equate to the four interlocking sets of relationships, described in Chapter 5, that constitute the church: with the Trinity, within the gathering, with the world and with the wider church. Such '360 degrees research' will help the mission community, however small, to be a thorough expression of church.

The context

Apart from conversing with God, the most important research partners are the people the mission community is called to. This presupposes that the community is clear about its mission focus, discussed in the previous chapter. Initially, the community may need to research more widely to discern its mission context, but once that focus is clear it can listen in greater depth.

Even if the community knows the people well, research will involve discovering more about their lives. If it knows them less well, some new relationships may have to be made. These may include (depending on what sort of initiative)

- *Networkers* – individuals with lots of contacts. They are 'persons of peace', who open the door to God's messengers. They will describe their networks and put the mission community in touch with others.
- *Agencies* – community and voluntary groups, and statutory agencies. We might extend the term to include the local head teacher, for example, medical practitioners, police and the local authority. Alongside their knowledge and contacts, individuals within agencies can prove invaluable in winning the support of permission-givers (and may be permission-givers themselves).
- *Businesses*, such as a corner shop or the local hairdresser. They will have useful insights into people's lifestyles.

The mission community will be wise to avoid a rescue-mission mentality – 'We're here to help you.' Such a mindset puts the community in a superior position: 'We have something you don't.' The community should take seriously Jesus' statement in Matthew 25.40, 'Whatever you did for the least of these brothers of mine, you did for me.' This will encourage members to ask: 'If Jesus is already present in the people we seek to serve, how might they be a blessing to us?' Researching should open the door to mutual relationships.

Christian friends and the local church

The concept of '360 degrees research' includes the mission community's immediate Christian circle. Who is the mission community acting on behalf of? Has anyone authorized what it is doing? If so, the community should spend time sharing its journey with them. In some situations, a community's ideas will change substantially as its understanding grows. If it wants the continued blessing of those to whom it is accountable, it will need to keep them in touch with its learning, listen to their feedback and take their responses seriously.

New contextual churches are far too important to be initiated without prayer support, which may come from the community's local church and/ or Christian friends. God may speak through prayer partners to help the community's discernment. So it will be important for the community to update them regularly on its learning and its evolving ideas, and to seek their reactions. Prayer partners may be a source of wisdom, knowledge, skills, time, money or contacts. Listening to them carefully at every stage will keep them engaged and perhaps secure offers of help.

Some founders find that a big headache is relationships with the local church. They encounter misunderstanding, unrealistic expectations and often suspicion, such as the belief that the initiative is not proper church but a bridge into existing church. These difficulties may not be readily overcome, but they can be eased if the mission community explains repeatedly what it is doing, attends to the reaction and shows it has heard this response. Trust grows when people feel understood. Attentiveness builds up the body of Christ.

The wider church

Using '360 degrees research' will encourage listening to the wider church, which contains a library of wisdom and experience. Listening to other church founders is probably the most natural place to start. But this immediately encounters the question Mair and Marti pose in relation to social entrepreneurs: 'If context and embeddedness is so important, to what extent is it possible to transfer practice and scale out initiatives across geographic and community borders?' (2006, p. 43).

David Snowden's Cynefin framework, discussed in Chapter 11, provides a partial response. Good practice can be transferred in relation to 'simple contexts' and the principles of good practice in relation to 'complicated' ones. In the case of 'complex contexts', the experience of others can enthuse a mission community, spark thoughts, increase confidence, legitimize ideas ('If they were allowed to be radical, why can't we?'), alert members to pitfalls and illustrate some of the dynamics involved in starting a new church.

Mission communities might visit other contextual churches, read case studies[2] and explore stories of church planting in other traditions and times. What can be learnt from church planting in Africa or from the eighteenth-century Wesleyan revival? What about resources in the wider church for introducing people to the gospel?

What should be researched?

The mission community will be asking: 'How can we best serve the context with the resources available?' Finding the answer will include prayerful attention to the local and wider church, but will focus on researching opportunities in the context. The community may have

---

2 For example www.freshexpressions.org.uk/stories and the 'Encounters on the Edge' series, published by the Church Army's Sheffield Centre.

some initial ideas. In which case, it will need to test these on others, and discover who else shares and wants to shape them. If the community starts with a vision for its work, giving the vision to those who will be served by it and letting them develop it is crucial. Only then will become *their* vision.

Discovering how best to serve the context will entail 'cultural exegesis', which sees culture as a piece of communication, like a text, that calls for interpretation (Vanhoozer, 2007, pp. 35–59). Cultural exegesis asks 'What is this context "saying" and what does it mean?' It can be approached through three questions:

- *What's going on?* seeks information about the surface of people's lives, such as where they meet, where they work and what leisure activities they enjoy.
- *What's going on behind what's going on?* probes beneath the surface to the underlying processes shaping people's lives – such as the distribution and exercise of power, past events with a continuing influence, people's shared assumptions and untapped resources within the locality or network. It involves reading culture like a book (see Box).
- *What's going on for God in what's going on?* looks for traces of God's image in the context and for signs of the Spirit's redemptive activity.

Reading cultural texts (such as film, TV commercial, brand name) like a book

'*What's going* behind *the work?*' refers to the cultural context in which a 'text' emerges.
'*What's going on* in *the work?*' refers to how a text makes its point and projects its vision.
'*What's going on* in front of *the work?*' refers to how the audience/consumer responds.

Source: Vanhoozer (2007, pp. 48–54).

Just as readers bring their own experiences and assumptions to a text, so will mission communities when they read their contexts. There is no value-free exegesis of a culture. By talking about their hopes, fears and assumptions, members of mission communities will become more aware of how these affect both what they choose to notice and their interpretation of what they see.

Draw on what you know

Members' existing knowledge will be an important resource for the mission community. If a couple of friends are hoping to start a church in their network, they are likely to know a great deal about the people involved. Even if the mission focus is less familiar, members may be surprised by how much they already know. Pooling existing knowledge is like a researcher's literature review. It provides a platform for considering what needs to be researched.

Mission communities will best capitalize on members' knowledge by concentrating on the following sources of information (Shane and Eckhardt, 2005, pp. 174–5):

- *Unique knowledge*: Everyone knows more about some things than other people because of their interests and circumstances – a person who loves cooking, for example, or lives in a particular area. Research can tap into this knowledge where relevant.
- *Local search*: Searching for information close to what members already know tends to be quicker and easier than branching into a completely new field. 'Individuals are likely to discover opportunities within a close proximity to their knowledge base' (Shane and Eckhardt, 2005, p. 174). A nurse might explore church pioneering round healthcare, for example.
- *Social ties*: Individuals uncover information through the structure and content of their networks. If members are connected to the same networks, they will receive less information than if some are plugged into very different ones. Mission communities wanting to scan widely for opportunities will need a diversity of social ties, which may require forming new networks (Vyakarnam and Myint, 2006).

Opportunities and resources

Having started with what they already know, mission communities will begin to dig beneath the surface. What are the needs and aspirations of people in the context? Often these will be clearly expressed and obvious, but sometimes this will not be the case.

In the world of entrepreneurship, research shows that innovation frequently lies with consumers who cannot articulate their needs for not-yet-developed solutions to problems. A firm that listens carefully to its customers and knows them well may articulate these barely formed needs and generate solutions to them (Wiklund and Shepherd, 2003, p. 1309). This was famously expressed by Henry Ford: 'If I'd asked customers what they'd wanted, they would have said faster horses.' Part of attending to 'what is going on behind what is going on' involves helping to surface half-buried desires and needs.

Helpful questions might include

How do people spend their time?
Where do they meet?
What are the joys and pleasures, hardships and difficulties in people's lives?
What do people value and what do they put a low value on?
What works and doesn't work round here?
Who is most effectively solving the sort of problems faced by these people, and why?
Who are the key networkers?
Who are the leaders and how do they exercise their leadership?
What do people think about church, God and spirituality? Do they pray?
How might people connect with the gospel, which aspects would challenge them, and who is likely to be most open?
What are the evident needs?
What resources can we draw on?

This does not mean naively assuming that, because people do not always know what they need, 'we' can find out for them and produce the solution. A mission community should presume that people are 'competent interpreters' of their own lives (Mulgan, 2009, p. 164). Individuals may need help in accessing the relevant information. But once they have it, they can interpret it in and for their context. The community therefore should work with them, and with professionals and others who know the context, to identify challenges and possible responses.

Mission communities should take seriously the notion of 'resilience' – the idea that people who have been marginalized and socially oppressed can persevere over hardship. They have skills, resources and knowledge to transform their lives (Hardina, 2002, pp. 47–8). Mission communities might study situations where individuals and groups have successfully dealt with similar challenges – where drug use has been sharply reduced, for example. What lessons can be learned?

Indigenous leadership

Communities will pay special attention to the exercise and distribution of power (see Box), and in particular to leadership. Who are the natural leaders? How is leadership exercised? As Chapter 1 noted, first-century house churches formed round social units that had indigenous leadership built in. To be sustainable, contextual churches similarly will need to work with the context's leadership resources and styles, even though locating and empowering leadership in areas of poverty may be difficult. Giving close attention to the available leadership is a vital part of researching opportunities.

For reflection: Seven sources of power

- *Coercive power* can sanction an individual/group for non-compliant behaviour.
- *Reward power* can provide a benefit for appropriate behaviour.
- *Legitimate power* derives from positions of authority, professional status or public recognition, and can reward/sanction behaviours and make certain decisions.
- *Positional power* derives from one's position in the social structure – such as gender, race, education, wealth.
- *Expert power* derives from recognition that the person has the experience or education to make certain decisions.
- *Personal power* derives from the individual's personal attributes – such as personal attractiveness, charisma, celebrity.
- *Referent power* derives from a subordinate's desire to identify with the power holder, due to personal admiration.

Source: Hardina (2002, pp. 159–60).

What research methods should be used?

Researching the context is best undertaken by using and adapting methods of community research. Stuart Murray (2008, pp. 84–94) has described five methods – observation, conversation, investigation, interpretation and application. I have added experimentation, participation and imagination, and have omitted interpretation and application which are addressed in the next section. These form six methods of research that combine both recognizing and creating opportunities.

Observation

Looking will reveal a great deal about a network or neighbourhood – what people do, where they gather, what they value, who relates to whom and lots more. 'Being attentive to what is known as "spatial symbolism" is important' (Murray, 2008, p. 88). It involves discerning the historical, cultural and spiritual messages conveyed by buildings and locations.

Observation has been important in entrepreneurial innovation. Howard Shultz hit on the idea for Starbucks by observing the characteristics of espresso bars in Italy. Scott Cook, founder and CEO of Intuit, which provides financial management software, came up with the idea for the initial product by watching his wife struggle with the mechanics of paying the bills (Dyer, Gregersen and Christensen, 2008, p. 325).

Members of a mission community might observe by

- walking round the area alone or with others in the community, at different times of day and night, perhaps praying as they go;
- sitting watchfully in public spaces, parks or cafes;
- using a camera to record significant places, buildings, people or activities;
- spending a day in a local community project or with a professional, such as a police officer.

A small group of Christians in the Hythe area of Colchester 'began to prayer walk around the area regularly and "notice" things. We saw the two pubs trying to attract more customers, a newly-opened wine bar, local businesses struggling to stay afloat and the coffee shops, cafes and benches where people ate their lunch. We also saw rubbish, rubbish and more rubbish. All over the Hythe people had just dropped their litter. So our first attempt at something "missional" was to begin to take care of our local environment by organizing a litter pick and clearing up one area of the Hythe . . .' (www.freshexpressions.org.uk/stories).

Conversation

Conversations allow the mission community to listen to people's stories, ask probing but non-intrusive questions and develop mutually enriching relationships. Murray (2008, p. 89) lists some ways of being attentive through conversation, which include

- *inviting people to complete a questionnaire* about their lives or their neighbourhood, which can lead into a conversation;
- *convening a focus group* by inviting people to someone's home, extending hospitality and asking them to talk about local issues;
- *interviewing a range of people* to understand the mission context from different perspectives;
- *using the 'snowball' approach*, whereby initial conversation partners suggest others to approach;
- *chatting to key networkers*, who know lots of people and have their finger on their network's pulse.

Dyer, Gregersen and Christensen (2008) found that innovative entrepreneurs were more likely to ask questions that challenge the status quo than managers. 'As they think and brainstorm, they like to ask *if we did this, what would happen?*' (p. 323, authors' italics). 'What if' questions generate novel ideas.

Mark Berry, Pioneer Leader of Safespace, a new monastic community in Telford, has described how

> [w]e took Luke 10 very seriously – Jesus sent his disciples out in small groups to offer peace to households. We began by asking the questions: 'Where are the communities in need of peace? Where are the households?' . . . We spoke directly to key people, leaders, gatekeepers face to face, in their places, and simply asked, 'What would peace look like/mean for you and your community?' And then we offered that to them. (Goodhew, Roberts and Volland, 2012, forthcoming)

Experimentation

Amar Bhide remarks that 'businesses cannot be launched like space shuttles, with every detail of the mission planned in advance . . . Entrepreneurs should play with and explore ideas, letting their strategies evolve through a seamless process of guesswork, analysis, and action' (1999, p. 84). Entrepreneurs can undertake only so much research. Indeed, returns from additional analysis diminish. Effective entrepreneurs screen out unpromising ideas as early as possible, and concentrate on the most promising ones. 'In fact, analyzing and acting are tough to separate in entrepreneurial environments. Smart founders dive in and improvise . . .'(Bhide, 1999, p. 58)

Many pioneers find that experimentation is one of the best forms of research. They learn by doing. A mission community might open a stall in a farmers' market and give the other stallholders free refreshments during the day. As members chat to customers, ideas might form, such as a 'welcome lunch' in the local cafe with a discussion about spirituality. So they give it a try – a second experiment. In time they offer a Christianity discovery course, and this becomes a third experiment.

American Jonathan Wilson-Hartgrove (2008, p. 87) describes how he and a friend invited local Christians to study Mark's Gospel with a group of homeless people. At first individuals in the hostel were slow to join in. 'What would it take to get more people?' they asked. 'Fried chicken' one man quipped. Next week there were 50 pieces of chicken. By the time they finished the Gospel, 20 people were enthusiastically involved – half of them were from local churches and the other half from the hostel.

Especially when it draws on observation and conversation, experimentation has a number of strengths. It allows activist types to get on and do something; it involves learning by doing, which can be highly effective; it fits a step-by-step, act–reflect–act approach; it avoids wasteful research – you cannot learn everything before you do anything. But experimentation is not without risks.

If the experiment goes wrong, will people be hurt and the initiative's reputation suffer? If it goes well, will the mission community hurry on enthusiastically to the next step, short-circuiting deep and extensive listening?

Participation

One version of participation is for the mission community's members to take part in the activities of the people they feel called to and get immersed in their lives. They join the social committee at work, the residents' association or a school governing body. If they are starting a neighbourhood church and do not already live in the area, moving there will be indispensable. They research the context by becoming part of it.

Participation includes receiving from the context. This can make the mission community dependent in some way on the people it intends to serve. The 72 sent out by Jesus were to take nothing with them (Luke 10.4). Each pair was to rely on the hospitality of the village it entered. This dependence would have drawn individuals into the village's life as they were fed, given shelter and made welcome. When you make yourself dependent, you give other people permission to include you in their lives, which is an important step to identifying with them. Might mission communities ask for help before they offer help?

An alternative form of participation is to invite others to join in what you are doing. Janet started a fresh expression of church based on her hobby, which was making greeting cards. Around 40 people met regularly. In time, when they made cards connected with Advent, Christmas, Mothering Sunday and so on, Janet would explain what the season or occasion meant to her as a Christian. This sparked enough interest for her to start two lunch-time discussion groups before the card-making session. Some of those involved began to find that the card-making group was church for them (Potter, 2009, pp. 107–8).

A third form of participation is to spend time in a new contextual church elsewhere, preferably among people in a similar context. An in-depth study of successful social entrepreneurs was 'struck by the general tendency of this group to be able to identify and learn so much from example, and to continue to use and develop the learning that had arisen from close and powerful observation of someone else successfully at work' (Chambers and Edwards-Stuart, 2007, p. 21).

Investigation

This involves researching relevant issues in more depth. It includes finding out more about the mission context, as well as learning from the experience of the wider church. To avoid too much information, the mission community should investigate only the key issues emerging from other forms of research.

If the aim is to start a small contextual church among friends and peers, the mission community might read up on the cultural influences shaping their lives. If the envisaged church is a geographical community, members might visit council offices, the local library and websites to learn more about demographic trends, building development plans, social needs, types of employment, local history and such like. The local newsagent will know which newspapers and magazines people read, and these can be a valuable source of insight too.

Imagination

This is the reflective part of research, whereas the other methods generally entail doing something. Imagination gets the most out of active forms of attentiveness. It helps individuals to process what they are learning. Imagination is the laboratory in people's minds. Individuals can conduct experiments in their heads. 'What would happen if . . .?' Ideas can be as off-the-wall as you like. If an idea lingers, it can be tested on other people. Most of what Einstein achieved came through what he called 'thought experiments' (Hirsch and Ferguson, 2011, p. 56). 'Innovation is imagination put to work' (p. 207).

Summary of research methods

- Observation
- Conversation
- Experimentation
- Participation
- Investigation
- Imagination

How might the results of research be processed?

Though research will be ongoing, at some point the mission community will draw the threads together and prayerfully consider what God is calling it to do and with whose help. What vision is the Spirit generating? If the community consists of a couple of friends, this part of researching will probably occur during their everyday exchanges. If the group is more formal, it will put aside time – perhaps in a quiet day or retreat – to pool what's been learnt and draw conclusions. Even if a new church seems to just happen, almost by surprise, the community will want to link this emergence to their other learning. Does it reflect God's will? How can it be steered in a fruitful direction?

Might these four questions help to turn the fruits of research into a vision?

What's going on here?
What shall we do in response?
How can we make it happen?
What will be the result?

Source: Robinson (2006, p. 98).

Corporate alertness

'Pulling everything together' should be a team exercise rather than a task for a single person. Processing what is being learnt is a creative activity that relies on the combination of different ideas, insights and pieces of information. Combinations will be richer if several people are involved. In particular, the process demands 'alertness'. Alertness is the individual's and the community's capacity to use bits of information to create new frameworks for thinking about means and ends. Information can be used to imagine different ways of achieving a desired end or for thinking afresh about the goal.

Individuals are alert to certain kinds of information, but not others. What they notice depends on their circumstances, existing knowledge and prior experience (Shane and Eckhardt, 2005, p. 176). So pooling members' experiences of the research process will widen the mission community's field of vision and extend its corporate alertness. Broadening the community's experience – by visiting other contextual churches for example – may increase this awareness further.

The community will be alert to the emergence of:

- *Individuals* to work with. As conversations take place with research partners, the latter hopefully will warm to the mission community and be willing to help. Members will be prayerfully alert to what assistance is available and to the strengths and weaknesses of the individuals involved.
- *Ideas* for what to do, which are generated as members attend to the context, talk with research partners and discuss what they see and hear.
- *Insights* into the context – into what makes the people tick – fertilize the initiative with understanding.

How might a vision emerge?

Claus Otto Scharmer (2000, pp. 17–9) has described six 'redirections of attention' that allow individuals and groups in organizations to move from seeing and sensing to enacting and embodying change. These 'redirections' describe how a vision for the contextual church can emerge through the researching process.

- *Suspension* is the sine qua non of effective observation. Instead of projecting mental models on to the world, the person opens up to what is happening in the world.
- *Redirection* shifts attention from the current reality to the emergent one. Members of a mission community focus on the vision that is beginning to take shape.
- *Letting go* surrenders to what is emerging. Theologically, it comes from recognizing that what is emerging is from the Spirit, and involves a willingness to go with the Spirit.
- *Letting come* is less about surrender and more about quickening the coming new. How can we crystallize the vision?
- *Bringing forth* involves enactment. How can we turn our conversation about the new into reality? Individuals become instruments of the emerging new as they discuss what each can do to make the vision happen.
- *Institutional embodiment* involves creating the organizational arrangements that will sustain what is emerging. What organizational routines will support the new?

As these processes are reflected in conversations within the mission community, attending to the context will be mirrored by attentiveness to what is happening within the community. Over a series of conversations, attentiveness will move from 'suspension' through to 'institutional embodiment', though probably not in a neat linear way! The result will be an emerging vision for what God is calling the community to undertake and some plans for taking the vision forward.

The nature of the vision

Building on Sarasvathy et al. (2005, pp. 143–58), the vision will take one of three forms. A vision will be based on *opportunity recognition* when both the demand for something and the means of supplying it already exist. (The term is used differently here to elsewhere in the chapter.) The creative work lies in recognizing an opportunity to bring the demand and the supply together, and realizing this through an appropriate vehicle. A mission community may recognize that parents would welcome a chance to support each other and learn about parenting. It knows a Christian with the expertise to facilitate such a group. The challenge becomes how to enable the 'expert' to meet the demand.

A vision based on *opportunity discovery* will emerge when only one side of the supply–demand equation exists. There may be a demand but no current means of meeting it, or vice versa. Perhaps the demand for a parenting support group exists, but the mission community does not know anyone equipped to facilitate it. The right person has to be discovered, or someone within the community may need to acquire the necessary expertise.

A vision will be based on *opportunity creation* when neither the supply nor the demand exists in an obvious way. The mission community may be working with parents who do not have the confidence to join a support group and where there is no Christian with the expertise to convene one. Both supply and demand would have to be 'created'. Perhaps the community knows a health visitor with the contacts and skills to gather a group, and maybe one of the community's members has the skills to lead the group in 'mission worship' (discussed in Chapter 11). Might the two work together?

Opportunity recognition and *discovery* are likely to be more common in church pioneering than *opportunity creation*, which is more demanding. Novelty is involved in all three, however. This highlights again how researching opportunities is much more than listening. It generates a vision for something new.

As the vision forms, the mission community will share its emerging thoughts with its prayer partners and those to whom it is accountable, with appropriate people whose advice it has sought (do they think the community is on the right track?), and – most important of course – with the people it is called to serve. Are the latter starting to own the vision?

Conclusion

Researching opportunities is a vital and dynamic activity that generates novelty. It consists of conversations with four sets of research partners – the Trinity, the mission context, Christian partners and the wider church. It involves building on members' existing knowledge to understand the possibilities and needs of the context. It may include observation, conversation, experimentation, participation, investigation and imagination. Through corporate alertness, the community at the core of the initiative will recognize the individuals, ideas and insights that are needed to develop a vision for the venture. The vision will emerge by means of six 'redirections of attention' that move the mission community from sensing and seeing to enacting and embodying change.

Research is far from complete once a vision emerges and starts to be acted upon. Throughout the ensuing journey, the mission community will need to remain attentive to all its 'research partners'. Through this attentiveness, the Spirit will enable the vision – step by step – to evolve. Researching opportunities should be a continuing process.

Ann Morisy (2004, pp. 26–41) warns against mission being focused too heavily on meeting others' needs. Preoccupation with needs can mask a host of graceful, kingdom dynamics that are set in train when secure and apparently competent individuals allow themselves to be transformed by the people they serve. Through empathy, they share in others' lives by proxy. By reflecting on their experience with others, they come to see God in a new light. People who may once have been viewed as strangers are now regarded as brothers and sisters.

Researching opportunities, therefore, is not only about needs and opportunities to serve. It is also about discerning what God is doing, joining in, receiving from people in the context, participating in their activities and learning new things. To test the effectiveness of its research, a mission community should ask how far it has been changed by the process.

Further reading

Donovan, Vincent J., *Christianity Rediscovered: An Epistle from the Masai*, London: SCM Press, 2001 [1978].

Murray, Stuart, *Planting Churches: A Framework for Practitioners*, Milton Keynes: Paternoster, 2008.

Vanhoozer, Kevin J., 'What Is Everyday Theology? How and Why Christians Should Read Culture', in Kevin J. Vanhoozer, Charles A. Anderson and Michael J. Sleasman (eds), *Everyday Theology: How to Read Cultural Texts and Interpret Trends*, Grand Rapids, MI: Baker, 2007, pp. 15–60.

Questions for discussion

- What examples of fruitful attending to context can you think of? What can be learnt from them?
- How much of this chapter applies to contextual church within personal networks (for example among a group of friends)?
- Are individuals always 'competent interpreters' of their own lives? What is the role of outside or newly arrived interpreters?
- As part of '360 degrees research', how much attention should be paid to existing church? Are its views always helpful?

14

Engaging Partners

Engaging partners (those with a stake in the contextual church) is about forming a 'web of belief' – belief by partners in the initiative and in those who lead it (Dunham, 2003). This web comprises the bonds between a contextual church and its partners, and is critical for mobilizing external resources such as offers of help, permission, goodwill, financial support in some cases, collaboration with others and much else. These resources become available through relationships with partners that are based on emotional feelings, beliefs and commitments.

Building a web of belief is crucial for starting a contextual church, yet receives scant attention in the church planting literature. Murray, for example, discusses the value of cooperative planting and the need to consult other churches (2008, pp. 77–9, 95–6), but does not treat engaging partners as a subject in its own right. However, the importance of relationships with 'stakeholders' is recognized in the entrepreneurship literature, which considers these to be vital for raising money, identifying opportunities and securing other ingredients of success (Dougan and Tourigny, 2004; Vandekerckhove and Dentchev, 2005). In a similar way, contextual churches do not emerge in a vacuum: they depend on networks of support, which have to be encouraged into existence and sustained.

If Chapters 11 and 12 were about making concrete the idea of mission in community and the last chapter was about laying the foundations for being contextual, 'Engaging partners' provides support for communal and contextual mission. It is not a hermetically sealed process, distinct from other sets of methodologies. Rather, like all the methodologies, it weaves in and out of the others and is connected to them. It is tied especially closely to 'Researching Opportunities', which involves initiating relationships with potential partners. It is treated separately for analytical purposes.

Still remembering that we have much to learn, the treatment here is in two parts. The first highlights the importance of the topic by discussing key partners that a mission community – the founding core of the new church – may need to engage. The second draws on some of the entrepreneurship literature to propose a model for understanding these partner relationships.

How the relationships are conducted should be at the forefront of practitioners' minds.

Partners

A wide range of groups and individuals will have a potential stake in the initiative. They could be affected by it or have a contribution to make. The church will largely emerge from conversations between these stakeholders and members of the mission community. So the community needs to be alert not only to the range of potential partners, but to some of the issues that will be involved. The treatment that follows is not meant to be exhaustive, nor will all the categories discussed contribute to the birth of every church.

Prayer partners

Prayer support is easily forgotten, but is vital. Of course, Christians at the core of the initiative will be praying for it, but their prayers should be supported by others. Pioneering can be hard work and face many obstacles. Prayer support is vital. In his study of church planting movements, David Garrison found that prayer played a key role in protecting church founders from spiritual attack, in enabling them to establish networks of partners quickly, in bringing forth more workers, in modelling to non-believers the importance of prayer, in bringing people to faith and in enabling new believers to mature in their faith.

> Prayer permeates Church Planting Movements. Whether it's Koreans rising at four in the morning for a two-hour prayer time, or Spanish Gypsies *'going to the mountain'*, as they call their all night prayer vigils, Church Planting Movements are steeped in prayer. Consequently, prayer has become the first priority of every Church Planting Movement strategist. (Garrison, 2004, pp. 172–3)

Prayer partners may include Christian friends, the church that is sponsoring the initiative, individuals with a special call to pray or a nearby religious order. A regular flow of information and stories from the mission community will provide fuel for prayer, but the communication should be two-way. Prayer partners may have helpful inputs to make.

In addition to the benefits Garrison lists, a wide circle of prayer partners will

- strengthen the spiritual heart of the venture;
- open more channels for the Spirit's guidance;

- assist the mission community to remain connected to the living Christian tradition;
- expand the potential for practical support. This may include being a source of advice and expertise, introducing the community to gatekeepers and widening the community's networks.

The people the venture is called to serve

A mission community will want to cement relationships that have begun to form among people who are its mission focus. As trust grows, the community will invite these people to shape its vision further and help in planning for it. Encouraging volunteers from the context will increase commitment to the venture, and volunteers will be likely to invite their friends.

Mission communities can include or exclude people. Inclusion immediately distinguishes an 'in' group from an 'out'. The ability to define who is and who is not 'in' is the prerogative of the more powerful and essential to their self-identity. A mission community will want to think carefully about which individuals, from those it seeks to serve, it is including in its conversations and why. How will others' views be taken into account?

From 30 years of experience, Bob Hopkins urges that converts from the mission culture should be brought into the 'planting team' before developing patterns of community and worship. They should play a decisive role in forming these aspects of the new church (Hopkins, 2008, p. 30). Well before they are converted, volunteers from the context will be making important practical contributions. In some circumstances, might they make spiritual contributions as well?

A community of artists, for example, could have a spiritual zone where they meet. Why should not someone without obvious Christian faith populate the zone with books showing European religious art? The convener of a spirituality group in a leisure centre might lead members through an Ignatian exercise, using a book bought for the purpose, in the first couple of sessions. A member with no overt faith might be asked to lead the third session, if they were willing, using the same book.

Sharing leadership will help individuals grow in confidence, be a first step toward making the church self-sustaining and will express faith that the Spirit has been preparing the heart of the person involved. Good leaders do more than win followers: they breed other leaders, and this process can start in the early stages of a new church. Individuals quickly become dependent on their leaders. So countering that dependence is vital. Jesus shared his ministry with his disciples, including Judas Iscariot who betrayed him. Good leaders take risks.

Permission-givers

Entrepreneurship research emphasizes the importance of connecting to networks of established and prestigious actors. Support from strongholds of power contributes significantly to success. To mobilize resources from these power holders, however, the entrepreneur may have to accept certain constraints (Rindova, Barry and Ketchen, 2009, p. 483). Because human relationships tend to be reciprocal, mission communities must weigh up the freedom they want against the support they desire.

Permission-givers are individuals whose permission is needed if the mission community's vision is to be achieved. They may be outside or inside the church. To gain their support, the initiative must be relevant to their objectives and priorities. A proposal for a school-based church, for instance, would need to relate to the school's values (such as its desire to serve the community), its strategic plan or a challenge the staff face.

If the proposed church is linked to a denomination, permission-givers will be especially concerned about accountability. This should be based on

- *Trust.* The Father trusts his Son to advance the kingdom (1 Cor. 15.24), the Son trusted his disciples to take forward his work after the ascension, the apostles trusted Saint Paul with his mission to the Gentiles, and Saint Paul trusted the leaders he appointed to look after his new churches through the Spirit. He neither retained tight control nor abandoned his oversight. Trusting the mission community is the starting line for accountability.
- *Risk*, which is the companion to trust. There is no risk-free mission. Much went wrong in Paul's churches, but he continued to start more churches and hand their leadership over to new converts. A key issue is who is exposed to risks. It should not be those the church serves. It should not *only* be the initiative's leadership. Ecclesial permission-givers should share the risks too.
- *Mutual accountability*, which is the outworking of trust and risk. Jesus felt accountable to his Father and his Father provided him with support. This two-way relationship should exist between mission communities and their local church or denomination. 'Low control, high accountability' is often held up as the ideal. But notions of support and interdependence need to be in there as well. Though it trips off the tongue less easily, might 'high support/low control, accountability/mutuality' capture better what is involved? This will be expressed through the institution's delegation and support, and through the mission community's reciprocal willingness to evaluate progress (perhaps with the aid of a third party) and to share fully in the denomination's life.

In a denominational context, the ideal is a culture of provisional recognition that allows the emerging church to be progressively recognized in a light-touch manner. Ecclesial authorities should give plenty of support, but also allow the initiative to develop in unexpected ways. For instance, it should not be pressured into becoming a church if the Spirit is leading in a different direction.

Good practice in accountability

In the context of a local church/denomination, it will be wise for those in authority to

- appoint a church founder they can trust;
- agree with the founder what will be expected of him/her and what support will be available;
- separate accountability from support. Combining the two allows one element to undermine the other;
- make sure meetings between the line manager and founder are regular, and that together they periodically evaluate this relationship;
- use the four constituent relationships of the church (with God, the world, the wider church and between members of the gathering) to monitor the initiative's progress, and entrust this evaluation to a third party (evaluation is discussed more fully in the next chapter);
- expect the line manager to champion the initiative.

Early conversations around questions such as those below can be helpful. Where answers are not yet clear, agreeing when the questions will be revisited, by whom and how will help to avoid misunderstandings later.

- How will the initiative be governed?
- How will leaders be appointed and for how long?
- What are the financial expectations?
- How will the venture be safeguarded if leaders of the sponsoring church/denomination change (often a problem)?
- How will progress be reviewed?
- How will the sacraments be celebrated (in the case of denominations where only ordained ministers can preside)?

An alternative or complementary approach involves sharing support and accountability with those who do not have a direct stake in the project. For example the Order of Mission (TOM), which includes church founders, encourages members to join an accountability group of up to 12 peers and to lead one. It is also developing biannual learning communities of leaders and potential leaders for discipleship and accountability (Kershaw, 2010, p. 85).

Holders of purse strings

Though contextual churches may be started by lay people in everyday settings and be financially lightweight, they also include larger church-starts with paid staff and other costs. Questions of finance are especially important for them. Finance is an enabler of mission when handled well. On the other hand, poor financial planning can hurt people served by the initiative and leave them disillusioned, jeopardize the livelihoods of people employed and waste resources when the church as a whole is financially stretched.

A simple ecclesial (or business) plan will usually be necessary if the mission community approaches charitable trusts and foundations for money (see Box). Members will want to consider the time it will take to become financially self-supporting, how this squares with the time frames of potential funders and what alternative sources of finance will be available when the initial funding ends:

- Will the mission community and some of their friends be the mainstay of financial support?
- Will funding from the parent church (where relevant) be available on an ongoing basis?
- Can the community develop a network of financial supporters, perhaps starting with its prayer partners?
- Can it ask for donations from the people the initiative serves, or introduce a charge?
- As individuals come to faith, what role will Christian giving play in their discipleship?
- What combination of these streams might be possible?

Potential ingredients of an 'ecclesial plan'

- **Aim**: Can the mission community express in a few words what it is seeking to achieve?
- **Opportunity**: Who will the initiative serve? In what ways? What is the potential for sustainability and growth? How will leaders evaluate whether the aim has been achieved?
- **Context**: What is the evidence that the opportunity exists to serve people in this way? Who has been consulted? Is anyone else doing something similar?
- **People**: Who is leading the initiative? Who else is involved? What specialist expertise can the initiative draw on, such as financial and legal advice?

- **Costs**: What will be the start-up and ongoing costs? How will they be met?
- **Risks**: What could go wrong? What steps will be taken to minimize these risks? How often will a risk assessment be undertaken?

Source: Adapted from Sahlman (1999, p. 32).

Donors will almost certainly want to know how fruitfulness will be measured. As suggested in the next chapter, a 'theology of evaluation' can be based on the concept of discernment. Evaluating the results of a contextual church can be a means of discerning whether and how the Spirit has been at work. Learning from this discernment can guide the initiative's development, and if the learning is shared, add to the wisdom of the whole church.

Funders and others in authority should have realistic expectations. A church started by someone who is new to the area and has to draw together a team will take longer to become financially self-sustaining (if that is the aim) than one that is led by a person inheriting a team with strong networks. Initiatives relying on grants or loans may require several years to develop income streams that cover their ongoing costs.

Partnerships

Organizations collaborate for a variety of reasons. Sometimes they do so to gain efficiency (Williamson, 1991). Local churches, for example, can reduce the time and cost of organizing similar events separately or of being in dispute with each other. At other times they cooperate to get greater control over scarce resources (Pfeffer and Salancik, 1978). A joint grant application avoids the risk that one organization will be successful and the other not. Extending this perspective, some theorists emphasize how networks generate additional resources, including information. Entrepreneurship becomes a collective process (Conway and Jones, 2006).

Ann Morisy writes that when people, motivated by 'venturesome love', embrace a struggle for the well-being of others, it can prompt an often unexpected 'cascade of grace'. A simple act of volunteering may spark conversations that result in an invitation to a Christian event, which leads to a deeper pondering about spiritual issues. A small expression of love may ripple through a network with amplifying effects (2004, p. 32).

This suggests a key theological reason to collaborate with others. Networking across organizational boundaries multiplies the opportunity for grace to cascade. These networks may include formal or informal partnerships with organizations inside the church or outside. As partnerships form to share resources, coordinate complementary activities, leverage in additional resources, expand networks and increase impact, relationships form that can become carriers of grace.

The benefits of these partnerships must outweigh the costs, such as the time involved and the possible loss of focus if partners have disparate goals and values. A secular agency may have a diversity agenda, for instance, that constrains the initiative's expression of faith. An imbalance of power, perhaps because the partner is putting in most of the resources, creates a risk that the initiative's interests become subordinate to its partner's.

Research confirms everyday experience that successful collaboration depends on having a shared mission and values, on personal connection and relationship, on an expectation of mutual benefit, on shared power and risk, and on mutual trust (Foster and Meinhard, 2002, p. 551).

The public

Enjoying 'the goodwill of all the people' (Acts 2.47) witnesses to the kingdom, opens doors and makes it easier to win backing for the initiative. A good reputation is a priceless asset. To be 'a good citizen', a mission community will need to think about:

- *legal requirements*, such as child protection, health and safety, employment law, third party insurance and charitable status;
- *organizations and churches*, ranging from the police, to the school, to local voluntary groups and churches nearby. Who needs to be informed or consulted as the initiative develops?
- *representatives*, such as the residents association, local councillors or representatives of local retailers;
- *ethical boundaries*, which may apply especially to a workplace expression of church. A teacher planning an initiative at school, for example, would need to think carefully about what can be said and done during school hours.

Six types of stakeholder

- Prayer partners
- The people the mission community serves
- Permission-givers
- Holders of purse strings
- Partnering organizations
- The public.

Building a web of belief

Laura Dunham (2003) has described stakeholder networks in early-stage entrepreneurial ventures as 'webs of belief'. These are relationships between the entrepreneur and those with a stake in the venture, such as providers of financial support. The relationships are largely based on stakeholders' belief in the entrepreneur. Dunham's model is striking for emphasizing the ethical and non-financial components of this belief. It thus suggests a helpful framework for understanding how mission communities can fruitfully engage with their partners as they birth a contextual church.

Forming relationships of trust

On the basis of empirical study, Dunham (2003, pp. 133–97) describes a process of 'expressive embedding' that enables entrepreneurs and prospective stakeholders to quickly form close, personal, trust-based ties. Relationships are formed not by individuals who are rationally calculating, but through a process that is value-led and identity-driven. The process is characterized by the development of 'swift trust' and by strong emotional and moral commitments. It is driven more by a sense of social affiliation between the entrepreneur and the resource giver than by mutual self-interest. Both parties speedily recognize that they have shared values – 'a sense that both are similar in terms of what is most important to them, about how they think about problems, and about what they want to achieve through their involvement in the venture' (p. 24).

On the basis of Dunham's research, three elements are likely to be involved in the formation of strong relationships between the mission community and its partners. The first is the perceived character of the initiative's leader. This includes the person's apparent trustworthiness, such as their competence, integrity and goodwill, and their authentic 'embodiment' of the initiative: the leader's personal story and stated purposes make the person the obvious one to run it.

A second element is the 'venture narrative' – the story that is told about the initiative. The narrative will appeal to the partner at emotional, moral and even aesthetic levels. The initiative will come to have a moral legitimacy because of its ethical stance, or a pragmatic legitimacy because it adds moral value to the partner or both. In the context of ecclesial pioneering, a school might want to be associated with a church-run after-school club. Perhaps the church is an important player in the community and the school wants to strengthen its community credentials.

Teasdale (2010) has described how social entrepreneurs may construct a narrative that responds to the expectations, interests and agendas of potential stakeholders. They may start with a 'script' that worked in a previous conversation, but modify the script in the light of the other person's verbal and non-verbal reactions. This means that being able to read people becomes an important skill. However, if stakeholders are diverse, there may be a temptation to stretch the narrative to accommodate a wide range of audiences. Stretch too far and the entrepreneur's integrity will be at risk.

This will undermine the person's moral credibility, which – according to Dunham – is critical for establishing trusting relationships. Moral consistency in the 'venture narrative' is therefore essential.

To make themselves plausible, founders need much more than a compelling idea. Credibility depends on being clear about processes, pointing to relevant experience, obtaining persuasive endorsements and putting in place appropriate structures. All these are part of the venture narrative.

A third element is a set of strategies that the leader uses to add a personal dimension to the partner relationship. In Dunham's research, these strategies included casual meeting places, peppering conversations with life stories, discussing the stakeholder's personal goals and aspirations, and getting to know prospective stakeholders' families. If done without integrity, these strategies will ring hollow and fail to convince. But if they are authentic, they can be very persuasive. In a kingdom context, these strategies are about being other directed – being genuinely concerned about the partner's welfare and looking out for their interests.

Once relationships have formed, regular engagement in open, trust-based communication maintains the tie. So does an ethic of care; the mission community shows concern for the partner in appropriate ways. In addition, following Huy and Zott (2007, pp. 11–5), the leader (or representative of the mission community) will pay attention to the partners' emotions by putting minds at rest (such as assuaging fears that the initiative will 'steal' other churches' members), being upbeat about the initiative to generate enthusiasm, and displaying self-control in meetings to calm agitated feelings. Emotionally versatile church founders can be effective in a variety of contexts. But this versatility will need an ethical framework – a concern for genuineness and integrity.

Relationships of trust

They are established through
- a shared identity between the entrepreneur and the resource-giver;
- a convincing 'venture narrative';
- the personalizing of relationships.

They are maintained by
- regular communication;
- an ethic of care;
- attention to partners' emotions.

What influences success?

What enables mission communities to create shared identity, develop an attractive 'venture narrative' and personalize relationships? One part of the answer, drawing on Dunham, is the community's stock of 'ethical capital' – its moral assets. A mission community should be *credible* – there is congruity between its aspirations and its capacity; members are not 'all talk'. It should be *consistent* – members do what they say. It should be *concerned* – for other people and the environment. And it should have *compelling ideals*, which others respect. As it develops and displays these qualities, the community will be trusted, it will forge fruitful bonds with partners and its reputation will grow.

Dunham found that certain qualities encourage stakeholder relationships. These include qualities like integrity and goodwill, which are kingdom virtues. If we extrapolate Dunham's findings, we might suggest that when mission communities and their leaders embody the kingdom, the virtues they display will appeal to at least some people outside the church. 'Webs of belief' will draw in, alongside those within the church, partners who are attracted to the kingdom. They will create clusters of supporters who, without necessarily being aware of it, are in some way in favour of God's reign.

Displaying kingdom virtues – or, in Dunham's language, maintaining a stock of ethical capital – thus becomes vital to birthing church. This resonates with Alasdair MacIntyre's concept of practice, discussed in Chapter 11. The chapter argued that birthing contextual churches should be seen as a practice, whose goal is set within the larger Christian story. It noted MacIntyre's emphasis on qualities of character that sustain a practice. To practise well requires virtues that are learnt within the community of practitioners.

Kingdom virtues are nurtured as members of the Christian body read Scripture, pray and worship, discern the Spirit, share their gifts, and provide mutual support and accountability. It is vital, therefore, that as they bring a church to birth mission communities develop a rich spiritual life, which will include remaining well connected to the living Christian tradition.

Second, mission communities are enabled to create and maintain bonds of trust if they possess one virtue in particular – humility. In conveying their narrative about the initiative, mission communities are likely to find themselves on a strategic spectrum. At one end is the 'salesman' approach based on the heroic pioneer. The pioneer has lots of charisma and uses it to pitch for help from whoever matters. The pioneer, or mission community, comes up with the vision. All that is then needed is to drum up support.

Charismatic leaders can develop amazing ventures by being effective sales people. But the approach can produce an attitude of superiority. 'We've got a great vision. Will you get behind it?' rather than 'We've got some ideas. Will you help to shape them?' There is a danger that the leader's enthusiasm will sweep others along and silence warning voices. Someone outside the team may be aware of a change in circumstances or have an idea that could improve the proposal. This feedback is hard to hear if the leader and the community are in selling rather than listening mode. If a selling approach appears to be the only model, potential but less charismatic founders of church may be put off.

At the other end of the spectrum, a 'testing' approach seeks not mainly to sell a vision to partners but to involve them in developing it. 'This is where our thinking has got to. How do you react?' The mission community garners support by engaging others in 'co-producing' the vision. Persuasion occurs as partners work together. The personal qualities of a charismatic founder can still come into play, but there is room for less charismatic leaders. They enlist help not by being good at selling, but by patiently developing ideas with people outside the mission community.

The process may be slower than 'selling' because the community more frequently goes back to partners as ideas evolve. But partners will feel they have a stronger stake in the vision. This will increase trust, respect and friendliness, all of which enlarges support for the initiative. The input of others will expand the pool of wisdom, knowledge and personal contacts available to the community. The community itself will keep open to new ideas and alternative solutions. Opposition from a partner will be seen as an opportunity for learning rather than being viewed negatively: negotiation may produce an outcome better than the original idea.

Testing requires humility. It involves recognizing the limitations of one's own perspective. It demands a willingness to give what seems a good idea to someone else and allow them to reshape it. It is a self-emptying process – 'what is mine I hand over to you.' This may prolong uncertainty. The mission community thought it had a clear vision, but finds that some of its partners have reservations. Perhaps different possibilities compete with each other, clouding the way ahead. This can feel uncomfortable. On the other hand, through the Spirit, novelty is more likely to emerge. People may come up with creative ideas to combine possibilities or to solve problems that critics have identified. When things are buttoned up, there is less space for innovative thought. Humility keeps the future open.

Third, mission communities are enabled to create and maintain bonds of trust if those who represent them, usually their leaders, possess social competence. This is the ability to relate well to others by using social skills – in particular:

- *Social perception*: an ability to read other people.
- *Social adaptability*: the person can relate well to people in a variety of social contexts.
- *Expressiveness*: the person expresses emotions clearly to evoke enthusiasm in others.
- *Positive impression management*: others see the person in a positive way.

A study of business entrepreneurs found that their financial success was related to social competence (Baron and Markman, 2003, pp. 41–60). Social perception was especially important, followed by social adaptability and expressiveness. The results for positive impression management were less conclusive. The authors noted (p. 58) that techniques for enhancing such skills have had considerable success, and argued that training entrepreneurs in social skills might help them to exploit opportunities and launch new ventures. Might this have implications for how church founders are supported and trained?

Mission communities will be likely to form webs of belief if they possess

- kingdom virtues;
- humility in particular;
- social competence.

What do webs of belief deliver?

Dunham found that forming relationships of trust produced positive outcomes for entrepreneurs and their ventures, such as reducing the need for legal agreements (2003, pp. 180–94). In the context of giving birth to church, the benefits of creating a web of belief can be understood in terms of the gifts received by the mission community on behalf of the initiative. These gifts will normally be received on a reciprocal basis. Partners get something back in return, such as identifying with a cause they believe in.

In the secular world, a number of writers have discussed entrepreneurial capital, which is the variety of assets and resources used in the entrepreneurial process (Firkin, 2001, p. 1). 'Pioneer gifts' can be seen as the ecclesial equivalent. It is the stock of gifts, or resources, that the initiative receives. A web of belief increases pioneer gifts by adding to one or more of the following:[1]

- *Economic gifts*, such as loans and grants. Prayer or other partners may provide financial support.
- *Social gifts*, which are the ability to secure resources through membership of social networks and other social structures. Partners, such as permission-givers, may introduce the mission community to their networks – 'I'm sure our treasurer could give you some advice'.
- *Ethical gifts*, which include norms such as accountability, transparency, reciprocity and fairness that can be used to create social gifts. Ethical gifts also include the moral goals of the initiative. The mission com-

---

1 The list is based on Firkin (2001, pp. 2–4) and, in the case of ethical capital, Ridley-Duff and Bull (2011, pp. 94–6).

munity may increase its stock of these gifts by gaining the support of professionals, like medical practitioners, whose practices rub off on the community. The community may learn about accountability and transparency, for example, by working with professionals.

- *Human gifts*, which are all the attributes and abilities, from family background to education and experience to personality traits, that enable the mission community's members to be effective. They include volunteers with their attributes and abilities.
- *Cultural gifts*, such as knowledge, books and machines. Partners may be sources of information and may offer cultural goods, such as a room to meet in or the loan of equipment.

The task for the mission community is prayerfully to combine these gifts so that, through the Spirit, it can maximize what it offers the people it serves. As Chapter 6 emphasized, mission is essentially a process of giving – it flows out of the giving heart of God. Mission communities will therefore pray that through their ingenuity and hard work, the Spirit will magnify the gifts in their hands so that they can offer others abundantly more than they have received. Birthing a church becomes a process of multiplying talents (Luke 19.16, 18) and giving these talents away.

Conclusion

Contextual churches emerge through relationships with a range of partners such as prayer partners, the people the initiative serves, permission givers, holders of purse strings, partner organizations and the public. In a variety of ways, these partners make it possible for the church to be born. They do so through relationships with the mission community that form a web of belief.

The hypothesis here is that webs of belief come into being through the beliefs and values that church founders (and their mission communities) share with their partners. Through the Spirit, the process is pushed forward by the character of the founder and the mission community's members, the 'venture narrative' and a variety of personalizing strategies. Once underway, the process is maintained by trust-based communications, an ethic of care and attention to partners' emotions. Success depends on the possession of kingdom virtues, of humility in particular and of social competence. The result is an increase in gifts to the initiative. These enable the mission community to produce its own gifts to offer the people it serves.

Once the web of belief has formed, the new church must avoid an over-stable network of interactions. Stability certainly helps to create and maintain trust. But it can also lead to atrophy. As both the church and the context evolve, new relationships will breed fresh life into the community and renew its capacity to accompany the Spirit into the world. Persistent networking, flexibility and openness to the new will help the church neither to be stifled by the status quo, nor overwhelmed by novelty, but to occupy a space in which the Spirit can continue to surprise.

Further reading

Baron, Robert A. and Gideon D. Markman, 'Beyond Social Capital: the Role of Social Entrepreneurs' Social Competence in their Financial Success', *Journal of Business Venturing* 18 (1), 2003, pp. 41–60.

Ridley-Duff, Rory and Mike Bull, *Understanding Social Enterprise: Theory and Practice*, London: Sage, 2011.

Questions for discussion

- What should accountability and support look like? How might these differ for founders working within a denomination and those on the outside?
- How far are 'webs of belief' created intuitively? In what ways is it helpful to analyse the processes involved?
- What theological themes might illuminate the content of this chapter?

15

Action-based Learning

Reflecting on his extensive experience, Bob Hopkins comments, 'We're often invited to consultancies by weak or struggling church plants. Some of the most serious weaknesses exposed are failures in planning and preparation' (Hopkins, 2008, p. 35). Planning occurs throughout the life of the mission community, the founding core of a contextual church. But how to do so becomes a pressing question once the mission community has gathered, researched opportunities and begun to form relationships with key partners. Perhaps members have tested their emerging vision on others. They know it has support. Now they must turn it into reality. How do they plan for this?

There is not a lot about planning in emerging church or recent church planting literature. Indeed, for many church founders, 'planning' has mechanistic connotations they would reject. It is, however, discussed extensively in the business literature. The traditional approach understands planning in terms of analysis. In the light of a venture's purpose, vision and values, planning involves identifying goals, breaking a goal into steps, designing how to implement the steps and anticipating the consequences of each one. In much of the current literature, this planning-as-analysis approach is giving way to planning as learning. Planning is seen as a process of action-based learning, of learning by doing, of trial and error. But this learning does not always happen easily. Groups need practices that support it.

This chapter offers a pragmatic and theological rationale for planning as action-based learning, argues that looking forward and looking back are fundamental to the process, puts milestone reviews at the heart of what is involved and discusses evaluation as a means of learning. Whereas Chapters 11 to 13 considered methodologies that give concrete form to communal and contextual mission, this is the second of three chapters that discuss methodologies which facilitate the earlier ones. Engaging with partners provides resources for communal and contextual mission. Through the Spirit, action-based learning pulls the mission forward.

Planning as learning

Where planning is specifically discussed in the church planting literature, the taken-for-granted model is planning as analysis. For example, in *Be Fruitful and Multiply* (2006), Robert Logan devotes a chapter to 'Planning for church multiplication'. He recommends a framework of vision, goals, steps and individuals' tasks, which should be placed on a timeline (p. 89). Alan Hirsch veers in the same direction when he expounds the notion of 'managing from the future' (2006, pp. 233–5). He writes of the power of big visions to change the present. A big goal changes people as they seek to enact it.

However, this overlooks the iterative process whereby a vision influences action in the present, but enacting the present also influences the vision. As the vision is discussed, it is subtly changed. Some elements may be ignored, others reinterpreted and new ingredients may be added in. Conversations change the vision, just as the vision changes conversations. Hirsch makes vision sound static and solid, which gives his conception a rather traditional quality.

In relating to mission communities, denominations tend to incline toward this traditional approach. They ask for objectives, targets and timescales to see fruit from their investments and protect their reputations. This reinforces a sterile and outmoded approach to planning, which cements its bad name among some pioneers.

An unpredictable world

Planning as analysis is not as good as planning as learning – for three reasons. First, it assumes a stable context. In the analytic approach, a team may write down its purpose (to serve a specific group of people), its vision for how this is to be achieved, the values that underpin the vision and goals that must be reached for the vision to be realized. The intention is to hold the team on course and provide a focus for its work. To do this, the purpose, vision, values and goals must remain relatively fixed. If they keep changing, they will no longer provide clear points to guide the team.

Complexity theorists argue that much of today's world is intrinsically unpredictable (Holmdahl, 2005, pp. 4–5, 12). Though it is something of a myth that this was not so in the past, today's world has become even less stable. The network society is radically transforming social life. New forms of interconnectivity are multiplying the number of real life and online conversations between people. The world is perpetually being shaped and reshaped by these conversations. Time and again conversations have outcomes that cannot be anticipated. As these conversations flow in and out of each other, a small input into one may get amplified and transformed to produce a surprising result.

In this world, the emergence of churches tends to be fluid, haphazard and far from linear. A vision is not achieved through planned steps. Perhaps for example a vision has been discerned, but then a key person leaves; it is back to the drawing board. Life's unpredictability means that planning has to be approached in a different way. It must be seen as constantly provisional – as an ongoing response to new opportunities and changed circumstances.

Learning by doing

Second, planning as learning takes more seriously the learning dimension of human behaviour than planning as analysis. Modern learning theory emphasizes the vital role played by experience (Boud, Cohen and Walker, 1993). Ideas are not acquired in a vacuum. Relationships, personal interests, emotions and activity all play key parts in the assimilation and processing of information. Experience enables us to learn.

Henry Mintzberg argues that while we frequently think in order to act, sometimes we act in order to think. The essence of business strategy is learning as people act. 'Strategies can develop inadvertently, without the conscious intention of senior management, often through a process of learning . . . Learning inevitably plays *a*, if not *the*, crucial role in the development of novel strategies' (Mintzberg, 1994, p. 111; author's italics). In an earlier and influential article, Arie de Geus (1988, pp. 70–4) maintained that the real purpose of planning is to change the mental models of decision-makers. This happens through reflection on experience. Planning as changing your mind is very different to laying down fixed-in-stone courses of action.

This gives planning an experimental feel. Planners learn as they go. They try something. If it works they build on it. If it does not, they try something else. This view should not be a surprise because experimentation is intrinsic to being human. The history of civilization is the history of novelty, of experiments, of people trying an idea and seeing if it works. Experimentation has a playful dimension, akin to when children make up a game, or when a master chess player devises a new sequence of moves. The player experiments with the moves to see if they are effective. The children experiment with their new game to see how much fun they can have.[1]

Writing about play, Jürgen Moltmann describes the regularities of the laws of nature as the systemization of past adaptations. But patterns of adaptation are constantly interrupted by 'chance' – 'something underivable and undeducible from anything that already exists' (Moltmann, 1985, p. 312). These chance interruptions should not be seen as irritants for they prise open the regularities of existing laws. They create new situations to which living beings adapt through the free play of their energies. 'In play human beings display and maintain their own liberty . . . The kingdom of freedom is the kingdom of play' (p. 310).

On the basis of Proverbs 8.30ff, Moltmann argues that the creation of the world has the character of play. God created not out of necessity, but out of

---

1 When children explore, discover, create and innovate as they build pillow forts in the bedroom or sail away in a laundry basket to a foreign land, we call it play. But when adults explore, discover, create and innovate, we often say that they are experimenting. Play and experimentation are similar. From a psychoanalytic standpoint, Caper (1996) has explored some of the links between play, scientific experimentation and artistic creativity.

freedom. The process gave Wisdom delight. '[God] created what gave him pleasure, and what gives him pleasure is what accords with his inmost nature' (1985, p. 311). When humans experiment in the cause of the kingdom, they engage in a form of play that reflects the character of God. They enter zones of freedom that echo God's freedom. They use their freedom to try something new, something that reflects God, something that therefore brings pleasure to God. If it works, it gets caught up in and enriches the kingdom.

Planning as learning becomes part of human playfulness, a participation in divine play. This radically alters the experience of planning. Planning becomes more than a utilitarian exercise – what works best. It becomes an opportunity to join God in play, to create a world where freedom is used to bring divine delight. Changes in the context cease being irritants and become opportunities for creativity, for trying something different, for revelling in the freedom given by God.

Planning through conversations

Third, planning as learning puts a premium on learning through conversations. Actions emerge out of the story a group tells about itself. To learn, a group must process information in a way that changes the story. This requires conversations that generate a different story. Much learning founders because there is no space, permission or capability for different conversations to take place and new stories to emerge. A traditional strategic plan may contribute to this. It constrains conversations by squeezing them into a framework. The plan becomes a perceived reality 'out there' that puts boundaries round future exchanges.

This alters when purpose, vision, values, goals and next steps are seen as continuing outputs from and inputs into conversations. As a plan from earlier discussions is renegotiated in the light of new knowledge and experience, it becomes the subject of rather than a constraint on conversation. This encourages learning from experience. Space is created for the Spirit to bring something new. By keeping the plan constantly under review, individuals are allowed greater freedom in their contributions: they can say what they think about the plan. Conversations become more authentic.

This fits well with the relational essence of church described in Chapter 5. If church is a drama of four interlocking sets of relationships – with God, the living Christian tradition, the world and within the gathering – then conversations will be at the heart of the experience of church. Conversations about plans will occur in the context of these four sets of relationships as the mission community dialogues with God in prayer and study, consults prayer partners and appropriate ecclesial authorities, converses with other partners (especially the people it is called to serve) and discusses what is being learnt from all these interactions. Planning becomes strategic conversation about action-based learning.

Planning as learning

- works with the unpredictable nature of the world;
- takes seriously the experimental, even playful nature of much human activity;
- allows conversations to modify existing 'plans'.

Looking forward and looking back

Central to this view of planning is looking forward and looking back. As it helps to bring a church to birth, the mission community prayerfully looks forward in the light of its experience. This can be intuitive, but there are advantages – as we shall see – in being explicit about it. It is a learning process, enabled by the Spirit. Becoming aware of how they are learning helps mission communities to be more intentional about learning well.

Looking forward

In the early stages, the mission community draws on its emerging vision and its knowledge of the resources available to look ahead. It imagines the journey the initiative is likely to travel. This may be the *worship-first* or *serving-first journey* described in Chapter 11, or a variation on them. Looking forward is about envisaging the next stages of the journey and asking what the community must do to travel faithfully and fruitfully. It may include asking questions like those in the box below. Though the answers may not yet be clear, the questions may raise issues that help the mission community in its preparations.

Some questions for looking forward

- How might people experience community as the initiative develops?
- How would we put Jesus on to the agenda?
- How would we help people to explore discipleship?
- How will the way we introduce people to the faith affect their subsequent growth in the faith?
- As church begins to take shape, what might discipleship, worship and community look like?
- Are we starting in ways that will help the venture to be sustainable?
- How can we start to think about indigenizing leadership?
- How will the initiative stay missional and reproduce?

Looking forward is important because the kingdom comes to us from the future. Moltmann has differentiated between the future that develops out of the tendencies of the present and the future that is radically new. The first type of future is an extrapolation from the present: the second is known in anticipation. In his exposition of Moltmann, Paul Fiddes (2000b, pp. 167–8) distinguishes between potential and possibilities. When we extrapolate the future from the present, we think in terms of the present's potential. What in the present might be realized in the future? But when we anticipate the future, we think in terms of possibilities. What novelty from the future – from the kingdom – might the Spirit bring?

Anticipating possibilities is congruent with the view that novelty emerges from within conversations. As people talk, different ideas combine to produce new insights and proposals for action. Enacting these proposals also involves conversation, which modifies the plan (if only slightly) while giving effect to it. If the Spirit is present in human conversations and can nudge them toward the kingdom, conversations become one of the means by which the Spirit brings possibilities from the future into the present.

Drawing on Moltmann, Richard Bauckham (1987, p. 44) notes that planning which relies only on extrapolation can lose impetus and vision. It becomes constrained by the potentialities of the present. Vision shrinks and becomes less exciting. On the other hand, hope that reaches beyond the potential risks being unrealistic. It may be so unconstrained by the present as to become fantasy. Combining extrapolation and anticipation gives hope a realistic hue. Anticipation imagines a desirable future, shaped by the kingdom. Extrapolation looks for elements in the present that may support and be transformed by what is desired. This discernment must be ongoing. A mission community may spot new kingdom possibilities when it repeats the task of looking ahead.

Looking forward has a second purpose. It can help the mission community to think strategically. Peering down the path they hope to travel, members can ask, 'How might we move from one phase to the next?' 'What pitfalls must we avoid?' One risk for instance is that Christians will flood the new venture, change the atmosphere and reset the agenda. Several fresh expressions have experienced this problem, which might have been avoided if the danger had been considered in advance. Thinking strategically includes asking what principles should inform how the mission community addresses the challenges and tasks that lie ahead. These principles will relate to gathering, researching, engaging partners and the other processes involved in starting a new church.

Third, as members look ahead they can test the viability of their vision. 'Can we imagine how this initiative would become church for the people it serves?' If members cannot, it is possible that they are on the wrong track and should think again. Or they might conclude that they are being called to start not a church but a community project, an entirely valid contribution to the kingdom. Or they might start in the hope that the initiative becomes church, even though they are not clear how. Imagining the journey to church could spark some clarifying conversations.

Fourth, and perhaps most important, looking ahead can help the mission community to implant genetic material that will bring the initiative to a mature expression of church – 'what must we do now if the venture is to have the right DNA?' As Part 4 will argue, if the new church is to grow to maturity, the pathways to this end need to be considered early on. These will include forming disciples, worship, community and sustainability.

These pathways may be far from clear, but having some sense of direction will help the mission community to consider what next stone should be laid in each case. If there is no sense of direction, little attention will be paid to what should happen next. The initiative may stall because a vision for moving forward is absent. Thus if the vision includes birthing further churches, how this is built into the dynamics of the new church needs early thought. How would it affect the way disciples are formed, for instance? Though it may be too early to answer the question, keeping it in mind will alert members to pointers from the Spirit.

Looking forward should be a continuous activity throughout a contextual church's life. It will help leaders to avoid becoming so preoccupied with 'keeping the show on the road' that they settle into comfortable routines, allowing the venture to grow stale and failing to adapt to external changes. Looking for the next horizon will help to energize and renew the church's mission. It will keep the vision fresh.

Looking forward can enable the mission community

- to discern the kingdom as it comes from the future;
- to ask how the initiative can move from one phase of the journey to the next;
- to test the viability of its vision by imagining the future;
- to lay stepping stones to maturity;
- to keep the church fresh.

Looking back

Looking back is important even in a mission community's early days. It focuses on how God has been leading the initiative. This allows learning from experience and provides a perspective from which to look forward. Looking back can be based on the 'pastoral cycle', which is a way of prayerfully reflecting on experience. Paul Ballard and John Pritchard suggest a four-stage cycle, which may be better understood as an ongoing spiral (Ballard and Pritchard 2006, ch. 6.):

- *Experience*: What have we experienced on our journey, and how do our perceptions of this differ?
- *Exploration*: So what's been going on? In particular, what factors have shaped our experience?
- *Reflection*: How does God see this? What would delight and disappoint him? What would Jesus do in the light of the journey so far?
- *Action*: What should we do as a result of our exploration and reflection?

This spiral should be a continuous process. As members of a mission community take action, they begin to change the situation. New dynamics come into play which they experience, explore, reflect on and act upon, and these again alter the situation. Over time, both individuals and the community become different.

Using this spiral will include reviewing the principles the mission community previously identified when looking forward. What principles did the community think were relevant? How far did they steer what the community did? How were they adapted? Should they be modified further? Or were they not as relevant as the community thought? Is the community discovering new guiding principles?

Discerning the initiative's values

As the mission community gathers people round it and the initiative develops, the process of looking back can be used to discern the distinctive values of the emerging church. Chapter 12 described ethos as being how the group

The pastoral cycle

feels when members are together – the group's atmosphere. It is the group's 'spontaneous repeated behaviours' (Hirsch and Ferguson, 2011, p. 167). These behaviours give the group's its atmosphere and give rise to its values. Values identify who the group *is* (they are the group's fingerprints). Vision, which is shaped by values, expresses what the group *sees*. Purpose explains what the group wishes to *accomplish* to realize its vision.

As the mission community embarks on its work, it should be explicit about the values it holds dear. Only later will the *initiative's* values become clear. The mission community's values and the initiative's values should not be confused. The former only apply to the mission community and inform its activities and relationships. The latter apply to the initiative as a whole and describe what distinguishes it from other ventures of the same type. If the initiative is a youth church, the mission community's values describe the leaders' agreed bottom lines: the initiative's values describe what makes this youth church different to others. Though the mission community's values and the initiative's values are distinct, they are likely to overlap. The mission community's values will shape the initiative's ethos, out of which its values will arise.

Values of Potters House, Stoke-on-Trent

- A house of prayer
- Young at heart
- Friendly and welcoming
- Having high standards in all its activities
- Inclusive and compassionate
- Culturally relevant in the style of its activities
- Reaching the lost relationally.

Source: www.thepottershouse.org

The initiative's values are a gift from God. They contain charisms that give the emerging church its special flavour – that bless its members and people outside. Only as the initiative takes shape will these values become apparent. They emerge in retrospect. This is very different to stipulating them in advance, perhaps in a mission statement. Some groups are tempted to do this, but they risk closing down the future. Either the values put the initiative in a straitjacket and discourage it from growing in unexpected ways, or they are too general to steer the initiative's life and are ignored. When values are stipulated in advance, the people the initiative serves are denied room to shape these values.

Discerning the initiative's values in retrospect keeps the future open and places it in the hands of all involved. It ensures that the gift of being community with Jesus is a genuine gift. The manner of receiving the gift is placed into the hands of the recipients. This does not mean that members of a mission community will suppress their hopes for the venture. These hopes will properly be brought into conversations with others involved. But the hopes will be less prescriptive than approaches that seek to predetermine the incipient church's character.

As the mission community – in discussion with others – prayerfully looks back over the journey, it may discern the initiative's emerging values through the remarks of outsiders, visitors or new members. 'People always seem to be laughing.' 'You are such a generous group.' The aim should be to compile not a long list of values, but just a few statements that capture what is unique to the new church. A good test might be whether there is an 'aha' moment, when people say, 'Yes! That's us.'

Recognizing its distinctive values will strengthen the initiative's sense of identity. It will help the emerging church to nourish those aspects of its life members feel strongly about. The values may well evolve as the church continues its journey. If they do, it will be a sign that the church is very much alive.

Combining looking forward and looking back

When brought together, looking forward and looking back foster what is known as double-loop learning. This involves taking a double look at a situation by questioning what is given. If mission communities only learn from past experience, they risk getting trapped in single-loop learning. They accept the given parameters of the past, which then constrains how they think about the future. But if they also look forward, anticipating the possibilities of the kingdom, they allow these possibilities to challenge thinking entrenched in the past. The future can be viewed both realistically and creatively.

Milestone reviews

As a church is brought to birth, looking forward and looking back may seem obvious things to do. Yet it is remarkable how many leadership groups fail to do this regularly and systematically. To build them into a mission community's life, looking forward and back can be done in the context of milestone reviews (Block and MacMillan, 1999, pp. 117–33). These are opportunities to take stock and envisage the road ahead. They may be done by the mission community alone or include others who are part of the initiative. They can be undertaken informally during a communal meal or by two friends chatting over coffee, or they can be done formally as an agenda item in a team meeting.

Milestone reviews can have something of a eucharistic feel. In Holy Communion, the community looks back to what Jesus has done and looks forward to his return. Might milestone reviews be undertaken within the context of a Communion or agape supper? Worship, reflection and planning would be brought together. The story of the emerging church would be inserted into the heart of the Christian narrative.

The value of milestone reviews

Milestone reviews are important because they build discipline into the mission community's learning. Elaborating a 'constructivist view of learning', Jennifer Moon (2004, pp. 16–7) describes how new information is assimilated into an individual's network of knowledge, understanding and the associated emotions. This network is 'what is known' by the learner at a particular time. The new material of learning can both be changed by this network and bring changes to it.

Some people enjoy this process of being challenged and thinking afresh – of having their networks of knowledge reshaped. But others can find it uncomfortable. It may involve 'giving up' an established pattern of thought. This surrender can be painful in itself. It can also take time and energy that the person might rather use for something else. Groups sometimes collude with this reluctance to learn; they try to avoid the discomfort. Establishing a disciplined pattern of milestone reviews provides a counter weight to this temptation.

Through the Spirit, milestone reviews help the mission community to adapt to changes outside or inside the initiative. A new team member, a different venue or a change in the leadership of a key partner may have significant repercussions. Regular reviews provide a built-in way to reflect on such changes and adapt to them. In the absence of such reviews, members may have no forum in which to express concerns or explore new opportunities. Issues may get buried only to surface unhelpfully later, and possibilities contained in the new situation may be missed.

In particular, milestone reviews help communities to manage important transitions, such as the first public worship event, a change of leader or the decision to reproduce another contextual church. Transitions often follow the sequence – initial organization, mounting tension ('it's not really working', 'we need to move on'), resolution. How well these transitions are managed depends considerably on the quality of the conversations about them. Milestone reviews are a good context in which to start these conversations.

Milestone reviews are so pivotal for learning that, arguably, they should be central to the business side of the mission community's life. Looking forward and back can provide the engine for each meeting. Entire agendas, and some items within an agenda, can be framed around this dynamic. At the very least, therefore, they should be combined with Bible study, prayer and the exercise of spiritual gifts. When this happens, looking forward and looking back will be brought into the heart of the community's deliberations and be subject to the word and the Spirit.

Planning not plans

Dwight Eisenhower, the World War Two general and later US president, once said, 'In preparing for battle I have always found that plans are useless, but planning is indispensable.' (Quoted by Vincett and Farlow, 2008, p. 278) The same could be said for starting contextual churches. Though 'plans are useless' is an exaggeration, the thought captures the difficulty of working to fixed plans when mission communities are far from being in control of their destinies. Leadership by strategic plan should give way to leadership by discernment (Cray, 2010a). Mission communities go with what presents rather than with what members thought was going to happen, and revise their plans accordingly.

Planning becomes 'indispensable' when it is seen as Spirit-led and learning-based. Members of the mission community learn together. Like planning as analysis, the community will work with vision, goals, concrete steps and even time lines, but the process will feel very different. Instead of something fixed, it will be an exploration. Each step will be an experiment. If it works, it confirms that members are on track to achieve their goals. If not, it invites questions about whether there might be another approach or whether the goal should be revised. Learning occurs through feedback after each step. 'What worked? What didn't? What have we discovered?'

This takes success and failure out of the equation. Members no longer think mainly in terms of whether a planned activity succeeded. Their uppermost question is about what they have learnt – about the validity of their objectives, how things could be done differently and about their context. 'There is no such thing as failure, only feedback' keeps the group optimistic and alert. It shifts attention away from blame and makes discernment the community's central task – 'What is the Spirit saying?' Reflection becomes a community habit.

PEDALS (see Box) may provide a helpful framework for conducting milestone reviews. Though milestones will become millstones if the framework is applied too mechanically, PEDALS offers pegs on which the mission community can hang its reflections. It can open up discussion so that issues come to the surface. Next steps, perhaps as part of a Mission Action Plan (Ireland, 2009), can be agreed and reviewed within this framework.

Evaluation

Measurement and target-setting have had a bad press in the secular world, often because the targets are imposed from outside, are not owned by those involved and privilege some stakeholders (such as funders) over others (frequently those served by the venture). Surely we do not want the same culture creeping into church? On the other hand, evaluation can be seen as a

---

A possible framework for milestone reviews

- *Purposes*: What are we trying to achieve? Are we shifting from our original goals?
- *Environment*: Are we learning new things about the environment in which we are working?
- *Direction*: What was our original vision? Are we still travelling in that direction? Are we getting the necessary support?
- *Actions*: Have we taken the actions we agreed at our last milestone review? Why not? What have we done that we didn't expect?
- *Learning*: What have we learnt as a result of this review? Should we modify our purpose and priorities in the light of this?
- *So what?* In the light of this review, what specific steps should we take between now and the next review? Does this require an updated Mission Action Plan? When shall we hold our next review?

Source: Adapted from Mulgan (2009, p. 76).

---

vital form of learning. It is a way of discerning where and how the Spirit has been at work so that the new church can envisage how the Spirit might lead it in the future. A way through this debate is to ask, first, *who is the evaluation for?* Is it mainly for the initiative or to help partners keep an eye on the mission community, which leads the venture? If the evaluation is initiated by the mission community, it will feel under the community's control and be owned by it. If it is initiated by an external partner, it may seem more like an imposition. Where partners require an evaluation, therefore, they should make every effort to work with the mission community to agree its purpose and method. The evaluation itself should be a partnership.

Second and closely connected, *what is the evaluation for?* Is it primarily to hold the initiative – especially its leaders – to account, or is it for the purpose of learning? The two may not entirely overlap. If accountability is the aim, evaluation conventionally takes the form of assessing whether the initiative is achieving its declared objectives. But if learning is the purpose, evaluation can centre on feedback designed to help the initiative improve what it is doing. Though feedback may include whether the initiative is achieving its purpose, it can be wider, such as the leaders' willingness and capacity to learn.

Some external partners may want a combination of both. A denomination may welcome learning-centred evaluation, but also want an indication of progress toward agreed objectives, not least to decide what form of recognition to give the initiative: is it still on a journey to being church or has it become one?

Third, *what is to be measured?* Writing about social enterprise, Rory Ridley-Duff and Mike Bull (2011, p. 234) contrast relational and task perspectives. The former sees relationships as the 'ends' of the initiative rather than the 'means'. Relationships are valued for their own sake. Evaluation seeks to measure the quality of relationships within the initiative, and between the initiative and its external partners. The task view measures progress towards achieving the initiative's goals or targets. There is a place for the latter, but it should be combined with a relational perspective, so that volunteers and other contributors are seen as not just means but having intrinsic value.

This issue emerges in some of the questions denominations ask church founders to answer. Requests often derive from the inherited mode of the church and centre on information about attendance at meetings. Reflecting a relational understanding of the church, however, many contextual churches are more concerned about relationships through the week than meetings. Requests also typically ignore measurements of spiritual maturity and of the church's contribution to God's mission. Forms often require boxes to be ticked, whereas church founders prefer to tell illustrative stories.

One way of combining both relational and task perspectives might be to construct measurements round the four interlocking sets of relationships that constitute the church – within the gathering, with the wider church, with the world and with God. These would provide a relational framework within which to devise proxy measurements of the initiative's health and progress. These proxies would certainly not tell the whole story, but would be an improvement on many existing measurements. For example:[2]

- The size of the gathering might be measured by an affiliation list – a list of currently active members; the total would be used in denominational returns. The health of the gathering's relationships might be measured by proxies such as attendance at meetings and the numbers volunteering.
- Interaction with the wider body might be measured by the number and frequency of events in the wider church that the gathering's leaders and members attended during the year, and by the level of financial support for the larger church as a proportion of the gathering's budget.
- Mission might be measured by the proportion of affiliated members engaged in initiatives organized by the contextual church and the nature of these initiatives. It might also include the number of people who leave the initiative during the year (and why), and the number of people who join, including whether they came from another church, had a church background or were never-churched.

---

2 Thoughts in this paragraph (and they are very much first thoughts) have been stimulated by the unpublished paper by Bob Jackson, 'What is church and how do you measure it?', www.starttheweek.typepad.com/files/what-is-church-jan-12-2.pdf, but go considerably beyond it.

- The God-ward relationship might be measured by the proxies of financial giving, the numbers involved in the church's missional activities and the numbers in Christian discovery and formation or accountability groups.

Fourth, *how else might measurements be undertaken?* Possibilities include feedback through a simple questionnaire, or a focus group drawn from the wider neighbourhood or network, or the findings of a 'mystery visitor'. Charities often use quite sophisticated tools to evaluate softer outcomes,[3] and these might be adapted in some cases. Though both qualitative and quantitative methods can have a place, simplicity should be the watchword. Feedback is a means of learning from what the Spirit has been doing. How has the Spirit been blessing the initiative? What obstacles may the Spirit face? How can we find answers with our resources?

Finally, *when should evaluation be undertaken?* This largely depends on what the evaluation is for. If the purpose is to learn, evaluation can be undertaken at any stage – indeed, the earlier the better. It should be ongoing as part of milestone reviews, with more systematic forms of evaluation from time to time. If the purpose is to assess outcomes, evaluation will need to be undertaken later, when the initiative has had time to bear fruit.

Conclusion

As they help bring a church to birth, mission communities should learn from experience by looking forward and looking back. When combined, these two perspectives encourage innovative thought. They should take place within regular milestone reviews, which can also be the context for evaluation – another word for discerning how the Spirit has been at work. Action-based learning is a means for the community to keep fresh. How can new churches keep their missional edge and avoid slipping into maintenance mode? Part of the answer is for their leaders to conduct regular milestone reviews. As they do this, the possibilities of the kingdom will challenge the status quo. Leaders will be constantly open to innovations of the Spirit.

Further reading

Bauckham, Richard J., *Moltmann: Messianic Theology in the Making*, Basingstoke: Marshall Pickering, 1987.

De Geus, Arie P., 'Planning as Learning', *Harvard Business Review*, March 1988, pp. 70–4.

Ridley-Duff, Rory and Mike Bull, *Understanding Social Enterprise: Theory and Practice*, London: Sage, 2011, chapter 12.

---

3 See, for example, www.homelessoutcomes.org.ok.

Questions for discussion

- What lessons would you draw from your experience of planning in church and non-church contexts?
- What hinders learning among church founders, and how can barriers be overcome?
- How much attention should be paid to measuring outcomes, and for what reasons? What forms might measurement take in a contextual church that you know?

16

Team Awareness

Thomas Cooney claims that 'one of the great myths of entrepreneurship has been the notion of the entrepreneur as a lone hero . . . the reality is that successful entrepreneurs either built teams about them or were part of a team throughout'. He cites research that firms founded by entrepreneurial teams are more likely to grow rapidly than ones started by sole entrepreneurs. He argues that the 'lone hero' view of entrepreneurship may discourage potential entrepreneurs, who believe that they do not have the characteristics of entrepreneurs popularized by the media (Cooney, 2005, pp. 226–7). This resonates with Chapter 7's emphasis on the communal nature of mission.

The mission community is the team through which the Spirit brings the contextual church to birth and leads it thereafter. It is the heart of the initiative and sets its tone. Since God is revealed through healthy human relationships (John 17.20–3), the community is the evangelist. So forming a mission *community* is a mission activity its own right.

However, this task is often neglected in the church planting literature. For example, Ed Stetzer's chapter on teams is typical in its focus on the important issue of recruitment, but does not address the internal dynamics of the team (2006, pp. 198–206). The emerging church conversation lays greater emphasis on community, seeing this as central to ecclesial life, but has paid relatively little attention to community formation within groups bringing these churches to birth.

Hugh Halter and Matt Smay (2008), for instance, write insightfully about making the kingdom tangible through small faith communities meeting in homes, coffee shops and wherever space exists. They argue that the experience of authentic community is essential for contemporary people to discover Jesus, they describe a wide variety of missional and communal practices, but they devote hardly any attention to the 'nitty-gritty' of developing healthy relationships within these communities. Yet relational specifics are indispensable to authentic community.

This chapter begins to address a serious gap in the literature. It fleshes out Chapter 7's plea for mission to be undertaken in community. How can community be a positive reality? In seeking an answer, the chapter could use one or more of the standard theoretical perspectives on groups. Or it could engage with some of the rich theological reflections on community (such as Bonhoeffer, 1954; and Vanier, 2007). Instead, it develops an approach based on complex responsive process theory. It sets out a rationale for this, arguing that mission communities often pay insufficient attention to the minutiae of their conversations. The bulk of the chapter suggests ways for these communities both to encourage healthy conversations and to review periodically their conversational patterns. Attending to conversations is described here as 'team awareness'.

Some theoretical approaches to groups

- *Social conditioning theory* maintains that groups provide individuals with food, help, comfort, friendship and social approval.
- *Social comparison theory* claims that groups provide individuals with information about physical reality, which is ambiguous.
- *Social identity and self-categorization theories* discuss how self-image and self-esteem depend heavily on the groups individuals identify with.
- *Exchange theory* argues that people join groups that give them the greatest gains from membership.
- *Sociobiological theories* emphasize the survival value of groups for humans and other species.
- *Optimal distinctiveness theory* contends that individuals need to find a comfortable balance between their desires to be distinctive and to belong.

Source: Baron and Kerr (2003, pp. 2–5).

This is the last of six chapters on how contextual churches are brought to birth. The first two described methodologies that give concrete form to the theology of mission in community. The third discussed methodologies for laying the foundations of contextual mission. The next thee chapters are about methodologies that facilitate communal and contextual mission. Engaging with partners provides resources for this type of mission. Action-based learning pulls the mission forward. 'Team awareness' makes the mission more effective. The Spirit speaks with greater clarity – to the mission community and through it – as members pay attention to their conversations.

Conversations and community

The importance of conversations can be demonstrated by comparing three types of organization theory, acknowledging the dispersed nature of leadership, recognizing how a focus on conversations challenges three team temptations and considering some of the dynamics of conversations.

Understanding organizations

Patricia Shaw (2002) has described several ways of thinking about organizations. The traditional voice puts the emphasis on managers' agency. The manager stands outside the organization, which is seen as a pre-given reality that can be modelled, designed and controlled. It is a Newtonian approach, where movement results from the application of a set of forces to an object (Weick and Quinn, 1999, p. 372). Shaw likens it to a general on a hill, surveying the coming battlefield, developing strategies and commanding the troops (Shaw, 2002, p. 140). The difficulty with this is that managers are not outside the organization. They are inside, as much influenced by others within as influencing them. The organization is not a static entity that can be shaped. It is a vibrant reality of multiple relationships, which cannot be controlled or predicted.

A second view sees organizations as emergent and self-organizing. Change involves a redirection of what is already under way and is continuous. The role of the leader is to make sense of what is happening and redirect the momentum (Weick, 1995; Weick and Quinn, 1999, pp. 375–81). 'How actors frame events shapes how actors will enact change' (Baez and Abolafia, 2002, p. 527). The leader helps others to reframe the situation in a way that aids constructive change. Adapting Shaw, the general asks his fellow officers how they view the landscape, he suggests they move vantage point and the new perspective reveals alternative possibilities.

The problem is that the landscape is still 'out there'. Members of an organization make sense *of* experience, which is assumed to be a separate entity. But experience is not distinct. It is bound up with individuals in the organization and keeps changing as they reflect 'on' it. This is the conundrum: individuals' experience of their context changes the moment they make sense of it, and the experience changes again once individuals act on the basis of their understanding. No fixed meaning can be given to experience (Shaw, 2002, pp. 118–9; cf. p. 134). Meaning constantly evolves because humans are part of the context while they generalize about it. They immerse and abstract at the same time (Stacey, 2010, p. 178).

Shaw suggests a third approach, which she and her colleagues have described as complex responsive process theory. Rather than making sense *of* experience, sense-making is part of the movement *in* our experience (Shaw, 2002, p. 119). Individuals cannot stand outside the whole and describe it as a given because the very description changes what is described. The general and his commanders are not surveying a landscape 'out there': it is under their feet, changing as they walk. The territory of exploration is formed by the exploration itself (Shaw, 2002, p. 141).

This allows Shaw and her colleagues to see organizations as a series of conversations in which individuals seek to make sense of their experiences and discuss ways of acting upon their understandings. Meaning is never fixed but constantly on the move. Ideas lead to action, but in the network society actions themselves increasingly entail conversations. An activity may change from what is planned as individuals discuss what they are doing while carrying it out. Unlike the industrial model where much fixed capital was tied up in machinery and employees often worked silently, if you take away people's conversations little would be left of many of today's organizations. Organizations are conversations.

The emergent nature of leadership

Highlighting the importance of conversations provides a helpful perspective on the nature of leadership. The traditional view is that leaders emerge on the basis of their personal qualities – their personal traits and acquired characteristics. However, Benyamin Lichtenstein et al. argue that leadership is not 'in' a leader or 'done by' a leader. Leadership is an emergent event, an outcome of interactions between individuals. Leadership is distributed among members of a group. It involves 'an interactive dynamic, within which any particular person will participate as leader or a follower at different times and for different purposes' (Lichtenstein et al., 2006, p. 3).

Imagine a discussion, for example. The chair might initially take the lead by raising a problem. The lead passes to someone else who proposes a solution. A number of contributions follow, during which leadership as it were hangs in the air. Then someone intervenes decisively with an idea for taking the proposal forward, providing leadership at that point. The chair resumes leadership by summarizing the discussion and checking this is the group's view. Leadership shifts within the group. This does *not* mean that recognized leaders have no role. They can enable or constrain the conditions in which dispersed leadership occurs.

This view fits well with Saint Paul's teaching on the sharing of gifts in the body. Leadership moves as one person shares a message of wisdom, another offers a word of knowledge, another prophesies, someone else distinguishes between the spirits, while others speak in tongues and interpret tongues (1 Cor. 12.8–10). It follows that if leadership is dispersed within a mission community and emerges through its conversations, close attention should be paid to how the Spirit is working through members' conversational dynamics.

Three temptations

Homing in on conversations will challenge three team temptations. The first is to concentrate more on the team's external goals than its internal processes.

Members concentrate on doing certain tasks without paying much attention to how decisions about these tasks are taken. Yet complex responsive process theorists argue that when teams focus their attention differently, they are highly likely to act differently (Stacey, 2000, p. 9). Attending to the dynamics of a team discussion, for instance, may encourage a member to elicit an unexpressed view that changes the direction of the conversation and alters the task.

The second temptation is to deal with generalities rather than specifics. Team members may seek to improve their relationships by eating and socializing together, or – in a church context – by developing shared rhythms or 'rules' of life. While certainly helpful, these are not the same as noticing the details of how members relate when they get together. People may be together, but are they community? Does the language used invite dissenting views or close them down? Complex responsive process theory invites teams to go beyond thinking about their *relationships* (a comparatively abstract concept) to consider the patterns of *relating*, which are more concrete.

The third temptation is for leaders to think that they can shape their teams. They adopt a traditional view of organizations. They stand outside their teams and plot strategies to change them. They overlook the reality that teams cannot be moulded like clay. Leaders are participants in rather than instigators of change (Luoma, 2007, p. 292). Change emerges (or fails to emerge) through interactions within the team. The leader can propose different ways of conversing, for example, but the way others respond will determine how the proposals are received and enacted. Leaders do not act *on to* a team, they act *within* it.

The dynamics of conversations

Complex responsive process theory challenges these temptations by emphasizing the minutiae of conversational practice. The theory takes for granted that humans are thoroughly social. Life is full of interactions with others. These interactions consist of patterns of relating, such as role structure and behavioural norms, and patterns of meaning, including concepts and knowledge. Just as a piece of music exists only so long as musicians play new notes in each new moment, patterns of relating and meaning endure only so far as they are continuously re-enacted minute by minute (Suchman, 2006, p. 41).

These patterns self-organize in the back-and-forth exchanges of conversation. They form spontaneously without anyone's intention or direction. Though an individual can influence these patterns, ultimately they are unpredictable and beyond any one person's control. Through conversation, patterns of relating and meaning arise that did not exist for any of the participants before; no one could have created them on their own. Perhaps a person makes a comment that elicits a new idea for someone else. A third person develops the idea further. The idea is taken into a second conversation, where it is turned into a proposal for action. Enacting the proposal involves more conversations in which the idea is refined further. The outcome feeds into another series of conversations.

As they are continuously re-created, patterns of relating and meaning may exhibit stability (continuity) or novelty (when new patterns arise spontaneously). Self-organization requires the simultaneous presence of both – of order and disorder. 'Without freedom all processes would be deterministic with no possibility of spontaneous variation or change: without constraints patterns could not form and take hold' (Suchman, 2006, p. 41). Constraints arise from the past conversations that each individual – and the group – has been involved in. These histories create patterns of relating and thinking that are brought into each new conversation and place limits round the conversation. Words have particular meanings; there are acceptable ways of relating to the leader; the group must take account of its previous decisions.

Though patterns tend to repeat themselves, the dynamics of conversation are not linear (A causes B). They are non-linear: there is no equilibrium state and patterns can shift unpredictably. These shifts occur through the amplification of small differences. A new phrase or slightly different behaviour may elicit a response that carries the difference further. That in turn may spark a response which amplifies the difference further still. The amplification can sometimes escalate rapidly into an entirely new pattern, such as a solution to a problem.

Attending to conversations

Drawing on Griffin, Stacey and others, Anthony Suchman (2002) describes three qualities that enable conversations to generate fruitful novelty.

- *Diversity* makes it more likely that different contributions will spark novel ideas. It depends on both the heterogeneity of conversation partners and their willingness to make public their individual differences. Where little diversity exists, fewer serendipitous differences occur to spark cascades of change (Suchman, 2006, p. 42).
- *Responsiveness* reflects the ability and willingness of conversation partners to perceive and respond to each other, to be present to one another, and to invite and attend to each other's contributions. When individuals remain closed to or unaffected by one another, there will be little opportunity for an emerging new pattern to become amplified; existing patterns will be difficult to dislodge.
- *Associative capacity* is the willingness of participants to create and articulate novel associations. This will depend on their inherent creativity, how narrowly or broadly their attention is focused, the criteria by which they and others evaluate potential associations, and the

anticipated social consequences of expressing something new. Groups will vary in their capacity to create novel combinations of thought from the differences expressed.[1]

A team that generated no new patterns would be dead. A team that constantly produced new patterns would exhaust itself and disintegrate. There must be a balance. For mission communities starting a contextual church, the balance almost certainly needs to be tilted toward creating new ideas – toward flexibility of thought. Thinking back to the Cynefin framework in Chapter 11, this is because much of what mission communities do will involve either applying established principles to a new situation or facing situations where no established principles apply. Creativity will be vital. Hence this chapter's focus on encouraging patterns of conversation that allow novelty to emerge.

To help their members improve and pay attention to these patterns, the suggestion here is that mission communities periodically discuss five 'conversational themes' that they will typically engage in – forming, norming, storming, performing and adjourning. These are generally seen as stages in a group's life, with storming put second (Tuckman and Jensen, 1977, pp. 419–47). But as Baron and Kerr point out, some groups avoid certain stages, others change the sequence of stages and others recycle through the stages as new situations arise (2003, p. 17). There may be an element of 'forming' throughout a team's life, for example, as new members join. When existing ones leave, 'adjourning' will to some extent occur.

Here these categories are used to describe conversational themes within the mission community:

- *Forming*: discussions about the community's membership and purpose;
- *Norming*: discussions about how the community will work together;
- *Storming* (placed symbolically in the middle): discussions that arise from disagreements within the community;
- *Performing*: discussions about planning and implementing tasks;
- *Adjourning*: discussions and conversations that involve saying farewell.

---

1 A 1999 study, which recorded, coded and mathematically modelled the interactions of 60 teams, found that high-performing teams were more likely than others to display high levels of connectivity, a balance between enquiry (such as asking questions to elicit others' views) and advocacy (arguing your point), a tendency to be positive rather than negative (eg by appreciating and encouraging others in the team) and a balance between awareness of the external world and of the strengths and weaknesses of the team – the sort of characteristics that one would expect of teams with qualities of diversity, responsiveness and associative capacity (Losada, 1999, pp. 179–92).

Having fruitful conversations about each of these conversational themes will enhance the mission community's corporate life and enable it to better perform its tasks. These will not be conversations about the mechanics of performing, for example, nor the conversations that occur when people are in the midst of storming. They will be periodic conversations about the way the community discusses the things it must do to perform and about how it handles conflict. They will be conversations about the manner in which the mission community converses in relation to each of the forming, norming, storming, performing and adjourning processes.

Having such conversations periodically will enable the community to review how well individuals are talking together. What helpful patterns of conversation have been established, and what unhelpful ones need adjustment? In particular, how much diversity, responsiveness and associative capacity are being displayed? The mission community can learn to be more intentional about the ways it conducts its conversations.

Forming

Forming the mission community (the group that brings a church to birth) includes recruiting members, developing a shared concept of mission, discerning the community's mission focus and agreeing mission values – all intrinsic to the process of gathering discussed in Chapter 12. It is usually thought that once individuals come to see themselves as a group, the forming stage is complete. But especially in small teams, the departure of a member or the arrival of a new one inevitably alters the group's dynamics. As the mission community adjusts, some aspects of forming come back into play.

Size and composition

Decisions about the size and composition of the mission community will affect the nature of the conversations within it. A large team will be more likely to generate a plurality of ideas, which will cross-fertilize and produce novelty. But individuals must not be so different – in their theological views for example – that they do not trust each other enough to speak out. Nor must the community be so large that members struggle to manage their life together and some feel unable to contribute. 'Order' and 'chaos' should be balanced. Periodically, the mission community should ask whether this balance is being maintained.

Whether large or small, the mission community will need the appropriate range of gifts to fulfil its calling. This can be understood in terms of the fivefold ministries listed in Ephesians 4.11 – apostles, prophets, evangelists, pastors and teachers. The Belbin list of team roles (see box) offers an alternative – or complementary – approach (Belbin, 1981). Each role, and a balance between them, is thought to be essential for team success. Despite critiques of Belbin, a literature review concluded that there is substantial evidence for the validity of the model (Aritzeta, Swailes and Senior, 2005, pp. 22–3). The model's wide use testifies to its practical value.

Belbin Team Roles (role strengths)	
Completer Finisher	Painstaking, conscientious, searches out errors and omissions, delivers on time
Implementer	Disciplined, reliable, conservative and efficient, turns ideas into practical actions
Team worker	Cooperative, mild, perceptive and diplomatic, listens, builds, averts friction, calms the waters
Specialist	Single-minded, self-starting, dedicated; provides knowledge and skills in rare supply
Monitor Evaluator	Sober, strategic and discerning, sees all options, judges accurately
Coordinator	Mature, confident, a good chairperson, clarifies goals, promotes decision-making, delegates well
Plant	Creative, unorthodox, solves difficult problems
Shaper	Challenging, dynamic, thrives on pressure, has drive and courage to overcome obstacles
Resource Investigator	Extrovert, communicative, explores opportunities, develops contacts.

Source: Aritzeta, Swailes and Senior, 2005, p. 8.

Having *some* conceptual framework, be it the Ephesians or the Belbin list (or both), can help mission communities judge whether they have the variety of gifts and personal qualities they need. Few pioneering contexts allow the selection of ideal teams, but being aware of shortcomings can encourage a community to explore creative ways of filling the gaps, such as seeking aid from partners with capabilities the team lacks. This assistance may bring greater diversity into the community's conversations.

Becoming community

One of the aims of 'forming' should be to take initial steps toward turning the team into a community, even if just two or three people are involved. In a team, members concentrate mainly on the task: in a community, members are committed to each other. If the mission community sets the tone for the emerging church and community is essential to being church, then community must be at the heart of the founding team's life. Community also builds trust. The latter encourages conversation partners to express differences and to perceive and respond to each other, both of which are intrinsic to healthy conversations.

Forming community may be a new experience for some members. They may have been in hierarchical teams where the vertical reporting relationship (to the leader) predominated over horizontal relationships with other members. In a community, individuals don't just relate to the leader, they have strong ties to each other. They support each other and decision-making is shared. They walk in the way of Jesus, whose close fellowship with his disciples was echoed in the early church.

Shared lives are central to being community. The leader will play a key role by modelling openness, such as having the courage to admit mistakes. The first three gospels imply that Jesus did not hide his struggle in the Garden of Gethsemane – that's how we know! When leaders show they are incomplete, they open the door for others to help. The box below suggests additional steps to facilitate the sharing of lives. This sharing will encourage honesty, which is vital for diversity, responsiveness and associative capacity (the ability to combine thoughts creatively). Ideas can then 'ping-pong' within the community.

Sharing one another's lives might include

- doing a Myers-Briggs exercise to increase understanding of personality differences, and a Belbin Team Roles exercise to reveal members' preferred roles;
- using ice-breakers at the start of each meeting to encourage self-disclosure (a useful resource is Garry Poole, *The Complete Book of Questions: 1001 Conversation Starters for any Occasion*, Grand Rapids, MI: Zondervan, 2003);
- listening to one another's experiences of team working, both good and bad, and learning from them;
- fostering community-building rituals – ways of doing things that are particular to the community and give energy;
- sharing some meals and recreational activities.

Noting conversational patterns

Developing a sense of community will affect the patterns of conversation that start to be embedded. Ralph Stacey points out that these patterns involve sequences of turn-taking and turn-making. Individuals take turns in speaking, but they also make turns for themselves and others by asking questions, soliciting advice, clarifying issues, expressing opinions and so forth. These sequences largely structure the distribution of power within the group. They indicate who may talk and when, who is 'in' and who is 'out' (Stacey, 2010, pp. 150–1). In hierarchical teams, the leader tends to be central to conversations. In communities, conversations flow in less predictable and more varied directions.

Being alert to patterns of conversation before they become habitual can help members to develop healthy and inclusive traditions that aid the formation of community. Nominated leaders must ensure that they are not too dominant and that they create space for everyone to contribute. They should invite contributions to be made in ways that do not shut others out, but welcome a constructive response. When theological, personality and other differences emerge, the leader should encourage them to be explored even if it feels uncomfortable. Refusing to face conflict will establish a pattern of avoidance that reduces the mission community's ability to generate open and creative exchanges.

Establishing a pattern of periodic reflection on the mission community's conversations should be part of the forming process – 'Have we discussed the size and composition of the group?' 'How do we feel about our attempts to become community?' 'What do we notice about the way we talk together and handle differences?' 'Are we good at discussing uncomfortable truths, such as whether the time we are giving is putting a strain on our families and friendships?' As members become more conscious of their conversational patterns, they will modulate their contributions in response to what others find helpful.

Forming will involve conversations about

- the size and composition of the mission community;
- becoming a community rather than just a team;
- developing the habit of noting conversational patterns.

Norming

Norming involves establishing implicit and explicit rules for how members work and relate together. It occurs initially during the gathering process, but may restart when a new member joins the community or a significant transition occurs in the initiative's life.

Michael Frost (2006) argues that if you want 'the exquisite experience of rich, deep relationships', you need to belong to a group that is actively pursuing an end beyond itself (p. 111). In the context of church, this means being strongly engaged in mission. When people are thrown into a challenge, they develop a much deeper sense of communion. 'Building community for its own sake is like attending a cancer support group without having cancer' (p. 122). This should be balanced by Jean Vanier's observation,

> Co-operation without communion quickly becomes like a work camp or factory, where unity comes from an exterior reality . . . Communion is based on some common inner experience of love; it is the recognition of being one body, one people, called by God to be a source of love and peace . . . For this reason it is necessary to give priority in daily life to those realities, symbols, meetings and celebrations that will encourage a consciousness of communion. When a community is just a place of work, it is in danger of dying. (Vanier, 2007, p. 25)

Spiritual norms[2]

Central to norming is attending to the mission community's conversations. 'Where two or three are gathered in Jesus' name' (Matt. 18.20) . . . they talk. Since at the time of Jesus Jewish names conveyed the character of the person, the verse implies that participants must converse in the character of Jesus. Jesus' presence through the Spirit will enable mission communities to do this. Conversations will be graced with three particular spiritual norms.

First, members will be honest like Jesus, who said what he thought and allowed others to do the same. Savage and Boyd-MacMillan (2007, p. 89) note how Jesus adapted his communication style to different people. Towards the powerful, he could use forceful language, such as the seven woes directed at the religious authorities in Matthew 23. But to ordinary people, such as the woman at the well, Jesus used questions that permitted the other to choose their response. He taught in parables, which allowed listeners to reach their own conclusions about the story's meaning and implications.

Language exerts power. Tone of voice can close down or invite contributions from others. Honest communication includes attending to power dynamics so that others can speak openly. It also involves accurate communication. If truth and feelings are buried, issues may be unaddressed and the other person manipulated (Buck and Ginsburg, 1997, p. 33; Thomas and Fletcher, 1997, pp. 199–200). Innovative thinking may be stifled. Negotiating differences is an opportunity to generate unexpected ideas and solutions.

Second, like Jesus, members will respect others' boundaries. If people rejected him, Jesus was no doubt sad but he did not impose his will. Equally,

---

2 I am grateful to conversations with Dr Sara Savage, Senior Research Associate, Psychology and Religion Research Group, University of Cambridge and Roy Searle, one of the leaders of the Northumbria Community, whose insights have helped to inform this section.

he was robust in protecting his own boundaries. When the disciples tried to turn away the children, Jesus made clear where he stood (Matt. 19.13ff). He took time out to pray, even though he was sometimes interrupted. Perhaps using a facilitator, mission communities can role play situations where boundaries are being crossed and practise firmly but gently re-establishing them. Clear boundaries help to create the security people need if they are to speak their minds and be heard.

Third, members will be generous and forgiving, as Jesus was with his disciples. This may require attention to the inner heart, asking the Spirit to clear away the reluctance to forgive and other barriers to healthy relationships. The leader, or perhaps a recognized 'spiritual guide' within the mission community, can support the Spirit by encouraging members to spend time in prayer and to hold each other to account for being disciplined in spiritual practices. Generous hearts will help individuals to be responsive to one another.

Reframing conversations

Members can help each other to practice honesty, boundary-setting and generosity by reframing a conversation. If someone is grumbling about washing up, another person might say generously, 'Thank you. That's really helpful. You've identified what is obviously a problem' – an honest statement; nothing is swept under the carpet. 'Can I rephrase what you said to see if we can find a solution? For the last three weeks no one has volunteered to help with the washing up, which makes it a burden for Jane and James. Can anyone suggest what we should do?' This reaffirms the boundaries – that people will contribute to the group – but in a way that helps to energize rather than drain others.

Communal norms

Within this framework of honesty, boundary-setting and generosity are communal norms. These are what Ruth Blatt has called 'communal relational schemas' – norms that help to build relational capital in entrepreneurial teams (Blatt, 2009, pp. 539–42). Communal norms refer to how individuals give time, expertise, encouragement and the like to others in the team. Doing favours is a response to perceived needs and expresses members' commitment to the relationship (rather than just to the task). Individuals look out for each other, strengthening the team.

The concept can be applied to mission communities as they bring a church to birth. Members can be encouraged to go the extra mile for each other.

This will improve responsiveness within conversations, making honest exchanges more likely, in three ways:

- *By increasing trust.* People who are communal are more likely to express emotions and accept the emotional expressions of others. Open communications expand members' knowledge of others' motivations, goals and viewpoints. They reduce misunderstandings that undermine trust. Individuals will be more inclined to say what they think.
- *By increasing identification.* As members understand each other better, they identify more strongly with one another. They begin to see others' perspectives, resources and identities as extensions of their own. They can respond more empathetically to the other.
- *By strengthening the mutual sense of obligation.* Meeting someone else's needs creates a feeling of reciprocal obligation in the other person. Empathy for the other increases the willingness to help. Conversations become more collaborative.

It is important, therefore, that the group keeps working at their communal norms and does not take them for granted. Getting to know one another and sharing each others' lives, which is part of forming, should be central to the norming process too. The leader may want to draw attention to small acts of generosity within the group as an encouragement.

The danger is that mission communities become too 'communal'. Members may become more committed to each other than the task; they may avoid conflict to preserve supportive relationships; they may withhold critical feedback on others' performances, which impedes learning; they may be so comfortable together that newcomers struggle to belong. So, as Blatt points out, task norms must accompany communal ones. We might say that if communal norms refer to *community* and task norms to *mission*, mission communities need both.

Task norms

Task norms refer to what Blatt describes as 'contracting practices'. Established organizations normally have published policies and procedures for how employees should work. Entrepreneurial teams, by contrast, may be newly formed. 'Contracting serves as a proxy for the behavioural guidance that a large organization provides its employees' (2009, p. 542). Task norms also include the mission community's values. Discussing these norms stimulates conversations about specific issues, forces team members to articulate their views and encourages exchanges about how the team should function.

Mission communities can quickly slip into understandings of how members will work together without much discussion. But talking about these understandings will avoid the covert exercise of power and enable the group as a whole, whatever its size, to own them as fair. Task norms may initially cover simple things such as frequency of meetings, whether there will be an agenda, who will set it and how decisions will be recorded. Later, when members know each other better, issues like the community's values, the distribution of tasks and holding one another to account may be discussed. Periodically reviewing task norms will surface any difficulties and increase members' commitment to working arrangements. Norms will evolve as necessary, which is why norming is not a stage but a process.

The diagram below suggests how spiritual, communal and task norms relate to each other. Many teams base their lives on task norms, giving less attention to communal norms and even less (if any at all) to spiritual ones. The suggestion here is that mission communities should invert the order. They should base their lives on conversations about spiritual norms, use these as a foundation for conversations about communal norms and let conversations about task norms rest on the structure beneath.

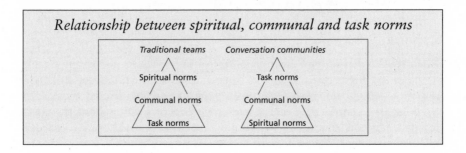

Talking about norms

Keeping a balance between the three sets of norms is vital. The mission community should not be so warm and friendly that nothing gets done, nor so goal-directed that fun and spontaneity evaporate, nor so spiritual that worldly wisdom is ignored. When members face uncertainty and disappointment, a balanced set of norms will sustain healthy conversations. It will encourage members to express differences of opinion, to be open to each other and to make connections between ideas and information – the diversity, responsive and associative qualities that encourage novelty to emerge.

A mission community should pay attention to the emergence of these norms. It will ask how they are being re-enacted in each moment, whether new patterns are forming and how healthy these patterns are. Explicitly reviewing norms will give the community a chance to review the conversations it has about them and perhaps change some of the patterns.

In particular, attention might be paid to how the community's statement of values starts to get used. Following Griffin (2002), if the statement is appealed to in an idealized manner, it can become a means of closing down disagreement. 'These are the values we agreed. We are a Bible-based community. We must read have a Scripture reading each time we meet. End of discussion.' By using the statement definitively, attention is diverted from how it might be understood in a variety of ways.

On the other hand, if the statement is used dynamically, the values will be open to interpretation, question and reassessment. 'What does it mean to be Bible-based?' 'Does how we have expressed ourselves really capture what we mean?' This empowers members to reshape the statement in the light of their conversations with each other and with people outside.

Norming will involve conversations about

- spiritual norms;
- communal norms;
- task norms.

Storming

The literature usually puts storming after forming because an uncomfortable period of jostling between members can occur before the group settles down. Here it is treated third, at the centre of the five conversational themes, to symbolize the central part that storming *should* play throughout the community's existence. Because it has an ongoing role, it should not be regarded as a discrete stage. 'Conflict can be defined as tension between two people or groups of people who disagree strongly on a topic or issue' (Savage and Boyd-MacMillan, 2007, p. 56). Inevitably, therefore, it can occur at any time.

Welcoming conflict

Most people try to avoid conflict, often because they fear rejection. This fear is compounded by the expectation that people will be 'nice' in church, translated as 'no anger, no disagreement, no problems, *no* conflict' (Savage and Boyd-MacMillan, 2007, p. 57). Savage and Boyd-MacMillan suggest that conflict is inevitable. Church headlines should read, *'Expect more – not less – conflict!'* (p. 56) Complex responsive process theorists go further. Conflict should be positively welcomed. It is a sign that diverse perspectives are on the table. They can be combined to spark further ideas and create novel thought.

Chapter 5 drew attention to Kathryn Tanner's view that church is a discussion – an argument, even – about practices. To see practices as subject to ongoing discussion and dispute is to suggest that difference rather than consensus is normal in the kingdom. When we pray 'Your kingdom come . . .', we are praying for continuing debate and discussion about what it means to be a follower of Jesus. Differences are the means by which human knowledge progresses. A new idea challenges the status quo. It is debated, perhaps modified, and then included in the body of human understanding.

Were such debate to cease, one might wonder whether humans had discovered all there is to know – a state of knowledge that only God can have. Or one might ask whether human creativity had blown itself out – that humans had ceased to be fully human. When the kingdom comes, differences, debate and even argument will not cease for they are intrinsic to human life. But they will be transformed. They will be encased in a spirit of generosity, kindness and attentiveness that will distinguish them from many human disputes today. Perhaps church headlines should read, '*Expect conflict, because that's what you'll find in heaven! (But it will be managed better.)*'

Conflict should therefore be welcomed as:

- *An opportunity to learn.* A range of perspectives allows issues to be considered from various angles. The community is less likely to overlook something important. Conflict feels less threatening when it is approached as learning – 'what can we discover from these different views?'
- *A sign that individuals are being given space.* Social workers recognize that unhealthy families silence certain members. When healthy communities allow – or even encourage – dissent, their members can flourish. Conflict indicates that members are not being suppressed and that power in the mission community is dispersed.
- *A means to build community.* 'Pseudo community' exists when everyone is polite to each other, individuals speak in generalities and platitudes, and real encounters are avoided. People are pretending to be community. True community starts when team members share their real thoughts and feelings, and risk the hurt of disagreement (Vanier, 2007, p. 33). Hurt is the growing pain of community.
- *A reflection of the pioneering task.* Because the mission community is engaged in something new, there will be times of uncertainty and confusion about what to do. Conflict will be more likely in these circumstances (Blatt, 2009, pp. 537–8). It can be welcomed as a sign that the community is breaking new ground.
- *An opportunity for transferable learning.* Experiencing well-managed conflict will school members of the mission community in how to respond to conflict in the church that is coming to birth. Handling conflict well in this wider setting will model for church members how to respond to disagreement at home, work and in other situations. This should be part of the church's mission to society.

Not just expecting but welcoming conflict goes against the grain of how many people think. But if individuals can see the positives and discuss how to manage disagreement, their fear of conflict is likely to diminish. This will lessen the emotional charge when conflict occurs and help issues to be approached dispassionately. Mission communities should therefore discuss how they can welcome and manage disagreement.

A case study: resolving conflict at the Council of Jerusalem (Acts 15)

- There was 'much discussion', which gave time to air different views.
- Both sides spoke openly and directly.
- People listened.
- Stories were told and interpreted in the light of Scripture.
- The Holy Spirit was seen to have been involved.
- A solution was reached that gave something to both parties – Gentiles did not have to be circumcised but were to observe some of the Jewish food laws.

The use of silence

Lengthy periods of dissent can be managed in several ways. One is to use prayerful silences. Interdependence theory suggests how the Spirit can make use of these silences (Rusbult and Van Lange, 2003, pp. 251–75). One version of the theory distinguishes between responses that the person would like to make based on *immediate* self-interest, and responses based on considering the *long-term* consequences for one's own well-being, the other person and for broader goals and norms.

Obviously it is desirable that individuals move from the first to the second type of response. This shift comes about via *meaning analysis*, in which the individual seeks to make the interaction predictable and so controllable.

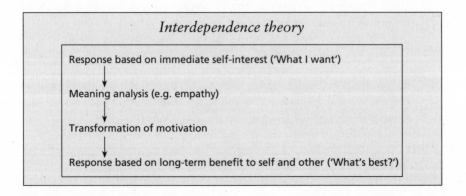

Interdependence theory

Response based on immediate self-interest ('What I want')

↓

Meaning analysis (e.g. empathy)

↓

Transformation of motivation

↓

Response based on long-term benefit to self and other ('What's best?')

Instead of feeling overwhelmed by anxiety and firing off in all directions, the person tries to get on top of their emotions. They interpret the immediate significance and wider implications of what is being discussed, relate this knowledge to personal needs and preferences, and react appropriately. The result is the *transformation of motivation*.

Accurately empathizing with the other person plays a central role in 'meaning analysis'. Individuals cannot pursue the well-being of the other person, the good of the relationship or other goals without knowing the concerns guiding the other's preferences and behaviour (Bissonnette, Rusbult and Kilpatrick, 1997, p. 256).

This model can be applied to conflicts within a mission community. It suggests that space may be needed for 'meaning analysis' to take place. When disagreement occurs, the self can become agitated and over-busy. Individuals find themselves talking a lot in their minds or speaking out loud a great deal. Sometimes they colonize God to their preferences. Instead of being open to the Spirit, God is used to justify what they want. They are dominated by their immediate self-interest.

Introducing a time of prayerful quiet can still some of this mental activity and give space for members to reconnect with God. The Spirit can help individuals to distance themselves from the issues and get a wider perspective. 'Meaning analysis' begins. During the silence, the leader (or perhaps a member with the role of 'spiritual guide') can encourage colleagues to pay attention to their inner hearts. What are they feeling strongly about? Where are their emotions coming from? Which motives should be taken to the cross?

As feelings start to settle, the 'transformation of motivation' begins and individuals become open to a wider view. This transformation can be encouraged by inviting members to share some of their reflections during the silence. Acknowledging vulnerabilities will help members to empathize with one another and support the 'meaning analysis' each is engaged in. A creative, Spirit-led resolution of the conflict becomes possible.

Articulating differences

The leader exercises a key role in managing conflict by articulating differences. When members disagree, leaders should keep re-expressing the different views, whether or not they are chairing the meeting and especially if they are a protagonist. It shows the parties that they have been understood. Sometimes, out of fear they have not been heard, individuals over-press their case, provoking a negative response. Knowing that the *leader* understands is affirming, which helps to reduce anxiety.

Reframing contributions helps the parties understand each other. Hearing the same point in different words can bring clarity. Hearing it expressed calmly can encourage a rational rather than emotional response. The leader may comment that a view is strongly held. Stating this dispassionately will encourage detachment by others. The discussion is not drained of feelings, but through the Spirit individuals are helped to process the group's feelings without being swamped by them. Reframing can be used to draw people together. A frustrated, 'That's wrong!' can be turned into, 'John feels that that misrepresents the situation. What other bits of the picture might we add in?'

Reframing is a skill. If someone other than the nominated leader is more gifted in this area, they might chair discussions. However, showing that individuals have been heard is a task that the leader cannot delegate. Chairing meetings, discerning vision and much else can be shared with others. But assuring individuals they have been understood cannot be handed over. The leader's status in the community gives the assurance particular weight.

Awareness of levels of conflict

1. Problem to solve – such as a church-sponsored café senses that they are becoming a church.
   Characteristics of conflict
   - General focus on problem itself;
   - Some risk-taking between sides;
   - Openness about people and information;
   - Language is clear, specific.
   Possible intervention strategies
   - Follow rules for good communication and collaboration.
   - Work at consensus-building and mutual problem-solving.

2. Disagreement – church leaders disagree that the cafe could be a church.
   Characteristics of conflict
   - Concerns for self-protection; pointing out inaccuracies of other side;
   - Growing emotional edginess;
   - Certain withholding of information;
   - Tendency to generalize in comments.
   Possible intervention strategies
   - Work at trust- and team-building;
   - Use a facilitator from within the organization.

3. Contest – both sides solidify their position, with no room for compromise.
   Characteristics of conflict
   - Determination to win the argument; dialogue is uneasy;
   - Perceptual distortions (seeing black or white) and false assumptions;
   - Personal attacks and emotional appeals;
   - Sub-groups and coalitions emerge.
   Possible intervention strategies
   - Use structure and ground rules for mutual problem-solving;
   - Use an insider-partial mediator if available;
   - Use an outsider-neutral mediator if insider not available.

4. Fight or flight – either 'side' gives an ultimatum: agreement with their view or severance of relationship.
   Characteristics of conflict
   - Desire to leave or cause other to leave;
   - Wanting to hurt or get rid of the other;
   - Try to win 'on principles' rather than problem-solving issues;
   - Factionalism and negative stereotyping of opponents.
   Possible intervention strategies
   - Possibly use leadership authority or majority vote;
   - Use a specialist outsider-neutral mediator.

5. Intractable – leaders caricature one another, question the other's faith commitments and denounce each other.
   Characteristics of conflict
   - Desire to destroy opponents;
   - Any means seem to justify the ends;
   - Feel compelled to fight at any cost;
   - Ideological warfare.
   Possible intervention strategies
   - Use outside adjudication;
   - Enforce separation;
   - Expel disruptive parties.

Based on Savage and Boyd-MacMillan, 2007, pp. 69–70.

Communities of grace

Conflict is best managed by fostering grace-full communities. As these communities bring a church to birth, individuals come to recognize their flaws, weaknesses and need of forgiveness, making them more ready to forgive others. 'To forgive is also to understand the cry behind the behaviour' (Vanier, 2007, p. 37). When we forgive, we cross over to the other person, as Jesus has crossed over to us, and enter their view of the world.

To make this journey, individuals need to tend their emotional lives so that they act and judge from their forgiven selves. If members of the mission community speak from their wounds, they condemn and hurt each other. But if they act from knowing they are accepted, they go out to the other in love. This requires members to pay continuing attention to their inner hearts, and to be willing to turn into their pains and anxieties rather than evade them. When we flee, we persuade ourselves that our hurts are too uncomfortable to face. This makes them even more forbidding, which strengthens the desire to turn away. The pain remains a disruptive force.

On the other hand, to be *filled* with the Spirit (Eph. 5.18) means that no part of a person's interior life is closed to God. Individuals encounter him in the midst of their hurts. When they turn into this pain, feeling and even magnifying it in their minds, they discover the welcoming arms of Jesus. The pain subsides, setting them free to forgive. Their view of the other is no longer clouded by their hurts: they recognize the true image the person has received from God. 'Thus this spiritual love will speak to Christ about a brother more than to a brother about Christ' (Bonhoeffer, 1954, p. 23).

Encouraging members of the mission community to cultivate their inner hearts may be the task of the leader, but some leaders excel in other areas. In these cases, the community can identify a spiritual guide to nurture this aspect of its life. The guide may be a member of the community or lead it in regular retreats.

How conflict is managed is so important that the mission community should keep this aspect of its life under review. 'Are we regularly expressing contrasting views? How are we handling these differences?' If members learn to deal with conflict constructively, the community will feel safe. Levels of honesty will rise, which will encourage members to express their differences (diversity), to be open to each other (responsiveness) and to make novel connections (associative capacity). The community's style of conversing will reflect more fully the mutual openness within the Godhead, which will strengthen its witness.

Handling conflict may involve

- periods of silence;
- affirming the contributions of others;
- attending to one's inner heart.

Performing

Performing is the aspect of the mission community's life that through the Spirit gets the task done. The focus is on agreeing and working toward shared goals. Performing will centre on the continuous looking forward and back, milestone review and evaluation processes described in the last chapter. Between meetings, individuals will perform a range of tasks generated by these processes. As mission communities help to birth contextual church, conversations about performing will pivot round the theme, 'How can we do things better?'

How do church founders learn?

To bring a church to birth, mission communities require ongoing training and support. This will include learning about the theology of mission, the principles behind starting and developing a contextual church, and specific issues like health and safety. Observation suggests that many contextual churches suffer because their mission communities have paid insufficient attention to learning. Putting learning at the centre of their conversations will help mission communities to avoid this mistake.

In summarizing the extensive literature on entrepreneurship education, David Rae (2007, p. 30) notes that while education can provide knowledge about entrepreneurship and skill development, the 'art' of entrepreneurial practice is learned mainly through experience. The London-based School for Social Entrepreneurs has explicitly set itself against traditional models of education. It provides opportunities to learn on the assumption that social entrepreneurs

> prefer action to reflection: they want to get on with it. They are willing to explore their environment for opportunities and resources, and to take risks. They are 'people' people. They aren't interested in learning programmes that don't seem relevant to them, and they often move straight into action without any educational preparation. They learn as they go. (www.sse.org.uk/programmes.php?sub=APPROACH)

A UK study found that social entrepreneurs tend to learn in three ways (Tomorrow Project, 2010). First, they search out helpful individuals, take advantage of chance encounters and plug into various informal networks. They are post-institutional in a post-institutional sector. However, they may exhaust or have limited networks. So they need support through national or regional themed conversations, where they can meet others from different backgrounds.

Second, they use communities of practice. These may be action learning sets (in which groups use questions to help members *explore* solutions to problems), or peer consulting groups (in which other members *advise* on possible solutions), or training courses, in which each cohort of students *learns together*.

Third, social entrepreneurs learn through coaching and mentoring. UnLtd, for instance, provides mentoring as part of a package of practical support for entrepreneurs receiving its Millennium Awards. Its research department gathers, systematizes and shares knowledge gleaned from entrepreneurs and their mentors. The Micro Coaches programme provides an online platform to match individuals wanting coaching in a skill with business leaders and social entrepreneurs offering to share their skills in one-off, one-to-one, three-hour sessions. Could both models play a role in supporting mission communities?

All this adds up to a preference for just-in-time learning (acquiring the knowledge you need at the moment) to just-in-case learning (ploughing through a syllabus, because you may need the knowledge at some stage). Observation suggests that church founders have a similar preference. A *coaching culture* takes this preference seriously.

Creating a coaching culture

The notion of a coaching culture can be used to describe a situation where just-in-time methods of learning are central to a mission community's conversational life. Writing from a business perspective, David Clutterbuck and David Megginson define a coaching culture as one where 'Coaching is the predominant style of managing and working together, and where a commitment to grow the organization is embedded in a parallel commitment to grow the people in the organization' (Clutterbuck and Megginson, 2005, p. 19). In a church context, a coaching culture is a relational way of growing people in the practice of the Christian faith.

As a central 'performing' practice, a mission community might commit itself to creating such a culture. Members would encourage each other to learn intentionally from one another and from elsewhere. They might use a team coach and peer-to-peer mentoring. They might see themselves as a community of practice, exchanging knowledge in ways that share many features of coaching and mentoring relationships (Clutterbuck and Megginson, 2005, p. 26–7). They would optimize their networks to learn from other people, engaging in one-off and serial conversations that would have, in effect, a coaching/mentoring dimension.

Through expert, peer-to-peer and informal coaching/ mentoring,[3] members of the mission community would prayerfully engage in conversations that enable them

- to gain insight into their interactions with their context and each other;
- to reflect theologically on the values involved in these interactions;

---

3 The terms coaching and mentoring are used interchangeably here.

- to come to appreciate the gifts and qualities they bring to these relationships;
- to learn how to make the most of opportunities as they emerge (including acquiring new skills).

What is learnt would be brought into and shaped by prayer, Bible study and worship, creating a strong discipleship culture within the mission community. This would prepare and equip the community for making disciples among the people it serves. The skills of coaching/mentoring and sharing experience-based learning would be transferred to the process of forming new believers. A platform would be laid for growing disciples within the church that is coming to birth.

By making learning highly intentional, a coaching/discipleship culture would reinforce the approach to planning described in the previous chapter and put learning at the centre of the mission community's life. Learning as a central topic of conversation would encourage members to make links between what each other are learning and discuss inputs that challenge the community's received wisdom. Periodically reviewing the quality of these learning conversations would keep them to the fore and enable members to discuss what forms of learning they find most effective. As a community learns about learning, through the Spirit its conversations and practice of mission will improve.

Performing will involve conversations about

- methods of just-in-time learning;
- the development of learning conversations within the mission community;
- the quality of these learning conversations

Adjourning

Adjourning happens if the mission community disbands after a time. This can occur when the mission community has given birth to a new church. In Urban Expression, a UK Baptist-based network of church planters in poor urban areas, teams disband when a new church has formed. Some members may remain in the new church, but they no longer function as a team. There is both joy and sadness at this point.[4]

Where attempts to start a church are not successful or the initiative has a limited though fruitful life, it is especially important that endings take place with dignity. The mission community should let go, grieve, give thanks for

---

4 I am grateful to Stuart Murray-Williams for drawing my attention to this.

what was, share any lessons and move on. This will help others involved to do the same. Members will be assisted in this if they reflect together on their journey and how they feel about its approaching end. Being honest about disappointments and jointly owning the responsibility for any shortcomings (rather than spreading blame) will help to ease the pain.

Sharing mistakes with the wider church can be a gift to the kingdom. 'These are things that we would have done differently' can assist others who are starting out. Making this a focus of the community's discussions will help to turn something that could feel quite negative into a positive experience. Mistakes can be 'redeemed' and become part of what the group celebrates and thanks God for. As members talk in these terms, they can display the responsive quality of being open with each other.

Mini 'adjournments' occur when individuals leave the mission community. Most teams are good at farewelling and thanking their members. But they are not always so good at learning from the departing person's experience of the team. Exit reviews, common in secular employment, can be used prayerfully to invite the colleague to describe what they have most enjoyed in the group, what they have learnt from their involvement and what issues they suggest the team give further thought to. Endings don't have to be loose ends. They can enrich the community's conversations, as well as those in the wider church.

Conclusion

Being intentional about forming, norming, storming, performing and adjourning will create opportunities for the mission community to review the quality of its conversations. Complex responsive process theory invites community members not to be so preoccupied with obtaining the desired results that they ignore their exchanges in the here and now. Without neglecting the task, the theory encourages members to pay close attention to conversations about the task. What are the current patterns of relating? How well does the team score on diversity, responsiveness and associative capacity? What is amplifying and diminishing these capabilities? Not just participating in forming and other conversations, but talking about the quality of the interactions involved will attune members to their conversational life. Team awareness will increase. Better conversations will produce more fruitful results.

Conversations are at the heart of church. There is much room for ethical and pastoral reflection on their style and content. Who is included and excluded, and when? What issues are allowed on to the table? How is language used to exercise power? What boundaries are set and by whom? How is conflict handled? What is the pattern of learning/coaching conversations? How can members create an environment that encourages them to talk honestly about these questions? Through the Spirit, members' interactions will strongly influence the venture that emerges and its fruitfulness. So conversations cannot be left to chance. They warrant focused and prayerful attention. The community's style of conversation will be in the DNA of the new church.

Further reading

Blatt, Ruth, 'Tough Love: How communal schemas and contracting practices build relational capital in entrepreneurial teams', *Academy of Management Review* 34 (3), 2009, pp. 533–51.

Bonheoffer, Dietrich, *Life Together*, trans. John W. Doberstein, London: SCM Press, 1954.

Shaw, Patricia, *Changing Conversations in Organizations: A complexity Approach to Change*, London: Routledge, 2002.

Vanier, Jean, *Community and Growth*, revised edition, London: Darton, Longman and Todd, 2007.

Questions for discussion

- What lessons would you draw from teams that you have belonged to – ones that have worked well and haven't? Which practices described in this chapter did the teams include?
- Who is responsible for the quality of a mission community's conversational life, and how should this responsibility be exercised?
- How can teams be encouraged to value conflict? What are the marks of a healthy disagreement?

Part 4

Growing to Maturity

17

Discipleship

Earlier chapters have looked at the past and present, the theological rationale and the bringing to birth of contextual church. Part 4 considers how, through the Spirit, these churches can be encouraged to grow to maturity. This challenge has been given added urgency by critics such as Martyn Percy, who suspects that fresh expressions of church are not a highway to mission, but 'a series of new intricate cul-de-sacs' (2010, p. 75).

Percy fears that these churches may be 'a form of collusion with a contemporary cultural obsession with newness, alternatives and novelty' (2010, p. 70). He fears that they may prove to be 'an expression of post-associationalism' and lack 'thick' connection – with a sense of obligation and duty – to their local contexts. They risk colluding with pluralism and individualism by focusing on 'niche spirituality'. They 'may represent a conservative, therapeutic and individualistic *retreat* from the world' (p. 73, author's italics). Their community-building efforts may be directed inward rather than toward the wider church.

There is a danger that they collude with the surrounding capitalism by being more obsessed with numerical growth than spiritual depth, and by preferring the promise of immediacy and a clear return on a focused investment than sustaining social and spiritual capital. While recognizing that these new forms of church may feed the institution, he warns that 'the church will need to avoid falling into the trap of imagining that spiritual forms of post-institutionalism hold out any long-term hope for the future' (Percy, 2010, p. 79).

Whether Percy's concerns are justified by experience is an empirical question that requires research. They certainly highlight the importance of contextual churches becoming mature. However, Chapter 5 cautioned against being too prescriptive about what maturity will look like. Existing church must not assume it knows best in this matter. As new Christians place themselves under Scripture and engage with the traditions of the church, defining maturity for a particular church will involve shared discernment between it and the wider body.

In making this point, Chapter 5 suggested that maturity will involve growth in Christ-likeness. This can be understood as movement toward the kingdom within each of the four interlocking sets of relationships that constitute the church – with the Trinity, the world, the living tradition and within the gathering. As this movement occurs, we would expect Percy's concerns to be met. The new church will become more like God in its character. It will embody the kingdom – by sacrificially serving its context, for example – in ways that mark it out from the world. Alongside growing fellowship within the community, ties to the whole Christian body will steadily deepen. The new church will become a vehicle not for satisfying the consumerist trinity of 'me, myself and I', but for social commitment and integration.

Maturity, therefore, goes to the heart of whether contextual churches are being shaped by the kingdom. Maturity is movement into God's reign, which is the *telos*, the goal of the church. When churches fail to mature, they fail to grow towards their purpose. It follows that members of a mission community, those people who lead a church to birth, should have maturity at the forefront of their minds. Each stage of their journey should be governed by the church's purpose. They should constantly ask, 'How would the initiatives we plan help the church on its journey towards the kingdom?'

The journey to maturity starts in the earliest days of an initiative. The life of the mission community and its first missional steps begin to set the direction of travel. The journey also requires intentionality. If there is no ambition to reach maturity and no 'straining' towards it (Phil. 3.13), the journey is unlikely to happen. Of course, the mission community will not know in advance the exact path. It will lay only the next stone in the light of the journey so far and of its perception of the *telos*, the church's destination. Through Scripture, prayer, the sharing of spiritual gifts and worship, the Spirit will enable the mission community to discern when each stone should be laid and what shape it should take.

This and the chapters that follow discuss four pathways to maturity – discipleship, worship, community and sustainability. Being mostly so new, especially in the setting of post-Christendom, we have more examples of contextual churches starting than growing to maturity. It is easier, therefore, to suggest what the practice of birthing a church might entail than what might be involved in these four pathways. Given the discussion about practice in Chapter 11, I am not even clear whether birthing should be seen as a practice distinct from leading to maturity (with overlaps between the two), or whether both should be seen as a single practice of birthing and nurturing.

Recognizing that it is too early to map the four pathways in detail, Chapters 17 to 20 provide an initial sketch of some of the theological and practical issues involved. Each pathway starts in the earliest stages of the initiative, underlining that maturity is not something you turn to when the church has come to birth. It must be considered from the outset.

This chapter, on making disciples, has three sections. The first addresses evangelism (which is the starting point for Christian formation), the second covers the process of conversion and initiation (which lays the foundations for formation), while the third suggests a framework for continuing formation. Evangelism, initiation and formation thus overlap. In the New Testament, they comprise the one commission to make disciples. The distinctions are used here for analytic convenience.

Inviting people into the kingdom

Laying down a pathway to mature discipleship starts with evangelism, which is not a popular word. For many it is associated with an over-narrow approach to the gospel and with a dogmatic, individualistic and insensitive focus on a moment of conversion. Yet the term is rooted in Scripture (for example Eph. 4.11). In a classic study, William Abraham defined evangelism as initiating people into the kingdom of God for the first time (Abraham, 1989, pp. 95–8).

This embraces a variety of understandings, from evangelism as the proclamation of the gospel (Watson, 1983), to evangelism as hospitality (Arias, 2008), to evangelism as liberation (Russell, 2008), to evangelism as an invitation to change identities – to switch stories that define the person (Brueggemann, 1993, pp. 10–1). Evangelism is a welcome to join the Spirit in making the lordship of Christ tangible throughout creation.

Can evangelism be justified?

In today's culture of tolerance, many Christians shy away from evangelism out of fear that to evangelize is to disregard the other person's difference. The Chief Rabbi of the United Hebrew Congregations of the Commonwealth, Jonathan Sacks, has expressed a widespread view: he worries that proselytizing in today's pluralistic society risks increasing conflict between the faiths. Yahweh's covenant with Israel, who was to be a holy (or different) people, was given as an exemplar 'to teach humanity the dignity of difference' (Sacks, 2002, p. 52). To be true to God is to respect difference. Many in the emerging church conversation would agree. Reflecting well-established mission theory, some maintain that respect for difference involves a willingness to be changed by the other person. The church must be evangelized by the world.[1]

However, this radical openness to the other need not imply a one-way conversation. Since mutual sharing is intrinsic to being human, humanity would be impaired if Christians could only listen to the other and not share their experiences too. The role of dialogue in evangelism is now widely

---

1 The Ikon collective in Belfast has an Evangelism Project that goes out to be evangelized. It visits other religious traditions within and outside Christianity in order to listen, learn and be transformed.

accepted. It avoids one-way traffic – from the Christian to the other or the other to the Christian – in favour of an exchange of views and experiences. Dialogue treats the other person as an equal. To the one who speaks about Jesus, listening can reveal how the Spirit has been at work in the other person. To the one who hears about Jesus, listening can lead to an expansion of understanding about the human condition. There is a mutual exchange of truth.

In today's society, organizations and groups are constantly offering invitations to people. 'Shop here!' 'Come to the barn dance in the village hall!' 'Join the parent/teacher association!' If faith groups failed to issue invitations in the public realm, the diversity on offer would diminish. The spirituality space would be left largely to those who profit financially from their offerings. Social exchange would become even more dominated by economics. When faith groups describe what they have to offer and create opportunities for people to taste and see, the public arena becomes more interesting, the diversity Sacks applauds increases and choice (a creation gift of God) expands.

Sacks' underlying concern, widely shared,[2] is that proselytizing shows insufficient respect for other people. Yet from a Christian standpoint, this depends on whether the style of evangelism is consistent with the kingdom. Saint Paul 'knew nothing else but "pluralism" in every city of the empire' (Thiselton, 2006, pp. 22–3). He responded not by vacating the public square, but by entering it in a distinctive way. He eschewed the audience-pleasing rhetoric that was common in places like Corinth and was more concerned with 'winning' than truth. Instead he used 'classical' rhetoric, which aimed to communicate the truth effectively (Thiselton, 2006, pp. 14–9). He avoided manipulation.

His approach to evangelism revealed the kingdom as a gift – the gift of life with God but also the gift of human freedom, the freedom to go further with God or not. In keeping with this, Mayo, Savage and Collins (2004, pp. 85–8) advocate the use of understatement, such as story, in evangelism with young people (but the principle applies more widely). Understatement creates room for listeners to reach out and interpret what is said for themselves. Unlike advertising, the audience keeps control.

Sometimes Christians draw back from evangelism, because they fear that it elevates one aspect of the gospel at the expense of others; witness through loving service and social action feels more important. Ecumenical discussions have addressed this through the concept of holistic mission, in which evangelism has a place alongside other aspects. As discussed in Chapter 6,

2 In a 2009–10 survey, only a sixth (17 per cent) of Britons thought that 'it is okay for religious people to try and convert other people to their faith', while 81 per cent took the opposite view (Voas and Ling, 2010, pp. 74–5).

the five marks of mission – proclamation, making disciples, loving service, justice and care for creation – are one way of expressing this.

Yet to claim that evangelism should sit alongside the other marks is not to say enough. How is evangelism to be related to them? Is it an equal, junior or senior partner? The common-sense experience of believers is that the answer depends on the context. There will be times when the Spirit calls Christians to invite others explicitly into God's reign. On other occasions, they will be called to witness through acts of care or through social and environmental concern.

Does this imply that evangelism is a parallel activity to the other marks – that evangelism, acts of kindness, and social and environmental initiatives can be boxed into discrete forms of mission? This is dangerous because it allows congregations to be content with focusing on one mark but not the others – 'we have a calling to social justice (but not to evangelism)', or vice versa. Mission ceases to be holistic and becomes lopsided.

The idea of completion may be more helpful. The different marks complete, or round out each other. The other marks authenticate Christian proclamation (words are backed by deeds), while proclamation points to the ultimate meaning of the other marks: it explains how loving care and social and environmental concern point to the kingdom. Proclamation gives them a distinctively Christian flavour (Jensen, 2007, pp. 286–7). The five marks encourage the church to engage in mission on a wide front, with evangelism as an integral component.

Evangelistic pointers to Christ

Chapter 11 suggested that mission communities can start to grow new churches by adopting one of two approaches, or perhaps combining both – *a worship first journey* or *a serving-first journey*. These are not the only paths to a contextual church, but the chapter argued that as groups of believers increasingly engage with people who have little or no Christian background, they are likely to embark on some variation of the second journey.

A serving-first journey

Source: Chapter 13.

The chapter suggested that within *a serving-first journey,* evangelism might take several forms:

- acts of kindness towards people outside the initiative (as well as those inside), which reveal the compassionate heart of Jesus;
- 'God talk', in which faith is shared through natural conversations or through events that provoke questions about Jesus;
- missional worship, which creates opportunities for people without Christian commitment to encounter God and engenders an appetite for more;
- the experience of answered prayer, including healing, which may open a person to God;
- creative expressions of spirituality, which can help to increase awareness of spiritual issues.

This approach to evangelism can be described in terms of the belonging–believing–behaving model that is widely favoured in Britain today. Communities are created around loving and serving. As individuals have a growing sense of belonging, evangelistic pointers such as acts of kindness, a testimony and missional worship draw their attention to Jesus. In the Spirit's time, individuals are offered more structured opportunities to explore becoming a disciple of Christ. Perhaps their belief grows, they embrace the faith and they begin to be formed within it. Belonging leads to belief, which is followed by changes in behaviour as the church takes shape.

In *a serving-first journey,* the model holds two strands in parallel – loving and serving plus community on the one hand, and the journey to faith on the other. Though the two cross over for those who become Christians and join the believing core of the initiative, for others the two strands can be kept separate. Individuals can learn English, enjoy a good lunch and meet with others to sew, while largely ignoring the evangelistic pointers.

The model has potential, but is it adequate on its own? Might the possibility exist for a behaving–belonging–believing approach alongside it? This involves closer integration between loving service and the Christian faith. Christian practices are used to address individuals' day-to-day concerns. Just as New Age spiritualities focus on the immanent life (and this may account for their growing popularity), in this second model mission communities use Christian practices to enhance the immanent lives of the people they serve. Loving service – with community – is not parallel to evangelism. They collapse into one.

Anecdotal evidence suggests that this model has potential. In Mind Body Spirit Fairs, which promote therapies, spirituality and other aspects of holistic lifestyles, often Christian stalls provide opportunities for prayer, talk and reflection. The Christian faith is directly connected to individuals' immanent concerns. A group of Church Army students took this idea to a local car boot sale and created a place where people could be prayed for

(Hollinghurst, 2010, p. 227). The challenge now 'is to move from what are becoming established mission presences to places where community can be formed' (p. 231).

A number of initiatives are beginning to connect individuals' immediate concerns to the experience of community and to Christian faith. On Wednesdays, Essence in Histon, near Cambridge, provides a crèche for young mothers who do not attend church. After coffee and croissants, there is some short input followed by discussion, in which individuals are encouraged to share their stories and to explore connections with the biblical one. After coffee and cake, the mothers move upstairs for quiet space. 'Although we didn't anticipate it, people have been keen to share what has happened in the quiet; God has done some amazing things and touched people at their point of need in quite wonderful ways' (www.freshexpressions.org.uk/ stories). Fruitful connections are being made between people's immanent lives and the transcendent.

Might it be possible for individuals to be introduced more intentionally to a Christian practice that will help them to better manage their lives? As they discuss it with other people, perhaps they increasingly feel that they belong to the group (and the group to them). They find the Christian practice helpful, enjoy the company of others and so become open to exploring further aspects of the Christian story. Their journey to faith starts with behaviour. Christian formation begins before they make a profession of faith.

The church would compete within the therapeutic market for spirituality, but not in a way that reinforces consumerist individualism and runs counter to Christian community. Rather, as with the twelve-steps programme of Alcoholics Anonymous, community would provide the context for individuals to discover practices that help them to counter habits that limit their lives. Learning these practices would introduce them to the thought and behaviour of Jesus.

The Christian tradition contains rich resources for addressing issues in people's everyday lives. The Sabbath theme can be applied to the time pressures many people experience. A group of parents might support each other in practising 'mini Sabbaths', short periods of rest, as well as more substantial Sabbath breaks during the week. A spirituality-at-work group might explore how Sabbath theology applies to work/life balance: what would be practical in its context?

In exploring how to manage conflict, members of a group might be introduced to the Christian discipline of silence. How can the Spirit be invoked during silence? Individuals might support each other as they learn, perhaps through role plays, to practise short Spirit-filled silences in the midst of conflict. Exploring longer periods of silence as part of a rhythm of life might be the next step. Other themes from the tradition also have considerable potential – confession and forgiveness, for instance, and stewardship in relation to managing personal finances and ecological concerns.

One example of a promising opportunity is the growing popularity of mindfulness training. Coming out of Buddhist meditation, mindfulness has been described as:

'affectionate attention'. It deepens our potential for kindness and understanding through developing our capacity to be present in each moment with an open-hearted attention to our experience. Mindfulness helps us to step back and see our situation more clearly. This allows us to make wiser choices and to take better care of ourselves . . . (www. mindfulnessforhealth.co.uk/mindfulness.html)

Those who seek mindfulness training do so to ease physical and psychological symptoms, cope better with stressful situations and generate greater energy and enjoyment of life. Why should not contextual churches respond to this demand but use resources from the Christian tradition? Individuals' immanent concerns and Christian practices would be clapped together.

Using Christian practices to serve people, introduce them to the kingdom and form their characters before they fully own the faith must be done with care. William Willimon has expressed second thoughts about Hauerwas's and his emphasis on practices in their books on 'resident aliens' (1989, 1996). Their attention to practices has been taken in ways that suggest a kind of Pelagianism – a faith based on human rather than divine activity (Willimon, 2010, pp. 22–5). To avoid this reliance on human efforts, practices must be combined with continual pointers to Jesus. They must be taught within a framework of grace, as well as with respect for people's right to disagree.

Evangelism within a kingdom narrative

Belonging–believing–behaving and behaving–belonging–believing can be seen as alternative, equally valid approaches, or as possible combinations. Whether either or both are involved, it is important that they be placed in a narrative that is faithful to the kingdom. This will not be a story mainly about self-fulfilment, which would collude with contemporary culture rather than help to subvert it. It will be a narrative that unfolds the possibilities of the kingdom for today's world. As individuals hear about, witness or experience interventions from God, these signs of the transcendent will be related to the kingdom.

In sketching a Pentecostal political theology, Luke Bretherton has suggested that miraculous 'healing is part of a repertoire of acts by which God establishes a community that can bear faithful witness to the coming kingdom' (Bretherton, 2011, p. 132). Jesus' acts of healing were public works. They unveiled the possibilities of the world as God intends it to be. They also revealed the inadequacy of those in power, who were shown to be unable to respond to the basic needs and dignity of people they claimed authority over.

Following the pattern of Christ's life, death and resurrection, healing today is an event that simultaneously ruptures what is normal and repairs it. It points to and is a foretaste of the world's destiny – to be refashioned by Jesus. Miraculous healing is not given for personal blessing. It must not collude with the contemporary illusion that we can cheat death (Bretherton, 2011, p. 139). Like all God's gifts, 'it is yet another way in which the Spirit acts among us to form a social body that bears witness to God's coming kingdom' (p. 138).

This is an appropriate narrative not only for healing, but for missional worship, creative expressions of spirituality, connections between the tradition and life concerns, and other evangelistic aspects of bringing a church to birth. A mission community will be an evangelizing community when it is explicit about this story and relates signs of God's activity to it.

Inviting believers into the kingdom

- Evangelism completes other aspects of mission and points to their ultimate meaning.
- It may include teaching Christian practices to help not-yet believers enhance their immanent lives – forming them in the faith, in effect, before they own the faith.
- It will include being explicit about the story of the kingdom and relating signs of God's activity to this story.

Initiating people into the kingdom

Having started with evangelism, laying a pathway to mature discipleship will involve putting down stepping stones that initiate the individual into God's family. These stones will be laid with one eye on the sort of journey to faith individuals may be inclined to make, and the other on habits of behaviour and thought that will support continuing discipleship thereafter.

Conversion within the evangelizing community

In Christendom, when the church had a dominant place in society, it was not unusual for there to be a *point* at which conversion occurred. With Saint Paul, Saint Augustine, Martin Luther, John Wesley and others as examples, the classic model of conversion centred on a 'crisis moment, in which an emotionally charged sinner [was] brought to release and sudden insight by the power of the Spirit' (Tomlin, 2002, p. 89).

During the 1990s there was a shift in emphasis.

It can be said that the 'evangelistic appeal' has changed from 'I want you to get up out of your seats and come forward now . . .' to 'we invite you to join a group that will be exploring the Christian faith over the coming weeks at . . .' Behind this shift in practice is a shift in perception . . . Coming to faith itself, not just the work of evangelism, is now seen as a process. (Warren, 1995, p. 65)

Having evolved from a point to a *process*, a third shift is underway – to conversion as a *pathway*. Chapter 4 noted that many people's preferred mode of spirituality – if they are interested in spirituality at all – is now the quest. They prefer to keep their options open rather than reach a destination. So when it occurs, the journey to Christian faith tends to be more prolonged. People also assume that individuals will travel their own paths and respect the paths of others. This puts greater emphasis on the personal nature of the journey than perhaps in the past. Individuals expect the uniqueness of their experiences to be respected. It means, too, that there will be a great plurality of journeys, just as there was an extraordinary range of encounters with Jesus in the gospels.

There are parallel changes in the corporate methods of evangelism. The *crusade*, or crusade-like event such as a guest service, assumed that people became Christians at a particular point, when they made a commitment. As process evangelism became popular in the 1990s, evangelistic *courses* spread, led by Alpha. The course, with its syllabus and structure, seemed a good platform from which to steer the conversion process. Now, with more attention to personal pathways, the *context* becomes crucial. What helps one person may not help another.

Alongside the changing balance between crusade, course and context is a change in style. In crusades (and crusade-like meetings) *exhortation* was common, with some apologetics. In evangelistic courses, the emphasis moved to *explanation*, with a focus on apologetics (coupled occasionally with some exhortation). In the current situation where context is vital, *exploration* becomes the key style. Mission teams prayerfully bring to birth communities in which individuals can explore their spiritual longings and experiences. Within these communities, a believer may explore with the other person as they walk together on the explorer's path.

It is important not to see these shifts from point/crusade/exhortation to process/course/explanation to pathway/context/exploration as a linear movement. They are changes in emphasis, but need not be mutually exclusive. Someone's pathway to faith may involve a course at some stage, and on the course the person may come to a point of commitment.

These changes can be connected to social developments such as the decline of church attendance, the emergence of the expressive self and, possibly, changes in consumption. In addition to mass consumption (which was conducive to mass, crusade-style evangelism), customization has segmented the market into groups of buyers with similar characteristics (resonant perhaps of courses). At the same time consumption is being personalized (though the recession has slowed the trend), and this may be encouraging individualized pathways.

Milestones to faith

One implication of changes in how individuals come to faith is that mission communities have to be quite sophisticated and patient in the support they offer. Different forms of support will be required to match the varied nature of people's journeys toward Jesus and to respect their expectations. In particular, communities must be sensitive to the milestones individuals have reached on their journeys. Support must be tailored to the different milestones.

These milestones have been conceptualized in various ways. The Engel Scale, of which there are slightly different versions, resembles a number line depicting a series of steps from complete unawareness and ignorance of the gospel to a maturing commitment to Christ (see box). Ed Stetzer (2006, pp. 187–91) offers an adaptation with a stronger communal focus, and suggests how to apply it to Muslims and postmodern people. A weakness in both the original and Stetzer's alternative is that they centre on knowledge of the gospel. Becoming a Christian is portrayed as a cognitive process, which underplays the emotional and relational aspects.

The Engel Scale

−8 Awareness of a supreme being but no effective knowledge of the gospel
−7 Initial awareness of the gospel
−6 Awareness of the fundamentals of the gospel
−5 Grasp implications of the gospel
−4 Positive attitude to the gospel
−3 Counting the cost
−2 Decision to act
−1 Repentance and faith in Christ

REGENERATION

+1 Post-decision evaluation
+2 Incorporation into the body
+3 A lifetime of growth in Christ – discipleship and service.

Source: Stetzer (2006, pp. 184–5).

Arising from their work among over 2,000 college students in North America and having tested their conclusions with colleagues, Don Everts and Doug Shaupp (2009) have described a 'postmodern path to faith', in which five thresholds are crossed: trusting a Christian, becoming curious, opening up to change, seeking after God and entering the kingdom, after which comes living in the kingdom (see Box below). Though based on college students, this path seems likely to apply more widely.

A postmodern path to faith

From distrust to trust – 'Christians are OK.'
From complacent to curious – 'Jesus is interesting.'
From curious to open – 'Jesus could be for me.'
From meandering to seeking – 'Jesus is worth taking seriously.'
From seeking to joining – 'I'll turn to Jesus.'
From joining to growing – 'Help me to live like Jesus.'

Source: Everts and Shaupp (2009) (slightly adapted).

The important thing is not to imagine that because it fits a model, one person's journey is the same as another's; each journey feels unique and has its own characteristics. Nor should we assume that 'a postmodern path to faith' applies to every context. Journeys to faith may be different in different situations. The value lies in having some sense of the paths people are likely to follow.

This awareness can help mission communities to be alert to where individuals are on their journeys and to offer appropriate support and encouragement.[3] The community can ask, 'What stages have people reached and what would help them to take the next step?' If people are learning to trust Christians, the type of support required will be very different to what is needed for individuals who are beginning to seek Jesus. Thinking about what is appropriate for different stages stops evangelism being a haphazard process. Both for individuals and the group, evangelism can be intentional and strategic.

Initiation into the evangelizing community

The change in how people are coming to faith reflects a missional context that increasingly has an early-church feel to it. As in the early centuries, more and more people have little or no Christian background and conversion can

---

3 For a model of what this support involves, see Croft (2005, pp. 132–41).

take considerable time. This trend is set to accelerate as we move further from Christendom. A growing number of writers, such as Martyn Atkins (2007, pp. 175–85), James Heard (2009, pp. 190–205) and Alan Kreider (1999, pp. 86–107), have suggested that practices of catechesis in the early church may contain lessons for today. What might these lessons be?

Various models of catechesis – religious instruction in preparation for baptism – were developed over the first four centuries. Collapsing them into a single and somewhat idealized model yields a four-stage process (Jones et al., 1992, pp. 129–44). The stages were:

- Pre-catechumenate, which was a time of enquiry into the Christian faith
- Catechemunate, which was a long process of instruction, sometimes up to three years. During that time, catechumens (those under instruction) belonged to the church but not fully. Alongside their instruction, they attended the service of the word and heard the sermon, but they were not admitted to the Eucharist.
- Sacramental initiation, which occurred during Lent and was the preparation for baptism, which took place at Easter
- Mystagogy, which was post-baptismal instruction that concentrated on the meaning of baptism and the Eucharist. It was only after the sacraments had been experienced that candidates were deemed ready to receive teaching about them.

Although this is probably not a model for today, three lessons stand out. First, it was a lengthy process – much longer than a term-long course! This is a helpful reminder as the church leaves behind expectations forged in an earlier period. When people were brought up in a Christian culture, it was natural to assume that a short period of instruction was enough to prepare adults for a commitment to faith. The cultural gap between the enquirer and the church was comparatively narrow, and the enquirer had considerable pre-knowledge of Christian belief. The situation today is very different as we become an increasingly post-Christian society.

In addition, the church has to contend with a culture of low commitment. This should not be exaggerated. Many people are highly committed to exercise regimes, their hobbies, work and their families. But there is a simultaneous reluctance to be tied down. Entering the kingdom is a big step. It is understandable that people who cherish open options often need time before making such a large commitment. Seeing initiation as a lengthy process works with this. Enquirers may need encouragement to take a series of small steps. Might they commit to an initial short period of exploration, then another and then perhaps to a longer period as their confidence and interest grow?

Secondly, Kreider (1999, p. 103) maintains that the early Christians encourage us to reconsider the balance of ingredients in conversion. They wrote relatively little about inner experience. They emphasized right belief, but it was not the centre of their attention. More important was transformed behaviour. This was the heart of catechism. As Jesus said, 'by their fruit you will recognize them' (Matt. 7.16). Emphasizing behaviour fits comfortably with the pragmatic strand of contemporary culture ('does it work?') and with the place of practice in education theory: learning starts with doing or experiencing something, on which the learner reflects, and this leads to a trying out of what has been learnt.

It is striking that the New Testament epistles originally addressed specific pastoral situations. The writers used their understanding of Jesus, his teachings and the Hebrew Scriptures to provide practical guidance to their readers. Christian doctrine later systematized this reflection, but the letters themselves were not systematic theology. Reflection on experience was the seedbed of doctrine. In a similar way, enquirers will learn essential doctrines most effectively as part of truthful reflection on life's experiences and how Jesus connects to them.

Thirdly, initiation happened in the context of church and was very much about church. Kreider notes that the early Christian liturgies emphasize a radical shift in believers' sense of belonging (Kreider, 1999, p. 103). There was a change of identity. Individuals retained their gender, family, ethnic and other identities, but acquired a new overarching allegiance. This loyalty was to Jesus and his kingdom, as embodied by the church.

Miroslav Volf has emphasized that individuals do not become Christians and then join the church. To believe means to enjoy fellowship with the triune God. But since God is also in fellowship with everyone else who believes, when the individual has fellowship with God he or she is drawn into fellowship with all believers. Communion with God 'is at once also communion with those others who have entrusted themselves in faith to the same God' (Volf, 1998, p. 173). The act of faith that joins a person to God joins that person to all others who stand in communion with God.

This does not mean that the church makes you a Christian. The believer does not receive faith as a gift of God from the church. Nor does salvation equate to belonging to the church. There must be a subjective appropriation of the faith. Individuals must believe in their hearts, and this is a gift through the Spirit. Volf argues (1998, p. 166) that believers do not receive faith *apart from* the church, nor *from* the church, but *through* the church. The church is both the means of salvation and the end. It brings people into the kingdom and at the end of history it will grow into the kingdom. It is therefore fundamental to believers' identity. They become who they are through the church, and the church is an integral part of who they are. The church is far more than a supportive aid to Christian living.

This understanding of Christian identity and the church should be at the forefront of the initiation process. Indeed, entry to the kingdom, the new identity this brings and ecclesial belonging may be appropriate pillars on which to construct for enquirers the story of faith. Grace, the cross, repentance, personal faith and other elements will be crucial ingredients too. But the story itself may best be structured round kingdom, identity and church because these themes challenge most radically the assumptions widespread today.

To work for the kingdom is to begin to turn away from consumerism and live for others. To become a Christian is to receive a kingdom identity that frames your other identities. To be part of the church is to forsake individualism in favour of a corporate life. All three are vital to following Jesus as Lord. If they shape the story about entering the faith, enquirers will be pointed in the direction they must walk for the rest of their lives. Foundations will be laid for ongoing discipleship.

Building instruction round these themes will require particular attention to the correct use of language – encouraging enquirers (and others) not to speak about going to church, most obviously, but about being church and expressing church. The importance of language is often overlooked in initiation. Yet how people talk influences how they think. Careful language will be one of the stepping stones to maturity.

Just as children's upbringing shapes them as adults, how believers are initiated into the faith does much to form them as Christians. So as mission communities lay down a path to maturity, they must consider what patterns of thought and behaviour their processes of initiation are encouraging.

Initiating believers into the kingdom – summary

- point → process → path;
- requires sensitivity to the milestones people have reached;
- initiation will often be lengthy, will connect belief to Christian behavior and will stress the communal nature of the Christian life.

Forming disciples within the kingdom

Once individuals have trod the path to initiation, mission communities – as the core of the nascent church – have a responsibility to help them grow in their faith. Traditionally, this has been largely a cognitive process. Individuals have learnt about the faith through sermons, small groups, conferences and so on. This has drawn them into the Christian story, but largely through the acquisition of knowledge. Christian visitors from the global South often comment on the extensive Christian knowledge of believers in the North, but ask questions about their strength of commitment as reflected in everyday life.

Engaging the world

Christian formation is primarily about changed lives. It is about learning to live the kingdom of God within the world. James Hunter has described three paradigms of Christian engagement with the world (2010, pp. 213–20). The *defensive against* paradigm is embraced by conservative Protestants and Catholics, who seek to retain the distinctiveness of Christian belief and practice, evangelize unbelievers and resist the erosion of Christian standards in the world, such as perceived assaults on the traditional family. The world tends to be seen as a threat, which needs converting. Formation concentrates on helping believers to preserve their Christian distinctiveness and engage in evangelism.

The *relevance to* paradigm was articulated by theological liberals and can be found today in the views of progressive evangelicals and Catholics. Being connected to the pressing issues of the world is the priority. The emphasis is less on the defence of truth than on being relevant to society. Priority is given to putting doctrine into practice. Often the church is more heavily criticized – for being out of touch with the world – than contemporary culture. There is a tendency to downplay the difference between the world and the church. Formation focuses on helping believers to lead pertinent lives.

The *purity from* paradigm emphasizes the church's task to live as a faithful community in the world. The church does not witness to the world mainly by trying to save souls or improve the social order, but by being the communal sign of the coming kingdom. 'Christians are responsible first of all for their own communities, not for the wider society. It is by the quality of their communal life that God wills them to be a light to the Gentiles' (Lindbeck, 1988 p. 194). The world tends to be construed as darkness, and formation concentrates on building the Christian community as a beacon of light.

Hunter proposes a fourth paradigm, *faithful presence within*, which draws together elements from the other three (2010, pp. 225–54). Recognizing the totality of the fall, the church must stand in antithesis to the world. It must always be a 'community of resistance'. This will include evangelism. The church must also be present in society in a way that constructively subverts all aspects of life that are incompatible with the well-being and flourishing of the world. It must, in addition, be present as a community within individual vocations and social institutions, offering an alternative vision and direction for them.

Jeremiah 29.4–7, addressed to the exiles from Jerusalem in Babylon, encapsulates what being a faithful presence involves. Christians are to 'seek the welfare of the city'. The church must therefore affirm the world – a world that has been created by God and is shared by believers and non-believers alike. Creation is fundamentally marred but is not negated by sin:

God's goodness remains in it. The church must play its part in continuing to fashion the world because 'world-making' 'is a work that God ordained to humankind at creation' (p. 232).

This will not involve Christians trying to 'take over' the culture, fashioning it in the image of the church. It is not another version of the Constantinian project, which can lead to the suppression of difference and abuses of power in God's name. Rather than seeking to establish the coming kingdom, Christians will provide foretastes of it by expressing its values as they serve the world. To enable them to so act, they will be formed through the community of the church, which seeks to embody the renewal of creation.

Four approaches to engaging with the world

- defensive against;
- relevance to;
- purity from;
- faithful presence within.

Being present in the world

This vision for discipleship has three implications for Christian formation. First, formation will teach Christians what working distinctively for the welfare of creation entails. It will help them to discover how to act in the manner of Jesus in their day-to-day contexts, such as in a work team or among friends. In Rowan Williams's phrase, believers will be shown what it means to put Jesus round the edges of life.[4]

Enacting Jesus involves going the second mile in relation to virtues already recognized by the world. If a workplace has values like, 'we work as a team', it means striving to create not just a team but a group that is a little closer to 'koinonia', the early Christian ideal of fellowship. Much of Saint Paul's ethics can be seen as raising the moral bar. He exhorted believers to go beyond what their contemporaries thought was moral – slaves were to obey their masters not just to win favours, but as if they were obeying Christ (Eph. 6.5–6).

In occupational psychology, the concept of 'occupational citizenship behaviour' refers to employees putting themselves out for each other and the organization (McBain, 2004). Individuals 'do the extra' in their jobs and for one another. This oils the wheels of a team, increases satisfaction with work, and promotes the welfare of the organization and the people

---

4 Presentation to 'Changing the landscape' conference, Lincoln, 5 March 2010.

it serves. In flourishing organizations, these behaviours are ubiquitous, so there is nothing specifically Christian about them. However, by being exceptionally diligent in their 'citizenship behaviours', Christians can go the second mile in going the second mile. Through the Spirit, they can become distinctive.

As another distinguishing feature, Christians are to bring a Christ-like humility into their everyday lives, reflected in a willingness to forgive others and to suffer for doing good. Tom Wright points out that in passages like Philippians 2.1–11, these are the main ways that the New Testament holds up Jesus as a model to follow. They are not examples of how to do it. 'They are indications that a new way of being human has been launched upon the world' (Wright, 2010, p. 113). The church is to form characters that express this different humanity.

It is also to nourish a willingness to side with the vulnerable. 'To be a disciple of the Markan Jesus meant that you had to follow Jesus in his mission to people at the bottom or at the fringes of society, to seek to bring some life to the outsiders of the world' (Vincent, 2006, p. 69). Today, this might involve asking questions like, 'Who can't afford to use this leisure centre, and how might access be extended to them?' 'How are the cleaners being treated here?' 'Who is being bullied in my workplace and how might they be supported?'

Formed in community

Second, to be a faithful presence in the world, Christians should see discipleship as a communal activity. Often discipleship is seen in individualistic terms – as equipping believers for their personal walks with God. Courses may be organized to provide the necessary knowledge. But Christians need far more than a course: they need community – in two ways. First, they must be formed by the Christian gathering to which they belong. Worship and teaching gain impact when they foster simple disciplines and rhythms of life, shared voluntarily by the community's members. A shared discipline can give preaching and teaching an applied focus. Individuals have the encouragement and support of others as they practise the discipline. Sharing practices builds community, which then builds the individual, who – in a virtuous circle – comes to value the community more highly.

Inspired possibly by the monastic tradition, these disciplines and rhythms might range from a daily call to prayer by text (Adams, 2010, p. 46), to members of the church – wherever they happen to be – saying the Lord's Prayer silently at a specific time of the day, to members sharing a simple rule of life (as in the Box below). To give concrete form to the missional nature of the church, these rhythms could include at least one regular corporate activity to serve others in the context. Reviewing these disciplines and perhaps expressing them differently can help to keep them fresh and relevant.

BELLS – Small Boat Big Sea's rhythm of life (practices by individuals)

B Bless × three	Three acts of blessing a week – to someone inside the community of faith, to someone outside, one spare to go either way.
E Eat × three	Table fellowship three times a week – with people inside the community of faith, with folks outside, one spare to go either way.
L Listen one hour	Spend at least one hour a week in contemplative prayer (knowing other forms of prayer will be practised along the way).
L Learn	Constantly (1) read and reread the Gospels, (2) read another book of the Bible, (3) read best books in any category, Christian or not. Give up trashy magazines.
S Sent	See yourself as 'sent' into every sphere and domain of life. At the end of the day, answer two questions in a journal reflection: (1) Where did I resist Jesus today? (2) Where did I work with Jesus today?

Source: Hirsch and Ferguson (2011, p. 182).

Experience suggests that formation best occurs through different sizes of community, including small groups. However, in a society that values personal networks, small groups in themselves are not counter-cultural. They become transformative when members hold each other to account for enacting Jesus. This mutual accountability requires honesty and challenge that many people are not used to. Individuals may have to be shown how to do it. A growing number of Christians are beginning to model and encourage this type of support, such as the 'huddle groups' practised by The Order of Mission (TOM). Simple methodologies are required that can be easily multiplied and adapted.

Alongside its main meeting, re:generation – a church among young people – formed small discipleship groups, run by the young people themselves, to encourage the sharing of personal issues, support and prayer. Though the groups have had natural ebbs and flows, in general they have proved effective, not over-'heavy' vehicles for individuals honestly to engage with issues they face as Christians. In addition, pairings have been encouraged between members of the same sex to encourage further sharing and support. While some pairings have not been effective and ceased to meet, others have stood the test of time and become a valuable tool of discipleship.

347

re:generation has also established an internship programme blending practical service, leadership training, character development and biblical study. Interns have worked alongside the 24/7 prayer movement delivering prayer rooms in schools, they have supported other Christian schools work in the locality and they have been involved in mission trips to Romania and the Ukraine. These programmes give expression to discipleship as practical mission, done communally, which is the second way in which community is central to following Jesus.[5]

The idea of an internship programme can be adapted to any age group. For instance, a team from a contextual church might form to organize a party for residents of an apartment block. During its short lifespan, members would study, pray and plan together, perhaps in parallel to the gathering's main meeting. After the party, they would meet one more time to reflect on their experience as a team – where had they encountered God? What had been the struggles? What had they learnt? What gifts had they seen in each other? What might they say to the gathering as a whole? An act of service would intentionally become a period of more intense discipleship formation.

Church in the midst of everyday life applies this principle over a longer period. Instead of one person, for example, imagining how a leisure centre might make its facilities available to unemployed people at certain times of the week, thinking through how this might actually work, having the courage to suggest it to the manager and helping with the organization to make it happen, all of which will be beyond most individuals acting alone, the person can do this with other Christians as part of a small church in the context.

Church in life allows members who know the context to support each other in applying the faith in concrete ways. When Christians are drawn from a variety of circumstances, they can discuss the application of faith only in general terms. But when they come from the same situation, they can help each other to be specific. 'If you are not part of a mutually discipling community, the culture will disciple you' (Cray, 2010b, p. 65).

Connected to the living tradition

Third, Christian formation will not be restricted to the individual gathering. Gatherings that are both in the multiple settings of life and strongly connected to the wider church have much greater formational promise. By connecting up, believers can enact their prime identities as members of God's family.[6]

---

5 Paper by Ruth Poch, 2011, available from the author, ruthpoch@ntlworld.com.

6 A fledgling church, however, should not be pressed to connect up till it has an identity of its own.

In particular, strengthening this identity will challenge two idols of consumerism – family and friendships.[7] Chapter 4 noted that Generation Y (and others) read life largely through the grid of family and friends. As a result, circles of altruism tend to be confined mainly to these 'personal communities'. The greater the distance a need is from these networks, the less willing individuals are to meet it. Identifying with the family of God has the potential to transform these loyalties. Suffering Christians in Bangladesh become as much 'family' as biological relatives. The villages in which they live, even though members are not all Christians, have a claim on believers elsewhere because their 'brothers' and 'sisters' reside there. Christian identity expands the individual's altruistic reach.

Connecting up also enables Christian character to be formed by the wider church. This includes approaches to learning not available in the gathering. The box below gives two models of learning. Like any typology, it simplifies reality. The models can best be seen as two ends of a spectrum. Both ends contribute to learning. Reflection on action may be enhanced if individuals have been instructed in the Christian story and can draw on it in their reflection. But instruction may seem irrelevant if it is far removed from practice.

Contrasting pedagogies

Cognitive	*Praxis*
Teacher instructs the group	The group shares insights
Learning by reflecting on teacher input	Learning by reflecting on action
Start with Scripture	Start with experience
Right truths matter	Right actions matter

If contextual churches veer towards the praxis end, they will leave space for more cognitive forms of learning, such as an evening course introducing the Old Testament or perhaps worship with a more traditional sermon. Through the wider body, individual churches can pool resources to provide these complementary approaches. The principle can be extended to different learning preferences. SIFT is a helpful acronym for four such preferences – sensing, intuition, feeling, thinking. A gathering should ideally take account of all four preferences (Francis, 2006, pp. 101–7). But if one is dominant, individuals favouring a different style may find that what is missing is catered for in the wider church.

---

7 Tony Walter (1979, pp. 47–66) has written persuasively about the family as a contemporary idol, and his sociological analysis can be extended to friendship networks. An idol can be understood as what you think about in your idle moments.

Pooling resources in the larger body, as emphasized in earlier chapters, enables specialist support for Christian formation way beyond the resources of a single gathering. The support can range from courses on specific biblical, doctrinal, ethical, spiritual and pastoral themes, to interest groups spanning evangelistic drama, ecological activism and prayer for the persecuted church, to Christian support groups for carers of relatives with disabilities or recovering drug addicts. Connecting to the other churches can help to deepen believers' roots in their spiritual tradition, but it can also enrich their Christian experience. Believers can graft into their tradition insights from other strands of the church, such as liberationist, Celtic or monastic spiritualities.

Three potentially overlapping models of connecting up appear to be emerging. *Ongoing* connections are maintained when an existing church forms missional communities that serve specific groups of people outside the church. These communities have their own worshipping lives, but come together with the rest of the church perhaps monthly. The Philadelphia network in Sheffield is developing a variation. Missional cells emerge and then meet together as a cluster, again perhaps monthly. In time, as clusters multiply, they can meet together for periodic celebrations and learning.

As described in Chapter 3, *occasional* connections occur when new churches belong to a network of churches sharing the same spiritual tradition, such as the network of church plants based on Holy Trinity, Brompton in London. The network has an annual holiday week. A variety of courses on work and family themes are open to people within the network and outside, and leaders share resources through learning communities.

'Coalitions of the willing' – local churches that collaborate on mission and discipleship – also encourage occasional connections, such as joint discipleship courses and 'street pastor' schemes (in which teams provide practical and pastoral support to those out in the town centre late at night). This local cooperation has many possibilities, not least because it is so easy to start.[8] Participating churches can advertise events that individual churches already organize, such as a weekend prayer retreat. As churches become used to sharing activities, they can try initiatives that may be too specialized for one church, but become viable when open to several churches.

Online connections refer to mushrooming opportunities on the Internet – blogging, websites, podcasts, a 'cathedral' in Second Life and much else. Though these links to the wider church can support Christian formation, believers may want to use them carefully. What values do the new media embody and where do these value stand in relation to the gospel?[9]

---

8 It is easy technically, but can be difficult emotionally if ministers fear that other churches will sheep steal. This is a theological and spiritual block: is the size of an individual church more important than the health of the kingdom?

9 Sherry Turkle (1995, 2011) argues that 'life on the screen' brings postmodernism down to earth. Using media that was meant to facilitate communication,

> ### 'Faithful presence within' the world requires formation that
>
> - helps Christians to learn what it means to enact Jesus in their daily lives;
> - occurs within the Christian community and as community;
> - involves active connections with the whole body.

Conclusion

To grow to maturity, contextual churches must lay down a pathway to discipleship. The pathway will start with evangelism, which may include teaching Christian practices as supports for everyday life before individuals come to faith. As individuals travel to faith, the mission community will provide support appropriate to the milestone each person has reached. It will stress the communal nature of life with Jesus, so that when individuals are born again they will be prepared to be discipled by the Spirit through the church. This formation will be a continuing process, undertaken within the gathering-in-life and in the church at large. Believers will live inside the inverted commas of Jesus.

Further reading

Cray, Graham, Ian Mobsby and Aaron Kennedy (eds), *New Monasticism as Fresh Expression of Church*, Norwich: Canterbury Press, 2010.

Everts, Don and Doug Shaupp, *Pathway to Jesus: Crossing the Thresholds of Faith*, Nottingham: InterVarsity Press, 2009.

Ward, Graham, *The Politics of Discipleship: Becoming Postmaterial Citizens*, Grand Rapids, MI: Baker and London: SCM, 2009.

Questions for discussion

- If members of your personal networks came to faith, what similarities and differences might exist between their journeys to Jesus and yours?
- Do published courses still have an important role in helping people come to faith and in what contexts?
- What should contextual churches do to support and encourage discipleship? Can you think of good examples?

---

individuals also end up being 'alone together' as they are pushed closer to their machines and further away from each other.

18

Worship

To grow to maturity, contextual churches must lay down a pathway not only to discipleship but to worship. This pathway will start in the worshipping life of the mission community that brings the church to birth. It will lead individuals served by the initiative gently towards Christian faith and play a key role in forming them in the faith thereafter. It will enable them to encounter God and be changed by him.

Worship in new contextual churches is a contested subject. Sceptics, such as Angela Tilby (2008), fear that new styles of church are 'worship-lite': their worship is too thin to immerse new believers deeply in the Christian story. Church founders wonder if critics have much experience of these communities and if they have engaged sufficiently with the challenge of contextualization. Understanding worship as a pathway may be a helpful perspective through which to engage with this debate. The pathway may appear undemanding when it helps people outside the church to experience God in an accessible way, but it makes increasing spiritual demands on worshippers as they are initiated into the faith and mature in it.

This chapter discusses some of the theological and practical stepping stones involved in this pathway. It covers the relationship between worship and mission, the place of worship in the journey to faith, the role of worship in Christian formation, the balance between tradition and context, worship and Christian identity, the role of authority and – briefly – worship online. Most of these issues are faced across the denominational spectrum, but some are especially problematic for traditions like the Roman Catholic and Anglican Churches, for whom conformity to prescribed liturgies has been a historic requirement. In relation to identity, the Church of England is used here as a case study. Non-Anglicans are invited to read the principles discussed through the lens of their own traditions.

We can distinguish between four approaches to worship:

- 'Inherited worship' relies on fixed liturgies or patterns of worship, drawn from the tradition. Contextualization occurs round a received core. Forms of inherited worship can emerge over quite a short period and become relatively fixed.

- 'Emerging worship' seeks to engage with postmodern culture. Gibbs and Bolger come close to identifying it with alt.worship, regularly describing practices – such as immersion in all forms of media (2006, p. 74) – that are associated with alt.worship. In 'emerging worship' approaches vary, but they have an alt-worship family likeness.
- 'Contextual worship' puts the main emphasis on indigenizing worship. It expects worship to look different in different contexts. No family likeness, beyond being recognizably Christian, can be expected because contexts vary so much.
- 'Blended worship' brings context and the ecclesial tradition of worship together. Worship is contextualized, but with a stronger eye to the tradition. Gifts from the tradition are indigenized to extend the context's worshipping repertoire, sometimes producing strikingly novel results. The chapter makes the case for this fourth type of worship.

Worship and mission

Until quite recently in the West, worship – giving worth to God – was a taken-for-granted activity of much of the population. The theological understanding of worship was in a mainly *inward* direction – towards the church. It focused on the incorporation of individuals into the church through baptism and on the church's nourishment through the Eucharist (Davies, 1966, p. 70). Vatican II could declare that 'the liturgy is the summit toward which the activity of the Church is directed' (*Sacrosanctum Concilium*, 1963, para. 10).

Central to traditional Catholic and Orthodox perspectives, shared by others, is that worship is a preparation for heaven – for some, the church is actually lifted into heaven. Worship is where we are corporately and individually formed for the vision of God – where we learn to rest in God and encounter him. Worship enables us to begin to live the life of heaven in the here and now. 'It is through the sacred liturgy that the joining of heaven to earth comes to be understood, and culminates in making present who the Christ is by giving us understanding and experience of him' (Hemming, 2008, p. 1).

Today in much of the global North, regular worship is a distinctly minority activity and mission is starting to rise up the agenda. Worship is now increasingly understood in the context of the *missio Dei,* as part of God's *outward* movement to creation. The World Council of Churches' *Baptism, Eucharist and Ministry* report declared that 'The very celebration of the eucharist is an instance of the Church's participation in God's mission to the world' (1982, para. 25).

As the result of God's mission, the Spirit brings us into the Trinity's conversation. The Spirit prompts the church to sing and say words that resonate with the words exchanged within the Godhead. These human words are the mouthpiece of creation. 'God made men and women in his own image to be the priests of creation and to express on behalf of all creatures the praises of God, so that through human lips the heavens might declare the glory of God' (Torrance, 1996, p. 1).

As worship draws creation into the conversation within God, the world is caught up in the divine mission. Chapter 6 argued that mission is an eternal first step for God and must therefore be a continuing first step for the church. Mission is the overarching framework within which God relates to the world. If the church is to correspond to God, mission must be the overarching framework of its life. The church is to be shaped by its participation in the *missio Dei*.

Participation includes worshipping God for God's own sake. This brings mission to the centre of worship. For if God is eternally a missionary God, to worship God for his sake is to worship a God who is perpetually in mission. Worship does not have a focus that is separate from mission. Worship and mission cannot be pulled apart, just as breathing in cannot be separated from breathing out. Worship is directed towards a God who has made mission his priority. Worshipping a missional God, therefore, must take missional form.

The relationship between mission and worship

Can we be more precise about how mission and worship relate? One possibility is that worship is *an act of mission*. First Corinthians 14.25 uses the Greek word *proskynesis* – 'worship that engages the affections and mobilizes the body'– in the context of worship that converts people (Kreider and Kreider, 2009, p. 5). Today, Holy Communion proclaims the Lord's death until he returns. This is a valid understanding of worship, but is too narrow.

Worship is also *a resource for mission*. 'By energizing and envisioning worshippers, by proclaiming the gospel, by shaping an alternative worldview and by modelling aspects of the kingdom, regular worship plays a significant part in the mission of a local church . . .' (Earey and Headley, 2002, p. 10). When we pray to God, listen to him, speak about him, praise him and remember him in worship, the words, material objects, songs and gestures that we use point to his missional movement. Worshippers are thus formed for mission by being drawn into the missionary God.

This can be broadened out further. Worship is *a life of mission*. This chimes with the Romans 12.1–2 exhortation, 'offer your bodies as living sacrifices . . . Do not conform any longer to the pattern of this world.' The Greek word, *latreia,* connoted formal religious acts, especially sacrifice, but Paul uses it here to describe an everyday life of worship. Worship and a missional life are tied together. However the problem, as with the other two views, is that worship is reduced to mission. Is worship *all* about mission?

A fourth view, therefore, is that worship *transcends mission*. Worship occurs within the flow of the church's missional life, but is not to be equated with it. It includes mission, yet goes beyond it. Worship has a richness that reaches beyond the practice of mission. To describe God as missionary is not all that can be said about him. He has qualities of beauty, faithfulness and much else, and these can be worshipped for their own sake too. Mission may be a recurring melody, but there is more to the music than that.

This can be extended to a fifth view: worship is *the goal of mission*. One of the purposes of mission is to bring people into a worshipping life with God. In worship, believers are enabled to gaze on God in all his glory. Though true, this makes the goal of mission unduly narrow. Just as the purpose of marriage goes beyond the partners' mutual devotion to include doing things together, so the purpose of mission goes beyond the devotion of God in worship to undertaking activities with God. This will continue into the kingdom. When the kingdom comes, worship will not exclude a practical life of creativity and service. The image of the multitude of worshippers in Revelation 7 is to be balanced by chapter 21's picture of active life in the new city – a life of continuing mission. There will be an eternal movement out toward others: the city's gates are always open (v. 25). Worship is *a* goal but not *the* goal of mission.

Thus account must be taken of all the ways in which worship relates to mission. The relationship is multifaceted. All five perspectives complement, qualify and elaborate each other. Just as the divine attributes have a missionary thrust but cannot be reduced to mission, worship takes place within the mission of God and contributes to it while offering a wider view. Worship and mission have an extremely close relationship, but are not the same.

Bringing worship and mission together

A number of contextual churches are exploring how worship can be linked more strongly to mission. If worship and mission are closely connected, can the link be made more visible? Examples include:

- St Laurence in Reading, a church with a particular calling to young people, which found that adults were coming in support as well. So they started Sunday morning worship for the adults, while their youth work continued in the evening. But the adult worship consumed steadily more of their resources, threatening to dilute their focus. Their solution was to move the adult service to the afternoon, with a cross-over time at the end. The adults have refreshments while the teenagers arrive for their activities. Adult worshippers can be more directly involved in the church's mission.

- Just Church in Bradford concentrates on peace, justice and human rights. The church began with members writing letters on behalf of Amnesty International as part of their worship. This was more than mission and worship being put next to each other, as in the previous example. Mission became an act of worship. Much the same happens when mission communities and other gatherings include planning for mission in their worship. Mission planning becomes a liturgical activity.
- A church plant in the West Midlands held a weekly gathering on mid Sunday afternoons. For a period, they worshipped together three weeks in four. On the fourth week they went out as a whole church to serve the wider community. They tidied up an older person's garden and decorated a care home. This was more than mission being done while the church gathered for worship. This was the church going out in mission during one of its worship slots. Worship and mission were integrated into a corporate rhythm of life.
- Third Place Communities in Tasmania, Australia are Christians who refuse to gather in sacred, isolated spaces. They meet in such places as pubs, bars, playgrounds and cafes, and worship in public in ways that are not off-putting to others using the facility. On average, curious non-churchgoers comprise about 60 per cent of each gathering (Hirsch, 2006, pp. 239–40). Rather than mission and worship occurring in a rhythm, the gathering goes out in worship and mission simultaneously. This has a New Testament ring about it. Not only did the very first Christians meet in the temple courts (Acts 2.46), but their joyful household gatherings (Acts 2.46) were also public affairs. As noted in Chapter 1, most urban houses were crammed together, walls were thin and the windows had no glass. Neighbours could hear what was going on.

Connecting worship to mission has considerable outreach potential, especially among men wanting to express spirituality through activity. A group of men might invite some non-believing friends to join them regularly in clearing up a neighbourhood, cleaning a dirty pond and other environmental improvements. After the activity, they might have a drink and discuss 'continuous improvement' in what they are doing and in their personal lives. The session might end with silent prayer. Over time, the spiritual component of the discussions might expand into a more recognizable form of Christian worship. As the group joins other Christians for worship perhaps monthly, it becomes a church whose life centres on community service connected to worship.

Worship and the journey to faith

The traditional approach to church planting has been to draw enquirers into a worshipping congregation. As Chapter 11 noted, this works especially well when churchgoers use their extensive networks to invite people with some Christian background who are open to returning to the faith. Experience shows that seeing God powerfully at work in worship can be a strong inducement to reconnect with him.

This is particularly the case when worship is led with an eye to the outsider, but not with evangelism mainly in mind. If worship becomes primarily a means to evangelism, its integrity as 'truthful liturgy' – worship that is true to God and done for God – will suffer. God will be less clearly present and so its evangelistic potential will be reduced (Hauerwas, 2008, pp. 205–14). Worship must be true to God before it can be true to the God-seeker.

The place of worship in evangelism

Chapter 11 went on to argue that increasing numbers of people have little or no church background. They are more likely to be drawn into faith through a process akin to *a serving-first journey*. Within this journey, the pathway to mature worship will start further back. It will centre on missional worship, which can help waken a desire to explore following Jesus.

Missional worship is Ann Morisy's notion of 'apt liturgy' applied to the birthing of contextual church. It takes into account people who only half believe, are confused or who have no more than a faint awareness of God. It involves the thoughtful introduction of symbols that resonate with people's concerns and connect these concerns to the transcendent. It provides a vehicle for individuals to encounter God, creating a hunger for more. It uses elements of worship in ways that help non-believers along a journey to faith (Morisy, 2004, pp. 156–67). The inclusion of physical objects as symbols introduces a sacramental element, which prepares for full sacramental worship later.

Missional worship differs from 'Christian worship' in having a specific evangelistic intent. In the UK, it takes forward a tradition of mission services that began in the 1870s and continued into 'family services', 'guest services' and 'seeker services' at the end of the last century (Jasper, 1989, pp. 57–8, 274–6). Examples would be a church-run cafe that has an adjacent prayer room with aids to prayer for customers to use, a luncheon club that introduces a short, accessible act of worship after the meal, a group of teenagers who use contemporary dance as a form of worship and a sewing circle that adds prayer to the end of its sessions.

In Mawsley village, Northamptonshire, a monthly 'cafe with a bit more', called SPACE, offers a quiet space to think, meditate or pray, a space for children with Bible-based activities and a common space for everyone to enjoy a coffee, bacon roll and a chat. The Goth Church in Coventry, for groups of young people who listen to heavy metal music and wear dark clothing, offers the ancient Office of Compline on Wednesday evenings. The service includes candles, prayer, silence and the Peace, tailored to the missional context.

At a local festival in 2010, Presence – based in Leicestershire – hosted a floating-lantern ceremony as the festival finale, with 1,000 lanterns on the canal. Hundreds of people took part during the day, making free lanterns for themselves, or writing a message for a friend or loved one. Others made statements about climate change. 'The ceremony was a moving and deeply spiritual moment for those who enjoyed the spectacle and allowed the spiritual to be at the heart of the festival.'[1]

The role of Holy Communion

Might Holy Communion have a place in missional worship? For most new contextual churches, making people welcome is a high value. They are reluctant to exclude people through their worship. But this runs up against the view that Communion should be restricted to people who have been baptized. Responses to this debate can be framed using three of the categories described by Stuart Murray (2004a, pp. 26–7).

An 'open set' approach is typical, for example, of many 'table churches', where a gathering centres on eating together. The bread and the wine are shared by all present, whether they profess the faith or not, as part of the meal. The sharing is seen as an act of worship, but not in a classical liturgical sense. Often the 'words of institution', which Christians since the fourth century have seen as constitutive of Holy Communion, are not used. This practice, and the extension of hospitality to everyone regardless of faith, is seen as consistent with what is imagined to have happened in the primitive church (1 Cor. 14.23–4).[2]

A 'centred-set' approach is not dissimilar, but places a greater emphasis on people's movement toward the centre. The centre is the core of the community, who are committed believers. Around them are people who are less committed, some of whom may be travelling toward faith – toward identifying with the centre. The invitation to share in Communion is extended to those who are travelling, and individuals decide whether they are on a journey toward Christian belief or not.

A 'bounded-set' approach puts boundaries round Communion. The community invites only those who have been baptized to participate, partly on the grounds that baptism otherwise does not make sense. What are the

---

1 These three stories, and other examples of missional worship, can be found at www.freshexpressions.org.uk/stories.

2 In v.23 Paul has in mind a situation when 'the whole church comes together'. This echoes 'when you come together as a church' in 11.18, where Paul is writing about the Lord's Supper. This would suggest that non-believers could be present at the supper, but there is no evidence that they actually received. Indeed, it seems that the practice quickly emerged that the non-baptized did not receive (Milavec, 2003, p. 354).

baptized being initiated into if it does not include Communion? Moreover, if Communion is an intimate way for believers to identify with Jesus' death and resurrection, in what way is it authentic for non-believers to take part? When believers receive the bread and the wine, non-participants are made comfortable, for instance by going forward for a blessing. Or they briefly pause and hold the elements while they are passed round the circle, as a mark of respect.

The place of worship in initiation

Traditionally of course, the church has seen baptism as the rite of initiation, a highly significant public entry into the community of faith. But the growing use of faith commitment prayers in evangelical circles has muddied the water. Popularized by Billy Graham, adapted by Norman Warren (1972, p. 13) and again by Alpha (Gumbel, p. 18), these brief prayers contain a confession, an acceptance of Jesus' salvific work and a future commitment. They are prayed by individuals who are committing themselves to the Christian faith for the first time or returning to it. They are widely seen as marking a point of conversion and often perform a de facto initiation into the faith.[3]

In Alpha, for instance, the prayer of commitment is an important part of the overall stress on experience. In his detailed study of Alpha, James Heard notes: 'While "becoming a Christian" on Alpha involves the matrix of repentance, faith, receiving the Holy Spirit and baptism, the main stress of initiation is on experience, a charismatic encounter with the Holy Spirit, which then brings assurance of salvation' (2009, p. 211).

This individualized initiation had a rationale when most converts had been baptized as infants, may have been attending church as 'nominal Christians' and had no liturgical provision for publicly renewing their baptism vows. A prayer of commitment, sometimes followed by a public 'testimony', seemed an appropriate way to mark a person's entry into the Christian life.

Might the balance have tilted too strongly toward the personal, interior aspect of conversion at the expense of its corporate, public dimension? When the corporate element is downplayed, the significance of the individual's new identity with the church is diminished. There is a risk that the subsequent faith journey will be skewed toward 'me and Jesus' rather than sustained through active involvement in the whole body.

Lurking behind this are important theological questions about the role of baptism in initiation. Is baptism to be understood in Zwinglian terms, as a visible sign that we make in response to an invisible grace, which means that baptism is not itself efficacious? Or does baptism actually accomplish

---

3 I am grateful to Nick Griffin, a student at Wycliffe Hall, Oxford, for drawing my attention to the significance of these prayers.

Points to keep in mind when preparing a 'welcome' service

- *Be sensitive to the context* – both the secular culture and the DNA of the emerging church. 'Welcome' should take place in the context of the church's worship, except where the local culture values an event in a more traditional church. In which case, a joint celebration can speak of catholicity – of joining the whole body.
- *Be counter-cultural.* The celebration is about entry into the life of Jesus, who has invited new believers to join his Spirit in transforming the world.
- *Keep in mind the wider church.* As part of catholicity, baptism, confirmation or the renewal of baptism vows should be recognizable to the church at large as a service of initiation.
- *Seek permission* from those in authority, if necessary. In the UK, the permission-giving culture continues to gain ground. Seeking authorization builds trust and is a means of identifying with the wider church.
- *Use prayerful imagination and creativity* to hold these considerations together! The gathering will thereby join other communities whose creativity and experience of contextual worship is a gift to the whole church.

something? In which case, what is the relationship between infant baptism (where it occurs) and subsequent parts of the initiation process, such as confirmation?[4]

Whatever view is taken, 'welcome' acts of worship should be seen as an important aspect of Christian formation. Initiation is a key stage on the pathway to mature worship, and so close attention should be given to what happens before, in and after the service. Normally stepping stones to faith, such as missional worship, will have been laid before the service. They will be responsive to the Spirit and the individual, and will clear a path toward a godly life. The 'welcome' will celebrate the journey travelled so far, highlight the meaning of this particular milestone and look forward to the pathway ahead. Subsequently, individuals should be supported in developing rhythms and practices that nurture a mature faith.

'Welcome' will take the form of baptism, confirmation or the renewal of baptism vows, as appropriate. For new believers who were baptized as children,

---

4 The issues are well discussed from an Anglican perspective in Avis (2011).

the latter is a helpful option since it avoids the theological difficulties of a second baptism while enabling individuals to publicly own what was said on their behalf as a child. Where allowed, the renewal of baptism vows *by immersion* can greatly enrich the experience, though it is advisable to hold the service separately from baptism to avoid confusion. Theologically, the two *are* different.

'Welcome' services will be faithful both to the context and the Christian story. They will be sensitive to the stages people have reached in their movement towards God and will encourage them to take a further step. At one Church of England service, some candidates were baptized and then confirmed, others were confirmed, several renewed their baptism vows and a few publicly committed themselves to a journey exploring the Christian faith.

All were given a narrative framework in which to interpret their experience, had the opportunity symbolically and publicly to mark a significant milestone, and were thereby enabled to take a step forward. Though some liturgists would object that combining these ingredients in one service confuses the differences between them, at least no one felt left out! Might putting the ingredients next to each other actually highlight the differences?

Worship and Christian formation

A pathway to mature worship must, of course, continue to be laid after initiation. Worship is so fundamental to the life of discipleship that many people (for example Smith, 2009) believe worship is the main sphere in which we encounter Christ. Though Jesus is present in the world through the Spirit, it is in worship that we experience him most intensely.

Yet, as Benedictine spirituality asserts, we can also have intense meetings with Jesus in everyday life (de Waal, 1999, pp. 83–98). We encounter him in other people, in a beautiful landscape or in a piece of music. An answered prayer strengthens faith. God is revealed particularly in acts of justice (Hull, 2008a, pp. 115–18). Both worship and life are contexts for spiritual growth. They feed and enable one another. Rather than privileging worship over everyday life, stepping stones to mature worship should help believers encounter God in ordinary life.

How far should worship be different to life?

Christian worship is 'movement into the new creation' (Williams, 2011, p. 5). 'It is an *event* in a physical space that has the effect of moving you from one context or condition of heart and imagination to another' (p. 2; author's italics). It is a transition into the kingdom. This holds together the immanent and transcendent dimensions of worship.

On the one hand, immanent worship embraces the culture and concerns of daily life. This is vital because

- *Humans are physical beings* who live in physical contexts. Disembodied worship is impossible. Nor can individuals be extracted from the settings in which they live. When we bring ourselves to God in worship, we bring our lives.
- *Intentionally connecting with life helps to make worship authentic.* If worshippers cannot come before God as they truthfully are in their lives, parts of the person and of their life are held back from God. Community is also impaired. The more open individuals are with each other, as well as with God, the closer they will be to one another. This is important because worship helps to form community (Church of England, 2007, pp. 5–6).
- *Worship must connect with life to transform it.* If worship seems to deal narrowly with 'churchy' things, Christians may separate their spirituality from the day to day. But if worship is linked to life, what happens in worship may sanctify the rest of the week. Worshippers will be made more like Jesus, whose kingdom transforms culture.

On the other hand, transcendent worship lifts us out of our daily lives so that our Christian identity, and how it is expressed in everyday life, can be reimagined from a divine perspective. As the conservative Catholic theologian, Laurence Hemming, notes: 'Every suggestion that the liturgy be "inculturated" confronts the awkwardness that the more the liturgy is accommodated to our own familiar lifeworld, its power to make visible the New Jerusalem is lessened' (Hemming, 2008, p. 153).

In a similar vein, Marva Dawn notes that 'worship that is too much like the world can hardly redescribe it!' (1999, p. 339). If worship becomes too 'relevant', the risk is that we end up worshipping ourselves, our aspirations and our dreams rather than having these desires or longings drawn toward God. Worship takes us into God's story, which is unlike the stories of our surrounding culture. It provides language, rituals and practices that uphold and nurture a different vision. It should help form communities of faith that, through the Spirit, enable God's story to enfold our stories (Dawn, 1999, pp. 333–44). By nurturing Christian character, worship becomes relevant to life by enabling believers to live distinctively.

Hemming and Dawn make an important point, but they assume the current structure of the church. Earlier chapters, especially Chapter 7, have asked whether that structure pulls the church too far from everyday life? 'Weekend church' is distant from many of the passions of believers and from many of the places where they conduct their lives. In today's multifaceted world, is the inherited church being asked to do too much? Can it fully combine the transcendent and the immanent? Can it both draw worshippers into the new creation and equip them to join God's mission in the old?

Temples, synagogues and tents

Chapter 3 described what seems to be an emerging reconfiguration of church. 'Tents' are starting to appear in everyday life – among groups of friends, in apartment blocks, in the workplace and elsewhere. These are small worshipping communities, sometimes pitched for a limited period, that concentrate on practical discipleship. They serve their contexts and draw others into the faith. 'Synagogues' are conventional local churches, which may continue to multiply through contextual forms of church planting. Like Jesus, believers attend 'synagogue' regularly, which immerses them in Scripture and the Christian tradition. 'Temples' are the various ways that believers connect to the whole body of Christ. Again like Jesus, believers go up to the 'temple' from time to time.

If this is what is starting to happen, new means may emerge to combine the relevance and distinctiveness of worship. Tents would include simple acts of worship that concentrate on the application of the Christian story to the context. Synagogues and temples would draw believers further into the story.

An example would be a local church that encourages mid-sized communities. These communities serve people in ordinary situations, have their own worshipping lives focused on the mission context, but join with other communities for worship once or twice a month. Another example might be a network (or 'order') of contextual churches that organized retreats to take its members deeper into the Christian story. A third might be local 'coalitions of the willing' that arranged retreats and specialist events, opening these up to 'tents' in the area. A fourth example might be a midweek 'tent' whose members also attended a variety of weekend churches.

If these examples multiply, might individual churches become more specialized, reflecting a wider trend in society? Each would concentrate on its strengths. Without over-drawing the distinction, some expressions of church would focus on transcendent worship, transforming individuals as they are drawn into the new creation. Others would practise more immanent worship, supporting and enabling worshippers to engage missionally with their contexts. Good connections between temples, synagogues and tents would allow individuals to take part in both types of worship.

As noted in Chapter 3, the possibility of increased specialization has been recognized by the Church of England's Liturgical Commission, though not specifically in this context. The Commission has called for worshippers to be able to 'attend more than one church regularly, for different occasions of worship, because excellence of different kinds is in different places' (Church of England, 2007, p. 25). Might different kinds of excellence include excellence at the immanent end of the spectrum and excellence at the transcendent one?

Context and tradition

Stepping stones to mature worship – to worship that forms Christian character – will include striking an appropriate balance between the context and the church's liturgical tradition. There is far from agreement, however, on what this should involve. For example, Davison and Milbank (2010, pp. 93–118) have accused fresh expressions of church of fleeing from the church's inheritance of worship – of seeking radically to reinvent the church in a form that repudiates the tradition. But this is a huge generalization. Mary Gray-Reeves and Michael Perham visited 14 Anglican emerging churches and fresh expressions. They found that they were perhaps more open to the liturgical tradition than the inherited church! 'There is no reluctance among emerging churches to search the tradition and to re-energize it' (Gray-Reeves and Perham, 2011, p. 4).

Nevertheless, some emerging church literature is hostile to the tradition. Frank Viola and George Barna, for example, argue that the church has degenerated from its first-century roots, when worship was fluid and highly participative. We should return to New Testament practices (Viola and Barna, 2008, pp. 47–83). Yet this is not as easy as it may seem. Paul Bradshaw has shown that relatively little is known about early Christian worship.[5] Different preferences for worship can be built on the same New Testament platform.

The church's heritage of worship cannot be lightly dismissed. Particularly for more catholic writers, the liturgical tradition confers identity. It opens up our life from narrow individuality to a common life pulsating through history. It helps to shape us as the people of God. As 'the critical memory of the church made alive by the Holy Spirit' (Lossky, quoted by Williams, 2008a, p. 37), it passes on truth from one generation to the next.

At the very least, it captures the church's learning about worship. Stuart Murray has commented:

> As a church planting consultant I frequently encounter young churches that dismantle inherited patterns of worship, then (usually about two years later) re-appropriate many abandoned practices. Exhausted by innovation and not fully satisfied with the results, they re-examine inherited forms of worship and begin to appreciate why these have stood the test of time. (Murray, 2004, p. 207)

However, tradition is tarnished by sin. If given too much weight, it can stifle the local gathering. This will weaken the universal church, whose life

---

5 He writes that a growing number of scholars accept 'that we know much, much less about the liturgical practices of the first three centuries of Christianity than we once thought that we did.' (Bradshaw, 2002, p. x)

flows through its congregations. Moreover, as argued in Chapter 8, God's story is not revealed separately from culture. The biblical texts are hardly culture free, and nor is the church's tradition. Tradition emerges from context, often by critiquing what went before. It must be open therefore to further interrogation, arising from the Spirit's presence in new settings. Indeed, as Chapter 5 pointed out, the very nature of the church's heritage invites engagement, discussion and variation in practice rather than consensus about it.

This means that the context of the worshipping community must be taken seriously. An international gathering of liturgists reported in 1989, 'From many parts of the world, we discovered afresh at York that liturgy to serve the contemporary church should be truly inculturated.' It noted that Jesus' earthly ministry included both the acceptance of a specific culture and confrontation with elements in that culture. When Jesus commissioned his disciples with 'As the Father has sent me, so I send you', he was commissioning them to be like him. In taking the gospel, they were both to adapt themselves to different cultures ('as a Jew to the Jews, as a Greek to the Greeks') and to confront those cultures (York Statement, 1989, paras 1, 2, 3).

Worship must be contextual if the church is to be truly catholic. To be inclusive of all, the body of Christ must embrace all within their cultures. It would hardly be hospitable to a child to say, 'You are welcome, but abandon your childish behaviour.' If the tradition consists of a series of 'local theologies' (Schreiter, 1985), why should it not also consist of a series of local patterns of worship? Contextual worship can then enrich the tradition that future generations inherit.

Distinctive expressions of worship

As with all churches, new contextual churches should create expressions of worship that bring context and the tradition together. Ingredients from the church's tradition should be blended with aspects of the context to create a distinctive pattern of worship. These distinctive expressions of worship will not be the same as the secular culture nor an imitation of another church's culture. They will be specific to the worshipping community. They will hint at what the surrounding culture might be like if it was redeemed by Christ. They will be events that invite God to be God – to do something in worship and change us.

One gathering might use an inherited confession or eucharistic prayer, play contemporary music while the words are spoken and show video clips at the same time to create a unique, worshipful ambience. Another might rewrite an ancient text to bring it closer to the everyday language of worshippers, or use it as a model to inspire members to produce their own version for the community's use. Another might play reflective music from the Christian tradition as an aid to quiet prayer. A meal-based church might light a candle and pray a traditional invocation of the Trinity as it gathers for worship.

The annual cycle of worship, for example in the Church of England, is full of English cultural associations. Think of Christmas carols like 'The Holly and the Ivy', Mothering Sunday (reinterpreted for a culture that clings self-consciously to the family), the Easter bunny (who comes out in some Easter all-age services) and Harvest. What would this cycle look like in an Asian community in Bradford, or on the Broadwater Farm Estate in Tottenham, London?

Distinctive expressions of worship should

- be recognizably Christian – part of the living tradition;
- be recognizably contextual;
- have something of the denomination's DNA (if they are part of a denomination), without being a clone.

Steven Bevans's six models of contextual theology, which Chapter 8 applied to contextual church in a general way, can also be used specifically in relation to worship. They provide a conceptual framework within which to integrate context and the tradition. Contextualization can take different forms to fit different aspects of worship and its preparation. Briefly:

- *The translation model* translates truths into contemporary culture. It is appropriate when Christian truths are being conveyed in worship, especially in word and song.
- *The anthropological model* assumes that God is active in culture and embraces a sacramental perspective (God is present in and revealed through the objects of everyday life). It will use cultural symbols as avenues of the Spirit to enhance the physicality of worship.
- *The praxis model* encourages prayerful reflection through an unending spiral of practice/reflection/practice. It can help a gathering to discern promptings of the Spirit as members reflect on their efforts to bring context and the tradition together.
- *The conversation model* is about engaging with Christians in different contexts (including history). It will encourage the community to attend to the wider church's experience of contextualizing worship.
- *The counter-cultural model* sees the gospel as a lens through which to interpret, critique and challenge culture. It will emphasize the transformational role of worship.
- *The subjective model* starts with the believer's interior experience of God. It will ask whether identities being formed in worship are not only Christ-like, but authentic to the individual. Are worshippers describing and expressing their experiences of God to help others on the journey?

A *liturgical supermarket?*

Some would worry that these distinctive expressions of worship risk treating tradition like a theme park or antique shop. 'You wander round, you pick and choose the pieces that attract; a bit of Celtic here, a bit of Syrian Orthodox there; *ancient is awesome*' (Tilby, 2008, pp. 78–9). Lost is an understanding of the element's significance and location in the tradition. It is less able to convey the story of God because it has been plucked out of the church's re-enactment of that story. Undermining the coherence of history weakens identity with the body as it has existed down the centuries.

In response, it is clearly impossible for any community to embrace the church's entire liturgical tradition. Selection has always been necessary. An 'artefact' of liturgy can be taken out of its historical context and put into a theological performance (worship), just as museums place historical objects into thematic contexts. The theological performance trumps the historical setting. Theological and liturgical coherence prevents selection from the tradition descending into thoughtless bricolage. An explanation of the origins of a text and why it is being used can enable worshippers to be mindful of its original context.

The idea that a gathering might rewrite a liturgical text such as a creed, or perform a eucharistic prayer extempore makes some people nervous, especially in Orthodox and Catholic traditions where authorized texts play an important role. The principle *lex orandi, lex credendi* (the law of believing following the law of prayer) assumes that how you worship shapes what you believe. This doctrinal role of worship will be undermined, some fear, if too much latitude is given to the local rewriting of texts. Truths may be lost, while if the liturgy keeps changing, worshippers may be hindered from learning doctrine through repetition. Others ask why words created by a gathering should be more beautiful and more faithful carriers of truth than words that have been prayed over down the centuries.

In practice, however, authorized liturgical texts are pragmatic compromises between different wings of the church. They frequently allow worshippers to say the same words but mean different things by them. Further ambiguity is introduced by the different ways in which a text may be performed, such as what manual actions accompany the eucharistic prayer. Contextualization recognizes that a text may mean something different to a congregation than to those who wrote it, and that a rewritten version may – in the context – be more faithful to the original intent. Why should extempore 'texts' not have a common doctrinal grammar while using different words? This would allow them to be faithful improvisations.

Moreover, liturgical texts are not the only means to preserve and pass on truth. Though repeating set liturgies may embed the truths they contain in worshippers' minds, this can equally be true of Scripture. Biblical passages that have particular salience for the community can be repeated, not least in song. Participative worship that allows plenty of space for individuals to contribute may appear to be 'liturgy-lite', but may in fact be the best setting for worshippers to build each other up in the faith. Robert Banks (1980, pp. 91–3) notes that this was a priority for Saint Paul.

Some good practice

To safeguard worship's integrity and coherence, worship coordinators must understand good practice. This will include being sensitive to the context, such as temperamental differences: some worshippers may find that texts are compelling when used sparingly; others may find that frequent use allows a text to get under their skin.

It will include striving for integrity and coherence, even in the simplest worship. This will involve keeping liturgical shape in mind. What must happen to move worshippers from one place to another, such as from dark to light if that is the theme? In gatherings that meet around a mission focus, the shape might comprise:

- Purpose – a review of their plans.
- Progress and problems since they last met – which might be opportunities for prayers of thanks, confession perhaps and intercession.
- Possibilities – centred on a Bible study around the question 'What is God saying to us about the week ahead?' This might include some silent prayer.
- Promise – jointly declaring, 'And surely I am with you always, to the very end of the age' (Matt. 28.20), as they conclude.

Good practice will include understanding the role of the core ingredients of worship such as the gathering, confession, the word, intercessions and so on. These ingredients have been widely used in Christian worship because they have been found helpful in opening doors to the Spirit. They can be incorporated imaginatively and beautifully in hosts of ways that fit the context. From time to time a community may want to ask:

- What elements recently have we hardly or never included in our worship – perhaps confession or the Lord's Prayer? Might it be a good idea to restore the balance?
- Are parts of our worship typically rather thin, such as the gathering or dismissal? Could they be enriched by learning from the practice of other Christians?
- Has some of the worship become routine in an unhelpful way – individuals are bored and not engaged? Might a different approach help to bring freshness?

Creating distinctive expressions of worship will take time as individuals tread the pathway through missional worship to faith, start to discover how to express their faith in worship that connects with their lives, and then explore the tradition to acquire a richer liturgical language. Leaders of the community and the wider church must be patient as this process unfurls.

Criteria for good practice

On the basis of 'by their fruits you shall know them', the following might indicate whether over a period a healthy balance has been struck between context and the tradition. (The criteria are based on the four interlocking sets of relationships that constitute the church.)

- Is the balance helping people to become more like Christ?
- Is it building up the community, such as encouraging individuals to share their gifts?
- Is it strengthening individuals' identity with the whole body of Christ?
- Is it energizing the community for mission?

Worship and identity

'When Christians meet for worship, they don't just share bread and wine; they gather to be told who they are, not only in action but in word, in story and song and above all in the story and song that is the Bible' (Williams, 2007, p. 121). Worship involves three ecclesial identities: with the whole body of Christ, the local Christian community and the denomination or network – the tradition – to which that community belongs. In some settings, striking a balance between local identity and the tradition's identity is especially contentious. How can the two be combined?

The identity of many traditions is tied, at least to some extent, to their worship – to their shapes of worship, the ingredients that they emphasize, the way these ingredients are enacted (such as how Holy Communion is celebrated) and the songs and hymns that they sing (particularly important in Methodism, for instance). The Church of England is unusual in that its identity has been linked especially closely to its liturgy. Its members 'have defined their beliefs to a significant extent by their public prayers rather than by formal statements of doctrine, like the Augsburg Confession for Lutherans or the documents of the *magisterium* for Roman Catholics' (Church of England, 2007, p. 7).

This means that issues of identity and worship that other denominations may face to some extent loom especially large for many in the Church of

England. If liturgy takes on the role of a founding document, inevitably liturgical texts become carriers of the church's identity. Yet enshrining identity in texts creates difficulties when a gathering wishes to deviate from the texts to contextualize its worship. Whose identity is to have priority – that of the tradition or the contextual church?

Texts as a source of identity?

Anglicans often exaggerate their shared inheritance of liturgical texts. Some parts of the Anglican Communion, such as Tanzania, have never used the Book of Common Prayer, which is often seen as foundational for Anglicanism. In the Church of England, there is little commonality now in how churches actually worship. With diversity ranging from 'low' church celebrations of Holy Communion to Anglo-Catholic, from 'all-age' services to Evensong, from some clergy robing to others not wearing dog collars, it is hard to find a common thread.

Some might say that this growing diversity represents a divergence from what is officially expected. Ad hoc practices are running ahead of the official mind of the church and should be discouraged. Others, however, would see these developments as a work of the Spirit. The Spirit is active in the official councils *and* the congregational life of the church. Both must be taken into account in the process of discernment.

Might increasing diversity be a gift of the Spirit? As Chapter 21 will argue, a tradition that takes seriously the doctrine of creation will have a strong theology of difference. Moreover, if relationships not practices are the essence of church, a tradition will be especially careful not to impose practices on a gathering so that the relationship between the tradition and the assembly becomes oppressive.

Shape as a source of identity?

Mark Earey and Philip Tovey have described how worship in the Church of England has evolved from conformity (Book of Common Prayer), to choice (the 1995 *Patterns for Worship* that offered liturgical alternatives) to creativity, reflected in the 2002 *New Patterns for Worship*. The latter encourages congregations to craft their own worship, using resource material in the book as sample 'off the peg' provisions (Earey and Tovey, 2009, pp. 8–12). In the Eucharistic Prayer, for example, set texts are required only to narrate the institution of the Lord's Supper, to offer the memorial prayer and to invoke the Spirit. The longer Preface can be composed locally, picking up issues that are live to the community at the time.

The focus is now on shared shapes of worship, with plenty of room to expand or contract the size of the shapes and be creative about their content. The Liturgical Commission is encouraging a common shape of worship as a way of maintaining some family likeness in the Church of England's practices.[6] Throughout *Common Worship,* a series of volumes that contain texts and resources for worship, an underlying fourfold structure is evident:

Gathering – Engaging – Responding – Sending

A common shape replaces a common text, though within this shape are certain 'authorized' and 'commended' texts which help bind the Church of England together. Despite the continuing importance of some texts, the balance has shifted from texts to shape as the bearer of identity.

Is liturgical shape, however, substantial enough to carry the weight of identity? The degree of diversity is now so great within the Church of England that a common shape of worship says little about who Anglicans are. Despite sharing the same fourfold structure, the feel of an Anglo-Catholic Eucharist may have more in common with Roman Catholic worship than with the fluid, spontaneous and highly participative celebration of an Anglican fresh expression.

Values as a source of identity?

Steven Croft has argued that the Church of England's identity should be sought in five common values (2006, pp. 178–82). They build on the values articulated for the Anglican Communion in 1888, which became known as the Chicago Lambeth Quadrilateral. Adding a fifth value, Croft proposes the following:

- a commitment to Scripture;
- a commitment to the dominical sacraments of baptism and Eucharist;
- a commitment to listening to the whole of the Christian tradition and seeing that tradition expressed in the historic creeds;
- a commitment to the ministry and mission of the whole people of God and to the ordering of the ministry through the threefold order of deacons, priests and bishops;
- a commitment to the mission to the whole of creation and to the whole of our society as defined and described in the Anglican Communion's five marks of mission (discussed in Chapter 6).

Angela Tilby (2008, p. 82) wonders whether an agreed set of values would too bland as to be helpful. In particular, she asks whether it would be feasible to agree a set of values – a good question in view of the bitterness of some of the current debates within the Anglican Communion. Even if a set was agreed, it would almost certainly be understood in different ways. Might there be a source of identity that takes account of division?

---

6 This is reflected in publications like *New Patterns for Worship*, which seek to provide 'for the diverse worshipping needs of our communities, within an ordered structure which affirms our essential unity and common life' (2002, p. ix).

Story as a source of identity

Perhaps the most fruitful approach is to think of identity in terms of the denomination's story (as those developed in Chapter 21). In the case of the Church of England, the story includes the Book of Common Prayer, liturgical shape in *Common Worship*, values that help to summarize the story and a great deal more. Seeing identity in terms of story takes account of how identity actually works. It allows for the reality that different people identify more strongly with different parts of the story. Thus it better accommodates diversity than is likely to be possible with, say, a set of values, which may not be universally owned.

In particular, identifying with the story includes identifying with debates within that story – they are seen as important; but identity is not required to depend on belonging to one side of the debate. So differences need not raise doubts about the right of any of the protagonists to belong. This is how the Davison and Milbank book has been read: in advancing their particular view, the authors seemed to deny a place within the Church of England for their opponents. But if the Anglican story embraces people on either side of the debate, both sides can see themselves as part of the same story despite their disagreement.

When worship no longer has to carry the whole load of identity, belonging can be more inclusive and the tone of debates, perhaps, more generous. Not least, if worship need not carry the weight of denominational identity, gatherings can be freer to contextualize their worship.

The role of authority

Stepping stones to mature worship will include exercising authority under Scripture in an appropriate way. This authority will empower gatherings to explore how they can worship in ways that are faithful to God and who they are.

Good practice within the gathering

Many new contextual churches are abandoning the default setting of inherited church, where worship has traditionally been led by an ordained minister with lay people contributing. Contextual churches are adopting more participative and spontaneous styles of worship. They seek to recapture something of the dispersed spiritual authority to be found in Saint Paul's congregations, where one person could have a hymn, another a word of instruction, another a revelation and someone else a tongue or interpretation (1 Cor. 14.26).

Worship of this kind requires a different style of leadership to that used in formal settings. It is more like this description of leadership: 'Leadership is not about giving commands, nor even about making decisions, it is quite literally about leading, clearing the way, making it possible for us to go where otherwise we could not.'[7] Worship leaders go beyond ensuring that all parts of the service hold together. They create space for members of the community to hear the Spirit and share what they have heard.

Jonny Baker (2010) has likened the process to curation in the art world. Rather than focusing on the role of presiding over liturgy or fronting a band, curation involves working off stage. The curator helps participants to create a communal offering to God. Though worship is ultimately the Spirit's work, those who plan and lead worship can do much to create channels for the Spirit. Competence in doing this is as much a gift as administration or pastoral care. Like other gifts, curating can be honed through learning and careful nurture. Ingredients of competence (which might double up as principles of good worship) are suggested in the box below.[8]

Marks of liturgical competence

- Understanding the cultural context, and what forms of worship will helpfully connect with believers and draw them to God;
- Attentiveness to the gathering and the Spirit during worship, and the ability to discern when to depart from what has been planned;
- The ability to draw out and coordinate gifts within the community in preparation for and during worship;
- A deepening awareness of the practices of worship in Christian history and across the globe;
- Appreciation of the sources from which patterns of prayer and liturgical forms of worship are derived;
- Sensitivity to a variety of 'liturgical languages' including the use of symbols in worship, measuring the pace and flow of worship and the use of silence, music and song;
- Skill in arranging liturgical space for worship, in positioning fittings and furniture, in using art, and in creating appropriate space for movement and bodily gesture in acts of corporate prayer;
- Competence in the use of material aids in worship – from candles to vestments and projectors.

Source: The last five elements are based on Church of England (2007, pp. 14–15).

---

7 Rowan Williams, The Archbishop's Retreat Addresses, V, Lambeth Conference of Bishops, 19 July 2008.

8 Note: For an overlapping but different list of liturgical principles, see Chatfield (2011, pp. 119–20).

Emphasizing competence in leading worship puts the accent on finding ways to encourage reflection on and education in good practice. As an example of how one denomination is seeking to approach this, the Church of England's Liturgical Commission wants diocesan liturgical groups to look for and promote good practice. It suggests that local churches invite a skilled individual or small group to observe their worship and make suggestions for development (Church of England, 2007, pp. 23–4, 26).

Might such groups contain a representative of contextual churches, so that they empathize with them and make it easier to cross-fertilize good practice between existing and new churches? Might young gatherings and established congregations be encouraged to visit and learn from each other? A heavy metal congregation in London, for example, has been enriched by sharing some worship with an Anglo-Catholic church. A number of emerging churches have developed imaginative worship that is both truthful and contextual. A liturgical group might ask whether their experience has something to offer the wider church.

Celebrating Holy Communion where there is no ordained minister

Holy Communion can be a thorny question for denominations that require an ordained minister to preside. A busy minister with several congregations may not have time for yet another act of worship. If a new church is lay led, worshippers may ask whether it is authentic for someone 'from outside' to lead such an important service. Where this is an issue, there are a number of possible ways through:

- *An 'outside' minister can symbolize the wider church*, adding a valuable element to a new church's celebration of Communion. The Anglican Province of Zambia, for instance, has congregations led by lay people. The priest (as a symbol of unity) visits roughly every couple of months to preside at Communion.
- *Communion might be celebrated jointly with the 'parent' church*, perhaps every month or two, with the minister presiding. The context could be a larger more upbeat celebration or a social function, such as a shared lunch, in which Communion was integrated. Care would be needed that the parent church did not dominate the proceedings.
- *'Agape suppers'* remember Christ's death and resurrection during a meal. They hark back to the communal meals of the first Christians. Some denominations do not recognize them as Holy Communion because the bread and wine are not consecrated. Where that is the case, 'agape suppers' might supplement the other possibilities. Making clear that they are not an authorized Communion would help worshippers understand that certain forms of worship are shared with the wider church, underlining the catholicity of Christian identity. Yet doing this

would also highlight that 'agape suppers' are a second best – they are not proper Communion. So they are not a solution on their own.

- *'Extended Communion'* in some traditions would allow the bread and wine to be consecrated at a regular service in the parent church, and be distributed when the new church met later. Communion would extend over time and place to strengthen the links between one gathering and another. Extended Communion has theological difficulties, centred on the nature of the connection between receiving the elements and the rest of the service (Hughes, 2002). Thus any risk of it becoming a normal practice meets resistance. But might it be permitted in mission situations that require it? If so, could Communion sometimes extend from the new to the parent church to symbolize a mutual relationship?

- *Local priests*, sometimes known as Ordained Local Ministers, can preside at Communion in the Church of England. Now widespread, they are ordained to serve in a specific locality. Churches that insist only ordained ministers can preside may need to be flexible in ordaining people within new churches for this purpose. The ordained person need not be the leader of the community, but would be someone anointed by the Spirit to act as a guardian of the faith tradition. Multiplying local priests would require a substantial reimagination of the ordained ministry, but would avoid the even greater problem of failing to provide adequately for a sacramental life (Tovey, 2001, p. 23).

- *Lay people* can be authorized to preside at Communion in certain circumstances in the Methodist church, which has a theology of exceptions. Might this be an example for other denominations where ordained ministers preside? Were these exceptions to become too frequent, however, there would be fears that this was a step toward lay presidency, to which strong opposition exists – not only in Methodism.

Generous exceptions

New contextual churches will inevitably stray across some demarcation lines. Lindsay Urwin, a Church of England bishop, has described an ordination he conducted in a youth congregation:

> As a strong believer in the 'take the risk and, if necessary, apologize afterwards' approach to life, I may have played a little fast and loose with the Canons at this ordination, but have no doubt that had second- or third-century Christians been present (and perhaps they were!) they would have known what we were doing. (Urwin, 2008, p. 33)

He suggests that there may be a need for a 'lively doctrine of exceptions', as growing numbers of new churches push the boundaries of accepted practice. The Methodist Church's practice of allowing exception may provide a helpful precedent. There would be fears in some quarters that this was just another way of tolerating the deviants; it would reinforce the marginal status of new contextual churches.[9] On the other hand, this might be a means of discerning whether God was calling the church to make changes in its regulations. Allowing exceptions, learning from them and seeing whether they are 'received' by the church would be a route to change.

Fears that today's exception will become tomorrow's norm can be addressed by stressing the shared nature of reception. Exceptions enable the church as a whole to prayerfully test the water and see what the Spirit is up to. Naming an exception can actually safeguard the norm by being explicit about what it is (Urwin, 2008, p. 35). A doctrine of exceptions appeals to the call to be merciful and forgiving, and to the urgency of mission: if new contextual churches are God's work, they must not be put in a straitjacket. Respect for church order will be increased when young churches believe they are being offered liturgical advice and resources that support them in mission and pastoral care (Vasey, 1993, p. 99).

Worship online

With steadily more Christians wanting to establish a missional presence on the Internet, worship online is becoming an important issue. Some would say that such worship is inappropriate. They believe that virtual relationships are inferior to real-life ones, and assume that online worship must be second best too.

Yet many Internet users find online relationships to be just as meaningful as those offline. Ordinary relationships often pass through technology, such as spectacles, and so mediating relationships through computers need not make them less real. Users may be as faintly aware of their computers as they are their glasses (Howe, 2007, p. 25). Of course individuals can use computers to mask who they really are. But this is an extreme form of the pretence that is often already part of everyday life. Online worshippers say that the great majority of fellow worshippers are genuine.[10]

What about celebrating Holy Communion online, such as in the virtual world, Second Life? Paul Fiddes has argued that an avatar can receive the bread and wine within the logic of the virtual world. The grace received, as it were, by the avatar will be shared by the person behind it.[11] Mark Howe has likened the complex relationship between an individual and their avatar

---

9 I am grateful to Mark Howe for making this point in correspondence.

10 In a survey of the online worshipping community, St Pixels, 93 per cent agreed that 'People at St Pixels are generally honest in what they say about themselves' (Howe, 2007, p. 10).

11 'Virtual Sacraments?', 22 June 2009, www.brownblog.info.

to the experience of cutting paper with scissors. The scissors are doing the cutting, but it can feel as if my fingers cut the paper. Although an avatar may receive Communion, the experience of the avatar's owner is that he or she is receiving.[12]

Would Christ be objectively present in such a Communion? Some believe that the Spirit works through God-given means as the priest lays hands on the bread and wine, which is consumed by worshippers afterwards. On the other hand, Cranmer's receptionist theology maintains that it is in the act of receiving that the bread and the wine become Christ's body and blood. Recent ecumenical discussions have highlighted the importance of the Holy Spirit in making Christ present in Communion, though points of significant disagreement remain. (Kasper, 2009, pp. 173, 182–3).

If the presence of the Spirit makes the sacrament effective, is there a need for worshippers to be physically in the same place? Can the Spirit not be powerfully at work through Communion even though the community is scattered? Some would fear that eating from the 'one' bread would be lost, allowing the whole to become an individual event. But others might ask whether oneness depends on sharing the same bread and wine. Might it not lie in being present at the same celebration, despite separation by distance?

As the 'net generation' matures and other generations immersed in the Internet follow behind, we should not assume that online Communion will be a rare event.[13] Increasing numbers will belong to virtual expressions of church. Perhaps the crucial question will become whether members of a virtual church should also belong to a physical one, so that they have an embodied as well as virtual experience of community?

Conclusion

Laying down a pathway to mature worship raises important questions about the relationship between worship and mission, worship's place in the journey to faith, worship and Christian formation, the balance between context and tradition, worship and ecclesial identity, authority in worship and worship online. Many of these issues are not unique to contextual churches, but are raised by them in new and often pressing ways. The issues represent a substantial agenda for further discussion and debate. It is important that they continue to be addressed because worship plays a key role in forming both the community and individuals within it. By inviting a fresh engagement with these issues, contextual churches are a gift to the whole body.

---

12 Communication with the author, 5 September 2009.

13 The 'net generation' is Don Tapscott's term for those aged 11 to 31 in 2008, the first generation to grow up surrounded by digital media (Tapscott, 2009, pp. 1–2).

Further reading

Baker, Jonny, *Curating Worship*, London: SPCK, 2010.

Gray-Reeves, Mary and Michael Perham, *The Hospitality of God: Emerging Worship for a Missional Church*, London: SPCK, 2011.

Kreider, Alan and Eleanor Kreider, *Worship and Mission after Christendom*, Milton Keynes: Paternester, 2009.

Tilby, Angela, 'What Questions Does Catholic Ecclesiology Pose for Fresh Expressions?', in Steven Croft (ed.), *Mission-shaped Questions*, London: Church House Publishing, 2008, pp. 78–89.

Questions for discussion

- What lessons for laying down a pathway to mature worship would you draw from your experiences of worship?
- Can you give examples of context and the tradition being blended together?
- How important is worship for the identity of contextual churches that you know? What issues relating to identity and worship should they address?

19

Community

'It would be hard to overstate the emphasis on the nature of the church as community and the importance of experiencing community in the church for those in the emerging church' (Hammett, 2009, p. 225). The same could be said of all new contextual churches. Despite their differences, they virtually all put community at the centre of their lives.

Does this stress on community represent collusion with a more widespread reaction against the depersonalizing trends of society? Molly Marshall has described how the church has often joined such a reaction. Calls for 'Christian community' represent a desire for the converse of what individuals experience elsewhere in their lives. Churchgoers want family-like communities in which they can be known in depth, trust and be trusted. Yet, idealizing this sort of community risks softening the church's call to be politically and publicly distinct. Comfortable intimacy can replace the hard grind of inventing new forms of church life that minister to a public in need (Marshall, 1996).

This chimes with an important strand of recent theology, which emphasizes the political nature of the Christian community. In Luke Bretherton's summary, an older generation of theologians saw the church as a constituency within civil society. The church was to address social and political problems through the state. By contrast, theologians such as Stanley Hauerwas, John Milbank and William Cavanaugh have argued that the church has a distinctive politics and is itself a political entity – it has structures for exercising power and it points to the kingdom, which is a political notion. Through its life as a political community, the church is to be a faithful witness to the world (Bretherton, 2010, pp. 16–17).

From this perspective, alongside pathways to discipleship and worship, laying a pathway to mature community involves digging in signposts that make a political statement – that point to the kingdom. Without pretending to be comprehensive, this chapter describes some of these signposts – community as a gift, hospitality, solidarity, power, engagement with life and identity. It uses the Old Testament as a primary resource, notes elements of continuity between the Old and the New Testaments and draws out some practical implications.

Turning to the Old Testament

In turning to the Old Testament, our interest lies in the texts as they have been received into the canon and the Christian tradition. The chapter, therefore, adopts a canonical reading of Scripture (Barton, 1996, pp. 77–103).[1] It focuses on the Old Testament for three reasons. First, as described in the Introduction, one of the book's aims is to encourage the integration of theory and practice across the theological disciplines. Using the Old Testament contributes to this and underscores how the whole of Scripture can be a resource for contextual churches. Relying on the New Testament alone brackets out much of what God has to say in the Bible.

Second, the New Testament sees the church as being in some way a continuation of Israel. This is reflected in the use of the Greek word *ekklesia*. In the Septuagint (LXX), a Greek version of the Old Testament translated in stages between the third and second centuries BC, *ekklesia* is used to describe the assembly of Israel. It refers to the event of gathering and also to the community, the people of God, who gathered. In the New Testament the word has the same two meanings, the assembly and God's people. Both of these are translated as 'church' (Giles, 1995, pp. 241–3).

This continuity of language reflects New Testament writers' strong sense of identity between Israel and the church, though their understandings of this differed. We can therefore learn from Old Testament insights into what it means to be the people of God. The assumption is not that the church replaces the Jewish people, but that it shares their vocation and looks forward to the day when they come to recognize Jesus (Goldingay, 2006, p. 253).

Third, Walter Brueggemann has suggested that, as depicted in the biblical texts, Israel before the time of David can be regarded as a 'new church start'. Israel was a new community with some parallels to the new Christian communities being started today.

> A new church start here means the planting of an alternative community among people who were ready for risk and shunned established social relations because such resources and patterns inevitably led to domestication and to bondage. It is a new church start that specialized in neighbor priorities and had at its centre the powerful voices of Moses and Joshua and Samuel, whose main work is voicing and revoicing and voicing

---

1 This approach does not mean that historical questions are excluded or that the original intentions of the texts are ignored (though much of what we know is provisional). It allows the material to be seen as a unity and to be recognized as having meaning that goes beyond its original purpose. Of course, in discerning such meaning we must keep in mind differences between the worlds of Scripture and our own – you cannot drag-and-drop Old Testament principles on to today. Equally, our context will influence our understanding of the text (McConville, 2006, pp. 1–11).

again the liturgy of liberation and the covenant of reshaping communal life, power, and vision. (Brueggemann, 1994, pp. 266–7)[2]

In words similar to how many pioneers of church describe their experiences, Brueggemann notes that Israel in this early period, guided by God, 'had to make up everything as it went along' (p. 268). Again like many church founders, this improvisation involved 'an enormous borrowing from the culture around it'. At the same time, mirroring the aspirations of many founders, Israel transformed what was borrowed 'according to its central passion for liberation and for covenant'.

Brueggemann (pp. 269–75) goes on to suggest that Israel represented a second 'new church start' in the post-exilic period. The model of 'establishment power', based on monarchy and Temple, had failed – not dissimilar, perhaps, to how some feel that today's established churches have failed. When the exiles went into Babylon and then returned, they had to rebuild community on the edges of society, as many contextual churches are doing now. In the process, Brueggemann claims, the returning exiles jumped over the monarchical period to find inspiration from the foundation narratives of their earlier history – echoing how today's new monastic communities are drawing from the earlier periods of church history.

If Israel can be seen as a church start, especially after the Exodus, what can we learn about laying down a pathway to community in contextual church?

Forming community

The pathway begins by recognizing that Christian community is a gift – a gift from God and a gift to the world. This is how the Old Testament understands the origins of Israel. In Genesis 12.1–3, God promises that he will make Abraham's descendants into a great nation and find them a place to inhabit. Nationhood, the form Abraham's community will eventually take, is something that *God* will accomplish.

This promise is enacted when God delivers Abraham's descendants from Egypt and leads them to the land they will occupy. The Lord says to Moses:

I have heard the groaning of the Israelites, whom the Egyptians are enslaving, and I have remembered my covenant. Therefore, say to the

---

2 The idea that the Israelites 'were ready for risk' may be something of an exaggeration. To the contrary, the risks of desert life prompted repeated demands to return to the safety of Egypt. It might be more accurate to say that there was strong dissatisfaction with life in Egypt, which resonates with the dissatisfaction many church founders feel with today's church.

Israelites: 'I am the LORD, and I will bring you out from under the yoke of the Egyptians. I will free you from being slaves to them, and I will redeem you with an outstretched arm and with mighty acts of judgement. I will take you as my own people, and I will be your God. Then you will know that I am the LORD your God, who brought you out from under the yoke of the Egyptians. And I will bring you to the land I swore with uplifted hands to give to Abraham, to Isaac and to Jacob. I will give it to you as a possession. I am the LORD.' (Exod. 6.5–8)

Being made God's people was to be a means by which God would bless the world. This purpose is expressed in the promise to Abraham and is repeated in Exodus 19.5, where the Lord says to the people through Moses:

Now if you obey me fully and keep my covenant, then out of all nations you will be my treasured possession. Although the whole earth is mine, you will be for me a kingdom of priests and a holy nation.

A priest in the Old Testament was a mediator between God and the people. He made God known to the people, especially in his teaching role (Deut. 33.10), and represented the people to God. By being a nation of priests, therefore, Israel was to represent God to the peoples of the world and be the means by which these peoples would be brought to God. God's character would be revealed in the nation's corporate life.

The church, with its origins in Israel, is also a gift. Writing about members of God's household (v. 20), Ephesians 2 emphasizes that being brought into union with Christ – and hence with others – is God's gift, not a reward for work done (vv. 8–9). To be in fellowship with Christ and with others in his body is something that only Jesus makes possible. The purpose of the church is to be a royal priesthood (1 Peter 2.9). Like ancient Israel, it is to make God known to the surrounding peoples and to bring them to God. It is a gift to the world.

In bringing churches to birth, mission communities give contemporary shape to this divine gift. As they express their dependence on God through prayer, Bible study, sharing spiritual gifts and worship, mission communities reflect the reality that these new churches are gifts from him. His Spirit brings them about. Equally, they are gifts for the world. They are gifts to serve the surrounding people.

Simply providing an opportunity for community to form can be a gift, as Michael Frost has pointed out. Drawing on the sociologist Ray Oldenburg, he notes that people have places in which to meet at home and work, but many lack 'third places' between the two. They lack hobbies, clubs and other opportunities to develop friendships, discuss issues and interact with other people (Frost, 2006, pp. 56–63). Contextual churches can help to fill the gap. For example, 'authentic (?)' [sic] found that in a Glasgow docklands regeneration project, there was a desire for community but no place for residents to meet. So some Christians moved into an apartment in the harbour to have a place on site where people could be invited for a meal and to practise hospitality (www.freshexpressions.org.uk/stories).

While many people long for the belonging and the friendships that can be found in community, there is a price to be paid for the commitments involved. The sociologist Zygmunt Bauman writes, 'The price is paid in the currency of freedom, variously called "autonomy", "right to self-assertion", "right to be yourself"' (Bauman, 2001, p. 4). For many people, the price appears to be too high. They would rather form less committed relationships. 'Technology and society specialist' Sherry Turkle (2011) has described how for many children and adults, relentless connection via the new media has led to a new solitude. Personal freedom is triumphing over community.

James Henley, team leader of The Lab, a missional community of young adults in Newport, Wales, has commented:

> One of the challenges we have encountered is people being interested in spirituality and faith – but as individuals not as part of a group. We think that perhaps this is the direction youth culture is going, as we seem to be meeting lots of young people whose reliance is not on a particular friendship group. (www.freshexpressions.org.uk/stories)

In some contexts, therefore, turning God's gift of community into reality may be a slow, step-by-step process of introducing people to the very idea of community. The first step may be one-to-one relationships, which are gradually joined together in groups of three, four and eventually larger. As this happens, individuals become familiar with some of the habits of Christian community – from meeting together and honest conversations to shared prayer and Bible study. Learning about community forms an important part of their journey to faith. The process may take a long time and require considerable patience.

Community is a gift

- from God;
- for the world.

Hospitality

If divine giving is the starting point for community, hospitality is the human response that enables community to begin to form. It is a second signpost along the pathway to mature community. The idea of hospitality is much valued within emerging church and fresh expressions circles and has an important place in the Christian tradition. But it runs into the question of identity. If the church is blissfully open to all and barriers to entry are removed, how can it preserve the distinctiveness of its life in Christ?

Is the church to be like a tennis club that restricts its facilities to those who play, but offers courses and coaching for people who want to learn? Or at the other extreme, is it to open its facilities to all comers, but do little to publicize the value of playing the game? Or, as a middle way, is it to be like a club that opens its facilities to everyone, but invites people who use them to discover the joys of tennis?

Exclusiveness and openness

Some Old Testament passages suggest that Israel was far from being an exclusive group, even in its early days. The crowd that left Egypt was diverse in its ethnic origins (Exod. 12.38). Throughout its history Israel assimilated foreigners. Leviticus 19.34 instructs the Israelites to love the resident alien 'as yourself, for you were aliens in Egypt'. Exodus 12.48–9 permits resident foreigners to take part in the Passover if they wish. Deuteronomy allows the descendants of certain resident foreigners to join the assembly of Israel, extending this right after three generations to Egyptians, even though they had enslaved the Israelites (Deut. 23.7–8).

How was this transcending of existing boundaries possible? On Israel's side, according to the narratives, it was feasible because the people's identity was based on their covenant relationship. The group that left Egypt could include non-Israelites because the latter shared Israel's separation from Egypt and its allegiance to Yahweh (McConville, 2006, p. 70). Resident foreigners could be treated considerately because they recognized some level of community membership and had obligations created by shared experiences. To varying degrees, they identified with the covenant community and subsumed their identities within Israel's larger vision (Nelson, 1997, p. 49). The inclusion of others rested on faithfulness to Yahweh.

Did this allegiance replace one cultural barrier with another? Some in Israel thought it should. In the exile a rigorist view, reflected in Ezra and Nehemiah for instance, argued that faithfulness to Yahweh could be maintained only by strict separation from the other nations. For support, rigorists could look back to Israel's apostasy, based on incorporating the religious practices of its neighbours.

Against this, however, was the view that Israel's religious identity not only permitted assimilation, but in time would require it. This liberal line was most fully developed in the Book of Isaiah, which sees the assimilation of foreigners as Israel's eschatological vocation. In submitting to Israel as God's instrument, all nations will unite under Yahweh and worship in

Jerusalem (Isa. 56.6–8; 66.18). Israel is to serve the nations, bringing justice to them (Isa. 42.1–7; 49.3; cf. 41.8–9). The idea is so important that it is worth suffering for (Isa. 50.6–7; 52.13 – 53.12).[3] When Israel is what it is meant to be, the Gentiles will join the people of God.

Kenton Sparks suggests that even when their boundaries were most rigid, at the time of Ezra, the Yahwistic communities could still make room for outsiders. This was because of 'the important place that religious assimilation had for their God, who desired that all human beings enjoy the benefits of covenant life' (Sparks, 1998, p. 331). By being ultimately affirming of others outside Israel, the liberal view tempered the exclusive one. It did this not by rejecting distinctiveness, but by helping to define it. Part of Israel's identity lay in including others within the covenant.

Some notable outsiders

It is intriguing that Israel took care when writing its foundation narratives to emphasize that individuals outside the nation could play an important role in the nation's affairs. Moses' father-in-law, Jethro, who was a Midianite, professed faith in Yahweh and then led Aaron, Moses and the elders of Israel in sacrificial worship (Exod. 18.9–12). Subsequently, he helped develop Israel's governance by advising Moses on how to share his administrative load, before returning home and apparently taking no further part in the nation's life (vv. 13–27). Much later the Moabite, Ruth, travelled to Israel with her mother-in-law, married Boaz and gave birth to Obed, the grandfather of David and ancestor of Jesus (Ruth 4.17; Matt. 1.1).

Especially remarkable are the stories of Rahab and Achan in Joshua. On the surface, the book describes the conquest of apparent religious outsiders (the Canaanites) by religious insiders, Israel. Yet the book also subverts the whole notion of religious ins and outs. Rahab was a prostitute and Canaanite, an outsider par excellence it would appear. Yet by protecting the men sent by Joshua to spy out Canaan, she contributed to Israel's advance and was drawn into the nation with her family. In particular, as Frank Spina shows, through her knowledge of the people's history and use of religious language, she is presented as an Israelite of the first order (Spina, 2005, pp. 53–63).

Achan, on the other hand, belonged to Judah, the tribe from which Israel's kings would be selected. He is presented as the quintessential representative of Israel. But by stealing some of the possessions taken during the earlier

---

3 I am following Brevard Childs who identifies the servant in Isaiah 42.1–4 with Israel, and argues that in the servant songs the figure of the servant evolves from being Israel to being an individual who embodies Israel (Childs, 2001, pp. 325, 384–5, 394–5, 412–18). For a different view, see Blenkinsopp (2002, pp. 118–20), who identifies the servant in Isaiah 45 with Cyrus and in 49–53 with a prophet.

destruction of Jericho rather than handing them over to Yahweh,[4] he brings about the nation's defeat at Ai. As a result Israel, who is guilty by association with Achan, is threatened with destruction, the same fate that awaits the Canaanites (Josh. 7.12). Spina suggests that by disobeying Yahweh, Achan – the archetypal Israelite – makes himself and the people little different to the Canaanites, and so in his punishment of death suffers the fate of a Canaanite (Spina, 2005, pp. 63–71).

Spina argues that the Rahab and Achan stories are intended to be read in the light of each other. Achan's story reverses the Rahab story. 'Just

---

How hospitable was Israel when the nation was commanded to slaughter the Canaanites? Some approaches to reading the conquest of Canaan

Evolutionary: The slaughter of the Canaanites belonged to an infantile stage in the moral evolution of Israel.

Biblical theology: The slaughter of the Canaanites must be understood in relation to God's progressive revelation of himself in Scripture, climaxing in Christ, who is himself slaughtered as he turns away from violence and vengeance.

Cultural relativist: The conquest of Canaan reflected the social and historical milieu of the time; each age must be understood by its own standards.

Canon within the canon: Some principles in Scripture have abiding value; others – like the slaughter of the Canaanites – are time-conditioned.

Canonical: Scripture contains a wide range of ethical viewpoints, which should be understood together; Israel's stance toward the Canaanites must dialogue with other ethical views.

Paradigmatic: It is the principles behind the conquest of Canaan that matter, such as God's judgement on the Canaanites for their violent way of life.

Reader-response: Readers should ethically critique accounts of the conquest, while celebrating ethical insights elsewhere in Scripture; as we critique the Bible, we allow it to critique us.

Source: Davies (2010) (the reference to biblical theology is additional).

---

4 This handing over might involve destruction. The aim, symbolically, was to prevent Israel being contaminated in any way by the Canaanites.

as Rahab's confession of faith got her and her family included, Achan's violation of faith got him and his family excluded. The outsider came in, and the insider was ousted: confessing faith and violating faith were the variables' (Spina, 2005, pp. 70–1). While it might seem that the Israelites were on the inside and the Canaanites on the outside, Rahab and Achan suggest that the boundary was highly porous.

Naaman illustrates the theme even more dramatically. He was the commander of the king of Aram's army in an enemy nation that had defeated Israel in battle (2 Kings 5.1–2). Through his encounter with Elisha and the cure of his leprosy, Naaman came to acknowledge the God of Israel (5.15). But with the prophet's approval, he returned to Aram, where he intended to practise Israel's faith (5.17–19). He planned to act as a member of Israel, while continuing to serve a king who was an enemy of Israel (Spina, 2005, p. 88). How much further can one blur the distinction between in and out!

Thus, alongside debates about the proper relationship between Israel and the nations, the Old Testament narratives describe different degrees of involvement with Israel. Individuals could be part of the community and devoted to Yahweh. They could be resident aliens, sharing Israel's life, taking part in certain religious festivals or remaining aloof from them as they wished, and in some cases joining the community if they chose. They could be outsiders who decided to become members of the community, or they could be outsiders who identified with the community but continued their life at a distance from it.

Jesus' welcome of outsiders

In parables such as the vineyard and its tenants, Jesus redefined Israel. Israel was not an entity based primarily on Torah, but comprised those who followed him (Matt. 21.33–44). Among Jesus' followers was a core who had left everything to be with him, such as the Twelve and Joseph Barsabbas and Matthias (Acts 1.23). Round them were disciples who stayed at home, including Martha and Mary and the secret disciple, Joseph of Arimathea (John 19.38). In addition, there were people outside the discipleship circle who acted in the name of Jesus (Mark 9.38–40). As with allegiance to Yahweh in the Old Testament, following Jesus could occur through different degrees of involvement in his community.

Jesus was adamant that the discipleship community must welcome others. His table fellowship was open to tax collectors and sinners (Mark 2.16). This was very different to the Pharisees who got their nickname, 'separated ones', by refusing to eat with people who had not strictly observed the food laws (Dunn, 1992, p. 112).[5] Jesus protested vigorously when his disciples tried to draw boundaries that would keep others out (Mark 9.39).

---

5 Baumgarten (1983, pp. 411–28) argues that in antiquity at least two names existed for the Pharisees – 'specifiers' (in the sense of being excellent, accurate and specific observers of the law) and 'separatists', which was used in a derogatory sense.

Indeed, like the Rahab/Achan and Naaman stories, Jesus subverted the notion of insiders and outsiders. Instead of family being based on biological boundaries, anyone who does the will of God could be part of his family (Mark 3.32–5). Those who care for people in need, with whom Jesus identifies, are welcomed by him, even though they do not see themselves as belonging to his community (Matt. 25.34–40). To human observers, it is unclear who are the wheat and the tares (Matt. 13.24–30). Jesus recognizes the reality of discipleship even when no profession of discipleship is made (Dunn, 1992, p. 113).

'Centred-set' communities

This offers a different vision of community to one having sharply defined boundaries that has been common in Christendom. Michael Frost and Alan Hirsch distinguish the latter's 'bounded-set' churches from 'centred-set' ones, which are defined by their core values. People are not in or out, but closer to or further away from the centre, whose values influence the whole (Frost and Hirsch, 2003, pp. 47–51). The notion is popular among practitioners of contextual church. At the extreme, it is reflected in 'liquid churches' that avoid fixed meetings, which make some people feel uncomfortable, in favour of ongoing one-to-one relationships. Community happens at the school gate and on the mobile phone. Outsiders are drawn in through osmosis, rather than being faced with the hurdle of a meeting.

Rather than being incompatible with religious distinctiveness, inclusivity becomes one of the marks of distinctiveness. Just as some Old Testament voices understood Israel's identity in this way, so when churches prioritize hospitality in their self-understanding, they bring openness to others and religious identity together. Being a Christian community means being hospitable.

This welcome begins in the earliest stages of bringing a church to birth. Peterson Feital has described how, before he had even gathered a mission community to help birth 'Something else' in Nottingham, he and his wife decided to make their home an open house for anyone at any time. Giving their time was counter-cultural in the British context because most people are often too busy to spend time with people other than friends and family.

> I had to make a continuing decision that people were more important than my diary and therefore I would drop almost anything I was doing every time someone knocked at the door. It was not easy all the time, but it was the price that we had to pay . . . After a year and a half, we had a constant flow of visitors who came for meals, Brazilian coffee, or just a chat and a laugh, which gradually resulted in conversations about their spiritual journeys or just the English's favourite topic, the weather. If people came while we were having dinner, they joined in, and before too

long they were washing up, cleaning and organizing birthday parties in our house for other people without telling us! (Feital, 2011, p. 109)

Having put up the signpost of hospitality, mission communities will be wise not to let outsiders smother the identity of the incipient church. As we noted in Chapter 12, an influx of well-meaning Christians can swamp an initiative that is still in the early stages of finding its spiritual feet. An Asian group exploring Christianity in relation to Eastern spiritualities will not be helped if it is joined by a growing number of white people, who like the curry but have different spiritual agendas.

Hospitality should be exercised sensitively, taking account of what will work for the community at the time and in particular what will be consistent with its identity. Sanctuary in Birmingham, for instance, used to describe itself as being 'for British Asians, their families and friends'. Later (when the group had a more settled sense of identity), it described itself as 'a safe space for British Asians or anyone interested in exploring eastern and western spiritualities in Christ'. This is more inclusive in the sense that anyone could say 'I'd like to go to that'. The church still has a clear identity, but the welcome has been broadened from British Asians to anyone who identifies with what the church is doing.

In time, a church's hospitality will extend to the provision of 'thick' connections to the wider church. Welcome will be offered not only to those who identify with the individual church, but to churches that are very different within the larger body. Welcome will be expressed by seeking to do things together. The church will demonstrate how to affirm the specific cultures of individual churches and to encourage these cultures to open their doors to each other. In doing this, it will form individuals in the values that support the embrace of difference.

Luke Bretherton maintains that hospitality is more than a private act – welcoming a stranger into your home. It is a political act. It is a disposition of heart that affects public life. In the institutions of society, it makes room for people who are different and includes building a shared existence with them (Bretherton, 2010, pp. 86–7). As the church models generous hospitality, first in a specific context and then by opening one context to another, it will point a world concerned about cultural diversity to the multi cultural kingdom.

Israel's practice of hospitality

- made space for outsiders;
- allowed outsiders to play crucial roles in its history;
- gave space to voices that defined its identity partly in terms of a commitment to outsiders.

Solidarity

In today's individualistic society, community involves more than people coming together as self-contained individuals. It involves solidarity – relationships of commitment to one another that bind members together, give individuals a stake in each other's lives and create a sense of oneness.

Having a stake

Some within ancient Israel held out an ideal of solidarity in which everyone had a roughly equal stake in the community. This was rooted in the nation's conception of itself as bound together in 'brotherly' ties of covenant solidarity – individuals belonged to each other. Members of the nation were brothers and sisters of each other. The idea motivated social ethics by levelling everyone to a common status – everyone was a 'brother' of everyone else – and emphasizing family-like solidarity (Nelson, 1997, p. 49). The king, for example, is not to consider himself better than his brothers and amass wealth for himself (Deut. 17.14–20).

Brueggemann suggests that this understanding was based in part on a God who broke with surrounding expectations. Though some other nations (such as Moab) envisaged covenant-style relationships with their gods, these gods were preoccupied with their rule, their majesty and their well-being. Yahweh was different. He made a move toward earth to identify a faithful covenant partner and respond to the groans of an oppressed people. He remained committed to Israel despite its infidelities, thereby dispensing with conventions to model a new kind of solidarity. This 'move to solidarity is a hint that solidarity on earth is possible' (Brueggemann, 1994, pp. 44–7).

Solidarity in Israel was reflected in the distribution of land. Unlike the Canaanite system where all land (as far as we know) was owned by the local kings or lords in each city, land in Israel – as portrayed in the narratives – was owned by Yahweh. Its possession by the people was to be as equitable and widespread as possible (Wright, 2004, p. 157). Joshua 13 – 19 repeatedly records that land was divided by tribe and 'according to their families'. Each tribe, clan and family was to have sufficient land according to its size and needs. Each family was to have a roughly equal economic stake in society.

When for reasons of greed, political displacement, natural disaster and personal misfortune families disposed of their land, they were to receive special protection under the law (Wright, 2004, pp. 157–8). The Jubilee regulations expressed the ideal that every 49 years land which had been sold was to be returned to its original owners (Lev. 15.28). The distribution of wealth, stored mainly in land, was to remain approximately equal.[6]

---

6 There is no historical record that the jubilee actually happened. Wright's view (2004, p. 205, n. 12) is that the jubilee was a very ancient law that fell into neglect during Israel's history in the land.

The same principle lies behind the legal aspiration of the seven-yearly cancellation (or suspension) of fellow Israelites' debts (Deut. 15.1–3). This 'probably meant that pledges taken as security for a loan were to be returned to the owner and the loan suspended for the year (or perhaps cancelled altogether). The pledge might be land mortgaged to the creditor, or it might be human dependents of the debtor working off his debts. The releasing of such pledges would bring substantial relief to the debtor and effectively check the rapacious expansion of unscrupulous creditors' (Wright, 2004, p. 165). By getting back untrammelled possession of his land or his family's labour, the debtor's shared access to economic resources would be restored.

Not only does the Old Testament imagine a community whose economic resources are shared almost equally and in which this economic stake could be restored if an individual fell on hard times, the essence of Old Testament justice 'is that no-one is forgotten and no-one is invisible' (Williams, 2008b, p. 117). Christopher Wright summarizes some of the provisions:

> Israel's law included a range of measures which, taken together, formed an impressive and systemic *welfare programme* for those who were truly destitute; that is, mainly the landless and familyless . . . The combination of all these [laws] would have meant that something was available every year for the benefit of those who truly had no means for their own economic support. (Wright, 2004, p. 173; author's italics)

No one was to be invisible before the law, even though punishments differed according to social status (as in the surrounding cuneiform laws). The Sabbath command in the Decalogue, the most basic of Israel's laws, explicitly applies to everyone, including slaves (Exod. 20.10). If an ox gores someone to death, the ox is to be stoned whether the person is a freeman or a slave. Though the slave owner is to be compensated, the law 'shows that the life of a slave has the same value as the life of a (free) man or a woman' (Ska, 2004, p. 153). Deuteronomy 10.17–19 affirms egalitarian justice as the crux of government that is divinely guided (McBride, 1987, p. 239).

By making sure that no one was forgotten, that economic misfortune could be reversed and that everyone had a stake in the land, the ideal was held out that everyone should be in a position to contribute to society. Individuals should be able to take part in economic exchange, freely offering their labour or selling the produce from their land, and in the socially important informal exchange of gifts. Solidarity involved enabling people to contribute.

Having a stake in the form of gifts

Notions of communal solidarity are also, of course, to be found in the New Testament church. Members were brothers and sisters of one another. They were to provide for each other when in need (James 2.14–17). Social hierarchies were to be levelled down within the community; members were to submit to one another whatever their social rank (Eph. 5.21). Not least, having a stake in the community is defined explicitly as being able to give to the community. The Spirit equips each person with a gift for the good of all (1 Cor. 12.7).

The logical implication, as Paul began to recognize, is that if every Christian is gifted for the good of every other Christian, when those gifts are not set free and permitted to work within the body everyone is diminished. 'If one part suffers, every part suffers with it' (1 Cor. 12.26). The verse comes at the end of a passage emphasizing that each person and their gifts are indispensable. Paul seems to be feeling toward an understanding of 'how the failure to give means somebody else's inability to receive, and how that inability to receive becomes itself a deprivation of the gift they might have been given' (Williams, 2008b, p. 122). When a gift is shared, the recipient in turn is enabled to share his or her gift (2 Cor. 8.14). This brings to the fore and develops what was implicit in the Old Testament's conception of solidarity in Israel.

Fostering this type of community will start within the missional core of the initiative, as members of the mission community share their gifts with each other. It will continue through the hospitality that is offered to the people the mission community serves. This hospitality will include welcoming the gifts that individuals bring.

Simple things may encourage people to share their gifts. One group of Christians held a summer party for their village. Participants were offered T-shirts on which they could have printed – free of charge – invitations to a group or activity that they were willing to run. As they circulated, others could talk to them about what was being offered and sign up for it. Breakfast @ 9 in Canford Magna, Dorset attracts 40 adults and children on three Sundays a month. It invites families to sit at individual tables, but puts two or three tables together to encourage families to talk to each other – the first step to the mutual sharing of gifts (www.freshexpressions.org.uk).

Members of the mission community may need to broker the offer and receipt of gifts. On a housing estate, a church founder puts individuals having skills to offer, such as fixing a computer, in touch with people who need those skills; leaders of a new church in a middle-class area invite members to help them repair or decorate someone's home. Often, however, sharing gifts will emerge spontaneously. In a fluid community based on a social enterprise in East London, individuals on low incomes help each other to find housing and pay part of one another's bills when they can't afford it.

All this suggests that church as community is more than warm relationships. It is intensely political because it makes a statement about how, in the will of God, society is to be ordered. By encouraging communities of mutual contribution, contextual churches can model the radical politics of the kingdom – a politics that the Old Testament points toward.

Solidarity

- The Old Testament pictures a community in which everyone is in a position to contribute.
- Paul enriches this picture into one of mutual giving within the church.
- As contextual churches model this mutual giving, they enact the radical politics of the kingdom.

Dispersing power

Signposts along the path to mature community include not only community as a gift to the context, hospitality and solidarity, but also the appropriate exercise of authority. Of course, leadership is under intense scrutiny in today's society. In the post-modern mood, it is often regarded with extreme suspicion. Against this background, what contribution might the Old Testament make to our understanding of leadership within contextual church?

Deuteronomy's ideal

Deuteronomy provides a major resource for an answer. Within the Pentateuch, Deuteronomy is 'the moment at which the nature of Israel and its mission is explored most extensively and profoundly' (McConville, 2006, p. 74). The book has been widely read as a programme for centralizing worship in a single place (Deut. 12). However, despite their differences, Norbert Lohfink and Peter Vogt take a different tack. They emphasize Deuteronomy's programme for the dispersal of power. They stress the position of authority given to Torah, Yahweh's revealed instructions to the Israelites.[7] Theirs is the view followed here.

Lohfink has argued against Levinson and others who associate Deuteronomy with Josiah's reforms. He plausibly maintains that in its final form the book dates probably from the beginning of the exile, was a statement of theory more than legal practice, and reflected a reaction against the concentration of power in the monarchy and priesthood.[8] As an alternative to centralization, Deuteronomy proposes a balance of power between four

---

7 The debate is extensively summarized by Vogt (2006, pp. 33–70).

8 As well as Lohfink, critics of a Josiah dating for Deuteronomy include McConville, who argues that the Pentateuch must be read canonically, which means taking seriously Deuteronomy's position ahead of Kings and Chronicles (McConville, 2000b; 2002). For a critique of McConville and defence of the majority view, see Levinson (2000).

different authorities – the judiciary, the king, the temple priesthood and the prophets (Lohfink, 1993, pp. 345–9). This Deuteronomic sequence has the king tucked in as one of the four authorities. He is not heading the list. He is not to be a centralizing figure.

An important theme of Deuteronomy is that another single ruler will not replace Moses (Vogt, 2006, p. 112). His roles of judge, mediator (between God and people), prophet and political leader are to be separated. They are to be distributed between judges appointed in every town (16.18), the priests who have liturgical and restricted legal functions (17.8–9), the prophets who from time to time are to be Yahweh's mouthpiece (18.17–18) and the king. Rather than gathering these threads into human hands, integration was to come through obeying the Torah.

Deuteronomy is noticeably cautious about these institutional authorities. It carefully builds in elements of self-correction. It recognizes, for example, that justice can be badly administered. So immediately after the command to appoint judges, it warns that they are not to pervert justice, show partiality or accept bribes (16.19). It gives judges an incentive to be fair – that the people may 'live and possess the land' (v. 20). The fallibility of judges, not their status or entitlements, is to the fore.

There is similar caution about the Levitical priests. Their hereditary dominance of Israel's worship is counterbalanced by allowing them no share in the land (McBride, 1987, p. 241). Their livelihood rests on the people's regular worship, to which individuals brought animals to be sacrificed; the priests were entitled to keep a portion of these sacrificial gifts. It also depended on the people obeying the Torah's command that they give the priests the first fruits of the harvest (18.1–4). The Levites are given a strong incentive, therefore, to encourage worship and respect for Torah. If they do not, they will not be paid. If they lead the people astray, a prophet may arise to call the nation back to Yahweh.

Likewise, the power of prophets is circumscribed. They have a right to command the nation's attention (18.15), which gives them precedence over the other offices. But this is offset by their provisional status. Who is a prophet is a matter of public discernment rather than legal recognition. It may take time for events to validate this discernment (18.21–2).

In Deuteronomy's idealized account, the king's powers are notably proscribed. He is not the supreme judge. Nowhere is he told to install officials or define their functions. No role in worship is envisaged for him. Far from having a standing army, he is forbidden to have too many horses (Deut. 17.16). Indeed, Deuteronomy contains 'the unprecedented notion' that the king is himself subject to the law (Levinson, 2000, p. 275). The king's tasks are whittled down to administration, which is so obvious as not to require mention (Lohfink, 1993, p. 349), and the exemplary reading of Torah (17.18–20). The notion of kingship subverts the whole idea of monarchy. By the standards of the day, the king looks most unlike a king.

This reflects ambivalence toward the idea of monarchy. Whereas judges, priests and prophets are mandated, a king is to be appointed only when the people express the need for one (Deut. 17.14). 'This implies that kingship is not compulsory, but permitted' (Scheffler, 2007, p. 775). It fits with the Old Testament's wider debate about kingship. The introduction of monarchy is preceded by deliberation about its pros and cons. Samuel predicts that the institution will become oppressive (1 Sam. 8.11–18). First and Second Kings of course describe how Samuel's fears are realized.

However, the alternative is not a success either. Judges reflects a decentralized governing structure, which at times works well. But the book descends toward chaos at the end, repeating the refrain, or variants on it, 'In those days Israel had no king; everyone did as he saw fit' (17.6; 21.25; cf 18.1; 19.1). This is widely regarded as an appeal for monarchy to bring order (McConville, 2006, p. 126). The book ends on this note, with the theme taken up again in 1 Samuel 8, when decentralized rule once again lets the people down (vv. 1–3).

Perhaps the conclusion from Israel's history, as the Old Testament narrates it, is that one should be hesitant about all forms of human governance. Judges often get it wrong, so do kings, so do the priests, while there are plenty of false prophets as well. Deuteronomy attempts to limit the damage by separating powers and using the dynamics of self-correction.

Extraordinarily for the time, responsibility is thrown back to the people as part of this distribution of power. Deuteronomy is addressed to the people, not as individuals but as a community. Hence the form of address can be both singular (which is appropriately dominant in the laws) and plural (McConville, 2000a, p. 43). The people are a corporate entity. As such, they are to take responsibility for administering and enforcing the law (16.18), identifying the Lord's choice of a king (17.14–15) and discerning a prophet (18.21–3).

The calendar of pilgrimage festivals is addressed to the community. It is not supervised by any official or public authority. It is a collective responsibility (Levinson, 2001, p. 523–4). The covenant is made with the nation as a whole, not with representatives of it, and the community is to make sure that each person observes it (26.17–18; 29.9–15, 18). Individuals are responsible for their own faith (29.19–20). Accordingly, the people are held accountable for the exile (31.14–30). If things go wrong, it is ultimately their responsibility.

Practising dispersed leadership

This picture of authority finds echoes in the New Testament. Christopher Burdon notes how Mark's Gospel subverts traditional notions of leadership. The first must be the last and servant of all (Mark 9.33–5). He suggests that Mark can inspire a process of learning that is not controlled by a leader but is thrown back to the group. This is more appropriate for learning wisdom – applying knowledge of God to the context – than the catechetical style, in which an instructor conveys information (Burdon, 2006, p. 180).

Though Jerusalem is initially the seat of authority, in the early church power is decentralized. Antioch has considerable autonomy and wins the argument at the Council of Jerusalem. Paul's churches have considerable autonomy as well. Within his communities, authority is distributed between apostles, prophets, evangelists, pastors and teachers (Eph. 4.11).

There is no single model of leadership, just as no one model was practised in the Old Testament. The epistles contain vivid descriptions of less than perfect leadership, as in Corinth. Human flaws are exposed, just as they are taken for granted in Deuteronomy. Though Paul appoints leaders, his churches are highly participative. A wide range of gifts are shared during worship (1 Cor. 12–14). There is a clear place for leadership 'from the top', but leadership is also side-by-side – shared and dispersed within each community and between communities.

This dispersal of leadership exists in many new contextual churches. Especially in the emerging church conversation, there has been a widespread reaction against the top-down CEO model, seen to have characterized inherited church. Tim Keel notes that in the early days of the emerging church, many wanted to jettison the notion of leadership altogether (Keel, 2007, p. 231). More realistic voices have called for emergent forms of leadership instead. For Keel, leaders must shape and create environments that nurture creativity and intuition. Sally Morgenthaler notes the 'wisdom of crowds' and the role of diversity in innovation. She argues that the future belongs to leaders 'who leave the addictive world of hierarchy to function relationally, intuitively, systematically, and contextually' (Morgenthaler, 2007, p. 188).

Community meals in new contextual churches have become an almost ubiquitous setting in which leadership is shared. Whether these churches are meal based, cafe style or incorporate meals within their main activities, eating together is a fundamental part of their lives. They represent a different understanding of community than the one in many inherited churches. Instead of community resting on common experience – saying the same hymns, listening to the same sermon and receiving the same distribution of bread and wine – community is based on interactions, on talking, laughing and sometimes crying together. In these types of community, dispersed leadership is most likely to be effective. The informal, conversational setting gives space for ideas to emerge bottom-up, and for individuals to run with them.

Feital has described how non-churchgoers he met in Nottingham were not attracted to worship services partly because there was nothing interactive or personal about their format. 'Something else' was intended to have the character of a close-knit family (2011, p. 109). Participants described it as more like a party, 'but we all had a feeling that, like any good party, it was up to us (the partygoers, not the event's organizers) to make it work' (p. 112). To bring this participative community to birth, Feital drew together a committed team in which members had an equal voice, served each other and modelled community.

GraceSpace in Bradford is 'a church for people who don't go to church'. By 2012, it had grown to 25 people of all ages, many of whom had been bruised by church in the past or had no experience of church. The church meets around different meal themes for each Sunday of the month – breakfast on the first Sunday, lunch on the second, tea on the third Sunday and supper on the fourth. The sharing of leadership extends to the children, who 'particularly like it when there is a fifth Sunday in the month because that's when they choose what the adults have to do . . . and tell us what the spiritual element is going to be' (www.freshexpressions.org.uk/stories).

Chapter 16 suggested that the quality of dispersed leadership within a mission community will be greatly influenced by the quality of members' conversations. This applies equally to the sharing of leadership in the church the community brings to birth. The chapter described conversation as a process of communicative action which patterns itself. No single individual or group has control over what emerges, yet participants are continually shaping and being shaped by their conversations. Continuity and change emerge not from top-down blueprints, but from conversations as a self-organizing process.

As participants seek to make sense of their experience, they engage in messy interactions, fraught with conflict and misunderstanding. The process is aided when people stay within the movement of communicating, learning and self-organizing, and when they allow conversations to develop their own dynamic. Leaders play an important part in helping fruitful conversations to take place. At their best, they subvert their own power by empowering others. They allow responsibility to lie with individuals as they talk to each other. Though using very different thought-forms to the Old Testament, the feel of what Chapter 16 described has close affinities to the multi-centred, self-correcting, flawed, participative and rather postmodern leadership envisaged in Deuteronomy.

Authority in Deuteronomy is

- dispersed;
- self-correcting;
- ultimately in the hands of the people.

Making a difference to life

Signposts to mature Christian community will include the clear expectation that the community will make a difference to everyday life. The community will stand in the tradition of Old Testament faith, which was to be lived out in everyday realities. Yahweh's word was to shape all aspects of the community. It was to be in the people's hearts (Deut. 6.5–6), but this inner spirituality was not to be separated from daily life; it was to be earthed in the everyday. This strong and explicit religious dimension to the ordinary, as revealed in Israel's narratives, appears to have distinguished the nation from the surrounding peoples.

A community in life

The nature of this distinction has been debated. H. W. F. Saggs argued that religion played a smaller part in the everyday existence of surrounding peoples than seems to have been the case in Israel (1978, pp. 160–3). John Walton argues that Saggs's view is probably not sustainable. The key difference between Israel and the surrounding cultures lay not in the importance of religion in people's lives, but in how serving the respective deities was understood.

Generally in the ancient Near East, the gods were served by being cared for through ritual and through preserving order in society and the cosmos. In Israel, Yahweh was served by obeying Torah, which showed the people how to love the Lord their God with all their hearts, minds and strength. It showed them how to be holy as Yahweh is holy. 'The high ideal of imitating the deity did not exist in any other ancient Near Eastern culture.' (Walton, 2007, p. 155)

Using illustrations from Babylon, Jacob Finkelstein argues that in the polytheistic nations the gods were one removed from ordinary life. The gods approved of order and were appeased when order was maintained. So the kings produced tightly regulated ethical systems that were concerned with maintaining order. But these systems reflected not the revelation of a god, but how the king understood the task of preserving orderliness. The king, not the gods, was the lawgiver (Finkelstein, 1991, pp. 375–6).

This meant that if individuals suffered for no apparent reason, they would not immediately assume that they had offended one of their gods through their everyday behaviour. They would most naturally assume that they were guilty of deficient worship. Ethical violations in everyday life were certainly possible, but because there was no *divinely* revealed code of conduct, there was often no obvious way of knowing how the individual had offended the gods. The only means was through divination. So if individuals could not identify any shortcoming in their worship, they would use divination to identify an offence in one of their day-to-day actions and offer an appropriate sacrifice (Walton, 2007, pp. 143–4, 306–7).

In ancient Israel, by contrast, Yahweh – not Moses – is described as the lawgiver and the laws extend to the details of ordinary life. What the Lord requires of individuals is made clear. Leviticus 19 'illustrates well the premise that God's authority is exercised over all of Israel's life . . .' (McConville 2006, p. 66). Children are to respect their parents (v. 3), leftovers from the harvest are for the poor and the alien (vv. 9–10), workers are to be fairly paid (v. 13), bodily appearance is regulated (vv. 27–8) and commercial dealings are to be scrupulously honest (vv. 35–6).

When the people settled in Canaan, they were not to have dealings with God in the place of worship, the sanctuary, and then work out how to pursue an orderly life for the rest of their time. The law made clear what daily practices Yahweh expected. The sanctuary was where transgressions of this law were confessed and sacrifices offered in penitence. Worship connected with the whole of life. If the sanctuary was too far away to attend, Deuteronomy 12.20–25 created a non-sacrificial ritual that highlighted the religious significance of ordinary life. Provision was made for disposing of blood when animals were slaughtered, so that individuals could demonstrate loyalty to Yahweh on a daily basis and be mindful of his sovereignty and presence (Vogt, 2006, p. 201).

The people were to imitate Yahweh's holiness in their day-to-day existence – they were to be holy because the Lord is holy (Lev. 19.2). Their ordinary lives were to show what God was like. They were to do this as a community. For it was as a community that they received God's law, the community as a whole was responsible for obeying the law, the law was to shape the community in its everyday existence, and it was in their communal existence that God was revealed. Israel was to be a faithful community in life.

Contextualizing the law

This meant that the law had to be practical. It had to take account of what the people could actually do in their context. The Old Testament frequently assimilates laws that were widely practised elsewhere, such as protection for widows, orphans and the poor; it takes over various taboos, including that on working on certain days or in certain years; it also incorporates certain cultic practices, such as killing and burning animals in worship. These laws are then set in a fundamentally new context – the covenant relationship with Yahweh (Goldingay, 1987, pp. 157–61). Being faithful in life required Israel to follow Yahweh in a manner that was appropriate to the historical time and place. The community was contextual.

Realism about the people's sinfulness was also necessary. Throughout the framework to Deuteronomy's laws, emphasis is placed on the sinfulness of those to whom they are given. The laws presuppose the realities of a sinful world, such as slavery through impoverishment (15.12–18), war (20.1–20), and marital and other family problems (21.10–21; 22.13–29; 24.1–4).

Practices like slavery, war, polygamy and divorce are not forbidden, but circumscribed by – and harnessed to – to the goal of being in covenant with Yahweh (Goldingay, 1987, pp. 155–6). Slavery has a time limit, for instance.

Alongside this accommodation to reality are the seeds of a critique of that reality. Children are to honour their fathers *and* mothers (Deut. 5.16), a hint that the husband's dominance of the home was not an ethical last word. Slaves are described as 'brothers', the literal translation of Deuteronomy 15.12, suggesting a relationship that makes slavery untenable. The preceding passage makes provision for the remission of debts if there is a poor person in the community (v. 7), and warns that there will always be poor people in the land (v. 11). But this accommodation is challenged in verses 4–5, which declare that there should be no poor among the people if the nation obeys God. Being a faithful community in life requires pragmatism, but that is not the end of the matter. Embedded in the law are resources for ethical reflection that pull toward a higher ideal.

New Testament and subsequent practice

The idea of being a godly community in everyday life is picked up in the very different circumstances of the New Testament. Primitive churches, as noted in Chapter 1, were located in the midst of ordinary life – in homes which were the centre of family, social networks and often work.

As in ancient Israel, norms governing everyday life were highly contextual – they had to be if they were to have an impact. The household codes in Colossians 3.18 – 4.1 and Ephesians 5.21 – 6.9 borrow heavily from secular codes, but are reinterpreted within the theology of the two letters. Married couples, children, parents, slaves and masters are all addressed in terms of reciprocal responsibilities towards one another. Rather than overthrow the prevailing order, the aim is to minimize the possibility of abusive behaviour by those in power (Harris, 2009, pp. 207–8).

Yet, as in the Old Testament, this accommodation to reality contains an implicit critique. A slave could be a 'dear brother' (Philemon 16). The husband is head of his wife, but in a self-giving way, like Christ, which redefines the nature of headship and opens the door to mutual submission (Eph. 5.22–33). As with ancient Israel, the church was to be a community living realistically but distinctly in the midst of daily life, yet having the resources to critique both its context and its accommodating stance.

By taking church into cafes, schools, leisure centres, workplaces and other settings, we have seen how some contextual churches are recapturing the notion that faithful community reveals God in the centre of daily existence. They make the church public in the nooks and crannies of society, testifying to Christ's lordship over the whole of life and visibly presenting the church as an alternative community. Encouraged and helped through mutual support, members can adopt personal and collective practices that resist, give new meaning to and subvert the existing order. They can echo the Old Testament ideal of a Godly community acting politically by shaping and critiquing ordinary life.

Israel was to be a community with a distinctive approach to life

- The community was to witness to God's holiness in everyday life.
- This witness was appropriate to the historical context.
- It contained the seeds of a critique of the context.

Identity

Travelling the pathway to mature community will inevitably raise questions of identity. Negotiating these questions may well be problematic. As we have seen in earlier chapters, if a contextual church belongs to a denomination or network, its identity may be in tension with that of the larger structure. Or if some members come to faith, they may begin to redefine the initiative in ways that make others uncomfortable.

Identity through story

Central to Israel's 'church start' in the desert was the formation of identity. At the nation's best, this was based on the people's experience of Yahweh. As presented in the Old Testament, identity was formed through a forward- and backward-looking process (perhaps resonant with that described in Chapter 15). The people were pulled along by the promises of Yahweh – that they would be freed from Egypt, would occupy 'a good and spacious land' (Exod. 3.8) and be blessed by Yahweh.

These promises only became plausible, however, in the light of events in the past. 'You yourselves have seen what I did to Egypt', the Lord reminds the people in Exodus 19.4. As they looked back on their past dealings with God and looked forward to a continuing relationship with him, the Israelites saw themselves as being embedded in and belonging to the ongoing story of God's dealings with them. They discovered their identity in their unfolding story.

At the heart of this story was their relationship to Yahweh, as it was disclosed through the accounts of Abraham, Isaac and Jacob and then in the people's liberation from Egypt. The memory of the Exodus, along with the gift of the covenant that followed, became central to the nation's identity. This identity was enacted in practices like the annual Passover celebration, when successive generations wrote themselves into the story, declaring it to be their story too.

As the story evolved, so did the people's identity. Deuteronomy, for example, is not just a book of laws. It presents itself as the speeches of Moses given to the people on the verge of entering the Promised Land. It has a narrative perspective, in which an important motif is journey. The early chapters recount the people's journeying in the desert, during which they have experienced the presence of Yahweh. Now much will change. The Israelites are about to enter the land. From being a nomadic people, they will become a settled nation. Their view of themselves will alter. Moses' speeches are designed to help them make the transition (Vogt, 2006, pp. 151–9).

There were other major transitions – from the decentralized social and political structures of the judges period to the centralizing tendencies of the monarchy, from national independence to exile and from exile to restoration to the land. These involved large shifts in the people's identity, in their self-understanding, alongside the continuing thread of their covenant relationship. Identity changed within the frame of Yahweh's faithfulness.

Contested identities

The development of identity was frequently contested. In his discussion of cultural memory and the Old Testament, J. W. Rogerson emphasizes that 'all communal memories are selective, and shaped by special interests' (Rogerson, 2009, p. 20). How a community sees itself will often be in dispute. A dominant conception, reflecting the interests of those in power, may compete with the alternative views of different groups.

This was certainly true of the birth of Israel, which entailed a painful and contentious process of 'individuation from Egypt' (Pardes, 2000, p. 33). As described in Exodus and Numbers, at times the people found the life of slavery behind them more attractive than the uncertainties of desert life ahead (for example, Exod. 16.2–3). Many Israelites wanted to cling on to their past identity, their home in Egypt, while others wanted to follow Moses in forging a new one. Identity was in dispute from the very beginning.

After the monarchy, as indeed throughout Israel's recorded history, rival notions of identity continued to jostle for influence. Steven Tuell, in just one example, argues that in the struggle for dominance between the Zadokite and Levite priestly parties, Ezekiel 44.1–14 reflects a Zadokite stance. It is a polemic against the Levites for allowing 'foreigners' to be in the shrine while the sacrificial liturgy was taking place. By contrast Isaiah 56.1–8 – which welcomes into the temple 'foreigners who bind themselves to the Lord' – expresses a more inclusive Levite view. Although neither party prevailed, these two passages preserve the debate 'and thus give us a window back on the divisive, conflicted world of postexilic Judah' (Tuell, 2005, p. 204).

As described in Chapter 1, disputes over identity are present also in the New Testament – notably at the Council of Jerusalem in Acts 15. Rival notions of Christian identity, based on different ways of incorporating Gentile converts, were openly debated. The dispute was resolved through a process of looking at God's activity now in the light of his actions in the past. By reflecting on the community's journey, the Council paved the way for a profound change in the church's identity.

Community identity today

That Israel discovered its identity by reflecting on its story with Yahweh resonates with James Hopewell's portrayal of congregations. Each congregation has its own identity, which it constructs through the stories it tells about itself. The identity of the congregation is always narrative in form, with its own plot, characterization and worldview. It is never final, but constantly evolving (Hopewell, 1987).

In the same way, the identity of a contextual church will emerge through its story with Jesus. Identity will be discerned through the Spirit largely by looking back over the story. Identity will never stand still, but be constantly evolving. This cautions against having a fixed destination too strongly in mind. Church authorities understandably ask what they must see before they can recognize a new church. Does it celebrate Holy Communion, for example? Has it got familiar forms of church government? Does it, indeed, look like the sort of church they are used to? This attention to what a church must be risks squeezing the initiative into a predetermined mould. Practitioners may be more concerned about meeting others' expectations than about letting the recipients of the gift of church prayerfully discern how the gift should be received.

However, if founders understand that, like ancient Israel, a contextual church's identity changes over time, they are likely to be less preoccupied with conforming to some stereotype of church. Even if the stereotype emerges, it may later change. Instead, they will focus on what it means to be a journeying, ever-changing community of God's people. Having a moving picture of the community rather than a fixed goal, they will be alert to transitions that bring shifts in the community's identity and may prompt disputes about identity. When laying down pathways to maturity, they will attend to the next step, keeping an eye on the long term but not being too prescriptive about it.

The contested nature of Israel's identity speaks to denominations and networks whose identities are challenged by new contextual churches. Competing ideas about Israel's self-understanding were included in the same canon. Sometimes the accounts describe how one identity prevails over another – following Moses overcomes the desire to return to Egypt. At other times, as in the Zadokite–Levite debate, opposing views are simply aired. Room is made for different voices. Diversity is preserved rather than being smoothed over. In a similar way, the mixed-economy church must allow space for groups with different outlooks to express their different identities within the denominational story that holds them together. When it does this, it will hold up an ideal for society.

Israel's identity

- grew out of its story with God;
- evolved and changed;
- was often contested;
- allowed space for rival conceptions of identity.

Conclusion

Signposts to mature community include, through the Spirit, offering Christian community as a divine gift to the world, the practice of hospitality, solidarity expressed in mutual giving, dispersed leadership, a contextualized faith that can subvert the existing order and make a difference to life, and a willingness to negotiate differences in identity. As a contextual church follows these signposts, it will witness to an alternative way of organizing social life. Contextual churches may often be small, but complexity theory says that small things can have big effects. Jesus put it better: the kingdom of God is like yeast. Unseen, it leavens the whole dough (Luke 13.20–1).

Further reading

Brueggemann, Walter, *A Social Reading of the Old Testament*, Minneapolis: Fortress Press, 1994.
Spina, Frank Anthony, *The Faith of the Outsider: Exclusion and Inclusion in the Biblical Story*, Grand Rapids, MI: Eerdmans, 2005.
Wright, Christopher J. H., *Old Testament Ethics for the People of God*, Downers Grove, IL: InterVarsity Press, 2004.

Questions for discussion

- What have your experiences of church taught you about community?
- What are the strengths and limitation of using ancient Israel to draw lessons for new contextual churches?
- What steps can a community take to preserve its Christian identity when adopting a 'centred-set' approach?
- How can participation in community be encouraged?

20

Sustainability[1]

How to sustain new contextual churches has risen up the agenda as increasing numbers are brought to birth. Sceptics wonder if these new types of church are durable. Dioceses, districts, synods and denominations seek to invest in initiatives that will last. Practitioners ask how they can keep their new churches fresh and fruitful, while visionaries speak of not just sustaining new communities but turning them into new movements.

Laying down a pathway to sustainability is vital for growth to maturity. As understood here, sustainability is an aspect of maturity. Unlike the latter, it does not include all the dimensions of a contextual church's life. It is about the durability of the container within which discipleship, worship, community and other ingredients of maturity are grown. It raises questions about whether the container is strong enough to last for the time intended. Working with this understanding, the chapter explores further the meaning of sustainability and then considers foundations for sustainability, transitioning leadership, keeping fresh, sustaining church reproduction and multiplying reproductive churches.

What do we mean by sustainability?

Often, such as in *Mission-shaped Church* (2004, pp. 120–3), sustainability is understood in terms of the 'three selfs'. These were formulated separately by the nineteenth-century missionary strategists, Henry Venn and Rufus Anderson. They refer to missionary ventures that become self-financing, self-governing and self-reproducing. Some people add a fourth 'self' – self-theologizing. A sustainable venture will develop a 'local theology' that responds to its context.

Are the 'four selfs' still valid?

This 'four selfs' approach has some advantages. Not least, assuming that initiatives should be self-supporting takes seriously their need for appropriate

---

1 Earlier versions of this chapter can be found in Moynagh (2011) and Moynagh with Freeman (2011b), but the material has been substantially revised and two sections added.

autonomy. But the approach meets problems if it is viewed through the lens of inherited church – if it is taken for granted that new types of church will be like existing ones.[2] Many contextual churches are not similar to inherited ones and so may not meet the 'four selfs' criteria. Some, like youth congregations, are unlikely to be self-financing. A small church emerging within a local church community project may not be self-governing, but continue to share its parent's administrative arrangements and be part of its oversight structure.

On the other hand, the 'four selfs' can be understood quite radically if they are applied contextually. A teenage congregation might interpret 'self-financing' to mean two part-time youth workers, both of whom are financially self-supporting because they have part-time jobs. A large church plant might understand self-reproducing not as giving birth to another similar church, but as new believers finding one or two other Christians in their work or street and starting church in the midst of life. Self-governing might not mean independence, but pooling administrative and other resources within a network of new churches.

However, even if applied contextually, the four selfs may not fit every situation. The language feels too static for churches that last for only a season. A community in a workplace or among film-goers may come to an end when a key member moves to another part of the country. A gathering on a campus may dissolve when the students graduate. A mid-sized community may run out of energy. In areas of social disadvantage, membership and attendance may be so fluid that the venture always feels fragile.

In particular, emphasizing 'self' sends an unhelpful message. The 'three selfs' were meant to encourage churches to stand on their own feet; missionaries were to move on. Though interdependence within the wider body was always assumed, the stress was on independence to counter dependence. Yet applied in today's individualistic culture, this emphasis comes at a cost. Independence is portrayed as a virtue, while connection to the whole church goes unmentioned. Is not mutual dependence more God-like and in keeping with the relational nature of church than heroic independence?

An alternative approach

Perhaps we should understand sustainability in a more flexible way – as four questions. First, is the initiative bearing *fruit*? Fruitfulness might be understood in terms of the four interlocking sets of relationships that constitute the church – with God, the world, the wider body and within the gathering. The fruitfulness question would be answered by looking for signs of

2 Bob Hopkins, 'The 3-Self Principle – which end of the telescope?', www.acpi. org.uk.

growing maturity in each of these four series of relationships. Because some new churches will be seasonal, the accent would be on the fruitfulness of the community while it lasts rather than on permanence.

Secondly, is the initiative paying attention to *flow*? Contextual churches will manage the flow of their members to other Christian communities so that individuals have a sustained church involvement. If members of a teenage congregation move away to college, as often happens now they will be put in touch with Christians in the places to which they go. If individuals need to move church as their spirituality evolves or circumstances alter, they will be helped to do so. In particular, if an initiative comes to the end of its natural life, members will be supported in finding an alternative community. In some contexts, sustainability will be more about maintaining church ties during transitions than durability.

This raises questions about the institutional solidity of contextual churches. If they can easily come and go, how can they build lasting commitments and durable relationships? The attention to flow responds to this. It is designed to encourage commitment in a culture that has become more fluid. Personal identities are more intentionally constructed than in the past, which introduces greater possibility of change and development; individuals are more likely to outgrow a congregation. Divorce and separation complicate family lives, often making it harder to sustain outside commitments over time. Mobility within jobs (if not between them) has increased (Moynagh and Worsley, 2005, pp. 93–109), causing more frequent change in individual circumstances. All this makes it more difficult to start churches that last especially when they are small.[3]

Thirdly, is the initiative well connected to the wider *family*? Connection to the whole church goes beyond facilitating movements from one expression of church to another. It includes both learning from the living tradition and giving to it. It entails being well networked so that resources can be shared. As Chapter 17 claimed, no single expression of church – even if it is quite large – can cater for all the spiritual and discipleship needs of its members. Churches must pool resources to offer specialist support – whether through a denomination, a theologically like-minded network or a coalitions of local churches. Sustained discipleship increasingly requires participation in the wider church.

Fourthly, does the initiative have an appropriate degree of *freedom*? The amount of financial, administrative and other independence will vary from one context to another, and may change over time. What matters is that each church has a proper amount of responsibility, and that this is negotiated

---

3 In Francis and Richter's summary of reasons people gave for leaving church, it is striking how often changes in life circumstances were cited (Francis and Richter, 2007, pp. 310–16). My point about flow ties in closely to Francis and Richter's concept of the multiplex church.

fairly. It will be important not to fill in the details too early. What is desirable may become apparent only as the church develops.

These 'four Fs' are not necessarily better than the 'four selfs', contextually applied. They probably relate best to situations that are fluid. Their strength includes the attention to fruitfulness and connection to the church family. A weakness is the omission of reproduction, though it might be said that reproduction is not appropriate in all circumstances; in some situations, sustaining one community – let alone reproducing it – is a big enough challenge. Might the two sets of criteria be useful in different contexts?

Facing in a sustainable direction

Like all the pathways to maturity, laying one to sustainability will begin in the very earliest stages of the contextual church. It will involve gathering the right sort of team ('the mission community'), researching the context carefully, engaging the appropriate partners and practising the other methodologies of starting a church. In addition, it will pay close attention to maturity from the outset, so pointing the initiative in a sustainable direction.

Sustaining the pioneer

Support for founders is often thought necessary to help them learn the basics and get through the early stages. But it is equally important for the long haul. Founders can be discouraged, burn out or be ill equipped for the next step. Putting in support at the beginning and refreshing it periodically will lay a pathway that sustains the leader. After seven years pioneering a church on a new housing estate, Charlie Noble commented that 'Without some wise people around me who were prepared to challenge my working patterns, I would not have made it this far' (Male, 2011, p. 29).

Where an existing church or group of churches is sponsoring an initiative, having selected the right person to lead it – obviously vital! – proper support should be made available. Depending on the scale and type of venture, the founder will need:

- someone to cry and laugh with;
- a spiritual director/companion;
- prayer support;
- training in the theology and practice of contextual church, including the methodologies and skills appropriate for the particular stage of the initiative;
- a coach or mentor who can not only listen, but advise, warn and not judge, but empower the other;

- advice from others in a similar field, preferably from someone who has started a church in a similar context or been involved in a comparable type of activity;
- peer support from other pioneers;
- specialist expertise in finance, legal and other matters.[4]

Though some of the sources may overlap, potentially this is a great deal of support. That should be no surprise. We live in an ever more sophisticated world, in which complex tasks are mushrooming. The challenges involved in leading a new church, even a small one, should not be underestimated. In addition, the skills required may change from one stage to another: 'settling' a church may demand different capabilities to birthing it. So, although a church or group of churches may want to provide some of the necessary support initially, it is normally best for founders to make their own arrangements in response to their perceived needs. It becomes *their* support. Coaches and mentors have a key role in helping founders to be aware of their evolving needs.

Size to fit the context

The initiative must also start on a sustainable scale. Thus from the earliest days, mission communities should ask, 'What sort of venture would be sustainable in this context? In particular, what sort of financial commitment will those involved be able to make?' The answer may warn against relying on outside finance to get the initiative started. Support from charitable trusts or public bodies will last for only a limited time. What happens when the money runs out? Will there be sufficient resources to keep the new church going?

Being realistic will discourage over-elaborate projects that cannot be sustained long term, and which produce heartache and disappointment when they eventually fold. Of course this presents an ethical dilemma. Outside grants help to redistribute wealth. If churches in poor neighbourhoods always accommodate themselves to what local people can afford, the spread of income will remain stubbornly skewed. But against this is the benefit of starting on a sustainable basis and scaling up step-by-step as each stage becomes financially self-supporting.

---

4 For an alternative list, with much overlap, see Kilpin and Murray (2007, p. 26).

Some questions to ask

- What are the financial resources of the people we are called to serve?
- What sized initiative could they realistically sustain?
- For how long will the initial funding last?
- Is outside replacement funding likely?
- Are we thinking on too large a scale?

Simplicity

'Simple church', which values small, multiplying, home-based communities and minimal structures, is one way of being financially sustainable. It differs from the typical church small group by having a strong mission focus. It serves its context and seeks to draw non-churchgoers into a relationship with Jesus. A simple church might comprise a weekly or fortnightly gathering round a bring-and-share meal. Members may discuss a film or the ethics of a news story.

One meal-based church among students in Paris started with the hors d'oeuvre, during which people caught up with each other. There was a short talk on a topic like forgiveness, which was discussed over the main course. Matters for prayer were collected over the dessert, and after prayer people had coffee. The convener's hope was that modelling something so simple would encourage students to start similar communities when they moved away.

Simple churches work with the grain of our busy culture. They suit contexts where resources are scarce and can fit easily into time-squeezed lives. They require less management time and skill than larger churches (which is not the same as needing no skill). They put smaller demands on leadership, making it easier to reproduce.

The more complex the church, the more sophisticated are the competences required to lead it. Compare what is involved in the Sunday worship of a typical inherited church with the meal-based worship of the one in Paris. Leadership skills in the economy at large are said to be in scarce supply.[5] So there is likely to be a shortage in the church as well. Competent lay people frequently have busy jobs, which limits the time they can give to the church. Lack of skills is a severe constraint on church reproduction. Simple church reduces the need for sophisticated management.

However, the danger is that simple churches forget their advantages and try to grow by adding new members instead. As the church expands, it seeks

---

5 In Aon Consulting's 2008 *Benefits and Talent Survey*, conducted in the US during the first year of the recession, 56 per cent of the respondents reported that they were experiencing a shortage of qualified leadership talent (www.aon.com/benefits_survey). Management shortages are regularly reported in Europe.

a building, employs a leader and loses its original simplicity (Lings, 2006b, pp. 21–2). Another danger is that they lose their missional focus. They become comfortable groups for Christians rather than communities with a commitment to others.

Simple churches are simple only in part. Honest relationships within the group have to be fostered. Their small size can make it difficult for outsiders to recognize them as church, which may complicate their relationships with the wider body. Language, such as the leader being 'spare time', may imply that leading these churches is 'akin to a hobby that can be done when convenient but stopped when bothersome' (Dalpra, 2011, p. 53). Might 'bi-vocational' better convey a simultaneous commitment to secular employment and church, as Claire Dalpra suggests?

Simple and clustered

Especially if the convener is untrained, the small size of simple churches may limit the range of spiritual input. Online and other published resources can help of course, but emerging Christians will be further enriched if they have the opportunity to meet with larger circles of believers. It may be that two or three small groups can 'cluster' together every few weeks to provide this wider experience. As groups multiply, additional clusters can be created, forming a network that pools resources and draws clusters together for occasional celebrations (Hopkins and Breen, 2007, p. 38).

Alternatively or in addition, a small group might periodically worship with a larger congregation nearby (such as its parent church, if it has one), take part in town-wide Christian events or attend a Christian festival. Coalitions of new and inherited local churches can share resources for mission and discipleship, helping simple churches to avoid being isolated. Might simple and connected be good words to keep together?

Transitioning from first- to second- generation leaders

Unless the church dies when its founder leaves, transitioning from one to another leader must occur at some stage. Surveying 57 stories of new churches since 1999, the Sheffield Centre found that 16 founders were 'still in the saddle'. In 21 cases, the founder was replaced and life continued well. Some were now with their third leader. On the other hand, 14 churches ceased to exist. In eight of these, either the founder was not replaced or a poor appointment was made. In nine of the 14 cases, the young church was too dependent on the founder to survive the person's departure.[6]

---

6 *TSC Research Bulletin*, Winter 2011/12, p. 2.

Transitioning leadership is a critical phase in the church's development. Sometimes founders leave because of their personal circumstances. Sometimes they move on because the founder is a natural pioneer and starts another church; the successor may need to be a 'settler', who helps the church bed down and grow roots that will sustain its future life. Arguably the best reason for leaving is to allow the church's indigenous leaders to flourish. The people have received the gift of being community with Jesus. Now they are given the opportunity, relying on the Spirit, to unwrap the gift fully in their context.

Three models

The New Testament contains three models for indigenizing leadership. The diaspora model is represented by the converts in Jerusalem at Pentecost (and the other major festivals), which attracted Jews from around the known world. As Chapter 1 pointed out, those from the diaspora who became believers appear to have returned home, shared the good news with their family and friends, and started churches in their households. Most would have remained in their new churches.

This model makes sense today for individuals who are starting contextual church among friends or among those who share their hobby or interest. Usually the church will be birthed and led in the founder's spare time. The founder remains because this is a personal network. Indigenization occurs as the leadership is shared. Sharing leadership means that the church does not depend on one individual. If personal circumstances change and the founder leaves, the transition has the potential to be stable.[7]

A second model is suggested by Saint Paul, who stayed with his new congregations for a relatively short time. He appointed elders for each house church, and these elders appear to have shared the leadership of the church in their town (Acts 20.17ff). The elders seem to have been drawn initially from converts among the Jews and 'God-fearing' Gentiles, who attended synagogue and were familiar with the Jewish Scriptures. Their pre-existing knowledge presumably made rapid indigenization possible. The equivalent today might be contextual churches among people with considerable church background.

A third model is provided by Jesus, who spent some three years with his closest disciples, day after day. This mentoring was highly intensive. Though like Paul's converts Jesus' followers attended synagogue, what Jesus was doing was so unprecedented that they needed extensive discipling before they could be entrusted with the church. This model perhaps speaks to situations where a church is birthed among the never or scarcely churched. Converts have too much to learn for indigenization to be rushed.

---

7 *TSC Research Bulletin*, Winter 2011/12, p. 2.

Preparation

Indigenizing leadership begins with the right mindset – not 'This is a project for other people' but 'This is a project *with*'. 'With' will affect every aspect of the initiative's life, including the basic strategy. Chapter 1 noted that Paul's churches were based on the most pervasive form of leadership within ancient society – leadership within the home. Was this partly because it made the indigenization of leadership more straightforward? Taking seriously the maxim, 'The resources are in the harvest', what would it mean for the leadership requirements of an envisaged church to shape how it is birthed?

Although not all eventualities can be anticipated, it may be helpful at the outset to identify some of the issues surrounding indenization and reach agreement on how they will be addressed. For example:

- If the church is being started by a 'mother church', when should the new church appoint its own leaders?
- If the church is being started by a team from a mission agency, should the team withdraw at some point so that indigenous leaders can emerge? If so, when?
- If the leadership of the 'mother church' changes and has different expectations of the initiative, how can the latter be safeguarded?
- If the founder is good at pioneering but not at settling a church, when and how should the founder be encouraged to move on? What kind of leadership is needed in the next phase?
- If the denomination redeploys staff at regular intervals, what will happen if the founder is redeployed at a critical stage for the initiative? Can an exception be made?
- What level of spiritual maturity is expected of potential leaders? Will they receive training or accreditation? What cultural assumptions are being made about the nature of leadership?[8]

Care should be taken that the initiative does not become over dependent on the founder and so finds it traumatic when the person withdraws. Professional clergy are especially prone to produce dependence. They see themselves as 'experts', which makes indigenizing leadership more difficult. Might this be one argument for new churches to be lay led, wherever possible?

Risk is always the big worry. Reflecting on their Welsh experience of pioneering a weekly all-age gathering of 40–50 people mainly with little or

---

8 This paragraph is based on Stuart Murray-Williams's contribution to *TSC Research Bulletin*, Winter 2011/12, p. 3.

no church background, Methodist ministers Michelle and David Legumi wrote:

> We have found it hard to entrust others with what has felt like our 'baby'. We have been reluctant to let people be involved in the leadership for fear of the vision being hijacked and 'churchified'. Pioneers are not often surrounded by like-minded people. It requires large amounts of trust to let go and let others grow into leadership. (Male, 2011, p. 65)

Paul faced risks that things would go wrong – and they did! Think of the church in Corinth. Leadership involves learning by experience, including mistakes. As with parents who give increasing freedom to their adolescent children, mistakes are the price of growth to maturity. It is a real price, but the gain is indigenous leaders who flourish.

As a stepping stone to indigenization, the people the initiative serves should be involved in the leadership as soon as possible. Focus Service: Sheffield Church 'is a church for people with learning difficulties and anyone else who enjoys an interactive experience of God'. From the beginning, everyone coming through the door was totally unchurched. When it became an official Baptist church in 2004 with an ordained minister, its leadership team included members of the church with learning difficulties. The church encouraged indigenization from the earliest days (www.fresh expressions.org.uk/stories).

Indigenizing leadership will influence how individuals are encouraged into the faith. Instead of fostering dependence on the founder, making it more difficult to leave, the process of initiation will model reliance on the Spirit and the community. The founder will be a facilitator rather than expert. Someone convening a spirituality group, for instance, might buy a book of Christian meditations, lead the first couple of sessions and then give the book to other members to lead subsequently. Weaning the group off the founder would start early. One person, working among poor people, resolved to answer as few of their questions as possible. To minimize their dependence on the leader, individuals were encouraged to google the information.

From the very beginning, a mission community might periodically review all elements of the emerging church's life. How far is leadership being shared? Are practices fostering dependence on the founder or the Spirit?

Who, when and how?

Leadership can be passed on to:

- *Another outsider*. This may happen when founders leave at an early stage and someone from the context is not yet ready to take over.

Dangers include the new leader lacking the church's DNA and failing to gel with the leadership team already in place.

- *Someone in the original mission community,* supported by the other members. This is likely to ensure a smooth transition, and may be necessary if indigenizing leadership has not progressed far. The danger is that this slow pace reflects a low commitment to indigenization and breeds continuing dependence on the missional core.
- *An indigenous leader,* supported by the original mission community. This will be a significant step toward indigenization, and will ensure that the new leader is surrounded by more mature Christians. The risk is that these Christians do not let go, the new leader is stifled and indigenizing the life of the church proceeds slowly or stalls.
- *An indigenous leader, supported by an indigenous leadership team.* This would be the natural outcome of bringing steadily more people from the context into the mission community, ensuring a relatively smooth transition. The danger is that the process occurs too quickly, leaving the church in spiritually immature hands. If members of the original mission community remain within the church, they may resist changes, mistaking indigenization for spiritually backward steps.
- *A combination of these,* such as an indigenous leader supported by a team containing a mixture of the original mission community and individuals from the context. This may reflect the ideal of steady progress toward indigenization. But circumstances do not always allow the ideal.

Dalpra maintains that 'a candidate's ability to understand a church's bespoke values should be the most important criteria in appointing them as a leader'.[9] But other factors are also important. When Jesus and Paul transitioned leadership, they left their new churches with

- the Holy Spirit;
- a basic understanding of the gospel;
- Scripture (our Old Testament);
- the sacraments of baptism and Holy Communion;
- leadership (Jesus left the apostles, Paul elders);
- ongoing support (Jesus instructed the Spirit; Paul revisited his churches when he could, sent members of his team to sort out problems and wrote pastoral letters).

---

9 *TSC Research Bulletin,* Winter 2011/12, p. 6.

As evidence of their spiritual maturity, potential leaders should demonstrate an ability to draw on these resources. This will be a sign that the time has come pass on the leadership.

When doing so, special sensitivity is required in areas of social disadvantage. Poor communities are used to individuals arriving from secular agencies, advancing their careers and then leaving. If the church repeats the pattern, cynicism about outsiders may be strengthened. The sudden departure of someone who has been the midwife of a new community can be profoundly painful.

Aware of these sensitivities, one ordained pioneer sought to manage the transition by withdrawing gradually. She shared more and more tasks with others in her team and continued to make herself available to the person who replaced her as leader. In contrast to her predecessor who had left the year before and avoided further contact, she stayed in touch with members of the community. Individuals felt less abandoned.

Keeping links with the departing founder can make practical sense. If serious problems arise, the founder will normally have the relationships and the authority to help sort them out. Maintaining the link would follow Paul's practice. Having left, he was forced to intervene in some of his new churches either through correspondence or by sending emissaries, such as Timothy.

Intervening like this in today's 'mixed economy', however, is problematic. A founder's responsibility for the church is expected to cease after moving away and the community comes under someone else's authority. This can be far from ideal. The new person may not have had enough time to build the necessary trust before a major difficulty arises, and so may not be as well placed as the founder to aid a resolution. Is this an example of how some traditional practices jar with what is needed in the missional contexts we now face? As 'serial pioneers' emerge, found one church after another and establish networks of new churches, how will their authority in the network square with denominational arrangements?

Keeping fresh

There is a well-known process by which churches become institutionalized. A magnetic leader forms a community round an inspirational vision. The community stabilizes in the second generation and formalizes criteria for membership. Subsequently, much of the energy goes in maintaining and protecting established structures to ensure the community survives. Ed Stetzer and Warren Bird comment, 'the institutionalizing of the church is essentially its immunization to an evangelistic impulse' (2010, p. 171). Can new contextual churches avoid the trend?

Drane has pointed to tendencies that threaten to suck the life out of contextual church (Drane, 2010, pp. 150–66). As part of a 'McDonaldization' process, he lists the concern for efficiency, such as succumbing to the temptation to replicate a fruitful model elsewhere; a trend toward calculability, as demands grow to see numerical results; a desire for predictability – conformity to some pattern or other; and a desire by existing churches to retain control. These represent an institutionalizing dynamic.

He suggests four values that can work in the opposite direction:

- creativity as opposed to efficiency;
- relationality instead of calculability;
- flexibility (or adaptability) rather than predictability;
- proactivity – straining forward instead of holding on to the past – in place of control.

He fails, however, to explain how these counter-values can become the heartbeat of a new church. To understand this, complexity theory would say that the aim should be to keep a young church at the 'edge of chaos', which is just on the safe side of the boundary between order and disorder. If there is too much order the church will ossify, but if it slides across the boundary it will disintegrate. Staying close to the line combines enough stability for the church to be viable with sufficient flexibility for it to remain innovative and fresh.

One approach suggests that in navigating transitions, organizations should push control downward. The system as a whole should be mobilized to find a solution to the problem. (This is a secular version of Paul's vision of shared ministry within the body.) The process includes[10]

- *Starting with values – the underlying rationale of the organization. What are we about? What do we want to achieve?* This gets back to basics, helps people focus on the essentials and allows fundamental change, if necessary, to be negotiated explicitly.
- *Agreeing the principles that will guide how these values are expressed –* A cell-based church wanting to grow further cells might agree four such principles: each cell will have a mission focus, it will meet at least three times a month, its leaders will meet regularly in an accountability group and the cells will cluster together monthly.
- *Allowing maximum flexibility within these principles –* Individuals can be creative within a framework that serves the organization's purpose. Energy is released and fresh thinking about how to make the transition is encouraged.

---

10 This is a schematized version of the insights discussed by Lichtenstein (2000, pp. 139–40).

Milestone reviews can make this self-organizing process an ongoing feature of a young church's life. Perhaps by involving the gathering as a whole, values and principles can be regularly reviewed and questions asked about whether there is enough flexibility. Picking up Drane's values, making this process continuous will engender flexibility, which will encourage creativity; the participation involved will promote relationality; the regular reviews of values and principles will foster proactivity.

One study of business entrepreneurs illustrates how participation, coupled with continuous small change, can keep an organization fresh. The authors found that the two 'visionary entrepreneurs' they observed prevented institutionalization by testing all proposals on the rest of the staff – '. . . we don't see anything as stupid.' This brought flexibility into the process and prevented habits. Making small changes regularly developed the business and kept it dynamic (Cantzler and Leijon, 2007, pp. 743–4).

Creativity and flexibility may mean bringing seasonality into the heart of a new church – activities are undertaken only for a period. The pattern of worship can be changed regularly. Social events can be varied. If constant flux within a church feels too unsettling, it may be helpful to remember that seasonality can be for a season too. 'We've had a period of constant change, now let us have a time of stability before we ask what God has next in store for us.'

Sustainability – key dynamics so far

- clarity of meaning – the '4 selfs' or '4 Fs';
- good foundations – support for the pioneer and sustainable scale;
- indigenized leadership – with preparation from the outset;
- staying fresh – participation and constant small changes.

Sustaining church reproduction

A new church will remain fresh and be sustainable par excellence if it reproduces. Despite exceptions (for example, Lings, 2010), there are not many instances of new contextual churches reproducing in the UK. Some apparently phenomenal examples exist in the United States. Neil Cole's Church Multiplication Associates planted 53 'organic' house-based churches before 2001. By 2008 this had risen to almost two new churches *a day* across the United States and overseas. (www.cmaresources.org/about/history).

Yet this, and the North American house church movement generally, 'has largely been a reform movement, drawing mostly from existing believers who want something "better" than and "different" from what they currently have . . . Too many house churches lack a heart or track record for outreach beyond the existing fold of disenchanted Christians' (Stetzer and Bird, 2010, pp. 123–4). Though we can learn from these reproducing churches, lessons from reaching disillusioned Christians may not apply to people with less Christian background.

We have much to learn about multiplying church in post-Christian societies. The seven principles that follow are drawn from literature about church multiplication in history, among North Americans with some church background and to some extent among people elsewhere. The literature, representing a wealth of learning, includes Addison (2011), Cole (2005, 2009), Comiskey (2009), Garrison (2004), Hirsch and Ferguson (2011), Logan (2006), Mannoia (2005), Roberts Jr (2008) and Stetzer and Bird (2010). The principles feel intuitively close to what is required for Christian communities to reproduce among the not-yet-churched in the global North, but we need more experience to be sure.

Encountering Jesus

Reproduction occurs when there has been an encounter with Jesus. The reproduction of New Testament churches was catalysed by the apostles who had met the risen Lord. Steve Addison uses examples from history, such as the Moravian missionary movement, John Wesley and the Azusa Street Pentecostal revival, to argue that this is the norm. He notes that profound encounters often arise from a personal *crisis* and are facilitated by the *process* of a disciplined life. They result in a passionate commitment to mission (Addison, 2011, pp. 36–54). These encounters are acts of grace. They can be prayed for but cannot be manufactured.

In describing the explosion of Christianity in the global South, Addison notes that Southern Christians have a much stronger sense of spiritual forces affecting everyday life than believers in the North (2011, p. 52). Might this hold the key to reproducing churches in a post-Christian society? When new believers have experienced the transforming impact of God on their immanent lives, they will have a convincing story to tell their friends.

Intentionality

As with all aspects of sustainability, being intentional about reproducing must exist from the outset. Among writers who stress this, Alan Hirsch and Dave Ferguson emphasize the need to start with the right paradigm of church. How we think shapes how we act. Our vision of church must not stem from an institutional paradigm, with its attention to buildings, clergy, programmes and so on. It must derive from the Great Commission, the practice of the New Testament church and, one might add, historical examples of the church at its missional best. Running through these is the multiplication of Christian communities. 'The work here is conceptual; we have to reframe assumptions and change imaginations.' (Hirsch and Ferguson, 2011, p. 112)

The idea of starting *a* new church belongs to a Christendom mindset. Christendom has a pedigree of founding churches in new population centres, such as a housing estate. The new church was expected to serve the surrounding area on an attractional basis – 'we'll invite those we serve to come to church.' It was not expected to grow by planting again.

The paradigm shift is to initiate a gathering that serves its neighbourhood or network partly by multiplying further gatherings.

> Instead of drawing people *out* of community and robbing what community already existed, Jesus' plan is to inject the Gospel into an existing community. Like a virus, the peace of the Good News infects and transforms the community so that the members become a church themselves.
>
> Most people setting out to start new churches automatically think of starting in their own home, but Jesus' idea of starting in the home of the new converts is a small shift with global implications. (Cole, 2005, p. 186)

As earlier chapters have stressed, the church is to multiply Christian communities, whether by founding a large church that gives birth to a further one, or initiating a large church that spawns a series of micro churches, or by starting a small church that produces other small communities. Founders are called not to start *a* church, but to catalyse a *process*. They are to initiate continuous reproduction. When they have made that mental shift, everything changes. Their goal will not be to launch a church that grows in size, nor even one that lasts (we live in a fluid society): it will be to birth a church that reproduces and whose offshoot reproduces again.

Everything is reproducible

In particular, churches that multiply will create 'simple structures that welcome reproducibility at every level' (Stetzer and Bird, 2010, p. 179). They will keep simplifying everything so that others can do it too. Using case studies from around the world, David Garrison makes a strong case for churches to be multiplied by unpaid, local, lay leaders (Garrison, 2004, pp. 189–91). Time-starved laity need simple ways of fostering community, leading worship, forming disciples and encouraging mission. They will not attend extended courses outside their contexts. They will learn best in situ, through apprenticeship. Through the Spirit, 'explosive growth often follows easily reproducible ministries' (Stetzer and Bird, 2010, p. 106).

The aim must be to reproduce, not replicate. Reproduction is sensitive to differences in context: replication ignores these differences. Reproducibility involves finding simple ways of doing things that can be adapted to new situations. An example would be forming disciples through one-to-one mentoring, which uses a simple framework. The framework can be adjusted when necessary. Another would be a rhythm of 'sermons', sometimes using a podcast or DVD, sometimes discussing input from a church member and sometimes breaking into small groups to discuss a Bible passage, using questions like: What can we learn from this passage? What difference will it make in the coming week? The rhythm and details can be varied as required.

Mentoring

When reproducibility saturates a new church's life, mentoring is a key leadership task. It is central to Christian formation and leadership training. Though group learning is also vital, mentoring has several advantages over groups. Learning can be personalized, which allows greater learning in depth. In a group, teaching has to be generalized: in a one-to-one, it can be specific to the individual. This makes it more time efficient. In an hour of group learning, an individual may find that just 20 minutes (if that) is absolutely relevant: in an hour of mentoring, the whole 60 minutes hits the target.

Just-in-time mentoring

- Never teach a skill until there is a need for it.
- Never teach a second skill till the first one is learned.
- Never assume a skill is learned till it is taught to another.

Source: Cole (2009, pp. 240–2).

Mentoring has been found to be especially effective in multiplying leaders. Through the Spirit, leaders are formed who are capable of shaping others. 'Thus the number of leaders increases exponentially as each new leader reproduces other leaders' (Cole, 2009, p. 249). Cole's astonishing multiplication of churches is based on mentoring. He tends to start informally. In the context of everyday relationships, he listens, asks a question or two and suggests a simple biblical practice relating to the person's spiritual experience to date. If the person takes the suggestion, he might offer something a little more challenging. Once a pattern of spiritual obedience emerges, he arranges formal appointments to meet up. This ensures he invests in what is proven, not in what is potential, which he claims is a good biblical principle (Luke 16.10).

Cole uses the MAWL method (see Box), and within that framework adopts the following principles (Cole, 2009, pp. 234–9):

- First things first – he addresses glaring areas of weakness first.
- One thing at a time – people learn best this way. They also learn at a different pace and have different styles of learning.
- Always one more thing – he keeps asking God what is next for the person.

The MAWL method of mentoring

Model: I do; you watch; we discuss.
Assist: We do; we discuss.
Watch: You do; I watch; we discuss.
Leave: You do; someone else watches . . . (The process begins again.)

Source: adapted from Cole (2009, p. 248).

Fundamental to Cole's approach is the integration of evangelism and leadership development. When people come to faith they are immediately baptized and drawn into Life Transformation Groups, which read Scripture, confess sin and pray for others. Those who are fruitful in seeing new groups get started are mentored to accelerate their leadership formation. 'By following people systematically, step-by-step through the process and starting with the end in mind, leaders are raised up. The process of leadership development is woven seamlessly into evangelism and discipleship' (Logan, 2006, p. 35).

Growth through networks

Churches grow by growing out – by spreading the gospel through networks. This is part of the church's genetic code. In the earliest days, the gospel rippled through converts' social ties. Where these networks were relatively open, the faith spread into adjacent networks as well (Stark, 2007, pp. 8–15, 119–39). To gain entry to networks, Paul relied on 'persons of peace', who made him welcome and put him in touch with their contacts. Churches that reproduce today use these same methods, as Cole exemplifies (Cole, 2005, pp. 175–86). Building relationships is a kingdom way of working, for the kingdom is relational by nature.

It may not be entirely straightforward, however. What happens when – often among the disadvantaged (McCulloch, 2003, pp. 1425–38) – individuals have too few contacts for the faith to spread, or when they do not stay long enough in the area to be drawn into church and travel to Jesus? Cole deals with these difficulties by looking for pockets of people who have a strong sense of community and social cohesiveness (Cole, 2005, pp. 176–7). That may be appropriate at times, but is not much help to founders called to isolated people. In these situations, bringing a church to birth may take a long time. Founders and those who support them must be realistic about this.

Growth through networks also has the idea of growing up – of maturing in the faith by connecting to the wider church. As earlier chapters have repeatedly stressed, being connected is vital for practical as well as theological reasons. Christian communities in the corners of life need the larger church to stay healthy. In today's educated and novelty driven world, individuals will value the informality and friendships of a small community, but they will also want a richer diet of worship, learning and openings for mission. They will want to be what they *are* – part of a larger family.

Learning from the context

To spread along networks, the church must keep learning from the people it serves. The more mission communities understand the context, the less likely they are to replicate an inappropriate model. DNA can be passed on from the mother church or from a network of churches. But in a customized society, 'it's one thing to pass on DNA; it's another to pass on skin tone, bone structure, and other biological features that will be shaped more by the context and era in which the church is planted.' (Roberts Jr, 2008, pp. 77–8) Each putative expression of church must discover how best to combine its inheritance with the requirements of the people it serves.

'Indigenization' will be the key step (Addison, 2011, p. 116). This will involve helping individuals through the Spirit to make personally authentic journeys to faith and take responsibility for their ensuing discipleship. As they do this, new converts – empowered by the Spirit, grounded in Scripture and informed by the tradition – will begin to show how the gospel (and church) can be contextualized in their situations.

Remaining missional

Keeping a mission focus is perhaps the most challenging of the seven principles. It is always tempting for relationships within the gathering and the larger body to take precedence over serving the context. This is reinforced if the gathering assumes that God is encountered primarily in corporate worship and only secondarily in everyday life. Yet if mission is not a second step for God and should not be for the church, contextual churches must pay special attention to retaining an outward focus.

This can be helped by ensuring that their spiritual rhythms and disciplines extend beyond personal practices and worship to shared missional activities. In particular, the mission emphasis can be reflected in the community's main meetings. Why should these not have an equal focus on mission planning and worship, perhaps integrating the two? Instead of the agenda sequence being Scripture, confession and prayer (as in Cole's Life Transformation Groups), it might be purpose (mission review and planning), problems (including confession), and prayer and praise (centred on Scripture). Scripture would be crucial, but it would be read explicitly in the light of the group's experience and be a resource for prayer and praise.

To keep reproducing, churches need

- encounters with Jesus;
- intentionality from the start;
- reproducible structures at every level;
- mentoring for Christian and leadership formation;
- growth by evangelizing networks and connecting to the wider church;
- continual learning from context;
- a constant mission focus.

Strategies to multiply reproducing churches

Pathways to sustainability will include supporting strategies that embed reproducing communities in the denominations or networks. Kevin Mannoia (2005) has proposed comprehensive systems for the regional multiplication of churches in North America. I made some suggestions for the UK in my 2004 book (pp. 206–37). *Mission-shaped Church* (2004, pp. 145–9) also contained a number of proposals, many of which have been acted upon. Recent British experience suggests that initiating an effective strategy will require action on a number of fronts. Though they will look different, these actions are likely to be similar in principle for both a local church and wider groupings of churches.

Leadership

The first is appropriate leadership. Using the words of Phil Potter, the Director of Pioneer Ministry in the Church of England's Liverpool Diocese, national or local church leaders can support new contextual churches along a spectrum of permission ('It's OK, but don't expect me to be much involved'), blessing ('I'll give you support'), passion ('I really believe in this and will be proactive in encouraging it') and paradigm shift ('I'll do more than encourage: I'll think and breathe it every day'). Paradigm shift may be unrealistic in the mixed economy, where leaders must show that they are passionate about both inherited and new expressions of church. But passion is essential.

Nominated leaders play a key role in fostering innovation. They can influence appointments. They can ask questions about the status quo. They can put issues on the agenda. They can stir the imagination. They can suggest experimentation. They can invite the institution to create protected spaces, where what emerges can be a source of learning and owned provisionally without making a final judgement. They can stimulate innovation by brokering connections between people and between individuals and contexts. They can amplify developments on the ground by commenting on them to other audiences, giving platforms to successful innovators and celebrating success. They can articulate the vision as it emerges. They can symbolize what they hope for (for example through photo opportunities). They can be advocates for pioneers when the latter face criticism.[11] All this requires leaders to be proactive. Might the starting point be to prioritize their diaries?

Definition

A second ingredient is an appropriate definition. In England, the 'fresh expressions' definition – cited in the Introduction – has sometimes been pulled so wide that almost anything seems to count. This has dulled the message about the urgency of mission. Churches can think that they are 'doing fresh expressions' when they start a service for churchgoers; they fail to engage with people outside the church. A vague definition lowers the bar. It avoids the challenge of equipping people to jump the bar at a more demanding level. Keeping the bar high will stretch the church in a missional direction.

Rationale

A third ingredient is a theological rationale. People will be more likely to take and support difficult decisions to encourage contextual churches if they believe in these churches as a matter of principle. The rationale should connect with the tradition of the local church and/or denomination. It should show how the envisaged communities are authentic to this tradition. It should also put some theological markers round new churches, such as criteria for discerning whether an initiative has the character of a church.

Lay led

Fourth, the strategy will have a lay focus. Financial constraints are one factor making it necessary to rediscover tent-making ministries. Contextual communities will never multiply at scale if the church relies on paid ministers. Lay-led initiatives, on the other hand, will model to other lay people that they too can found a Christian community. (Clergy-led churches encourage

---

11 For more on most of these ideas, see Bridges (1991, pp. 43–64).

the opposite assumption: that lay people would have to be ordained if they wanted to start a church.)

Existing churches may be able to give lay founders some financial help, perhaps by providing accommodation or paying their pension contributions. More important will be to employ lay or ordained persons to provide lay founders with pastoral encouragement, to connect them to each other and the wider body, to clear institutional road blocks, and to facilitate training and other forms of support.

Research

Fifth, an effective strategy will emphasize research. The denomination will want to know the number of new contextual churches, where they are located, how fruitful they are, and the factors behind 'success' and 'failure'; spreading the results widely will increase knowledge of good practice. A local church will research the opportunities for new contextual communities, and will want feedback on the latter's fruitfulness and on problems that need addressing.

Vision

Vision casting will be a sixth priority. This will include spreading stories of successful ventures, holding 'vision day' conferences to increase awareness among church members, enabling opinion formers to visit a new contextual church, holding teach-ins for ministers and their lay leaders, and hosting workshops for people wanting to explore specific issues in depth, such as contextual church in rural areas or among children.

Initiatives

The core of the strategy will be a series of initiatives. For example, a denomination or network might gather ministers who are interested in pioneering contextual churches. As they travel the journey, they would share together what they are learning and receive input on good practice. They would seek out and encourage potential lay practitioners, who would form a separate learning community, again sharing insights and receiving input. Members of the two groups would facilitate the same process with other ministers and lay people. In time, lay pioneers might be networked into a missional fellowship or order.

Another denomination might concentrate on the development of resource (or 'minster') churches, as the Anglican Diocese of Liverpool is beginning to do. These would be churches with a specific calling to multiply contextual communities. A minister with suitable gifts and experience would be appointed to lead such a church. Or a full-time pioneer would be temporarily appointed to a well-run church that wanted to move in this direction but lacked the know-how. Again, the leaders of these churches would meet regularly so that they could learn from and support each other.

A third denomination might bring together each month promising young adults from across a region to help them grow in their faith, and develop the skills and knowledge to start church in the contexts where they lead their lives. They would continue to meet as their initiatives flew or floundered, supporting and learning from one another. They too might be networked into a missional order.

A fourth denomination might put funds aside to select, equip and deploy a small group of full-time pioneers. A dedicated member of staff would provide oversight and support, draw the pioneers regularly together for mutual accountability and learning, and disseminate to the wider church the lessons being learned. Having gained experience, these pioneers would encourage others to do the same, perhaps on a part-time basis, and provide support. Britain's Methodist Church has an initiative on these lines called Venture FX, which aims over five years to appoint 20 missional leaders to start Christian communities among young adults not belonging to church.

Strategic initiatives

A denomination or network might

- form learning communities of ministers;
- develop resource churches;
- form a community of young adults with the potential to pioneer;
- employ a small group of pioneers, with intensive support;
- work in schools strategically.

A fifth denomination might concentrate on schools in an area. It might appoint first one and then a second children's/youth worker to form small communities of children with few church links, starting perhaps with seven-year-olds. The aim would be to keep the group together till the children left school (or thereafter if young people stayed in the locality). In year one the worker might start the first group of seven-year-olds, in year two a second group and in year three a third group. The first group might help with the youngest ones. The process would continue till there was a group for each age category. Appropriately aged groups might cluster together from time to time.

A local church might

- start with a fringe group, and encourage church to emerge gradually within it;
- enthuse networkers to draw together not-yet-Christians within their networks;

- work with two or three Christians in a missional context;
- encourage mid-sized missional communities;
- collaborate with other churches in the area to start a church (for example among youth);
- plant at scale, and then 'drill down' with smaller initiatives among networks it has not yet reached.

Support

These initiatives will require training and support in the context of accountability. This will include regular meetings with peers, weekend training events and possibly a course, such as Britain's *mission-shaped ministry* course (msm), which is being franchised to other countries. Practitioners will also need regular one-to-one coaching, or team coaching (in which a coach works with the pioneer and their team) or ad hoc coaching in conjunction with a learning community. The type of support will vary according to the stage of the venture. Initially, pioneers may need an inspirational and envisioning coach. Later, they may need someone who can help with practical issues.

Clergy will need training in the theology and practice of contextual church as part of their ministerial formation. This must extend beyond those who feel called to pioneering. All clergy should have a good understanding of contextual church. This will equip them to support and encourage lay people as the latter form Christian communities either within the orbit of the local church or beyond.

National and local strategies for multiplying churches

- proactive leadership;
- clear and challenging definition;
- theological rationale;
- lay focus;
- research;
- vision casting;
- strategic initiatives;
- training and support.

To implement a strategy with all these ingredients, one or more staff members in a denomination should act as a catalyst and coordinator. Creating teams of two or three staff to spark new churches in a particular area, such as a city's workplaces or a group of schools, could prove especially effective. This may require resources to be redeployed imaginatively. For instance, a Methodist Circuit replaced three ministers with eight part-time lay missioners, specializing in areas for which they were gifted. As existing posts become vacant, the new job descriptions might include a focus on contextual church.

The suggestions here have focused on how a denomination (or local church) might begin to initiate a strategy of church reproduction. A great deal more would be required if the strategy was to become the starting point of a self-sustaining movement. Steve Addison highlights five features of fruitful church movements: white hot faith, commitment to a cause, contagious relationships, rapid mobilization and adaptive methods. The typology in the box below contains much to ponder. It challenges to the core how church is widely practised in the global North.

Unsustainable church planting strategies	*Sustainable church planting strategies*
Fully fund every church plant	Train church planters to raise funds or become tentmakers
Require seminary training for every planter	Multiply trainers in the field
Provide a coach for every planter	Equip planters to coach the next wave of planters
Provide long-term subsidies for struggling church plants	Allow churches to take responsibility
Parent churches take responsibility for the budgeting and administration of church plants	Church plants set up their own arrangements
Centrally plan and coordinate where and when churches are to be planted	Expect churches and planters to seek God, do the research and multiply churches wherever there is a need
Start a church	Multiply churches
The denomination identifies and recruits church planters	Every church planter trains apprentices
Satellite congregations depend for ever on the sending church	Satellite congregations graduate quickly to interdependence and become multiplying hubs
A movement held together by tight systems of control	A movement held together by a common cause and relationships

Source: Addison (2011, p. 110).

Conclusion

Laying a pathway to sustainability begins with the intention to be sustainable. Understanding the concept, starting off on the right foot, indigenizing leadership, staying fresh and starting not just a church but *a process* of reproduction are not best dropped in as the initiative develops. They should be in mind from the earliest days. They should form part of a local and national strategy for reproducing church – a strategy that will create a sustaining environment for individual contextual churches. Nothing can substitute, however, for the Spirit's work. So nourishing the spiritual lives of all involved must be the absolute priority.

Further reading

Allen, Roland, *Missionary Methods – St Paul's or Ours?*, Cambridge: Lutterworth Press, 2006.

Cole, Neil, *Organic Leadership: Leading Naturally Right Where You Are*, Grand Rapids, MI: Baker, 2009.

Garrison, David, *Church Planting Movements: How God is Redeeming a Lost World*, Arkadelphia, AR: WIGTake Resources, 2004.

Stetzer, Ed and Warren Bird, *Viral Churches: Helping Church Planters Become Movement Makers*, San Francisco: Jossey-Bass, 2010.

Questions for discussion

- What are the arguments for and against founders staying in their new churches?
- What will keep founders and their churches spiritually fresh?
- Should a new contextual church always aim to reproduce? How can it be enabled to do so?
- How would you advise a church to multiply contextual churches (a) in a local church, and (b) in a denomination or network?

21

Towards the Mixed-economy Church

New contextual churches are expanding our understanding of what it means to be church. Often they look very different to inherited church and, as illustrated at the end of the last chapter, they ask some fundamental questions about the current life and organization of the church. Yet as Part 1 showed, they are not without precedent. They stand in the tradition of the New Testament and of missional expressions of church through history. They represent a serious attempt to engage with the contemporary missional context.

Part 2 proposed a theological rationale for these new churches. However unconventional, new expressions of Christian community can be understood to be church so long as they are engaged in the four interlocking sets of relationships that constitute the church – with God, the world, the living Christian tradition and within the gathering. Church is to be understood primarily not in terms of certain practices but as these four types of interconnected relationship.

Contextual churches are an expression of the mission of God. Mission is a first step for God and should always be a first step for the church. Wherever possible, mission should be undertaken in community. Churches in the multiple fragments of society are a form of communal mission. They allow believers to practise mission in their daily contexts not as individuals, but as Christians together.

These communities should be shaped by the context – they should be more like a bean bag than a chair – because God reveals himself through human contexts. This does not mean that anything goes. Faithfulness to Jesus is preserved by sitting under Scripture, drawing on the wisdom of the Christian tradition, listening to God through the spiritual gifts of the gathering, attending to the Spirit's activity in the world and using models of contextualization appropriately. Contextualization requires attention to a specific group of people. Churches that both emerge within a particular culture and are connected to the whole body reflect the New Testament pattern, embody God's will for creation, echo the dynamics of election, anticipate the new creation and safeguard justice.

Contextual churches correspond to the life of Jesus by nestling within a culture, by forming a community of disciples in the midst of everyday life, by suffering for the cause of mission, by joining Jesus in his transformation of centripetal into centrifugal mission and by anticipating his presence fully in every place. These characteristics of Jesus' life ricochet through the church's history, so that contextual churches are faithful not only to the founder of the tradition, but to the tradition itself.

As an outworking of this theological rationale, Part 3 suggested that bringing a church to birth should be seen as a church practice, with standards of excellence and a community of practitioners who teach, challenge and extend these standards. Central to this practice will be the birthing of church mainly through *a worship-first* or *a serving-first journey*. The latter is likely to become more common as the church increasingly serves people with little or no Christian background.

Through the Spirit, five groups of methodologies enable these *journeys*. Gathering mission communities requires attention to the identity voyages of the leader, potential members and of the community itself. Researching opportunities involves '360 degrees listening' – to God directly, the people the mission community is called to serve, the Christians the community represents and the wider church.

Engaging partners is enabled by the character of the founder, the 'venture narrative' and a variety of personalizing strategies. These in turn depend on kingdom virtues, especially humility, and social competence. Action-based learning uses planning as a process of learning, while team awareness involves attending carefully to the mission community's conversations, which set the tone of the nascent church.

Part 4 emphasized that pathways to maturity should be laid from the earliest stages. Making disciples involves connecting evangelism to life, walking with individuals on their 'postmodern' pilgrimages to faith and using communal resources to equip believers to go the extra mile in their ethical behaviour. The worship pathway includes missional worship, formational worship, contextual worship and worship that is not burdened with the weight of denominational identity. The community pathway includes hospitality, the exchange of gifts, dispersed forms of leadership, a distinctive engagement with life and the negotiation of differences about identity. Sustainability entails appropriate scale, indigenizing leadership, staying fresh, starting *a process* of reproduction (not just a church), and developing local and national strategies for reproducing church.

This chapter draws these threads together by pleading for contextual churches to be birthed within the mixed economy – Archbishop Rowan Williams's term for fresh expressions of church existing alongside inherited forms in relationships of mutual respect and support (Croft, 2008c, p. 5). The mixed economy contains the idea of bringing Christian communities to birth in different ways for different people, but as far as possible within the existing denominations and churches. Some prefer the phrase 'mixed ecology', which has a more organic ring.

Parts 1 to 4 can be seen as preparing the ground for answering: why the mixed economy? If contextual churches have precedents in the church's story and represent a response to today's missional situation, if they can be justified theologically, if bringing them to birth can be recognized as a church practice with clear, though provisional features and if we are beginning to understand what pathways to maturity might involve, a case can be made that they should be supported and encouraged by the inherited church.

Accordingly, the chapter starts by acknowledging critiques of the concept. It offers five theological arguments for the need to combine unity and diversity. The unity pole challenges those who start new contextual churches outside the denominations. The diversity pole challenges those who see little room for contextual churches within their denominations. In the light of these theological perspectives, the chapter responds to criticisms of the mixed economy idea and briefly suggests what the mixed economy might become.

Prophets, purists and pragmatists

The chapter assumes that the existing denominations, and networks such as Newfrontiers, cannot be discarded lightly. They reflect the Spirit's work, often over many years. They provide institutional and theological frameworks that help the local church connect to the church universal. They contain deposits of wisdom that enrich the wider body. While no denomination can grasp the whole of God, each has insights that fill out the picture. As they continue to be open to reformation in the light of Scripture, they remain living traditions. They evolve as they are led by the Spirit to adapt to new circumstances.

What's not to like?

From this standpoint, the mixed economy may seem a 'no brainer'. What is not to like in the idea of the old and the new existing harmoniously together within established denominations and networks? Unfortunately, it is not so straightforward. First, many contextual churches are coming to birth outside these structures. We do not have figures, but anecdotal evidence suggests that the proportion of these new churches could be significant in the UK and is much higher in the United States. Many founders of contextual church are voting with their feet.

Second, we know that in the past existing churches have not been very good at accommodating the new; the Church of England had no room for the Methodists. Third, despite gaining ground, the mixed economy ideal has yet to have substantial 'bite'. The denominations are still reluctant to fund new pioneering posts from their regular income. They say in effect, 'the mixed economy is a great idea, but don't expect us to shift resources into it.' Thus the mixed economy remains a concept that must be argued for. Fourth, critics have raised a number of objections, and these must be addressed.

Three types of critique

One group of critics, 'prophets', fears that the denominations will stifle new forms of church. Pete Rollins, for instance, believes that a variety of 'emerging groups' challenge the ecclesial structures of the mainline churches 'at their very core'. They are showing how the radical message of Christianity speaks to the church itself. The 'framework that the institutional church affirms is one that cannot be embraced by many of these emerging groups without them losing something substantive about their message' (Rollins, 2008, p. 75). Staying within the denominations would compromise the prophetic voice of these groups.

'Purists' worry about a watering down of the structures and practices they value in the church. For example, Davison and Milbank see fresh expressions as 'independent entities without any relation to the parish in which they operate . . . If Fresh Expressions is as equally valid a form of life for the Anglican Church as the parish, then what is common to both forms, the defining minimum of our identity, is greatly contracted' (Davison and Milbank, 2010, pp. vii–viii). Clearing space for very different-looking congregations becomes a challenge to the Church of England's self-understanding, as they perceive it.

Their book reflects the view of many Anglicans that the weekday activities of the parish church flow out of its Sunday eucharistic life. Activities that might be described as fresh expressions make ecclesial sense only if they are understood in that framework. They cannot be seen as churches in their own right. The practice of the Eucharist, the Church of England liturgical tradition and an authority structure of bishops, priests and deacons appear to constitute the core of what it means to be Anglican. This exemplifies an approach to denominational identity based on practices and church order. It is what we do and how we organize it that makes us who we are. This identity puts boundaries round acceptable innovation.

'Pragmatists' come to the mixed economy with practical questions. Some wonder whether traditional attitudes are sufficiently flexible to embrace the new. Can church structures adapt quickly enough? Others are concerned about diverting scarce resources into unproven experiments, weakening the existing church. They worry about how fresh expressions will be held to account, and whether pioneers really are committed to their sponsoring denominations. If they are not, 'how will the much vaunted "mixed economy" remain a single economy?' (Avis, 2005, p. 56)

Others again fear that all the emphasis on newness underestimates the resilience of 'inherited church'. As a supporter of fresh expressions, Robin Gamble pleads that 'it's about time we realized that there is still bags of mission, passion, energy and creativity left in "mother church"' (Gamble, 2008, p. 17). He points out that enthusiasm for the new may leave inherited church and its leaders feeling 'a bit neglected, slightly derided and rather like yesterday's model' (p. 16).

Five theological lenses

The mixed economy is about different pockets in the same pair of trousers. Unity and diversity flourish within the same denomination or local church. A collage of five rationales is offered here as a theological basis for the mixed economy.

A Trinitarian perspective

Aware of the suspicion of some postmodern writers that community can be a means of suppressing diversity, John Zizioulas asks how the one can avoid being submerged by the many. In *Communion and Otherness* he argues that God is not initially one and then three. He is both one and three simultaneously. 'Otherness, the Trinity, is built into the very oneness of divine being' (Zizioulas, 2006, p. 10).

Unity in the Godhead is not based on similarity, for the three persons are essentially different while remaining one. This is a difference not of qualities such as omniscience and omnipotence, for such qualities are common to all three. Difference in the Trinity derives from the relationships between the persons.

The Father would not be the Father if he did not relate to the second person as Father to Son. The Son would not be the Son if he did not have a Son-to-Father relationship with the first person. The Spirit relates to the Father in the mode of processing – of going out.[1] Zizioulas says that 'otherness is inconceivable apart from *relationship*. Father, Son and Spirit are all names indicating relationship. No person can be different unless he is related. Communion does not threaten otherness; it generates it' (2006, p. 5; author's italics).

If otherness and difference are fundamental to and constitutive of the Godhead, on what is the unity of the Trinity based? Zizioulas, from his Eastern Orthodox perspective, argues that it is based on the Father, who eternally causes the other two persons to exist as particular beings, to be whom they are in their unique identities (2006, pp. 113–54). Recent Western theologians, on the other hand, have tended to attribute the unity of the three persons to their interrelationships.

---

1 Western theologians have traditionally said, of course, that the Spirit relates to the Father *and Son* in the mode of processing.

Colin Gunton for example draws on the Fourth Gospel's language of mutual indwelling between the Father and Son to provide a 'conception of relatedness without absorption' (Gunton, 1993, p. 205). In a similar vein to Zizioulas, he speaks of the Godhead as 'shared being: the persons do not simply enter into relations with one another, but are constituted by one another in the relations. Father, Son and Spirit are eternally what they are by virtue of what they are from and to one another' (p. 214). However, unlike Zizioulas, for Gunton the Son and the Spirit are not constituted by the Father, but by all their Trinitarian relations. God is not a 'collectivity' nor an individual, but 'a unity of persons in relation' (p. 215).

In Gunton's perspective, the Trinity becomes not a model for us to copy (we look at the outline and fill in the details), but a life in which we participate. The Trinity is so committed to diversity that it opens itself to others. The Spirit brings us into the conversation of the Godhead. We are enabled to shape our relationships so that they start to echo the respect for difference and the oneness that epitomize God's own relationships.

A mixed-economy church will take its stand from the Trinity. It will recognize that difference is fundamental to its being. A denomination or network will be most like God when diversity and unity are combined. This does not in itself answer the question of how much difference is appropriate. But it does, perhaps, encourage a direction of travel: how can the denomination journey toward catholicity and oneness? How can its missional vocation prize open its inherited life to embrace converts who may see the church differently? How can those in control open up the denomination to those whom God might be calling to change it?

A creation perspective

Creation echoes the Trinity. Quoting John Macquarrie, Paul Fiddes points out that God's purpose in creation is the making of finite beings who can imitate their creator in the power of letting others be themselves. In giving freedom to creation while remaining involved in it, God has moved out from unity (retaining control) to diversity (allowing autonomy). 'With Macquarrie we must affirm that "the highest love is not the drive toward union, but rather letting-be"' (Fiddes, 1988, p. 108).

Francis and Richter have offered a vision for diversity and unity in the church based on a strong doctrine of creation. Genesis 1.27 recounts the creation of male and female in God's image. Being created male and female implies fundamental difference, and it is this *diversity* that reflects the divine image (Francis and Richter, 2007, p. 305). Diversity is expressed through the difference of gender, and this should be understood as a metaphor for other human differences coexisting within the unity of creation.

Francis and Richter suggest that we read Genesis 1.27 alongside Galatians 3.28: 'There is neither Jew nor Greek, slave nor free, male nor female, for you are all one in Christ Jesus.' Here Paul expands individual differences from the gender difference of Genesis 1.27 to ethnicity ('neither Jew nor Greek') and circumstances of life ('neither slave nor free'). Paul is not saying that Christ obliterates differences. After all, much of Paul's life was spent fighting for the right of Greek converts not to become Jews. He is claiming that Christ makes it possible for these differences to coexist with unity. Christ can bring about the unity with diversity envisaged at creation.

Just as Paul has extended the Genesis idea of difference, so – Francis and Richter argue – it is legitimate to extend the notion further. It includes all those fundamental personality differences that characterize the normal human population. In Christ all differences can be held together in unity. A church that takes this truth seriously will clear space for diversity.

On this basis the authors plea for a 'multiplex church', in which seekers after the kingdom will be able to enter 'through many different doors and celebrate their participation within the kingdom of God in many different ways' (Francis and Richter, 2007, p. 308). As well as many front doors, there will be many back doors leading into different expressions of church. As people develop and change, they will not be forced to leave church because they no longer feel at home in their congregation. Back doors will open the way to different congregations, where there will be new opportunities for giving and commitment. Church-switching (not to be undertaken lightly) can replace church-leaving.

Multiplex church does not describe a building.

> First and foremost, it is a new mindset that encourages churches to play to their strengths and to be aware of the niche markets for which they can, and cannot, cater. It encourages churches in a given locality to think of each other not as competitors but as collaborators, referring potential church-leavers on to other partner churches who can better meet their needs' – and, one might add, better create opportunities for Christian service. (Francis and Richter, 2007, p. 309)

Though Francis and Richter are discussing church leavers, their vision speaks to contextual communities serving people outside the church. It suggests what the ecclesial practice of diversity might involve. It invites 'purists' and 'pragmatists' to consider the price of failing to expand the diversity of the church through mission. Might the risk of switching resources to mission be outweighed by the danger that, over time, failing to do so will render the denomination too narrow to connect to people outside it? Might a risk-averse approach – 'let's not threaten the existing church' – be the very thing that endangers the denomination? As it decreasingly reflects the composition of society, might the denomination become less and less able to serve society?

A New Testament perspective

Loveday Alexander provides a New Testament rationale for the mixed economy. She maintains that Luke's vision of the church 'encompasses all the tensions inherent in the fresh expressions story – tensions between centre and periphery, between charisma and order, between "liquid church" and "solid church" – and refuses to allow us to be content with either end of the bi-polar division' (Alexander, 2008, p. 142). She sees a pattern of going out and referring back that is like the 'double helix' of the human genome.

Peter goes out to Cornelius and discovers what God is doing on the margins. He 'could have stayed there, doing his own thing, enjoying being a pioneer. But he doesn't. Something makes him go back to report on his actions to the folks back home – and face a very negative reaction.' (Alexander, 2008, p. 143) There follows a debate about the relationship between, in today's language, fresh expressions and traditional structures, during which the centre discovers the value of listening in order to hear what God is doing on the margins of the church (Acts 11.18). Peter also discovers something. In taking the risk of returning to the centre and submitting his experience to a process of shared discernment, he gains fuller insight into the significance of what has happened (Acts 11.16).

The founding of the Antioch church can be seen as a classic fresh expression, and the Jerusalem church responds by sending Barnabas to investigate (Acts 11.9–14). Through his gifts of discernment and encouragement, Barnabas helps the new community, while actively keeping links with the mother church (Acts 11.27–30; 12.24–5). The process of going out and reporting back is then repeated. The Antioch church sends out its own missionaries (Acts 13.1–3), and Paul and Barnabas later return home to describe what has happened (Acts 14. 26–8).

Although Antioch is now acting on its own initiative, fellowship with Jerusalem remains important. A 'hard-line directive' (implied by Acts 15.24) threatens the inclusive multicultural community created at Antioch. 'Again, it would have been easy for the fresh expression to go it alone, secure in its own conviction of the Spirit's leading.' (Alexander, 2008, p. 144) Instead, Paul and Barnabas 'take the risky step' of coming back to Jerusalem for a process of mutual discernment (Acts 15.5–18). Far from abandoning the old centre, 'the Spirit is part of the process of discernment (15.28), allowing the whole Church to move forward in a shared and costly commitment to catholicity' (p. 144).

Though beyond the scope of Alexander's chapter, this same going out and referring back occurs when Paul establishes a new mission centre at Ephesus. Epaphras, who was a native of Colossae (Col. 4. 12) and was most likely converted through Paul's preaching at Ephesus (cf Acts 19.10), returns to Colossae and evangelizes the region (Col. 1.7). When the faith of the new believers came under threat, he reports back to Paul. The apostle, who is in prison (possibly in Ephesus), responds – assuming he is the author – by writing to the Colossians. Paul himself continues to refer back to Antioch and Jerusalem (Acts 18.22; 21.17–26).

There is a pattern: led by the Spirit, pioneers go out and start new churches, sometimes in ways that the initiating centre does not expect. They report back to the centre what God is doing, and there follows a process of listening and shared discernment. The centre then blesses the initiative, puts fairly loose boundaries round it, such as the apostolic decree in Acts 15, and the work continues into its next phase, allowing new centres to emerge.

This is not an easy process. Vital to it is the centre's willingness to listen to those on the missional edge and be challenged by what they hear. Just as the Jewish believers were required to rethink fundamentally their understanding of what it meant to be a believing community, might new contextual churches be making similar demands of denominational purists? Equally, just as Peter and Paul returned to Jerusalem and dialogued with the leaders there, might God be summoning today's 'prophets' on the edge to come back to and engage in debate with the centre? There was plenty of heartache and struggle as the first Christians sought to discern what the Spirit was saying, but through it all the centre and edge remain in fellowship – a model of the mixed economy.

A sacramental perspective

Catholicity and unity are two means by which the church is a sacrament – a sign to the world of all cultures in their diversity being made one in Jesus. When the church's mission bears fruit this sign is strengthened. The church becomes more catholic by embracing a wider range of cultures, while also – through its relationships – bearing witness to the unity of all in Christ. Catholicity and unity, therefore, should not be pitched against each other, as sometimes happens: adding to the church's diversity is resisted out of fear it will threaten unity, or the demands of unity are subordinated to the pursuit of diversity. Both are equally important. Catholicity and unity are a sign together.

The sign is enacted in baptism. As individuals with their distinctive characteristics are baptized into Christ's body, the church visibly becomes more diverse. But this diversity combines with unity, symbolized through the use of names in the baptismal liturgy. The candidate is named (not given a name) as an acknowledgement of his or her uniqueness, and is then baptized in the name of the Father, the Son and the Holy Spirit. Different people are admitted to God's one family.

In Holy Communion, we celebrate this same unity and diversity. The church fathers spoke of the many grains that make up the one bread, and the many grapes that intermingle to form the one drink. Often for the fathers the grains and the grapes represent many people being united. Sometimes they have the idea of the scattered church being made one. But at times they symbolize differences being held together. Cyril of Alexandria wrote, 'Divided as it were into distinct personalities by which one is Peter or John or Thomas or Matthew, we are, so to say, molded into one sole body in Christ, feeding on one flesh alone' (quoted by De Lubac, 1988, p. 91).

Holy Communion is a sacrament of reconciliation. It not only brings people together, but witnesses to the fact. It demonstrates how people who are different – not just in their gender, age, background and interests, but also in their opinions – are joined to each other in Christ. When various churches within a denomination assemble round the Lord's Table, the fewer the differences among those who participate, the weaker will be the proclamation of reconciliation. The greater the diversity, on the other hand, the louder will be the sound of unity.

A prophetic perspective

The mixed economy has particular value when the church is understood from a prophetic angle. In his 'practical-prophetic' theology of the church, Healy rejects 'epic theologies' that step out of the drama to take an external, spectator's perspective on the completed play, the story of the church. This would be unrealistic because we cannot discern, more than in a glass darkly, the shape of the church at the end of the play. Nor can we imagine how the church should respond perfectly to all those future contexts we cannot now anticipate (Healy, 2000, p. 74).

Drawing on Hans Urs von Balthasar, he argues instead for a 'dramatic theology' that 'takes the perspective of a participant in the drama, of one who lives entirely within the movement of the play' (Healy, 2000, pp. 53–4). Participants do not know the script of the 'theodrama', the detailed unfolding of history between now and Christ's return, which means that their understanding is always provisional. The future will reveal more. As a result, 'ecclesial life takes the form of grand, never-ending experiment. If we are to play our evolving roles as we should, we should engage in ongoing self-critical evaluation of our ecclesial thought and action – i.e., practical-prophetic ecclesiology' (p. 75).

In the messiness of fallen people and a flawed church, conflict in the Christian community is to be expected. It should not be avoided by an enforced unity for it may frequently be fruitful. 'The church can be understood within a theodramatic horizon as the *locus* and embodiment of a set of ongoing arguments about how best to witness to Jesus Christ and to follow him in true discipleship' (Healy, 2000, p. 70). 'To repeat: truth is discerned through engagement with those who are other than "we" are: with the Spirit, with those Christians with whom we disagree; and with those outside the church' (p. 170). The church must therefore make space for 'solitary or minority forms of prophetic discipleship' (p. 72).

Thus within the mixed economy, encouraging communities of people from outside the church will create space for converts to bring new insights into the body. Conflict will be inevitable. Yet it is through engaging with these differences that the church will better understand its Lord, its mission and itself. The mixed economy becomes vital as the arena in which these disputes occur within relationships of love. As Rowan Williams puts it, 'The Church's work of judgement, its critical role in the world, is a nonsense (or worse) if criticism is not built into its own life and structures' (Williams, 1982, p. 53).

Five rationales for the mixed economy

- The Trinity models unity and diversity.
- God built unity and diversity into creation, including humanity.
- In the early church, the centre and the edge were in relationship with each other.
- Unity and diversity, celebrated in baptism and Holy Communion, are a sign to the world.
- Conflict in the church can be part of the process of discernment.

Responding to prophets, pragmatists and purists

These theological perspectives create foundations for a response to some of the concerns about the mixed economy.

Prophets

To the 'prophets' who believe that new contextual churches challenge the denominations, Healy's argument calls for these prophets to remain within. As a denomination navigates the conflicts these prophetic voices provoke, its real work of discernment begins. But will this work take place, will denominations heed prophetic challenges if the latter are presented from outside? The very methodology of contextual church argues for a staying in: you cannot speak the gospel *at* a culture, only from *within* the culture. Likewise, despite the historical exceptions, it can be less effective to be prophetic *at* the existing churches than to speak from *within* them. Is this why Old and New Testament prophets are always inside the people of God?

In 2002, Rowan Williams reviewed a book by the theologian Richard Roberts, who called for a distancing of new ecclesial activities from religious tradition and institutions in favour of looser, postmodern relationships (Roberts, 2002). Williams's counter arguments would apply to church founders tempted to leave the denominations. The latter contain traditions

441

steeped in prayer that can resource challenges to the consumerist assumptions of today's world. Will entrepreneurial communities outside the Christian mainstream have enough cultural capital to sustain their witness to society? And will they have real accountability? (Hobson, 2005, p. 91; Williams, 2002)

The logic of Healy's argument of course turns this last point on its head. If the denominations are to be communities of self-criticism, they need contextual churches to be among those holding *them* to account. Yet how can contextual churches do this if they are not involved in denominational structures? The mixed economy makes accountability two-way.

Purists

To the 'purists' worried about identity, the response is perhaps fourfold. First, how is identity understood? If it is tied to practices and structures, the denomination's identity will inevitably be at stake when new types of church with different practices emerge. But this is not the only way to conceive of identity. In writing about personal identity, Paul Ricœur says that it is the identity of the narrative that makes the identity of the character.[2] This applies as much to denominations and established networks as to individuals. The story links disparate practices (and persons) together. It gives them an overall meaning, which is the story's plot. It describes change over time. It places each denomination in a wider context, providing a reminder that denominational identities are not formed in isolation but in dialogue with other agents in society ('this is why we are not you').

Not least, narrative identity leaves room for conflict, including disagreements about identity. Much of the Church of England's story, for example, could be written in terms of disputes over identity. Seeing identity as story creates space for difference. To be a member of a denomination does not require you to agree with its current rules: you can belong because you identify with its narrative. Those who challenge the centre can be as much part of the denomination, provided they can see themselves in its story, as those who champion the centre.

The key question for 'purists', therefore, is what place diversity and unity have in the story they want to tell about the denomination. The more central the place of diversity alongside unity, the easier the denomination will find it to welcome new contextual churches. Might the five theological lenses on catholicity and oneness – the Trinity, creation, the early church, the sacraments and the church's prophetic role – encourage 'purists' to attach a higher value to diversity?

---

2 Paul Ricœur, *Oneself as Another*, trans. Kathleen Blamey, Chicago: University of Chicago Press, 1992 (1990), pp. 147–8, quoted in 'Paul Ricœur', *Stanford Encyclopedia of Philosophy*, www.plato.stanford.edu/ricoeur/entries/#3.4.

Second, Healy's 'practical–prophetic' theology reminds us that disagreement is very much part of the church's life. As Chapter 5 maintained, the church can be viewed as a debate over practices and structures. The church is fundamentally four sets of interlocking relationships. Maturity involves growth toward the kingdom within these relationships. If this is the case, unity will best be preserved not by seeking to limit diversity, but by attending to the quality of the conversations that diversity gives rise to. A denomination bears witness to the kingdom by the manner in which its differences are discussed.

Third, the forbearance of the Spirit provides a resource for handling these differences. In a meditation on some of the writings of early twentieth-century Russian Orthodox theologians, Williams highlights the patience of the Spirit. The Spirit teaches, warns and urges believers to follow a path of Christ-likeness. But when believers pursue a different course, the Spirit remains with, and open to them. 'The Holy Spirit is present in self-emptying and in patience – in self-forgetting – by being there alongside our fallibility, not overcoming it, not taking it over and ironing it out' (Williams, 2008a, p. 29).

In the mixed economy, Christians will have to live – sometimes painfully – with their differences. Having encouraged and exhorted one another, there may come a point when differences cannot be bridged. We must then entrust our differences to the Spirit of forbearance and stay in patient fellowship with each other, just as the Spirit walks with us. In so doing, the church reveals the goal of the kingdom, which is the restoration of all relationships in Christ.

Fourth, given our human frailty, there will be times when identities are perceived to be so different that they cannot be housed under the same denominational roof. Maybe a new contextual church cannot identify with a denomination's story, and despite strenuous efforts give-and-take fails to bridge the gap. We may wish that this was not the case, but the fallibility of our human structures mean that God's desire for unity and diversity is not always accomplished within them.

When denominations are unable to embrace diversity, the church's witness is weakened. This can be mitigated when different denominations and networks listen attentively to one another, seek to discern the Spirit in each other and maintain fellowship across their disagreements. A parting of the ways, therefore, may mean that instead of greater diversity and unity existing within one particular ecclesial stream, mixed economy values will extend to ecumenical relationships.

Pragmatists

To the 'pragmatists' who ask whether the mixed economy can be made to work, the answer is that for theological reasons the attempt should be a priority. When, through mission the church expands in diversity while re-taining its unity, it becomes more like the Trinity, it remains faithful to God's purposes in creation, it follows a pattern established by the very first Christians, it is authentic to what it celebrates in the sacraments and it takes seriously the task of becoming self-critical before being critical of the world.

Commitment to these values means more than paying lip service to the mixed economy. It means putting resources into it, making time for it and going out of one's way to help new types of church to emerge. If the mixed economy is part of what it means to be authentic church, making sacrifices so that the new can join the old, without either smothering the other, will be a sign of ecclesial integrity.

This is not easy because there are risks involved. Healy's pragmatic, experimental approach reminds us that, as participants within the drama, we may anticipate some of the problems but we cannot know in advance all of the answers. There has to be a trusting walk with the Spirit, often a groping toward the next step. Uncertainty about whether the path is feasible will be intrinsic to the journey. Pragmatists are understandably concerned about this uncertainty. If some resources are shifted from inherited to new forms of church, what happens if the new initiatives prove unfruitful? Will inherited church be weakened without a compensating gain?

The question is posed in terms of practical wisdom. But this wisdom must be balanced by faithfulness to the church's vocation. The church is called to grow, through mission, in diversity with unity. If this call is to be heeded, some risks will have to be taken. Risk is what it means to act in faith. The question becomes not how to avoid risk, but how to take risks for mission and for catholicity in a sensible way.

As Part 3 and Part 4 showed, taking these risks need not be foolhardy. Fruitful methodologies for contextual church are beginning to be developed. As denominations keep learning from experience, the practice of contextual church can be based on steadily greater understanding of what is likely to work. The more denominations gain experience and share what they learn, the more the church's understanding will grow. Conversely, of course, if the church does not try new things, it will never learn.

New Song Cafe in Warrington, Cheshire, meets monthly, attracting up to 125 worshippers, about a third of whom see this as their church. Between meetings, discipleship evenings attract 18 to 25 people. The initiative is developing into a network of churches, with a pub church and New Song Breakfast, which links to Latchford Methodist Church's traditional Holy Communion. The network has taken a deliberate decision to stay under the authority of Bold Street Methodist Church, who see their own future as being more secure as a result.

In a similar vein, Tas Valley Cell Church in South Norfolk has cells containing 50 adults, about half of whom would regard these cells as their church. (The other 25 also attend a Sunday congregation.) An additional 25 young people are in youth cells; about two-thirds would describe the cells as church for them. There is a growing cross-over with the long-established Sunday congregations, and the leaders encourage this mixing and supporting of each other. The cells and the congregations get together three times a year. These are examples of how the mixed economy, far from weakening existing church, is proving a source of strength.[3]

Questions for

- prophets: how will your voices be heard if you speak from outside the denominations?
- purists: is a denomination's call to diversity with unity best served by an identity based on practices and structures or on the denomination's story?
- pragmatists: if the goal of greater catholicity involves some risk, what arrangements will encourage the taking of sensible risks?

What can we hope for?

If the mixed economy proves resilient and flourishes, what might we hope and pray for? Anticipating the future is always dangerous, but as more diverse shapes of church emerge within the denominations, we are likely to see – as is beginning to happen – a growing variety of 'orders' and fellowships among these new churches.

By embracing churches with a similar outlook, these networks will offer support to church founders, and in time organize events and prepare resources for people who are coming, or have come to faith. In a post-denominational climate, a weakening of denominational ties is likely as individual churches increasingly identify with their network. Some in the denominations may regret this. But if networks of the like-minded allow gatherings space to grow and feel secure in their identities, members of denominations with different perspectives may find it easier to get along.

Of course, the networks could draw away and fracture the denominations. On the other hand, because contemporary people own a variety of identities, increasingly combine alternatives rather than choose between them, like to be part of a bigger whole and share a nostalgic mood that is not unreceptive to church tradition, the denominations may succeed in holding diverse streams together. Add in their institutional resources, and it is far from clear that the denominations have had their day.

---

3 Both stories are told at www.freshexpressions.org.uk/stories.

It is not difficult to imagine individuals coming to faith within a contextual church, identifying with the church and its network, and having some affiliation also with the denomination. This and earlier chapters have quoted examples of the old and new not just sitting alongside each other, but enriching one another – a traditional service of compline for Goth young people, a heavy-metal congregation meeting monthly with a nearby Anglo-Catholic church and New Song Cafe, Warrington deciding to stay within its Methodist circuit.

The prospect is not of contextual churches growing more like inherited church, as some may hope, nor traditional churches rushing to become something new. It is more likely that churches will bless each other *because of* their diversity. In the process, all concerned are bound to experience a change. The denomination will be different when new types of church contribute to its life. New churches will evolve as they are enriched by the denomination's story. Such mutual giving and receiving is at the heart of church life and of God himself. It is central to the promise of the mixed economy.

This exchange of gifts may also happen when new and older churches work together in an area. Though the mixed economy is about relations between emerging and inherited churches within the denominations, the idea can obviously be extended to geographical cooperation. So our prayerful hopes for the future can include greater collaboration between regional and local churches for mission and discipleship. Those who come into the faith would experience a rich ecclesial life and help to bridge social divides.

We can pray therefore that, aided by improving communications and the mosaic nature of people's lives, interactions between all kinds of churches will increase, that through these relationships the wealth of the tradition will be offered to new believers while the latter will bring their gifts to the tradition, and that the whole church will be strengthened and better equipped for its mission of service, witness and making disciples.

As Christian communities multiply in every context, the church will connect more closely to believers' everyday lives, its service to the world will be tailored more precisely to the needs of different settings and its presence will become more visible to the world at large. Instead of trying to bring change by seizing the commanding heights of power and influence, the Christendom model, the church will follow Jesus into the crevices of society. It will become a subversive influence from within.

Jesus first appears in John's Gospel in a crisis of ordinary life. The location is a village set among the Galilean peasantry, whose economic situation was at best precarious. In contrast to the ordinary people's limited resources, Jesus miraculously produces 180 gallons of wine! It is a symbolic announcement that amid the straitened conditions of everyday existence, he has come to give a profusion of life. As they serve the people round them, churches in every context enact a similar declaration. Through the Spirit, the abundance of Jesus can be available to all.

Further reading

Healy, Nicholas M., *Church, World and the Christian Life: Practical–Prophetic Ecclesiology*, Cambridge: Cambridge University Press, 2000.

Nelstrop, Louise and Martyn Percy (eds), *Evaluating Fresh Expressions: Explorations in Emerging Church*, Norwich: Canterbury Press, 2008, pp. 27–39.

Williams, Rowan, *A Margin of Silence: The Holy Spirit in Russian Orthodox Theology*, Quebec: Editions du Lys Vert, 2008.

Questions for discussion

- How much diversity of church practice can the denomination or network you know best tolerate? What factors aid or hinder this tolerance?
- How would you persuade sceptics in your denomination to provide more support for the mixed economy?
- How well are founders of contextual church providing prophetic critiques of existing church? What are the marks of an effective prophet-pioneer?

Bibliography

A Mixed Economy for Mission – the Journey so Far: Mission-shaped Church: Follow Up, Church of England, GS 1761, 2010.

Abraham, William, *The Logic of Evangelism*, London: Hodder & Stoughton, 1989.

Adams, Ian, 'Cave, Refectory, Road: The Monastic Life Shaping Community and Mission', in Graham Cray, Ian Mobsby & Aaron Kennedy (eds), *New Monasticism as Fresh Expression of Church*, Norwich: Canterbury Press, 2010, pp. 37–49.

Addison, Steve, *Movements That Change the World: Five Keys to Spreading the Gospel*, Downers Grove: InterVarsity Press, 2011 [2009].

Aldrich, Howard E., 'Facilitating a Rational Process Model of Entrepreneurial Team Formation through Designing Effective Social Networks', Paper prepared for the FSF Conference, September, 2008.

Alexander, Loveday, 'What patterns of church and mission are found in the Acts of the Apostles?', in Steven Croft (ed.), *Mission-shaped Questions. Defining Issues for Today's Church*, London: Church House Publishing, 2008, pp. 133–45.

Allen, Roland, *Missionary Methods – St Paul's or Ours?*, Cambridge: Lutterworth Press, 2006 [1912].

Allen, Roland, *The Spontaneous Expansion of the Church and the Causes which Hinder it*, Eugene: Wipf & Stock, 1997 [1927].

Amin, Ash, 'Post-Fordism: Models, Fantasies and Phantoms of Transition', in Ash Amin (ed.), *Post-Fordism: A Reader*, Oxford: Blackwell, 1994.

Anderson, Bernhard, 'The Babel Story: Paradigm of Human Unity and Diversity', in Andrew Greely (ed.), *Ethnicity*, New York: Seabury, 1977, pp. 63–70.

Anderson, Ray S., *An Emergent Theology for Emerging Churches*, Oxford: Bible Reading Fellowship, 2007.

Are We Yet Alive?, London: The Methodist Church, 2011.

Arias, Mortimer, 'Centripetal Mission, or Evangelization by Hospitality', in Paul W. Chilcote & Laceye C. Warner (eds), *The Study of Evangelism: Exploring a Missional Practice of the Church*, Grand Rapids, Eerdmans, 2008, pp. 424–35.

Aritzeta, Aitor, Stephen Swailes & Barbara Senior, 'Team Roles: Psychometric Evidence, Construct Validity and Team Building', *Research Memorandum* 51, 2005, Centre for Management and Organisational Learning, University of Hull.

Ashworth, Jacinta, Research Matters and Ian Farthing, *Churchgoing in the UK: A Research Report from Tearfund on Church Attendance in the UK*, Teddington: Tearfund, 2007, available on www.tearfund.org.

Atkins, Martyn, *Resourcing Renewal: Shaping Churches for the Emerging Future*, Peterborough: Inspire, 2007.

Atkins, Martyn, 'What is the essence of the Church?', in Steven Croft (ed.), *Mission-shaped Questions. Defining Issues for Today's Church*, London: Church House Publishing, 2008, pp. 16–28.

Audretsch, David B. & Max Keilbach, 'Does Entrepreneurship Capital Matter?', *Entrepreneurship Theory and Practice* 28 (5), 2004, pp. 419–29.

Avis, Paul, review of *Mission-shaped Church* in *Modern Believing* 46 (2), 2005, pp. 53–6.

Avis, Paul, *Reshaping Ecumenical Theology: The Church Made Whole?*, London: T & T Clark, 2010.

Avis, Paul (ed.), *The Journey of Christian Initiation: Theological and Pastoral Perspectives*, London: Church House Publishing, 2011.

Baez, Bien & Mitchel Y. Abolafia, 'Bureaucratic Entrepreneurship and Institutional Change: A Sense-Making Approach', *Journal of Public Administration Research and Theory* 12 (4), 2002, pp. 525–52.

Baillie, John, *Invitation to Pilgrimage*, London: Pelican, 1960 [1942].

Baker, Jonny, *Curating Worship*, London: SPCK, 2010.

Ballard, Paul & John Pritchard, *Practical Theology in Action*, 2nd edition, London: SPCK, 2006.

Banks, Robert, *Paul's Idea of Community: The Early House Churches in their Historical Setting*, Exeter: Paternoster, 1980.

Baron, Robert A. & Gideon D. Markman, 'Beyond Social Capital: the Role of Social Entrepreneurs' Social Competence in their Financial Success', *Journal of Business Venturing* 18 (1), 2003, pp. 41–60.

Baron, Robert S., *Group Process, Group Decision, Group Action*, 2nd edition, Buckingham: Open University Press, 2003 [1992].

Baron, Robert S. & Norbert L. Kerr, *Group Process, Group Decision, Group Action*, 2nd Edition, Buckingham: Open University Press, 2003 [1992.]

Barth, Karl, *Church Dogmatics*, IV/3.2, Edinburgh: T & T Clark, 1961.

Barton, John, *Reading the Old Testament: Method in Biblical Study*. 2nd ed., London: Darton, Longman & Todd, 1996.

Barton, Stephen, C., 'Paul as Missionary and Pastor', in James D. G. Dunn (ed.), *The Cambridge Companion to St Paul*, Cambridge: Cambridge University Press, 2003, pp. 34–48.

Baucum, Tory K., *Evangelical Hospitality: Catechetical Evangelism in the Early Church and Its Recovery for Today*, Plymouth, UK: The Scarecrow Press, 2008.

Bauckham, Richard J., *Moltmann: Messianic Theology in the Making*, Basingstoke: Marshall Pickering, 1987.

Bauckham, Richard J., *The Theology of Jurgen Moltmann*, London: T & T Clark, 1995.

Bauckham, Richard, 'The First Pioneers: Learning from the Acts of the Apostles', in Dave Male (ed), *Pioneers 4 Life. Explorations in Theology and Wisdom for Pioneering Leaders*, Abingdon: Bible Reading Fellowship, 2011, pp. 196–210.

Bauman, Zygmunt, *Community: Seeking Safety in an Insecure World*, London: Polity, 2001.

Baumgarten, A. I., 'The Name of the Pharisees', *Journal of Biblical Literature* 102 (3), pp. 411–28.

Bede, *Ecclesiastical History of the English People*, London: Penguin Books, 1990.

Becker, Jürgen, *Paul: Apostle to the Gentiles*, Louisville: Westminster John Knox, 1993.

Belbin, R. Meredith, *Management Teams: Why They Succeed or Fail*, Oxford: Butterworth-Heinemann, 1981.

Berry, Mark, 'New Monasticism and Engagement with Spiritual Seekers', in Graham Cray, Ian Mobsby and Aaron Kennedy, *New Monasticism as Fresh Expression of Church*, Norwich, Canterbury Press, 2010, pp. 56–66.

Bevans, Stephen B., 'God Inside Out: Toward a Missionary Theology of the Holy Spirit', *International Bulletin of Missionary Research* 22 (3), 1998, pp. 102–5.

Bevans, Stephen B., 'Letting Go and Speaking Out: A Spirituality of Inculturation', in Stephen Bevans, Eleanor Droidge & Robert Schreiter (eds), *The Healing Circle: Essays in Cross-Cultural Mission Presented to The Rev. Dr. Claude Marie Barbour*, Chicago: CCGM Publications, 1999, pp. 133–46.

Bevans, Stephen B., *Models of Contextual Theology*, revised edition, Maryknoll: Orbis, 2002.

Bevans, Stephen B., 'Ecclesiology since Vatican II: From a Church with a Mission to a Missionary Church', *Verbum SVD* 46 (1), 2005, pp. 27–56.

Bevans, Stephen B. & Roger P. Schroeder, *Constants in Context: A Theology of Mission for Today*, Maryknoll: Orbis, 2004.

Bhide, Amar, 'How Entrepreneurs Craft Strategies That Work', in *Harvard Business Review on Entrepreneurship*, Boston: Harvard Business Review, 1999, pp. 57–88.

Bird, Michael F., 'Jesus and the Gentiles after Jeremias: Patterns and Prospects', *Currents in Biblical Research* 4 (1), 2005, pp. 83–108.

Bird, Michael F., *Crossing over Sea and Land: Jewish Missionary Activity in the Second Temple Period*, Peabody: Hendrickson, 2010.

Bissonnette, Victor L., Caryl E. Rusbult & Shelley D. Kilpatrick, 'Empathic Accuracy and Marital Conflict Resolution', in William Ickes (ed.), *Empathic Accuracy*, New York: Guildford Press, 1997, pp. 251–81.

Blatt, Ruth, 'Tough Love: How Communal Schemas and Contracting Practices Build Relational Capital in Entrepreneurial Teams', *Academy of Management Review* 34 (3), 2009, pp. 533–51.

Blenkinsopp, Joseph, *Isaiah 40—55: A New Translation with Introduction and Commentary*, The Anchor Bible, New York: Doubleday, 2002.

Bliese, Richard, 'The Mission Matrix: Mapping Out the Complexities of a Missional Ecclesiology', *Word & World*, 26 (3) 2006, pp. 237–48.

Block, Zenas & Ian C. MacMillan, 'Milestones for Successful Venture Planning', in *Harvard Business Review on Entrepreneurship*, Boston: Harvard Business Review, 1999.

Bockmuehl, Markus, 'God's Life as a Jew: Remembering the Son of God as Son of David', in Beverly Roberts Gaventa & Richard B. Hays (eds), *Seeking the Identity of Jesus: A Pilgrimage*, Grand Rapids: Eerdmans, 2008, pp. 60–78.

Boff, Leonardo, *Ecclesiogenesis: The Base Communities Reinvent the Church*, Maryknoll: Orbis, 1986.

Boff, Leonardo, *Holy Trinity, Perfect Community*, Maryknoll, NY: 2000.

Bolger, Ryan, 'Following Jesus into Culture. Emerging Church as Social Movement', in Doug Pagitt & Tony Jones (eds), *An Emergent Manifesto of Hope*, Grand Rapids: Baker, 2007.

Bolton, Bill, *The Entrepreneur and the Church*, Cambridge: Grove Books, 2006.

Bolton, Bill & John Thompson, *Entrepreneurs: Talent, Temperament, Technique*, 2nd ed., Oxford: Elsevier, 2004 [2000].

Bonhoeffer, Dietrich, *Life Together*, tr. John W. Doberstein, London: SCM, 1954.

Bosch, David J., 'The Structure of Mission: An Exposition of Matthew 28:16–20', in Wilbert K. Shenk (ed.), *Exploring Church Growth*, Grand Rapids: Eerdmans, 1983, pp. 218–48.

Bosch, David J., *Transforming Mission: Paradigm Shifts in Theology of Mission*, Maryknoll, NY: Orbis, 1991.

Boud, David, Ruth Cohen & David Walker, *Using Experience for Learning*, Buckingham: Open University Press, 1993.

Bradley, Ian, *Colonies of Heaven: Celtic Christian Communities*, Kelowna, BC: Northstone Publishing, 2000.

Bradshaw, Paul F., *The Search for the Origins of Christian Worship*, second edition, Oxford: Oxford University Press, 2002.

Bradshaw, Paul F. *Reconstructing Early Christian Worship*, London: SPCK, 2009.

Breen, Mike & Alex Absalom, *Launching Missional Communities: A Field Guide*, 3DM, Kindle version, 2010.

Bretherton, Luke, *Christianity and Contemporary Politics: The Conditions and Possibilities of Faithful Witness*, Chichester: Wiley-Blackwell, 2010.

Bretherton, Luke, 'Pneumatology, Healing and Political Power: Sketching and Pentecostal Political Theology', in Jane Williams (ed.), *The Holy Spirit in the World Today*, London: Alpha International, 2011.

Brewin, Kester, *The Complex Christ. Signs of Emergence in the Urban Church*, London: SPCK, 2004.

Bridges, William, *Managing Transitions: Making the Most of Change*, Reading, MA: Perseus Books, 1991.

Brierley, Peter, *The Tide is Running Out: What the English Church Attendance Survey Reveals*, London: Christian Research, 2000.

Brierley, Peter, *Steps to the Future*, London: Christian Research & Scripture Union, 2000.

Brierley, Peter, *Pulling out of the Nosedive: A Contemporary Picture of Churchgoing*, London: Christian Research, 2006.

Brown, Callum, *The Death of Christian Britain: Understanding Secularisation, 1800–2000*, 2nd edition, Abingdon: Routledge, 2009 [2001].

Brown, David, 'The Political Role of the Church: The Form of a Servant', *International Review of Missions* 51 (203), 1962, pp. 265–71.

Brown, Raymond E & John P. Meier, *Antioch and Rome: New Testament Cradles of Catholic Christianity*, New York: Paulist Press, 1982.

Brown, Rupert, *Group Processes: Dynamics Within and Between Groups*, 2nd edition, Oxford: Blackwell, 2000 [1988].

Bruce, Steve, 'The Curious Case of the Unnecessary Recantation: Berger and Secularization', in Linda Woodhead with Paul Heelas & David Martin (eds), *Peter Berger and the Study of Religion*, London: Routledge, 2001, pp. 87–111.

Bruce, Steve, *God is Dead: Secularization in the West*, Oxford: Blackwell, 2002.

Brueggemann, Walter, *Biblical Perspectives on Evangelism: Living in a Three-Storied Universe*, Nashville: Abingdon, 1993.

Brueggemann, Walter, *A Social Reading of the Old Testament*, ed. Patrick D. Miller, Minneapolis: Fortress Press, 1994.

Brueggemann, Walter, *Theology of the Old Testament: Testimony, Dispute, Advocacy*, Minneapolis: Augsburg Fortress, 1997.

Buck, Ross & Benson Ginsburg, 'Communicative Genes and the Evolution of Empathy', in William Ickes (ed.), *Empathic Accuracy*, New York: Guildford Press, 1997, pp. 17–43.

Bulgakov, Sergius, *The Orthodox Church* (trans. Elizabeth S. Cram), London: Centenary Press, 1935.

Burdon, Christopher, 'Mark and the Formation of Community', in John Vincent (ed.), *Mark: Gospel of Action: Personal and Community Responses*, London: SPCK, 2006, pp. 176–87.

Burgess, Andrew, *The Ascension in Karl Barth*, Aldershot: Ashgate, 2004.

Bynum, Caroline Walker, 'Religious Women in the Later Middle Ages', in Jill Raitt, John Meyendorff, and Bernard McGinn (eds), *Christian Spirituality* Vol. II, *High Middle Ages and Reformation*, New York: Crossroad/Herder & Herder, 1989, pp. 121–39.

Cantalamessa, Raniero, *Come, Creator Spirit. Meditations on the* Veni Creator, Collegeville: The Liturgical Press, 2003.

Cantzler, Ingmari & Svante Leijon, 'Team-oriented Women Entrepreneurs: a Way to Modern Management', *Journal of Small Business and Enterprise Development* 14 (4), 2007, pp. 732–46.

Caper, Robert, 'Play, Experimentation and Creativity', *International Journal of Psycho-analysis* 1996, 77 (5), pp. 859–69.

Carroll R, M. Daniel, 'Blessing the Nations: Toward a Biblical Theology of Mission from Genesis', *Bulletin for Biblical Research* 10 (1), 2000, pp. 17–34.

Carson, D. A., *Becoming Conversant with the Emerging Church*, Grand Rapids: Zondervan, 2005.

Carter, Jane Frances Mary & Thomas Thellusson Carter, *Nicholas Ferrar, His Household and His Friends*, London: Longmans, Green, & Co., 1892.

Carter, Sara & Dylan Jones-Evans, *Enterprise and Small Business: Principles, Practice and Policy*, 2nd edition, Harlow: Prentice Hall, 2006.

Casey, Michael, *Strangers to the City: Reflections on the Beliefs and Values of the Rule of Saint Benedict*, Brewster, Mass: Paraclete Press, 2005.

Castells, Manuel, *The Rise of the Network Society: The Information Age: Economy, Society and Culture Volume I*, Oxford: Blackwell, 2000 [1996].

Castells, Manuel, *The Power of Identity: The Information Age: Economy, Society and Culture Volume II*, Oxford: Blackwell, 2010 [1997].

Castells, Manuel, *End of Millennium: The Information Age: Economy, Society and Culture Volume III*, Oxford: Blackwell, 2000 [1998].

Castells, Manuel, *The Internet Galaxy: Reflections on the Internet, Business, and Society*, Oxford: Oxford University Press, 2001.

Castells, Manuel, *Communication Power*, Oxford: Oxford University Press, 2009.

Catto, Stephen K., *Reconstructing the First-Century Synagogue: A Critical Analysis of Current Research*, London: T & T Clark, 2007.

Cavanaugh, William T., *Torture and Eucharist: Theology, Politics, and the Body of Christ*, Oxford: Blackwell, 1998.

Chambers, Charlotte & Fiona Edwards-Stuart, *Leadership in the Social Economy: Research Report*, London: School for Social Entrepreneurs, 2007.

Chandra, Yanto & Nicole Coviello, 'Broadening the concept of international entrepreneurship: "Consumers as International Entrepreneurs"', *Journal of World Business* 45, 2010, pp. 228–36.

Chatfield, Adrian, 'Form and Freedom: Creating Pioneer Worship', in David Male (ed.), *Pioneers 4 Life. Explorations in Theology and Wisdom for Pioneering Leaders*, Abingdon: Bible Reading Fellowship, 2011, pp. 115–26.

Childs, Brevard S., *Isaiah*, Louisville: Westminster John Knox, 2001.

Chiles, Todd H. & Alan D. Meyer, 'Managing the Emergence of Clusters: An Increasing Returns Approach to Strategic Change', *Emergence* 3 (3), 2001, pp. 58–89.

Chiles, Todd H., Alan D. Meyer & Thomas J. Hench, 'Organizational Emergence: The Origin and Transformation of Branson, Missouri's Musical Theaters', *Organizational Science* 15 (5), 2004, pp. 499–519.

Christakis, Nicholas & James Fowler, *Connected: The Amazing Power of Social Networks and How they Shape Our Lives*, London: Harper, 2010.

Church of England Liturgical Commission, *Transforming Worship: Living the New Creation*, London: General Synod, GS 1651, 2007.

Clutterbuck, David & David Megginson, *Making Coaching Work. Creating a Coaching Culture*, London: CIPD, 2005.

Cole, Neil, *Organic Church. Growing Faith Where Life Happens*, San Francisco: Jossey-Bass, 2005.

Cole, Neil, *Organic Leadership: Leading Naturally Right Where You Are*, Grand Rapids: Baker, 2009.

Collins, Paul M., *The Trinity: A Guide for the Perplexed*, London: T & T Clark, 2008.

Collins-Mayo, Sylvia, Bob Mayo, Sally Nash with Christopher Cocksworth, *The Faith of Generation Y*, London: Church House Publishing, 2010.

Comiskey, Joel, *Planting Churches that Reproduce. Starting a Network of Simple Churches*, Moreno Valley, CA: CCS Publishing, 2009.

Conn, Harvie M., *Eternal Word and Changing Worlds: Theology, Anthropology, and Mission in Trialogue*, Grand Rapids: Academie Books, 1984.

Conway, Steve & Oswald Jones, 'Networking and the small business', in Sara Carter & Dylan Jones-Evans, *Enterprise and Small Business: Principles, Practice and Policy*, 2nd edition, Harlow: Pearson Education, 2006, pp. 305–23.

Cook, Matthew, 'Contextual But Still Objective?', in Matthew Cook, Rob Haskell, Ruth Julian & Natee Tanchanpongs (eds), *Local Theology for the Global Church. Principles for an Evangelical Approach to Contextualization*, Pasadena: William Carey, 2010, pp. 75–89.

Cooney, Thomas M., 'Editorial: What is an Entrepreneurial Team?' *International Small Business Journal* 23(3), 2005, pp. 226–35.

Cox, Harvey G., *God's Revolution and Man's Responsibility*, Valley Forge: Judson, 1965.

Cox, Joanne, 'Fresh Churches and Emerging Expressions: Current Currents in the Ocean of Liquid Churches', in Rob Frost, David Wilkinson & Joanne Cox (eds), *The Call and the Commission. The Challenge of How the Church Equips a New Generation of Leaders for a Different World*, Milton Keynes: 2009, pp. 130–55.

Cray, Graham, *Disciples and Citizens. A Vision for Distinctive Living*, Nottingham: Inter-Varsity Press, 2007.

Cray, Graham, *Discerning Leadership: Cooperating with the Go-Between God*, Cambridge: Grove Books, 2010.

Cray, Graham, *Who's Shaping You? 21st Century Disciples*, Harpenden: Cell UK, 2010.

Cray, Graham, 'Why is New Monasticism Important to Fresh Expressions?', in Graham Cray, Ian Mobsby & Aaron Kennedy (eds), *New Monasticism as Fresh Expression of Church*, Norwich: Canterbury Press, 2010, pp. 1–11.

Cray, Graham, Ian Mobsby & Aaron Kennedy (eds), *New Monasticism as Fresh Expression of Church*, Norwich: Canterbury, 2010.

Croft, Steven, 'Transforming Evangelism', in Steven Croft, Rob Frost, Mark Ireland, Anne Richards, Yvonne Richmond & Nick Spencer, *Evangelism in a Spiritual Age: Communicating Faith in a Changing Culture*, London: Church House Publishing, 2005, pp. 126–47.

Croft, Steven, 'Conclusion', in Steven Croft (ed.), *The Future of the Parish System*, London: Church House Publishing, 2006, pp. 178–82.

Croft, Steven, 'Formation for Ministry in a Mixed economy Church: the Impact of Fresh Expressions of Church on Patterns of Training', in Louise Nelstrop and Martyn Percy (eds), *Evaluating Fresh Expressions: Explorations in Emerging Church*, Norwich: Canterbury Press, 2008, pp. 40–54.

Croft, Steven (ed.), *Mission-shaped Questions. Defining Issues for Today's Church*, London: Church House Publishing, 2008.

Croft, Steven, 'What Counts as a Fresh Expression of Church and Who Decides?', in Louise Nelstrop and Martyn Percy (eds), *Evaluating Fresh Expressions: Explorations in Emerging Church*, Norwich: Canterbury Press, 2008, pp. 3–14.

Croft, Steven, Claire Dalpra & George Lings, *Starting a Fresh Expressions*, Fresh Expressions, 2006.

Croft, Steven, Freddy Hedley & Bob Hopkins, *Listening for Mission*, London: Church Publishing House, 2007.

Cunningham, David S., *These Three Are One: The Practice of Trinitarian Theology*, Oxford: Blackwell, 1998.

Dalpra, Claire, 'Keeping Church Simple? The Perceived Ingredients of Sustainability in Spare-Time Led Fresh Expressions of Church, MA dissertation, Cliff College, 2011.

Davie, Grace, 'The Persistence of Institutional Religion in modern Europe', in Linda Woodhead with Paul Heelas & David Martin (eds), *Peter Berger and the Study of Religion*, London: Routledge, 2001, pp. 101–11.

Davie, Grace, *The Sociology of Religion*, London: Sage, 2007.

Davies, Eryl W., *The Immoral Bible. Approaches to Biblical Ethics*, London: T & T Clark, 2010.

Davies, J. G., *Worship and Mission*, London: SCM, 1966.

Davies, Philip R., *Memories of Ancient Israel. An Introduction to Biblical History – Ancient and Modern*, Louisville: Westminster John Knox, 2008.

Davison, Andrew & Alison Milbank, *For the Parish: A Critique of Fresh Expressions*, London: SCM, 2010.

Dawn, Marva J., *A Royal "Waste" of Time. The Splendor of Worshipping God and Being Church for the World*, Grand Rapids/Cambridge: Eerdmans, 1999.

Day, Dorothy, *The Long Loneliness: The Autobiography of Dorothy Day*, New York: Harper, 1997 [1952].

Deakins, David & Mark Freel, *Entrepreneurship and Small Firms*, 5th edition, Maidenhead: McGraw-Hill Education, 2009.

De Geus, Arie P., 'Planning as Learning', *Harvard Business Review* March 1988, pp. 70–4.

De Lubac, Henri, *Catholicism: Christ and the Common Destiny of Man*, tr. Lancelot C. Sheppard & Elizabeth Englund, OCD, San Francisco: Ignatius Press, 1988 [1950].

Demson, David E., *Hans Frei and Karl Barth: Different Ways of Reading Scripture*, Grand Rapids: Eerdmans, 1997.

De Ridder, Richard R., *Discipling the Nations*, Grand Rapids: Baker, 1975.

De Waal, Esther, *The Celtic Way of Prayer: The Recovery of the Religious Imagination*, New York: Doubleday, 1997.

De Waal, Esther, *Seeking God: The Way of St Benedict*, Norwich: Canterbury Press, 1999 [1984].

De Wolf, Tom & Tom Holvoet, 'Emergence Versus Self-organisation: Different Concepts but Promising When Combined', in Sven A. Brueckner, Giovanna Di Marzo Serugendo, Anthony Karageorgos, Radhika Nagpal (eds), *Engineering Self-Organising Systems: Methodologies and Applications*, Berlin: Springer, 2005, pp. 1–15.

Dietz, Thomas, Tom R. Burns & Federick H. Buttel, 'Evolutionary Theory in Sociology: An Examination of Current Thinking', *Sociological Forum* 5 (2), 1990, pp. 155–71.

Donovan, Vincent J., *Christianity Rediscovered: An Epistle from the Masai*, London: SCM, 2001 [1978].

Dougan, William L. & Louise Tourigny, 'Inducing Faith: How Novice, Nascent Entrepreneurs Can Convince Reluctant Stakeholders', paper presented to United States Association of Small Businesses and Entrepreneurs 2004 Conference, Dallas, Texas.

Down, Simon & James Reveley, 'Generational Encounters and the Social Formation of Entrepreneurial Identity: "Young Guns" and "Old Farts"', *Organization* 11 (2), 2004, pp. 233–50.

Drane, John, 'What Does Maturity in the Emerging Church Look Like?', in Steven Croft (ed.), *Mission-shaped Questions. Defining Issues for Today's Church*, London: Church House Publishing, 2008, pp. 90–101.

Drane, John, *The World of the Bible*, Oxford: Lion, 2009.

Drane, John, 'Resisting McDonaldization: Fresh Expressions of Church for a New Millennium', in Viggo Mortensen & Andreas Osterlund Nielsen (eds), *Walk Humbly with the Lord: Church and Mission Engaging Plurality*, Grand Rapids: Eerdmans, 2010, pp. 150–66.

Drane, John, 'From One Pioneer to Another: Insights from St Paul', in Dave Male (ed) *Pioneers 4 Life: Explorations in Theology and Wisdom for Pioneering Leaders*, Abingdon: Bible Reading Fellowship, 2011, pp. 149–67.

Drane, John & Olive Fleming Drane, *Reformed, Reforming, Emerging and Experimenting*, Report for the Church of Scotland, 2010.

Drori, Gili S., John W. Meyer & Hokyu Hwang, 'Introduction', in Gili S. Drori, John W. Meyer & Hokyu Hwang, *Globalization and Organization*, Oxford: Oxford University Press, 2006.

Dunham, Laura Catherine, 'Building the Web of Belief: The Emergence of Stakeholder Networks in Early Stage Ventures', PhD dissertation, The Darden Graduate School of Business Administration, University of Virginia, 2003.

Dunn, James D. G., *Jesus' Call to Discipleship*, Cambridge: Cambridge University Press, 1992.

Dunn, James D. G., *The Partings of the Ways Between Christianity and Judaism and their Significance for the Character of Christianity*, London: SCM, 2nd ed., 2006.

Dunn, James D. G., 'Is there Evidence for Fresh Expressions of Church in the New Testament?', in Steven Croft (ed.), *Mission-shaped Questions. Defining Issues for Today's Church*, London: Church House Publishing, 2008, pp. 54–65.

Dunn, James D G., *Beginning from Jerusalem*, Grand Rapids: Eerdmans, 2009.

Dyer, Anne, 'Repairing the Breach: Developing a Spirituality for Leadership Today', in Rob Frost, David Wilkinson & Joanne Cox (eds), *The Call and the Commission: The Challenge of How the Church Equips a New Generation of Leaders for a Different World*, Milton Keynes: 2009, pp. 180–93.

Dyer, Jeffrey H., Hal B. Gregersen & Clayton Christensen, 'Entrepreneur Behaviors, Opportunity Recognition, and the Origins of Innovative Ventures', *Strategic Entrepreneurship Journal* 2, 2008, pp. 317–38.

Earey, Mark & Carolyn Headley, *Mission and Liturgical Worship*, Cambridge: Grove Books, 2002.

Earey, Mark & Phillip Tovey, *Liturgical Formation and Common Worship*, Cambridge: Grove Books, 2009.

Edelman, Linda & Helena Yli-Renko, 'The Impact of Environment and Entrepreneurial Perceptions on Venture-Creation Efforts: Bridging the Discovery and Creation Views of Entrepreneurship', *Entrepreneurship Theory and Practice* 34 (5), 2010, pp. 8334–56.

Eisenstadt, S. N., 'Multiple Modernities', *Daedalus*, 129 (1), 2000, pp. 1–29.

Ellul, Jacques, *The Meaning of the City*, trans. by Dennis Pardee, Grand Rapids: Eerdmans, 1970.

Elmore, Tim, 'A New Kind of Leader: Leading Effectively as Our Culture Evolves', www.growingleaders.com/www.iequip.org.

Enns, Peter, *Inspiration and Incarnation: Evangelicals and the Problem of the Old Testament*, Grand Rapids: Baker, 2005.

Everts, Don & Doug Shaupp, *Pathway to Jesus. Crossing the thresholds of faith*, Nottingham: InterVarsity Press, 2009.

Farmer, Steven M., Xin Yao & Kate Kung-Mcintyre, 'The Behavioral Impact of Entrepreneur Identity and Aspiration and Prior Entrepreneurial Experience', *Entrepreneurship Theory and Practice* 35 (2), 2011, pp. 245–73.

Farrow, Douglas, *Ascension and Ecclesia: On the Significance of the Doctrine of the Ascension for Ecclesiology and Christian Cosmology*, Edinburgh, T & T Clark, 1999.

Farrow, Douglas, 'Between the Rock and a Hard Place: In Support of (something like) a Reformed View of the Eucharist', *International Journal of Systematic Theology* 3 (2), 2001, pp. 167–86.

Farrow, Douglas, *Ascension Theology*, London: T & T Clark, 2011.

Feital, Peterson, 'Breaking free from individualism: discipleship and community', in David Male (ed.), *Pioneers 4 Life: Explorations in Theology and Wisdom for Pioneering Leaders*, Abingdon: Bible Reading Fellowship, 2011, pp. 105–14.

Felstead, Alan, Duncan Gallie & Francis Green, *Work Skills in Britain 1986–2001*, London: DfES, 2002.

Fergusson, David, 'Another Way of Reading Stanley Hauerwas', *Scottish Journal of Theology* 50 (2), 1997, pp. 242–9.

Ferrar, John, *Life of Nicholas Ferrar*, ed. J. E. B. Mayor, Cambridge: Cambridge University Press, 1855.

Fiddes, Paul S., *The Creative Suffering of God*, Oxford: Clarendon, 1988.

Fiddes, Paul S., *Participating in God: A Pastoral Doctrine of the Trinity*, London: Darton, Longman & Todd, 2000.

Fiddes, Paul S., *The Promised End: Eschatology in Theology and Literature*, Oxford: Blackwell, 2000.

Fiensy, David A., 'The Composition of the Jerusalem Church', in Richard Bauckham (ed.), *The Book of Acts in its First Century Setting Vol. 4: Palestinian Setting*, Grand Rapids: Eerdmans, 1995, pp. 213–36.

Finger, Reta Halteman, *Of Widows and Meals: Communal Meals in the Book of Acts*, Grand Rapids: Eerdmans, 2007.

Finkelstein, Jacob J., 'Bible and Babel: A Comparative Study of the Hebrew and Babylonian Religious Spirit', in Frederick E. Greenspahn, *Essential Papers on Israel and the Ancient Near East*, New York: New York University Press, 1991, pp. 355–79.

Firkin, Patrick, 'Entrepreneurial Capital: A Resource-Based Conceptualisation of the Entrepreneurial Process', Albany and Palmerston North Labour Market Dynamic Research Programme, 2001.

Flemming, Dean, *Contextualization in the New Testament. Patterns for theology and mission*, Leicester: Apollos, 2005.

Flett, John G., *The Witness of God: The Trinity, Missio Dei, Karl Barth, and the Nature of Christian Community*, Grand Rapids: Eerdmans, 2010.

Forbes, Daniel P., Patricia S. Borchert, Mary E. Zellmer-Bruhn, Harry J. Sapienza, 'Entrepreneurial Team Formation: An Exploration of New Member Addition', *Entrepreneurship Theory and Practice*, 30 (2), 2006, pp. 225–44.

Foster, M. John, 'Scenario Planning for small businesses', *Long Range Planning* 26 (1), 1993, pp. 123–9.

Foster, Mary & Agnes G. Meinhard, 'A Regression Model Explaining Predispositions to Collaborate,' *Non-Profit and Voluntary Sector Quarterly* 31 (4), 2002, pp. 549–64.

Francis, Leslie J., 'Mark and Psychological Type', in John Vincent (ed.), *Mark: Gospel of Action: Personal and Community Responses*, London: SPCK, 2006, pp. 98–108.

Francis, Leslie J. & Philip Richter, *Gone for Good? Church-Leaving and Returning in the 21st Century*, Peterborough: Epworth, 2007.

Freeman, Andy, 'New Monasticism, Mission and Young People', in Graham Cray, Ian Mobsby & Aaron Kennedy (eds), *New Monasticism as Fresh Expression of Church*, Norwich: Canterbury, 2010, pp. 50–6.

Friesenhahn, Jacob H., *The Trinitarian Theology of von Balthasar and the Problem of Evil*, Farnham: Ashgate, 2011.

Frost, Michael, *Exiles: Living Missionally in a Post-Christian Culture*, Peabody: Hendrickson, 2006.

Frost, Michael & Alan Hirsch, *The Shaping of Things to Come: Innovation and Mission for the 21st-Century Church*, Peabody: Hendrickson, 2003.

Gaillardetz, Richard R., 'The Reception of Doctrine: New Perspectives', in Bernard Hoose (ed.), *Authority in the Roman Catholic Church: Theory and Practice*, Aldershot: Ashgate, 2002

Gamble, Robin, 'Mixed Economy: Nice Slogan or Working Reality?', in Louise Nelstrop and Martyn Percy (eds), *Evaluating Fresh Expressions: Explorations in Emerging Church*, Norwich: Canterbury Press, 2008, pp. 15–23.

Garrison, David, *Church Planting Movements: How God is Redeeming a Lost World*, Arkadelphia, AR: WIGTake Resources, 2004.

Garvey, Robert, Paul Stokes & David Megginson, *Coaching and Mentoring: Theory and Practice*, London: Sage, 2009.

Gay, Doug, *Remixing the Church:. The Five Moves of Emerging Ecclesiology*, London: SCM, 2011.

Gehring, Roger W., *House Church and Mission: The Importance of Household Structures in Early Christianity*, Peabody: Hendrickson, 2004.

Gibbs, Eddie, *I Believe in Church Growth*, London: Hodder, 1981.

Gibbs, Eddie & Ryan K. Bolger, *Emerging Churches: Creating Christian Communities in Postmodern Cultures*, London: SPCK, 2006.

Giddens, Anthony, *Modernity and Self-Identity: Self and Society in the Late Modern Age*, Stanford: Stanford University Press, 1991.

Giles, Kevin, *What on Earth Is the Church? An Exploration in New Testament Theology*, Downers Grove, IL: InterVarsity Press, 1995.

Gill, Robin, *The 'Empty' Church Revisited*, Aldershot: Ashgate, 2003.

Gill, Robin, 'The Cultural Paradigm: Declines in Belonging and Then Believing', in Detlef Pollack & Daniel V. A. Olson (eds), *The Role of Religion in Modern Societies*, New York: Routledge, 2008, pp. 177–89.

Glasson, Barbara, *Mixed-up Blessing: A New Encounter with Being Church*, Peterborough: Inspire, 2006.

Goddard, Andrew, *Living the Word, Resisting the World. The Life and Thought of Jacques Ellul*, Carlisle: Paternoster, 2002.

Goldingay, John, *Theological Diversity and the Authority of the Old Testament*, Grand Rapids: Eerdmans, 1987.

Goldingay, John, *Old Testament Theology: Volume Two. Israel's Faith*, Downers Grove/ Milton Keynes: InterVarsity Press/Paternoster, 2006.

Goldstein, Jeffrey A., James K. Hazy & Joyce Silberstang, 'Complexity and Social Entrepreneurship: A Fortuitous Meeting', *Emergence: Complexity and Organization* 10 (3), 2008, pp. 9–24.

Goldstein, Jeffrey A., James K. Hazy & Joyce Silberstang, 'A Complexity Science Model of Social Innovation in Social Enterprise', *Journal of Social Entrepreneurship* 1 (1), 2010, pp. 101–25.

Gooder, Paula, 'In Search of the Early "Church": The New Testament and the Development of Christian Communities', in Gerard Mannion & Lewis Mudge (eds), *The Routledge Companion to the Christian Church*, Abingdon: Routledge, 2008, pp. 9–25.

Goodhew, David, Andrew Roberts & Michael Volland, *Fresh! An Introduction to Fresh Expressions and Pioneer Ministry*, London: SCM, 2012.

Goodman, Martin, *Mission and Conversion: Proselytizing in the Religious History of the Roman Empire*, Oxford: Clarendon, 1994.

Gorringe, Timothy J., *God's Theatre: A Theology of Providence*, London: SCM, 1991.

Gottwald, Norman K., *The Tribes of Yahweh: A Sociology of the Religion of Liberated Israel, 1250–1050 BCE*, Maryknoll: Orbis, 1979.

Granovetter, Mark, 'The Strength of Weak Ties: A Network Theory Revisited', *Sociological Theory* 1, 1983, pp. 201–33.

Gray-Reeves, Mary & Michael Perham, *The Hospitality of God. Emerging Worship for a Missional Church*, London: SPCK, 2011.

Green, Joel B., & Mark D. Baker, *Recovering the Scandal of the Cross. Atonement in New Testament and Contemporary Contexts*, Carlisle: Paternoster, 2003 [2000].

Gregersen, Niels Henrik, 'Laws of Physics, Principles of Self-Organization, and Natural Capacities: On Explaining a Self-Organizing World', in Fraser Watts (ed.), *Creation: Law and Probability*, Aldershot: Ashgate, 2008, pp. 81–100.

Grey, Chris & Christina Garsten, 'Trust, Control and Post-Bureaucracy', *Organization Studies* 22 (2), 2001, pp. 229–50.

Griffin, Douglas, *The Emergence of Leadership. Linking Self-organization and Ethics*, London: Routledge, 2002.

Griffin, Douglas & Ralph Stacey (eds), *Complexity and the Experience of Leading Organizations*, Abingdon: Routledge, 2005.

Grindheim, Sigurd, *The Crux of Election. Paul's Critique of the Jewish Confidence in the Election of Israel*, Tübingen: Mohr Siebeck, 2005.

Guenther, Bruce L., 'The "Enduring Problem" of Christ and Culture', *Direction* 34 (2), 2005, pp. 215–27.

Gumbel, Nicky, *Questions of Life*, Eastbourne: Kingsway, 1993.

Gunton, Colin E., *The One, the Three and the Many: God, Creation and the Culture of Modernity*, Cambridge: Cambridge University Press, 1993.

Halter, Hugh and Matt Smay, *The Tangible Kingdom: Creating Incarnational Community*, San Francisco: Jossey-Bass, 2008.

Hammett, John, 'The Church According to Emergent/Emerging Church', in William D. Henard & Adam W. Greenway (eds), *Evangelicals Engaging Emergent. A Discussion of the Emergent Church Movement*, Nashville, TN: B&H Publishing, 2009, pp. 219–60.

Hardina, Donna, *Analytical Skills for Community Organization Practice*, New York: Columbia University Press, 2002.

Harris, Geoffrey, 'Mark and Mission', in John Vincent (ed.), *Mark. Gospel of Action. Personal and Community Responses*, London: SPCK, 2006.

Harris, Geoffrey, *SCM Core Text Paul*, London: SCM, 2009.

Hauerwas, Stanley, *A Community of Character: Toward a Constructive Christian Social Ethic*, Indiana: University of Notre Dame Press, 1981.

Hauerwas, Stanley, *With the Grain of the Universe*, Grand Rapids: Brazos, 2001.

Hauerwas, Stanley, 'Worship, Evangelism, Ethics: On Eliminating the "And"', in Paul W. Chilcote & Laceye C. Warner (eds), *The Study of Evangelism: Exploring a Missional Practice of the Church*, Grand Rapids: Eerdmans, 2008, pp. 205–14.

Hauerwas, Stanley, 'Beyond the Boundaries: The Church Is Mission', in Viggo Mortensen & Andreas Osterlund Nielsen (eds), *Walk Humbly with the Lord: Church and Mission Engaging Plurality*, Grand Rapids: Eerdmans, 2010, pp. 53–69.

Hauerwas, Stanley & William H. Willimon, *Resident Aliens: Life in the Christian Colony*, Nashville: Abingdon, 1989.

Hauerwas, Stanley & William H. Willimon, *Where Resident Aliens Live: Exercises for Christian Practice*, Nashville: Abingdon, 1996.

Healy, Nicholas M., 'Communion Ecclesiology: A Cautionary Note', *Pro Ecclesia* 4 (4), 1995, pp. 442–53.

Healy, Nicholas M., *Church, World and the Christian Life. Practical–Prophetic Ecclesiology*, Cambridge: Cambridge University Press, 2000.

Heard, James, *Inside Alpha: Explorations in Evangelism*, Milton Keynes: Paternoster, 2009.

Hebblethwaite, Margaret, *Base Communities: An Introduction*, London: Geoffrey Chapman, 1993.

Heelas, Paul, *Spiritualities of Life: New Age Romanticism and Consumptive Capitalism*, Oxford: Blackwell, 2008.

Heelas, Paul & Linda Woodhead with Benjamin Seel, Bronislaw Szerszynski & Karin Tusting, *The Spiritual Revolution: Why Religion is Giving Way to Spirituality*, Oxford: Blackwell, 2005.

Hemer, Colin J., *The Book of Acts in the Setting of Hellenistic History*, WUNT 49, Tübingen: Mohr Siebeck, 1989.

Hemming, Laurence Paul, *Worship as a Revelation: The Past, Present and Future of Catholic Liturgy*, London/New York: Burns & Oates, 2008.

Hengel, Martin, *Acts and the History of Earliest Christianity*, London: SCM, 1979.

Hiebert, Paul G., 'Evangelism, Church, and Kingdom', in Charles van Engen, Dean S. Gilliland & Paul Pierson (eds), *The Good News of the Kingdom*, Maryknoll NY: Orbis, 1993, pp. 153–61.

Higgins, Gregory C., 'The Significance of Postliberalism for Religious Education', in Jeff Astley, Leslie Francis & Colin Crowder (eds), *Theological Perspectives on Christian Formation. A Reader on Theology and Christian Education*, Leominster: Gracewing, 1996, pp. 135–45.

Higton, Mike, *SCM Core Text Christian Doctrine*, London: SCM, 2008.

Hill, Craig C., *Hellenists and Hebrews: Reappraising Division with the Earliest Church*, Minneapolis: Fortress, 1992.

Hills, Matt, *How To Do Things With Cultural Theory*, London: Hodder Education, 2005.

Hirsch, Alan, *The Forgotten Ways: Reactivating the Missional Church*, Grand Rapids: Brazos, 2006.

Hirsch, Alan & Dave Ferguson, *On the Verge: a Journey into the Apostolic Future of the Church*, Grand Rapids: Zondervan, 2011.

Hoang, Ha & Javier Gimeno, 'Becoming a Founder: How Founder Role Identity Affects Entrepreneurial Transitions and Persistence in Founding', *Journal of Business Venturing* 25 (1), 2010, pp. 41–53.

Hobson, Theo, *Anarchy, Church and Utopia: Rowan Williams on Church*, London: Darton, Longman & Todd, 2005.

Hock, Ronald F., *The Social Context of Paul's Ministry: Tentmaking and Apostleship*, Minneapolis: Fortress, 2007 [1980].

Hoekendijk, Hans, 'The Church in Missionary Thinking', *International Review of Missions* XLI (163), 1952, pp. 324–36.

Hofsted, Geert, Gert Jan Hofstede & Michael Minkov, *Cultures and Organizations. Software of the Mind*, New York: McGraw Hill, 2010.

Hollinghurst, Steve, *Mission-Shaped Evangelism: The Gospel in Contemporary Culture*, Norwich: Canterbury Press, 2010.

Holmdahl, Lars, 'Complexity Theory and Strategy: A Basis for Product Development', 2005, www.complexityforum.com/articles/complexity-strategy.pdf.

Holmes, Stephen R., 'Trinitarian Missiology: Towards a Theology of God as Missionary', *International Journal of Systematic Theology* 8 (1), 2006, pp. 72–90.

Hope, Susan, *Mission-shaped Spirituality: The Transforming Power of Mission*, London: Church House Publishing, 2006.

Hopewell, James F., *Congregation: Stories and Structures*, Minneapolis: Fortress, 1987.

Hopkins, Bob, *Church Planting 1 : Models for Mission in the Church of England*, Bramcote: Grove Books, 1988.

Hopkins, Bob, *Planters Problems: Assessing the Challenges of Planting New Churches*, Sheffield: Anglican Church Planters Initiative, 2008.

Hopkins, Bob & Mike Breen, *Clusters. Creative Mid-sized Missional Communities*, 3DM Publications, 2007.

Hopkins, Bob & Freddy Hedley, *Coaching for Missional Leadership: Growing and Supporting Pioneers in Church Planting and Fresh Expressions*, Sheffield: ACPI Books, 2008.

Houston, Walter J., *Contending for Justice: Ideologies and Theologies of Social Justice in the Old Testament*, London: T & T. Clark, 2006.

Howe, Mark, *Online Church? First Steps Towards Virtual Incarnation*, Cambridge: Grove, 2007.

Howkins, John, *The Creative Economy: How People Make Money From Ideas*, London: Penguin, 2007 [2002].

Howsare, Rodney A., *Balthasar: A Guide for the Perplexed*, London: T & T Clark, 2009.

Howson, Chris, *A Just Church: 21st Century Liberation Theology in Action*, London: Continuum, 2011.

Hughes, Alex, *Public Worship and Communion by Extension: Some Pastoral and Theological Issues*, Cambridge: Grove, 2002.

Hull, John M., *Mission-Shaped Church: A Theological Response*, London: SCM, 2006.

Hull, John M., 'Mission-shaped and Kingdom focused?', in Steven Croft (ed.), *Mission-shaped Questions. Defining Issues for Today's Church*, London: Church House Publishing, 2008, pp. 114–32.

Hull, John M., 'Only One Way to Walk with God: Christian Discipleship for New Expressions of Church', in Louise Nelstrop and Martyn Percy (eds), *Evaluating Fresh Expressions: Explorations in Emerging Church*, Norwich: Canterbury Press, 2008, pp. 105–20.

Hunter III, George G., *The Celtic Way of Evangelism: How Christianity Can Reach the West... Again*, Nashville: Abingdon Press, 2000.

Hunter, James Davison, *To Change the World: The Irony, Tragedy, and Possibility of Christianity in the Late Modern World*, Oxford: Oxford University Press, 2010.

Hunter, Todd D., *Christianity Beyond Belief: Following Jesus for the Sake of Others*, Downers Grove: IVP, 2009.

Hütter, Reinhard, *Suffering Divine Things: Theology as Church Practice*, Grand Rapids: Eerdmans, 2000.

Huy, Quy & Christoph Zott, 'How Entprepreneurs Regulate Stakeholders' Emotions To Build New Organizations', Best Paper Proceedings, Academy of Management Meeting, 2007.

Ibarra, Herminia, *Working Identity: Unconventional Strategies for Reinventing Your Career*, Boston: Harvard Business School, 2004 [2003].

Inglehart, Ronald F., 'Changing Values among Western Publics from 1970 to 2006', *West European Politics* 31 (1–2), 2008, pp. 130–46.

Inglehart, Ronald & Christian Welzel, *Modernization, Cultural Change and Democracy: The Human Development Sequence*, Cambridge: Cambridge University Press, 2005.

Ireland, Mark, *How to do Mission Action Planning: A Vision Centred Approach*, London: SPCK, 2009.

Iremonger, F. A., *William Temple: Archbishop of Canterbury—His Life and Letters,* Oxford: Oxford University Press, 1949.

Jackson, Bob, *Hope for the Church,* London: Church House Publishing, 2002.

Jackson, Bob, *The Road to Growth: Towards a Thriving Church,* London: Church House Publishing, 2005.

Jasper, R. C. D., *The Development of the Anglican Liturgy, 1662–1980.* London: SPCK, 1989.

Jensen, Michael P., 'Mission Recalibrated – Chris Wright's *The Mission of God*', *Anvil* 24 (4), 2007, pp. 279–88.

Jenson, Matt & David Wilhite, *The Church: A Guide for the Perplexed,* London: T & T Clark, 2010.

Jewett, Robert, *Romans: A Commentary,* Minneapolis: Fortress, 2007.

Johnson, Bradford C., James Manyika & Lareina A. Yee, 'The Next Revolution in Interactions', *The McKinsey Quarterly* 4, 2005.

Johnson, D. Paul, 'From Religious Markets to Religious Communities: Contrasting Implications for Applied Research', *Review of Religious Research* 44 (4), 2003, pp. 325–40.

Johnson, Steven, *Emergence: The Connected Lives of Ants, Brains, Cities and Software,* Penguin, 2002 [2001].

Jones, Cheslyn, Geoffrey Wainwright, Edward Yarnold SJ & Paul Bradshaw (eds), *The Study of Liturgy,* revised edition, London: SPCK, 1992 [1978].

Jones, Robert, James Lathan & Michela Betta, 'Narrative Construction of the Social Entrepreneurial Identity', *International Journal of Entrepreneurial Behaviour and Research* 14(5), 2008, pp. 330–45.

Jones, Tony, *The New Christians: Dispatches from the Emergent Frontier,* San Francisco: Jossey-Bass, 2008.

Kaiser, Walter C., *Mission in the Old Testament: Israel as a Light to the Nations,* Grand Rapids: Baker, 2000.

Kandori, Michihiro, George J. Mailath & Rafael Rob, *Econometrica* 61 (1), 1993, pp. 29–56.

Kavanagh, Aidan, *On Liturgical Theology: The Hale Memorial Lectures of Seabury-Western Theological Seminary, 1981,* Collegeville: Liturgical Press, 1984.

Kasper, Walter, *Harvesting the Fruits: Aspects of Christian Faith in Ecumenical Dialogue,* London & New York: Continuum, 2009.

Keel, Tim, 'Leading from the Margins: The Role of Imagination in Our Changing Context', in Doug Pagitt & Tony Jones (eds), *An Emergent Manifesto of Hope,* Grand Rapids: Baker Books, 2007, pp. 225–33.

Keown, Mark J., *Congregational Evangelism in Philippians: The Centrality of an Appeal for Gospel Proclamation to the Fabric of Philippians,* Carlisle: Paternoster, 2008.

Kershaw, Diane, 'The Order of Mission: Being a Sent People', in Graham Cray, Ian Mobsby & Aaron Kennedy (eds), *New Monasticism as Fresh Expression of Church,* Norwich: Canterbury Press, 2010, pp. 80–91.

Kilpin, Juliet & Stuart Murray, *Church Planting in the Inner City: The Urban Expression Story,* Cambridge: Grove Books, 2007.

Kingsley, Charles, *The Works of Charles Kingsley,* Vol. 1, Letters and Memories, Philadelphia: John D. Morris & Company, 1899.

Kirby, David A, *Entrepreneurship,* Maidenhead: McGraw-Hill Education, 2003.

Kirk, Kenneth E., *The Vision of God. The Christian Doctrine of the Summum Bonum,* London: Longmans, Green & Co., 1932 [1931].

Kolb, David A., *Experiential Learning: Experience as the Source of Learning and Development,* Upper Saddle River: Prentice Hall, 1984.

Kumar, Krishan, *From Post-Industrial to Post-Modern Society: New Theories of the Contemporary World*, Oxford: Blackwell, 1995, pp. 36–65.

Kraft, Charles H., *Christianity and Culture: A Study in Dynamic Biblical Theologizing*, Maryknoll: Orbis, 1979.

Kreider, Alan, *Worship and Evangelism in Pre-Christendom*, Grove Books, 1995.

Kreider, Alan, *The Change of Conversion and the Origin of Christendom*, Eugene, OR: Wipf & Stock: 1999.

Kreider, Alan & Eleanor Kreider, *Worship and Mission after Christendom*, Milton Keynes: Paternoster, 2009.

Langmead, Ross, *The Word Made Flesh: Towards an Incarnational Missiology*, Lanham, ML: United Press of America, 2004.

Lauffer, Armand, 'Fundraising, Programming, and Community Organizing: Working With Donors, Investors, Collaborators, and Purchasers', in Marie Weil (ed.), *The Handbook of Community Practice*, Thousand Oaks: Sage, 2005, pp. 582–603.

Lawrence, C. H., *Medieval Monasticism: Forms of Religious Life in Western Europe in the Middle Ages*, 3rd edition, Harlow: Pearson Education, 2001.

Leclercq, O.S.B., Jean, *The Love of Learning and the Desire for God: A Study of Monastic Culture*, trans. Catharine Misrahi, New York: Fordham University Press, 1961.

Lee, Andrew, 'Executive Coaching and Leading', in Douglas Griffin and Ralph Stacey, *Complexity and the Experience of Leading Organisations*, Abingdon: Routledge, 2005, pp. 153–78.

Leifer, Richard, 'Understanding Organizational Transformation Using a Dissipative Structure Model', *Human Relations* 42 (10), 1989, pp. 899–916.

Levinson, Bernard M., 'The Hermeneutics of Tradition in Deuteronomy: A Reply to J. G. McConville', *Journal of Biblical Literature* 119 (2), 2000, pp. 269–86.

Levinson, Bernard M., 'The Reconceptualization of Kingship in Deuteronomy and the Deuteronomistic History's Transformation of Torah', *Vetus Testamentum* 51 (4), 2001, pp. 511–34.

Lichtenstein, Benyamin Bergmann, 'Self-Organized Transitions: A Pattern Amid the Chaos of Transformative Change', *The Academy of Management Executive (1993–2005)* 14 (4), 2000, pp. 128–41.

Lichtenstein, Benyamin B., Mary Uhl-Bieny, Russ Marionz, Anson Seers, James Douglas Ortonyy & Craig Schreiberzz, 'Complexity Leadership Theory: An Interactive Perspective on Leading in Complex Adaptive Systems', Management Department Faculty Publications, University of Nebraska, 2006.

Lichtenstein, Benyamin B. & Donde Ashmos Plowman, 'The Leadership of Emergence: A Complex Systems Leadership Theory of Emergence at Successive Organizational Levels', *The Leadership Quarterly* 20 (2009), pp. 617–30.

Lindbeck, George, *The Nature of Doctrine: Religion and Theology in a Postliberal Age*, Philadelphia: Westminster Press, 1984.

Lindbeck, George, 'The Church', in Geoffrey Wainwright (ed.), *Keeping the Faith: Essays to Mark the Centenary of Lux Mundi*, Philadelphia: Fortress Press, 1988, pp. 179–208.

Lings, George, 'Fresh Expressions Growing to Maturity', in Steven Croft (ed.), *The Future of the Parish System: Shaping the Church of England for the 21st Century*, London: Church House Publishing, 2006, pp. 138–51.

Lings, George, *Simpler Church: Where Time is at a Premium*, The Sheffield Centre: Encounters on the Edge 32, 2006.

Lings, George, *Leading Fresh Expressions: Lessons from Hindsight*, The Sheffield Centre: Encounters on the Edge, 36, 2007.

Lings, George, 'The Church's Calling and Capacity to Reproduce', thesis submitted to University of Manchester for the degree of Doctor of Philosophy, November 2008.

Lings, George, *That's 'Sorted' Then: Start, Sustain . . . and Begin Again*, The Sheffield Centre: Encounters on the Edge, 48, 2010.

Lings, George, 'Looking in the Mirror: What Makes a Pioneer?', in David Male (ed.), *Pioneers 4 Life. Explorations in Theology and Wisdom for Pioneering Leaders*, Abingdon: Bible Reading Fellowship, 2011, pp. 30–47.

Lings, George & Stuart Murray, *Church Planting: Past, Present and Future*, Cambridge: Grove Books, 2003.

Little, Lester, K., *Religious Poverty and the Profit Economy in Medieval Europe*, Ithaca, New York: Cornell University Press, 1978.

Logan, Robert E., *Be Fruitful and Multiply: Embracing God's Heart for Church Multiplication*, St. Charles, IL: ChurchSmart Resources, 2006.

Logan, Robert E. & Steve L. Ogne, *The Church Planters Toolkit*, Carol Stream, IL.: ChurchSmart Resources, 2nd edition, 1991.

Lohfink, Norbert, 'Distribution of the Functions of Power: The Laws Concerning Public Offices in Deuteronomy 16:18 – 18:22', in Duane L. Christensen (ed.), *A Song of Power and the Power of Song: Essays on the Book of Deuteronomy*, Winona Lake: Eisenbrauns, 1993, pp. 336–52.

Lomax, Tim & Michael Moynagh, *Liquid Worship*, Cambridge: Grove Books, 2004.

Lonergan, Bernard, *Method in Theology*, 2nd edition, London: Darton, Longman & Todd, 1973.

Losada, Marcial, 'The Complex Dynamics of High Performance Teams', *Mathematical and Computer Modelling* 30 (9–10), 1999, pp. 179–92.

Lumpkin, G. T., G. E. Hills & R. C. Shrader, 'Opportunity Recognition', in H. P. Welsch, *Entrepreneurship: The Way Ahead*, New York: Routledge, 2004, pp. 73–90.

Luoma, Jukka, 'Systems Thinking in Complex Responsive Processes and Systems Intelligence', in Raimo P. Hamalainen & Esa Saarinen (eds), *Systems Intelligence in Leadership and Everyday Life*, Espoo: Systems Analysis Laboratory, Helsinki University of Technology, 2007, pp. 281–94.

Mair, Johanna & Ignasi Marti, 'Social entrepreneurship research: A source of explanation, prediction, and delight, *Journal of World Business*, 41 (1), 2006, pp. 36–44.

Male, David, *Church Unplugged: Remodelling Church Without Losing Your Soul*, Milton Keynes: Authentic Media, 2008.

Male, David (ed.), *Pioneers 4 Life: Explorations in Theology and Wisdom for Pioneering Leaders*, Abingdon: Bible Reading Fellowship, 2011.

Malphurs, Aubrey, *Planting Growing Churches for the 21st Century*, 3rd edition, Grand Rapids: Baker, 2004 [1992].

Mannoia, Kevin W., *Church Planting: The Next Generation*, third edition, Toronto: Clements Publishing, 2005 [1994].

Marshall, I. Howard, 'Who Were the Evangelists?', in Jostein Ådna & Hans Kvalbein (eds), *The Mission of the Early Church to Jews and Gentiles*, Tübingen: Mohr Siebeck, 2000, pp. 251–64.

Marshall, Molly, 'Going Public: A Bold Church in Changing Culture', *Christian Ethics Today* 6 (5), 1996, available on www.christianethicstoday.com/Issue/006.

Martin, David, *On Secularization: Towards a Revised General Theory*, Aldershot: Ashgate, 2005.

Matthey, Jacques, 'Missiology in the World Council of Churches: Update', *International Review of Mission* 90 (4), 2001, pp. 427–43.

Mayo, Bob with Sara Savage & Sylvie Collins, *Ambiguous Evangelism*, London: SPCK, 2004.

McBain, Richard, 'Developing Organisational Citizenship Behaviour (OCB)', *Henley Manager Update* 16 (2), 2004, pp. 25–33.

McBride Jr, S. Dean, 'Polity of the Covenant People: The Book of Deuteronomy', *Interpretation* 41 (3), 1987, pp. 229–44.

McClintock, Waynes, 'Sociological Critique of the Homogeneous Unit Principle', *International Review of Mission* 77 (305), 1988, pp. 107–16.

McConville, J. G., 'Deuteronomy: Torah for the Church of Christ', *European Journal of Theology* 9 (1), 2000, pp. 33–47.

McConville, J. G, 'Deuteronomy's Unification of Passover and *Massot*: A Response to Bernard M. Levinson', *Journal of Biblical Literature* 119 (1), 2000, pp. 47–58.

McConville, J. Gordon, 'Law and Monarchy in the Old Testament', in Craig Bartholomew, Jonathan Chaplin, Robert Song & Al Wolters (eds), *A Royal Priesthood? The Use of the Bible Ethically and Politically: A Dialogue with Oliver O'Donovan*, Carlisle: Paternoster, 2002, pp. 67–88.

McConville, J. G., *God and Earthly Power: An Old Testament Political Theology*, London: T & T Clark, 2006.

McCulloch, Andrew, 'An Examination of Social Capital and Social Disorganisation in Neighbourhoods in the British Household Panel Study', *Social Science & Medicine*, 56 (7), 2003, pp. 1425–38.

McDonough, William K., *The Divine Family: The Trinity and Our Life in God*, Cincinnati: St Anthony Messenger Press, 2005.

McGavran, Donald A., *Understanding Church Growth*, 2nd edition, Grand Rapids: Eerdmans, 1980 [1970].

McKelvey, 'Toward a complexity science of entrepreneurship', *Journal of Business Venturing* 19, 2004, pp. 313–41.

McLaren, Brian, 'One, Holy, Catholic and Fresh?', in Steven Croft and Ian Mobsby (eds), *Fresh Expressions in the Sacramental Tradition*, Norwich: Canterbury Press, 2009, pp. 16–26.

McLeod, Hugh, *Religion and the People of Western Europe: 1789–1989*, 2nd ed. Oxford, Oxford University Press, 1997.

McMichael, Ralph, *Eucharist: A Guide for the Perplexed*, London: T & T Clark, 2010.

McPherson, Miller, Lynn Smith-Lovin & Matthew E. Brashears, 'Social Isolation in America: Changes in Core Discussion Networks over Two Decades', *American Sociological Review* 71 (3), 2006, pp. 353–75.

Meeks, Wayne A., *The First Urban Christians: The Social World of the Apostle Paul*, 2nd edition, Newhaven: Yale University Press, 2003 [1983].

Meisel, Anthony C. & M. L. Del Mastro (trans. and intro.), *The Rule of St. Benedict*, New York: Image Books-Doubleday, 1975.

Milavec, Aaron, *The Didache: Faith, Hope, and Life of the Earliest Christian Communities, 50–70 C. E.*, New Jersey: Newman Press, 2003.

Milbank, John, 'Stale Expressions: the Management-Shaped Church', *Studies in Christian Ethics* 21 (1), 2008, pp. 117–28.

Miles, Todd L., 'A Kingdom Without a King? Evaluating the Kingdom Ethic(s) of the Emerging Church', 2007 ETS National Conference, paper available from author.

Miller, Daniel, *A Theory of Shopping*, Cambridge: Polity Press, 1998.

Miller, Patrick D., 'Divine Command and Beyond: The Ethics of the Commandments', in William P. Brown (ed.), *The Ten Commandments: The Reciprocity of Faithfulness*, Louisville: Westminster John Knox, 2004, pp. 12–29.

Minear, Paul S., *Images of the Church in the New Testament*, Louisville: Westminster John Knox, 2004 [1960].

Mintzberg, Henry, 'The Fall and Rise of Strategic Planning', *Harvard Business Review* January–February, 1994, pp. 107–14.

Mission-shaped Church: Church Planting and Fresh Expressions of Church in a Changing Context, London: Church House Publishing, 2004.

Mitchell, J. Robert & Dean A Shepherd, 'To Thine Own Self Be True: Images of Self, Images of Opportunity, and Entrepreneurial Action', *Journal of Business Venturing* 25 (1), 2010, pp. 138–54.

Mitchelmore, Siwan & Jennifer Rowley, 'Entrepreneurial Competencies: A Literature Review and Development Agenda', *International Journal of Entrepreneurial Behaviour & Research* 16 (2), 2010, pp. 92–111.

Mobsby, Ian, *Emerging and Fresh Expressions of Church: How Are They Authentically Church and Anglican?*, London: Moot, 2007.

Mobsby, Ian, *The Becoming of G-D*, Haverhill: YTC, 2008.

Mobsby, Ian, 'The Importance of New Monasticism as a Model for Building Ecclesial Communities out of Contextual Mission', in Graham Cray, Ian Mobsby & Aaron Kennedy (eds), *New Monasticism as Fresh Expression of Church*, Norwich: Canterbury Press, 2010, pp. 12–18.

Moltmann, Jürgen, *Theology of Hope: On the Ground and the Implications of a Christian Eschatology*, trans. James W. Leitch, London: SCM, 1967.

Moltmann, Jürgen, *The Church in the Power of the Spirit: A Contribution to Messianic Ecclesiology*, trans. M. Kohl, London: SCM, 1977.

Moltmann, Jürgen, *God in Creation. An Ecological Doctrine of Creation*, trans. M. Kohl, London: SCM, 1985.

Moltmann, Jürgen, *The Coming of God: Christian Eschatology*, trans. Margaret Kohl, Minneapolis: Fortress Press, 1996.

Moltmann, Jürgen, *The Spirit of Life. A Universal Affirmation*, trans. M. Kohl, Minneapolis: Fortress, 2001 [1992].

Moon, Jennifer A., *A Handbook of Reflective and Experiential Learning: Theory and Practice*, Abingdon: RoutledgeFarmer, 2004.

Moore, Lucy, *Messy Church: Fresh Ideas for Building a Christ-centred Community*, Oxford: Bible Reading Fellowship, 2006.

Moore, Lucy, 'Leading the Way: Pioneering Women', in David Male (ed.), *Pioneers 4 Life. Explorations in Theology and Wisdom for Pioneering Leaders*, Abingdon: Bible Reading Fellowship, 2011, pp. 90–101.

Moorman, John R. H, *A History of the Church in England*, 3rd ed., Harrisburg, PA: Morehouse Publishing, 1980 [1952].

Morgan, Gareth, *Images of Organization*, revised edition, Thousand Oaks: Sage, 2006.

Morgenthaler, Sally, 'Leadership in a Flattened World. Grassroots Culture and the Demise of the CEO Model', in Doug Pagitt & Tony Jones (eds), *An Emergent Manifesto of Hope*, Grand Rapids: Baker Books, 2007, pp. 175–88.

Morisy, Ann, *Journeying Out: A New Approach to Christian Mission*, London: Morehouse, 2004.

Morris, Jeremy and Hugh Macleod, 'Scholars, Slums and Socialists', in Henry Chadwick (ed.), *Not Angels, But Anglicans: A History of Christianity in the British Isles*, Eugene, OR: Wipf & Stock, 2000, pp. 226–8.

Moynagh, Michael, *Changing World, Changing Church*, London: Monarch, 2001.

Moynagh, Michael, *Emergingchurch.intro*, Oxford: Monarch, 2004.

Moynagh, Michael, 'In for the long haul? Sustaining Fresh Expressions of Church', in David Male (ed.), *Pioneers 4 Life. Explorations in Theology and Wisdom for Pioneering Leaders*, Abingdon: Bible Reading Fellowship, 2011, pp. 130–48.

Moynagh, Michael with Andy Freeman, *How can Fresh Expressions Emerge?*, Fresh Expressions, 2011.

Moynagh, Michael with Andy Freeman, *How Can We Be Sustainable?* Fresh Expressions, 2011.

Moynagh, Michael and Richard Worsley, *Working in the Twenty-First Century*, Leeds: ESRC Future of Work Programme, 2005.

Mulgan, Geoff, *The Art of Public Strategy: Mobilizing Power and Knowledge for the Common Good*, Oxford: Oxford University Press, 2009.

Murphy, Nancey, 'Divine Action in the Natural Order: Buridan's Ass and Schrodinger's Cat', in Robert John Russell, Nancey Murphy & Arthur R. Peacocke (eds), *Chaos and Complexity. Scientific Perspectives on Divine Action*, Vatican/Berkeley: Vatican Observatory & Centre for Theology & the Natural Sciences, 1995, pp. 325–57.

Murphy-O'Connor, Jerome, *St Paul's Corinth. Texts and Archaeology*, Collegeville: Liturgical Press, 3rd ed., 2002.

Murray, Stuart, *Post-Christendom: Church and Mission in a Strange New World*, Carlisle: Paternoster, 2004.

Murray, Stuart, *Church After Christendom*, Carlisle: Paternoster, 2004.

Murray, Stuart, *Changing Mission: Learning from the Newer Churches*, London: CTBI, 2006.

Murray, Stuart, *Planting Churches. A Framework for Practitioners*, Milton Keynes: Paternoster, 2008.

Myers, Glenn, E., *Seeking Spiritual Intimacy: Journeying Deeper with Medieval Women of Faith*, Downers Grove: InterVarsity Press, 2011.

Nelson, Richard D., '*Herem* and the Deuteronomic Social Conscience', in *Deuteronomy and Deuteronomic Literature*, Festschrift C. H. W. Brekelmans, Leuven: Leuven University Press, 1997, pp. 39–54.

Nelstrop, Louise and Martyn Percy (eds), *Evaluating Fresh Expressions: Explorations in Emerging Church*, Norwich: Canterbury Press, 2008.

Nelstrop, Louise, 'Learning from Practitioners Experiences of "Fresh Expressions". A Report on the Fresh Expressions Initiative', unpublished report submitted to Church of England Ministry Division, June 2008, available from author.

New Patterns for Worship, London: Church House Publishing, 2002.

Newbigin, Lesslie, *The Household of God*, London: SCM, 1953.

Newbigin, Lesslie, 'All in One Place or All of One Sort? On Unity and Diversity in the Church', in Richard W. A. McKinney (ed.), *Creation, Christ and Culture*, Edinburgh; T & T Clark, 1976, pp. 288–306.

Newbigin, Lesslie, 'What is "a local church truly united"?', *Ecumenical Review* 29, 1977, pp. 115–28.

Newbigin, Lesslie, 'Evangelism in the City', *Reformed Review* 41, autumn, 1987, pp. 3–8.

Newbigin, Lesslie, *The Gospel in a Pluralist Society*, London: SPCK, 1989.

Niebuhr, H. Richard, *Christ and Culture*, New York: Harper Torchbooks, 1975 [1951].

Nilges, Mathias, 'The Anti-Oedipus: Representing Post-Fordist Subjectivity', *Mediations* 23 (2), 2008, pp. 26–69.

Norris, Pippa & Ronald Inglehart, *Sacred and Secular: Religion and Politics Worldwide*, Cambridge: Cambridge University Press, 2004.

Null, Ashley, 'Thomas Cranmer and Tudor Evangelicalism', in Michael A. G. Haykin and Kenneth J. Stewart (eds), *The Advent of Evangelicalism: Exploring Historical Continuities*, Nashville, Tennessee: B&H Academic, 2008, pp. 221–51.

O'Donnell, John, *Hans Urs von Balthasar*, London: Continuum, 1991.

O'Donovan, Oliver, 'What Kind of Community is the Church? The Richard Hooker Lectures 2005', *Ecclesiology* 3 (2), 2007, pp. 171–93.

O'Loughlin, Thomas, *The Didache: A Window on the Earliest Christians*, Grand Rapids: Baker Academic, 2010.

Olson, Daniel V. A., 'Quantitative Evidence Favoring and Opposing the Religious Econo-mies Model', in Detlef Pollack & Daniel V. A. Olson (eds), *The Role of Religion in Modern Societies*, New York: Routledge, 2008, pp. 95–113.

Osiek, Carolyn & Margaret Y. MacDonald with Janet H. Tulloch, *A Woman's Place. House Churches in Earliest Christianity*, Minneapolis: Fortress, 2006.

Ozkazanc-Pan, Banu, 'Globalization and Identity Formation: A Postcolonial Analysis of the International Entrepreneur', 2009, *Open Access Dissertations*, Paper 48, http://scholarworks.umass.edu/open_access_dissertations/48.

Pardes, Ilarna, *The Biography of Ancient Israel: National Narratives in the Bible*, Berke-ley: University of California, 2000.

Park, Alison & Ceridwen Roberts, 'The Ties that Bind', in Alison Park, John Curtice, Katarina Thomson, Lindsey Jarvis & Catherine Bromley (eds), *British Social Attitudes: The 19th Report*, London: Sage, 2002, pp. 185–212.

Parry, Graham, *The Arts of the Anglican Counter-Reformation: Glory, Laud, and Hon-our*, Woodbridge: Boydell Press, 2006.

Paton, David M., *Reform of the Ministry: A Study in the Work of Roland Allen*, Cam-bridge: Lutterworth Press, 1968.

Patzia, Arthur G., *The Emergence of the Church: Context, Growth, Leadership & Wor-ship*, Downers Grove: InterVarsity Press, 2001.

Peacocke, Arthur R., 'Chance and Law in Irreversible Thermodynamics, Theoretical Biol-ogy, and Theology', in Robert John Russell, Nancey Murphy & Arthur R. Peacocke (eds), *Chaos and Complexity. Scientific Perspectives on Divine Action*, Vatican/Berkeley: Vatican Observatory & Centre for Theology & the Natural Sciences, 1995, pp. 123–43.

Percy, Martyn, 'Old Tricks for New Dogs? A Critique of Fresh Expressions', in Louise Nelstrop and Martyn Percy (eds), *Evaluating Fresh Expressions: Explorations in Emerging Church*, Norwich: Canterbury Press, 2008, pp. 27–39.

Percy, Martyn, *Shaping the Church: The Promise of Implicit Theology*, Farnham: Ash-gate, 2010.

Perkins, Pheme, 'The Gospel of Mark', in Leander E. Keck et al (eds), *The New Inter-preter's Bible: A Commentary in Twelve Volumes*, Vol. 8, Nashville: Abingdon, 1995, pp. 507–733.

Perry, John, 'Gentiles and Homosexuals: A Brief History of an Analogy', *Journal of Reli-gious Ethics* 38 (2), 2010, pp. 321–48.

Pfeffer, Jeffrey & Richard Salancik, *The External Control of Organizations: A Resource Dependency Perspective*, New York: Harper & Row, 1978.

Pointers, Bulletin of the Christian Research Association, 20 (2). June 2010.

Poitras, Edward W., 'St Augustine and the *Missio Dei*: A Reflection on Mission at the Close of the Twentieth Century', *Mission Studies* 16 (2), 1999, pp. 28–46.

Polkinghorne, 'The Metaphysics of Divine Action', in Robert John Russell, Nancey Mur-phy & Arthur R. Peacocke (eds), *Chaos and Complexity. Scientific Perspectives on Divine Action*, Vatican/Berkeley: Vatican Observatory & Centre for Theology & the Natural Sciences, 1995, pp. 147–56.

Potter, Phil, *The Challenge of Cell Church*, Abingdon: Bible Reading Fellowship, 2001.

Potter, Phil, *The Challenge of Change*, Abingdon: Bible Reading Fellowship, 2009.

Rae, David, *Entrepreneurship: From Opportunity to Action*, Basingstoke: Palgrave, 2007.

Rahner, Karl, 'Trinity, Divine' and 'Trinity in Theology', in Kahl Rahner et al (eds), *Sacramentum Mundi: An Encyclopedia of Theology*, Volume Six, London: Burns & Oates, 1970.

Rahner, Karl, 'Towards a Fundamental Theological Interpretation of Vatican II', *Theological Studies* 40 (4), 1979, pp. 716–27.

Ratzinger, Cardinal Joseph, 'Notification to Father Leonardo Boff', issued by the Vatican Congregation of the Doctrine of the Faith, 11 March 1985.

Reynolds, Barbara, *Dorothy L. Sayers: Her Life and Soul*, New York: St. Martin's Griffin, 1993.

Reynolds, Barbara (ed.), *The Letters of Dorothy L. Sayers*, Vol. II: 1937–1943, *From Novelist to Playwright*, New York: St. Martin's Press, 1997.

Richardson, Neil, *Paul for Today: New Perspectives on a Controversial Apostle*, London: Epworth, 2008.

Richmond, Yvonne, 'A Spiritual Snapshot', in Steven Croft, Rob Frost, Mark Ireland, Anne Richards, Yvonne Richmond & Nick Spencer, *Evangelism in a Spiritual Age: Communicating Faith in a Changing Culture*, London: Church House Publishing, 2005, pp. 3–15.

Riddell, Michael, *Threshold of the Future: Reforming the Church in the Post-Christian West*, London: SPCK, 1998.

Ridley, Charles R., *How to Select Church Planters: A Self-study Manual for Recruiting, Screening, Interviewing and Evaluating Qualified Church Planters*, Pasadena: Fuller Evangelistic Association, 1988.

Ridley-Duff, Rory & Mike Bull, *Understanding Social Enterprise: Theory and Practice*, London: Sage, 2011.

Riesner, Rainer, 'A Pre-Christian Jewish Mission?,' in Jostein Ådna & Hans Kvalbein (eds), *The Mission of the Early Church to Jews and Gentiles*, Tübingen: Mohr Siebeck, 2000.

Riesner, Rainer, *Paul's Early Period: Chronology, Mission Strategy, Theology*, [tr. Doug Stott], Grand Rapids: Eerdmans, 1998.

Rindova, Violina, David Barry & David J. Ketchen, Jr, 'Entrepreneurship as Emancipation', *Academy of Management Review* 34 (3), 2009, pp. 477–91.

Ringe, Sharon H., 'A Gentile Woman's Story', in Letty M. Russell (ed.), *Feminist Interpretation of the Bible*, Philadelphia: Westminster Press, 1985, pp. 67–8.

Roberts Jr, Bob, The Multiplying Church: The New Math for Starting New Churches, Grand Rapids: Zondervan, 2008.

Roberts, Richard H., *Religion, Theology and the Human Sciences*, Cambridge: Cambridge University Press, 2002.

Robinson, Martin, *Planting Mission-Shaped Churches Today*, Oxford: Monarch, 2006.

Robinson, Martin & Dwight Smith, *Invading Secular Space: Strategies for Tomorrow's Church*, London: Monarch, 2003.

Robinson, Stuart P., *Starting Mission-Shaped Churches*, Chatswood: St Paul's, 2007.

Robinson, Stuart & Wayne Brighton, 'Fresh Expressions of Church', in Stephen Hale & Andrew Curnow (eds), *Facing the Future: Bishops Imagine a Different Church*, Brunswick East, Victoria: Acorn Press, 2009, pp. 21–31.

Rogerson, J. W., *A Theology of the Old Testament: Cultural Memory, Communication and Being Human*, London: SPCK, 2009.

Rollins, Pete, 'Biting the Hand that Feeds: an Apology for Encouraging Tensions between the Established Church and Emerging Collectives', in Louise Nelstrop and Martyn Percy (eds), *Evaluating Fresh Expressions: Explorations in Emerging Church*, Norwich: Canterbury Press, 2008, pp. 71–84.

Roxburgh, Alan J., *Missional Map-Making. Skills for Leading in Times of Transition*, San Francisco: Jossey-Boss, 2010.

Rusbult, Caryl E. & Paul A. M. Van Lange, 'Interdependence, Interaction and Relationships', *Annual Review of Psychology* 54, 2003, pp. 351–75.

Russell, Letty M., 'Liberation and Evangelization – A Feminist Perspective', in Paul W. Chilcote & Laceye C. Warner (eds), *The Study of Evangelism: Exploring a Missional Practice of the Church*, Grand Rapids, Eerdmans, 2008, pp. 416–23.

Sacks, Jonathan, *The Dignity of Difference: How to Avoid the Clash of Civilizations*, London: Continuum, 2002.

Sacrosanctum Concilium, Constitution on the Sacred Liturgy of the Second Vatican Council, 4 December 1963, www.vatican.va/archive/hist_councils/ii_vatican_council/documents/vat-ii_const_19631204_sacrosanctum-concilium_en.html.

Saggs, H. W. F., *The Encounter with the Divine in Mesopotamia and Israel*, London: Athlone Press, 1978.

Sahlman, William H., 'How to Write a Great Business Plan' in *Harvard Business Review on Entrepreneurship*, Boston: Harvard Business Review, 1999, pp. 29–56.

Sanneh, Lamin, *Translating the Message: The Missionary Impact on Culture*, Maryknoll: Orbis, 1989.

Sarasvathy, Saras D., Nicholas Dew, S. Ramakrishna Velamuri & Sankaran Venkataraman, 'Three Views of Entrepreneurial Opportunity', in Zoltan J. Acs & David B. Audretsch (eds), *Handbook of Entrepreneurship Research: An Interdisciplinary Survey and Introduction*, New York: Springer, 2005 [2003], pp. 141–60.

Savage, Sara & Eolene Boyd-MacMillan, *The Human Face of Church: A Social Psychology and Pastoral Theology Resource for Pioneer and Traditional Ministry*, Norwich: Canterbury Press, 2007.

Savage, Sara, Sylvia Collins-Mayo, Bob Mayo with Graham Cray, *Making Sense of Generation Y: The World View of 15–16-Year-Olds*, London: Church House Publishing, 2006.

Scharmer, Claus Olto 'Presencing: Learning From the Future As It Emerges. On the Tacit Dimension of Leading Revolutionary Change', Paper presented to the Conference on Knowledge and Innovation, Helsinki School of Economics, 25–26 May 2000.

Scheffler, Eben, 'Criticising Political Power: The Challenge of Deuteronomy 17:14–20', *Journal of the Old Testament Society of South Africa* 20 (3), pp. 772–85.

Scherer, James A., 'Church, Kingdom, and *Missio Dei*', in Charles van Engen, Dean S. Gilliland & Paul Pierson (eds), *The Good News of the Kingdom*, Maryknoll, NY: Orbis, 1993, pp. 82–8.

Schnabel, Eckhard J., *Paul the Missionary: Realities, Strategies and Methods*, Downers Grove: InterVarsity Press, 2008.

Schreiter, Robert J., *Constructing Local Theologies*, London: SCM, 1985.

Schuster, Jürgen, *Christian Mission in Eschatological Perspective. Lesslie Newbigin's Contribution*, Nürnberg & Bonn: VTR & VKW, 2009.

Schwarz, Christian A., *Natural Church Development. A Guide to Eight Essential Qualities of Healthy Churches*, St Charles, IL: 2006 [1996].

Scola, Angelo, *Hans Urs von Balthasar: A Theological Style*, Grand Rapids: Eerdmans, 1995.

Shah, Sonali K. & Mary Tripsas, 'The Accidental Entrepreneur: the Emergent and Collective Process of User Entrepreneurship', *Strategic Entrepreneurship Journal* 1, 2007, pp. 123–40.

Shane, Scott & Jonathan Eckhardt, 'The Individual-Opportunity Nexus', in Zoltan J. Acs & David B. Audretsch (eds), *Handbook of Entrepreneurship Research: An Interdisciplinary Survey and Introduction*, New York: Springer, 2005 [2003], pp. 161–11.

Shaw, Patricia, *Changing Conversations in Organizations: A Complexity Approach to Change*, London: Routledge, 2002.

Sheldrake, Philip, *Living Between Worlds: Place and Journey in Celtic Spirituality*, Boston: Cowley Publications, 1996.

Shier-Jones, Angela, *Pioneer Ministry and Fresh Expressions of Church*, London: SPCK, 2009.

Shirky, Clay, *Here Comes Everybody: How Change Happens When People Come Together*, London: Penguin, 2009 [2008].

Shorter, Aylward & Edwin Onyancha, *Secularism in Africa*, Nairobi: Paulines Publications Africa, 1997.

Ska, Jean Louis, 'Biblical Law and the Origins of Democracy', in William P. Brown (ed.), *The Ten Commandments: The Reciprocity of Faithfulness*, Louisville: Westminster John Knox, 2004, pp. 146–58.

Skipton, H. P. K., *The Life and Times of Nicholas Ferrar*, London: A. R. Mowbray & Co., 1907.

Smith, James K. A., *Desiring the Kingdom: Worship, Worldview and Cultural Formation*, Grand Rapids: Baker, 2009.

Smith, Peter A. C. & Abby Day, 'Strategic Planning as Action Learning', *Organization and People* 7 (1), 2000, pp. 1–11.

Snowden, David J. & Mary E. Boone, 'A Leader's Framework for Decision Making', *Harvard Business Review*, November 2007, pp. 1–8.

Sorensen, Knut H., 'Domestication: the Enactment of Technology', in Thomas Berker, Maren Hartmann, Yves Punie & Katie J. Ward (eds), *Domestication of Media and Technology*, Maidenhead: Open University Press, 2006, pp. 40–61.

Sparks, Kenton L., *Ethnicity and Identity in Ancient Israel*, Winona Lake: Eisenbrauns, 1998.

Spencer, Nick, 'Attitudes to Christianity and the Church', in Steven Croft, Rob Frost, Mark Ireland, Anne Richards, Yvonne Richmond & Nick Spencer, *Evangelism in a Spiritual Age: Communicating Faith in a Changing Culture*, London: Church House Publishing, 2005, pp. 41–53.

Spencer, Nick, 'Beyond the Fringe?', in Steven Croft, Rob Frost, Mark Ireland, Anne Richards, Yvonne Richmond & Nick Spencer, *Evangelism in a Spiritual Age: Communicating Faith in a Changing Culture*, London: Church House Publishing, 2005, pp. 16–40.

Spina, Frank Anthony, *The Faith of the Outsider: Exclusion and Inclusion in the Biblical Story*, Grand Rapids: Eerdmans, 2005.

Stacey, Ralph D., *Strategic Management and Organisational Dynamics: The Challenge of Complexity*, 3rd edition, London: Pearson Education, 2000 [1993].

Stacey, Ralph D., *Complexity and Organizational Reality*, 2nd ed., Abingdon: Routledge, 2010.

Stacey, Ralph D., Douglas Griffin & Patricia Shaw, *Complexity and Management: Fad or Radical Challenge to Systems Thinking?*, London: Routledge, 2000.

Stalder, Felix, 'The Space of Flows: Notes on Emergence, Characteristics and Possible Impact on Physical Space', August/September 2001, http://felix.openflows.com/html/space_of_flows.html.

Stalder, Felix, *Manuel Castells. The Theory of the Network Society*, Cambridge: Polity, 2006.

Standage, Tom (ed.), *The Future of Technology*, London: The Economist, 2005.

Stanley, Brian, 'Inculturation: Historical Background, Theological Foundations and Contemporary Questions', *Transformation: An International Journal of Holistic Mission Studies* 24 (1), 2007, pp. 21–7.

Stark, Rodney, *Cities of God: The Real Story of How Christianity Became an Urban Movement and Conquered Rome*, New York: HarperOne, 2007 [2006].

Starkey, Ken & Sue Tempest, 'Late Twentieth-Century Management, the Business School, and Social Capital', in Cary L. Cooper (ed.), *Leadership and Management in the 21st Century: Business Challenges of the Future*, Oxford: Oxford University Press, 2004, pp. 139–59.

Stetzer, Ed, *Planting Missional Churches*, Nashville: B&H Publishing, 2006.

Stetzer, Ed, 'The Emergent/Emerging Church: A Missiological Perspective', in William D. Henard & Adam W. Greenway (eds), *Evangelicals Engaging Emergent: A Discussion of the Emergent Church Movement*, Nashville: B&H Publishing, 2009, pp. 47–90.

Stetzer, Ed & Warren Bird, *Viral Churches: Helping Church Planters Become Movement Makers*, San Francisco: Jossey-Bass, 2010.

Stone, Bryan, *Evangelism after Christendom: The Theology and Practice of Christian Witness*, Grand Rapids: Brazos Press, 2007.

Stone, Matt, *Fresh Expressions of Church: Fishing Nets or Safety Nets?*, Cambridge: Grove Books, 2010.

Suchman, Anthony L., 'An Introduction to Complex Responsive Process: Theory and Implications for Organizational Change Initiatives', 2002, unpublished paper available from asuchman@rochester.rr.com.

Suchman, Anthony L., 'A New Theoretical Foundation for Relationship-centred Care. Complex Responsive Processes of Relating', *Journal of Internal Medicine*, 21 (1), 2006, pp. 40–4.

Sykes, S. W., 'The Strange Persistence of Kenotic Christology', in Alistair Kee and Eugene T. Long (eds), *Being and Truth: Essays in Honour of John Macquarrie*, London: SCM, 1986, pp. 349–75.

Tanner, Kathryn, *Theories of Culture: A New Agenda for Theology*, Minneapolis: Fortress Press, 1997.

Tapscott, Don, *Grown Up Digital: How the Net Generation is Changing Your World*, New York: McGraw Hill, 2009.

Taylor, Charles, *A Secular Age*, Cambridge, MA: Belknap Press, 2007.

Taylor, John V., *The Go-Between God: The Holy Spirit and the Christian Mission*, London: SCM, 2004 [1972].

Teasdale, Simon, 'Explaining the Multifaceted Nature of Social Enterprise: Impression Management as (Social) Entrepreneurial Behaviour', paper presented to the International Social Innovation Research Conference, Oxford University, 13–15 September 2010.

The Nature and Mission of the Church: A Stage on the Way to a Common Statement, Faith and Order Paper 198, Geneva: World Council of Churches, 2005.

Thiselton, Anthony C., *1 Corinthians: A Shorter Exegetical and Pastoral Commentary*, Grand Rapids: Eerdmans, 2006.

Thomas, Geoff & Garth J. O. Fletcher, 'Empathic Accuracy in Close Relationships', in William Ickes (ed.), *Empathic Accuracy*, New York: Guildford Press, 1997, pp. 194–217.

Thomson, John B., *The Ecclesiology of Stanley Hauerwas: A Christian Theology of Liberation*, Aldershot: Ashagate, 2003.

Thomson, John B., *Living Holiness: Stanley Hauerwas and the Church*, London: Epworth, 2010.

Thompson, John, *Modern Trinitarian Perspectives*, Oxford: Oxford University Press, 1994.

Thompson, Michael B., 'The Holy Internet: Communication Between Churches in the First Christian Generation', in Richard Bauckham (ed.), *The Gospels for All Christians: Rethinking the Gospel Audiences*, Grand Rapids: Eerdmans, 1998, pp. 49–70.

Tilby, Angela, 'What Questions Does Catholic Ecclesiology Pose for Fresh Expressions?', in Steven Croft (ed.), *Mission-shaped Questions*, London: Church House Publishing, 2008, pp. 78–89.

Tomlin, Graham, *The Provocative Church*, London: SPCK, 2002.

Tomorrow Project, 'Knowledge exchange among social entrepreneurs: a report by the Tomorrow Project', November 2010, www.socialenterprise.org.uk.

Torrance, James B., *Worship, Community and the Triune God of Grace*, Carlisle: Paternoster, 1996.

Tovey, Phillip, *Public Worship with Communion by Extension: A Commentary*, Cambridge: Grove Books, 2001.

Tuckman, Bruce W. & Mary Ann C. Jensen, 'Stages of small group development revisited', *Group and Organization Studies* 2 (4), 1977, pp. 419–27.

Tuell, Steven, 'The Priesthood of the "Foreigner": Evidence of Competing Polities in Gzekiel 44:1–4 and Isiah 56:1–8' in *Constituting the Community: Studies on the Policy of Ancient Israel in Honor of S. Deen McBride Jr.*, Winona Lake: Eisenbrauns, 2005, pp. 185–206.

Turkle, Sherry, *Life on the Screen: Identity in the Age of the Internet*, New York: Simon & Schuster, 1995.

Turkle, Sherry, *Alone Together: Why We Expect More from Technology and Less from Each Other*, New York: Basic Books, 2011.

Urban Church Project, 'Let My People Grow', Workpaper No. 1, presented to General Synod of the Church of England, November 1974.

Urban Church Project, 'Divide and Conquer', Workpaper No. 2, prepared as background to 'The Survival of Mission' presentation to the Annual General Meeting of the Archbishops' Council on Evangelism, 13 November 1975.

Urwin, Lindsay, 'What is the Role of Sacramental Ministry in Fresh Expressions of Church?', in Steve Croft (ed.), *Mission-shaped Questions*, London: Church House Publishing, 2008, pp. 29–41.

Vaghely, Ivan P. & Pierre-André Julien, 'Are Opportunities Recognized or Constructed? An Information Perspective on Entrepreneurial Opportunity Identification', *Journal of Business Venturing* 25 (1), 2010, pp. 73–86.

Vandekerckhove, Wim & Nikolay A. Dentchev, 'A Network Perspective on Stakeholder Management: Facilitating Entrepreneurs in the Discovery of Opportunities', *Journal of Business Ethics* 60, 2005, pp. 221–32.

Van den Toren, Benno, 'Can We See the Naked Theological Truth?', in Matthew Cook, Rob Haskell, Ruth Julian & Natee Tanchanpongs (eds), *Local Theology for the Global Church: Principles for an Evangelical Approach to Contextualization*, Pasadena: William Carey, 2010, pp. 91–108.

Van der Heijden, Kees, *Scenarios: The Art of Strategic Conversation*, Chichester: John Wiley, 1996.

Van Gelder, Craig, *The Essence of the Church: A Community Created by the Spirit*, Grand Rapids: Baker Books, 2000.

Vanhoozer, Kevin J., 'What Is Everyday Theology? How and Why Christians Should Read Culture', in Kevin J. Vanhoozer, Charles A. Anderson & Michael J. Sleasman (eds), *Everyday Theology: How to Read Cultural Texts and Interpret Trends*, Grand Rapids: Baker, 2007, pp. 15–60.

Vanier, Jean, *Community and Growth*, revised edition, London: Darton, Longman & Todd, 2007 [1979].

Vasey, Michael, 'Promoting a Common Core', in Michael Perham (ed.), *The Renewal of Common Prayer. Unity and Diversity in Church of England Worship*, London: SPCK, 1993, pp. 81–101.

Vincent, John, 'Losing Life, Gaining Life', in John Vincent (ed.), *Mark: Gospel of Action: Personal and Community Responses*, London: SPCK, 2006, pp. 68–78.

Vincett, Paul S. & Steve Farlow, "Start-a-Business": an Experiment in Education through Entrepreneurship', *Journal of Small Business and Enterprise Development* 15 (2), 2008, pp. 274–88.

Viola, Frank & George Barna, *Pagan Christianity?*, Barna Books, 2008.

Voas, David, 'The Rise and Fall of Fuzzy Fidelity in Europe', *European Sociological Review* 25 (2), 2009, pp. 155–68.

Voas, David & Rodney Ling, 'Religion in Britain and the United States', in Alison Park, John Curtice, Katarina Thomson, Miranda Phillips, Elizabeth Clery & Sarah Butt (eds), *British Social Attitudes 2009–2010. The 26th Report*, London: Sage, 2010, pp. 65–86.

Vogt, Peter T., *Deuteronomic Theology and the Significance of Torah: A Reappraisal*, Winona Lake: Eisenbrauns, 2006.

Volf, Miroslav, *Work in the Spirit: Toward a Theology of Work*, Oxford: Oxford University Press, 1991.

Volf, Miroslav, *After Our Likeness: The Church as the Image of the Trinity*, Grand Rapids: Eerdmans, 1998.

Volf, Miroslav, 'Enter into Joy! Sin, Death, and the Life of the World to Come', in John Polkinghorne & Michael Welker (eds), *The End of the World and the Ends of God. Science and Theology on Eschatology*, Harrisburg: Trinity Press, 2000, pp. 256–78.

Volland, Michael, *Through the Pilgrim Door: Pioneering a Fresh Expression of Church*, Eastbourne: Survivor Books, 2009.

Von Rad, Gerhard, *Genesis: A Commentary*, revised edition, London: SCM, 1972.

Vyakarnam, S. and Y. M. Myint, 'Becoming a global entrepreneur: it takes networks, passion and experience', The Institute of Small Business and Enterprise (ISBE), Annual Conference, 2006.

Wack, Pierre, 'Scenarios: uncharted waters ahead', *Harvard Business Review* 63 (1985), pp. 72–89.

Wagner, Peter C., *Our Kind of People: The Ethical Dimensions of Church Growth in America*, Atlanta: John Knox, 1979.

Wagner, Peter C., *Church Growth and the Whole Gospel: A Biblical Mandate*, London: MARC Europe/British Church Growth Association, 1987 [1981].

Walls, Andrew F., *The Missionary Movement in Christian History: Studies in the Transmission of Faith*, New York: Orbis, 1996.

Walls, Andrew F., *The Cross-Cultural Process in Christian History: Studies in the Transmission and Appropriation of Faith*, Maryknoll: Orbis, 2002.

Walter, J. A., *A Long Way from Home: Sociological Exploration of Contemporary Idolatry*, London: Paternoster, 1980.

Walton, John H., *Ancient Near Eastern Thought and the Old Testament: Introducing the Conceptual World of the Hebrew Bible*, Nottingham: Apollos, 2007.

Walton, Roger, 'Have we got the *Missio Dei* right?', *Epworth Review* 35 (3), 2008, pp. 39–51.

Walton, Steve, "The Heavens Opened": Cosmological and Theological Transformation in Luke and Acts', in Jonathan T. Pennington & Sean M. McDonough (eds), *Cosmology and New Testament Theology*, London: T & T Clark, 2008, pp. 60–73.

Walton, Steve, 'Paul, Patronage and Pay: What do we Know about the Apostle's Financial Support?', in Trevor J. Burke & Brian S. Rosner, *Paul as Missionary: Identity, Activity, Theology and Practice*, T & T Clark, 2011, pp. 220–33.

Wang, Hua & Barry Wellman, 'Social Connectivity in America: Changes in Adult Friendship Network Size From 2002 to 2007', *American Behavioural Scientist* 53(8), 2010, pp. 1148–69.

Wannenwetsch, Bernd, *Political Worship*, Oxford: Oxford University Press, 2004.

Ward, Graham, 'BODIES: The Displaced Body of Jesus Christ', in John Milbank, Catherine Pickstock & Graham Ward (eds), *Radical Orthodoxy: A New Theology*, London: Routledge, 1999, pp. 163–81.

Ward, Graham, *The Politics of Discipleship: Becoming Postmaterial Citizens*, Grand Rapids: Baker and London: SCM, 2009.

Ward, Pete, *Liquid Church*, Carlisle: Paternoster, 2002.

Ward, Pete, *Participation and Mediation: A Practical Theology for the Liquid Church*, London: SCM, 2008.

Warren, Norman, *Journey into Life*, Eastbourne: Kingsway, 1972.

Warren, Robert, *Signs of Life: How Goes the Decade of Evangelism?*, London: Church House Publishing, 1995.

Wasdell, David, 'The evolution of missionary congregations', *International Review of Mission* 66 (264), 1977, pp. 366–72.

Wasdell, 'Long Range Planning and the Church', *Long Range Planning* 13 (3), 1980, pp. 99–108.

Watson, David Lowes, 'The Church as Journalist: Evangelism in the Context of the Local Church in the United States, *International Review of Mission* 72 (285), 1983, pp. 57–74.

Weick, Karl E., *Sensemaking in Organizations*, Thousand Oaks: Sage, 1995.

Weick, Karl E. & Robert E. Quinn, 'Organizational Change and Development', *Annual Review of Psychology*, 50 (1), 1999, pp. 361–86.

Wells, David F., *Above All Earthly Pow'rs. Christ in a Postmodern World*, Grand Rapids: Eerdmans, 2005.

Wesley, John, 'A Plain Account of the People Called Methodists', in *The Works of the Reverend John Wesley*, New York: J. Emory and B. Waugh, 1831, pp. 176–90.

Wesley, John, 'A Short Account of the Life and Death of the Reverend John Fletcher', in *The Works of the Rev. John Wesley*, Vol. XI, London: Wesleyan Conference Office, 1872.

Wesley, John, *The Journal Of John Wesley*, Introduction by Hugh Price Hughes, ed. Percy Livingstone Parker, Chicago: Moody Press, 1951.

Weston, Paul (ed.), *Lesslie Newbigin: Missionary Theologian. A Reader*, Grand Rapids: Eerdmans, 2006.

Wheatley, Margaret J., *Leadership and the New Science: Discovering Order in a Chaotic World*, 3rd ed., San Francisco: Berrett-Koehler, 2006.

Wiklund, Johan & Dean Shepherd, 'Knowledge-based Resources, Entrepreneurial Orientation, and the Performance of Small and Medium-sized Businesses', *Strategic Management Journal* 24 (13), 2003, pp. 1307–14.

Williams, Eleanor, *Fresh Expressions in the Urban Context*, Haverhill: YTC, 2007.

Williams, Rowan, *Resurrection: Interpreting the Easter Gospel*, London: Darton, Longman & Todd, 1982.

Williams, Rowan, *A Ray of Darkness. Sermons and Reflections*, London: Darton, Longman & Todd, 1994.

Williams, Rowan, 'Mission and Christology', J. C. Jones Memorial Lecture, Church Missionary Society, Welsh Members Council, 1994.

Williams, Rowan, *On Christian Theology*, Oxford: Blackwell, 2000.

Williams, Rowan, 'Against the Market', review of Richard H. Roberts, *Religion, Theology and the Human Sciences* in *Times Literary Supplement*, 29 March 2002.

Williams, Rowan, 'Balthasar and the Trinity', in Edward T. Oakes & David Moss (eds), *The Cambridge Companion to Hans Urs Von Balthasar*, Cambridge: Cambridge University Press, 2004, pp. 37–50.

Williams, Rowan, *Why Study the Past? The Quest for the Historical Church*, Grand Rapids: Eerdmans, 2005.

Williams, Rowan, 'Theological Resources for Re-examining Church', in Steven Croft (ed.), *The Future of the Parish System: Shaping the Church of England for the 21st Century*, London: Church Publishing House, 2006, pp. 49–60.

Williams, Rowan, *Tokens of Trust: An Introduction to Christian Belief*, Norwich: Canterbury Press, 2007.

Williams, Rowan, *A Margin of Silence: The Holy Spirit in Russian Orthodox Theology*, Quebec: Editions du Lys Vert, 2008.

Williams, Rowan, 'No-one can be forgotten in God's Kingdom', *Anvil*, 25 (2), 2008, pp. 117–28.

Williams, Rowan, 'The "strength" of the church is never anything other than the strength of the Risen Jesus', *Mixed Economy*, Fresh Expressions, Autumn/Winter 2008/09, pp. 12–13.

Williams, Rowan, 'Address to the Fresh Expressions National Pilgrimage, Coventry Cathedral, December 2008', in Steven Croft & Ian Mobsby (eds), *Fresh Expressions in the Sacramental Tradition*, Norwich: Canterbury Press, 2009, pp. 1–8.

Williams, Rowan, 'Introduction. *Common Worship*, common life: defining liturgy for today', in Nicholas Papadopulos (ed.), *God's Transforming Work: Celebrating Ten Years of* Common Worship, London: SPCK, 2011, pp. 1–13.

Williamson, Oliver E, 'Comparative Economic Organization: The Analysis of Discreet Structural Alternatives, *Administrative Science Quarterly* 36 (2), 1991, pp. 269–96.

Willimon, William H., 'Too Much Practice: Second Thoughts on a Theological Movement', *The Christian Century*, 127 (5), 2010, pp. 22–5.

Wilson, Bryan, 'The Secularization Thesis: Criticisms and Rebuttals', in Laermans, Rudi, Bryan Wilson & Jaak Billiet, *Secularization and Social Integration*, Leuven, Belgium: 1998, pp. 45–65.

Wilson-Hartgrove, Jonathan, *New Monasticism*, Grand Rapids: Brazos Press, 2008.

Wimber, John, *Power Evangelism*, London: Hodder, 1985.

Winter, Ralph D., *The Two Structures of God's Redemptive Mission*, address first given to All-Asia Mission Consultation in Seoul, Korea in August 1973 and republished by the Presbyterian Centre for Mission Studies, Pasadena, California.

Witherington III, Ben, *The Acts of the Apostles: A Socio-Rhetorical Commentary*, Grand Rapids: Eerdmans, 1997.

Wolf, William J. (ed.), *The Spirit of Anglicanism: Hooker, Maurice, Temple*, Wilton, Conn.: Morehouse-Barlow Co., 1979.

Wood, Susan K., 'The Liturgy: Participatory Knowledge of God in the Liturgy', in James J. Buckley and David S. Yeago (eds), *Knowing the Triune God: The Work of the Spirit in the Practices of the Church*, Grand Rapids: Eerdmans, 2001, pp. 95–118.

World Council of Churches, *The Church for Others and The Church for the World. A Quest for Structures for Missionary Congregations*, Geneva: World Council of Churches, 1968.

World Council of Churches, *Baptism, Eucharist and Ministry*, Faith and Order Paper No. 111, Geneva: World Council of Churches, 1982.

Wright, Christopher J. H., *Old Testament Ethics for the People of God*, Downers Grove: InterVarsity Press, 2004.

Wright, Christopher J. H., *The Mission of God: Unlocking the Bible's Grand Narrative*, Nottingham: InterVarsity Press, 2006.

Wright, N. T., *The New Testament and the People of God*, London: SPCK, 1992.

Wright, Robert, *The Moral Animal. Evolutionary Psychology and Everyday Life*, London: Abacus, 1996 [1994].

Wright, Tom, *Virtue Reborn*, London: SPCK, 2010.

Yoder, John Howard, *The Royal Priesthood: Essays Ecclesiological and Ecumenical*, ed. Michael G. Cartwright, Grand Rapids: Eerdmans, 1994.

Yoder, John Howard, 'How H. Richard Niebuhr Reasoned: A Critique of *Christ and Culture*', in Glen H. Stassen, D. M. Yeager & John Howard Yoder (eds), *Authentic Transformation: A New Vision of Christ and Culture*, Nashville: Abingdon, 1996, pp. 31–90.

York Statement, The, 'Down to Earth Worship': the Statement of the Third International Anglican Liturgical Consultation, York, 1989, in David R. Holeton (ed.), *Liturgical Inculturation in the Anglican Communion*, Nottingham: Grove Books, 1990.

Zafirovski, Milan, 'Some Amendments to Social Exchange Theory: A Sociological Perspective', *Theory and Science* 4 (2), 2003, http://theoryandscience.icaap.org/content/vol004.002/01_zafirovski.html

Zizioulas, John, *Being as Communion: Studies in Personhood and the Church*, London: Darton, Longman & Todd, 1985.

Zizioulas, John, *Communion and Otherness*, London: T & T Clark, 2006.

Zuboff, Shoshana, 'Creating Value in the Age of Distributed Capitalism', *McKinsey Quarterly*, September 2010, available on www.mckinseyquarterly.com/Creating_value_in_the_age_of_distributed_capitalism_2666.

Zuboff, Shoshana & James Maxmin, *The Support Economy: Why Corporations are Failing Individuals and the Next Episode of Capitalism*, New York: Viking Penguin, 2002.

Author Index

Subject Index

3DM 144
360 degree listening 252–5

Abraham, God's promise to 381–2
accountability 271–2
Achan 385–6
action-based learning 283–98
adjourning 323–4
Agape meals 30–1, 374
Aidan (monk) 32
Alpha course 56, 57, 338, 359
amplification 58–63
Anderson, Rufus 405
Anglicanism 434
anthropological model of
    contextualization 162–3
Antioch, church in 7–12, 21, 28–31
apostles (the Twelve) 5
  role of 24
art 128
ascension 187–8
assimilation 384–5
attractors 63–6
Augustine of Canterbury 33–4
Augustine of Hippo 122, 140–1
authentic (?) (Glasgow) 382–3
authority
  in the early church 396
  in worship 372–7

Babel 173–4
baptism 359–60
Barnabas 9, 11
base communities 137
Beguines 37–40
Benedictines 34–7

Bible
  contextual nature 154
  transformative effect of reading 41
  vernacular 39
Birmingham 389
Bishops' Mission Orders 61, 65
Blair, Patrick xiv
blended worship 353
Bradford 356, 397
Breakfast @ 9 (Canford Magna) 392
Bristol xviii–xix
broadcasting 47–9

cafe churches 178, 208, 215, 219, 357
call to mission 240
Canaan, conquest of 386–7
Canford Magna 392
catechesis 341
catholicity 439
Celtic mission 32–3
chaos theory 53, 64
Chester-le-Street xiv
Chicago Lambeth Quadrilateral 371
Chichester 57
choice 77–8
Christian socialism 46
church
  attendance 55–6, 73, 75–7
  buildings 78
  catholicity 439
  as community 379–404
  culture 158
  de-centring 116–17
  dual membership 148–9
  essence 104–14
  as gathering 380